**United Health Foundation**

9900 Bren Road East
Minnetonka, MN 55343

July, 2004

Dear Colleague:

On behalf of United Health Foundation, I am pleased to provide you with this edition of *Clinical Evidence Concise*, Issue 11. This distribution stems from the ongoing partnership between our Foundation and the BMJ Publishing Group to provide our nation's physicians with this essential resource of the best available evidence for effective health care. Considerable feedback continues to indicate that physicians and other health professionals appreciate this evidence-based information and regularly use it to inform their clinical practice.

Over the years, *Clinical Evidence* has benefited from the scientific and clinical expertise of an extraordinary team of international experts, many of whom are from the United States. In recent years, as the evidence-based clinical literature has become more robust, so too have the challenges faced by the BMJ Publishing Group in organizing it into an efficient and convenient document. This edition of *Clinical Evidence Concise* represents another impressive achievement in this regard.

I am pleased to note that the *Concise* format has proven to be widely accepted by practicing clinicians. Please note that the enclosed CD-ROM includes all of the relevant background material and supporting documentation relevant to each topic. In addition, as one of the 500 000 recipients of our Foundation's distribution, you also have free access to the online version, which can be accessed at www.clinicalevidence.com. Once there, click "Free Access – UHF".

I hope this edition of *Clinical Evidence Concise* will provide you with a resource that meaningfully supports your efforts to provide the best quality of care to your patients.

Sincerely,

William W. McGuire, M.D.
Chairman
United Health Foundation

# BMJ

# clinical
# evidence
## *concise*

**The international source of the
best available evidence for
effective health care**

# 11

JUNE 2004

**Editorial Office**
BMJ Publishing Group, BMA House, Tavistock Square, London, WC1H 9JR, United Kingdom. Tel: +44 (0)20 7387 4499 • Fax: +44 (0)20 7383 6242 • www.bmjpg.com

**Subscription prices for *Clinical Evidence***
*Clinical Evidence* and *Clinical Evidence Concise* (with companion CD-ROM) are both published six monthly (June/December) by the BMJ Publishing Group. The annual subscription rates (for June, Issue 11 and December, Issue 12) are:

**Concise edition**
Personal: £90 • €145 • US$145 • Can$200
Institutional: £190 • €305 • US$305 • Can$420
Student/nurse: £40 • €65 • US$65 • Can$90

**Full edition**
Personal: £100 • €160 • US$160 • Can$220
Institutional: £210 • €335 • US$335 • Can$460
Student/nurse: £45 • €70 • US$70 • Can$100

All individual subscriptions (personal, student, nurse) include online access at no additional cost. Institutional subscriptions are for print editions only. Institutions may purchase online site licences separately. For information on site licences and individual electronic subscriptions please visit the subscription pages of our website www.clinicalevidence.com or email us at CEsubscriptions@bmjgroup.com (UK and ROW) or clinevid@pmds.com (Americas). You may also telephone us or fax us on the following numbers:

**UK and ROW** Tel: +44 (0)20 7383 6270 • Fax: +44 (0)20 7383 6402
**Americas** Tel: +1 800 373 2897/240 646 7000 • Fax: +1 240 646 7005

**Bulk subscriptions for societies and organisations**
The Publishers offer discounts for any society or organisation buying bulk quantities for their members/ specific groups. Please contact Miranda Lonsdale, Sales Manager (UK) at mlonsdale@bmjgroup.com or Maureen Rooney, Sales Manager (USA) at mrooney@bmjgroup.com.

**Rights and permission to reproduce**
For information on translation rights, please contact Daniel Raymond-Barker at draymond-barker@bmjgroup.com. To request permission to reprint all or part of any contribution in *Clinical Evidence* please contact Alan Thomas at athomas@bmjgroup.com.

British Library Cataloguing in Publication Data. A catalogue record for this book is available from the British Library. ISSN 1475-9225, ISBN 0-7279-1806-0.

Printed by Cadmus Communications Corporation, Richmond, VA, USA
Designed by Pete Wilder, The Designers Collective, London, UK

# Team and Advisors

# Acknowledgements

The BMJ Publishing Group would like to thank United Health Foundation for their advice and support.

The BMJ Publishing Group thanks the following people and organisations for their advice and support: The Cochrane Collaboration, and especially Iain Chalmers, Mike Clarke, Phil Alderson, Peter Langhorne, and Carol Lefebvre; the National Health Service (NHS) Centre for Reviews and Dissemination, and especially Jos Kleijnen and Julie Glanville; the NHS, and especially Tom Mann, Sir John Patteson, Ron Stamp, Ben Toth, Veronica Fraser, Muir Gray, and Nick Rosen; the British National Formulary, and especially Dinesh Mehta, Eric Connor, and John Martin; Martindale: The Complete Drug Reference, and especially Sean Sweetman; the Health Information Research Unit at McMaster University, and especially Brian Haynes and Ann McKibbon; the United Health Foundation (UHF), and especially Reed Tuckson and Yvette Krantz; Bazian Ltd, and especially Anna Donald and Vivek Muthu; Paul Dieppe, Tonya Fancher, and Richard Kravitz who are working with Clinical Evidence to explore ways of presenting evidence on the usefulness of diagnostic test; previous staff who have contributed to this issue; the clinicians, epidemiologists, and members of patient groups who have acted as contributors, advisors, and peer reviewers; and members of our user panels: Lis Hawthorne and colleagues at Didcot Health Centre, Murray Lough and colleagues at Airdrie Health Centre, Alex Potter and colleagues at Clydebank Health Centre, Aimee Brame, Chris Clark, Gloria Daly, Hilary Durrant, Sarah Gwynne, James Harper, Diane Hickford, Sarosh Irani, Alison Kedward, Denise Knight, Sarah Lourenco, Vina Mayor, Michael Murphy, Ross Overshott, Deborah Rigby, and Catherine Tighe.

The BMJ Publishing Group values the ongoing support it has received from the global medical community for *Clinical Evidence*. We are grateful to the clinicians and patients who have taken part in focus groups, which are crucial to the development of *Clinical Evidence*. Finally, we would like to acknowledge the readers who have taken the time to send us their comments and suggestions.

The BMJ Publishing Group wishes to thank United Health Foundation for its efforts in providing educational funding which has allowed the wide dissemination of this valuable resource to millions of physicians and health professionals in the USA.

# Contents

*These topics appear on the website but not in this paper edition.

# Welcome to Issue 11

**Welcome to Issue 11 of *Clinical Evidence*, the international source of the best available evidence on the effects of common clinical interventions. *Clinical Evidence* summarises the current state of knowledge and uncertainty about the prevention and treatment of clinical conditions, based on thorough searches and appraisal of the literature. It is neither a text book of medicine, nor a set of guidelines. It describes the best available evidence from systematic reviews, RCTs, and observational studies where appropriate, and if there is no good evidence it says so.**

## SUPPORTING EVIDENCE BASED DECISIONS

*Clinical Evidence* is intended as a tool for clinicians, and thereby patients, to help them make evidence based healthcare decisions. Our task is to provide information that is as accessible as possible without undue simplification. We aim to support the partnership between clinicians and patients that lies at the heart of good health care. We are working towards a future in which the information in *Clinical Evidence* can be personalised and synchronised with the electronic patient record, acknowledging that most interactions between patients and clinicians are complex and that 'evidence' is only one part of the equation.

In a truly knowledge based health system, the flow of knowledge would form a virtuous circle or (as characterised in figure 1) a figure of eight. Healthcare providers and patients generate questions during consultations. If there aren't ready answers in evidence based guidelines or handbooks, questions should be assessed by systematic review of the literature. Systematic reviews may identify good evidence to support clinical decisions, in which case this can be fed into practice. If a systematic review finds insufficient evidence to support a clinical decision, this represents a gap in our knowledge base, which should be fed into the research agenda. Ultimately, new research should be incorporated into further systematic reviews and the results of these used to guide practice. And so the cycle continues. The quality of information available at each stage depends on the quality of the information provided by the stage before.

Figure 1

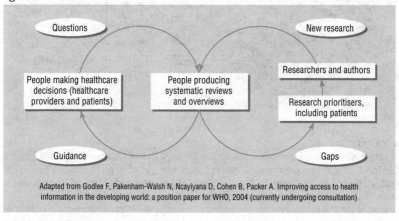

Adapted from Godlee F, Pakenham-Walsh N, Ncayiyana D, Cohen B, Packer A. Improving access to health information in the developing world: a position paper for WHO, 2004 (currently undergoing consultation)

What is presented in the figure as a unidirectional flow is in reality much more complex. Information flows within and between groups in ways that are now being characterised as local information cycles. A completely inclusive information cycle exists within the world of academic research, where all authors are readers and all readers potential authors.

But information cycles also exist, or can be established, between researchers, systematic reviewers, funders of research, healthcare providers, and patients. These information cycles have the potential to greatly increase the relevance and reliability of information about health care, and to build skills, understanding, and 'buy in' that will encourage the use of that information.

*Clinical Evidence* aims to establish and strengthen such information cycles. It works closely with users to identify clinical questions, and it is now working with the UK National Coordinating Centre for Health Technology Assessment to feed the gaps it identifies in the evidence back into the UK research agenda.

## HOW MUCH DO WE KNOW?

So what can *Clinical Evidence* tell us about the state of our current knowledge? What proportion of commonly used treatments are supported by good evidence, what proportion should not be used or used only with caution, and how big are the gaps in our knowledge? A quick scan of the 2148 treatments covered in Issue 11 shows that 329 (15%) are rated as beneficial, 457 (21%) likely to be beneficial, 164 (8%) as trade off between benefits and harms, 106 (5%) unlikely to be beneficial, 94 (4%) likely to be ineffective or harmful, and 998 (47%), the largest proportion) as unknown effectiveness (see figure 2). Dividing treatments into categories is never easy. It always involves a degree of subjective judgement and is sometimes controversial. We do it because users tell us it is helpful. The figures above suggest that the research community has a large task ahead and that most decisions about treatments still rest on the individual judgements of clinicians and patients.

Figure 2

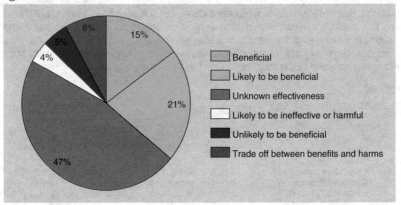

ACCESSIBILITY

*Clinical Evidence* is currently available in five formats: the full text and Concise books; the CD-ROM, which is supplied with Concise; a version for PDA; and the website (www.clinicalevidence.com). Our website has just been redesigned and improved in response to user feedback, and further enhancements are planned throughout this year.

Whichever the format, we recognise that accessing the sort of information contained in *Clinical Evidence* can be challenging, even for experienced users. We are therefore working on making the text as readable as possible. Future issues of *Clinical Evidence* will see more of the numbers presented in data tables rather than in the text, and more use of expert commentary to highlight the main clinical messages. We would welcome your views on other ways in which we can make the information as accessible as possible.

## UPDATE CYCLE

We update the *Clinical Evidence* website monthly, and produce twice yearly paper versions: full text and Concise. Each chapter is now updated every 12 months, and we will shortly be adding clinical alerts to the website to let users know about important studies that are published between updates. With each update we increase the coverage and include stronger information about the adverse effects of treatments.

The content of *Clinical Evidence* Issue 11 is a snapshot of all content that was ready for publication in February 2004. Fourteen new chapters have been added since Issue 10: acute cholecystitis, altitude sickness, athlete's foot, cataract, constipation in adults, dengue fever, ectopic pregnancy, irritable bowel syndrome, jet lag, neonatal jaundice, *Pneumocystis carinii* pneumonia in people with HIV, postnatal depression, stress incontinence, and varicocele. In addition, 109 chapters have been updated, and by the time this reaches you more new and updated chapters will have been posted on the website (www.clinicalevidence.com).

## INTERNATIONAL REACH

*Clinical Evidence* has an international circulation. In the USA 500 000 copies of Concise are circulated by United Health Foundation. The UK NHS distributes 50 000 copies of the Concise edition to clinicians in England. This is accompanied by free online access to everyone in England and Wales. *Clinical Evidence* is now complemented by free access to *Best Treatments* through NHS Direct Online (www.besttreatments.co.uk). *Best Treatments* contains 60 chronic conditions comprehensively rewritten from the patient perspective and also provides information on operations and tests.

Thanks to the BMA, 14 000 UK medical students receive a copy of the full text edition. And thanks to the Italian Ministry of Health and the work of the Italian Cochrane Centre, 300 000 Italian doctors receive a copy of *Clinical Evidence Conciso* and CD-ROM,[1] both translated into Italian.

*Clinical Evidence* is also available in other non-English language editions. The Spanish translation (thanks to the Iberoamerican Cochrane Centre and MediLegis) now comes in all formats—full, concise, CD-ROM, and online.[2] The full text is available in Japanese,[3] and Russian (seven broad specialty editions).[4] The Concise edition is available in German,[5] and French (both with CD-ROM in English).[6]

Finally, *Clinical Evidence* online continues to be available free to people in developing countries as part of the HINARI initiative by the World Health Organization and the BMJ Publishing Group. Details of those countries that qualify are available from the *Clinical Evidence* website (www.clinicalevidence.com).

## FEEDBACK

Our newly enhanced website aims to encourage feedback, all of which we welcome. If you have any comments on any of the material in *Clinical Evidence*, think that any important evidence has been missed, or have suggestions for new topics or questions please let us know. You can contact us at CEfeedback@bmjgroup.com or contact the deputy editor, David Tovey, on +44 (0)20 7383 6043. Many thanks to all of you who have already sent in your comments. Readers who would like to contribute either as authors or peer reviewers are invited to send their CV to Claire Folkes at cfolkes@bmjgroup.com

### References

1. *Clinical Evidence Conciso: La fonte delle migliori prove de efficacia per la pratica clinica.* Milan, Italy: Centro Cochrane Italiano/Editore Italiano/Editore Zadig, 2003.
2. *Evidencia Clínica.* Barcelona, Spain/Bogotá , Colombia: Asociacón Colaboración Cochrane Iberoamerican/Legis, 2004.
3. *Clinical Evidence* (Japanese edition). Tokyo, Japan: Nikkei Medical, 2004.
4. *Dokazatel'naya meditsina.* Moscow, Russia: Media Sphera Publishing Group, 2003.
5. *Kompendium evidenzbasierte Medizin.* Bern, Switzerland Verlag Hans Huber, 2004.
6. *Décider pour traiter abrégé.* Meudon, France: RanD, 2004.

# A Guide to Clinical Evidence Concise

*Clinical Evidence Concise* is an index of the summary information from each chapter in *Clinical Evidence* Issue 11. It contains evidence relating to hundreds of therapeutic or preventative interventions, derived from thousands of original studies, and presents it in around 500 pages. For each condition, interventions are categorised according to whether they have been found to be effective or not. The full evidence detail behind these summaries, including clinical questions, figures, tables, and appendices, are featured on the accompanying CD-ROM, along with quantified, referenced, and up to date information about each condition. The full evidence is also available by subscription to our full text paper version.

Making summaries involves discarding detail, and users of *Clinical Evidence Concise* need to be aware of the limitations of the evidence that is presented. It is not possible to make global statements that are both useful and apply to every patient or clinical context that occur in practice. For example, when stating that we found evidence that a drug is beneficial, we mean that there is evidence that the drug has been shown to deliver more benefits than harms when assessed in at least one subgroup of people, using at least one outcome at a particular point in time. It does not mean that the drug will be effective in all people given that treatment or that other outcomes will be improved, or even that the same outcome will be improved at a different time after the treatment.

## MEASURE OF TREATMENT EFFECTS

The dilemma is how to present summaries that are useful but not misleading. We have experimented with providing statements with no numerical information at all, with NNTs only, with a batch of absolute and relative risks, or with just the odds ratio. Each measure has its advantages and disadvantages, and not all are available from the included studies. Quantitative results may be misleading in the absence of discussion of their precision, reliability, and applicability. In *Clinical Evidence Concise*, we present non-numerical information only. Detailed quantitative results are presented on the CD-ROM, where we are able to discuss their interpretation in more detail. Your suggestions on improvements are welcome.

## USING CLINICAL EVIDENCE CONCISE AND COMPANION CD-ROM

*Clinical Evidence Concise* is intended to be used as a first point of call when trying to decide what the options for treatment might be. A detailed exploration of the evidence will require looking up the detail on the CD-ROM, the full print version, or *Clinical Evidence* online. The electronic versions link, whenever possible, to abstracts of the original research in PubMed or published online versions. In this way, *Clinical Evidence* is also designed to act as a pointer, connecting the clinician rapidly to the relevant original evidence.

## INDEX PAGE

Each topic on the CD-ROM contains an index page listing interventions within their assigned categories of whether they have been found to be effective or not. Key messages summarising the evidence for each intervention are listed below the categorisation table. The full evidence detail supporting the categorisation, consisting of the question, a summary statement, benefits, harms, and a comment can be accessed by a hyperlink from the categorisation table. We would value your feedback on the presentation of interventions in future issues.

## CATEGORISATION

We have developed these categories of effectiveness from one of the Cochrane Collaboration's first and most popular products, *A guide to effective care in pregnancy and childbirth*.[1] The categories are explained in the table below.

| TABLE | Categorisation of treatment effects in *Clinical Evidence* |
|---|---|
| **Beneficial** | Interventions for which effectiveness has been demonstrated by clear evidence from RCTs, and for which expectation of harms is small compared with the benefits. |
| **Likely to be beneficial** | Interventions for which effectiveness is less well established than for those listed under "beneficial". |
| **Trade off between benefits and harms** | Interventions for which clinicians and patients should weigh up the beneficial and harmful effects according to individual circumstances and priorities. |
| **Unknown effectiveness** | Interventions for which there are currently insufficient data or data of inadequate quality. |
| **Unlikely to be beneficial** | Interventions for which lack of effectiveness is less well established than for those listed under "likely to be ineffective or harmful". |
| **Likely to be ineffective or harmful** | Interventions for which ineffectiveness or harmfulness has been demonstrated by clear evidence. |

Fitting interventions into these categories is not always straightforward. For one thing, the categories represent a mix of several hierarchies: the level of benefit (or harm), the level of evidence (RCT or observational data), and the level of certainty around the finding (represented by the confidence interval). Another problem is that much of the evidence that is most relevant to clinical decisions relates to comparisons between different interventions rather than to comparison with placebo or no intervention. Where necessary, we have indicated the comparisons. A third problem is that interventions may have been tested, or found to be effective, in only one group of people, such as those at high risk of an outcome. Again, we have indicated this where possible. But perhaps most difficult of all has been trying to maintain consistency across different topics. We are working on refining the criteria for putting interventions under each category.

## REFERENCES
Full references to the individual studies cited in *Clinical Evidence Concise* are available on the accompanying CD-ROM.

References cited in the definition, incidence/prevalence, aetiology/risk factors, and prognosis sections are listed in the text but are available as hyperlinks from the equivalent section on the CD-ROM.

## TOPIC GLOSSARY
Topics may contain glossary listings; these are available in full on the CD-ROM and can be accessed from the index page of each topic or as hyperlinks from the equivalent section on the CD-ROM. Terms with corresponding CD-ROM definitions will be flagged up with a symbol **G**.

## MAIN GLOSSARY
Words and terms that are used throughout *Clinical Evidence* are listed in the main glossary on the companion CD-ROM.

## TABLES AND FIGURES
The presence of figures and tables on the CD-ROM are flagged up in a similar way to the glossary with the use of **F** for figures and **T** for tables.

**FEEDBACK**

We would like feedback from CD-ROM users, in order to improve future releases. Simply follow the guidance on the CD-ROM welcome page. This process should take up just 10 minutes of your time.

The design of *Clinical Evidence Concise* will change progressively over the next few years. We will perform evaluation studies ourselves to measure the relevance of the material to the questions that are being asked in practice, the ease of use, and to check that the message extracted from the summary corresponds closely with that intended. If you have any comments, suggestions, or detect any errors, please let us know at CEfeedback@bmjgroup.com.

For more information on any of our methods or processes, please visit our website at www.clinicalevidence.com.

Please refer to the CD-ROM for more information about *Clinical Evidence*.

**REFERENCES**

1. Enkin M, Keirse M, Renfrew M, et al. *A guide to effective care in pregnancy and childbirth*. Oxford: Oxford University Press, 1998.

### Search date October 2002

*Graham Mead, James Woodcock, and Charles Young*

## Effects of treatments for early stage aggressive non-Hodgkin's lymphoma (NHL) in younger adults

### LIKELY TO BE BENEFICIAL

### Short schedule CHOP plus radiotherapy versus longer schedule CHOP alone

One RCT found that short schedule CHOP🅖 plus radiotherapy significantly improved 5 year survival with the addition of radiotherapy compared with longer schedule CHOP alone. It included many older people. Longer schedule CHOP increased the risk of congestive heart failure and possibly the risk of myelosuppression.

### UNKNOWN EFFECTIVENESS

### ACVBP versus m-BACOD

One RCT, mostly in people with early stage🅖 disease, found no significant difference in 5 year survival between ACVBP🅖 and m-BACOD🅖.

### Chemotherapy versus radiotherapy

We found no systematic review or RCTs of chemotherapy compared with radiotherapy.

### CVP versus BACOP

Subgroup analysis in one RCT found no significant difference in complete remission between CVP🅖 and BACOP🅖.

## Effects of treatments for advanced stage aggressive NHL in younger adults

### LIKELY TO BE BENEFICIAL

### CHOP versus BCOP

One RCT compared CHOP with BCOP🅖. Subgroup analysis of people with advanced stage🅖 disease found significantly higher complete response with CHOP. Subgroup analysis in people younger than 60 years found similar results but the difference was not significant. However, 20% of people were excluded for poorly defined reasons.

### CHOP versus HOP

One poorly reported RCT, including people with all grades of NHL, found significantly higher complete response with CHOP with HOP🅖. However, 20% of people were excluded for a variety of reasons.

### CHOP versus MEV

One RCT, including some older people and people who relapsed after treatment for early stage disease, found weak evidence of a survival benefit with CHOP compared with MEV🅖. Subgroup analysis in people with advanced disease found that more people achieved complete response with CHOP. ▶

# Non-Hodgkin's lymphoma

## TRADE OFF BETWEEN BENEFITS AND HARMS

### CHOP versus MACOP-B

One RCT, including some people aged over 65 years, found no significant difference in 3 year survival between four chemotherapy regimens: CHOP, MACOP-B⊙, m-BACOD⊙, and ProMACE-CytaBOM⊙. It found limited evidence of greater toxicity with MACOP-B and m-BACOD compared with CHOP and ProMACE-CytaBOM. A second RCT, including some people with early disease and some older people, found no significant difference in complete response. Subgroup analysis in younger people found significantly improved 5 year survival with MACOP-B. A third RCT, including people with stage II disease, found no significant difference in complete response. Subgroup analysis from one centre found better quality of life and physical function with MACOP-B compared with CHOP. These two RCTs found a different range of adverse events with CHOP compared with MACOP-B.

## UNKNOWN EFFECTIVENESS

### CHOP versus CHOP-B

One RCT in a population of mixed ages found no significant difference in 5 year mortality between CHOP and CHOP-B⊙.

### CHOP versus CHOP-M

One poorly reported RCT in a population of mixed ages and disease stages found similar mortality at 36 months with CHOP and CHOP-M⊙.

### CHOP versus CHOP plus interferon

We found no systematic review or RCTs of CHOP versus CHOP plus interferon.

### CHOP versus CHOP plus monoclonal antibodies

We found one systematic review, which found no RCTs of CHOP versus CHOP plus monoclonal antibodies.

### CHOP versus CHOP/VIA

One RCT, including people with stage II disease, found no significant difference in 3 year survival between CHOP and CHOP/VIA⊙.

### CHOP versus CIOP

One RCT of people with Kiel classification intermediate grade lymphoma, including some people with stage II disease and some people over 65 years of age, found similar overall survival at 42 months with CHOP and CIOP⊙.

### CHOP versus m-BACOD

We found one RCT comparing four different chemotherapy regimens (see CHOP versus MACOP-B above). A second RCT comparing CHOP with m-BACOD, including older adults and with a high withdrawal rate, found no significant difference in mortality at 4 or 5.3 years.

### CHOP versus PACEBOM

One RCT of people with intermediate grade lymphoma, including some people with stage II disease, found no difference in 5 or 8 year mortality in the total population. Subgroup analysis found mortality was lower with PACEBOM⊙ than CHOP in people with stage IV disease at 8 years' follow up, but the difference was not significant.

### CHOP versus ProMACE-CytaBOM

We found one RCT comparing four different chemotherapy regimens (see CHOP v MACOP-B above). A second RCT, including some people with stage II disease and some people over 65 years of age, found longer median survival with CHOP compared with ProMACE-CytaBOM, but significance was not assessed.

**DEFINITION**

NHL consists of a complex group of cancers arising mainly from B lymphocytes and occasionally from T lymphocytes (15% of cases). NHL usually develops in lymph nodes but can arise in other tissues almost anywhere in the body. NHL is divided according to histology and stage (spread). Histology: Historically histology was divided into aggressive and low grade disease. This chapter focuses on the most common aggressive lymphoma — diffuse large B cell lymphoma in the WHO❶,[1] and REAL classification systems❶. Interpretation of older studies is complicated by changes in classification systems and diagnostic techniques. We have included studies using older systems if they are primarily in people with the following types of aggressive lymphoma: Working Formulation classification — primarily intermediate grades (grades E–H❶);[2] Kiel classification — centroblastic, immunoblastic, and anaplastic❶;[3] Rappaport classification — diffuse histiocytic, diffuse lymphocytic poorly differentiated, and diffuse mixed (lymphocytic and histiocytic❶).[4] There is no direct correspondence between the terms used in the different classification systems and attempts to generalise results must be treated with caution.[1–4] Stage: Historically, NHL has been staged according to disease spread using the Ann Arbor❶ system❶.[5] Ann Arbor stages I and II correspond to early disease, whereas stages III and IV are advanced disease. However, people with bulky disease will usually be treated as having advanced disease even if the stage is only I or II. There is also substantial variation in prognosis within each stage. More recent studies assess stage using a prognostic indicator. We excluded RCTs that were primarily in children (< 16 years old), older people (> 65 years old), people with HIV infection, and people who had received prior treatment except local radiotherapy. We also excluded RCTs of maintenance treatment and RCTs with fewer than 50 people in each arm. In RCTs of mixed populations we have reported subgroup analysis in the population of interest, if available.

**INCIDENCE/ PREVALENCE**

NHL occurs more commonly in males than females, and is increasing in incidence in the Western world at about 4% a year. It is the seventh most common cancer in the UK consisting of 8680 new cases in 1998 (3% of cancers) and causing 4500 deaths in 2000.[6]

**AETIOLOGY/ RISK FACTORS**

Unknown for most people. Surveys have implicated pesticides and hair dyes. Incidence is higher in people who are immunosuppressed.

**PROGNOSIS**

Relates to histological type, stage, age, performance status, and lactate dehydrogenase levels. High grade lymphomas, particularly diffuse large B cell lymphoma and Burkitt's lymphoma, have a high cure rate, with both initial and salvage (high dose) chemotherapy.[7] CHOP is the standard treatment for aggressive❶ NHL and placebo controlled trials would be considered unethical.

Please refer to CD-ROM for full text and references.

# Sickle cell disease

Search date January 2003

*Martin M Meremikwu*

---

## *What are the effects of interventions to prevent sickle cell crisis and other acute complications of sickle cell disease?*

### BENEFICIAL

**Penicillin prophylaxis in children under 5 years of age**

One systematic review found that penicillin prophylaxis in children younger than 5 years reduced the risk of invasive pneumococcal infections and related deaths.

### LIKELY TO BE BENEFICIAL

**Hydroxyurea**

Two RCTs found that hydroxyurea reduced the risk of acute chest syndrome and the need for blood transfusion in people with sickle cell disease. A non-significant reduction was also found for stroke, hepatic sequestration, and death related to sickle cell disease. Hydroxyurea has been associated with neutropenia, hair loss, skin rash, and gastrointestinal disturbances. We found no evidence on the long term effects of hydroxyurea.

### UNKNOWN EFFECTIVENESS

**Pneumococcal vaccine**

One RCT found insufficient evidence to determine whether polysaccharide pneumococcal vaccine is effective. We found no RCTs of conjugate pneumococcal vaccine in sickle cell disease. Three RCTs found that pneumococcal vaccines caused local reaction and fever but no severe adverse events.

**Malaria chemoprophylaxis**

We found no RCTs of malaria chemoprophylaxis in people with sickle cell disease.

**Avoidance of cold environment; limiting physical exercise**

We found no RCTs or observational studies of sufficient quality about the effects of this intervention in preventing sickle cell crisis and other life threatening complications.

---

## *What are the effects of interventions to treat pain in sickle cell crisis?*

### LIKELY TO BE BENEFICIAL

**Controlled release oral morphine given after an intravenous bolus dose of morphine**

One RCT found that controlled release oral morphine was as effective as intravenous morphine after an intravenous loading dose of morphine at onset of treatment.

### TRADE OFF BETWEEN BENEFITS AND HARMS

**Corticosteroid as adjunct to narcotic analgesics**

One RCT found that intravenous methylprednisolone improved pain relief as an adjunct to intravenous morphine, but was associated with a high rate of recurrence of crisis.

◀ **Patient controlled analgesia**

Two small RCTs have found no significant difference between patient controlled analgesia discussing either meperidine or morphine and intermittent parenteral treatment. The incidence of adverse effects was also equal in both regimens.

## UNKNOWN EFFECTIVENESS

### Acupuncture

We found no systematic reviews or RCTs on the effects of acupuncture in sickle cell disease.

### Codeine

We found no systematic reviews or RCTs on the effects of codeine in sickle cell disease.

### Diflunisal

One RCT found no significant difference between oral diflunisal and placebo as an adjunct to meperidine in sickle cell crisis.

### Ketorolac

Four RCTs found insufficient and conflicting evidence on the pain relieving effect of ketorolac in sickle cell crisis.

### Oxygen

Two RCTs found insufficient evidence on the effects of oxygen therapy as an adjunct to analgesics. The RCTs excluded patients with acute chest syndrome.

### Rehydration

We found no systematic reviews or RCTs on the effects of rehydration in sickle cell crisis.

### Aspirin; ibuprofen; paracetamol

We found no RCTs on the effects of these analgesics in sickle cell crisis.

**DEFINITION**    **Sickle cell disease** refers to a group of disorders caused by inheritance of a pair of abnormal haemoglobin genes, including the sickle cell gene. It is characterised by chronic haemolytic anaemia and episodic clinical events called "crises". [1] Vaso-occlusive painful crisis is the most common and occurs when abnormal red cells clog small vessels causing tissue ischaemia. The others are hyper haemolytic crisis (excessive haemolysis), acute chest syndrome🅖, sequestration crisis🅖, and aplastic crisis🅖. Infections such as pneumonia, septicaemia, meningitis, and osteomyelitis are common in people with sickle cell disease. A common variant of sickle cell disease, also characterised by haemolytic anaemia, occurs in people with one sickle and one thalassaemia gene. **Sickle cell trait** occurs in people with one sickle gene and one normal gene. People with sickle cell trait do not have any clinical manifestation of illness. This topic covers people with sickle cell disease with or without thalassaemia.

**INCIDENCE/**    Sickle cell disease is most common among people living in or originating from
**PREVALENCE**    sub-Saharan Africa.[2] The disorder also affects people of Mediterranean, Caribbean, Middle Eastern, and Asian origin. The sickle ceel gene is most common in areas where malaria is endemic: sickle cell trait affects about 10–30% of people in tropical Africa.[3] Sickle cell disease affects and estimated 1–2% (120 000) of new borns in Africa[3] and 250 000 newborns worldwide. About 60 000 people in the USA[4] and 10 000 in the UK[5] suffer from the disease. ▶

# Sickle cell disease

**AETIOLOGY/ RISK FACTORS**

Factors that precipitate or modulate the occurrence of sickle cell crisis are not fully understood, but infections, hypoxia, dehydration, acidosis, stress (such as major surgery or childbirth), and cold are believed to play some role. In tropical Africa, malaria is the most common cause of anaemic and vaso-occlusive crisis.[3] High levels of fetal haemoglobin Ⓖ is known to ameliorate the severity and incidence of sickle cell crisis and other complications of the disease.

**PROGNOSIS**

People affected by sickle cell disease are predisposed to bacterial infections, especially to those caused by encapsulated organisms such as *Pneumococcus*, *Haemophilus influenzae*, *Meningococcus*, and *Salmonella* species. Severe bacterial infections such as pneumonia, meningitis, and septicaemia are common causes of morbidity and mortality, especially among young children.[6] About 10% of children with sickle cell anaemia may develop a stroke, and more than half of these may suffer recurrent strokes.[7] Abnormal features of cerebral blood vessels shown by transcranial Doppler scan predict a high risk of stroke in children with sickle cell disease.[8] Frequent episodes of crisis, infections, and organ damage reduce the quality of life of people with sickle cell disease. High rate of painful crisis is an index of clinical severity that correlates with early death. Life expectancy remains low, especially in communities with poor access to health services. In some parts of Africa, about 50% of children with sickle cell disease die before their first birthday.[3] The average life expectancy for men and women with sickle cell disease in the USA is about 42 and 48 years, respectively.[9] Frequent blood transfusions could increase the risk of immune reactions and infections, such as HIV and hepatitis B or C viruses, and Chagas' disease.

Please refer to CD-ROM for full text and references.

### Search date February 2003

*Nicolas Danchin, Edoardo De Benedetti, and Philip Urban*

## What treatments improve outcomes in acute myocardial infarction?

### BENEFICIAL

#### Angiotensin converting enzyme inhibitors

One systematic review in people treated within 14 days of acute myocardial infarction has found that angiotensin converting enzyme inhibitors reduce mortality after 6 weeks compared with placebo. However, a non-systematic review found that angiotensin converting enzyme inhibitors increase persistent hypotension and renal dysfunction at 6 weeks compared with placebo.

#### Aspirin

One systematic review in people with acute myocardial infarction has found that aspirin reduces mortality, reinfarction, and stroke at 1 month compared with placebo.

#### β Blockers

We found evidence from systematic reviews and one subsequent RCT that β blockers reduced mortality compared with no β blockers. One RCT in people receiving thrombolytic treatment found that immediate treatment with metoprolol reduced rates of reinfarction and chest pain at 6 days compared with delayed treatment, but had no significant effect on mortality at 6 days or at 1 year.

#### Primary percutaneous transluminal coronary angioplasty versus thrombolysis (performed in specialist centres)

One systematic review has found that primary percutaneous transluminal coronary angioplasty reduces a combined outcome of death, non-fatal reinfarction, and stroke compared with thrombolysis.

#### Thrombolysis

Two non-systematic reviews in people with acute myocardial infarction and ST elevation or bundle branch block on their initial electrocardiogram found that prompt thrombolytic treatment (within 6 hours and perhaps up to 12 hours and longer after the onset of symptoms) reduces mortality compared with placebo. RCTs comparing different types of thrombolytic agents with each other found no significant difference in mortality. One non-systematic review found that thrombolytic treatment increased the risk of stroke or major bleeding compared with control. The review also found that intracranial haemorrhage is more common in people of advanced age and low body weight; those with hypertension on admission, and those given tissue plasminogen activator rather than another thrombolytic agent. One non-systematic review found conflicting results for intracerebral haemorrhage with bolus treatment compared with infusion of thrombolytic agents.

### LIKELY TO BE BENEFICIAL

#### Nitrates (in the absence of thrombolysis)

One systematic review of the trials conducted in the prethrombolytic era found that nitrates reduced mortality in people with acute myocardial infarction compared with placebo.

# Acute myocardial infarction

## UNLIKELY TO BE BENEFICIAL

### Nitrates (in addition to thrombolysis)

Two RCTs in people with acute myocardial infarction (after thrombolysis was introduced) found no significant difference in mortality between nitrates and placebo.

## TRADE OFF BETWEEN BENEFITS AND HARMS

### Glycoprotein IIb/IIIa inhibitors

Two large RCTs have found that combined treatment with half dose thrombolysis plus abciximab does not reduce mortality at 1 month compared with full dose thrombolysis in people with acute myocardial infarction, but may prevent non-fatal cardiovascular events. However, the RCTs found that combined treatment with abciximab increased bleeding complications, particularly extracranial haemorrhage. Three RCTs found conflicting evidence about the benefits of adding abciximab to primary coronary angioplasty or stenting in people with acute myocardial infarction, although all found that adding abciximab increased bleeding risk.

## LIKELY TO BE INEFFECTIVE OR HARMFUL

### Calcium channel blockers

We found evidence that neither dihydropyridines nor verapamil reduce mortality compared with placebo. One RCT found limited evidence that, in people with left ventricular dysfunction, nifedipine given in the first few days after myocardial infarction may increase mortality compared with placebo.

---

## Which treatments improve outcomes for cardiogenic shock after acute myocardial infarction?

## BENEFICIAL

### Early invasive cardiac revascularisation

One large RCT has found that early invasive cardiac revascularisation❻ reduces mortality after 6 and 12 months compared with medical treatment alone in people with cardiogenic shock within 48 hours of acute myocardial infarction. A second smaller RCT found similar results, although the difference was not significant.

## UNKNOWN EFFECTIVENESS

### Intra-aortic balloon counterpulsation

We found limited evidence from an abstract of an RCT of no significant difference in mortality at 6 months between intra-aortic balloon counterpulsation plus thrombolysis versus thrombolysis alone in people with cardiogenic shock.

### Early cardiac surgery; positive inotropes and vasodilators; pulmonary artery catheterization; ventricular assistance devices and cardiac transplantation

We found no evidence from RCTs about the effects of these interventions.

## UNLIKELY TO BE BENEFICIAL

### Thrombolysis

Subgroup analysis of one RCT found no significant difference in mortality after 21 days between thrombolysis and no thrombolysis in people with cardiogenic shock.

# Acute myocardial infarction

◀ **DEFINITION**   **Acute myocardial infarction (AMI):** The sudden occlusion of a coronary artery leading to myocardial cell death. **Cardiogenic shock:** Defined clinically as a poor cardiac output plus evidence of tissue hypoxia that is not improved by correcting reduced intravascular volume.[1] When a pulmonary artery catheter is used, cardiogenic shock may be defined as a cardiac index❻ below 2.2 L/minute/m$^2$ despite an elevated pulmonary capillary wedge pressure ($\geq$ 15 mm Hg).[1–3]

**INCIDENCE/**   **AMI:** Acute myocardial infarction is one of the most common causes of
**PREVALENCE**   mortality worldwide. In 1990, ischaemic heart disease was the world's leading cause of death, accounting for about 6.3 million deaths. The age standardised incidence varies among and within countries.[4] Each year, about 900 000 people in the USA experience AMI, about 225 000 of whom die. About half of these people die within 1 hour of symptoms and before reaching a hospital emergency room.[5] Event rates increase with age for both sexes and are higher in men than in women and in poorer than richer people at all ages. The incidence of death from AMI has fallen in many Western countries over the past 20 years. **Cardiogenic shock:** Cardiogenic shock occurs in about 7% of people admitted to hospital with AMI.[6] Of these, about half have established cardiogenic shock at the time of admission to hospital, and most of the others develop it during the first 24–48 hours after their admission.[7]

**AETIOLOGY/**   **AMI:** See aetiology/risk factors under primary prevention, p 28. The immediate
**RISK FACTORS**   mechanism of AMI is rupture or erosion of an atheromatous plaque causing thrombosis and occlusion of coronary arteries and myocardial cell death. Factors that may convert a stable plaque into an unstable plaque (the "active plaque") have yet to be fully elucidated. Shear stresses, inflammation, and autoimmunity have been proposed. The changing rates of coronary heart disease in different populations are only partly explained by changes in the standard risk factors for ischaemic heart disease (particularly a fall in blood pressure and smoking). **Cardiogenic shock:** Cardiogenic shock after AMI usually follows a reduction in functional ventricular myocardium, and is caused by left ventricular infarction (79% of people with cardiogenic shock) more often than by right ventricular infarction (3% of people with cardiogenic shock).[8] Cardiogenic shock after AMI may also be caused by cardiac structural defects, such as mitral valve regurgitation due to papillary muscle dysfunction (7% of people with cardiogenic shock), ventricular septal rupture (4% of people with cardiogenic shock), or cardiac tamponade after free cardiac wall rupture (1% of people with cardiogenic shock). Major risk factors for cardiogenic shock after AMI are previous myocardial infarction, diabetes mellitus, advanced age, hypotension, tachycardia or bradycardia, congestive heart failure with Killip class II–III❻, and low left ventricular ejection fraction (ejection fraction < 35%).[7,8]

**PROGNOSIS**   **AMI:** May lead to a host of mechanical and cardiac electrical complications, including death, ventricular dysfunction, congestive heart failure, fatal and non-fatal arrhythmias, valvular dysfunction, myocardial rupture, and cardiogenic shock. **Cardiogenic shock:** Mortality rates for people in hospital with cardiogenic shock after AMI vary between 50–80%.[2,3,6,7] Most deaths occur within 48 hours of the onset of shock ❻. People surviving until discharge from hospital have a reasonable long term prognosis (88% survival at 1 year).[10]

---

Please refer to CD-ROM for full text and references.

# Angina (unstable)

**Search date November 2002**

*Madhu Natarajan*

---

## What are the effects of treatments?

### BENEFICIAL

**Aspirin**

One systematic review has found that aspirin reduces the risk of death, myocardial infarction, and stroke compared with placebo in people with unstable angina. The evidence suggests no added cardiovascular benefit, and possible added harm, from doses of aspirin over 325 mg daily.

### LIKELY TO BE BENEFICIAL

**Clopidogrel/ticlopidine**

Two RCTs have found that clopidogrel or ticlopidine reduce mortality and myocardial infarction compared with placebo or conventional treatment alone. One RCT found that clopidogrel increased major bleeding, but not haemorrhagic strokes compared with placebo after 6–9 months. Ticlopidine may cause reversible neutropenia. These drugs may be an alternative in people who are intolerant of or allergic to aspirin.

**Direct thrombin inhibitors**

One systematic review has found that treatment with direct thrombin inhibitors for 7 days reduces death and myocardial infarction compared with heparin after 30 days.

**Intravenous glycoprotein IIb/IIIa inhibitors**

One systematic review found that intravenous glycoprotein IIb/IIIa inhibitors reduced the risk of death or myocardial infarction compared with placebo but increased the risk of major bleeding complications.

**Low molecular weight heparins**

One systematic review in people taking aspirin has found that adding low molecular weight heparin reduces the risk of death or myocardial infarction compared with placebo or no treatment and does not significantly increase bleeding complications in the first 7 days after unstable angina. However, it found that longer term treatment with low molecular weight heparin did not significantly reduce death or myocardial infarction compared with placebo. One systematic review found no significant difference between low molecular weight heparin and unfractionated heparin in death or myocardial infarction. Long term low molecular weight heparin increased major bleeding compared with placebo, but not compared with unfractionated heparin.

**Unfractionated heparin added to aspirin**

One systematic review has found that adding unfractionated heparin to aspirin for 7 days in people with unstable angina reduced death or myocardial infarction at 1 week. However, a second review found no significant effect after 12 weeks.

### UNKNOWN EFFECTIVENESS

**β Blockers; nitrates**

We found insufficient evidence of effects of these interventions on myocardial infarction or death rates. However, RCTs found that these interventions may reduce frequency and severity of chest pain.

◀ **Routine early invasive treatment**

We found five RCTs that reported on different composite outcomes. Two of these found that early invasive treatment reduced death and other cardiac events compared with conservative treatment at 6 months. However, the remaining three RCTs found no significant difference in death or other cardiac events between early invasive treatment and conservative treatment at 12 months or more.

## UNLIKELY TO BE BENEFICIAL

### Calcium channel blockers

One systematic review found no significant difference between calcium channel blockers and either placebo or standard treatment on mortality or myocardial infarction. Observational studies suggest that short acting dihydropyridine calcium channel blockers may increase mortality.

### Warfarin

One RCT found that adding warfarin to aspirin reduced cardiac events and death after 12 weeks. However, four RCTs found no significant effect after 5 months or more and one RCT found that warfarin was associated with an increase in major bleeding.

## LIKELY TO BE INEFFECTIVE OR HARMFUL

### Oral glycoprotein IIb/IIIa inhibitors

One systematic review found that the oral glycoprotein IIb/IIIa inhibitor sibrafiban did not reduce the combined outcome of death, myocardial infarction, and recurrent ischaemia compared with aspirin. However, it found that oral glycoprotein IIb/IIIa inhibitors with or without aspirin increased bleeding compared with aspirin alone.

**DEFINITION**  Unstable angina is distinguished from stable angina, acute myocardial infarction, and non-cardiac pain by the pattern of symptoms (characteristic pain present at rest or on lower levels of activity), the severity of symptoms (recently increasing intensity, frequency, or duration), and the absence of persistent ST segment elevation on a resting electrocardiogram. Unstable angina includes a variety of different clinical patterns: angina at rest of up to 1 week of duration; angina increasing in severity to moderate or severe pain; non-Q wave myocardial infarction; and post-myocardial infarction angina continuing for longer than 24 hours.

**INCIDENCE/**  In industrialised countries, the annual incidence of unstable angina is about
**PREVALENCE**  6/10 000 people in the general population.

**AETIOLOGY/**  Risk factors are the same as for other manifestations of ischaemic heart
**RISK FACTORS**  disease: older age, previous atheromatous cardiovascular disease, diabetes mellitus, smoking cigarettes, hypertension, hypercholesterolaemia, male sex, and a family history of ischaemic heart disease. Unstable angina can also occur in association with other disorders of the circulation, including heart valve disease, arrhythmia, and cardiomyopathy.

**PROGNOSIS**  In people taking aspirin, the incidence of serious adverse outcomes (such as death, acute myocardial infarction, or refractory angina requiring emergency revascularisation) is 5–10% within the first 7 days and about 15% at 30 days. Between 5% and 14% of people with unstable angina die in the year after diagnosis, with about half of these deaths occurring within 4 weeks of diagnosis. No single factor identifies people at higher risk of an adverse event. Risk factors include severity of presentation (e.g. duration of pain, speed of progression, evidence of heart failure), medical history (e.g. previous unstable angina, ▶

# Angina (unstable)

acute myocardial infarction, left ventricular dysfunction), other clinical parameters (e.g. age, diabetes), electrocardiogram changes (e.g. severity of ST segment depression, deep T wave inversion, transient ST segment elevation), biochemical parameters (e.g. troponin concentration), and change in clinical status (e.g. recurrent chest pain, silent ischaemia, haemodynamic instability).

Please refer to CD-ROM for full text and references.

## What are the effects of interventions to prevent embolism?

### UNKNOWN EFFECTIVENESS

**Antithrombotic treatment before cardioversion**

We found no RCTs on use of aspirin, heparin, or warfarin as thromboprophylaxis before attempted cardioversion in acute atrial fibrillation.

## What are the effects of interventions for conversion to sinus rhythm?

### TRADE OFF BETWEEN BENEFITS AND HARMS

**Flecainide**

One RCT found that intravenous flecainide increased the proportion of people who reverted to sinus rhythm within 1 hour and in whom the sinus rhythm was maintained after 6 hours compared with placebo. Flecainide has been associated with serious adverse events such as severe hypotension and torsades de point. Two RCTs found that oral flecainide increased the proportion of people who reverted to sinus rhythm within 8 hours compared with intravenous amiodarone. We found insufficient evidence to draw any conclusions about comparisons between intravenous flecainide and intravenous amiodarone and between flecainide and quinidine. Three RCTs found no significant difference in rates of conversion to sinus rhythm between flecainide and propafenone. Flecainide and propafenone are not used in people with known or suspected ischaemic heart disease because they may cause arrhythmias.

**Propafenone**

One systematic review and subsequent RCTs have found that propafenone increased the proportion of people converting to sinus rhythm within 1–4 hours compared with placebo. One RCT in people with onset of atrial fibrillation of less than 48 hours found no significant difference between intravenous propafenone and amiodarone in the proportion of people who converted to sinus rhythm within 1 hour. Another RCT in people with onset of atrial fibrillation of less than 2 weeks found that a higher proportion of people converted to sinus rhythm with oral propafenone within 2.5 hours compared with amiodarone but the difference did not remain significant at 24 hours. Three RCTs found insufficient evidence to compare rates of conversion to sinus rhythm between propafenone and flecqinide. Propafenone and flecainide are not used in people with known or suspected ischaemic heart disease.

### UNKNOWN EFFECTIVENESS

**Amiodarone**

We found insufficient evidence from three RCTs about the effects of amiodarone as a single agent compared with placebo for conversion to sinus rhythm in people with acute atrial fibrillation in people who are haemodynamically stable. Four small RCTs found no significant difference in rate of conversion to sinus rhythm at 24–48 hours for amiodarone compared with digoxin, although the studies may have lacked power to exclude clinically important differences. One small RCT found that amiodarone increased rate of cardioversion compared with verapamil at 3 hours. One RCT in people with onset of atrial fibrillation of less than 48 hours found no ▶

# Atrial fibrillation (acute)

significant difference between intravenous propafenone and amiodarone in conversion to sinus rhythm within 1 hour. Another RCT in people with onset of atrial fibrillation of less than 2 weeks found that a higher proportion of people converted to sinus rhythm with oral propafenone within 2.5 hours compared with amiodarone but the difference did not remain significant at 24 hours. Two RCTs found that intravenous amiodarone reduced the proportion of people who reverted to sinus rhythm within 8 hours compared with oral flecainide. We found insufficient evidence to draw any conclusion between intravenous flecainide compared with intravenous amiodarone. We found no RCTs comparing amiodarone with either DC cardioversion or diltiazem.

### DC cardioversion

W We found no RCTs of DC cardioversion in acute atrial fibrillation in people who are haemodynamically stable.

### Quinidine

We found no RCTs of DC cardioversion that compared quinidine versus placebo. One small RCT in people with onset of atrial fibrillation of less than 48 hours found that quinidine plus digoxin increased the proportion of people converting to sinus rhythm within 12 hours compared with sotalol. We found insufficient evidence to draw any conclusions about comparisons between flecainide and quinidine.

### Sotalol

We found no RCTs comparing sotalol versus placebo. One small RCT in people with onset of atrial fibrillation of less than 48 hours found that quinidine plus digoxin increased the proportion of people who converted to sinus rhythm within 12 hours compared with sotalol.

## UNLIKELY TO BE BENEFICIAL

### Digoxin

We found no placebo controlled RCTs limited to people with acute atrial fibrillation. Three RCTs in people with atrial fibrillation of up to 7 days' duration found no significant difference between digoxin and placebo in conversion to sinus rhythm. Four RCTs found no significant difference between amiodarone and digoxin in conversion to sinus rhythm at 24–48 hours, although these trials may have lacked power to detect clinically important differences.

## What are the effects of interventions to control heart rate?

## LIKELY TO BE BENEFICIAL

### Digoxin

We found no placebo controlled RCTs limited to people with acute atrial fibrillation. Two RCTs found that compared with placebo, digoxin reduced ventricular rate after 30 minutes and after 2 hours in people with atrial fibrillation of up to 7 days' duration. One RCT found that compared with digoxin, intravenous diltiazem reduced heart rate within 5 minutes in people with acute atrial fibrillation and atrial flutter.

### Diltiazem

One RCT in people with atrial fibrillation (of unspecified duration) or atrial flutter❸ found that intravenous diltiazem reduced heart rate in people within 15 minutes compared with placebo. One RCT found that in people with acute atrial fibrillation and atrial flutter, intravenous diltiazem reduced heart rate within 5 minutes compared with intravenous digoxin. One RCT found no significant difference ▶

between intravenous verapamil and intravenous diltiazem in rate control or measures of systolic function in people with acute atrial fibrillation or atrial flutter, but verapamil caused hypotension in some people.

## Timolol

OWe found no RCTs limited to people with acute atrial fibrillation. One small RCT in people with atrial fibrillation of unspecified duration found that intravenous timolol (a   blocker) reduced ventricular rate within 20 minutes compared with placebo.

## Verapamil

Two RCTs found that intravenous verapamil reduced heart rate at 10 or 30 minutes compared with placebo in people with atrial fibrillation or atrial flutter. One RCT in people with atrial fibrillation or acute atrial flutter found no significant difference between intravenous verapamil and intravenous diltiazem in rate control or measures of systolic function, but verapamil caused hypotension in some people. The RCT found that amiodarone increased the rate of cardioversion compared with verapamil at 3 hours.

### UNKNOWN EFFECTIVENESS

## Amiodarone

We found no RCTs examining effects of amiodarone alone on heart rate in people with acute atrial fibrillation.

## Sotalol

We found no RCTs comparing sotalol versus placebo.

| | |
|---|---|
| DEFINITION | **Acute atrial fibrillation** is rapid, irregular, and chaotic atrial activity of less than 48 hours' duration. It includes both the first symptomatic onset of chronic, or persistent, atrial fibrillation**G** and episodes of paroxysmal atrial fibrillation**G**. It is sometimes difficult to distinguish new onset of atrial fibrillation from long standing atrial fibrillation that was previously undiagnosed. Atrial fibrillation within 72 hours of onset is sometimes called recent onset atrial fibrillation. By contrast, **chronic atrial fibrillation G** is more sustained and can be described as paroxysmal (with spontaneous termination and sinus rhythm between recurrences), persistent, or permanent atrial fibrillation**G**. This review deals only with people with acute atrial fibrillation who are haemodynamically stable. The consensus is that people who are not haemodynamically stable should be treated with immediate DC cardiversion. We have excluded studies in people with atrial fibrillation arising during or soon after cardiac surgery. |
| INCIDENCE/ PREVALENCE | We found limited evidence of the incidence or prevalence of acute atrial fibrillation. Extrapolation from the Framingham study suggests an incidence in men of 3/1000 person years at age 55 years, rising to 38/1000 person years at 94 years.[1] In women, the incidence was 2/1000 person years at age 55 years and 32.5/1000 person years at 94 years. The prevalence of atrial fibrillation ranged from 0.5% for people aged 50–59 years to 9% in people aged 80–89 years. Among acute emergency medical admissions in the UK, 3–6% had atrial fibrillation, and about 40% were newly diagnosed.[2,3] Among acute hospital admissions in New Zealand, 10% (95% CI 9% to 12%) had documented atrial fibrillation.[4] |
| AETIOLOGY/ RISK FACTORS | Common precipitants of acute atrial fibrillation are acute myocardial infarction and the acute effects of alcohol. Age increases the risk of developing acute atrial fibrillation. Men are more likely to develop atrial fibrillation than women (38 years' follow up from the Framingham Study, RR after adjustment for age and known predisposing conditions 1.5).[5] Atrial fibrillation can occur in association with underlying disease (both cardiac and non-cardiac) or can arise in the absence of any other condition. Epidemiological surveys have found that risk ▶ |

# Atrial fibrillation (acute)

factors for the development of acute atrial fibrillation include ischaemic heart disease, hypertension, heart failure, valve disease, diabetes, alcohol abuse, thyroid disorders, and disorders of the lung and pleura.[1] In a British survey of acute hospital admissions of patients with atrial fibrillation, a history of ischaemic heart disease was present in 33%, heart failure in 24%, hypertension in 26%, and rheumatic heart disease in 7%.[3] In some populations, the acute effects of alcohol explain a large proportion of the incidence of acute atrial fibrillation. Paroxysms of atrial fibrillation are more common in athletes.[6]

PROGNOSIS **Spontaneous reversion:** Observational studies and placebo arms of RCTs have found that more than 50% of people with acute atrial fibrillation revert spontaneously within 24–48 hours, especially if atrial fibrillation is associated with an identifiable precipitant such as alcohol or myocardial infarction. **Progression to chronic atrial fibrillation:** We found no evidence about the proportion of people with acute atrial fibrillation who develop more chronic forms of atrial fibrillation (e.g. paroxysmal, persistent, or permanent atrial fibrillation). **Mortality:** We found little evidence about the effects on mortality and morbidity of acute atrial fibrillation where no underlying cause is found. Acute atrial fibrillation during myocardial infarction is an independent predictor of both short term and long term mortality.[7] **Heart failure:** Onset of atrial fibrillation reduces cardiac output by 10–20% irrespective of the underlying ventricular rate[8,9] and can contribute to heart failure. People with acute atrial fibrillation who present with heart failure have worse prognoses. **Stroke:** Acute atrial fibrillation is associated with a risk of imminent stroke.[10,11,12,13] One case series used transoesophageal echocardiography in people who had developed acute atrial fibrillation within the preceding 48 hours; 15% had atrial thrombi.[14] An ischaemic stroke associated with atrial fibrillation is more likely to be fatal, have a recurrence, and leave a serious functional deficit among survivors than a stroke not associated with atrial fibrillation.[15]

---

Please refer to CD-ROM for full text and references.

### Search date January 2003

*Margaret Thorogood, Melvyn Hillsdon, and Carolyn Summerbell*

## What are the effects of interventions?

### BENEFICIAL

**Advice from physicians and trained counsellors to quit smoking**

Systematic reviews have found that simple, one off advice from a physician during a routine consultation is associated with 2% of smokers quitting smoking without relapse for 1 year. Advice from trained counsellors who are neither doctors nor nurses also increases quit rates compared with minimal intervention.

**Advice on cholesterol lowering diet**

Systematic reviews have found that advice on cholesterol lowering diet (i.e. advice to lower total fat intake or increase the ratio of polyunsaturated : saturated fatty acid) leads to a small reduction in blood cholesterol concentrations in the long term (≥ 6 months).

**Advice on diet and exercise supported by behavioural therapy for the encouragement of weight loss**

Systematic reviews and subsequent RCTs have found that a combination of advice on diet and exercise supported by behavioural therapy is probably more effective than either diet or exercise advice alone in the treatment of obesity, and might lead to sustained weight loss.

**Advice on reducing sodium intake to reduce blood pressure**

One systematic review has found that, compared with usual care, intensive interventions to reduce sodium intake, unsuited to primary care or population prevention programmes, provide only small reductions in blood pressure. Effects on deaths and cardiovascular events are unclear.

**Bupropion as part of a smoking cessation programme**

One systematic review of antidepressants used as part of a smoking cessation programme has found that bupropion increases quit rates at 1 year.

**Counselling people at high risk of disease to quit smoking**

Systematic reviews and one subsequent RCT have found that antismoking advice improves smoking cessation in people at high risk of smoking related disease.

**Counselling pregnant women to quit smoking**

Two systematic reviews have found that antismoking interventions in pregnant women increase abstinence rates during pregnancy. Interventions without nicotine replacement were as effective as nicotine replacement in healthy non-pregnant women.

**Exercise advice to women over 80 years of age**

One RCT found that exercise advice delivered in the home by physiotherapists increased physical activity and reduced the risk of falling in women over 80 years.

**Nicotine replacement in smokers who smoke at least 10 cigarettes daily**

One systematic review and one subsequent RCT have found that nicotine replacement is an effective additional component of cessation strategies in smokers who smoke at least 10 cigarettes daily. We found no evidence that any method of delivery of nicotine is more effective than others. We found limited evidence from three RCTs with follow up of 2–6 years that the additional benefit of nicotine replacement treatment on quit rates reduced with time. ▶

# Changing behaviour

## LIKELY TO BE BENEFICIAL

### Advice from nurses to quit smoking
One systematic review has found that advice to quit smoking increased quitting at 1 year compared with no advice.

### Counselling sedentary people to increase physical activity
We found weak evidence from systematic reviews and subsequent RCTs that counselling sedentary people increases physical activity compared with no intervention. Limited evidence from RCTs suggests that consultation with an exercise specialist rather than a physician may increase physical activity at 1 year. We found limited evidence that interventions delivered by new media can lead to short term changes in physical activity.

### Self help materials for people who want to stop smoking
One systematic review found that self help materials slightly improve smoking cessation compared with no intervention. It found that individually tailored materials were more effective than standard or stage based materials and that telephone counselling increased the effectiveness of postal self help materials.

## UNKNOWN EFFECTIVENESS

### Physical exercise to aid smoking cessation
One systematic review found limited evidence that exercise might increase smoking cessation.

### Training health professionals to give advice on smoking cessation (increases frequency of antismoking interventions, but may not improve effectiveness)
One systematic review has found that training professionals increases the frequency of antismoking interventions being offered. It found no good evidence that antismoking interventions are more effective if the health professionals delivering the interventions received training. One RCT found that a structured intervention delivered by trained community pharmacists increased smoking cessation rates compared with usual care delivered by untrained community pharmacists.

## LIKELY TO BE INEFFECTIVE OR HARMFUL

### Acupuncture for smoking cessation
One systematic review has found no significant difference between acupuncture and control in smoking cessation rates at 1 year.

### Anxiolytics for smoking cessation
One systematic review found no significant difference in quit rates with anxiolytics compared with control.

Categorisation relates to producing the intended behavioural change.

**DEFINITION** Cigarette smoking, diet, and level of physical activity are important in the aetiology of many chronic diseases. Individual change in behaviour has the potential to decrease the burden of chronic disease, particularly cardiovascular disease. This topic focuses on the evidence that specific interventions lead to changed behaviour.

**INCIDENCE/ PREVALENCE** In the developed world, the decline in smoking has slowed and the prevalence of regular smoking is increasing in young people. A sedentary lifestyle is becoming increasingly common and the prevalence of obesity is increasing rapidly.

Please refer to CD-ROM for full text and references.

## What are the effects of treatments?

### BENEFICIAL

#### Angiotensin converting enzyme inhibitors

Systematic reviews and RCTs have found that angiotensin converting enzyme inhibitors reduce ischaemic events, mortality, and hospital admission for heart failure compared with placebo. Relative benefits are similar in different groups of people, but absolute benefits are greater in people with severe heart failure. RCTs in people with asymptomatic left ventricular systolic dysfunction and in people with other risk factors have found that angiotensin converting enzyme inhibitors delay the onset of symptomatic heart failure and reduce cardiovascular events compared with placebo.

#### β Blockers

Systematic reviews have found strong evidence that adding a β blocker to an angiotensin converting enzyme inhibitor decreases mortality and hospital admission. Limited evidence from a subgroup analysis of one RCT found no significant effect on mortality in black people.

#### Digoxin (improves morbidity in people already receiving diuretics and angiotensin converting enzyme inhibitors)

One large RCT in people already receiving diuretics and angiotensin converting enzyme inhibitors found that digoxin reduced the proportion of people admitted to hospital for worsening heart failure at 37 months compared with placebo, but found no significant difference between groups in mortality.

### LIKELY TO BE BENEFICIAL

#### Angiotensin II receptor blockers

One systematic review found no significant difference between angiotensin receptor blockers and placebo in all cause mortality and hospital admission in people with New York Heart Association❻ class II–IV heart failure, although a smaller proportion of people died or were admitted with heart failure with angiotensin receptor blockers. This lack of significant effect may be explained by the small number of deaths and admissions reported. The review found no significant difference between angiotensin receptor blockers and angiotensin converting enzyme inhibitors in all cause mortality or hospital admission. It found that angiotensin receptor blockers plus angiotensin converting enzyme inhibitors reduced admission for heart failure compared with angiotensin converting enzyme inhibitors alone, but found no significant difference between groups in all cause mortality.

#### Eplerenone (in people with myocardial infarction complicated by left ventricular dysfunction and heart failure already on medical treatment)

One large RCT in people with recent myocardial infarction complicated by left ventricular dysfunction and clinical heart failure already on medical treatment (which could include angiotensin converting enzyme inhibitors, angiotensin receptor blockers, diuretics, β blockers, or coronary reperfusion therapy) found that adding eplerenone (an aldosterone receptor antagonist) reduced mortality compared with placebo.

# Heart failure

### Exercise

One systematic review found that exercise training improved physiological measures compared with control. One included RCT that assessed clinical outcomes found that exercise improved quality of life, and reduced cardiac events, mortality, and hospital admission for heart failure at 12 months compared with control. One subsequent RCT found no significant difference between 3 months of supervised aerobic plus resistance training followed by 9 months of home based training and usual care in 6 minute walk distance, total mortality, or quality of life at 12 months.

### Implantable cardiac defibrillators (in people with heart failure and near fatal arrhythmia)

One RCT has found good evidence that an implantable cardiac defibrillator reduces mortality in people with heart failure who have experienced a near fatal ventricular arrhythmia.

### Multidisciplinary interventions

One systematic review has found that multidisciplinary programmes reduce admissions to hospital compared with conventional care, but found no significant difference in mortality. The review found that telephone contact plus improved coordination of primary care had no significant effect on admission rate. Two RCTs included in the review found that that home based support reduced cardiovascular events at 3–6 years compared with usual care. Subsequent RCTs found that education, nurse led support, and multidisciplinary programmes reduced death and hospital readmission and improved quality of life at 12 weeks to 1 year compared with usual care.

### Prophylactic use of implantable cardiac defibrillators in people at high risk of arrhythmia

Two RCTs have found that implantable cardiac defibrillators reduce mortality compared with medical treatment in people with heart failure and at high risk of arrhythmia, whereas one RCT found no significant difference in mortality.

### Spironolactone in people with severe heart failure

One large RCT in people with severe heart failure taking diuretics, angiotensin converting enzyme inhibitors, and digoxin has found that adding spironolactone compared with placebo reduces mortality after 2 years.

## UNKNOWN EFFECTIVENESS

### Amiodarone

Systematic reviews found weak evidence suggesting that amiodarone may reduce mortality compared with placebo. However, we were not able to draw firm conclusions about the effects of amiodarone in people with heart failure.

### Anticoagulation

A preliminary report from one RCT found no significant difference between warfarin and no antithrombotic treatment or between warfarin and aspirin in the combined outcome of death, myocardial infarction, and stroke after 27 months. However, the RCT may have lacked power to detect a clinically important difference.

### Antiplatelet agents

A preliminary report from one RCT found no significant difference between aspirin and no antithrombotic treatment or between aspirin and warfarin in the combined outcome of death, myocardial infarction, and stroke after 27 months. However, the RCT may have lacked power to detect a clinically important difference.

### Treatments for diastolic heart failure

We found no RCTs in people with diastolic heart failure.

◄ UNLIKELY TO BE BENEFICIAL

### Calcium channel blockers

One systematic review has found no significant difference in mortality between second generation dihydropyridine calcium channel blockers and placebo. RCTs comparing other calcium channel blockers versus placebo also found no evidence of benefit.

LIKELY TO BE INEFFECTIVE OR HARMFUL

### Non-amiodarone antiarrhythmic drugs

Evidence extrapolated from one systematic review in people treated after a myocardial infarction suggests that other antiarrhythmic drugs (apart from β blockers) may increase mortality.

### Positive inotropes (other than digoxin)

RCTs in people with heart failure found that positive inotropic drugs other than digoxin (ibopamine, milrinone, and vesnarinone) increased mortality over 6–11 months compared with placebo. One systematic review in people with heart failure found a non-significant increase in mortality with intravenous inotropic drugs that act through the adrenergic pathway compared with placebo or control, and insufficient data to determine whether symptoms improved. It suggested that their use may not be safe.

| | |
|---|---|
| **DEFINITION** | Heart failure occurs when abnormality of cardiac function causes failure of the heart to pump blood at a rate sufficient for metabolic requirements under normal filling pressure. It is characterised clinically by breathlessness, effort intolerance, fluid retention, and poor survival. It can be caused by systolic or diastolic dysfunction and is associated with neurohormonal changes.[1] Left ventricular systolic dysfunction (LVSD) is defined as a left ventricular ejection fraction below 0.40. It may be symptomatic or asymptomatic. Defining and diagnosing diastolic heart failure can be difficult. Recently proposed criteria include: (1) clinical evidence of heart failure; (2) normal or mildly abnormal left ventricular systolic function; and (3) evidence of abnormal left ventricular relaxation, filling, diastolic distensibility, or diastolic stiffness.[2] However, assessment of some of these criteria is not standardised. |
| **INCIDENCE/ PREVALENCE** | Both the incidence and prevalence of heart failure increase with age. Studies of heart failure in the USA and Europe found that under 65 years of age the incidence is 1/1000 men a year and 0.4/1000 women a year. Over 65 years, incidence is 11/1000 men a year and 5/1000 women a year. Under 65 years the prevalence of heart failure is 1/1000 men and 1/1000 women; over 65 years the prevalence is 40/1000 men and 30/1000 women.[3] The prevalence of asymptomatic LVSD is 3% in the general population.[4–6] The mean age of people with asymptomatic LVSD is lower than that for symptomatic individuals. Both heart failure and asymptomatic LVSD are more common in men.[4–6] The prevalence of diastolic heart failure in the community is unknown. The prevalence of heart failure with preserved systolic function in people in hospital with clinical heart failure varies from 13–74%.[7,8] Less than 15% of people with heart failure under 65 years have normal systolic function, whereas the prevalence is about 40% in people over 65 years.[7] |
| **AETIOLOGY/ RISK FACTORS** | Coronary artery disease is the most common cause of heart failure.[3] Other common causes include hypertension and idiopathic dilated congestive cardiomyopathy. After adjustment for hypertension, the presence of left ventricular hypertrophy remains a risk factor for the development of heart failure. Other risk factors include cigarette smoking, hyperlipidaemia, and diabetes mellitus.[4] The common causes of left ventricular diastolic dysfunction are coronary artery disease and systemic hypertension. Other causes are hypertrophic cardiomyopathy, restrictive or infiltrative cardiomyopathies, and valvular heart disease.[8] ▶ |

**Cardiovascular disorders**

# Heart failure

**PROGNOSIS**   The prognosis of heart failure is poor, with 5 year mortality ranging from 26–75%.[3] Up to 16% of people are readmitted with heart failure within 6 months of first admission. In the USA, heart failure is the leading cause of hospital admission among people over 65 years of age.[3] In people with heart failure, a new myocardial infarction increases the risk of death (RR 7.8, 95% CI 6.9 to 8.8). About a third of all deaths in people with heart failure are preceded by a major ischaemic event.[9] Sudden death, mainly caused by ventricular arrhythmia, is responsible for 25–50% of all deaths, and is the most common cause of death in people with heart failure.[10] The presence of asymptomatic LVSD increases an individual's risk of having a cardiovascular event. One large prevention trial found that for a 5% reduction in ejection fraction, the risk ratio for mortality was 1.20 (95% CI 1.13 to 1.29). For hospital admission for heart failure, the risk ratio was 1.28 (95% CI 1.18 to 1.38) and the risk ratio for heart failure was 1.20 (95% CI 1.13 to 1.26).[4] The annual mortality for people with diastolic heart failure varies in observational studies (1.3–17.5%).[7] Reasons for this variation include age, the presence of coronary artery disease, and variation in the partition value used to define abnormal ventricular systolic function. The annual mortality for left ventricular diastolic dysfunction is lower than that found in people with systolic dysfunction.[11]

Please refer to CD-ROM for full text and references.

Cardiovascular disorders

## What are the effects of treatments for chronic peripheral arterial disease?

### BENEFICIAL

**Antiplatelet treatment**

Systematic reviews have found strong evidence that antiplatelet agents reduce major cardiovascular events over an average of 2 years compared with control treatment. Systematic reviews have found that antiplatelet agents reduce the risk of arterial occlusion and revascularisation procedures compared with placebo or no treatments. The balance of benefits and harms is in favour of treatment for most people with symptomatic peripheral arterial disease, because as a group they are at much greater risk of cardiovascular events.

**Exercise**

Systematic reviews and subsequent RCTs in people with chronic stable claudication have found that regular exercise at least three times weekly for between 3 and 6 months improves total walking distance and maximal exercise time after 3–12 months compared with no exercise. One RCT found that a "stop smoking and keep walking" intervention increased the maximal walking distance at 12 months compared with usual care.

### LIKELY TO BE BENEFICIAL

**Bypass surgery (v thrombolysis in people with acute limb ischaemia)**

One systematic review found that surgery reduced amputation rate and pain compared with thrombolysis, but found no significant difference in mortality after 1 year.

**Percutaneous transluminal angioplasty (transient benefit only)**

Two small RCTs in people with mild to moderate intermittent claudication🄖 found limited evidence that percutaneous angioplasty improved walking distance after 6 months compared with no angioplasty but found no significant difference after 2 or 6 years. Two small RCTs identified by a systematic review and three small additional RCTs in people with femoro–popliteal artery stenoses found no significant difference between angioplasty alone and angioplasty plus stent placement in patency rates, occlusion rates, or clinical improvement. The RCTs may lack power to rule out an important clinical effect.

**Smoking cessation***

RCTs of advice to stop smoking would be considered unethical. The consensus view is that smoking cessation improves symptoms in people with intermittent claudication. One systematic review of observational studies found inconclusive results from stopping smoking, both in terms of increasing absolute claudication distance and reducing the risk of symptom progression compared with people who continue to smoke.

*Based on observational evidence and consensus.

### TRADE OFF BETWEEN BENEFITS AND HARMS

**Cilostazol**

RCTs found that cilostazol improved initial claudication distance🄖 at 12–24 weeks compared with placebo. However, adverse effects of cilostazol were common in ▶

# Peripheral arterial disease

the RCTs, and included headache, diarrhoea, and palpitations. We found limited evidence from one RCT that pentoxifylline reduced absolute claudication distance© compared with cilostazol.

## UNKNOWN EFFECTIVENESS

### Bypass surgery (v percutaneous transluminal angioplasty)

One systematic review found that surgery improved primary blood vessel patency after 12–24 months compared with percutaneous transluminal angioplasty, but found no significant difference after 4 years. The review found no significant difference in mortality after 12–24 months. Although the consensus view is that bypass surgery is the most effective treatment for people with debilitating symptomatic peripheral arterial disease, we found inadequate evidence from RCTs reporting long term clinical outcomes to confirm this view.

### Pentoxifylline

One systematic review and one subsequent RCT found insufficient evidence to compare pentoxifylline with placebo. One RCT found limited evidence that pentoxifylline reduced absolute claudication distance compared with cilostazol.

**DEFINITION**     Peripheral arterial disease arises when there is significant narrowing of arteries distal to the arch of the aorta. Narrowing can arise from atheroma, arteritis, local thrombus formation, or embolisation from the heart or more central arteries. This topic includes treatment options for people with symptoms of reduced blood flow to the leg that are likely to arise from atheroma. These symptoms range from calf pain on exercise (intermittent claudication©) to rest pain, skin ulceration, or symptoms of ischaemic necrosis (gangrene) in people with critical limb ischaemia©.

**INCIDENCE/**    Peripheral arterial disease is more common in people aged over 50 years than
**PREVALENCE**   in younger people, and is more common in men than women. The prevalence of peripheral arterial disease of the legs (assessed by non-invasive tests) is about 3% in people under the age of 60 years, but rises to over 20% in people over 75 years.[1] The overall annual incidence of intermittent claudication is 1.5–2.6/1000 men a year and 1.2–3.6/1000 women.[2]

**AETIOLOGY/**     Factors associated with the development of peripheral arterial disease include
**RISK FACTORS** age, gender, cigarette smoking, diabetes mellitus, hypertension, hyperlipidaemia, obesity, and physical inactivity. The strongest association is with smoking (RR 2.0–4.0) and diabetes (RR 2.0–3.0).[3] Acute limb ischaemia© may result from thrombosis arising within a peripheral artery or embolic occlusion.

**PROGNOSIS**     The symptoms of intermittent claudication can resolve spontaneously, remain stable over many years, or progress rapidly to critical limb ischaemia©. About 15% of people with intermittent claudication eventually develop critical leg ischaemia, which endangers the viability of the limb. The annual incidence of critical limb ischaemia in Denmark and Italy in 1990 was 0.25–0.45/1000 people.[4,5] Coronary heart disease is the major cause of death in people with peripheral arterial disease of the legs. Over 5 years, about 20% of people with intermittent claudication have a non-fatal cardiovascular event (myocardial infarction or stroke).[6] The mortality rate of people with peripheral arterial disease is two to three times higher than that of age and sex matched controls. Overall mortality after the diagnosis of peripheral arterial disease is about 30% after 5 years and 70% after 15 years.[6]

Please refer to CD-ROM for full text and references.

### Search date November 2002

*Charles Foster, Michael Murphy, Julian J Nicholas, Michael Pignone, and Bazian Ltd*

## LIKELY TO BE BENEFICIAL

### Eating more fruit and vegetables

Observational studies have found limited evidence that eating fruit and vegetables reduces ischaemic heart disease and stroke. The size and nature of effects are uncertain.

### Physical activity

One RCT and many observational studies have found that moderate to high physical activity reduces coronary heart disease and stroke. They also found that sudden death soon after strenuous exercise was rare, more common in sedentary people, and did not outweigh the benefits.

### Smoking cessation

We found no direct evidence from RCTs that advice to stop smoking reduces cardiovascular risk compared with no advice. However, we found robust evidence from observational studies that smoking is an important risk factor for overall mortality, coronary heart disease, and stroke, and that smoking cessation should therefore be encouraged. The evidence is strongest for stroke.

## TRADE OFF BETWEEN BENEFITS AND HARMS

### Anticoagulant treatment (warfarin)

One RCT found that the benefits and harms of oral anticoagulation (to a target international normalised ratio of 1.5) among people without symptoms of cardiovascular disease were finely balanced, and that net effects were uncertain.

### Aspirin in low risk people

We found insufficient evidence to identify which asymptomatic individuals would benefit overall and which would be harmed by regular treatment with aspirin. Benefits are likely to outweigh risks in people at higher risk.

## UNKNOWN EFFECTIVENESS

### Antioxidants (other than β carotene and vitamin E)

We found insufficient evidence on the effects of vitamin C, copper, zinc, manganese, or flavonoids.

## LIKELY TO BE INEFFECTIVE OR HARMFUL

### β carotene

Systematic reviews of RCTs found no evidence of benefit from β carotene supplements, and RCTs suggest that they may be harmful.

### Vitamin E

Systematic reviews of RCTs found no evidence of benefit from vitamin E supplements, and RCTs suggest that they may be harmful

# Primary prevention

## What are the effects of interventions aimed at lowering blood pressure?

### Antihypertensive drug treatments in people with hypertension

Systematic reviews have found that initial treatment with diuretics, angiotensin converting enzyme inhibitors, or β blockers reduce morbidity and mortality compared with placebo, with minimal adverse effects. RCTs found no significant differences in morbidity or mortality among these agents. We found limited evidence from two systematic reviews that diuretics, β blockers, and angiotensin converting enzyme inhibitors reduced coronary heart disease and heart failure more than calcium channel antagonists. However, calcium channel antagonists reduced risk of stroke more than the other agents. One RCT found that a thiazide diuretic reduced cardiovascular events, particularly congestive heart failure, compared with an α blocker. One RCT found that losartan (an angiotensin receptor blocker) reduced cardiovascular events compared with atenolol in people with hypertension and left ventricular hypertrophy.

### Diuretics in high risk people

Systematic reviews have found that diuretics decrease the risk of fatal and non-fatal stroke, cardiac events, and total mortality compared with placebo. The biggest benefit is seen in people with the highest baseline risk. Systematic reviews have found no significant difference in mortality or morbidity between diuretics and β blockers.

### Dietary salt restriction

We found no RCTs of the effects of salt restriction on morbidity or mortality. One systematic review has found that a low salt diet may lead to modest reductions in blood pressure compared with a usual diet, with more benefit in people older than 45 years than in younger people❶.

### Fish oil supplementation

We found no RCTs examining the effects of fish oil supplementation on morbidity or mortality in people with primary hypertension. One systematic review has found that fish oil supplementation in large doses of 3 g daily modestly lowers blood pressure.

### Low fat, high fruit and vegetable diet

We found no systematic review and no RCTs examining the effects of low fat, high fruit and vegetable diet on morbidity or mortality of people with raised blood pressure. One RCT found that a low fat, high fruit and vegetable diet modestly reduced blood pressure compared with control diet.

### Physical activity

We found no RCTs in people with primary hypertension examining the effects of exercise on morbidity or mortality. One systematic review has found that aerobic exercise reduces blood pressure compared with no exercise.

### Potassium supplementation

We found no RCTs examining the effects of potassium supplementation on morbidity or mortality in people with primary hypertension. One systematic review has found that a daily potassium supplementation of about 60 mmol (2 g, which is about the amount contained in 5 bananas) reduces blood pressure by small amounts.

◀ **Smoking cessation**

Observational studies have found that smoking is a risk factor for cardiovascular disease. We found no direct evidence in people with hypertension that stopping smoking decreases blood pressure.

**Weight loss**

We found no RCTs examining the effects of weight loss on morbidity and mortality. One systematic review and additional RCTs have found that modest weight reduction in obese people with hypertension leads to a modest reduction in blood pressure.

**UNKNOWN EFFECTIVENESS**

**Calcium supplementation**

We found insufficient evidence about effects of calcium supplementation on blood pressure, morbidity, or mortality specifically in people with hypertension. One systematic review in people with and without hypertension found that calcium supplementation may reduce systolic blood pressure by a small amount.

**Magnesium supplementation**

We found no RCTs examining the effects of magnesium supplementation on morbidity or mortality in people with hypertension. We found limited and conflicting evidence on the effect of magnesium supplementation on blood pressure in people with hypertension and normal magnesium concentrations.

**Reduced alcohol consumption**

We found no RCTs examining the effects of reducing alcohol consumption on morbidity or mortality. One systematic review in moderate drinkers (25–50 drinks/week) found inconclusive evidence regarding effects of alcohol reduction on blood.

---

## What are the effects of interventions aimed at lowering cholesterol?

**LIKELY TO BE BENEFICIAL**

**Cholesterol reduction in high risk people**

Systematic reviews have found that reducing cholesterol concentration in asymptomatic people lowers the rate of cardiovascular events. RCTs have found that the magnitude of the benefit is related to an individual's baseline risk of cardiovascular events, and to the degree of cholesterol lowering, rather than to the individual's cholesterol concentration.

**Low fat diet**

Systematic reviews and RCTs have found that combined use of cholesterol lowering diet and lipid lowering drugs reduces cholesterol concentration more than lifestyle interventions alone.

**DEFINITION** Primary prevention in this context is the long term management of people at increased risk but with no evidence of cardiovascular disease. Clinically overt ischaemic vascular disease includes acute myocardial infarction, angina, stroke, and peripheral vascular disease. Many adults have no symptoms or obvious signs of vascular disease, even though they have atheroma and are at ▶

# Primary prevention

increased risk of ischaemic vascular events because of one or more risk factors (see aetiology below). In this topic, we have taken primary prevention to apply to people who have not had clinically overt cardiovascular disease, or people at low risk of ischaemic cardiovascular events. Prevention of cerebrovascular events is discussed in detail elsewhere in *Clinical Evidence* (see stroke prevention topic, p 36).

**INCIDENCE/ PREVALENCE** According to the World Health Report 1999, ischaemic heart disease was the leading single cause for death in the world, the leading single cause for death in high income countries and second to lower respiratory tract infections in low and middle income countries. In 1998 it was still the leading cause for death, with nearly 7.4 million estimated deaths a year in member states of the World Health Organization. This condition had the eighth highest burden of disease in the low and middle income countries (30.7 million disability adjusted life years).[1]

**AETIOLOGY/ RISK FACTORS** Identified major risk factors for ischaemic vascular disease include increasing age, male sex, raised low density lipoprotein cholesterol, reduced high density lipoprotein cholesterol, raised blood pressure, smoking, diabetes, family history of cardiovascular disease, obesity, and sedentary lifestyle. For many of these risk factors, observational studies show a continuous gradient of increasing risk of cardiovascular disease with increasing levels of the risk factor, with no obvious threshold level. Although by definition event rates are higher in high risk people, most ischaemic vascular events that occur in the population are in people with intermediate levels of absolute risk because there are many more of them than there are people at high risk; see Appendix 1.[2]

**PROGNOSIS** A study carried out in Scotland found that about half of people who suffer an acute myocardial infarction die within 28 days, and two thirds of acute myocardial infarctions occur before the person reaches hospital.[3] The benefits of intervention in unselected people with no evidence of cardiovascular disease (primary prevention) are small because in such people the baseline risk is small. However, absolute risk of ischaemic vascular events varies widely, even among people with similar levels of blood pressure or cholesterol. Estimates of absolute risk can be based on simple risk equations or tables; see Appendix 1.[4,5]

Please refer to CD-ROM for full text and references.

# Secondary prevention of ischaemic cardiac events

Search date November 2002

*Michael Pignone, Charanjit Rihal, and Bazian Ltd*

## What are the effects of treatments?

### BENEFICIAL

**Amiodarone in people at high risk of arrhythmic death**

Two systematic reviews have found that amiodarone reduces the risk of sudden cardiac death and overall mortality at 1 year compared with placebo in people at high risk of arrhythmic death after myocardial infarction.

**Angiotensin converting enzyme inhibitors in high risk people without left ventricular dysfunction**

One large RCT in high risk people without left ventricular dysfunction found that ramipril reduced the combined outcome of cardiovascular death, stroke, and myocardial infarction compared with placebo after about 5 years.

**Angiotensin converting enzyme inhibitors in people with left ventricular dysfunction**

One systematic review has found that, in people who have had a myocardial infarction and have left ventricular dysfunction, angiotensin converting enzyme inhibitors reduce mortality, admission to hospital for congestive heart failure, and recurrent non-fatal myocardial infarction compared with placebo after 2 years' treatment.

**Anticoagulants in the absence of antiplatelet treatment**

One systematic review and subsequent RCTs have found that high or moderate intensity oral anticoagulants given alone reduce the risk of serious vascular events compared with placebo or no anticoagulants in people with coronary artery disease, but are associated with substantial risk of haemorrhage.

**Any oral antiplatelet treatment**

One systematic review has found that prolonged antiplatelet treatment compared with placebo or no antiplatelet treatment reduces the risk of serious vascular events in people at high risk of ischaemic cardiac events.

**Aspirin**

One systematic review has found that, for prolonged use, aspirin 75–150 mg daily is as effective as higher doses, but found insufficient evidence that doses below 75 mg daily are as effective.

**β Blockers**

Systematic reviews in people after myocardial infarction have found that long term β blockers reduce all cause mortality, coronary mortality, recurrent non-fatal myocardial infarction, and sudden death. One RCT found that about 25% of people suffer adverse effects.

**Cardiac rehabilitation**

One systematic review has found that cardiac rehabilitation including exercise reduces the risk of major cardiac events. One subsequent RCT found no significant difference in quality of life between standard rehabilitation and early return to normal activities, although the study may have lacked power to detect a clinically important difference between groups.

▶

# Secondary prevention of ischaemic cardiac events

### Cholesterol lowering drugs

Systematic reviews and large subsequent RCTs have found that lowering cholesterol in people at high risk of ischaemic coronary events substantially reduces overall mortality, cardiovascular mortality, and non-fatal cardiovascular events. We found good evidence from systematic reviews and subsequent RCTs that statins were the only non-surgical treatment for cholesterol reduction that reduced mortality. One systematic review has found that the absolute benefits increase as baseline risk increases, but are not additionally influenced by the person's absolute blood cholesterol concentration.

### Coronary artery bypass grafting versus medical treatment alone

One systematic review found that coronary artery bypass grafting reduced the risk of death from coronary artery disease at 5 and 10 years compared with medical treatment alone. Greater benefit occurred in people with poor left ventricular function. One subsequent RCT in people with asymptomatic disease found that revascularisation with coronary artery bypass grafting or coronary percutaneous transluminal angioplasty reduced mortality at 2 years compared with medical treatment alone.

### Coronary percutaneous transluminal angioplasty versus medical treatment alone in people with stable coronary artery disease

One systematic review found that coronary percutaneous transluminal angioplasty improved angina compared with medical treatment alone, but was associated with a higher rate of coronary artery bypass grafting. The review found higher mortality and rates of myocardial infarction with percutaneous transluminal angioplasty than with medical treatment but the difference was not significant. RCTs have found that percutaneous transluminal angioplasty is associated with increased risk of emergency coronary artery bypass grafting and myocardial infarction during and soon after the procedure. One RCT found that percutaneous transluminal angioplasty reduced cardiac events and improved angina severity compared with medical treatment alone in people over the age of 75 years.

### Exercise without cardiac rehabilitation

One systematic review has found that exercise alone reduces mortality compared with usual care.

### Intracoronary stents (better than coronary percutaneous transluminal angioplasty alone)

One systematic review found that intracoronary stents reduce the need for repeat vascularisation compared with coronary percutaneous transluminal angioplasty alone. It found no significant difference in mortality or myocardial infarction, but crossover rates from angioplasty to stent were high. RCTs found that intracoronary stents improved outcomes after 4–9 months compared with percutaneous transluminal angioplasty in people with previous coronary artery bypass grafting, chronic total occlusions, and for treatment of restenosis after initial percutaneous transluminal angioplasty.

## LIKELY TO BE BENEFICIAL

### Blood pressure lowering in people at high risk of ischaemic coronary events

We found no direct evidence of the effects of blood pressure lowering in people with established coronary heart disease. Observational studies, and extrapolation of primary prevention trials of blood pressure reduction, support the lowering of blood pressure in those at high risk of ischaemic coronary events. The evidence for benefit is strongest for β blockers, although not specifically in people with ▶

hypertension. The optimum target blood pressure in people with hypertention is not clear. Effects of angiotensin converting enzyme inhibitors, calcium channel blockers, and β blockers are discussed separately.

### Coronary artery bypass grafting versus percutaneous revascularisation for multivessel disease (less need for repeat procedures)

One systematic review has found no significant difference between coronary artery bypass grafting and percutaneous transluminal angioplasty in death, myocardial infarction, or quality of life. Percutaneous transluminal angioplasty is less invasive but increased the number of repeat procedures.

### Eating more fish (particularly oily fish)

One RCT has found that advising people with coronary heart disease to eat more fish (particularly oily fish) reduced mortality at 2 years. A second RCT found that fish oil capsules reduced mortality at 3.5 years.

### Mediterranean diet

One RCT has found that advising people with coronary artery disease to eat more bread, fruit, vegetables, and fish, and less meat, and to replace butter and cream with rapeseed margarine reduces mortality at 27 months.

### Psychosocial treatment

RCTs found limited evidence that psychosocial treatments reduced cardiac events or cardiac death compared with no psychosocial treatment in people with coronary heart disease. Two RCTs found that psychological treatments improved quality of life compared with no psychological treatment.

### Smoking cessation

We found no RCTs of the effects of smoking cessation on cardiovascular events in people with coronary heart disease. Moderate quality evidence from epidemiological studies indicates that people with coronary heart disease who stop smoking rapidly reduce their risk of recurrent coronary events or death. Treatment with nicotine patches seems safe in people with coronary heart disease.

### Stress management

One systematic review of mainly poor quality RCTs found that stress management may decrease rates of myocardial infarction or cardiac death in people with coronary heart disease.

### Thienopyridines

One systematic review has found that clopidogrel is at least as safe and effective as aspirin in people at high risk of cardiovascular events.

## UNKNOWN EFFECTIVENESS

### Advice to eat less fat

RCTs found no strong evidence that low fat diets reduced mortality at 2 years.

### Vitamin C

We found insufficient evidence about effects of vitamin C alone.

### Vitamin E

We found no consistent evidence from four RCTs about effects of vitamin E versus placebo or other antioxidants in people with high cardiovascular risk.

## UNLIKELY TO BE BENEFICIAL

### Hormone replacement therapy

Large RCTs found no significant difference between hormone replacement therapy and placebo in major cardiovascular events in postmenopausal women with ▶

established coronary artery disease. Observational studies and one large RCT found that hormone replacement therapy increased risk of breast cancer, venous thromboembolism, and gall bladder disease compared with placebo.

### Oral glycoprotein IIb/IIIa receptor inhibitors

Systematic reviews in people with acute coronary syndromes or undergoing percutaneous coronary interventions have found that oral glycoprotein IIb/IIIa receptor inhibitors (with or without aspirin) increase risk of mortality and bleeding compared with aspirin alone.

### Sotalol

One RCT found limited evidence that sotalol increased mortality within 1 year compared with placebo.

## LIKELY TO BE INEFFECTIVE OR HARMFUL

### Adding anticoagulants to antiplatelet treatment

One systematic review and subsequent RCTs found no consistent evidence that addition of oral anticoagulation at low (INR⊕ < 1.5) or moderate (INR 1.5–3.0) intensity to aspirin reduced risk of death or recurrent cardiac events, but found an increased risk of major haemorrhage compared with aspirin alone.

### β Carotene

Four large RCTs of β carotene supplementation in primary prevention found no cardiovascular benefits, and two of the RCTs raised concerns about increased mortality.

### Calcium channel blockers

One systematic review found non-significantly higher mortality with dihydropyridines compared with placebo. One systematic review found no benefit from calcium channel blockers in people after myocardial infarction or with chronic coronary heart disease. Diltiazem and verapamil may reduce rates of reinfarction and refractory angina in people after myocardial infarction who do not have heart failure.

### Class I antiarrhythmic agents

One systematic review has found that class I antiarrhythmic agents given after myocardial infarction increase the risk of cardiovascular mortality and sudden death compared with placebo.

**DEFINITION**  Secondary prevention in this context is the long term management of people with a prior acute myocardial infarction, and of people at high risk of ischaemic cardiac events for other reasons, such as a history of angina or coronary surgical procedures.

**INCIDENCE/**  Coronary artery disease is the leading cause of mortality in developed
**PREVALENCE**  countries and is becoming a major cause of morbidity and mortality in developing countries. There are pronounced international, regional, and temporal differences in death rates. In the USA, the prevalence of overt coronary artery disease approaches 4%.[1]

**AETIOLOGY/**  Most ischaemic cardiac events are associated with atheromatous plaques that
**RISK FACTORS**  can cause acute obstruction of coronary vessels. Atheroma is more likely in elderly people, in those with established coronary artery disease, and in those with risk factors (such as smoking, hypertension, high cholesterol, diabetes mellitus).

**AETIOLOGY/**  Of people admitted to hospital with acute myocardial infarction, 7–15% die in
**RISK FACTORS**  hospital and another 7–15% die during the following year. People who survive the acute stage of myocardial infarction fall into three prognostic groups, based ▶

on their baseline risk❶;[2-4] high (20% of all survivors), moderate (55%), and low (25%) risk. Long term prognosis depends on the degree of left ventricular dysfunction, the presence of residual ischaemia, and the extent of any electrical instability. Further risk stratification procedures include assessment of left ventricular function (by echocardiography or nuclear ventriculography) and of myocardial ischaemia (by non-invasive stress testing).[4-8] Those with low left ventricular ejection fraction, ischaemia, or poor functional status can be assessed further by cardiac catheterisation.[9]

---

Please refer to CD-ROM for full text and references.

# Stroke management

Search date May 2003

*Elizabeth Warburton*

## What are the effects of medical treatments for acute ischaemic stroke?

### BENEFICIAL

#### Aspirin

One systematic review in people with ischaemic stroke confirmed by computerised tomography scan has found that aspirin within 48 hours of stroke onset reduces death or dependency at 6 months and increases the number of people making a complete recovery compared with placebo.

#### Specialised care (specialist stroke rehabilitation)

One systematic review has found that specialist stroke rehabilitation reduces death or dependency after a median follow up of 1 year compared with conventional (less specialised) care. Prospective observational data suggest that these findings may be reproducible in routine clinical settings. A second systematic review found no significant difference between care based on in-hospital care pathways and standard care in death or dependency rates. However, these results were based on one small RCT, which may have lacked power to detect clinically important effects. One small subsequent pilot study found no significant difference between intensive monitoring and usual stroke unit care in rates of poor outcome at 3 months but found that intensive monitoring significantly reduced mortality.

### TRADE OFF BETWEEN BENEFITS AND HARMS

#### Thrombolysis

One systematic review in people with confirmed ischaemic stroke has found that thrombolysis reduces the risk of the composite outcome of death or dependency after 1–6 months compared with placebo, but increases the risk of death from intracranial haemorrhage in the first 7–10 days and the risk of death after 1–6 months. The excess of deaths is offset by fewer people being alive but dependent 6 months after stroke onset, and the new effect was a reduction in people who were dead or depedent.

### UNLIKELY TO BE BENEFICIAL

#### Neuroprotective agents (calcium channel antagonists, γ-aminobutyric acid agonists, lubeluzole, glycine antagonists, tirilazad, N-methyl-D-aspartate antagonists)

RCTs found no evidence that, compared with placebo, calcium channel antagonists, tirilazad, lubeluzole, γ-aminobutyric acid agonists, glycine antagonists, or N-methyl-D-aspartate antagonists☉ improve clinical outcomes. One systematic review found that lubeluzole was associated with a significant increase in the risk of having Q-T prolongation to more than 450 ms on electrocardiography compared with placebo.

### LIKELY TO BE INEFFECTIVE OR HARMFUL

#### Acute reduction in blood pressure

One systematic review in people with acute stroke found insufficient evidence about the effects of lowering blood pressure compared with placebo on clinical outcome, but RCTs have suggested that people treated with antihypertensive agents may have a worse clinical outcome and increased mortality.

◄ **Immediate systemic anticoagulation**

One systematic review comparing systemic anticoagulants (unfractionated heparin, low molecular weight heparin, heparinoids, oral anticoagulants, or specific thrombin inhibitors) with usual care without systemic anticoagulants has found no significant difference in death or dependence after 3–6 months. One systematic review found no significant difference between anticoagulants (unfractionated and low molecular weight heparin) and aspirin in death or dependency at 3–6 months for all people with stroke or for the subset of people who also had atrial fibrillation. Systematic reviews provided evidence that systemic anticoagulation reduces the risk of symptomatic deep venous thrombosis in people with ischaemic stroke, but increases the risk of intracranial haemorrhage or extracranial haemorrhage.

## What are the effects of surgical treatments for intracerebral haematomas?

**UNKNOWN EFFECTIVENESS**

### Evacuation

We found that the balance between benefits and harms has not been clearly established for the evacuation of supratentorial haematomas. We found no evidence from RCTs on the role of evacuation or ventricular shunting in people with infratentorial haematoma whose consciousness level is declining.

**DEFINITION** Stroke is characterised by rapidly developing clinical symptoms and signs of focal, and at times global, loss of cerebral function lasting more than 24 hours or leading to death, with no apparent cause other than that of vascular origin.[1] Ischaemic stroke is stroke caused by vascular insufficiency (such as cerebrovascular thromboembolism) rather than haemorrhage.

**INCIDENCE/ PREVALENCE** Stroke is the third most common cause of death in most developed countries.[2] It is a worldwide problem; about 4.5 million people die from stroke each year. Stroke can occur at any age, but half of all strokes occur in people over 70 years old.[3]

**AETIOLOGY/ RISK FACTORS** About 80% of all acute strokes are ischaemic, usually resulting from thrombotic or embolic occlusion of a cerebral artery.[4] The remainder are caused either by intracerebral or subarachnoid haemorrhage.

**PROGNOSIS** About 10% of all people with acute ischaemic strokes will die within 30 days of stroke onset.[5] Of those who survive the acute event, about 50% will experience some level of disability after 6 months.[6]

Please refer to CD-ROM for full text and references.

**Cardiovascular disorders**

# Stroke prevention

### Search date January 2003

*Bethan Freestone, Gregory YH Lip, Peter Rothwell, and Cathie Sudlow*

## What are the effects of preventive interventions in people with prior stroke or transient ischaemic attack?

### BENEFICIAL

#### Antiplatelet treatment
One systematic review has found that antiplatelet treatment reduces the risk of serious vascular events in people with prior stroke or transient ischaemic attack compared with placebo or no antiplatelet treatment.

#### Blood pressure reduction
One systematic review and one subsequent RCT found that antihypertensive treatment reduced stroke among people with a prior stroke or transient ischaemic attack, whether or not they were hypertensive.

#### Carotid endarterectomy in people with moderately severe (50–69%) symptomatic carotid artery stenosis
Evidence from a pooled analysis of individual patient data from three RCTs found that carotid endarterectomy reduced stroke and death compared with no endarterectomy in symptomatic people with 50–69% carotid stenosis.

#### Carotid endarterectomy in people with severe (> 70%) symptomatic carotid artery stenosis
Evidence from three RCTs has found that carotid endarterectomy reduces stroke and death compared with no endarterectomy in symptomatic people with more than 70% stenosis, although no benefit was found in people with near-occlusion. Benefit in symptomatic people with more than 70% stenosis is greater than in people with lower grade stenosis.

#### Cholesterol reduction
One large RCT has found that, compared with placebo, simvastatin reduced major vascular events, including stroke, in people with prior stroke or transient ischaemic attack. RCTs found no evidence that non-statin treatments reduced stroke compared with placebo or no treatment.

### LIKELY TO BE BENEFICIAL

#### Carotid endarterectomy in people with asymptomatic but severe carotid artery stenosis
Two systematic reviews found that carotid endarterectomy reduced perioperative stroke, death, and subsequent ipsilateral stroke in people with asymptomatic but severe stenosis. However, because the risk of stroke without surgery in asymptomatic people is relatively low, the benefit from surgery is small.

### UNKNOWN EFFECTIVENESS

#### Carotid or vertebral angioplasty
We found insufficient evidence about the effects of carotid or vertebral percutaneous transluminal angioplasty or stenting compared with medical treatment or carotid endarterectomy in people with a recent carotid or vertebral territory transient ischaemic attack or non-disabling ischaemic stroke who have severe stenosis of the ipsilateral carotid or vertebral artery.

◀ **Different blood pressure lowering regimens (no evidence that any regimen more or less effective than any other)**

Systematic reviews found no clear evidence of a difference in effectiveness between different antihypertensive drugs. One systematic review found that more intensive treatment reduced stroke and major cardiovascular events, but not mortality, compared with less intensive treatment.

## UNLIKELY TO BE BENEFICIAL

**Alternative antiplatelet agents to aspirin (no evidence that any more or less effective than aspirin)**

Systematic reviews have found no good evidence that any antiplatelet treatment is superior to aspirin for long term secondary prevention of serious vascular events.

**Carotid endarterectomy in people with moderate (30–49%) symptomatic carotid artery stenosis**

Evidence from a pooled analysis of individual patient data from three RCTs suggests that carotid endarterectomy is of no benefit in symptomatic people with 30–49% stenosis.

**Carotid endarterectomy in people with symptomatic near-occlusion of the carotid artery**

We found limited evidence from three RCTs that carotid endarterectomy increases the risk of stroke or death due to surgery in symptomatic people with near occlusion of the ipsilateral carotid artery.

**High dose versus low dose aspirin (no additional benefit but may increase harms)**

One systematic review and one subsequent RCT have found that low dose aspirin (75–150 mg/day) is as effective as higher doses for preventing serious vascular events. It found insufficient evidence that doses lower than 75 mg daily are as effective. Systematic reviews found no evidence of an association between aspirin dose and risk of intracranial, major extracranial, or gastrointestinal haemorrhage. RCTs found that high dose aspirin (500–1500 mg/day) increased the risk of upper gastrointestinal upset compared with medium dose aspirin (75–325 mg/day).

## LIKELY TO BE INEFFECTIVE OR HARMFUL

**Carotid endarterectomy in people with less than 30% symptomatic carotid artery stenosis**

Evidence from a pooled analysis of individual patient data from three RCTs suggests that carotid endarterectomy increases the risk of stroke or death due to surgery in symptomatic people with less than 30% carotid stenosis.

**Oral anticoagulation in people with prior cerebrovascular ischaemia and sinus rhythm**

Systematic reviews found no significant difference between anticoagulation and placebo or antiplatelet treatment for preventing recurrent stroke after presumed ischaemic stroke in people in normal sinus rhythm. Anticoagulants increased the risk of fatal intracranial and extracranial haemorrhage compared with placebo. High intensity anticoagulation increased the risk of major bleeding compared with antiplatelet treatment.

# Stroke prevention

*What are the effects of preventive interventions in people with atrial fibrillation and prior stroke or transient ischaemic attack?*

## BENEFICIAL

### Aspirin in people with contraindications to anticoagulants

Systematic reviews have found that aspirin reduces the risk of stroke compared with placebo, but found that aspirin is less effective than anticoagulants. These findings support the use of aspirin in people with atrial fibrillation and contraindications to anticoagulants.

### Oral anticoagulation

Systematic reviews have found that adjusted dose warfarin reduces the risk of stroke compared with placebo. Systematic reviews have also found that warfarin reduces the risk of stroke in people with previous stroke or transient ischaemic attack compared with aspirin.

---

*What are the effects of preventive interventions in people with atrial fibrillation but no other major risk factors for stroke?*

## LIKELY TO BE BENEFICIAL

### Aspirin in people with contraindications to anticoagulants

One systematic review has found that aspirin reduces the risk of stroke compared with placebo, but another review found no significant difference. These findings support the use of aspirin in people with atrial fibrillation and contraindications to anticoagulants.

### Oral anticoagulation

One systematic review has found that warfarin reduces fatal and non-fatal ischaemic stroke compared with placebo, provided there is a low risk of bleeding and careful monitoring. The people in the review had a mean age of 69 years. One overview in people less than 65 years old has found no significant difference in the annual stroke rate between warfarin and placebo.

DEFINITION      Prevention in this context is the long term management of people with a prior stroke or transient ischaemic attack, and of people at high risk of stroke🔵 for other reasons such as atrial fibrillation. **Stroke:** See definition under stroke management, p 35. **Transient ischaemic attack:** This is similar to a mild ischaemic stroke except that symptoms last for less than 24 hours.[1]

INCIDENCE/      See incidence/prevalence under stroke management, p 35.
PREVALENCE

AETIOLOGY/      See aetiology under stroke management, p 35. Risk factors for stroke include
RISK FACTORS   prior stroke or transient ischaemic attack, increasing age, hypertension, diabetes, cigarette smoking, and emboli associated with atrial fibrillation, artificial heart valves, or myocardial infarction. The relation with cholesterol is less clear. One overview of prospective studies among healthy middle aged people found no association between total cholesterol and overall stroke risk.[2]

◀ However, one review of prospective observational studies in eastern Asian people found that cholesterol was positively associated with ischaemic stroke but negatively associated with haemorrhagic stroke.[3]

**PROGNOSIS**  People with a history of stroke or transient ischaemic attack are at high risk of all vascular events, such as myocardial infarction, but are at particular risk of subsequent stroke (about 10% in the first year and about 5% each year thereafter); see figure 1❻, and figure 1 in secondary prevention of ischaemic cardiac events, p 29.[4,5] People with intermittent atrial fibrillation treated with aspirin should be considered at similar risk of stroke, compared to people with sustained atrial fibrillation treated with aspirin (rate of ischaemic stroke/year: 3.2% with intermittent v 3.3% with sustained).[6]

Please refer to CD-ROM for full text and references.

# Thromboembolism

Search date November 2002

*David Fitzmaurice, FD Richard Hobbs, and Richard McManus*

## What are the effects of treatments for proximal deep vein thrombosis?

### TRADE OFF BETWEEN BENEFITS AND HARMS

#### Unfractionated and low molecular weight heparin

Systematic reviews have found that low molecular weight heparin◉ reduces the incidence of recurrent thromboembolic disease and decreases the risk of major haemorrhage◉ compared with unfractionated heparin. One systematic review found no significant difference between long term low molecular weight heparin and oral anticoagulation in recurrent thromboembolism, major haemorrhage, or mortality. One systematic review of RCTs found no significant difference in recurrence of thromboembolism between heparin treatment at home and in hospital.

#### Warfarin

We found no RCTs comparing warfarin versus placebo. One RCT found that fewer people had recurrence of proximal deep vein thrombosis within 6 months with combined acenocoumarol (nicoumalone) plus intravenous unfractionated heparin than with acenocoumarol alone; as a result, the trial was stopped. Systematic reviews have found that longer duration of anticoagulation reduces recurrence of deep vein thrombosis compared with shorter duration of anticoagulation. One non-systematic review found limited evidence that longer compared with shorter duration of warfarin was associated with an increased risk of major haemorrhage, but another non-systematic review found no significant difference in major haemorrhage. The absolute risk of recurrent venous thromboembolism decreases with time, but the relative risk reduction with treatment remains constant. Harms of treatment, including major haemorrhage, continue during prolonged treatment. Individuals have different risk profiles and it is likely that the optimal duration of anticoagulation will vary.

### UNKNOWN EFFECTIVENESS

#### Compression stockings

We found no RCTs of standard compression stockings for treating people with proximal deep vein thrombosis. One RCT found that made to measure knee length graduated compression stockings reduced post-thrombotic syndrome over 5–8 years compared with no stockings.

## What are the effects of treatments for isolated calf vein thrombosis?

### TRADE OFF BETWEEN BENEFITS AND HARMS

#### Warfarin plus heparin

One unblinded RCT found no significant difference in recurrent thromboembolism or rates of major haemorrhage between 6 and 12 weeks of anticoagulation. One RCT found that warfarin plus intravenous unfractionated heparin (international normalised ratio◉ > 2.5–4.2) reduced the rate of proximal extension compared with heparin alone.

▶

Cardiovascular disorders

# What are the effects of treatments for pulmonary embolism?

## TRADE OFF BETWEEN BENEFITS AND HARMS

### Oral anticoagulants
We found no direct evidence about the optimum intensity and duration of anticoagulation in people with pulmonary embolism. The best available evidence requires extrapolation of results from studies of people with proximal deep vein thrombosis.

### Unfractionated and low molecular weight heparin
One small RCT in people with pulmonary embolism found that heparin plus warfarin reduced mortality compared with no anticoagulation at 1 year. One RCT in people with symptomatic pulmonary embolism who did not receive thrombolysis or embolectomy found no significant difference between low molecular weight heparin and unfractionated heparin in mortality or new episodes of thromboembolism. Another RCT in people with proximal deep vein thrombosis without clinical signs or symptoms of pulmonary embolism but with high probability lung scan findings found that fixed dose low molecular weight heparin reduced the proportion of people with new episodes of venous thromboembolism compared with intravenous heparin.

## UNLIKELY TO BE BENEFICIAL

### Thrombolysis
RCTs identified by one systematic review found no significant difference in mortality between thrombolysis plus heparin and heparin alone, and found that thrombolysis may increase the incidence of intracranial haemorrhage. One small RCT identified by the review found limited evidence that adding thrombolysis to heparin may reduce mortality in people with shock due to massive pulmonary embolism.

# What are the effects of computerised decision support on oral anticoagulation management?

## UNKNOWN EFFECTIVENESS

### Computerised decision support in oral anticoagulation management
We found no RCTs comparing computerised decision support❻ versus usual management of oral anticoagulation that used clinically important outcomes (major haemorrhage or death).

One systematic review and three subsequent RCTs have found that, compared with usual care, computerised decision support in oral anticoagulation increases time spent in the target international normalised ratio range. Another subsequent RCT found no significant difference between computerised decision support and standard manual support in the time spent in the target international normalised ratio range. A subsequent RCT of initiation of warfarin found that computerised decision support reduced the mean time taken to reach therapeutic levels of anticoagulation compared with usual care. Most RCTs were small and brief.

DEFINITION   **Venous thromboembolism** is any thromboembolic event occurring within the venous system, including deep vein thrombosis and pulmonary embolism. **Deep vein thrombosis** is a radiologically confirmed partial or total thrombotic occlusion of the deep venous system of the legs sufficient to produce symptoms of pain or swelling. **Proximal deep vein thrombosis** affects the veins above the knee (popliteal, superficial femoral, common femoral, and iliac veins). **Isolated calf vein thrombosis** is confined to the deep veins of the calf and does not affect the veins above the knee. **Pulmonary embolism** ▶

# Thromboembolism

is radiologically confirmed partial or total thromboembolic occlusion of pulmonary arteries, sufficient to cause symptoms of breathlessness, chest pain, or both. **Post-thrombotic syndrome** is oedema, ulceration, and impaired viability of the subcutaneous tissues of the leg occurring after deep vein thrombosis. **Recurrence** refers to symptomatic deterioration because of a further (radiologically confirmed) thrombosis, after a previously confirmed thromboembolic event, where there had been an initial, partial, or total symptomatic improvement. **Extension** refers to a radiologically confirmed new, constant, symptomatic intraluminal filling defect extending from an existing thrombosis.

**INCIDENCE/ PREVALENCE** We found no reliable study of the incidence/prevalence of deep vein thrombosis or pulmonary embolism in the UK. A prospective Scandinavian study found an annual incidence of 1.6–1.8/1000 people in the general population.[1,2] One postmortem study estimated that 600 000 people develop pulmonary embolism each year in the USA, of whom 60 000 die as a result.[3]

**AETIOLOGY/ RISK FACTORS** Risk factors for deep vein thrombosis include immobility, surgery (particularly orthopaedic), malignancy, smoking, pregnancy, older age, and inherited or acquired prothrombotic clotting disorders.[4] The oral contraceptive pill is associated with death due to venous thromboembolism (ARI with any combined oral contraception: 1–3/million women a year).[5] The principal cause of pulmonary embolism is a deep vein thrombosis.[4]

**PROGNOSIS** The annual recurrence rate of symptomatic calf vein thrombosis in people without recent surgery is over 25%.[6,7] Proximal extension develops in 40–50% of people with symptomatic calf vein thrombosis.[8] Proximal deep vein thrombosis may cause fatal or non-fatal pulmonary embolism, recurrent venous thrombosis, and the post-thrombotic syndrome. One case series (462 people) published in 1946 found 5.8% mortality from pulmonary emboli in people in hospital with untreated deep vein thrombosis.[9] One non-systematic review of observational studies found that, in people after recent surgery who have an asymptomatic deep calf vein thrombosis, the rate of fatal pulmonary embolism was 13–15%.[10] The incidence of other complications without treatment is not known. The risk of recurrent venous thrombosis and complications is increased by thrombotic risk factors.[11]

Please refer to CD-ROM for full text and references.

## What are the effects of treatments in adults with varicose veins?

### LIKELY TO BE BENEFICIAL

#### Surgery

We found no RCTs comparing surgery versus no treatment or compression stockings. RCTs have found that surgery reduced varicose vein recurrence and incidence of new varicose veins at 1 to 10 years compared with injection sclerotherapy.

### UNKNOWN EFFECTIVENESS

#### Compression stockings

One crossover RCT found no significant difference in symptoms between compression stockings for 4 weeks and no treatment in people with varicose veins. However, the study may have lacked power to detect clinically important effects.

#### Injection sclerotherapy

One RCT found no significant difference between polidocanol and sodium tetradecyl sulphate for improving the appearance of varicose veins at 16 weeks. One RCT reported a similar incidence of new varicose veins at 5 or 10 years with standard dose sclerotherapy, high dose sclerotherapy, and foam sclerotherapy❻.

| | |
|---|---|
| **DEFINITION** | Although we found no consistent definition of varicose veins,[1] the term is commonly taken to mean veins that are distended and tortuous. Any vein may become varicose, but the term "varicose veins" conventionally applies to varices of the superficial leg veins. The condition is caused by poorly functioning valves within the lumen of the veins. Blood flows from the deep to the superficial venous systems through these incompetent valves, causing persistent superficial venous hypertension, which leads to varicosity of the superficial veins. Common sites of valvular incompetence include the saphenofemoral and saphenopopliteal junctions and perforating veins connecting the deep and superficial venous systems along the length of the leg. Sites of venous incompetence are determined by clinical examination handheld Doppler, or by duplex ultrasound. Symptoms of varicose veins include distress about cosmetic appearance, pain, itch, limb heaviness, and cramps. This review focuses on uncomplicated, symptomatic varicose veins. We have excluded treatments for chronic venous ulceration and other complications. We have also excluded studies that solely examine treatments for small, dilated veins in the skin of the leg, known as thread veins, spider veins, or superficial telangiectasia. |
| **INCIDENCE/ PREVALENCE** | One large US cohort study found the biannual incidence of varicose veins to be 2.6% in women and 2.0% in men.[2] Incidence was constant over the age of 40 years. The prevalence of varicose veins in Western populations has been estimated in one study to be about 25–30% among women and 10–20% in men.[3] A recent Scottish cohort study has, however, found a higher prevalence of varices of the saphenous trunks and their main branches in men than in women (40% men and 32% women).[4] |
| **AETIOLOGY/ RISK FACTORS** | One large case control study found that women with two or more pregnancies were at increased risk of varicose veins compared with women with fewer than two pregnancies (RR about 1.2–1.3 after adjustment for age, height, and weight).[2] It found that obesity was also a risk factor, although only among ▶ |

**Cardiovascular disorders**

# Varicose veins

women (RR about 1.3). One narrative systematic review found insufficient evidence on the effects of other suggested risk factors, including genetic predisposition; prolonged sitting or standing; tight undergarments; low fibre diet; constipation; deep vein thrombosis, and smoking.[3]

**PROGNOSIS**  We found no reliable data on prognosis, nor on the frequency of complications, which include chronic inflammation of affected veins (phlebitis), venous ulceration, and rupture of varices.

Please refer to CD-ROM for full text and references.

## What are the effects of treatments for typical absence seizures in children?

TRADE OFF BETWEEN BENEFITS AND HARMS

### Ethosuximide*

We found one systematic review. It found no RCTs comparing ethosuximide versus placebo. There is, however, consensus that ethosuximide is beneficial, although it is associated with rare but serious adverse effects, including aplastic anaemia, skin reactions, and renal and hepatic impairment. The review found three small RCTs comparing ethosuximide versus valproate. It found no significant difference between ethosuximide and valproate in clinical response (as determined by either electroencephalogram or telemetry recordings, or observer reports of seizure frequency). The review found no RCTs comparing ethosuximide versus other anticonvulsants.

### Lamotrigine

One RCT in children and adolescents who had previously benefited from lamotrigine found that lamotrigine increased the proportion of children who remained seizure free compared with placebo. However, lamotrigine is associated with serious skin reactions. We found no RCTs comparing lamotrigine versus other anticonvulsants.

### Valproate*

We found one systematic review. It found no RCTs comparing valproate versus placebo. There is, however, consensus that valproate (sodium valproate or valproic acid) is beneficial, although it is associated with rare but serious adverse effects, including behavioural and cognitive abnormalities, liver necrosis, and pancreatitis. The review found three small RCTs comparing valproate versus ethosuximide. It found no significant difference between valproate and ethosuximide in clinical response (as determined by either electroencephalogram or telemetry recordings, or observer reports of seizure frequency). The review found no RCTs comparing valproate versus other anticonvulsants.

*We found no RCT evidence for valproate or ethosuximide versus placebo but there is consensus belief that valproate and ethosuximide are beneficial in typical absence seizures.

UNKNOWN EFFECTIVENESS

### Gabapentin

One small RCT found no significant difference between gabapentin versus placebo in the frequency of typical absence seizures. However, the study may have lacked power to detect clinically important effects.

**DEFINITION**    Absence seizures are sudden, frequent episodes of unconsciousness lasting a few seconds and are often accompanied by simple automatisms. Typical absence seizures display a characteristic electroencephalogram showing regular symmetrical generalised spike and wave complexes with a frequency of 3 Hz. Typical absence seizures should not be confused with atypical absence seizures, which differ markedly in electroencephalogram findings and ictal behaviour, and usually present with other seizure types in a child with a background of learning disability and severe epilepsy.[1] Childhood absence epilepsy is an epileptic syndrome**ⓖ** whereby typical absence seizures are the ▶

# Absence seizures in children

only type of seizures experienced by a child of otherwise normal development in the absence of any structural lesions. However, in many children, typical absence seizures coexist with other types of seizures and constitute a number of distinct epileptic syndromes such as juvenile myoclonic epilepsy or juvenile absence epilepsy. This differentiation into typical versus atypical seizures is important, as the natural history and response to treatment varies in the two groups. Interventions for atypical absence seizures are not included in this chapter.

**INCIDENCE/** About 10% of seizures in children with epilepsy are typical absence seizures.[1]
**PREVALENCE** Annual incidence has been estimated at 0.7–4.6/100 000 people in the general population and 6–8/100 000 in children aged 0–15 years. Prevalence is 5–50/100 000 people in the general population.[2] Age of onset ranges from 3–13 years with a peak at 6–7 years.

**AETIOLOGY/** The cause of childhood absence epilepsy is presumed to be genetic. Seizures
**RISK FACTORS** can be triggered by hyperventilation in susceptible children.

**PROGNOSIS** In childhood absence epilepsy, in which typical absence seizures are the only type of seizures suffered by the child, seizures generally cease spontaneously by 12 years of age or sooner. Less than 10% of children develop infrequent generalised tonic-clonic seizures and it is very rare for them to continue having absence seizures.[3] In other epileptic syndromes (in which absence seizures may coexist with other types of seizure) prognosis is varied, depending on the syndrome. Absence seizures have a significant impact on quality of life. The episode of unconsciousness may occur at any time, and usually without warning. Affected children need to take precautions to prevent injury during absences and refrain from activities that would put them at risk if seizures occurred (e.g. climbing heights, swimming unsupervised, or cycling on busy roads). Often, school staff members are the first to notice the recurrent episodes of absence seizures, and treatment is generally initiated because of the adverse impact on learning.

---

Please refer to CD-ROM for full text and references.

## What are the effects of treatments?

### LIKELY TO BE BENEFICIAL

**Ibuprofen**

One RCT in children aged 1–6 years receiving antibiotic treatment found that ibuprofen reduced earache as assessed by parental observation after 2 days compared with placebo.

**Paracetamol**

One RCT in children aged 1–6 years receiving antibiotic treatment found that paracetamol reduced earache as assessed by parental observation after 2 days compared with placebo.

### TRADE OFF BETWEEN BENEFITS AND HARMS

**Antibiotics compared with placebo**

We found four systematic reviews comparing antibiotics versus placebo in acute otitis media but using different inclusion criteria and outcome measures. One review in children aged 4 months to 18 years found a reduction in symptoms with a range of antibiotics (cephalosporins, erythromycin, penicillins, trimethoprim–sulfamethoxazole [co-trimoxazole]) after 7–14 days of treatment compared with placebo. Another review in children younger than 2 years found no significant difference in clinical improvement between antibiotics (penicillins, sulphonamides, amoxicillin/clavulanic acid [co-amoxiclav]) and placebo alone or placebo with myringotomy❻ after 7 days. A third review in children aged 4 weeks to 18 years found that antibiotics (ampicillin, amoxicillin) reduced clinical failure rate within 2–7 days compared with placebo or observational treatment. The fourth review in children aged 6 months to 15 years found that, compared with placebo, the early use of antibiotics (erythromycin, penicillins) reduced the proportion of children still in pain 2–7 days after presentation, and reduced the risk of developing contralateral acute otitis media. This review also found that antibiotics increased the risk of vomiting, diarrhoea, or rashes.

**Choice of antibiotic regimen**

One systematic review in children aged 4 months to 18 years found no significant difference between a range of antibiotics in rate of treatment success at 7–14 days or of middle ear effusion at 30 days. Another systematic review in children aged 4 weeks to 18 years found no significant difference between antibiotics in clinical failure rates within 3–14 days. The second review also found that adverse effects, primarily gastrointestinal, were more common with cefixime compared with amoxicillin or ampicillin, and were more common with amoxicillin/clavulanate (original formulation) compared with azithromycin.

**Immediate compared with delayed antibiotic treatment**

One RCT in children aged 6 months to 10 years found that immediate compared with delayed antibiotic treatment reduced the number of days of earache, ear discharge, and amount of daily paracetamol used after the first 24 hours of illness, but found no significant difference between groups in daily pain scores. It also found that immediate antibiotic treatment increased diarrhoea compared with delayed antibiotic treatment. ▶

# Acute otitis media

### Short compared with longer courses of antibiotics

One systematic review and two subsequent RCTs have found that 10 day compared with 5 day courses of antibiotics reduce treatment failure, relapse, and reinfection at 8–14 days, but found no significant difference between groups at 20–42 days.

### LIKELY TO BE INEFFECTIVE OR HARMFUL

### Myringotomy

One RCT in infants aged 3 months to 1 year found no significant difference in resolution of clinical symptoms between groups receiving myringotomy only, antibiotic only, and myringotomy plus antibiotic, but found higher rates of persistent infection with myringotomy only. A second RCT in children aged 2–12 years found no significant difference between myringotomy and no treatment in reduction of pain at 24 hours or 7 days. A third RCT in children aged 7 months to 12 years found higher rates of initial treatment failure (resolution of symptoms within 12 hours) for severe episodes of acute otitis media treated by myringotomy and placebo compared with antibiotic.

## What are the effects of interventions to prevent recurrence?

### LIKELY TO BE BENEFICIAL

### Xylitol chewing gum or syrup

One RCT found that xylitol syrup or chewing gum reduced the proportion of children with at least one episode of acute otitis media compared with control. It found no significant difference between xylitol lozenges and control gum. It found that more children taking xylitol withdrew because of abdominal pain or other unspecified reasons compared with control.

### TRADE OFF BETWEEN BENEFITS AND HARMS

### Antibiotic prophylaxis (long term)

One systematic review in children and adults found that long term antibiotic prophylaxis reduced recurrence of acute otitis media compared with placebo. However, one subsequent RCT in children aged 3 months to 6 years found no significant difference between antibiotic prophylaxis and placebo in preventing recurrence. The RCTs provided insufficient evidence on adverse effects of long term antibiotic prophylaxis. We found insufficient evidence on which antibiotic to use, for how long, and how many previous episodes of acute otitis media justify starting preventive treatment.

### LIKELY TO BE INEFFECTIVE OR HARMFUL

### Tympanostomy (ventilation tubes)

One small RCT found that tympanostomy❻ tube insertion reduced the mean number of acute otitis media episodes during the first 6 month period after treatment compared with myringotomy alone or no surgery, but not during the subsequent 18 months. It also found a non-significant trend for more recurrent infections and worse hearing, after tube extrusion, in those treated with tympanostomy. It found more tympanosclerosis in ears that received ventilating tubes compared with myringotomy alone or no surgery.

**DEFINITION**   Otitis media is an inflammation in the middle ear. Subcategories include acute otitis media (AOM), recurrent AOM, and chronic suppurative otitis media. AOM is the presence of middle ear effusion in conjunction with rapid onset of one or more signs or symptoms of inflammation of the middle ear. Uncomplicated AOM is limited to the middle ear cleft.[1] AOM presents with systemic and local signs, and has a rapid onset. The persistence of an effusion beyond 3 months without signs of infection defines otitis media with effusion (also known as "glue ear"; see otitis media with effusion, p 124). Chronic suppurative otitis media is characterised by continuing inflammation in the middle ear causing discharge (otorrhoea) through a perforated tympanic membrane (see chronic suppurative otitis media, p 116).

**INCIDENCE/ PREVALENCE**  AOM is common and has a high morbidity and low mortality in otherwise healthy children. In the UK, about 30% of children under 3 years of age visit their general practitioner with AOM each year, and 97% receive antimicrobial treatment.[2] By 3 months of age, 10% of children have had an episode of AOM. It is the most common reason for outpatient antimicrobial treatment in the USA.[3]

**AETIOLOGY/ RISK FACTORS**  The most common bacterial causes for AOM in the USA and UK are *Streptococcus pneumoniae*, *Haemophilus influenzae*, and *Moraxella catarrhalis*.[2] Similar pathogens are found in Colombia.[4] The incidence of penicillin resistant *S pneumoniae* has risen, but rates differ between countries. The most important risk factors for AOM are young age and attendance at daycare centres, such as nursery schools. Other risk factors include being white; male sex; a history of enlarged adenoids, tonsillitis, or asthma; multiple previous episodes; bottle feeding; a history of ear infections in parents or siblings; and use of a soother or pacifier. The evidence for an effect of environmental tobacco smoke is controversial.[2]

**PROGNOSIS**  In about 80% of children, the condition resolves in about 3 days without antibiotic treatment. Serious complications are rare in otherwise healthy children but include hearing loss, mastoiditis🅖, meningitis, and recurrent attacks.[2] The World Health Organization estimates that each year 51 000 children under the age of 5 years die from complications of otitis media in developing countries.[5]

Please refer to CD-ROM for full text and references.

# Asthma and other wheezing disorders in children

Search date June 2003

*Duncan Keeley and Michael McKean*

## What are the effects of treatments for acute asthma in children?

### BENEFICIAL

**Oxygen***

An RCT comparing oxygen treatment with no oxygen treatment in acute severe asthma would be considered unethical. One prospective cohort study and clinical experience support the need for oxygen in acute asthma.

**High dose inhaled corticosteroids**

We found one systematic review that identified four RCTs comparing high dose inhaled with oral corticosteroids in children. Three RCTs found no significant difference in hospital admission with nebulised budesonide or dexamethasone compared with oral prednisolone in children with mild to moderate asthma. One RCT in children with moderate to severe asthma found that, compared with inhaled fluticasone, oral prednisolone reduced hospital admission and improved lung function at 4 hours. A subsequent RCT in children aged 4–16 years found that, compared with oral prednisolone, nebulised fluticasone improved lung function over 7 days. Another RCT in children aged 5–16 years admitted to hospital with severe asthma found no significant difference with nebulised budesonide compared with oral prednisolone in lung function at 24 hours or 24 days after admission.

**Inhaled ipratropium bromide added to $\beta_2$ agonists (in emergency room)**

One systematic review has found that, compared with $\beta_2$ agonist alone, multiple doses of inhaled ipratropium bromide plus an inhaled $\beta_2$ agonist (fenoterol or salbutamol) reduced hospital admissions and improved lung function in children aged 18 months to 17 years with severe asthma exacerbations. In children with mild to moderate asthma exacerbations, a single dose of inhaled ipratropium bromide plus a $\beta_2$ agonist (fenoterol, salbutamol, or terbutaline) compared with a $\beta_2$ agonist alone improved lung function for up to 2 hours, but did not reduce hospital admissions

**Metered dose inhaler plus spacer devices for delivery of $\beta_2$ agonists (as effective as nebulisers)**

One systematic review in children with acute but not life threatening asthma, who were old enough to use a spacer, has found no significant difference in hospital admission rates with a metered dose inhaler plus a spacer versus nebulisation for delivering $\beta_2$ agonists (fenoterol, salbutamol, or terbutaline) or $\beta$ agonist (orciprenaline❻). Children using a metered dose inhaler with a spacer may have shorter stays in emergency departments, less hypoxia, and lower pulse rates compared with children receiving $\beta_2$ agonist by nebulisation.

**Systemic corticosteroids**

One systematic review has found that systemic corticosteroids increase the likelihood of early discharge and reduce the frequency of relapse within 1–3 months in children hospitalised with acute asthma.

*In the absence of RCT evidence, categorisation based on observational evidence and strong consensus belief that oxygen is beneficial.

Child health

◀ **LIKELY TO BE BENEFICIAL**

## Intravenous theophylline

One systematic review found that in children aged 1–19 years admitted to hospital with severe asthma, intravenous theophylline improved lung function and symptom scores 6–8 hours after treatment compared with placebo, but found no significant difference in number of bronchodilator treatments required or length of hospital stay. A subsequent RCT in children aged 1–17 years admitted to an intensive care unit with severe asthma found that, compared with controls, intravenous theophylline decreased the time to reach a clinical asthma score of 3 or less but found no significant difference in length of stay in the intensive care unit.

**UNKNOWN EFFECTIVENESS**

## Inhaled ipratropium bromide added to salbutamol (after initial stabilisation)

One RCT in children admitted to hospital with initially stabilised severe asthma found no significant difference in clinical asthma scores**☉** during the first 36 hours with nebulised ipratropium bromide compared with placebo added to salbutamol**☉** (a $\beta_2$ agonist) and corticosteroid (hydrocortisone or prednisone).

## What are the effects of single agent prophylaxis in childhood asthma?

**BENEFICIAL**

## Inhaled corticosteroids

One systematic review has found that, compared with placebo, prophylactic inhaled corticosteroids improve symptoms and lung function in children with asthma. Several RCTs have found that inhaled corticosteroids slightly reduce growth rate compared with placebo, although studies with long term follow up suggest attainment of normal adult height. Inhaled corticosteroids have been associated with rare reports of adrenal suppression. One RCT in children aged 6–16 years found no significant difference in improvement of asthma symptoms with inhaled beclometasone compared with theophylline, but found less use of bronchodilators and oral corticosteroids with inhaled beclometasone. Small RCTs have found inhaled corticosteroids to be more effective than sodium cromoglicate in improving symptoms and lung function. RCTs in children aged 5–16 years have found that, compared with inhaled long acting $\beta_2$ agonists (salmeterol) or inhaled nedocromil, inhaled corticosteroids (beclometasone, budesonide, or fluticasone) improve symptoms and lung function in children with asthma. RCTs in children aged 5–16 years have found that inhaled corticosteroids (beclometasone, budesonide, or fluticasone) versus inhaled long acting $\beta_2$ agonists (salmeterol) or inhaled nedocromil improve symptoms and lung function in children with asthma.

## Inhaled nedocromil

Two RCTs in children aged 6–12 years found that, compared with placebo, inhaled nedocromil reduces asthma symptom scores, asthma severity, and bronchodilator use, and improves lung function. One large RCT in children aged 5–12 years with mild to moderate asthma found no significant difference between nedocromil and budesonide or placebo in lung function, hospital admission rate, or the symptom score on diary cards, but found that budesonide was superior to nedocromil, and that nedocromil was superior to placebo in several measures of asthma symptoms and morbidity.

# Asthma and other wheezing disorders in children

### Oral montelukast

One RCT in children aged 6–14 years found that, compared with placebo, oral montelukast (a leukotriene receptor antagonist) increased from baseline the mean morning forced expiratory volume in 1 second and reduced the total daily $\beta_2$ agonist use, but found no significant difference in daytime asthma symptom score or in nocturnal awakenings with asthma. Another RCT in children aged 2–5 years found that, compared with placebo, oral montelukast improved average daytime symptom scores and reduced the need for rescue oral steroid courses, but found no significant difference in average overnight asthma symptom scores. We found no RCTs directly comparing oral montelukast with inhaled corticosteroids.

## TRADE OFF BETWEEN BENEFITS AND HARMS

### Inhaled salmeterol

Two RCTs in children aged 4–14 years found that, compared with placebo, inhaled salmeterol improved lung function but found conflicting evidence about reduced use of salbutamol⊙. One RCT comparing inhaled salmeterol with beclometasone found that salmeterol was associated with a significant deterioration in bronchial reactivity.

### Oral theophylline

One small RCT in children aged 6–15 years found that, compared with placebo, oral theophylline increased mean morning peak expiratory flow rate and reduced the mean number of acute night time attacks and doses of bronchodilator used. Another RCT in children aged 6–16 years found no significant difference in improvement of asthma symptoms with oral theophylline compared with inhaled beclometasone, but found greater use of bronchodilators and oral corticosteroids with theophylline over 1 year. Theophylline has serious adverse effects (cardiac arrhythmia, convulsions) if therapeutic blood concentrations are exceeded.

## UNKNOWN EFFECTIVENESS

### Inhaled sodium cromoglicate

One systematic review found insufficient evidence for prophylactic treatment with sodium cromoglicate in children aged less than 1 year to 18 years. Several small comparative RCTs found sodium cromoglicate to be less effective than inhaled corticosteroids in improving symptoms and lung function.

---

## What are the effects of additional prophylactic treatments in childhood asthma inadequately controlled by standard dose inhaled corticosteroids?

## UNKNOWN EFFECTIVENESS

### Increased dose of inhaled beclometasone

One RCT in children aged 6–16 years taking inhaled beclometasone (a corticosteroid) comparing the addition of a second dose of inhaled beclometasone with placebo found no significant difference in lung function, symptom scores, exacerbation rates, or bronchial reactivity but found a reduction in growth velocity at 1 year.

### Inhaled salmeterol

One RCT in children aged 6–16 years found that addition of salmeterol (a long acting $\beta_2$ agonist) increased peak expiratory flow rates in the first few months of treatment but found no increase after 1 year. A second short term RCT in children aged 4–16 years also found increased morning peak expiratory flow rates and more symptom free days at 3 months with addition of salmeterol.

◄ **Oral montelukast**

One crossover RCT in children aged 6–14 years with persistent asthma who had been taking inhaled budesonide for at least 6 weeks found that, compared with addition of placebo, oral montelukast (a leukotriene receptor antagonist) improved lung function and decreased the proportion of days with asthma exacerbations over 4 weeks. These differences were statistically significant but modest in clinical terms.

**Oral theophylline**

One small RCT found that addition of theophylline, compared with placebo, to previous treatment increased the proportion of symptom free days and reduced the use of additional orciprenaline (a β agonist) and additional corticosteroid (beclometasone or prednisolone) over 4 weeks. We found insufficient evidence to weigh these short term benefits and possible long term harms.

## What are the effects of treatments for acute wheezing in infants?

**LIKELY TO BE BENEFICIAL**

### Addition of ipratropium bromide to fenoterol

One RCT identified by a systematic review in infants aged 3–24 months found that addition of ipratropium bromide to fenoterol (a long acting $\beta_2$ agonist) compared with fenoterol alone reduced the proportion of infants receiving further treatment 45 minutes after initial treatment.

### Inhaled salbutamol

One RCT in infants aged 3 months to 2 years found that, compared with placebo, nebulised salbutamol❻ (a short acting $\beta_2$ agonist) improved respiratory rate but found no significant difference in hospital admission. Another RCT that included infants aged less than 18 months to 36 months found no significant difference in change from baseline in clinical symptom scores with nebulised salbutamol versus placebo.

### Short acting $\beta_2$ agonists delivered by metered dose inhaler/spacer versus nebuliser

Two RCTs in children aged up to 5 years found no significant difference in hospital admissions with delivery of salbutamol through a metered dose inhaler plus spacer compared with nebulised salbutamol. Another RCT in infants aged 1–24 months found no significant difference in improvement of symptoms with delivery of terbutaline through a metered dose inhaler plus spacer compared with nebulised terbutaline. Nebulised $\beta_2$ agonists may cause tachycardia, tremor, and hypokalaemia.

**UNKNOWN EFFECTIVENESS**

### High dose inhaled corticosteroids

One systematic review found that high dose inhaled corticosteroids compared with placebo reduced the requirement for oral corticosteroids, but the difference was not statistically significant. The review also found a clear preference for the inhaled corticosteroids by the children's parents over placebo. The clinical importance of these results is unclear.

### Inhaled ipratropium bromide

We found no RCTs comparing inhaled ipratropium bromide compared with placebo for treating acute wheeze.

◄ **Oral prednisolone**

One small RCT found no significant difference in daily symptom scores with oral prednisolone (a corticosteroid) versus placebo.

## What are the effects of prophylaxis in wheezing infants?

**LIKELY TO BE BENEFICIAL**

### Oral salbutamol

One RCT identified by a systematic review in infants aged 3–14 months found that oral salbutamol (a short acting $\beta_2$ agonist) compared with placebo reduced treatment failures.

**TRADE OFF BETWEEN BENEFITS AND HARMS**

### Higher dose inhaled budesonide

One RCT in infants aged 6–30 months found that higher prophylactic doses of inhaled budesonide (a corticosteroid) compared with placebo reduced symptoms and the proportion of children with acute wheezing episodes during a 12 week period but found no significant reduction in the proportion of wheezing episodes per infant. Another RCT in infants aged 11–36 months found that higher prophylactic doses of inhaled budesonide significantly reduced the proportion of days requiring oral prednisolone, and symptoms of wheezing and sleep disturbance, but found no significant improvement for cough. Higher doses of inhaled corticosteroids have the potential for adverse effects.

**UNKNOWN EFFECTIVENESS**

### Inhaled ipratropium bromide

One small RCT identified by a systematic review found no significant difference in relief of symptoms with nebulised ipratropium bromide compared with placebo. The study may have lacked power to exclude a clinically important difference between treatments.

### Inhaled salbutamol

Two RCTs identified by a systematic review in infants aged up to 2 years found no significant improvement in symptoms with inhaled salbutamol (a short acting $\beta_2$ agonist)compared with placebo.

### Lower dose inhaled budesonide

Three RCTs found no clear evidence of effectiveness with lower prophylactic doses of inhaled budesonide (a corticosteroid) in children aged 1 week to 6 years with recurrent wheeze.

**UNLIKELY TO BE BENEFICIAL**

### Addition of inhaled beclometasone to salbutamol

One RCT found no significant improvement in symptoms with addition of inhaled beclometasone compared with placebo to inhaled salbutamol.**Ⓖ**

**DEFINITION**   Differentiation between asthma and non-asthmatic viral associated wheeze may be difficult; persisting symptoms and signs between acute attacks are suggestive of asthma, as are a personal or family history of atopic conditions such as eczema and hay fever. **Childhood asthma** is characterised by chronic or recurrent cough and wheeze. The diagnosis is confirmed by demonstrating reversible airway obstruction, preferably on several occasions over time, in children old enough to perform peak flow measurements or spirometry. Diagnosing asthma in children requires exclusion of other causes of recurrent respiratory symptoms. Acute asthma is a term used to describe a ▶

severe exacerbation of asthma symptoms accompanied by tachycardia and tachypnoea. The aim of prophylactic treatments in asthma is to minimise persistent symptoms and prevent acute exacerbations. **Wheezing in infants** is characterised by a high pitched purring or whistling sound produced mainly on the out breath and is commonly associated with an acute viral infection such as bronchiolitis (see bronchiolitis, p 56) or asthma. These are not easy to distinguish clinically.

**INCIDENCE/ PREVALENCE**

**Childhood asthma:** Surveys have found an increase in the proportion of children diagnosed with asthma. The increase is higher than can be explained by an increased readiness to diagnose asthma. One questionnaire study from Aberdeen, Scotland, surveyed 2510 children aged 8–13 years in 1964 and 3403 children in 1989. Over the 25 years, the diagnosis of asthma rose from 4% to 10%.[1] The increase in prevalence of childhood asthma from the 1960s to 1980s was accompanied by an increase in hospitals admissions over the same period. In England and Wales this was a sixfold increase.[2] **Wheezing in infants** is common and seems to be increasing, although the magnitude of any increase is not clear. One Scottish cross-sectional study (2510 children aged 8–13 years in 1964 and 3403 children in 1989) found that the prevalence of wheeze rose from 10% in 1964 to 20% in 1989, and episodes of shortness of breath rose from 5% to 10% over the same period.[1] Difficulties in defining clear groups (phenotypes) and the transient nature of the symptoms, which often resolve spontaneously, have confounded many studies.

**AETIOLOGY/ RISK FACTORS**

**Childhood asthma:** Asthma is more common in children with a personal or family history of atopy, increased severity and frequency of wheezing episodes and presence of variable airway obstruction or bronchial hyperresponsiveness. Precipitating factors for symptoms and acute episodes include infection, house dust mites, allergens from pet animals, exposure to tobacco smoke, and anxiety. **Wheezing in infants:** Most wheezing episodes in infancy are precipitated by viral respiratory infections.

**PROGNOSIS**

**Childhood asthma:** A British longitudinal study of children born in 1970 found that 29% of 5 year olds wheezing in the past year were still wheezing at the age of 10 years.[3] Another study followed a group of children in Melbourne, Australia from the age of 7 years (in 1964) into adulthood. The study found that a large proportion (73%) of 14 year olds with infrequent symptoms had few or no symptoms by the age of 28 years, whereas two thirds of those 14 year olds with frequent wheezing still had recurrent attacks at the age of 28 years.[4] **Wheezing in infants:** One cohort study (826 infants followed from birth to 6 years) suggests that there may be at least three different prognostic categories for wheezing in infants: "persistant wheezers" (14% of total, with risk factors for atopic asthma such as elevated immunoglobulin E levels and a maternal history of asthma), who initially suffered wheeze during viral infections, and in whom the wheezing persisted into school age; "transient wheezers" (20% of total, with reduced lung function as infants but no early markers of atopy), who also suffered wheeze during viral infections but stopped wheezing after the first 3 years of life; and "late onset wheezers" (15% of total), who did not wheeze when aged under 3 years but had developed wheeze by school age.[5] Another retrospective cohort study found that 14% of children with one attack and 23% of children with four or more attacks in the first year of life had experienced at least one wheezing illness in the past year at age 10 years.[3] Administering inhaled treatments to young children can be difficult. Inconsistencies in results could reflect the effects of the differences in the drugs used, delivery devices used, dosages used, and the differences in the pattern of wheezing illnesses and treatment responses among young children.

Please refer to CD-ROM for full text and references.

# Bronchiolitis

Search date February 2003

*Juan Manuel Lozano*

## What are the effects of preventive interventions?

### BENEFICIAL

**Respiratory syncytial virus immunoglobulins or palivizumab (monoclonal antibody) in children at high risk**

One systematic review has found that, in children born prematurely, in children with bronchopulmonary dysplasia, and in children with a combination of risk factors, prophylactic respiratory syncytial virus immunoglobulin or palivizumab (monoclonal antibody) reduces admission rates to hospital and intensive care units compared with placebo or no prophylaxis.

### UNKNOWN EFFECTIVENESS

**Nursing interventions (cohort segregation⊕, handwashing, gowns, masks, gloves, and goggles) in children admitted to hospital**

We found no RCTs about the effects of these interventions to prevent spread of bronchiolitis to other children.

## What are the effects of treatments?

### UNKNOWN EFFECTIVENESS

**Bronchodilators (inhaled salbutamol, inhaled adrenaline [epinephrine])**

Systematic reviews have found that, inhaled bronchodilators achieve short term improvement in overall clinical scores compared with placebo in children treated in hospital, emergency departments, and outpatient clinics. They have found no evidence that bronchodilators reduce admission rates or produce a clinically important improvement in oxygen saturation. Subsequent RCTs found no evidence that nebulised adrenaline, changed short term outcomes during the first 4 days of illness in infants or the duration of hospital stay compared with 0.9% sodium chloride. One small RCT found that nebulised adrenaline reduced the rate of hospital admission compared with salbutamol. However, we were unable to draw reliable conclusions from this small study.

**Corticosteroids**

One systematic review and 10 additional RCTs found limited and conflicting evidence on the effects of corticosteroids compared with placebo.

**Routine broad spectrum antibiotics**

We found no evidence in children with bronchiolitis alone. One unblinded RCT in children with bronchiolitis and uncomplicated pneumonia (crackles on auscultation or consolidation on a chest radiograph) found no significant difference in clinical scores with routine use of antibiotics (ampicillin, penicillin, or erythromycin) compared with placebo. However, the RCT may have lacked power to exclude a clinically important effect.

**Ribavirin**

One systematic review found insufficient evidence that ribavirin reduced mortality, risk of respiratory deterioration, or duration of hospital stay in children admitted to hospital with respiratory syncytial virus bronchiolitis. It found some evidence that ▶

ribavirin reduced the duration of mechanical ventilation. Two subsequent RCTs found no evidence that ribavirin reduced duration of hospital stay, admission rate because of lower respiratory tract symptoms during the first year after the acute episode, or the frequency of recurrent wheezing illness over 1 year of follow up.

## Respiratory syncytial virus immunoglobulins, pooled immunoglobulins, or palivizumab (monoclonal antibody)

RCTs found insufficient evidence on the effects of immunoglobulin treatment.

**DEFINITION**     Bronchiolitis is a virally induced acute bronchiolar inflammation that is associated with signs and symptoms of airway obstruction. Diagnosis is based on clinical findings. Clinical manifestations include fever, rhinitis (inflammation of the nasal mucosa), tachypnoea, expiratory wheezing, cough, rales, use of accessory muscles, apnoea (absence of breathing), dyspnoea (difficulty in breathing), alar flaring (flaring of the nostrils), and retractions (indrawing of the intercostal soft tissues on inspiration). Disease severity $\textbf{G}$ of bronchiolitis may be classified clinically as mild, moderate, or severe.

**INCIDENCE/**     Bronchiolitis is the most common lower respiratory tract infection in infants,
**PREVALENCE**     occurring in a seasonal pattern with highest incidence in the winter in temperate climates,[1] and in the rainy season in warmer countries. Each year in the USA, about 21% of infants have lower respiratory tract disease and 6–10/1000 infants are admitted to hospital for bronchiolitis (1–2% of children < 12 months of age).[2] The peak rate of admission occurs in infants aged 2–6 months.[3]

**AETIOLOGY/**     Respiratory syncytial virus is responsible for bronchiolitis in 70% of cases. This
**RISK FACTORS**    figure reaches 80–100% in the winter months. However, in early spring, parainfluenza virus type 3 is often responsible.[1]

**PROGNOSIS**     **Morbidity and mortality:** Disease severity is related to the size of the infant, and to the proximity and frequency of contact with infective infants. Children at increased risk of morbidity and mortality are those with congenital heart disease, chronic lung disease, history of premature birth, hypoxia, and age less than 6 weeks.[4] Other factors associated with a prolonged or complicated hospital stay include a history of apnoea or respiratory arrest, pulmonary consolidation seen on a chest radiograph, and (in North America) people of Native American or Inuit race.[5] The risk of death within 2 weeks is high for children with congenital heart disease (3.4%) or chronic lung disease (3.5%) as compared with other groups combined (0.1%).[4] Rates of admission to intensive care units (range 31–36%) and need for mechanical ventilation (range 11–19%) are similar among all high risk groups.[4] The percentage of these children needing oxygen supplementation is also high (range 63–80%).[4] In contrast, rates of intensive care unit admission (15%) and ventilation (8%) in such children are markedly lower.[6] **Long term prognosis:** Information on long term prognosis varies among studies. One small prospective study of two matched cohorts (25 children with bronchiolitis; 25 children without) found no evidence that bronchiolitis requiring outpatient treatment is associated with an increased risk of asthma in the long term.[7] Possible confounding factors include variation in illness severity, smoke exposure, and being in overcrowded environments.[8] We found one prospective study in 50 randomly selected infants admitted with bronchiolitis, followed up by questionnaire for 5 years and a visit in the fifth year. It found a doubling of asthma incidence compared with the general population, although there was large (30%) loss to follow up and no matched control group.[9]

Please refer to CD-ROM for full text and references.

# Cardiorespiratory arrest in children

Search date June 2003

*Kate Ackerman and David Creery*

## What are the effects of treatments for non-submersion out of hospital cardiorespiratory arrest?

### LIKELY TO BE BENEFICIAL

**Bag–mask ventilation**

We found no RCTs. One controlled clinical trial in children requiring airway management in the community found no significant difference in survival or neurological outcome between endotracheal intubation and bag–mask ventilation in children with non-submersion cardiorespiratory arrest.

**Bystander cardiopulmonary resuscitation**

It is widely accepted that cardiopulmonary resuscitation and ventilation should be undertaken in children who have arrested. Placebo controlled trials would be considered unethical. One systematic review of observational studies has found that children whose arrest was witnessed and who received bystander cardiopulmonary resuscitation were more likely to survive to hospital discharge compared with no bystander cardiopulmonary resuscitation. We found no RCTs on the effects of training parents to perform cardiopulmonary resuscitation.

**Intubation**

We found no RCTs. One controlled trial found no significant difference in survival or neurological outcome between endotracheal intubation and bag–mask ventilation in children with non-submersion cardiorespiratory arrest.

**Airway management and ventilation; direct current cardiac shock (for ventricular fibrillation or pulseless ventricular tachycardia❸); standard dose intravenous adrenaline (epinephrine)**

Although we found no direct evidence to support their use, widespread consensus based on indirect evidence and extrapolation from adult data holds that these interventions should be universally applied to children who have arrested. Placebo controlled trials would be considered unethical.

### UNKNOWN EFFECTIVENESS

**High dose intravenous adrenaline; intravenous sodium bicarbonate; intravenous calcium; training parents to perform cardiopulmonary resuscitation**

We found no RCTs or prospective observational studies on the effects of these interventions in children who have arrested in the community.

**DEFINITION**　　The chapter deals with non-submersion out of hospital cardiorespiratory arrest in children, which is defined as a state of pulselessness and apnoea occurring outside of a medical facility and not caused by submersion in water.[1]

**INCIDENCE/**　　We found 12 studies (3 prospective, 9 retrospective) reporting the incidence
**PREVALENCE**　of non-submersion out of hospital cardiorespiratory arrest in children❶.[2–13] Eleven studies reported the incidence in both adults and children, and eight reported the incidence in children.[2–9,11–13] Incidence of arrests in the general population ranged from 2.2–5.7/100 000 people a year (mean 3.1, 95% CI ▶

2.1 to 4.1). Incidence of arrests in children ranged from 6.9–18.0/100 000 children a year (mean 10.6, 95% CI 7.1 to 14.1).[8] One prospective study (300 children) found that about 50% of out of hospital cardiorespiratory arrests occurred in children under 12 months, and about two thirds occurred in children under 18 months.[11]

**AETIOLOGY/ RISK FACTORS**  We found 26 studies reporting the causes of non-submersion pulseless arrests𝐆 in a total of 1574 children. The commonest causes were undetermined (as in sudden infant death syndrome𝐆) (39%), trauma (18%), chronic disease (7%), and pneumonia (4%)𝐓.[1,3–12,14–28]

**PROGNOSIS**  We found no observational studies that investigated non-submersion arrests alone. We found 27 studies (5 prospective, 22 retrospective; total of 1754 children) that reported out of hospital arrest.[1–12,14–28] The overall survival rate following out of hospital arrest was 5% (87 children). Nineteen of these studies (1140 children) found that of the 48 surviving children, 12 (25%) had no or mild neurological disability and 36 (75%) had moderate or severe neurological disability. We found one systematic review (search date 1997), which reported outcomes after cardiopulmonary resuscitation for both in hospital and out of hospital arrests in children of any cause, including submersion.[29] Studies were excluded if they did not report survival. The review found evidence from prospective and retrospective observational studies that out of hospital arrest of any cause in children carries a poorer prognosis than arrest within hospital (132/1568 children [8%] survived to hospital discharge after out of hospital arrest v 129/544 children [24%] after in hospital arrests). About half of the survivors were involved in studies that reported neurological outcome. Of these, survival with "good neurological outcome" (i.e. normal or mild neurological deficit) was higher in children who arrested in hospital compared with those who arrested elsewhere (60/77 surviving children [78%] in hospital v 28/68 [41%] elsewhere).[29]

---

Please refer to CD-ROM for full text and references.

# Constipation in children

**Search date August 2003**

*Gregory Rubin*

## What are the effects of treatments?

**TRADE OFF BETWEEN BENEFITS AND HARMS**

### Cisapride with or without magnesium oxide

Two RCTs in people aged 2–18 years found that cisapride improved stool frequency and symptoms of constipation after 8–12 weeks of treatment in an outpatient setting compared with placebo. One RCT in children aged 1–7 years with chronic constipation found that combined treatment with cisapride and magnesium oxide significantly improved stool frequency after 3–4 weeks of treatment in an outpatient setting compared with magnesium oxide alone. We found no evidence from primary care settings. Use of cisapride has been restricted in some countries because of adverse cardiac effects.

**UNKNOWN EFFECTIVENESS**

### Biofeedback training

One systematic review found no significant difference between biofeedback plus conventional treatment and conventional treatment alone in persisting defecation disorders at 12 months.

### Increased dietary fibre

We found no systematic review or RCTs in children on the effects of increasing dietary fibre.

### Osmotic laxatives

We found no RCTs that compared osmotic laxatives versus placebo in children. Two small RCTs found no significant difference in stool frequency or consistency between lactulose and lactitol after 2–4 weeks in children aged 8 months to 16 years. One of the RCTs found that lactulose increased abdominal pain and flatulence compared with lactitol. A third RCT in non-breastfed constipated infants found no difference between different strengths of lactulose.

### Stimulant laxatives

One systematic review found no reliable RCTs comparing stimulant laxatives versus placebo or other treatments.

**DEFINITION**  **Constipation** is characterised by infrequent bowel evacuations; hard, small faeces; or difficult or painful defecation. The frequency of bowel evacuation varies from person to person.[1] According to the Rome II diagnostic criteria for childhood defecation disorders, functional constipation can be defined as "either having hard or pellet-like stools for the majority of stools or firm stools two or less times per week in the absence of structural, endocrine or metabolic diseases".[2] Some studies reported in this chapter used other diagnostic criteria.[3] **Encopresis** is defined as involuntary bowel movements in inappropriate places at least once a month for 3 months or more, in children aged 4 years and older.[4]

**INCIDENCE/**  Constipation with or without encopresis is common in children. It accounts for
**PREVALENCE**  3% of consultations to paediatric outpatient clinics and 25% of paediatric gastroenterology consultations in the USA.[5] Encopresis has been reported in 2% of children at school entry. The peak incidence is at 2–4 years of age. ▶

◀ **AETIOLOGY/** No cause is discovered in 90–95% of children with constipation. Low fibre
**RISK FACTORS** intake and a family history of constipation may be associated factors.[6] Psychosocial factors are often suspected, although most children with constipation are
developmentally normal.[5] Chronic constipation can lead to progressive faecal
retention, distension of the rectum, and loss of sensory and motor function.
Organic causes for constipation are uncommon, but include Hirschsprung's
disease (1/5000 births; male to female ratio of 4 : 1; constipation invariably
present from birth), cystic fibrosis, anorectal physiological abnormalities, anal
fissures, constipating drugs, dehydrating metabolic conditions, and other forms
of malabsorption.[5] This chapter aims to cover children in whom no underlying
cause is identified.

**PROGNOSIS** Childhood constipation can be difficult to treat and often requires prolonged
support, explanation, and medical treatment. In one long term follow up study
of children presenting under the age of 5 years, 50% recovered within 1 year
and 65–70% recovered within 2 years; the remainder required laxatives for
daily bowel movements or continued to soil for several years.[5] It is not known
what proportion continue to have problems into adult life, although adults
presenting with megarectum or megacolon often have a history of bowel
problems from childhood.

Please refer to CD-ROM for full text and references.

# Depression in children and adolescents

Search date May 2003

*Philip Hazell*

---

## What are the effects of treatments?

### BENEFICIAL

**Cognitive behavioural therapy (in children and adolescents with mild to moderate depression)**

One systematic review in children and adolescents with mild to moderate depression has found that cognitive behavioural therapy⊙ improves symptoms compared with non-specific support.

### LIKELY TO BE BENEFICIAL

**Interpersonal therapy (in adolescents with mild to moderate depression)**

Two RCTs found that interpersonal therapy⊙ versus clinical monitoring or waiting list control increased recovery rate over 12 weeks in adolescents with mild to moderate depression.

### TRADE OFF BETWEEN BENEFITS AND HARMS

**Selective serotonin reuptake inhibitors**

We found limited evidence that selective serotonin reuptake inhibitors improved symptoms of depression compared with placebo; one RCT found no significant difference, one RCT found significant results on some depression measures but not others, while one RCT found improvement in depressive symptoms with fluoxetine compared with placebo after 8–9 weeks. One RCT found that, in adolescents with major depression, paroxetine improved remission after 8 weeks compared with placebo. Another RCT found no significant difference in effects on outcomes between paroxetine and clomipramine, although it may have lacked power to detect clinically important effects. We found no RCTs on other selective serotonin reuptake inhibitors. Selective serotonin reuptake inhibitors are frequently associated with dizziness, light-headedness, drowsiness, poor concentration, nausea, headache, and fatigue if treatment is reduced or stopped.

### UNKNOWN EFFECTIVENESS

**Cognitive behavioural therapy (in depressed adolescents with depressed parent)**

One RCT in depressed adolescents with depressed parents found no significant difference in recovery from depression between cognitive behavioural therapy plus usual care and usual care alone over 2 years.

**Electroconvulsive therapy**

We found no RCTs on electroconvulsive therapy in children and adolescents with depression.

**Intravenous clomipramine (in adolescents)**

One small RCT found that, in non-suicidal adolescents, intravenous clomipramine improved depression scores at 6 days compared with placebo. However, the trial was too small and brief for us to draw reliable conclusions.

▶

### Lithium

One Small RCT in children with depression and a family history of bipolar affective disorder found no significant difference between lithium and placebo in global assessment or depression scores after 6 weeks. However, the study may have lacked power to detect clinically important effects.

### Monoamine oxidase inhibitors

One RCT found insufficient evidence to compare the reversible monoamine oxidase inhibitor moclobemide versus placebo in children aged 9–15 years with major depression, some of whom had a comorbid disorder. We found no RCTs on non-reversible monoamine oxidase inhibitors in children or adolescents.

### St John's Wort

We found no RCTs on St John's Wort (Hypericum perforatum) in children or adolescents with depression.

### Venlafaxine

One small RCT in children and adolescents with major depression receiving psychotherapy found no significant difference between venlafaxine and placebo in improvement of depressive symptoms after 6 weeks. However, the study may have lacked power to detect clinically important effects.

### Family therapy; specific pyschological treatments other than cognitive behavioural therapy

We found insufficient evidence in children and adolescents about the effects of these interventions.

### UNLIKELY TO BE BENEFICIAL

### Tricyclic antidepressants (in adolescents)

One systematic review in adolescents and children found no significant difference in depression scores between oral tricyclic antidepressants (amitriptyline, desipramine, imipramine, nortriptyline) and placebo after 4–10 weeks. However, subgroup analyses found that oral tricyclic antidepressants improved symptoms compared with placebo in adolescents but not children. There was no significant difference in rates of remission. The review also found that oral tricyclic antidepressants were associated with adverse effects. One RCT found no significant difference in improvement rates between oral clomipramine and paroxetine after 8 weeks.

### LIKELY TO BE INEFFECTIVE OR HARMFUL

### Tricyclic antidepressants (in children)

Subgroup analyses in one systematic review found no significant difference between oral tricyclic antidepressants (amitriptyline, desipramine, imipramine, nortriptyline) and placebo in children with depression. The review also found that oral tricyclic antidepressants were associated with adverse effects.

**DEFINITION**  Compared with adult depression (see depressive disorders, p 249), depression in children (6–12 years) and adolescents (13–18 years) may have a more insidious onset, may be characterised more by irritability than sadness, and occurs more often in association with other conditions such as anxiety, conduct disorder, hyperkinesis, and learning problems.[1] The term "major depression" is used to distinguish discrete episodes of depression from mild, chronic (1 year or longer) low mood or irritability, which is known as "dysthymia".[1] The severity of depression may be defined by the level of impairment and the presence or absence of psychomotor changes and somatic symptoms (see depressive disorders, p 249). In some studies, ▶

# Depression in children and adolescents

severity of depression is defined according to cut off scores on depression rating scales. A manic episode is defined by abnormally and persistently elevated, expansive, or irritable mood. Additional symptoms may include grandiosity, decreased need for sleep, pressured speech, flight of ideas, distractibility, psychomotor agitation, and impaired judgement.[2]

**INCIDENCE/ PREVALENCE** Estimates of prevalence of depression among children and adolescents in the community range from 2–6%.[3,4] Prevalence tends to increase with age, with a sharp rise at around the onset of puberty. Pre-adolescent boys and girls are affected equally by the condition, but depression is seen more frequently among adolescent girls than boys.[5]

**AETIOLOGY/ RISK FACTORS** The aetiology is uncertain, but may include genetic vulnerability,[6] childhood events, and current psychosocial adversity.[1]

**PROGNOSIS** In children and adolescents, the recurrence rate after a first depressive episode is 70% by 5 years, which is similar to the recurrence rate in adults. It is not clear whether this is related to the severity of depression.[1] Young people experiencing a moderate to severe depressive episode may be more likely than adults to have a manic episode within the following few years.[1,7] Trials of treatments for child and adolescent depression have found high rates of response to placebo (as much as two thirds of people in some inpatient studies).[8] A third of young people who experience a depressive episode will make a suicide attempt at some stage, and 3–4% will die from suicide.[1]

Please refer to CD-ROM for full text and references.

### Search date February 2003

*Jacqueline Dalby-Payne and Elizabeth Elliott*

## What are the effects of treatments?

**BENEFICIAL**

### Oral rehydration solutions (as effective as iv fluids)

One systematic review and two additional RCTs in children with mild to moderate dehydration in developed countries found no significant difference between oral rehydration solutions versus intravenous fluids in duration of diarrhoea, time spent in hospital, or weight gain at discharge. One small RCT in children with mild to moderate dehydration managed in the emergency department found that oral rehydration reduced length of stay in the department but did not significantly reduce admission to hospital compared with intravenous fluids. One RCT in children with severe dehydration in a developing country found that oral rehydration solutions reduced the duration of diarrhoea and increased weight gain at discharge, and was associated with fewer adverse effects compared with intravenous fluids.

**LIKELY TO BE BENEFICIAL**

### Lactose-free feeds (for duration of diarrhoea)

We found evidence from one systematic review and subsequent RCTs that lactose-free feeds versus feeds containing lactose reduce the duration of diarrhoea in children with mild to severe dehydration.

### Loperamide (reduces duration of diarrhoea, but adverse effects are unclear)

Two RCTs found that, in children with mild to moderate dehydration, loperamide versus placebo significantly reduces the duration of diarrhoea. Another RCT found no significant difference with loperamide versus placebo in the duration of diarrhoea. We found insufficient evidence about adverse effects.

**UNKNOWN EFFECTIVENESS**

### Clear fluids for rehydration (other than oral rehydration solutions)

We found no systematic review or RCTs on "clear fluids" (water, carbonated drinks, and translucent fruit juices) versus oral rehydration solutions for treatment of mild to moderate dehydration caused by acute gastroenteritis.

**DEFINITION**  Acute gastroenteritis is characterised by rapid onset of diarrhoea with or without vomiting, nausea, fever, and abdominal pain.[1] In children, the symptoms and signs can be non-specific.[2] Diarrhoea is defined as the frequent passage of unformed liquid stools.[3]

**INCIDENCE/ PREVALENCE**  Worldwide, about 3 billion–5 billion cases of acute gastroenteritis occur in children under 5 years of age each year.[4] In the UK, acute gastroenteritis accounts for 204/1000 general practitioner consultations each year in children under 5 years of age.[5] Gastroenteritis leads to hospital admission in 7/1000 children under 5 years of age a year in the UK[5] and 13/1000 in the USA.[6] In Australia, gastroenteritis accounts for 6% of all hospital admissions in children under 15 years of age.[7]

**AETIOLOGY/ RISK FACTORS**  In developed countries, acute gastroenteritis is predominantly caused by viruses (87%), of which rotavirus is most common;[8-11] bacteria cause most of the remaining cases, predominantly Campylobacter, Salmonella, Shigella, and *Escherichia coli*. In developing countries, bacterial pathogens are more frequent, although rotavirus is also a major cause of gastroenteritis.

**Child health**

# Diarrhoea in children

**PROGNOSIS**  Acute gastroenteritis is usually self limiting but if untreated can result in morbidity and mortality secondary to water and electrolyte losses. Acute diarrhoea causes 4 million deaths a year in children under 5 years of age in Asia (excluding China), Africa, and Latin America, and over 80% of deaths occur in children under 2 years of age.[12] Although death is uncommon in developed countries, dehydration secondary to gastroenteritis is a significant cause of morbidity and need for hospital admission.[6,7,13]

Please refer to CD-ROM for full text and references.

# Gastro-oesophageal reflux in children

## Search date September 2003

*Yadlapalli Kumar and Rajini Sarvananthan*

## What are the effects of treatments?

### LIKELY TO BE BENEFICIAL

#### Feed thickeners in infants

One systematic review of feed thickeners found no RCTs in newborn infants. One RCT in infants aged 14–120 days found that a pre-thickened infant formula reduces regurgitation, choking and gagging, and coughing within a week without causing constipation. One small RCT in infants aged 1–6 weeks found no significant difference between carob flour and placebo thickening after 1 week, although the study may have lacked power to detect a clinically important difference.

#### Sodium alginate

Two RCTs in infants and in children under 2 years found that sodium alginate reduced the frequency of regurgitation at 8–14 days compared with placebo. A third small RCT of children under 17 years of age comparing sodium alginate with metoclopramide and with placebo found no significant difference between treatments.

### UNKNOWN EFFECTIVENESS

#### Domperidone

One small RCT provided insufficient evidence about the effects of domperidone in children with gastro-oesophageal reflux.

#### $H_2$ antagonists

Two small RCTs provided insufficient evidence about the effects of $H_2$ antagonists in children with gastro-oesophagael reflux. Neither RCT reported clinically meaningful results.

#### Metoclopramide

We found insufficient evidence from three small RCTs about the clinical effects of metoclopramide compared with placebo or other treatments.

#### Proton pump inhibitors

We found no RCTs of proton pump inhibitors for gastro-oesophageal reflux in children.

#### Surgery

We found no RCTs of surgery for gastro-oesophageal reflux in children.

### TRADE OFF BETWEEN BENEFITS AND HARMS

#### Positioning (left lateral or prone)

Three crossover RCTs in children aged under 6 months found limited evidence that prone or left lateral positioning improved oesophageal pH variables compared with supine positioning. Both prone and left lateral positions may be associated with a higher risk of sudden infant death syndrome compared with supine positioning. ▶

# Gastro-oesophageal reflux in children

## LIKELY TO BE INEFFECTIVE OR HARMFUL

### Cisapride
One systematic review found no significant difference between cisapride and placebo in the proportion of children with improved symptoms at the end of treatment. Cisapride has been withdrawn or restricted in several countries because of an association with life-threatening heart rhythm abnormalities.

**DEFINITION**   Gastro-oesophageal reflux disease is the passive transfer of gastric contents into the oesophagus due to transient or chronic relaxation of the lower oesophageal sphincter.[1] A survey of 69 children (median age 16 months) with gastro-oesophageal reflux disease attending a tertiary referral centre found that presenting symptoms were recurrent vomiting (72%), epigastric and abdominal pain (36%), feeding difficulties (29%), failure to thrive (28%), and irritability (19%).[2] However, results may not be generalisable to younger children or children presenting in primary care, who make up the majority of cases. Over 90% of children with gastro-oesophageal reflux disease have vomiting before 6 weeks of age.[1]

**INCIDENCE/ PREVALENCE**   Gastro-oesophageal regurgitation is considered a problem if it is frequent, persistent, and is associated with other symptoms such as increased crying, discomfort with regurgitation, and frequent back arching.[1,3] A cross-sectional survey of parents of 948 infants attending 19 primary care paediatric practices found that regurgitation of at least one episode a day was reported in 51% of infants aged 0–3 months. "Problematic" regurgitation occurred in significantly fewer infants (14% $v$ 51%; P < 0.001).[3] Peak regurgitation reported as "problematic" was reported in 23% of infants aged 6 months.[3]

**AETIOLOGY/ RISK FACTORS**   Risk factors for gastro-oesophageal reflux disease include immaturity of the lower oesophageal sphincter, chronic relaxation of the sphincter, increased abdominal pressure, gastric distension, hiatus hernia, and oesophageal dysmotility.[1] Premature infants and children with severe neurodevelopmental problems or congenital oesophageal anomalies are particularly at risk.[1]

**PROGNOSIS**   Regurgitation is considered benign, and most cases resolve spontaneously by 12–18 months of age.[4] In a cross-sectional survey of 948 parents, the peak age for reporting four or more episodes of regurgitation was at 5 months of age (23%), which decreased to 7% at 7 months (P < 0.001). One cohort study found that those infants with frequent spilling**ⓖ** in the first 2 years of life (90 days or more in the first 2 years) were more likely to have symptoms of gastro-oesophageal reflux at 9 years of age than those with no spilling (RR 2.3, 95% CI 1.3 to 4.0).[5] The prevalence of "problematic" regurgitation also reduced from 23% in infants aged 6 months to 3.25% in infants aged 10–12 months.[3] Rare complications of gastro-oesophageal reflux disease include oesophagitis with haematemesis and anaemia, respiratory problems (such as cough, apnoea, and recurrent wheeze), and failure to thrive.[1] A small comparative study (40 children) suggested that, when compared with healthy children, infants with gastro-oesophageal reflux disease had slower development of feeding skills and had problems affecting behaviour, swallowing, food intake, and mother–child interaction.[6]

Please refer to CD-ROM for full text and references.

### Search date September 2003

*Teresa Kilgour and Sally Wade*

## What are the effects of treatments?

### LIKELY TO BE BENEFICIAL

**Whey hydrolysate milk**
One small RCT found limited evidence that replacing cows' milk formula with whey hydrolysate formula🟢 reduced crying recorded in a parental diary.

### TRADE OFF BETWEEN BENEFITS AND HARMS

**Dicycloverine (dicyclomine)**
Two systematic reviews of RCTs of variable quality found limited evidence that dicycloverine🟢 reduced crying in infants with colic compared with placebo. RCTs found that dicycloverine increased drowsiness, constipation, and loose stools compared with placebo, but the difference did not reach significance. Case reports of harms in infants have included breathing difficulties, seizures, syncope, asphyxia, muscular hypotonia, and coma.

### UNKNOWN EFFECTIVENESS

**Advice to reduce stimulation**
One RCT found limited evidence that advice to reduce stimulation (by not patting, lifting, or jiggling the baby, or by reducing auditory stimulation) reduced crying after 7 days in infants under 12 weeks of age compared with an empathetic interview giving no advice. However, we were unable to draw reliable conclusions from this small study.

**Car ride simulation**
One RCT found no significant difference between a car ride simulation plus reassurance; counselling mothers about specific management techniques plus reassurance; and reassurance alone, in terms of maternal anxiety or hours of infant crying over 2 weeks.

**Casein hydrolysate milk**
Two RCTs found insufficient evidence about the effects of replacing cows' milk formula with casein hydrolysate hypoallergenic formula🟢.

**Cranial osteopathy**
We found no RCTs about the effects of cranial osteopathy🟢 in infants with colic.

**Counselling**
One RCT found no significant difference between counselling mothers about specific management techniques (responding to crying with gentle soothing motion, avoiding over stimulation, using a pacifier, and prophylactic carrying) plus reassurance🟢; car ride simulation plus reassurance; and reassurance alone, in terms of maternal anxiety or hours of infant crying over 2 weeks. Another small RCT found that counselling decreased duration and extent of crying compared with substitution of soya or cows' milk with casein hydrolysate formula.

**Herbal tea**
One small RCT found that herbal tea (containing extracts of camomile, vervain, liquorice, fennel, and balm mint in a sucrose solution) improved symptoms of colic rated by parents at 7 days compared with sucrose solution alone. However, we were unable to draw reliable conclusions from this small study. ▶

# Infantile colic

### Infant massage

One RCT found no significant difference between massage and a crib vibrator in colic related crying or parental rating of symptoms of infantile colic, but it may have lacked power to detect a clinically important difference.

### Low lactose (lactase treated) milk

Four small crossover RCTs found insufficient evidence on the effects of low lactose milk in infants with colic.

### Soya based infant feeds

One small RCT found that soya based infant feeds☉ reduced the duration of crying in infants with colic compared with standard cows' milk formula. However, we were unable to draw reliable conclusions from this small study.

### Spinal manipulation

Two RCTs found insufficient evidence about the effects of spinal manipulation☉.

### Sucrose solution

One small crossover RCT found limited evidence that sucrose solution improved symptoms of colic as rated by parents after 12 days compared with placebo. However, we were unable to draw reliable conclusions from this small study.

### UNLIKELY TO BE BENEFICIAL

### Advice to increase carrying

One RCT found no significant difference in daily crying time between advice to carry the infant, even when not crying, for at least an additional 3 hours a day, and general advice (to carry, check baby's nappy, feed, offer pacifier, place baby near mother, or use background stimulation such as music). The "advice to carry" group carried their babies for 4.5 hours daily compared with 2.6 hours daily in the general advice group.

### Simethicone (activated dimeticone)

One RCT found no significant difference between simethicone and placebo in colic rated by carers. Another RCT found no significant difference between simethicone and placebo in improvement as rated by parental interview, 24 hour diary, or behavioural observation. Another poor quality RCT found that simethicone reduced the number of crying attacks on days 4–7 of treatment compared with placebo.

**DEFINITION**     Infantile colic is defined as excessive crying in an otherwise healthy baby. The crying typically starts in the first few weeks of life and ends by 4–5 months. Excessive crying is defined as crying that lasts at least 3 hours a day, for 3 days a week, for at least 3 weeks.[1] Due to the natural course of infantile colic, it can be difficult to interpret trials which do not include a placebo or no treatment group for comparison.

**INCIDENCE/**     Infantile colic causes one out of six families (17%) to consult a health
**PREVALENCE**   professional. One systematic review of 15 community based studies found a wide variation in prevalence, which depended on study design and method of recording.[2] Two prospective studies identified by the review yielded prevalence rates of 5% and 19%.[2] One RCT (89 breast and formula fed infants) found that, at 2 weeks of age, the prevalence of crying more than 3 hours a day was 43% among formula fed infants and 16% among breast fed infants. The prevalence at 6 weeks was 12% (formula fed) and 31% (breast fed).[3] ▶

◀ **AETIOLOGY/**    The cause is unclear and, despite its name, infantile colic may not have an
**RISK FACTORS**   abdominal cause. It may reflect part of the normal distribution of infantile
crying. Other possible explanations are painful intestinal contractions, lactose
intolerance, gas, or parental misinterpretation of normal crying.[1]

**PROGNOSIS**    Infantile colic improves with time. One study found that 29% of infants aged
1–3 months cried for more than 3 hours a day, but by 4–6 months of age the
prevalence had fallen to 7–11%.[4]

Please refer to CD-ROM for full text and references.

# Measles (prevention)

**Search date March 2003**

*Helen Bedford, Nitu Sengupta, David Elliman, and Robert Booy*

## What are the effects of measles vaccination?

### BENEFICIAL

**Monovalent measles vaccine or combined MMR vaccine versus placebo or no vaccine**

We found no RCTs comparing the clinical effects of combined measles, mumps, and rubella (MMR)🅖 versus no vaccine or placebo. One large RCT, one quasi randomised trial, a large retrospective cohort study, and several observational studies have found that monovalent vaccine reduces the incidence of measles. Mass population cohort studies and other observational studies have also consistently found important child mortality reductions after measles vaccination. Observational studies have found that measles vaccination programmes have been followed by a reduction in the incidence of subacute sclerosing panencephalitis. Several of the known harms of measles disease occur or are suspected to occur after the vaccine, but we found no studies comparing the rates of adverse events between people with naturally acquired measles and those who have been vaccinated. Severe complications are rare with measles immunisation. One non-systematic review found that, compared with placebo, measles vaccination increases the incidence of fever and febrile seizures, although febrile seizures are rare and do not progress into afebrile seizures. Observational studies found that aseptic meningitis, a rare complication, increased after mass vaccination with the L-Z and Urabe strains of MMR, but no increased incidence has been reported with Jeryl Lynn, Hoshino, or Rubini strains. Observational studies have found that both measles vaccination and naturally acquired measles increase the incidence of idiopathic thrombocytopenic purpura. Observational studies found no significant change in the incidence of asthma in healthy children or in the frequency of acute exacerbation children with asthma. They also found no significant change in the incidence of Guillain–Barré syndrome, autism, or inflammatory bowel disease. Anaphylaxis has been reported after vaccination with MMR, but this is extremely rare.

### UNKNOWN EFFECTIVENESS

**Comparative effects of combined MMR and monovalent measles vaccine**

We found no RCTs comparing the clinical effects of MMR versus monovalent vaccines in children. Seroconversion rates are similar with both vaccines.

**DEFINITION**   Measles is an infectious disease caused by a ribonucleic acid paramyxovirus. The illness is characterised by an incubation period of 6–19 days (median 13);[1] a prodromal period of 2–4 days with upper respiratory tract symptoms; conjunctivitis, Koplik's spots on mucosal membranes, and high fever; followed by a widespread maculopapular rash that persists, with fever, for 5–6 days.

**INCIDENCE/ PREVALENCE**   Incidence varies according to vaccination coverage. Worldwide, there are an estimated 30 million cases of measles each year,[2] but an incidence of only 0–10/100 000 people in countries with widespread vaccination programmes such as the USA, UK, Mexico, India, China, Brazil, and Australia.[3] In the USA, before licensing of effective vaccines, over 90% of people were infected by the ▶

Child health

age of 15 years. After licensing in 1963, incidence fell by about 98%.[4] Mean annual incidence in Finland was 366/100 000 in 1970,[5] but declined to about zero by the late 1990s.[6] Similarly, annual incidence declined to about zero in Chile, the English speaking Caribbean, and Cuba during the 1990s when vaccination programmes were introduced.[7,8]

**AETIOLOGY/ RISK FACTORS**
Measles is highly contagious and spread through airborne droplets. As with most other infectious diseases, risk factors include overcrowding and low herd immunity🅖. Immunosupressed people have a higher morbidity and mortality. Newborn babies have a lower risk of measles than older infants, owing to protective maternal antibodies although, in recent US outbreaks, maternal antibody protection was lower than expected.[4] Antibody levels are lower in babies born to immunised mothers compared with offspring of naturally infected mothers.[9,10]

**PROGNOSIS**
The World Health Organization estimated that in 2000, measles caused 777 000 deaths and 27.5 million disability adjusted life years.[11] **Disease in healthy people:** In developed countries, most prognostic data come from the pre-vaccination era and from subsequent outbreaks in non-vaccinated populations. The overall rate of complications in the UK was 6.7% before the introduction of measles vaccination. Encephalitis affected 1.2/1000 diseased people, and respiratory complications in 38/1000 diseased people.[12] Other complications before the introduction of the vaccine included seizures, with or without fever, affecting five out of every 1000 people with measles.[13] Idiopathic thrombocytopenic purpura (ITP)🅖 has been reported, but the frequency is not known. Subacute sclerosing panencephalitis (SSPE)🅖 is an inevitably fatal, progressive degenerative disorder of the central nervous system with a mean onset 7–10 years after measles infection. It is more common when measles occurs under the age of 1 year (18/100 000 in children < 1 year of age v 4/100 000 overall), as identified by a passive reporting system set up in England and Wales to monitor the incidence of SSPE.[14] Between 1989–1991 in the USA, measles resurgence among young children (< 5 years) who had not been immunised led to 55 622 cases, with more than 11 000 hospital admissions and 166 deaths.[15–17] Measles complications include diarrhoea (9%), pneumonia (6%), and acute encephalitis (about 0.14%).[17] Measles during pregnancy results in higher risk of premature labour,[18] but no proven increase in congenital anomalies.[19] **Disease in malnourished or immuno-compromised people:** In malnourished people, particularly those with vitamin A deficiency, measles case fatality can be as high as 25%. Immuno-compromised people have a higher morbidity and mortality. Children younger than 5 years, and adults older than 20 years, have a higher risk of severe complications and death.[15,20] In the period 1974–1984, four UK centres reported that 15/51 (29%) deaths in children in their first remission from leukaemia resulted from measles.[21] Another report reviewing cases from the same four UK centres between 1973 and 1986 found that five out of 17 cases of measles in children with malignancies proved fatal.[22] At least 5 out of 36 (14%) measles associated deaths in 1991 in the USA were in HIV infected persons.[15] Worldwide, measles is a major cause of blindness, and causes 5% of deaths in young children (< 5 years). [23]

Please refer to CD-ROM for full text and references.

# Migraine headache in children

**Search date September 2003**

*Nick Barnes, Guy Millman, and Elizabeth James*

## What are the effects of treatment for acute attacks of migraine headache in children?

### UNKNOWN EFFECTIVENESS

**Antiemetics; codeine phosphate; non-steroidal anti-inflammatory drugs; paracetamol; 5HT$_1$ antagonists**

We found insufficient evidence to compare these interventions with each other or with placebo in children with migraine headache.

## What are the effects of prophylaxis for migraine in children?

### LIKELY TO BE BENEFICIAL

**Stress management**

We found limited evidence from one small RCT that self administered stress management☉ improved headache severity and frequency compared with no stress management.

### UNKNOWN EFFECTIVENESS

**β Blockers**

We found insufficient evidence from small RCTs about effects of β blockers compared with placebo in children with migraine headache

**Dietary manipulation☉; pizotifen; progressive muscle relaxation☉; thermal biofeedback☉**

We found insufficient evidence about effects of these interventions to prevent migraine in children.

**DEFINITION**  Migraine is defined by the International Headache Society (IHS) as a recurrent headache that occurs with or without aura☉ and lasts 2–48 hours.[1] It is usually unilateral in nature, pulsating in quality, of moderate or severe intensity, and is aggravated by routine physical activity. Nausea, vomiting, photophobia, and phonophobia are common accompanying symptoms❶. This topic focuses on children younger than 18 years. Diagnostic criteria for children are broader than criteria for adults, allowing for a broader range of duration and a broader localisation of the pain.[2] Diagnosis is difficult in young children, because the condition is defined by subjective symptoms. Studies that do not explicitly use criteria that are congruent with IHS diagnostic criteria (or revised IHS criteria in children under 15 years of age) have been excluded from this topic.

**INCIDENCE/ PREVALENCE**  Migraine occurs in 3–10% of children,[3–7] and currently affects 50/1000 school age children in the UK and an estimated 7.8 million children in the European Union.[8] Studies in developed countries suggest that migraine is the most common diagnosis among children presenting with headache to a medical practitioner. It is rarely diagnosed in children under 2 years of age because of the symptom based definition, but increases steadily with age thereafter.[1,9,10] It affects boys and girls similarly before puberty, but after puberty girls are more likely to suffer from migraine.[4,6,10] See incidence/ prevalence of migraine headache, p 320.

**AETIOLOGY/ RISK FACTORS** The cause of migraine headaches is unknown. We found few reliable data identifying risk factors or quantifying their effects in children. Suggested risk factors include stress, foods, menses, and exercise in genetically predisposed children and adolescents.[10,11]

**PROGNOSIS** We found no reliable data about prognosis of childhood migraine headache diagnosed by IHS criteria. It has been suggested that more than half the children will have spontaneous remission after puberty.[10] It is believed that migraine that develops during adolescence tends to continue in adult life, although attacks tend to be less frequent and severe in later life.[12] We found one longitudinal study from Sweden (73 children with "pronounced" migraine and mean age onset 6 years) with over 40 years follow up, which predated the IHS criteria for migraine headache.[13] It found that migraine headaches had ceased before the age of 25 years in 23% of people. However, By the age of 50 years, more than 50% of people continued to have migraine headaches. We found no prospective data examining long term risks in children with migraine.

Please refer to CD-ROM for full text and references.

# Neonatal jaundice

Search date March 2003

*Anthony Kwaku Akobeng*

## What are the effects of treatments for unconjugated hyperbilirubinaemia in term and preterm infants? New

Most RCTs did not report kernicterus as an outcome.

### BENEFICIAL

#### Exchange transfusion*

We found no RCTs on the effects of exchange transfusion versus no treatment or versus phototherapy. There is general consensus that exchange transfusion is effective in reducing serum bilirubin levels and in preventing neuro-developmental sequelae. In most of the RCTs comparing other interventions, exchange transfusion was used successfully to reduce serum bilirubin levels when those interventions failed to control the rise of serum bilirubin.

#### Phototherapy

Two RCTs have found that both conventional phototherapy and fibreoptic phototherapy reduce neonatal jaundice more effectively than no treatment. One systematic review (which included quasi-randomised as well as randomised controlled trials) and one subsequent RCT found that conventional phototherapy is more effective than fibreoptic phototherapy, although subgroup analysis in the systematic review found no significant difference between groups in preterm infants. No trials included in the review evaluated the impact of either phototherapy method on parent-infant bonding. One RCT found a greater effect with double conventional compared with single conventional phototherapy, whilst another RCT found no significant difference between double fibreoptic and single conventional phototherapy. One systematic review (which included quasi-randomised as well as randomised controlled trials) found no significant difference between fibreoptic plus conventional and conventional phototherapy alone in additional phototherapy, exchange transfusion, or percentage change in bilirubin after 24 hours, although it noted a trend favouring the fibreoptic plus conventional group. We found insufficient evidence on the adverse effects of phototherapy.

*Although we found no RCTs, there is a general consensus that exchange transfusion is effective in reducing serum bilirubin levels.

### UNKNOWN EFFECTIVENESS

#### Albumin infusion

We found no RCTs on the effects of albumin infusion versus no treatment or versus other treatment.

#### Home phototherapy versus hospital phototherapy

We found no RCTs on the effects of home phototherapy versus no treatment or versus hospital phototherapy.

**DEFINITION** Neonatal jaundice refers to the yellow colouration of the skin and sclera of newborn babies that results from hyperbilirubinaemia.

**INCIDENCE/ PREVALENCE** Jaundice is the most common condition requiring medical attention in newborn babies. About 50% of term and 80% of preterm babies develop jaundice in the first week of life.[1] Jaundice is also a common cause of ▶

readmission to hospital after early discharge of newborn babies.[2] Jaundice usually appears 2–4 days after birth and disappears 1–2 weeks later, usually without the need for treatment.

**AETIOLOGY/ RISK FACTORS**  In most infants with jaundice, there is no underlying disease and the jaundice is termed physiological. Physiological jaundice occurs when there is accumulation of unconjugated bilirubin in the skin and mucous membranes. It typically presents on the second or third day of life and results from the increased production of bilirubin (due to increased circulating red cell mass and a shortened red cell lifespan), and the decreased excretion of bilirubin (due to low concentrations of the hepatocyte binding protein, low activity of glucuronyl transferase, and increased enterohepatic circulation) which normally occurs in newborn babies. In some infants, unconjugated hyperbilirubinaemia may be associated with breast feeding (breast milk jaundice), and this typically occurs after the third day of life. Although the exact cause of breast milk jaundice is not clear, it is generally believed to be due to an unidentified factor in breast milk. Other causes are non-physiological such as blood group incompatibility (Rhesus or ABO problems) causing haemolysis, other causes of haemolysis, sepsis, bruising, and metabolic disorders. Gilbert's and Crigler-Najjar syndromes are rare causes of neonatal jaundice.

**PROGNOSIS**  In the newborn baby, unconjugated bilirubin can penetrate the blood–brain barrier and is potentially neurotoxic. Unconjugated hyperbilirubinaemia can, therefore, result in neuro-developmental sequelae including the development of kernicterus. Kernicterus is brain damage arising from the deposition of bilirubin in brain tissue. However, the exact level of bilirubin that is neurotoxic is unclear, and kernicterus at autopsy has been reported in infants in the absence of markedly elevated levels of bilirubin.[3] Recent reports suggest a resurgence of kernicterus in countries in which this complication had virtually disappeared.[4] This has been attributed mainly to early discharge of newborns from hospital.

Please refer to CD-ROM for full text and references.

# Nocturnal enuresis

**Search date February 2003**

*Natalie Lyth and Sara Bosson*

## What are the effects of interventions?

### BENEFICIAL

**Enuresis alarm plus dry-bed training (as effective as enuresis alarm alone)**

One systematic review has found limited evidence that a higher proportion of children achieve 14 consecutive dry nights with alarm plus dry bed training than with no treatment. A second systematic review found no significant difference between alarm plus dry bed training and alarm alone for achieving 14 consecutive dry nights.

**Desmopressin (in short term)**

One systematic review has found that desmopressin reduces bedwetting by at least one night per week and increases the chance of attaining initial success (14 consecutive dry nights) compared with placebo. The review found insufficient evidence comparing either intranasal versus oral administration of desmopressin or desmopressin versus tricyclic drugs. There was some evidence that higher doses of desmopressin were more likely to reduce the number of wet nights during treatment compared with lower doses. The review found no difference between desmopressin and enuresis alarms in the number of children achieving initial success, although one RCT found that, after 3 months of treatment, enuresis alarms were better than desmopressin at reducing the number of wet nights per week.

**Dry bed training (in short term)**

One systematic review has found that a greater proportion of children achieved 14 consecutive dry nights with dry bed training than with no treatment.

**Enuresis alarm (in short and long term)**

One systematic review has found that enuresis alarms increase initial success rates compared with no treatment, and that 31–61% of children using alarms were still dry at 3 months. We found limited evidence from one small RCT that dry bed training reduced bedwetting compared with an enuresis alarm after initial treatment and after 6 months. One systematic review found no significant difference between alarm plus dry bed training and alarm alone for achieving 14 consecutive dry nights. One systematic review found that desmopressin plus alarm was better at reducing the number of wet nights per week during treatment compared with alarm alone or alarm plus placebo, although there was no significant difference in the rate of initial success.

### LIKELY TO BE BENEFICIAL

**Laser acupuncture (as effective as desmopressin in one RCT)**

One RCT found no difference between laser acupuncture and intranasal desmopressin in the number of wet nights in children aged over 5 years.

**Standard home alarm clock (in short term)**

One RCT found that a higher proportion of children achieved 14 consecutive dry nights with standard home alarm clock than with waking after 3 hours' sleep.

◄ UNKNOWN EFFECTIVENESS

### Adding desmopressin to an alarm (in long term)

One systematic review found that desmopressin plus alarm was better at reducing the number of wet nights per week during treatment compared with alarm alone or alarm plus placebo, although there was no significant difference in the rate of initial success.

### Dry bed training (in long term)

One systematic review has found no significant long term difference in the proportion of dry nights between dry bed training and no treatment. However, one small RCT showed some long-term advantages of dry bed training.

### Standard home alarm clock (in long term)

One RCT found no significant difference in the proportion of dry nights achieved at 3 months between standard home alarm clock and waking after 3 hours' sleep.

### Ultrasound

We found no RCTs. One small controlled trial in children aged 6–14 years found that ultrasound increased the proportion of dry nights for up to 12 months compared with control.

TRADE OFF BETWEEN BENEFITS AND HARMS

### Tricyclic drugs (imipramine, desipramine)

One systematic review has found that tricyclic drugs (imipramine, desipramine) increase the chance of attaining 14 consecutive dry nights compared with placebo, although tricyclic drugs increased adverse effects such as anorexia, anxiety reaction, constipation, depression, diarrhoea, dizziness, drowsiness, dry mouth, headache, irritability, lethargy, sleep disturbance, upset stomach, and vomiting compared with placebo. We found no good studies comparing tricyclic drugs versus desmopressin. The review found no significant difference between imipramine and an enuresis alarm during the treatment period, but it found limited evidence that an alarm reduced bedwetting after the treatment had stopped compared with imipramine.

**DEFINITION**  Nocturnal enuresis is the involuntary discharge of urine at night in the absence of congenital or acquired defects of the central nervous system or urinary tract in a child aged 5 years or older.[1] Disorders that have bedwetting as a symptom (termed "nocturnal incontinence") can be excluded by a thorough history, examination, and urinalysis. "Monosymptomatic" nocturnal enuresis is characterised by night time symptoms only and accounts for 85% of cases. Nocturnal enuresis is defined as primary if the child has not been dry for a period of more than 6 months, and secondary if such a period of dryness preceded the onset of wetting.

**INCIDENCE/**  Between 15% and 20% of 5 year olds, 7% of 7 year olds, 5% of 10 year olds,
**PREVALENCE**  2–3% of 12–14 year olds, and 1–2% of people aged 15 years and over wet the bed twice a week on average.[2]

**AETIOLOGY/**  Nocturnal enuresis is associated with several factors, including small functional
**RISK FACTORS**  bladder capacity, nocturnal polyuria, and arousal dysfunction. Linkage studies have identified associated genetic loci on chromosomes 8q, 12q, 13q, and 22q11.[3–6]

▶

# Nocturnal enuresis

**PROGNOSIS**   Nocturnal enuresis has widely differing outcomes, from spontaneous resolution to complete resistance to all current treatments. About 1% of adults remain enuretic. Without treatment, about 15% of children with enuresis become dry each year.[7] We found no RCTs on the best age at which to start treatment in children with nocturnal enuresis. Anecdotal experience suggests that reassurance is sufficient below the age of 7 years. Behavioural treatments, such as alarms, require motivation and commitment from the child and a parent. Anecdotal experience suggests that children under the age of 7 years may not exhibit the commitment needed.

Please refer to CD-ROM for full text and references.

## What are the effects of treatments for recurrent idiopathic epistaxis in children?

### LIKELY TO BE BENEFICIAL

**Antiseptic cream**
One RCT found that chlorhexidine/neomycin cream reduced nosebleeds compared with no treatment at 8 weeks.

### UNKNOWN EFFECTIVENESS

**Antiseptic cream versus cautery**
One small RCT found no significant difference in nosebleeds between chlorhexidine/neomycin cream and silver nitrate cautery at 8 weeks. However, the study may have lacked power to detect clinically important differences between treatments. Some children found the smell and taste of the antiseptic cream unpleasant. All children found cautery painful, despite the use of local anaesthesia.

**Cautery plus antiseptic cream**
One small RCT found insufficient evidence about the effects of silver nitrate cautery plus chlorhexidine/neomycin cream compared with chlorhexidine/neomycin cream alone.

**Cautery versus no treatment**
We found no RCTs about the effects of this intervention.

**DEFINITION**     Recurrent idiopathic epistaxis is recurrent, self limiting, nasal bleeding in children for which no specific cause is identified. There is no consensus on the frequency or severity of recurrences.

**INCIDENCE/**     A cross sectional study of 1218 children (aged 11–14 years) found that 9%
**PREVALENCE**  had frequent episodes of epistaxis.[1] It is likely that only the most severe episodes are considered for treatment.

**AETIOLOGY/**     In children, most epistaxis occurs from the anterior part of the septum in the
**RISK FACTORS** region of Little's area.[2] Initiating factors include local inflammation, mucosal drying, and local trauma (including nose picking).[2] Epistaxis caused by other specific local (e.g. tumours) or systemic factors (e.g. clotting disorders) is not considered here.

**PROGNOSIS**     Recurrent epistaxis is less common in adolescents over 14 years and many children "grow out" of this problem.

Please refer to CD-ROM for full text and references.

Child health

# Reducing pain during blood sampling in infants

**Search date May 2003**

*Deborah Pritchard*

## What are the effects of interventions to reduce pain related distress during heel puncture?

**LIKELY TO BE BENEFICIAL**

### Holding (skin to skin) versus swaddling in term infants
RCTs found that holding reduced crying during heel puncture compared with swaddling in term infants.

### Oral glucose
RCTs found that oral glucose reduced pain responses (particularly the duration of crying) in preterm and term infants compared with water or no treatment.

### Oral sucrose
Systematic reviews and additional RCTs found good evidence in preterm infants and limited evidence in term infants that oral sucrose reduced pain responses (particularly the duration of crying) compared with water or no treatment. One RCT found that sucrose did not appear to increase the benefit of holding. Three RCTs in term infants found that sucrose plus pacifier was more effective than pacifier alone, although one RCT in preterm infants found no significant difference in pain score between a pacifier❻ dipped in sucrose and pacifier alone. One RCT found insufficient evidence about the effects of oral sucrose compared with lidocaine–prilocaine emulsion in term infants undergoing heel puncture.

### Other sweeteners
RCTs have found that other sweeteners (hydrogenated glucose❻ or an artificial sweetener, 10 parts cyclamate and 1 part saccharin) reduce pain scores and the percentage of time spent crying in term infants compared with water.

### Pacifiers
RCTs in term and preterm infants have found that pacifiers given before heel puncture reduce pain responses compared with no treatment.

### Positioning (tucking arms and legs) in preterm infants
One RCT found limited evidence that pain responses were reduced by tucking the arms and legs into a mid-line flexed position during heel puncture.

### Rocking
We found limited evidence that rocking reduces pain related stress compared with placebo.

**UNKNOWN EFFECTIVENESS**

### Multiple doses of sweet solution
One small RCT found no significant difference with multiple versus single doses of sucrose in pain scores for heel puncture.

### Swaddling
One small RCT found no significant difference in pain responses from swaddling compared with no swaddling.

### UNLIKELY TO BE BENEFICIAL

**Breast milk or breast feeding**

RCTs found no evidence that breast milk or breast feeding during heel puncture reduced pain responses or crying in neonates compared with water.

**Prone position**

One RCT found no significant difference in pain score between prone position and either side or supine position during heel puncture.

**Topical anaesthetics**

Systematic reviews and additional RCTs found no evidence of reduced pain responses, particularly crying, following heel puncture with topical anaesthetic (lidocaine, lidocaine–prilocaine emulsion, or tetracaine [amethocaine]) compared with placebo.

**Warming**

Two RCTs in term infants found no benefit of warming before heel puncture.

---

## What are the effects of interventions to reduce pain related distress during venepuncture?

### LIKELY TO BE BENEFICIAL

**Breast feeding**

One RCT found that breast feeding during venepuncture reduced pain responses compared with oral water or being held. The RCT found no significant difference in pain response between breast feeding and oral glucose.

**Oral glucose**

RCTs have found that oral glucose reduces pain responses (particularly the duration of crying) in term and preterm infants compared with water or no treatment. One RCT found no significant difference in pain scores between sucrose and glucose.

**Oral sucrose**

RCTs have found that oral sucrose reduces pain responses (particularly the duration of crying) in term and preterm infants compared with water or no treatment. One RCT found no significant difference in pain between sucrose and glucose.

**Pacifiers**

One RCT found that pacifiers reduced pain responses compared with water or no treatment in term infants undergoing venepuncture.

**Topical anaesthetics**

Four RCTs found limited evidence that lidocaine–prilocaine emulsion reduced pain responses to venepuncture compared with placebo. Two RCTs found that tetracaine (amethocaine) gel reduced pain and crying during venepuncture compared with placebo.

### UNKNOWN EFFECTIVENESS

**Other sweeteners**

We found no RCTs of other sweeteners for venepuncture.

# Reducing pain during blood sampling in infants

**DEFINITION**  Methods of sampling blood in infants include heel puncture, venepuncture, and arterial puncture. Heel puncture involves lancing of the lateral aspect of the infant's heel, squeezing the heel, and collecting the pooled capillary blood. Venepuncture involves aspirating blood through a needle from a peripheral vein. Arterial blood sampling is not discussed in this review. RCTs in this review were performed in a hospital care setting and the evidence relates to preterm and ill infants who have multiple blood tests, rather than infants undergoing heel puncture tests for routine screening. The results therefore cannot be applied to routine screening heel puncture tests in healthy infants.

**INCIDENCE/ PREVALENCE**  Almost every infant in the developed world undergoes heel puncture to screen for metabolic disorders (e.g. phenylketonuria). Many infants have repeated heel punctures or venepunctures to monitor blood glucose or haemoglobin. Preterm or ill neonates may undergo 1–21 heel punctures or venepunctures per day.[1–3] These punctures are likely to be painful. Heel punctures comprise 61–87% and venepunctures comprise 8–13% of the invasive procedures performed on ill infants. Analgesics are rarely given specifically for blood sampling procedures, but 5–19% of infants receive analgesia for other indications.[2,3] In one study, comfort measures were provided during 63% of venepunctures and 75% of heel punctures.[3]

**AETIOLOGY/ RISK FACTORS**  Blood sampling in infants can be difficult to perform, particularly in preterm or ill infants. Young infants may have increased sensitivity and more prolonged responses to pain than older age groups.[4] Factors that may affect the infant's pain responses include postconceptional age, previous pain experience, and procedural technique.

**PROGNOSIS**  Pain caused by blood sampling is associated with acute behavioural and physiological deterioration.[4] Experience of pain during heel puncture seems to heighten pain responses during subsequent blood sampling.[5] Other adverse effects of blood sampling include bleeding, bruising, haematoma, and infection.

---

Please refer to CD-ROM for full text and references.

## What are the effects of interventions to reduce the risk of sudden infant death syndrome?

### BENEFICIAL

**Advice to avoid prone sleeping**

Several observational studies found that campaigns involving advice to encourage non-prone sleeping positions❺ were followed by a reduced incidence of sudden infant death syndrome. RCTs are unlikely to be conducted.

### LIKELY TO BE BENEFICIAL

**Advice to avoid tobacco smoke exposure**

Several observational studies found limited evidence that campaigns to reduce several risk factors for sudden infant death, which included tobacco smoke exposure, were followed by a reduced incidence of sudden infant death syndrome. RCTs are unlikely to be conducted.

### UNKNOWN EFFECTIVENESS

**Advice to avoid bed sharing**

One observational study found that a campaign to reduce several risk factors for sudden infant death, which included advice to avoid bed sharing, was followed by a reduced incidence of sudden infant death syndrome. RCTs are unlikely to be conducted.

**Advice to avoid over heating or over wrapping**

Three observational studies found limited evidence that campaigns to reduce several risk factors for sudden infant death, which included over wrapping❺, were followed by a reduced incidence of sudden infant death syndrome. RCTs are unlikely to be conducted.

**Advice to avoid soft sleeping surfaces**

We found no evidence on the effects of avoiding soft sleeping surfaces in the prevention of sudden infant death syndrome.

**Advice to breastfeed**

One non-systematic review of observational studies and three additional observational studies found that campaigns to reduce several risk factors for sudden infant death, which included advice to breastfeed, were followed by a reduced incidence of sudden infant death syndrome. In some countries, however, incidence had begun to fall before the national advice campaigns. RCTs are unlikely to be conducted.

**Advice to promote soother use**

We found insufficient evidence on soother use in the prevention of sudden infant death syndrome.

**DEFINITION**  Sudden infant death syndrome (SIDS) is the sudden death of an infant aged under 1 year that remains unexplained after review of the clinical history, examination of the scene of death, and postmortem.

**INCIDENCE/**  The incidence of SIDS has varied over time and among nations (incidence per
**PREVALENCE**  1000 live births of SIDS in 1996: Netherlands 0.3, Japan 0.4, Canada 0.5, England and Wales 0.7, USA 0.8, and Australia 0.9).[1] ▶

# Sudden infant death syndrome

**AETIOLOGY/ RISK FACTORS** By definition, the cause of SIDS is not known. Observational studies have found an association between SIDS and several risk factors including prone sleeping position,[2,3] prenatal or postnatal exposure to tobacco smoke,[4] soft sleeping surfaces,[5,6] hyperthermia/over wrapping❶,[7,8] bed sharing (particularly with mothers who smoke),[9,10] lack of breastfeeding,[11,12] and soother❸ use.[7,13]

**PROGNOSIS** Although by definition prognosis is not applicable for an affected infant, the incidence of SIDS is increased in the siblings of that infant.[14,15]

Please refer to CD-ROM for full text and references.

Search date May 2003

*James Larcombe*

## What are the effects of treatment of acute urinary tract infection in children?

### LIKELY TO BE BENEFICIAL

**Antibiotics**

There is consensus that antibiotics are likely to be beneficial compared with placebo. Placebo controlled trials of antibiotics for symptomatic acute urinary tract infection in children are considered unethical.

**Oral antibiotics (as effective as initial intravenous antibiotics in children without severe vesicoureteric reflux or renal scarring)**

One RCT found no significant difference between oral cephalosporins alone and initial intravenous plus continued oral cephalosporins in duration of fever, reinfection, renal scarring, or extent of scarring in children aged 2 years or younger with first confirmed urinary tract infection. The RCT found weak evidence that, in children with grades III–IV❻ reflux, renal scarring at 6 months may be more common with oral compared with initial intravenous treatment.

### UNKNOWN EFFECTIVENESS

**Immediate empirical antibiotic treatment (unclear benefit compared with treatment based on microscopy and culture)**

We found no RCTs comparing early empirical treatment with awaiting the results of microscopy or culture in acute urinary tract infection in children. Retrospective analysis of one RCT found no significant difference in risk of renal scarring between cephalosporin treatment within 24 hours compared with 24 hours after the onset of fever in children under 2 years of age with urinary tract infections.

### UNLIKELY TO BE BENEFICIAL

**Longer (7–10 days) courses of initial intravenous antibiotics (no more effective than shorter [3 days] courses for non-recurrent lower urinary tract infections in the absence of renal tract abnormality in children with acute pyelonephritis)**

Two RCTs found no significant difference between long (7–10 days) and short (3 days) courses of initial cephalosporins in renal scarring in children with acute pyelonephritis.

**Longer (7–14 days) courses of oral antibiotics (no more effective than shorter [2–4 days] courses for non-recurrent lower urinary tract infections in the absence of renal tract abnormality)**

One systematic review found no significant difference between longer courses (7–14 days) and shorter courses (2–4 days) of the same antibiotic in cure rate at 7 days after treatment in children with no history of renal tract abnormality and judged not to have acute pyelonephritis❻. However, longer courses may be associated with more adverse effects.

### LIKELY TO BE INEFFECTIVE OR HARMFUL

**Prolonged delay in treatment (> 7 days)**

We found no RCTs. Five retrospective studies found that medium to long term delays (4 days–7 years) in treatment may be associated with an increased risk of renal scarring.

▶

◄ **Single dose of oral amoxicillin (less effective than longer course [10 days] of oral amoxicillin)**

One systematic review has found that single dose amoxicillin reduces cure rate at 3–30 days compared with a longer (10 days) course of amoxicillin.

## What are the effects of interventions to prevent recurrence?

**LIKELY TO BE BENEFICIAL**

### Immunotherapy

One systematic review in premature and low birth weight neonates has found that intravenous immunoglobulins⊕ reduce serious infections, including urinary tract infections, compared with placebo. One RCT in children with recurrent urinary tract infection found that adding pidotimod (an immunotherapeutic agent) to antibiotic treatment reduced recurrence compared with adding placebo.

### Prophylactic antibiotics

One systematic review found limited evidence that prophylactic antibiotics (co-trimoxazole, nitrofurantoin) reduced recurrence of urinary tract infection in children compared with placebo or no treatment. One RCT found that nitrofurantoin reduced recurrence of urinary tract infection over 6 months compared with trimethoprim. However, more children discontinued treatment with nitrofurantoin because of adverse effects. We found no RCTs evaluating the optimum duration of prophylactic antibiotics.

**UNKNOWN EFFECTIVENESS**

### Surgical correction of moderate to severe bilateral vesicoureteric reflux (grades III–IV) with bilateral nephropathy

One small RCT found a steady, but not statistically significant, decline in glomerular filtration rate over 10 years with medical treatment compared with surgery in children with moderate to severe bilateral vesicoureteric reflux and bilateral rephropathy.

**UNLIKELY TO BE BENEFICIAL**

### Surgical correction of minor functional anomalies

We found no RCTs. One observational study suggested that children with minor anomalies do not develop renal scarring and therefore may not benefit from surgery.

### Surgical correction of moderate to severe vesicoureteric reflux with adequate glomerular filtration rate (similar benefits to medical management)

One systematic review and two subsequent RCTs found that, although surgery abolished reflux, there was no significant difference between surgical and medical management (prophylactic antibiotic treatment) in preventing complications from urinary tract infection after 6 months to 5 years in children with moderate to severe vesicoureteric reflux. There was insufficient evidence of any difference between the two groups in preventing recurrent urinary tract infection.

**DEFINITION**   Urinary tract infection (UTI) is defined by the presence of a pure growth of more than $10^5$ colony forming units of bacteria per millilitre of urine. Lower counts of bacteria may be clinically important, especially in boys and in specimens obtained by urinary catheter. Any growth of typical urinary pathogens is considered clinically important if obtained by suprapubic aspiration. In ►

practice, three age ranges are usually considered on the basis of differential risk and different approaches to management: children under 1 year; young children (1–4, 5, or 7 years, depending on the information source); and older children (up to 12–16 years). Recurrent UTI is defined as a further infection by a new organism. Relapsing UTI is defined as a further infection with the same organism.

**INCIDENCE/ PREVALENCE**  Boys are more susceptible before the age of 3 months; thereafter the incidence is substantially higher in girls. Estimates of the true incidence of UTI depend on rates of diagnosis and investigation. At least 8% of girls and 2% of boys will have a UTI in childhood.[1]

**AETIOLOGY/ RISK FACTORS**  The normal urinary tract is sterile. Contamination by bowel flora may result in urinary infection if a virulent organism is involved or if the child is immunosuppressed. In neonates, infection may originate from other sources. *Escherichia coli* accounts for about 75% of all pathogens. *Proteus* is more common in boys (about 30% of infections). Obstructive anomalies are found in 0–4% and vesicoureteric reflux in 8–40% of children being investigated for their first UTI.[2] One meta-analysis of 12 cohort studies (537 children admitted to hospital for UTI, 1062 kidneys) found that 36% of all kidneys had some scarring on DMSA scintigraphy🅖 and that 59% of children with vesicoureteric reflux on micturating cystourethography had at least one scarred kidney (pooled positive likelihood ratio 1.96, 95% CI 1.51 to 2.54; pooled negative likelihood ratio 0.71, 95% CI 0.58 to 0.85). There was evidence of heterogeneity in likelihood ratios among studies. The authors concluded that vesicoureteric reflux is a weak predictor of renal damage in children admitted to hospital.[3] Thus although vesicoureteric reflux is a major risk factor for adverse outcome, other as yet unidentified triggers may also need to be present.

**PROGNOSIS**  After first infection, about 50% of girls have a further infection in the first year and 75% within 2 years.[4] We found no figures for boys, but a review suggests that recurrences are common under 1 year of age, but rare subsequently.[5] Renal scarring occurs in 5–15% of children within 1–2 years of their first UTI, although 32–70% of these scars are noted at the time of initial assessment.[2] The incidence of renal scarring rises with each episode of infection in childhood.[6] Retrospective analysis of an RCT comparing oral versus intravenous antibiotics found that new renal scarring after a first UTI was more common in children with vesicoureteric reflux than in children without reflux (logistic regression model; AR of scarring: 16/107 [15%] with reflux v 10/165 [6%] without reflux; RR 2.47, 95% CI 1.17 to 5.24).[7] A study (287 children with severe vesicoureteric reflux treated either medically or surgically for any UTI) evaluated the risk of renal scarring with serial DMSA scintigraphy over 5 years. It found that younger children (aged < 2 years) were at greater risk of renal scarring than older children regardless of treatment for the infection (AR for deterioration in DMSA scan over 5 years: 21/86 [24%] for younger children v 27/201 [13%] for older children; RR 1.82, 95% CI 1.09 to 3.03).[8] One prospective study found that children of all ages who presented with symptoms of pyelonephritis🅖, were likely to have renal abnormalities (abnormal initial scans in 34/65 [52%] children).[9] Another prospective study found that the highest rates of renal scarring after pyelonephritis occurred between 1–5 years of age.[10] A further prospective study by the same team found that children aged over 1 year had more abnormalities on DMSA scans at 3 months after an episode of pyelonephritis (54/129 [42%] of older children v 22/91 [24%] of younger children; RR 1.73, 95% CI 1.14 to 2.63).[11] They noted conflicting results in previous literature on this subject.[11] They also found that girls were more likely than boys to develop scarring on DMSA scan 3 months after an episode of pyelonephritis (67/171 [39%] girls v 9/49 [18%] boys; RR 2.13, 95% CI 1.15 to 3.96).[11] Renal scarring is associated with future complications: poor renal growth, recurrent adult pyelonephritis, impaired glomerular function, early hypertension, and end stage renal failure.[12–15] A combination of recurrent ▶

# Urinary tract infection in children

UTI, severe vesicoureteric reflux, and the presence of renal scarring at first presentation is associated with the worst prognosis. One prospective observational study assessed the persistence of scarring on DMSA scans in children with a first UTI.[16] Grading of scars was as follows: mild (< 25% of kidney affected), moderate (25–50% of kidney), and severe (> 50% of kidney). The study found that vesicoureteric reflux was associated with more persistent scarring at 6 months (in children with severe scarring on initial scan: 7/8 [88%] with reflux had a persisting lesion v 1/7 [14%] without reflux; RR 6.13, 95% CI 0.98 to 38.00; in children with mild to moderate scarring on initial scan: 3/8 [38%] with reflux had a persisting lesion v 5/31 [16%] without reflux; RR 2.70, 95% CI 0.81 to 9.10).[16] The study also found that vesicoureteric reflux was associated with a higher risk of pyelonephritis on the initial scan (RR for pyelonephritis with reflux v without reflux 1.62, 95% CI 1.14 to 2.31).

Please refer to CD-ROM for full text and references.

---

## What are the effects of treatments for acute cholecystitis?
New

### BENEFICIAL

### Early cholecystectomy

Four RCTs found that operation before the scheduled date because of recurrent or worsening symptoms was necessary in 13–19% of people receiving delayed cholecystectomy (open or laparoscopic cholecystectomy☉ after 6–8 weeks). The RCTs found no significant difference between early (within 72 hours) and delayed cholecystectomy (open or laparoscopic) in intraoperative or postoperative complications, but found that early cholecystectomy reduced hospital stay. Two RCTs found that early laparoscopic cholecystectomy increased duration of operation compared with delayed laparoscopic cholecystectomy but reduced use of analgesics. The RCTs found no significant difference between early and delayed laparoscopic cholecystectomy in the rate of conversion to open cholecystectomy☉.

### Laparoscopic cholecystectomy

Two RCTs found that laparoscopic cholecystectomy reduced duration of surgery, use of nasogastric tube, duration of antibiotic treatment, use of analgesia, and hospital stay. One RCT found no significant difference in rates of postoperative complications between laparoscopic and open cholecystectomy. The other RCT found fewer major and minor postoperative complications with laparoscopi cholecystectomy. The rate of conversion from laparoscopic to open cholecystectomy was 16–27%.

### Minilaparoscopic cholecystectomy

One RCT found that minilaparoscopic☉ and conventional laparoscopic cholecystectomy were associated with similar use of analgesics, hospital stay, and rates of conversion to open cholecystectomy. Minilaparoscopic cholecystectomy marginally increased duration of surgery.

### TRADE OFF BETWEEN BENEFITS AND HARMS

### Open cholecystectomy

Two RCTs found that open cholecystectomy increased duration of surgery, use of nasogastric tube, duration of antibiotic treatment, use of analgesia, and hospital stay. One RCT found that no significant difference in rates of postoperation complications between open and laparoscopic cholecystectomy. The other RCT found more postoperative complications with open cholecystectomy. The rate of conversion from laparoscopic to open cholecystectomy was 16–27%. Conversion from laparascopic to open cholecystectomy is needed if the laparoscopic procedure cannot be completed without risking injury to surrounding structures or when bleeding cannot be stopped. Open cholecystectomy is required in people who have a fistula from the gallbladder into the bile duct or intestine, and in some people who have perforation and abscess in the right upper quadrant.

DEFINITION     **Acute cholecystitis** results from obstruction of the cystic duct usually by a gallstone, followed by distension and subsequent chemical or bacterial inflammation of the gallbladder. People with acute cholecystitis usually have unremitting right upper quadrant pain, anorexia, nausea, vomiting, and fever. About 95% of people with acute cholecystitis have gallstones (calculous ▶

# Acute cholecystitis

cholecystitis) and 5% lack gallstones (acalculous cholecystitis).[1] **Acute cholangitis** is a severe complication of gallstone disease and is generally a result of bacterial infection. People with acute cholangitis often have jaundice, haemodynamic instability, and mental status changes in addition to right upper quadrant pain and fever. This review does not include people with acute cholangitis.

**INCIDENCE/ PREVALENCE**
The incidence of acute cholecystitis among people with gallstones is unknown. Twenty per cent of people admitted to hospital for biliary tract disease have acute cholecystitis.[1] The number cholecystectomies carried out for acute cholecystitis has increased from the mid 1980s to the early 1990s, especially in elderly people.[2] Acute calculous cholecystitis is three times more common in women than men up to the age of 50 years, and about 1.5 times more common in women than men thereafter.[1]

**AETIOLOGY/ RISK FACTORS**
Acute calculous cholecystitis seems to be caused by obstruction of the cystic duct by a gallstone or local mucosal erosion and inflammation caused by a stone, but cystic duct ligation alone does not produce acute cholecystitis in animal studies. The role of bacteria in the pathogenesis of acute cholecystitis is not clear; positive cultures of bile or gallbladder wall are found in 50–75% of cases.[3,4] The cause of acute acalculous cholecystitis is uncertain and may be multifactorial, including increased susceptibility to bacterial colonisation of static gallbladder bile.[1]

**PROGNOSIS**
Complications of acute cholecystitis include perforation of the gallbladder, pericholecystic abscess, and fistula caused by gallbladder wall ischaemia and infection. In the USA, the overall mortality from complications is about 20%.[5]

---

Please refer to CD-ROM for full text and references.

Search date May 2003

Marion Jonas and John Scholefield

## What are the effects of treatments for chronic anal fissure?

### BENEFICIAL

#### Internal anal sphincterotomy

One systematic review found no significant difference between internal anal sphincterotomy⊕ and anal stretch⊕ in persistence of fissures. Both procedures healed 70–95% of fissures. It found no significant difference between open and closed internal anal sphincterotomy in persistence of fissures. Four RCTs have found that sphincterotomy improved fissure healing compared with topical glyceryl trinitrate⊕ after 6 weeks to 2 years.

### LIKELY TO BE BENEFICIAL

#### Anal advancement flap (as effective as internal anal sphincterotomy based on 1 small RCT)

One small RCT found no significant difference between lateral internal anal sphincterotomy and anal advancement flap⊕ in patient satisfaction or fissure healing.

#### Botulinum A toxin-haemagglutinin complex

RCTs found that botulinum A toxin-haemagglutinin complex⊕ increased fissure healing at 2 months compared with placebo or topical glyceryl trinitrate. Two RCTs found no significant difference between high dose and low dose botulinum A toxin-haemagglutinin complex in healing rates after 2–3 months. One RCT found that compared with botulinum A toxin-haemagglutinin complex, sphincterotomy increased fissure healing at 12 months. It also increased time taken to return to daily activities.

#### Topical glyceral trinitrate

RCTs comparing topical glyceryl trinitrate versus placebo found mixed results for healing and pain, and results were difficult to interpret owing to differing durations and doses of treatments. However, consensus opinion still regards glyceryl trinitrate as an effective first line treatment for chronic anal fissure. One RCT found no significant difference between glyceryl trinitrate ointment and a glyceryl trinitrate patch in fissure healing at 8 weeks. One RCT found no significant difference between topical glyceryl trinitrate and topical diltiazem in fissure healing at 8 weeks. One RCT, identified by a systematic review, found that botulinum A toxin-haemagglutinin complex increased fissure healing after 2 months compared with glyceryl trinitrate. Four RCTs found that internal anal sphincterotomy improved fissure healing compared with topical glyceryl trinitrate after 6 weeks to 2 years.

### TRADE OFF BETWEEN BENEFITS AND HARMS

#### Anal stretch (as effective as internal anal sphincterotomy but higher rates of flatus incontinence)

One systematic review found no significant difference between internal anal sphincterotomy and anal stretch in persistence of fissures. It found that both procedures healed 70–95% of fissures. Anal stretch increased rates of flatus incontinence compared with internal anal sphincterotomy. ▶

# Anal fissure

**UNKNOWN EFFECTIVENESS**

### Botulinum A toxin-haemagglutinin complex (botulinum A toxin-hc) plus nitrates

We found no RCTs comparing botulinum A toxin-haemagglutinin complex plus nitrates versus placebo. One small RCT found that botulinum A toxin-haemagglutinin complex plus topical isosorbide dinitrate three times daily increased fissure healing at 6 weeks compared with botulinum A toxin-haemagglutinin complex alone. It found no significant difference at 8 or 12 weeks.

### Diltiazem

We found no placebo controlled RCTs. One RCT found no significant difference in healing rates between topical diltiazem and topical glyceryl trinitrate at 8 weeks. One small RCT found no significant difference in fissure healing after 8 weeks between oral diltiazem and topical diltiazem.

### Indoramin

One RCT found no significant difference between oral indoramin and placebo in fissure healing at 6 weeks.

**DEFINITION**   Anal fissure is a split or tear in the lining of the distal anal canal. It is a painful condition often associated with fresh blood loss from the anus and perianal itching. **Acute anal fissures** have sharply demarcated, fresh mucosal edges, often with granulation tissue at the base. **Chronic anal fissures** margins are indurated, there is less granulation tissue, and muscle fibres of the internal anal sphincter may be seen at the base. Fissures persisting for longer than 6 weeks are generally defined as chronic.

**INCIDENCE/**   Anal fissures are common in all age groups, but we found no evidence to
**PREVALENCE**   measure incidence.

**AETIOLOGY/**   Low intake of dietary fibre may be a risk factor for the development of acute anal
**RISK FACTORS** fissure.[1] People with anal fissure often have raised resting anal canal pressures with anal spasm.[2,3] Men and women are equally affected by anal fissure, and up to 11% of women develop anal fissure after childbirth.[4]

**PROGNOSIS**   Placebo controlled studies found that 70–90% of untreated "chronic" fissures did not heal during the study.[5,6]

Please refer to CD-ROM for full text and references.

## What are the effects of treatments?

### BENEFICIAL

**Adjuvant antibiotics**

One systematic review and one subsequent RCT in children and adults with simple🅖 or complicated appendicitis🅖 undergoing appendicectomy have found that prophylactic antibiotics reduce wound infections and intra-abdominal abscesses compared with no antibiotics. Subgroup analysis from the systematic review has found that antibiotics reduce the number of wound infections in children with complicated appendicitis compared with no antibiotics. However, subgroup analysis from the systematic review found no significant difference in the number of wound infections between antibiotics and no antibiotics in children with simple appendicitis. One subsequent RCT in children with simple appendicitis found no significant difference with antibiotic prophylaxis compared with no antibiotic prophylaxis in wound infections, but the RCT may have been too small to exclude a clinically important difference.

### LIKELY TO BE BENEFICIAL

**Laparoscopic surgery versus open surgery (in children)**

One systematic review has found that, in children, laparoscopic surgery reduced the number of wound infections and the length of hospital stay compared with open surgery, but found no significant difference in postoperative pain, time to mobilisation, or proportion of intra-abdominal abscesses.

### TRADE OFF BETWEEN BENEFITS AND HARMS

**Antibiotics versus surgery**

One small RCT in adults with suspected appendicitis found that conservative treatment with antibiotics reduced pain and morphine consumption for the first 10 days compared with appendicectomy. However, the RCT found that 35% of people treated with antibiotics were readmitted within 1 year with acute appendicitis and subsequently had an appendicectomy.

**Laparoscopic surgery versus open surgery (in adults)**

One systematic review and one subsequent RCT have found that laparoscopic surgery in adults reduces wound infections, postoperative pain, duration of hospital stay, and time taken to return to work compared with open surgery. However, the systematic review found that laparoscopic surgery increased post-operative intra-abdominal abscesses compared with open surgery.

### UNKNOWN EFFECTIVENESS

**Open surgery versus no treatment**

We found no RCTs comparing open surgery with no surgery.

**Stump inversion at open appendicectomy**

One RCT found no significant difference between stump inversion and simple ligation in wound infection, length of hospital stay, or intra-abdominal abscesses. Another RCT found that stump inversion increased wound infections compared with simple ligation, but found no significant difference between groups for intra-abdominal abscesses or length of hospital stay. ▶

# Appendicitis

**DEFINITION**  Acute appendicitis is acute inflammation of the vermiform appendix.

**INCIDENCE/ PREVALENCE**  The incidence of acute appendicitis is falling, although the reason for this is unclear. The reported lifetime risk of appendicitis in the USA is 8.7% in men and 6.7% in women,[1] and there are about 60 000 cases reported annually in England and Wales. Appendicitis is the most common surgical emergency requiring operation.

**AETIOLOGY/ RISK FACTORS**  The cause of appendicitis is uncertain, although various theories exist. Most relate to luminal obstruction, which prevents escape of secretions and inevitably leads to a rise in intraluminal pressure within the appendix. This can lead to subsequent mucosal ischaemia, and the stasis provides an ideal environment for bacterial overgrowth. Potential causes of the obstruction are faecoliths, often because of constipation, lymphoid hyperplasia, or caecal carcinoma.[2]

**PROGNOSIS**  The prognosis of untreated appendicitis is unknown, although spontaneous resolution has been reported in at least 1/13 (8%) episodes.[3] The recurrence of appendicitis after conservative management,[3,4] and recurrent abdominal symptoms in certain people,[5] suggests that chronic appendicitis and recurrent acute or subacute appendicitis may also exist.[6] The standard treatment for acute appendicitis is appendicectomy. RCTs comparing treatment with no treatment would be regarded as unethical. The mortality from acute appendicitis is less than 0.3%, rising to 1.7% after perforation.[7] The most common complication of appendicectomy is wound infection, occurring in between 5 and 33% of cases.[8] Intra-abdominal abscess formation occurs less frequently in 2% of appendicectomies.[9] A perforated appendix in childhood does not appear to have subsequent negative consequences on female fertility.[10]

---

Please refer to CD-ROM for full text and references.

## What are the effects of treatments for uncomplicated diverticular disease?

### LIKELY TO BE BENEFICIAL

**Rifaximin (plus dietary fibre supplementation v dietary fibre supplementation alone)**

One RCT in people with uncomplicated diverticular disease⊙ has found that rifaximin⊙ plus dietary fibre supplementation improved symptoms compared with dietary fibre supplementation alone after 12 months of treatment.

### UNKNOWN EFFECTIVENESS

**Bran and ispaghula husk**

Two small RCTs found no consistent effect of bran or ispaghula husk compared with placebo on symptom relief after 12–16 weeks.

**Elective surgery**

We found no RCTs of elective open or laparoscopic colonic resection.

**Lactulose**

One small RCT found no significant difference between lactulose and a high fibre diet in self rated improvement after 12 weeks.

**Methylcellulose**

One small RCT found no significant difference between methylcellulose and placebo in mean symptom score after 3 months.

## What are the effects of treatments to prevent complications of diverticular disease?

### UNKNOWN EFFECTIVENESS

**Increased fibre intake**

We found no RCTs of advice to consume a high fibre diet or of dietary fibre supplementation.

**Mesalazine (after an attack of acute diverticulitis)**

One methodologically flawed RCT provided insufficient evidence about effects of mesalazine compared with no treatment in people previously treated for an episode of acute diverticulitis⊙.

## What are the effects of treatments for acute diverticulitis?

### UNKNOWN EFFECTIVENESS

**Medical treatment**

We found no RCTs comparing medical treatment versus placebo. One small RCT found no significant difference between intravenous cefoxitin and intravenous gentamicin plus intravenous clindamycin in rates of clinical cure. Observational studies in people with acute diverticulitis have found low mortality with medical treatment, but found that recurrence rates may be high.

Digestive system disorders

# Colonic diverticular disease

## Surgery (for diverticulitis complicated by generalised peritonitis)

We found no RCTs comparing surgery verus no surgery or versus medical treatment. One RCT found no significant difference in mortality between acute resection and transverse colostomy of the sigmoid colon. A second RCT found no significant difference in mortality between primary and secondary sigmoid colonic resection, but found that primary resection reduced rates of postoperative peritonitis and emergency reoperation. We found no RCTs comparing open versus laparoscopic surgery.

**DEFINITION**  Colonic diverticula are mucosal out pouchings through the large bowel wall. They are often accompanied by structural changes (elastosis of the taenia coli, muscular thickening, and mucosal folding). They are usually multiple and occur most frequently in the sigmoid colon. If diverticula are associated with symptoms, then this is termed diverticular disease🅖.

**INCIDENCE/**  In the UK, the incidence of diverticulosis🅖 increases with age; about 5% of
**PREVALENCE**  people are affected in their fifth decade of life and about 50% by their ninth decade.[1] Diverticulosis is common in developed countries, although there is a lower prevalence of diverticulosis in Western vegetarians consuming a diet high in roughage.[2] Diverticulosis is almost unknown in rural Africa and Asia.[3]

**AETIOLOGY/**  There is an association between low fibre diets and diverticulosis of the colon.[3]
**RISK FACTORS**  Prospective observational studies have found that both physical activity and a high fibre diet are associated with a lower risk of developing diverticular disease🅖.[4,5] One case control study found an association between the ingestion of non-steroidal anti-inflammatory drugs and the development of severe diverticular complications, including pericolic abscess, generalised peritonitis, bleeding, and fistula formation.[6] People in Japan, Singapore, and Thailand develop diverticula that affect mainly the right side of the colon.[7]

**PROGNOSIS**  Symptoms will develop in 10–25% of people with diverticula at some point in their lives.[1] It is unclear why some people develop symptoms and some do not. Even after successful medical treatment of acute diverticulitis🅖 almost two thirds of people suffer recurrent pain in the lower abdomen.[8] Recurrent diverticulitis is observed in 7–42% of people with diverticular disease, and after recovery from the initial attack, the calculated yearly risk of suffering a further episode is 3%.[9] About half of recurrences occur within 1 year of the initial episode and 90% occur within 5 years.[10] Complications of diverticular disease (perforation, obstruction, haemorrhage, and fistula formation) are each seen in about 5% of people with colonic diverticula when followed up for 10–30 years.[11] Intra-abdominal abscess formation may also occur.

Please refer to CD-ROM for full text and references.

*Charles Maxwell-Armstrong and John Scholefield*

## What are the effects of treatments?

### BENEFICIAL

#### Adjuvant chemotherapy

Three systematic reviews and one subsequent RCT have found that adjuvant chemotherapy reduces mortality compared with surgery alone in people with Dukes'🅖 A, B, and C colorectal cancer. One RCT found that adding levamisole to adjuvant fluorouracil did not significantly reduce mortality or recurrence compared with adjuvant fluorouracil alone in people with Dukes' A, B, and C colorectal cancer. One RCT found that mortality and recurrence rates were similar with adjuvant fluorouracil plus high or low dose folinic acid in people with Dukes' A, B, and C colorectal cancer.

### UNKNOWN EFFECTIVENESS

#### Routine intensive follow up

One systematic review and one subsequent RCT have found that intensive follow up increases survival compared with less intensive follow up in people treated surgically with curative intent.

### TRADE OFF BETWEEN BENEFITS AND HARMS

#### Preoperative radiotherapy

Two systematic reviews and two subsequent RCTs found that adding preoperative radiotherapy to surgery is at least as effective as surgery alone for mortality and recurrence in people with rectal cancer. One RCT found no significant difference in mortality between preoperative and postoperative radiotherapy but preoperative radiotherapy reduced local tumour recurrence. One systematic review has found that preoperative radiotherapy increases early postoperative morbidity.

#### Total mesorectal excision

We found no RCTs of total mesorectal excision🅖 in people with rectal cancer. Observational studies suggest that total mesorectal excision may reduce the rate of local recurrence compared with conventional surgery.

**DEFINITION** Colorectal cancer is a malignant neoplasm arising from the lining (mucosa) of the large intestine (colon and rectum). Nearly two thirds of colorectal cancers occur in the rectum or sigmoid colon. Colorectal cancer may be categorised as A, B, or C Dukes'.

**INCIDENCE/ PREVALENCE** Colorectal cancer is the third most common malignancy in the developed world. It accounts for about 20 000 deaths each year in the UK and 60 000 deaths each year in the USA. Although the incidence of, and mortality from, colorectal cancer has changed little over the past 40 years, the incidence of the disease has fallen recently in both the UK and the USA.[1,2] In the UK, about a quarter of people with colorectal cancer present as emergencies with either intestinal obstruction or perforation.[3,4]

**AETIOLOGY/ RISK FACTORS** Colon cancer affects almost equal proportions of men and women, most commonly between the ages of 60 and 80 years. Rectal cancer is more common in men.[1] The pathogenesis of colorectal cancer involves genetic and environmental factors. The most important environmental factor is probably diet.[5]

▶

# Colorectal cancer

**PROGNOSIS**   Overall 5 year survival is about 50% and has not changed over the past 40 years. Disease specific mortality in both USA and UK cancer registries is decreasing but the reasons for this are unclear.[1,2] Surgery is undertaken with curative intent in over 80% of people, but about half experience cancer recurrence.

Please refer to CD-ROM for full text and references.

## What are the effects of lifestyle advice in adults with idiopathic chronic constipation? *New*

### UNKNOWN EFFECTIVENESS

**Lifestyle advice**

We found no RCTs in adults with idiopathic chronic constipation.

## What are the effects of bulking agents in adults with idiopathic chronic constipation? *New*

### LIKELY TO BE BENEFICIAL

**Ispaghula husk (psyllium)**

One RCT identified by a systematic review found that ispaghula husk increased the frequency of bowel movements and improved overall symptoms compared with placebo after 2 weeks. We found limited evidence from two RCTs that ispaghula husk improved symptoms compared with lactulose at 4 weeks. One RCT provided insufficient evidence to compare ispaghula husk versus macrogol 3350. One RCT found no clinically important difference between ispaghula husk and docusate in frequency of bowel movements, stool consistency, straining, or pain after 2 weeks.

### UNKNOWN EFFECTIVENESS

**Bran**

We found no RCTs of sufficient quality comparing bran versus placebo in adults with idiopathic chronic constipation.

## What are the effects of stool softeners in adults with idiopathic chronic constipation? *New*

### UNKNOWN EFFECTIVENESS

**Paraffin; seed oils/arachis oil**

We found no RCTs in adults with idiopathic chronic constipation.

## What are the effects of osmotic laxatives in adults with idiopathic chronic constipation? *New*

### BENEFICIAL

**Macrogols**

Three RCTs identified by a systematic review found that macrogols (polyethylene glycols) improved symptoms after 2–20 weeks compared with placebo. One RCT provided insufficient evidence to compare macrogol 3350 versus ispaghula husk. One systematic review found that macrogol 3350 improved global satisfaction and the frequency of bowel movements at 4 weeks compared with lactulose. ▶

*Clin Evid Concise* 2004;11:101–103.

# Constipation in adults

**LIKELY TO BE BENEFICIAL**

## Lactulose

We found limited evidence from two RCTs that lactulose improved symptoms compared with placebo. We found limited evidence from two RCTs that lactulose was less effective in improving symptoms at 4 weeks than ispaghula husk. Three RCTs identified by systematic reviews compared lactulose versus lactitol and found different results. Two RCTs found no significant difference in effectiveness at 2–4 weeks and one RCT found that lactulose was less effective than lactitol in increasing bowel movement frequency at 2 weeks. One RCT identified by a systematic review found that lactulose was less effective than macrogol 3350 in improving global satisfaction and the frequency of bowel movements at 4 weeks.

**UNKNOWN EFFECTIVENESS**

## Lactitol

One small crossover RCT identified by a systematic review found that lactitol increased the frequency of bowel movements compared with placebo after 4 weeks. Three RCTs identified by systematic reviews compared lactitol versus lactulose and found different results. Two RCTs found no significant difference in frequency of bowel movements at 2–4 weeks and one RCT found that lactitol increased frequency of bowel movements at 2 weeks compared with lactulose.

## Magnesium salts; phosphate enemas; sodium citrate enemas

We found no RCTs in adults with idiopathic chronic constipation.

---

## What are the effects of stimulant laxatives in adults with idiopathic chronic constipation? New

**UNKNOWN EFFECTIVENESS**

## Docusate

One systematic review identified no RCTs of sufficient quality comparing docusate versus placebo. One RCT identified by a systematic review found that docusate was less effective than ispaghula husk in increasing the frequency of bowel movements after 2 weeks. It found no significant difference between treatments in stool consistency, straining, or pain.

## Bisacodyl; dantron; glycerol/glycerin suppositories; picosulphate (picosulfate); senna

We found no RCTs in adults with idiopathic chronic constipation.

**DEFINITION**    Bowel habits and perception of bowel habit vary widely within and among populations, making constipation difficult to define strictly. The Rome II criteria ❻ is a standardised tool which diagnoses chronic constipation on the basis of two or more of the following symptoms for at least 12 weeks in the preceding year: straining at defecation on at least a quarter of occasions; stools that are lumpy/hard on at least a quarter of occasions; sensation of incomplete evacuation on at least a quarter of occasions; and three or fewer bowel movements a week.[1] In practice, however, diagnostic criteria are less rigid and are in part dependent on perception of normal bowel habit. Typically, chronic constipation might be diagnosed when a person has bowel actions twice a week or less, for two consecutive weeks, especially in the presence of features such as straining at stool, abdominal discomfort, and sensation of incomplete evacuation. In this chapter, we have included all RCTs that stated that all participants had chronic constipation. Where the definitions of constipation in the RCTs differ markedly from those presented here, we have ▶

made this difference explicit. In this chapter, we deal with chronic constipation that is not caused by a specific underlying disease (sometimes known as idiopathic constipation) in adults aged over 18 years. We have excluded studies in pregnant women and in people with constipation associated with underlying specific organic diseases such as autonomic neuropathy, spinal cord injury, bowel obstruction, and paralytic ileus.

**INCIDENCE/ PREVALENCE**  Twelve million general practitioner prescriptions were written for laxatives in England in 2001.[2] Prevalence data are limited by small samples and problems with definition. One UK survey of 731 women found that 8.2% had constipation meeting Rome II criteria, and 8.5% defined themselves as being constipated.[3] A larger survey (1892 adults) found that 39% of men and 52% of women reported straining at stool on more than a quarter of occasions.[4] Prevalence rises in the elderly. Several surveys from around the world suggest that in a community setting, prevalence among the elderly is about 20%.[4–7]

**AETIOLOGY/ RISK FACTORS**  One systematic review found that factors associated with increased risk of constipation included low fibre diet, low fluid intake, reduced mobility, and consumption of drugs such as opioids and anticholinergic antidepressants.[8]

**PROGNOSIS**  Untreated constipation may lead to faecal impaction, particularly in elderly and confused people.[9] Constipation has been suggested as a risk factor for haemorrhoids and colorectal cancer, but evidence of causality is lacking.[9]

---

Please refer to CD-ROM for full text and references.

# Gastro-oesophageal reflux disease

Search date July 2003

*Paul Moayyedi, Brendan Delaney, and David Foreman*

## What are the effects of initial treatment of gastro-oesophageal reflux disease (GORD) associated with oesophagitis?

### BENEFICIAL

#### H₂ receptor antagonists

One systematic review has found that $H_2$ receptor antagonists reduce the risk of persisting oesophagitis compared with placebo, but are not as effective as proton pump inhibitors.

#### Proton pump inhibitors

One systematic review, one additional RCT, and one subsequent RCT found that proton pump inhibitors increase healing compared with placebo or $H_2$ receptor antagonists. One systematic review found that esomeprazole 40 mg daily increased healing at 4 weeks compared with omeprazole 20 mg daily. RCTs have found no significant differences in clinical benefit among other proton pump inhibitors.

### UNKNOWN EFFECTIVENESS

#### Antacids/alginates

Two RCTs provided limited evidence that antacids reduced symptom scores at 4–8 weeks compared with placebo, but neither found a significant difference in endoscopic healing. We found limited evidence on the effects of antacids compared with $H_2$ receptor antagonists. The first RCT found no significant difference between antacids compared with cimetidine in endoscopic healing at 8 weeks. The second RCT found that antacids were less effective for heartburn symptoms compared with ranitidine at 12 weeks.

#### Lifestyle advice

Small RCTs provided insufficient evidence on the effects of raising the head of the bed or weight loss for the treatment of reflux oesophagitis. We found no RCTs on the effects of reducing coffee intake, stopping smoking, reducing alcohol intake, or reducing fatty food intake.

### LIKELY TO BE INEFFECTIVE OR HARMFUL

#### Motility stimulants

One RCT found that cisapride increased endoscopic healing compared with placebo at 12 weeks. The use of cisapride has been restricted in some countries because of concerns about heart rhythm abnormalities. We found no RCTs of domperidone or metoclopramide.

## What are the effects of maintenance treatment of GORD associated with oesophagitis?

### BENEFICIAL

#### Proton pump inhibitors

RCTs have found that proton pump inhibitors reduce relapse in people with healed reflux oesophagitis compared with placebo or $H_2$ receptor antagonist at 6–18 months. One systematic review has found that standard dose lansoprazole ▶

(30 mg/day) was as effective as omeprazole (20 mg/day) for maintaining healing at 12 months. However, the systematic review and one subsequent RCT provided evidence that lower dose lansoprazole (15 mg/day) was less effective than higher dose lansoprazole (30 mg/day), omeprazole, or esomeprazole for maintaining healing for up to 12 months.

## TRADE OFF BETWEEN BENEFITS AND HARMS

### Laparoscopic surgery

One systematic review found no fully published RCTs comparing laparoscopic surgery versus medical treatment for maintenance of remission. Two RCTs found no significant difference between open and laparoscopic fundoplication for remission at 3 months to 2 years. One RCT found that laparoscopic treatment was associated with surgical complications, although the rate was lower than with open surgery.

### Open surgery

RCTs have found that open Nissen fundoplication compared with medical treatment improved the endoscopic grade of oesophagitis in people with chronic gastro-oesophageal reflux disease and oesophagitis at between 3 and 38 months. However, longer term follow up from one of these RCTs found no significant difference in endoscopic appearance between surgery and medical treatment at 10 years. Two RCTs found no significant difference between open and laparoscopic fundoplication for remission at 3 months to 2 years. One RCT found that mortality was higher with open surgery than with medical treatment. One RCT found that complication rates were higher with open than with laparoscopic surgery.

## UNKNOWN EFFECTIVENESS

### Antacids/alginates

We found no RCTs on the effects of antacids/alginates on the long term management of reflux oesophagitis.

### $H_2$ receptor antagonists

One RCT found no significant difference between ranitidine and placebo for relapse of oesophagitis at 6 months in people with previously healed reflux oesophagitis. RCTs have found that $H_2$ receptor antagonists are less effective than proton pump inhibitors for maintaining remission up to 12 months.

### Lifestyle advice

We found no RCTs on the effects of lifestyle advice on the long term management of reflux oesophagitis.

## LIKELY TO BE INEFFECTIVE OR HARMFUL

### Motility stimulants

Three RCTs have found that cisapride compared with placebo improved maintenance of healing at 6–12 months. Two further RCTs found no evidence of a difference, but they might have lacked power to detect a clinically significant effect. The use of cisapride has been restricted in some countries because of concerns about effects on heart rhythms. We found no RCTs comparing other prokinetic drugs with placebo or each other in people with gastro-oesophageal reflux disease and oesophagitis.

**DEFINITION**    Gastro-oesophageal reflux disease (GORD) is defined as reflux of gastroduo-denal contents into the oesophagus, causing symptoms that are sufficient to interfere with quality of life.[1] People with GORD often have symptoms of heartburn and acid regurgitation.[2] GORD can be classified according to the results of upper gastrointestinal endoscopy. Currently the most validated ▶

# Gastro-oesophageal reflux disease

method is the Los Angeles classification, where an endoscopy showing mucosal breaks in the distal oesophagus indicate the presence of oesophagitis, which is graded in severity from grade A (mucosal breaks of < 5 mm in the oesophagus) to grade D (circumferential breaks in the oesophageal mucosa).[1,3] Alternatively, severity may be graded according to the Savary–Miller classification (grade I: linear, non-confluent erosions, to grade IV: severe ulceration or stricture).

**INCIDENCE/ PREVALENCE**  Surveys from Europe and the USA suggest that 20–25% of the population have symptoms of GORD, and 7% have heartburn daily.[4,5] In primary care settings, about 25–40% of people with GORD have oesophagitis on endoscopy, but most have endoscopy negative reflux disease.[3]

**AETIOLOGY/ RISK FACTORS**  We found no evidence of clear predictive factors for GORD. Obesity is reported to be a risk factor for GORD but epidemiological data are conflicting.[6,7] Smoking and alcohol are also thought to predispose to GORD, but observational data are limited.[7,8] It has been suggested that some foods, such as coffee, mints, dietary fat, onions, citrus fruits, or tomatoes, may predispose to GORD.[9] However, we found insufficient data on the role of these factors. We found limited evidence that drugs that relax the lower oesophageal sphincter, such as calcium channel blockers, may promote GORD.[10] Twin studies suggest that there may be a genetic predisposition to GORD.[8]

**PROGNOSIS**  GORD is a chronic condition, with about 80% of people relapsing once medication is discontinued.[11] Many people therefore require long term medical treatment or surgery. Endoscopy negative reflux disease remains stable, with a minority of people developing oesophagitis over time.[12] However, people with severe oesophagitis may develop complications such as oesophageal stricture and Barrett's oesophagus.[1]

Please refer to CD-ROM for full text and references.

## What are the effects of treatments?

BENEFICIAL

### *H pylori* eradication for healing and preventing recurrence of duodenal ulcer

Systematic reviews and one subsequent RCT have found that *H pylori* eradication increases ulcer healing at 6 weeks and reduces 1 year recurrence compared with acid suppression or antisecretory treatment**G**. One systematic review found that *H pylori* eradication compared with ulcer healing alone, or compared with ulcer treatment plus subsequent acid suppression maintenance treatment reduced the risk of rebleeding.

### *H pylori* eradication for healing and preventing recurrence of gastric ulcer

One systematic review found no good evidence on endoscopic healing of gastric ulcers. One systematic review has found that *H pylori* eradication treatment compared with antisecretory treatment reduces recurrent ulcers at 1 year. Observational evidence identified by the review found that eradication treatment heals 83% of gastric ulcers within 6 weeks of starting treatment. We found no RCTs of *H pylori* eradication treatment on preventing complications of gastric ulcers.

### *H pylori* eradication for non-ulcer dyspepsia

One systematic review in people with non-ulcer dyspepsia has found that *H pylori* eradication significantly reduces dyspeptic symptoms compared with placebo at 3–12 months.

LIKELY TO BE BENEFICIAL

### *H pylori* eradication rather than empirical acid suppression for uninvestigated dyspepsia

One RCT found that *H pylori* eradication increased relief from dyspeptic symptoms compared with placebo after 1 year.

### *H pylori* eradication rather than endoscopy in people with uninvestigated dyspepsia not at risk of malignancy

One RCT has found that *H pylori* eradication increased relief from dyspeptic symptoms after 1 year compared with placebo. One systematic review and one subsequent RCT have found no significant difference between *H pylori* testing plus eradication compared with management based on initial endoscopy in dyspepsia after 1 year. The review found that H pylori testing plus eradication reduced the need for requiring endoscopy compared with endoscopy based management.

### Three day quadruple regimen (*v* 1 week triple regimen)

One RCT comparing a 3 day quadruple regimen versus a 1 week triple regimen found no significant difference in *H pylori* eradication at 6 weeks, but found that people taking the 3 day quadruple regimen experienced fewer days of adverse effects.

### Triple regimen (*v* dual regimen)

We found no systematic review or RCTs of the effects of dual regimen**G** compared with triple regimens**G** on dyspeptic symptom scores, proportion of subjects with symptoms, quality of life, or mortality. One systematic review has found that dual versus triple regimens eradicate *H pylori* from fewer people.   ▶

# *Helicobacter pylori* infection

## Two week triple regimen (v 1 week triple regimen)

One systematic review found that 14 days treatment with proton pump inhibitor based treatment increased *H pylori* cure rates compared with 7 days treatment.

### UNKNOWN EFFECTIVENESS

### *H pylori* eradication for gastric B cell lymphoma

We found no RCTs of *H pylori* eradication treatment in people with B cell gastric lymphoma❻. Observational studies found limited evidence that 60–93% of people with localised, low grade B cell lymphoma respond to *H pylori* eradication treatment possibly avoiding, or delaying the need for radical surgery, radiotherapy, or chemotherapy.

### *H pylori* eradication for prevention of gastric cancer (adenocarcinoma)

We found no RCTs of *H pylori* eradication in people at risk of gastric cancer. One RCT in people with gastric atrophy or intestinal metaplasia found that *H pylori* eradication increased the regression of high risk lesions compared with no eradication. We found consistent evidence from observational studies of an association between *H pylori* infection and increased risk of distal gastric adeno-carcinoma.

### One triple regimen versus another

We found no systematic review or RCTs of the effects of different triple regimens on symptoms, quality of life, or mortality. One systematic review has found that clarithromycin 500 mg twice daily versus clarithromycin 250 mg twice daily plus a proton pump inhibitor❻ plus amoxicillin significantly increases *H pylori* eradication, but found no significant difference between clarithromycin 500 mg twice daily compared with clarithromycin 250 mg twice daily plus a proton pump inhibitor plus metronidazole in *H pylori* eradication rates. Another systematic review has found that a triple regimen containing ranitidine bismuth❻ plus clarithromycin plus metronidazole versus a triple regimen containing ranitidine bismuth plus clarithromycin plus amoxicillin significantly increases eradication at 5–7 days.

### UNLIKELY TO BE BENEFICIAL

### *H pylori* eradication in people with gastro-oesophageal reflux disease

One RCT in people with gastro-oesophageal reflux disease found no significant difference between *H pylori* eradication treatment and placebo in symptomatic relapse.

**DEFINITION** *Helicobacter pylori* is a Gram negative flagellated spiral bacterium found in the stomach. Infection with *H pylori* is predominantly acquired in childhood. The organism is associated with lifelong chronic gastritis and may cause other gastroduodenal disorders.[1]

**INCIDENCE/ PREVALENCE** *H pylori* prevalence rates vary with birth cohort and social class in the developed world. Prevalence rates in many developed countries tend to be much higher (50–80%) in those born before 1950 in comparison to rates (< 20%) in individuals born more recently.[2] In many developing countries the infection has a high prevalence (80–95%) irrespective of the period of birth.[3] Adult prevalence is believed to represent the persistence of a historically higher rate of infection acquired in childhood, rather than increasing acquisition of infection during life.

**AETIOLOGY/ RISK FACTORS** Overcrowded conditions associated with childhood poverty lead to increased transmission and higher prevalence rates. Adult reinfection rates are low — less than 1% a year.[3]

▶

**◄ PROGNOSIS**    *H pylori* infection is believed to be causally related to the development of duodenal and gastric ulceration, gastric B cell lymphoma, and distal gastric cancer. About 15% of people infected with *H pylori* will develop a peptic ulcer, and 1% of people will develop gastric cancer during their lifetime.[4] *H pylori* infection is not associated with a specific type of dyspeptic symptom.

Please refer to CD-ROM for full text and references.

# Irritable bowel syndrome

Search date October 2002

*Thomas M Kennedy, Gregory Rubin, and Roger H Jones*

## What are the effects of treatments in people with irritable bowel syndrome? New

### LIKELY TO BE BENEFICIAL

#### Antidepressants (amitriptyline, clomipramine, desipramine, doxepin, mianserin, trimipramine)

One systematic review found limited evidence from low to moderate quality RCTs that antidepressants (amitriptyline, clomipramine, desipramine, doxepin, mianserin, trimipramine) reduced symptoms of irritable bowel syndrome compared with placebo in the short term. It was not clear whether effects on irritable bowel syndrome were independent of effects on psychological symptoms.

#### Smooth muscle relaxants (cimetropium bromide, hyoscine butyl bromide, mebeverine hydrochloride, otilonium bromide, pinaverium bromide, trimebutine)

One systematic review found limited evidence that smooth muscle relaxants (cimetropium bromide, hyoscine butyl bromide, mebeverine hydrochloride, otilonium bromide, pinaverium bromide, trimebutine) improved symptoms compared with placebo. One subsequent RCT found no significant difference between alverine and placebo in improvement in abdominal pain, although the study may have lacked power to exclude a clinically important effect.

### TRADE OFF BETWEEN BENEFITS AND HARMS

#### Alosetron

RCTs have found that alosetron (a $5HT_3$ receptor antagonist) improves symptoms in women with diarrhoea predominant or alternating irritable bowel syndrome compared with placebo. However, it is associated with adverse effects, particularly constipation, and has been restricted in some countries because of concerns that it may be associated with ischaemic colitis.

#### $5HT_4$ receptor agonists (tegaserod)

One large RCT in people with constipation predominant irritable bowel syndrome found that tegaserod improved overall symptoms. It was more likely to cause diarrhoea compared with placebo.

### UNKNOWN EFFECTIVENESS

#### $5HT_3$ receptor antagonists other than alosetron

We found no RCTs examining $5HT_3$ receptor antagonists other than alosetron.

### UNLIKELY TO BE BENEFICIAL

#### Fibre supplementation

Limited evidence from small RCTs suggests that fibre supplementation does not improve symptoms compared with placebo.

▶

◄ **DEFINITION**    Irritable bowel syndrome (IBS) is a chronic non-inflammatory condition characterised by abdominal pain, altered bowel habit (diarrhoea or constipation), and abdominal bloating, but with no identifiable structural or biochemical disorder. Symptom based criteria, such as the Manning criteria❶,[1] the Rome I criteria❶,[2] and the Rome II criteria❶,[3] aid diagnosis but their main use is in defining populations in clinical trials. IBS is often categorised according to predominant symptoms (diarrhoea, constipation, or alternating between diarrhoea and constipation).

**INCIDENCE/**    Estimates of incidence and prevalence vary depending on the diagnostic
**PREVALENCE**    criteria used to define IBS. One cross-sectional postal survey (4476 people aged 20–69 years) in Teeside, UK, defined IBS as recurrent abdominal pain on more than six occasions during the previous year plus two or more of the Manning criteria.[4] It estimated prevalence in the UK to be 16.7% (95% CI 15.4% to 18.0%) overall, with a prevalence of 22.8% (95% CI 20.8% to 24.8%) among women, and 10.5% (95% CI 8.9% to 12.1%) among men.[4] A cross-sectional postal survey (4500 people aged > 17 years) in Australia found prevalences of IBS of 13.6% (95% CI 12.3% to 14.8%) using the Manning criteria, 6.9% (95% CI 6.0% to 7.8%) using the Rome I criteria, and 4.4% (95% CI 3.5% to 5.1%) using the Rome II criteria.[5]

**AETIOLOGY/**    The pathophysiology of IBS is not certain. Studies on the aetiology of IBS have
**RISK FACTORS** been descriptive or retrospective, and are of limited reliability. Suggested aetiological factors include: abnormal gastrointestinal motor function;[6–8] enhanced visceral perception;[9–11] psychosocial factors such as a history of childhood abuse;[12] genetic predisposition,[13–15] and a history of enteric mucosal inflammation.[16,17] We found no reliable prospective data to measure these associations.

**PROGNOSIS**    A retrospective study reviewed the medical records of people with IBS (112 people aged 20–64 years when diagnosed with IBS at the Mayo Clinic, USA, in 1961–1963). IBS was defined as the presence of abdominal pain associated with either disturbed defecation or abdominal distension and the absence of organic bowel disease.[18] Over a 32 year period, death rates were similar among people with IBS compared with age and gender matched controls. One postal survey (4432 adults aged 20–69 years) found that people with IBS are significantly more likely to have had a cholecystectomy than controls (OR 1.9, 95% CI 1.2 to 3.2).[4] A paper reporting on the same survey population (2238 women aged 20–69 years) found that women with IBS were significantly more likely to have had a hysterectomy than controls (OR 1.6, 95% CI 1.1 to 2.2).[19]

Please refer to CD-ROM for full text and references.

# Pancreatic cancer

Search date May 2003

*Bazian Ltd*

## What are the effects of surgical treatments in people with pancreatic cancer that is considered suitable for complete tumour resection?

### UNKNOWN EFFECTIVENESS

**Pancreaticoduodenectomy (Whipple's procedure)**

We found no RCTs comparing pancreaticoduodenectomy (Whipple's procedure) with non-surgical treatment in people with resectable pancreatic cancer, although such studies may be considered unethical. Observational data provide limited evidence that surgery may reduce mortality compared with non-surgical treatment, although results may be confounded by differences in disease stage. Small RCTs found no significant difference in quality of life or survival at 5 years between pancreaticoduodenectomy and pylorus preserving pancreaticoduodenectomy.

**Pylorus preserving pancreaticoduodenectomy (compared with Whipple's procedure)**

Small RCTs found no significant difference between pylorus preserving surgery and classical pancreaticoduodenectomy (Whipple's procedure☉) for overall quality of life at 1 year or survival at 5 years in people with resectable tumours. However, the studies may have lacked power to exclude clinically important differences for these outcomes.

## What are effects of adjuvant treatments in people with completely resected pancreatic cancer?

### TRADE OFF BETWEEN BENEFITS AND HARMS

**Systemic fluorouracil based chemotherapy**

One RCT has found that adjuvant fluorouracil based chemotherapy improves median survival compared with no adjuvant chemotherapy in people with resected pancreatic cancer. This RCT and a second RCT found no significant difference in 5 year survival between adjuvant chemotherapy with fluorouracil based chemotherapy and no chemotherapy but the RCTs may have lacked power to detect a clinically important effect. The second RCT found that adjuvant fluorouracil based chemotherapy increased ≥ Grade 2 leukopenia, anorexia, and nausea or emesis compared with no chemotherapy. A third RCT did not compare chemotherapy alone with no chemotherapy directly.

### UNKNOWN EFFECTIVENESS

**Systemic gemcitabine based chemotherapy**

One systematic review found insufficient evidence about effects of adjuvant gemcitabine compared with no adjuvant chemotherapy in people with resected pancreatic cancer.

**DEFINITION**     In this chapter, the term "pancreatic cancer" refers to primary adenocarcinoma of the pancreas. Other pancreatic malignancies, such as carcinoid tumour, are not considered. Symptoms of pancreatic cancer include pain, jaundice, nausea, weight loss, loss of appetite, and symptoms of gastrointestinal obstruction and diabetes. Pancreatic cancer is staged from I to IV according to disease spread. Stage I disease is limited to the pancreas, ▶

duodenum, bile duct, or peri-pancreatic tissues, with no distant metastases or regional lymph node involvement. Stages II–IV describe disease that has spread more extensively or become metastatic. A pancreatic tumour is considered resectable if there is a possibility that surgery could remove all cancerous tissue completely. Early stage tumours in the tail or body of the pancreas are more likely to be resectable than the more common, later stage cancers in the head of the pancreas. Other factors that influence resectability include proximity of the tumour to major blood vessels and perceived peri-operative risk.

**INCIDENCE/ PREVALENCE**  Pancreatic cancer is the eighth most common cancer in the UK with an annual incidence in England and Wales of about 12/100 000.[1] It is the fourth most common cause of cancer death in higher income countries, responsible for about 30 000 deaths each year in the USA.[2] Prevalence is similar in men and women, with 5–10% presenting with resectable disease.[3]

**AETIOLOGY/ RISK FACTORS**  Pancreatic cancer is more likely in people who smoke and have high alcohol intake. Dietary factors, such as lack of fruit and vegetables, are also reported risk factors.[4] One meta-analysis of observational studies found that people with diabetes mellitus of more than 5 years' duration are more likely to develop pancreatic cancer compared with the general population.[5] However, estimates of the magnitude of increased risk vary. Additional risk factors include pancreatitis and, in some cases, a family history.[1]

**PROGNOSIS**  Prognosis is poor. One year survival is about 12%, with 5 year survival ranging from less than 1% in those with advanced cancer at presentation to 5% in those with early stage cancer at presentation.[1,6]

---

Please refer to CD-ROM for full text and references.

_Digestive system disorders_

# Stomach cancer

Search date January 2003

_Charles Bailey_

---

## What are the effects of treatments?

### LIKELY TO BE BENEFICIAL

**Complete surgical resection***

RCTs of complete surgical resection are unlikely to be conducted. Observational studies and multivariate analysis of RCTs have found a strong association between survival and complete resection of the primary tumour.

**Subtotal gastrectomy (as effective as total gastrectomy) for resectable distal tumours**

RCTs in people with primary tumours in the distal stomach have found no significant difference with total❻ versus subtotal❻ gastrectomy in 5 year survival or postoperative mortality.

*Observational evidence only; RCTs unlikely to be conducted.

### UNKNOWN EFFECTIVENESS

**Adjuvant chemotherapy**

Systematic reviews and subsequent RCTs have found conflicting evidence that adjuvant chemotherapy❻ increases survival compared with surgery alone. Two RCTs found that adjuvant chemotherapy increased postoperative complications. The size of any benefit remains uncertain, and many recent adjuvant chemotherapy regimens have not been evaluated fully in RCTs.

**Radical versus conservative lymphadenectomy**

Two large RCTs found no significant difference in 5 year survival rates between radical and conservative lymphadenectomy. However, confounding factors may have affected reliability of results, and we found conflicting data from subgroup analyses of prospective cohort studies.

### LIKELY TO BE INEFFECTIVE OR HARMFUL

**Removal of adjacent organs**

One RCT found no significant difference between radical gastrectomy plus splenectomy and radical gastrectomy alone in 5 year survival rates or postoperative mortality. The RCT found that radical gastrectomy plus splenectomy significantly increased the number of postoperative infections compared with radical gastrectomy alone. Retrospective analyses of observational studies and RCTs in people with stomach cancer found that removal of additional organs (spleen and distal pancreas) increased morbidity and mortality compared with no organ removal.

**DEFINITION**
Stomach cancer is usually an adenocarcinoma arising in the stomach and includes tumours arising at or just below the gastro-oesophageal junction (type II and III junctional tumours). Tumours are staged according to degree of invasion and spread❶. Only non-metastatic stomach cancers are considered in this topic.

**INCIDENCE/ PREVALENCE**
The incidence of stomach cancer varies among countries and by sex (incidence per 100 000 population a year in Japanese men is about 80, Japanese women 30, British men 18, British women 10, white American men 11, white American women 7).[1] Incidence has declined dramatically in North America, Australia, and New Zealand since 1930, but the decline in Europe has been ▶

slower.[2] In the USA, stomach cancer remains relatively common among particular ethnic groups, especially Japanese–Americans and some Hispanic groups. The incidence of cancer of the proximal stomach and gastro-oesophageal junction is rising rapidly in many European populations and in North America.[3,4] The reasons for this are poorly understood.

**AETIOLOGY/ RISK FACTORS**  Distal stomach cancer is strongly associated with lifelong infection with *Helicobacter pylori* and poor dietary intake of antioxidant vitamins (A, C, and E).[5,6] In Western Europe and North America, distal stomach cancer is associated with relative socioeconomic deprivation. Proximal stomach cancer is strongly associated with smoking (OR about 4),[7] and is probably associated with gastro-oesophageal reflux, obesity, high fat intake, and medium to high socioeconomic status.

**PROGNOSIS**  Invasive stomach cancer (stages T2–T4) is fatal without surgery. Mean survival without treatment is less than 6 months from diagnosis.[8,9] Intramucosal or submucosal cancer (stage T1) may progress slowly to invasive cancer over several years.[10] In the USA, over 50% of people recently diagnosed with stomach cancer have regional lymph node metastasis or involvement of adjacent organs. The prognosis after macroscopically and microscopically complete resection (R0) is related strongly to disease stage❻, particularly penetration of the serosa (stage T3) and lymph node involvement. Five year survival rates range from over 90% in intramucosal cancer to about 20% in people with stage T3N2 disease❶. In Japan, the 5 year survival rate for people with advanced disease is reported to be about 50%, but the explanation for the difference remains unclear. Comparisons between Japanese and Western practice are confounded by factors such as age, fitness, and disease stage, as well as by tumour location, because many Western series include gastro-oesophageal junction adenocarcinoma with a much lower survival after surgery.

Please refer to CD-ROM for full text and references.

# Chronic suppurative otitis media

Search date March 2003

*Jose Acuin*

## What are the effects of treatments in adults?

We found no RCTs with long term follow up.

### LIKELY TO BE BENEFICIAL

**Topical antibiotics**

We found no RCTs with long term follow up. Two RCTs found limited evidence that topical quinolone antibiotics improved otoscopic appearances compared with placebo in adults with chronic suppurative otitis media. Six RCTs found no clear evidence of clinically important differences among topical antibiotics in adults. One systematic review found that topical antibiotics were more effective than systemic antibiotics for reducing otoscopic features of chronic suppurative otitis media. One RCT found no significant effect of adding topical ceftizoxime to systemic ceftizoxime compared with systemic ceftizoxime alone. One RCT found no significant effect of preoperative topical antibiotics compared with no preoperative treatment in people undergoing tympanoplasty. Short term topical antibiotics have been associated with few adverse events in RCTs. Uncontrolled case studies have reported vestibular ototoxicity after topical non-quinolone antibiotics.

### UNKNOWN EFFECTIVENESS

**Ear cleansing (aural toilet)**

We found no RCTs comparing ear cleansing❻ versus no treatment.

**Systemic antibiotics**

We found insufficient evidence about the effects of systemic antibiotics compared with placebo, no treatment, or topical antiseptics. One systematic review found that systemic antibiotics were less effective than topical antibiotics in reducing otoscopic features of chronic suppurative otitis media. We found no evidence about long term treatment.

**Topical antibiotics plus topical steroids**

One systematic review found insufficient evidence from three RCTs about effects on symptoms of topical antibiotics plus topical steroids versus placebo or topical steroids alone.

**Topical antiseptics**

We found no RCTs comparing topical antiseptics versus placebo or no treatment. One RCT compared topical antiseptics plus ear cleansing under microscopic control versus topical antibiotics alone or versus oral antibiotics. It found no significant difference in the rate of persistent activity on otoscopy. However, the RCT was too small to exclude a clinically important difference.

**Topical steroids**

We found no RCTs comparing topical steroids versus placebo or no treatment.

**Tympanoplasty with or without mastoidectomy**

We found no RCTs comparing tympanoplasty❻ with or without mastoidectomy❻ versus no surgery for chronic suppurative otitis media without cholesteatoma❻. ▶

◀ *What are the effects of treatments in children?*

UNKNOWN EFFECTIVENESS

**Ear cleansing**
One systematic review found no significant difference in persistent otorrhoea or tympanic perforations with a simple form of ear cleansing versus no ear cleansing. However, a clinically important effect cannot be excluded.

**Systemic antibiotics**
RCTs found insufficient evidence about the effects of systemic antibiotics in children with chronic suppurative otitis media.

**Topical antibiotics**
We found no RCTs comparing topical antibiotics versus placebo.

**Topical antibiotics plus topical steroids**
We found insufficient evidence from small RCTs to compare topical antibiotics plus topical steroids versus cleansing only or topical antiseptics. We found no RCTs comparing topical antibiotics plus topical steroids versus either topical treatment alone.

**Topical antiseptics**
Two RCTs found no significant reduction in otorrhoea with topical antiseptics versus placebo after 2 weeks. One RCT found no significant difference in otorrhoea with topical antiseptics versus topical antibiotic plus steroid. However, the RCTs were too small to exclude a clinically important effect.

**Topical steroids**
We found no RCTs comparing topical steroids versus placebo.

**Tympanoplasty with or without mastoidectomy**
We found no RCTs comparing tympanoplasty with or without mastoidectomy versus no surgery for chronic suppurative otitis media without cholesteatoma.

**DEFINITION**  Chronic suppurative otitis media is persistent inflammation of the middle ear or mastoid cavity. Synonyms include "chronic otitis media (without effusion)", chronic mastoiditis, and chronic tympanomastoiditis. Chronic suppurative otitis media is characterised by recurrent or persistent ear discharge (otorrhoea) over 2–6 weeks through a perforation of the tympanic membrane. Typical findings also include thickened granular middle ear mucosa, mucosal polyps, and cholesteatoma**ⓖ** within the middle ear. Chronic suppurative otitis media is differentiated from chronic otitis media with effusion, in which there is an intact tympanic membrane with fluid in the middle ear but no active infection. Chronic suppurative otitis media does not include chronic perforations of the eardrum that are dry, or only occasionally discharge, and have no signs of active infection.

**INCIDENCE/**  The worldwide prevalence of chronic suppurative otitis media is 65–330
**PREVALENCE**  million people. Between 39–200 million (60%) suffer from clinically significant hearing impairment. Otitis media was estimated to have caused 28 000 deaths and loss of over 2 million Disability Adjusted Life Years**ⓖ** in 2000,[1] 94% of which were in developing countries. Most of these deaths were probably due to chronic suppurative otitis media because acute otitis media is a self limiting infection. Estimates of prevalence are shown in table A on web extra.[2–32]

**AETIOLOGY/**  Chronic suppurative otitis media is assumed to be a complication of acute otitis
**RISK FACTORS**  media, but the risk factors for chronic suppurative otitis media are not clear. Frequent upper respiratory tract infections and poor socioeconomic conditions ▶

# Chronic suppurative otitis media

(overcrowded housing,[33] hygiene, and nutrition) may be related to the development of chronic suppurative otitis media.[34,35] Improvement of housing, hygiene, and nutrition in Maori children was associated with a halving of the prevalence of chronic suppurative otitis media between 1978 and 1987.[36] See also acute otitis media, p 47.

**PROGNOSIS**  Most children with chronic suppurative otitis media have mild to moderate hearing impairment (about 26–60 dB increase in hearing thresholds) based on surveys among children in Africa, Brazil,[37] India,[38] and Sierra Leone,[39] and among the general population in Thailand.[40] In many developing countries, chronic suppurative otitis media represents the most frequent cause of moderate hearing loss (40–60 dB).[41] Persistent hearing loss during the first 2 years of life may increase learning disabilities and poor scholastic performance.[42] Spread of infection may lead to life threatening complications such as intracranial infections and acute mastoiditis.[43] The frequency of serious complications fell from 20% in 1938 to 2.5% in 1948 and is currently estimated to be about 0.24% in Thailand and 1.8% in Africa. This is believed to be associated with increased use of antibiotic treatment, tympanoplasty, and mastoidectomy.[44–46] Cholesteatoma is another serious complication that has been found in a variable proportion of people with chronic suppurative otitis media (range 0–60%).[47–50] In the West, the incidence of cholesteatoma is low (in 1993 in Finland the age standardised incidence of cholesteatoma was eight new cases per 100 000 population/year).[51]

---

Please refer to CD-ROM for full text and references.

Search date June 2003

*Adrian James and Marc Thorp*

## What are the effects of treatments for acute attacks?

**UNKNOWN EFFECTIVENESS**

**Anticholinergics; benzodiazepines; betahistine**
We found no RCTs on the effects of these interventions.

## What are the effects of interventions to prevent attacks and delay progression?

**UNKNOWN EFFECTIVENESS**

**Betahistine (for vertigo or tinnitus)**
Seven RCTs provided insufficient evidence to compare the effects of betahistine versus those of placebo on the frequency and severity of attacks of vertigo, tinnitus, and aural fullness. Two small RCTs in people with definite or possible Menière's disease found no significant difference in tinnitus between betahistine and trimetazidine. One of these RCTs found that trimetazidine reduced the intensity of vertigo compared with betahistine, but the other RCT found no significant difference in vertigo intensity between trimetazidine and betahistine.

**Diuretics**
One small crossover RCT provided insufficient evidence about the effects of triamterene plus hydrochlorothiazide on hearing, vertigo, or tinnitus.

**Trimetazidine**
We found no RCTs comparing trimetazidine versus placebo in Menière's disease. Two small RCTs in people with definite or possible Menière's disease found no significant difference in tinnitus between betahistine and trimetazidine. One of these RCTs found that trimetazidine reduced the intensity vertigo compared with betahistine, but the other RCT found no significant difference in vertigo intensity between trimetazidine and betahistine.

**Dietary modification; psychological support; aminoglycosides; vestibular rehabilitation☺**
We found no RCTs on the effects of these interventions.

**UNLIKELY TO BE BENEFICIAL**

**Betahistine (for hearing loss)**
Four RCTs in people with possible Menière's disease found no significant difference between betahistine and placebo in change in hearing assessed by pure tone audiograms. Two small RCTs in people with definite or possible Menière's disease found no significant difference in hearing between betahistine and trimetazidine.

**LIKELY TO BE INEFFECTIVE OR HARMFUL**

**Lithium**
Two small crossover RCTs in people with possible Menière's disease provided insufficient evidence to compare effects of lithium versus those of placebo on vertigo, tinnitus, aural fullness, or hearing, although they found that lithium was associated with tremor, thirst, and polyuria in some people.

▶

*Clin Evid Concise* 2004;11:119–120.

# Menière's disease

**DEFINITION**     Menière's disease is characterised by recurrent episodes of spontaneous rotational vertigo and sensorineural hearing loss with tinnitus, and a feeling of fullness or pressure in the ear. It may be unilateral or bilateral. Acute episodes can occur in clusters of about 6–11 a year, although remission may last several months.[1] The diagnosis is made clinically.[2] It is important to distinguish Menière's disease from other types of vertigo that might occur independently with hearing loss and tinnitus, and respond differently to treatment (e.g. benign positional vertigo, acute labyrinthitis). Strict diagnostic criteria help to identify the condition. In this chapter we applied the classification of the American Academy of Otolaryngology–Head and Neck Surgery to indicate the diagnostic rigour used in RCTs**❶**.

**INCIDENCE/**     Menière's disease is most common between 40–60 years of age, although
**PREVALENCE**   younger people may be affected.[6,7] In Europe, the incidence is about 50–200/100 000 a year. A survey of general practitioner records of 27 365 people in the UK found an incidence of 43 affected people in a 1 year period (157/100 000).[8] Diagnostic criteria were not defined in this survey. A survey of over 8 million people in Sweden found an incidence of 46/100 000 a year with diagnosis strictly based on the triad of vertigo, hearing loss, and tinnitus.[9] From smaller studies, the incidence appears lower in Uganda[10] and higher in Japan (350/100 000, based on a national survey of hospital attendances during a single week).[7]

**AETIOLOGY/**     Menière's disease is associated with endolymphatic hydrops (raised endol-
**RISK FACTORS** ymph pressure in the membranous labyrinth of the inner ear),[11] but a causal relationship remains unproven.[12] Specific disorders associated with hydrops (such as temporal bone fracture, syphilis, hypothyroidism, Cogan's syndrome**❻**, and Mondini dysplasia**❻**) can produce symptoms similar to those of Menière's disease.

**PROGNOSIS**     Menière's disease is progressive but fluctuates unpredictably. It is difficult to distinguish natural resolution from the effects of treatment. Significant improvement in vertigo is usually seen in the placebo arm of RCTs.[13,14] Acute attacks of vertigo often increase in frequency during the first few years after presentation and then decrease in frequency in association with sustained deterioration in hearing.[6] In most people, vertiginous episodes eventually cease completely.[15] In one 20 year cohort study in 34 people, 28 (82%) people had at least moderate hearing loss (mean pure tone hearing loss > 50 dB)[1] and 16 (47%) developed bilateral disease. Symptoms other than hearing loss improve in 60–80% of people irrespective of treatment.[16]

---

Please refer to CD-ROM for full text and references.

# Middle ear pain and trauma during air travel

**Search date July 2003**

*Simon Janvrin*

## What are the effects of preventive interventions?

### LIKELY TO BE BENEFICIAL

**Oral decongestants in adults**

One RCT in adult passengers with a history of ear pain during air travel found limited evidence that oral pseudoephedrine decreased symptoms of barotrauma⊙ during air travel compared with placebo. One other RCT in adult passengers with a history of ear pain during air travel found limited evidence that oral pseudoephedrine decreased ear pain and hearing loss compared with placebo.

### UNKNOWN EFFECTIVENESS

**Oral decongestants in children**

One small RCT in children up to the age of 6 years found no significant difference between oral pseudoephedrine and placebo in ear pain at take off or landing.

**Topical nasal decongestants**

One small RCT in adults with a history of ear pain during air travel found no significant difference with oxymetazoline nasal spray and placebo in symptoms of barotrauma.

| | |
|---|---|
| **DEFINITION** | The effects of air travel on the middle ear can include ear drum pain, vertigo, hearing loss, and ear drum perforation. |
| **INCIDENCE/ PREVALENCE** | The prevalence of symptoms depends on the altitude, type of aircraft, and characteristics of the passengers. One point prevalence study found that 20% of adult and 40% of child passengers had negative pressure in the middle ear after flight, and that 10% of adults and 22% of children had auroscopic evidence of damage to the ear drum.[1] We found no data on the incidence of perforation, which seems to be extremely rare in commercial passengers. |
| **AETIOLOGY/ RISK FACTORS** | During aircraft descent, the pressure in the middle ear drops relative to that in the ear canal. A narrow, inflamed, or poorly functioning Eustachian tube impedes the necessary influx of air. As the pressure difference between the middle and outer ear increases, the ear drum is pulled inward. |
| **PROGNOSIS** | In most people, symptoms resolve spontaneously. Experience in military aviation shows that most ear drum perforations will heal spontaneously.[2] |

Please refer to CD-ROM for full text and references.

# Otitis externa

Search date July 2003

*Daniel Hajioff*

## What are the effects of empirical treatment?

### LIKELY TO BE BENEFICIAL

**Topical aluminium acetate drops (as effective as topical anti-infective agents)**

We found no RCTs that compared topical aluminium acetate versus placebo. One RCT in people with acute diffuse otitis externa found no significant difference between aluminium acetate drops and topical polymyxin–neomycin–hydrocortisone drops in clinical cure rate at 4 weeks.

**Topical anti-infective agents (antibiotics or antifungals with or without steroids)**

One RCT found that methylprednisolone–neomycin drops improved symptoms and signs compared with placebo at 28 days. Two RCTs found no significant difference in cure rate between topical quinolones and other topical anti-infective agents. One RCT found that triamcinolone–neomycin drops improved resolution rates compared with hydrocortisone–neomycin–polymyxin B drops. Two RCTs found limited evidence that neomycin–dexamethasone–acetic acid spray improved clinical cure compared with topical anti-infective drops that did not contain acetic acid. We found no RCTs on the effects of topical anti-infective agents versus oral antibiotics.

**Topical steroids**

One RCT in people with mild or moderate, acute or chronic otitis externa found that topical budesonide improved symptoms and signs compared with placebo. We found no RCTs of topical steroids compared with topical anti-infective agents. One RCT found no significant difference in symptom scores between low potency steroid(topical hydrocortisone) and high potency steroid (topical hydrocortisone butyrate) after 1 week.

### UNKNOWN EFFECTIVENESS

**Oral antibiotics**

We found no RCTs of oral antibiotics compared with placebo or topical anti-infective agents.

**Specialist aural toilet**

We found no RCTs that compared specialist aural toilet❸ versus no aural toilet. One RCT found no significant difference between an ear wick with anti-infective drops versus ribbon gauze impregnated with anti-infective ointment in resolution rates after 4 weeks.

### UNLIKELY TO BE BENEFICIAL

**Oral antibiotics plus topical anti-infective agents (no better than topical anti-infective agents alone)**

One RCT found limited evidence of no significant difference between oral co-trimoxazole plus topical anti-infective ointment and topical anti-infective ointment alone in symptom severity, symptom duration, and cure rate.

**DEFINITION** ◀ Otitis externa is inflammation, often with infection, of the external ear canal. This inflammation is usually generalised throughout the ear canal so it is often referred to as "diffuse otitis externa". The present topic excludes localised inflammations such as furuncles. Otitis externa has acute (< 6 weeks), chronic (> 3 months), and necrotising (malignant) forms. Acute otitis externa may present as a single episode, or recur. It causes severe pain with aural discharge and associated hearing loss.[1] If the ear canal is visible, it appears red and inflamed. Chronic otitis externa may result in canal stenosis with associated hearing loss, for which it may be difficult to fit hearing aids. Necrotising otitis externa is defined by destruction of the temporal bone, usually in people with diabetes or in people who are immunocompromised, and can be life-threatening.[2] In this review we look at empirical treatment of acute and chronic otitis externa only.

**INCIDENCE/** Otitis externa is common in all parts of the world. The incidence is not known
**PREVALENCE** precisely, but 10% of people are thought to have been affected at some time.[3] The condition affects children but is more common in adults. It accounts for a large proportion of the workload of otolaryngology departments, but milder cases are often managed in primary care.[3]

**AETIOLOGY/** Otitis externa may be associated with local or generalised eczema of the ear
**RISK FACTORS** canal. It is more common in swimmers, in humid environments, in people with an absence of ear wax or narrow external ear canals, in hearing aid users, and after mechanical trauma.[4]

**PROGNOSIS** We found few reliable data. Many cases of otitis externa resolve spontaneously over several weeks or months. Acute episodes have a tendency to recur, although the risk of recurrence is unknown. Experience suggests that chronic inflammation affects a small proportion of people after a single episode of acute otitis externa, and may rarely lead to canal stenosis.[1]

---

Please refer to CD-ROM for full text and references.

# Otitis media with effusion

Search date July 2003

*Ian Williamson*

## What are the effects of preventive interventions?

### UNKNOWN EFFECTIVENESS

**Modifying risk factors to prevent otitis media with effusion**

We found no RCTs on the effects of risk factors interventions aimed at modifying, such as passive smoking and bottle feeding, in preventing otitis media with effusion.

## What are the effects of pharmacological, mechanical and surgical treatments?

### LIKELY TO BE BENEFICIAL

**Autoinflation (with purpose-manufactured nasal balloon)**

One systematic review has found that autoinflation with a purpose-manufactured nasal balloon significantly improves effusion compared with no treatment. Some children may find autoinflation difficult. We found no evidence on other methods of autoinflation.

**Grommets plus adenoidectomy/adenotonsillectomy**

We found one systematic review, which found that grommets and adenoidectomy alone or in combination were equally effective and reduced mean hearing impairment by less than 12 decibels. The clinical significance of this hearing improvement was variable. One RCT from the review, which subsequently reported outcomes after 5 years, found that grommets plus adenoidectomy/ adenotonsillectomy was more effective than adenoidectomy/adenotonsillectomy or grommets alone; all of these surgical interventions were more effective than no treatment in reducing duration of otitis media with effusion. Two subsequent RCTs found different effects on language development with grommets compared with watchful waiting. A fourth subsequent RCT found that early insertion of grommets reduced behavioural problems at 9 months compared with watchful waiting.

### UNKNOWN EFFECTIVENESS

**Corticosteroids (intranasal)**

One small RCT found no significant difference between intranasal corticosteroids alone compared with placebo for resolution of effusion. A second small RCT found limited evidence that intranasal corticosteroids plus antibiotics improved symptoms compared with antibiotics alone.

**Adenoidectomy alone; adenotonsillectomy alone; autoinflation (with other devices); grommets alone; tonsillectomy**

We found insufficient evidence on the effects of these interventions.

### UNLIKELY TO BE BENEFICIAL

**Antimicrobial drugs**

One systematic review found limited evidence that antibiotics compared with placebo or no treatment improved short term outcomes. However, a second systematic review of higher quality and incorporating six RCTs from the first review found no significant difference between antibiotics and placebo. A third systematic ▶

review found limited evidence from four RCTs that antibiotics plus oral cortico-steroids improved resolution rates compared with antibiotics alone. Another small RCT in the same review found limited evidence that intranasal corticosteroids plus antibiotics improved symptoms compared with antibiotics alone. Adverse effects with antibiotics (mainly nausea, vomiting, and diarrhoea) were reported in 2–32% of children.

## Mucolytics

One systematic review found no significant difference between 1–3 month courses of carbocisteine or carbocistine lysine and placebo or no treatment in resolution of effusion. Three small RCTs of bromhexine versus placebo found inconclusive results.

### LIKELY TO BE INEFFECTIVE OR HARMFUL

## Antihistamines plus oral decongestants

One systematic review found no significant difference between antihistamines plus oral decongestants compared with placebo in clearance of effusion after 4 weeks.

## Corticosteroids (oral)

One systematic review found no significant difference between oral corticosteroids and placebo in clearance of effusion after 2 weeks. It found limited evidence that oral corticosteroids plus antibiotics improved resolution rates compared with antibiotics alone. Oral corticosteroids may cause behavioural changes, increased appetite, and weight gain.

**DEFINITION**   Otitis media with effusion (OME), or "glue ear", is serous or mucoid but not mucopurulent fluid in the middle ear. Children usually present with hearing loss and speech problems. In contrast to those with acute otitis media (see chapter, p 47), children with OME do not suffer from acute ear pain, fever, or malaise. Hearing loss is usually mild and often identified when parents express concern regarding their child's behaviour, performance at school, or language development. See acute otitis media, p 47.

**INCIDENCE/**   One study in the UK found that, at any time, 5% of children aged 5 years had
**PREVALENCE**   persistent (at least 3 months) bilateral hearing loss associated with OME.[1] The prevalence declines considerably beyond 6 years of age.[2] About 50–80% of children aged 4 years have been affected by OME some time in the past.[2,3] OME is the most common reason for referral for surgery in children in the UK. Middle ear effusions also occur infrequently in adults after upper respiratory tract infection or after air travel, and may persist for weeks or months after an episode of acute otitis media.[4]

**AETIOLOGY/**   Contributory factors include upper respiratory tract infection and narrow upper
**RISK FACTORS** respiratory airways.[5,6] Case control studies have identified risk factors, includ-ing age 6 years or younger at first onset, day care centre attendance, large number of siblings, low socioeconomic group, frequent upper respiratory tract infection, bottle feeding, and household smoking.[2,5] These factors may be associated with about twice the risk of developing OME.[6]

**PROGNOSIS**   In 5% of preschool children, OME (identified by tympanometric screening) persists for at least 1 year.[7,8] The disease is ultimately self limiting in most cases.[1,4,9] However, one large cohort study (534 children) found that middle ear disease increased reported hearing difficulty at 5 years of age (OR 1.44, 95% CI 1.18 to 1.76) and was associated with delayed language development in children up to 10 years of age.[10]

Please refer to CD-ROM for full text and references.

# Seasonal allergic rhinitis

Search date September 2003

*Aziz Sheikh, Sukhmeet Singh Panesar, and Sangeeta Dhami*

## What are the effects of treatments on quality of life?

**BENEFICIAL**

### Oral fexofenadine
Of all the oral antihistamines, only fexofenadine has been shown in RCTs to improve quality of life as well as rhinitis symptoms compared with placebo.

**LIKELY TO BE BENEFICIAL**

### Oral leukotriene receptor antagonists
One systematic review provides good evidence that montelukast improves quality of life compared with placebo.

### Oral leukotriene receptor antagonists plus oral antihistamines
One systematic review has found that montelukast plus loratadine improves quality of life compared with placebo. However, it found no evidence that combined treatment was any more effective than loratadine or montelukast alone.

**UNKNOWN EFFECTIVENESS**

### Intranasal antihistamines; intranasal ipratropium bromide; oral decongestants; oral decongestants plus oral antihistamines; other oral antihistamines
We found no RCTs evaluating the effects of these interventions on quality of life.

## What are the effects of treatments on rhinitis symptoms?

**BENEFICIAL**

### Oral antihistamines
Numerous RCTs have found that oral antihistamines (acrivastine, azatadine, brompheniramine, cetirizine, ebastine, loratadine, desloratadine, or mizolastine) improve rhinitis symptoms compared with placebo. Drowsiness, sedation, and somnolence were the most commonly reported adverse effects.

### Oral pseudoephedrine plus oral antihistamines
RCTs have found that pseudoephedrine plus oral antihistamines (fexofenadine, acrivastine, cetirizine, terfenadine, triprolidine, loratadine, or azatadine) improve overall symptoms of seasonal allergic rhinitis compared with pseudoephedrine or oral antihistamine or placebo alone. The most common adverse effects reported with combination treatment were headache and insomnia.

**LIKELY TO BE BENEFICIAL**

### Intranasal levocabastine
RCTs found that intranasal levocabastine improved symptoms of seasonal allergic rhinitis compared with placebo.

### Oral leukotriene receptor antagonists
One systematic review provided good evidence that montelukast improved nasal symptoms compared with placebo. One RCT provided inconclusive evidence about effects of pranlukast compared with placebo.

◀ **Oral leukotriene receptor antagonists plus oral antihistamines**

One systematic review has found that montelukast plus loratadine improves nasal symptoms compared with placebo. However, it found no evidence that combined treatment was any more effective than loratadine or montelukast alone.

## TRADE OFF BETWEEN BENEFITS AND HARMS

### Oral astemizole

RCTs have found that astemizole improves rhinitis symptoms compared with placebo but astemizole has been associated with prolongation of the QTc interval, and may induce ventricular arrhythmias.

### Oral terfenadine

RCTs have found conflicting results about the effectiveness of terfenadine compared with placebo on rhinitis symptoms. Terfenadine is associated with risk of fatal cardiac toxicity if used in conjunction with macrolide antibiotics, oral antifungal agents, or grapefruit juice.

## UNKNOWN EFFECTIVENESS

### Intranasal azelastine

RCTs have found conflicting results about effectiveness of intranasal azelastine compared with placebo on symptoms of seasonal allergic rhinitis. Two small RCTs found no significant difference in nasal symptoms between intranasal antihistamines (azelastine, levocabastine) and oral antihistamines (cetirizine, terfenadine).

### Intranasal ipratropium bromide

We found no systematic review or published RCTs.

**DEFINITION** Seasonal allergic rhinitis is a symptom complex that may affect several organ systems. Symptoms will typically consist of seasonal sneezing, nasal itching, nasal blockage, and watery nasal discharge.[1] Eye symptoms (red eyes, itchy eyes, and tearing) are common. Other symptoms may include peak seasonal coughing, wheezing, and shortness of breath, oral allergy syndrome (manifesting as an itchy swollen oropharynx on eating stoned fruits), and systemic symptoms such as tiredness, fever, a pressure sensation in the head, and itchiness. Confirming the presence of pollen hypersensitivity using objective allergy tests such as skin prick tests, detection of serum specific IgE, and nasal provocation challenge testing may improve diagnostic accuracy.

**INCIDENCE/ PREVALENCE** Seasonal allergic rhinitis is found throughout the world. Epidemiological evidence suggests that there is considerable geographical variation in its prevalence. Prevalence is highest in socioeconomically developed countries, where the condition may affect as much as 25% of the population.[2–4] Prevalence and severity are increasing. It is thought that improved living standards and reduced risk of childhood infections may lead to immune deviation of T helper cells in early life, which may increase susceptibility to seasonal allergic rhinitis (the so called "hygiene hypothesis").[5,6] Although people of all ages may be affected, the peak age of onset is adolescence.[7]

**AETIOLOGY/ RISK FACTORS** The symptoms of seasonal allergic rhinitis are caused by an IgE mediated type 1 hypersensitivity reaction to grass, tree, or weed pollen. Allergy to other seasonal aeroallergens such as fungal spores may also provoke symptoms. Typically, symptoms become worse during the relevant pollen season and in the open, when pollen exposure is increased. Risk factors include a personal or family history of atopy or other allergic disorders, male sex, birth order (increased risk being seen in first born), and small family size.[8,9]

# Seasonal allergic rhinitis

**PROGNOSIS**  Seasonal allergic rhinitis may impair quality of life, interfering with work, sleep, and recreational activities.[10] Other allergic problems such as asthma and eczema frequently coexist, adding to the impact of rhinitis.[11]

Please refer to CD-ROM for full text and references.

## What are the effects of treatments in people with clinically diagnosed acute sinusitis?

### UNKNOWN EFFECTIVENESS

#### Antibiotics

Two RCTs found no evidence that amoxicillin reduced or cured symptoms compared with placebo in people with clinically diagnosed acute sinusitis, who had not had radiological or bacteriological confirmation of disease. One RCT has found that diarrhoea was more common with amoxicillin than with placebo. We found no RCTs examining effects of other antibiotics (amoxicillin–clavulanate, co-trimoxazole, cephalosporins, azithromycin, and erythromycin) compared with placebo or each other.

#### Antihistamines; decongestants; steroids (topical)

We found no RCTs examining clinical effects of topical or systemic decongestants, topical steroids, or antihistamines in people with clinically diagnosed acute sinusitis.

## What are the effects of treatments in people with radiologically or bacteriologically confirmed acute sinusitis?

### LIKELY TO BE BENEFICIAL

#### Cephalosporins and macrolides (fewer adverse effects than amoxicillin or amoxicillin–clavulanate)

One systematic review in people with radiologically or bacteriologically confirmed acute sinusitis found no significant difference in clinical resolution between amoxicillin or amoxicillin–clavulanate and cephalosporins or macrolides. However, cephalosporins and macrolides caused fewer adverse effects than amoxicillin and amoxicillin–clavulanate. One RCT found no significant difference in clinical improvement or clinical cure between cefaclor (a cephalosporin) and azithromycin (a macrolide).

### TRADE OFF BETWEEN BENEFITS AND HARMS

#### Amoxicillin and amoxicillin–clavulanate (more adverse effects than cephalosporins or macrolides)

One systematic review identified two RCTs in people with radiologically or bacteriologically confirmed acute maxillary sinusitis, which found that amoxicillin improved early clinical cure rate compared with placebo, but was associated with more frequent adverse effects, mainly gastrointestinal. One systematic review in people with radiologically or bacteriologically confirmed acute sinusitis found no significant difference in clinical resolution between amoxicillin or amoxicillin–clavulanate and cephalosporins or macrolides. However, amoxicillin and amoxicillin–clavulanate caused more adverse effects.

### UNKNOWN EFFECTIVENESS

#### Different dosages of antibiotics

One RCT in people with radiologically or bacteriologically confirmed acute sinusitis found no significant difference in clinical resolution rates or adverse events between two and three daily doses of cefaclor (a cephalosporin).

▶

# Sinusitis (acute)

◀ **Antihistamines; decongestants; steroids (topical)**

We found no RCTs examining effects of antihistamines, decongestants, or topical steroids in people with radiologically or bacteriologically confirmed acute sinusitis.

## UNLIKELY TO BE BENEFICIAL

**Long course antibiotic regimens (no more effective than short course regimens, and more adverse effects)**

RCTs in people with confirmed acute sinusitis found no significant difference in clinical resolution rates between a 10 day course and 3–5 day courses of either co-trimoxazole or cefuroxime (a cephalosporin) up to 3 weeks after treatment. One RCT found that adverse effects, which were mainly gastrointestinal, were more frequent with longer course cefuroxime than with shorter course cefuroxime.

**DEFINITION**  Acute sinusitis is defined pathologically, by transient inflammation of the mucosal lining of the paranasal sinuses lasting less than 4 weeks. Clinically, it is characterised by nasal congestion, rhinorrhoea🔘, facial pain, hyposmia🔘, sneezing, and, if more severe, additional malaise and fever. The diagnosis is usually made clinically (on the basis of history and examination, but without radiological or bacteriological investigation). Clinically diagnosed acute sinusitis is less likely to be due to bacterial infection than is acute sinusitis confirmed by radiological or bacteriological investigation.[1] In this chapter, we have excluded studies in children, in people with symptoms for more than 4 weeks (chronic sinusitis), and in people with symptoms after facial trauma. We have made it clear in each section whether we are dealing with clinically diagnosed acute sinusitis or acute sinusitis that has been confirmed by bacteriological or radiological investigation, because the effects of treatment may be different in these groups.

**INCIDENCE/ PREVALENCE**  Each year in Europe, 1–5% of adults are diagnosed with acute sinusitis by their general practitioner.[2] Extrapolated to the British population, this is estimated to cause 6 million restricted working days a year.[3,4] Most people with acute sinusitis are assessed and treated in a primary care setting. The prevalence varies according to whether diagnosis is made on clinical grounds or on the basis of radiological or bacteriological investigation.

**AETIOLOGY/ RISK FACTORS**  One systematic review (search date 1998) reported that about 50% of people with a clinical diagnosis of acute sinusitis have bacterial sinus infection.[1] The usual pathogens in acute bacterial sinusitis are *Streptococcus pneumoniae* and *Haemophilus influenzae*, with occasional infection with *Moraxella catarrhalis*. Preceding viral upper respiratory tract infection is often the trigger for acute bacterial sinusitis,[5] with about 0.5% of common colds becoming complicated by the development of acute sinusitis.[6]

**PROGNOSIS**  One meta-analysis of RCTs found that up to two thirds of people with acute sinusitis had spontaneous resolution of symptoms without active treatment.[7] One non-systematic review reported that people with acute sinusitis are at risk of chronic sinusitis and irreversible damage to the normal mucociliary mucosal surface.[8] One further non-systematic review reported rare life-threatening complications such as orbital cellulitis🔘 and meningitis after acute sinusitis.[9] However, we found no reliable data to measure these risks.

Please refer to CD-ROM for full text and references.

## What are the effects of treatments for chronic tinnitus?

### TRADE OFF BETWEEN BENEFITS AND HARMS

**Tricyclic antidepressants**

One systematic review in people with depression and chronic tinnitus found that tricyclic antidepressants (nortriptyline) improved tinnitus related disability, audiometric tinnitus loudness matching, and symptoms of depression at 6 weeks, but found no significant difference in self reported tinnitus severity compared with placebo. One small RCT in people with tinnitus but without depression found that a greater proportion of people rated themselves as improved with tricyclic antidepressants (amitriptyline) compared with placebo at 6 weeks.

### UNKNOWN EFFECTIVENESS

**Benzodiazepines (alprazolam)**

One systematic review found limited evidence that alprazolam, a benzodiazepine, improved self reported tinnitus severity after 12 weeks. Benzodiazepines can have side effects that may outweigh potential benefits.

**Psychotherapy**

One systematic review found insufficient evidence about effects of cognitive behavioural treatment, relaxation therapy, education, or biofeedback compared with other or no treatment in people with chronic tinnitus.

**Acupuncture; baclofen; cinnarizine; electromagnetic stimulation; hyperbaric oxygen; hypnosis; lamotrigine; low power laser; nicotinamide; tinnitus masking devices; zinc**

We found insufficient evidence about the effects of these interventions.

### LIKELY TO BE INEFFECTIVE OR HARMFUL

**Carbamazepine**

One systematic review found no significant difference between carbamazepine and placebo in tinnitus severity at 30 days. Treatment with carbamazepine was associated with an increased risk of dizziness, nausea, and headaches

**Ginkgo biloba**

One systematic review and one subsequent RCT found no significant difference between ginkgo biloba and placebo in tinnitus symptoms.

**Tocainide**

One systematic review found no significant difference between tocainide and placebo in improving symptoms, but found evidence that tocainide increased adverse effects after 30 days' treatment.

**DEFINITION**     Tinnitus is defined as the perception of sound, which does not arise from the external environment, from within the body (e.g. vascular sounds), or from auditory hallucinations related to mental illness. This review is concerned with tinnitus, where tinnitus is the only, or the predominant, symptom in an affected person.

**INCIDENCE/**     Up to 18% of the general population in industrialised countries are mildly
**PREVALENCE**   affected by chronic tinnitus, and 0.5% report tinnitus having a severe effect on their ability to lead a normal life.[1]

# Tinnitus

**AETIOLOGY/ RISK FACTORS**
Tinnitus may occur as an isolated idiopathic symptom or in association with any type of hearing loss. Tinnitus may be a particular feature of presbyacusis**G**, noise induced hearing loss, Menière's disease**G** (see Menière's disease, p 119), or the presence of an acoustic neuroma. In people with toxicity from aspirin or quinine, tinnitus can occur while hearing thresholds remain normal. Tinnitus is also associated with depression, although it may be unclear whether the tinnitus is a manifestation of the depressive illness or a factor contributing to its development.[2]

**PROGNOSIS**
Tinnitus may have an insidious onset, with a long delay before clinical presentation. It may persist for many years or decades, particularly when associated with a sensorineural hearing loss. In Menière's disease, both the presence and intensity of tinnitus can fluctuate. Tinnitus may cause disruption of sleep patterns, an inability to concentrate, and depression.[3]

Please refer to CD-ROM for full text and references.

## What are the effects of tonsillectomy for severe tonsillitis in children and adults?

### TRADE OFF BETWEEN BENEFITS AND HARMS

**Tonsillectomy versus antibiotics in children**

Two systematic reviews found insufficient evidence to compare surgical versus medical treatment. One subsequent RCT in less severely affected children found that surgery significantly reduced the frequency of tonsillitis compared with medical treatment over 3 years. The modest benefit may be outweighed by morbidity associated with the operation in populations with a low incidence of tonsillitis.

### UNKNOWN EFFECTIVENESS

**Tonsillectomy versus antibiotics in adults**

We found no RCTs evaluating tonsillectomy in adults.

DEFINITION   Tonsillitis is infection of the parenchyma of the palatine tonsils. The definition of severe recurrent tonsillitis is arbitrary, but recent criteria have defined tonsillitis as five or more episodes of true tonsillitis a year, symptoms for at least a year, and episodes that are disabling and prevent normal functioning.[1] The definition does not include tonsillitis occurring as a manifestation of the viral illness infectious mononucleosis, which usually occurs as a single episode. However, acute tonsillitis in this situation may be followed by recurrent tonsillitis in some patients. Infection of the palatine tonsils may occur in isolation or as part of the clinical picture of a generalised pharyngitis. The clinical distinction between tonsillitis and pharyngitis is unclear in the literature and the condition is often referred to simply as "acute sore throat". A sore throat lasting for 24–48 hours as part of the prodrome of minor upper respiratory tract infection is excluded from this definition. The diagnosis of acute tonsillitis is primarily clinical, with the main interest of the clinician being in whether the illness is viral or bacterial, this information being of relevance if the prescription of antibiotics is being considered. Several authors have attempted to distinguish viral from bacterial sore throat on clinical grounds but the results of these studies are conflicting, suggesting a lack of reliable diagnostic criteria. Investigations to assist with this distinction include throat swabs and serological tests, including the rapid antigen test and the antistreptolysin O (ASO) titre. Of these, throat swabs and the ASO titre are of less practical value because of the time lag before results are obtainable. Throat swabs are also potentially misleading, as their sensitivity and specificity is low. There is a high asymptomatic carrier rate of up to 40% for potentially pathogenic bacteria such as group A β haemolytic streptococcus, and the results of surface swab bacteriology may be irrelevant to the deeper flora which may be responsible for the clinical infection. Rapid antigen testing is convenient and popular in North America but also has doubtful sensitivity (61–95%), at least when measured against throat swab results, although specificity is higher (88–100%).[1] The monospot test, Epstein-Barr virus serology, and occasional other viral serology may be of assistance in the diagnosis of infectious mononucleosis

INCIDENCE/   Recurrent sore throat has an incidence in general practice in the UK of 100
PREVALENCE   per 1000 population a year.[2] Acute tonsillitis is more common in childhood. ▶

# Tonsillitis

**AETIOLOGY/ RISK FACTORS**

Common bacterial pathogens include β haemolytic and other streptococci. Bacteria are cultured successfully only from a minority of people with tonsillitis. The role of viruses is uncertain in most cases of acute tonsillitis. In the tonsillitis associated with infectious mononucleosis, the most common infective agent is the Epstein-Barr virus (present in 50% of children and 90% of adults with the condition). Cytomegalovirus infection may also result in the clinical picture of infectious mononucleosis, and the differential diagnosis also includes toxoplasmosis, HIV, hepatitis A, and rubella.[3]

**PROGNOSIS**

We found no good data on the natural history of tonsillitis or recurrent sore throat in children or adults. Participants in RCTs who were randomised to medical treatment (courses of antibiotics as required) have shown a tendency towards improvement over time.[4,5] Recurrent severe tonsillitis results in significant morbidity, including time lost from school or work. The most common complication of acute tonsillitis is peritonsillar abscess, but we found no good evidence on the incidence of this condition. Rheumatic fever and acute glomerulonephritis are recognised complications of acute tonsillitis associated with group A β haemolytic streptococci. These diseases are rare in developed countries, but do occasionally occur sporadically. They are still a common problem in certain populations, notably Australian Aboriginals, and may be effectively prevented in closed communities by the use of penicillin. A systematic review found that there is no evidence that aggressive antibiotic treatment of acute sore throat in the developed world is useful in the prevention of these diseases.[6]

Please refer to CD-ROM for full text and references.

## What are the effects of methods to remove symptomatic ear wax?

### TRADE OFF BETWEEN BENEFITS AND HARMS

**Ear syringing***

There is consensus that ear syringing is effective but we found no RCTs comparing ear syringing versus no treatment or versus other treatment. Reported complications of ear syringing include otitis externa, perforation of the ear drum, damage to the skin of the external canal, tinnitus, pain, and vertigo.

### UNKNOWN EFFECTIVENESS

**Manual removal (other than ear syringing)***

We found no RCTs about other mechanical methods of removing ear wax.

**Wax softeners**

One small RCT in people with impacted wax found that active treatment (with a proprietary softening agent, sodium bicarbonate, or sterile water) reduced the risk of persisting impaction after 5 days compared with no treatment, but found no significant difference among active treatments. Three RCTs found no consistent evidence that any one type of wax softener was superior to the others. RCTs found insufficient evidence to assess the effects of wax softeners prior to syringing.

*Although many practitioners consider these to be standard treatments, we found no RCTs of these interventions.

| | |
|---|---|
| **DEFINITION** | Ear wax is normal and becomes a problem only if it produces deafness, pain, or other aural symptoms. Ear wax may also need to be removed if it prevents inspection of the ear drum. The term "impacted" **G** is used in different ways and can merely imply the coexistence of wax obscuring the ear drum with symptoms in that ear.[1,2] |
| **INCIDENCE/ PREVALENCE** | We found four surveys of the prevalence of impacted wax **T**.[3-6] The prevalence was higher in men than in women, in the elderly than in the young, and in people with intellectual impairment.[7] One survey found that 289 Scottish general practitioners each saw an average of nine people a month requesting removal of ear wax.[1] |
| **AETIOLOGY/ RISK FACTORS** | Factors that prevent the normal extrusion of wax from the ear canal (e.g. wearing a hearing aid, using cotton buds) increase the chance of ear wax accumulating. |
| **PROGNOSIS** | Most ear wax emerges from the external canal spontaneously. Without impaction or adherence to the drum, there is likely to be minimal, if any, hearing loss. |

Please refer to CD-ROM for full text and references.

# Foot ulcers and amputations in diabetes

**Search date September 2003**

*Dereck Hunt and Hertzel Gerstein*

## What are the effects of preventive interventions?

### LIKELY TO BE BENEFICIAL

**Screening and referral to foot care clinics**
One RCT found that a diabetes screening and protection programme (involving referral to a foot clinic if high risk features were present) reduced the risk of major amputation⦿ compared with usual care after 2 years.

### UNKNOWN EFFECTIVENESS

**Education**
One systematic review found insufficient evidence about the effects of patient education for preventing foot ulcers, serious foot lesions, or amputation.

**Therapeutic footwear**
In people with diabetes and previous diabetic foot ulcer, one RCT found no significant difference in rates of foot ulceration between therapeutic footwear and usual footwear.

## What are the effects of treatments?

### BENEFICIAL

**Pressure off-loading with non-removable cast**
RCTs found that pressure off-loading with total contact casting or non-removable fibreglass casts improved healing of non-infected diabetic foot ulcers compared with traditional dressing changes, removable cast or half shoes, or specialised cloth shoes.

### LIKELY TO BE BENEFICIAL

**Human skin equivalent**
One RCT found that human skin equivalent⦿ increased ulcer healing rates compared with saline moistened gauze in people with chronic neuropathic non-infected foot ulcers.

**Systemic hyperbaric oxygen (for infected ulcers)**
One RCT identified by a systematic review found that systemic hyperbaric oxygen⦿ plus usual care reduced amputation rates at 10 weeks compared with usual care alone in people with severely infected diabetic foot ulcers, but one small RCT found no significant difference between treatments in major amputation rates. The second RCT but may have been too small to detect a clinically important difference.

**Topical growth factors**
One systematic review found that topical growth factors⦿ increased healing rates compared with placebo in people with non-infected diabetic foot ulcers.

### UNKNOWN EFFECTIVENESS

**Cultured human dermis**
One systematic review found insufficient evidence of the effects of cultured human dermis ⦿ on ulcer healing in people with non-infected diabetic foot ulcers.

▶

◄ **Pressure off-loading with felted foam versus pressure relief half shoe**
One RCT found no significant difference in time to ulcer healing between a pressure off-loading felted foam dressing and a pressure relief half shoe.

## Systemic hyperbaric oxygen (for non-infected, non-ischaemic ulcers)
One small RCT found no significant difference between hyperbaric oxygen plus usual care and usual care alone in ulcer healing at 4 weeks in people with non-infected, neuropathic, non-ischaemic ulcers.

DEFINITION
Diabetic foot ulceration is full thickness penetration of the dermis of the foot in a person with diabetes. Ulcer severity is often classified using the Wagner system. Grade 1 ulcers are superficial ulcers involving the full skin thickness but no underlying tissues. Grade 2 ulcers are deeper, penetrating down to ligaments and muscle, but not involving bone or abscess formation. Grade 3 ulcers are deep ulcers with cellulitis or abscess formation, often complicated with osteomyelitis. Ulcers with localised gangrene are classified as grade 4 and those with extensive gangrene involving the entire foot are classified as grade 5.

INCIDENCE/
PREVALENCE
Studies conducted in Australia, Finland, the UK, and the USA have reported the annual incidence of foot ulcers among people with diabetes as 2.5–10.7%, and the annual incidence of amputation as 0.25–1.8%.[1–10]

AETIOLOGY/
RISK FACTORS
Long term risk factors for foot ulcers and amputation include duration of diabetes, poor glycaemic control, microvascular complications (retinopathy, nephropathy, and neuropathy) and peripheral vascular disease. The strongest predictors of foot complications are altered foot sensation, foot deformities, and previous foot ulcer or amputation.[1–10]

PROGNOSIS
People with diabetes are at risk of foot ulcers, infections, and vascular insufficiency. Amputation is indicated if these are severe or do not improve with conservative treatment. As well as affecting quality of life, these complications account for a large proportion of the healthcare costs of diabetes. For people with healed diabetic foot ulcers, the 5 year cumulative rate of ulcer recurrence is 66% and of amputation is 12%.[11]

---

Please refer to CD-ROM for full text and references.

# Glycaemic control in diabetes

Search date December 2002

*Bazian Ltd*

## What are the effects of intensive versus conventional glycaemic control?

### Intensive control of hyperglycaemia in people aged 13–75 years

Large RCTs have found that diabetic complications increase with HbA1c concentrations above the non-diabetic range.

One systematic review and large subsequent RCTs in people with type 1 or type 2 diabetes have found strong evidence that intensive versus conventional glycaemic control significantly reduces the development and progression of microvascular and neuropathic complications. A second systematic review has found that intensive versus conventional treatment is associated with a small reduction in cardiovascular risk.

RCTs have found that intensive treatment increases the incidence of hypoglycaemia and weight gain, without adverse impact on neuropsychological function or quality of life.

The benefit of intensive treatment is limited by the complications of advanced diabetes (such as blindness, end stage renal disease, or cardiovascular disease), major comorbidity, and reduced life expectancy.

### Intensive control of hyperglycaemia in people with frequent severe hypoglycaemia

The benefits of intensive treatment of hyperglycaemia are described above.

It is difficult to weigh the benefit of reduced complications against the harm of increased hypoglycaemia. The risk of intensive treatment is increased by a history of severe hypoglycaemia or unawareness of hypoglycaemia, advanced autonomic neuropathy or cardiovascular disease, and impaired ability to detect or treat hypoglycaemia (such as altered mental state, immobility, or lack of social support). For people likely to have limited benefit or increased risk with intensive treatment, it may be more appropriate to negotiate less intensive goals for glycaemic management that reflect the person's self determined goals of care and willingness to make lifestyle modifications.

**DEFINITION**    Diabetes mellitus is a group of disorders characterised by hyperglycaemia (definitions vary slightly, one current US definition is fasting plasma glucose $\geq 7.0$ mmol/L or $\geq 11.1$ mmol/L 2 h after a 75 g oral glucose load, on 2 or more occasions). Intensive treatment is designed to achieve blood glucose values as close to the non-diabetic range as possible. The components of such treatment are education, counselling, monitoring, self management, and pharmacological treatment with insulin or oral antidiabetic agents to achieve specific glycaemic goals.

**INCIDENCE/**    Diabetes is diagnosed in about 5% of adults aged 20 years or older in the
**PREVALENCE**    USA.[1] A further 2.7% have undiagnosed diabetes on the basis of fasting glucose. The prevalence is similar in men and women, but diabetes is more common in some ethnic groups. The prevalence in people aged 40–74 years has increased over the past decade.

**AETIOLOGY/ RISK FACTORS**  Diabetes results from deficient insulin secretion, decreased insulin action, or both. Many processes can be involved, from autoimmune destruction of the β cells of the pancreas to incompletely understood abnormalities that result in resistance to insulin action. Genetic factors are involved in both mechanisms. In type 1 diabetes there is an absolute deficiency of insulin. In type 2 diabetes, insulin resistance and an inability of the pancreas to compensate are involved. Hyperglycaemia without clinical symptoms but sufficient to cause tissue damage can be present for many years before diagnosis.

**PROGNOSIS**  Severe hyperglycaemia causes numerous symptoms, including polyuria, polydipsia, weight loss, and blurred vision. Acute, life threatening consequences of diabetes are hyperglycaemia with ketoacidosis or the non-ketotic hyperosmolar syndrome. There is increased susceptibility to certain infections. Long term complications of diabetes include retinopathy (with potential loss of vision), nephropathy (leading to renal failure), peripheral neuropathy (increased risk of foot ulcers, amputation, and Charcot joints), autonomic neuropathy (cardiovascular, gastrointestinal, and genitourinary dysfunction), and greatly increased risk of atheroma affecting large vessels (macrovascular complications of stroke, myocardial infarction, or peripheral vascular disease). The physical, emotional, and social impact of diabetes and the demands of intensive treatment can also create problems for people with diabetes and their families. One systematic review (search date 1998) of observational studies in people with type 2 diabetes found a positive association between increased blood glucose concentration and mortality.[2] It found no minimum threshold level.

Please refer to CD-ROM for full text and references.

# Obesity

Search date September 2003

*David E Arterburn*

---

## What are the effects of drug treatments in adults?

For information on the effects of lifestyle interventions to achieve weight loss see changing behaviour, p 17

### TRADE OFF BETWEEN BENEFITS AND HARMS

**Diethylproprion**

One systematic review found that diethylpropion promotes modest weight loss compared with placebo in healthy obese adults. We found two case reports describing pulmonary hypertension and psychosis with diethylpropion. We found insufficient evidence on weight regain and long term safety. A European Commission review concluded that a link between diethylpropion and heart and lung problems could not be excluded.

**Fluoxetine**

One systematic review found that fluoxetine promotes modest weight loss compared with placebo in healthy obese adults. We found insufficient evidence on weight regain and long term safety of fluoxetine in obesity. One systematic review of antidepressant treatment has found an association between selective serotonin reuptake inhibitors and uncommon but serious adverse events, including bradycardia, bleeding, granulocytopenia, seizures, hyponatraemia, hepatotoxicity, serotonin syndrome●, and extrapyramidal effects●.

**Mazindol**

One systematic review found that mazindol promotes modest weight loss compared with placebo in healthy obese adults. We found one case report of pulmonary hypertension diagnosed 1 year after stopping treatment with mazindol. We found one case series of mazindol in people with stable cardiac disease that reported cardiac events such as atrial fibrillation and syncope. We found insufficient evidence on weight regain and long term safety.

**Orlistat**

Systematic reviews and subsequent RCTs have found that, in addition to a low energy diet, orlistat modestly increases weight loss compared with placebo in healthy obese adults and in obese people with diabetes, hyperlipidaemia, and hypertension. One RCT in people with hypercholesterolaemia found that orlistat plus fluvastatin increased weight loss compared with orlistat or fluvastatin alone. Adverse effects such as oily spotting from the rectum, flatulence, and faecal urgency occurred in a high proportion of people taking orlistat. We found insufficient evidence on weight regain and long term safety.

**Phentermine**

One systematic review found that phentermine promotes modest weight loss compared with placebo in healthy obese adults. We found insufficient evidence on weight regain and long term safety. A European Commission review concluded that a link between phentermine and heart and lung problems could not be excluded.

**Sibutramine**

Systematic reviews and RCTs have found that sibutramine promotes modest weight loss compared with placebo in healthy obese adults and in obese people with diabetes and hypertension. One RCT has found that sibutramine is more effective than placebo for weight maintenance after weight loss in healthy obese adults, but weight regain occurs when sibutramine is discontinued. Sibutramine ▶

was temporarily suspended from the market in Italy for use in obesity because of concerns about severe adverse reactions, including arrhythmias, hypertension, and two deaths resulting from cardiac arrest. Two RCTs found no difference in the incidence of valvular heart disease between sibutramine and placebo, although these trials may have been too small to detect clinically important differences. One RCT found that sibutramine achieved greater weight loss than either orlistat or metformin.

## UNKNOWN EFFECTIVENESS

### Sibutramine plus orlistat
We found insufficient evidence about the effects of sibutramine plus orlistat and sibutramine alone.

## LIKELY TO BE INEFFECTIVE OR HARMFUL

### Dexfenfluramine
One systematic review has found that dexfenfluramine promotes weight loss compared with placebo in healthy obese adults. Dexfenfluramine has been associated with valvular heart disease and pulmonary hypertension.

### Fenfluramine
One systematic review found that fenfluramine promotes modest weight loss compared with placebo in healthy obese adults. Fenfluramine has been associated with valvular heart disease and pulmonary hypertension.

### Fenfluramine plus phentermine
One RCT has found that fenfluramine plus phentermine promotes weight loss compared with placebo. The combination of fenfluramine plus phentermine has been associated with valvular heart disease and pulmonary hypertension.

### Phenylpropanolamine
One systematic review has found that phenylpropanolamine promotes modest weight loss compared with placebo in healthy obese adults. One case control study found that phenylpropanolamine increased risk of haemorrhagic stroke in the first 3 days of use.

**DEFINITION** Obesity is a chronic condition characterised by an excess of body fat. It is most often defined by the body mass index (BMI) ⓖ a mathematical formula that is highly correlated with body fat. BMI is weight in kilograms divided by height in metres squared ($kg/m^2$). Worldwide, people with BMIs between 25–30 $kg/m^2$ are categorised as overweight, and those with BMIs above 30 $kg/m^2$ are categorised as obese.[1,2] Nearly 5 million US adults used prescription weight loss medication between 1996 and 1998. A quarter of users were not overweight, suggesting that weight loss medication may be inappropriately used. This is thought to be especially the case among women, white people, and Hispanic people.[3] The National Institutes of Health has issued guidelines for obesity treatment, which indicate that all obese adults (BMI ≥ 30 $kg/m^2$) and all adults with a BMI of 27 $kg/m^2$ or more and concomitant risk factors or diseases are candidates for drug treatment.[1]

**INCIDENCE/ PREVALENCE** Obesity has increased steadily in many countries since 1900. In the UK in 2001, it was estimated that 21% of men and 24% of women were obese.[4] In the past decade alone, the prevalence of obesity in the USA has increased from 22.9% between 1988 and 1994, to 30.5% between 1999 and 2000.[5]

**AETIOLOGY/ RISK FACTORS** Obesity is the result of long term mismatches in energy balance where daily energy intake exceeds daily energy expenditure.[6] Energy balance is modulated by a myriad of factors, including metabolic rate, appetite, diet, and physical activity.[7] Although these factors are influenced by genetic traits, the increase in ▶

# Obesity

obesity prevalence in the past few decades cannot be explained by changes in the human gene pool, and is more often attributed to environmental changes that promote excessive food intake and discourage physical activity.[7,8] Obesity may also be induced by drugs (e.g. high dose glucocorticoids), or be secondary to a variety of neuroendocrine disorders such as Cushing's syndrome and polycystic ovary syndrome.[9]

**PROGNOSIS**  Obesity is a risk factor for several chronic diseases, including hypertension, dyslipidaemia, diabetes, cardiovascular disease, sleep apnoea, osteoarthritis, and some cancers.[1] The relationship between increasing body weight and mortality is curvilinear, where mortality is highest among adults with low body weight (BMI☉ < 18.5 kg/m$^2$) and among adults with the highest body weight (BMI > 35 kg/m$^2$).[2] Results from five prospective cohort studies and 1991 national statistics suggest that the number of annual deaths attributable to obesity among US adults is about 280 000.[10] Obese adults also have more annual admissions to hospital, more outpatient visits, higher prescription drug costs, and worse health related quality of life than normal weight adults.[11,12]

---

Please refer to CD-ROM for full text and references.

# Prevention of cardiovascular events in diabetes

**Search date October 2003**

*Ronald Sigal, Janine Malcolm, and Hilary Meggison*

## What are the effects of promoting smoking cessation in people with diabetes?

### LIKELY TO BE BENEFICIAL

**Smoking cessation\***

We found no RCTs on promotion of smoking cessation specifically in people with diabetes. Observational evidence and extrapolation from evidence in people without diabetes suggest that promotion of smoking cessation is likely to reduce cardiovascular events.

\*No RCT but observational evidence suggests some benefit.

## What are the effects of controlling blood pressure in people with diabetes?

### BENEFICIAL

**Antihypertensive treatment (compared with no antihypertensive treatment)**

One systematic review and RCTs have found that blood pressure lowering with antihypertensive agents in people with diabetes and hypertension reduces cardiovascular morbidity and mortality compared with no antihypertensive treatment.

**Lower target blood pressures**

Large RCTs including people with diabetes and hypertension have found that control of blood pressure to a target diastolic blood pressure of no more than 80 mm Hg reduces the risk of major cardiovascular events. One RCT in normotensive people with diabetes found that intensive blood pressure lowering reduced cerebral vascular events but found no significant difference in cardiovascular death, myocardial infarction, congestive heart failure, or all cause mortality.

### TRADE OFF BETWEEN BENEFITS AND HARMS

**Different antihypertensive drugs**

Systematic reviews and RCTs have found that angiotensin converting enzyme inhibitors, diuretics, β blockers, and calcium channel blockers all reduce cardiovascular morbidity and mortality in people with diabetes and hypertension. However, there are differences in the types of adverse effects reported with different antihypertensive drugs. RCTs have found that people taking atenolol gained more weight than those taking captopril, an increase in risk of congestive heart failure with lisinopril or amlodipine compared with chlorthalidone, a higher frequency of headache with diltiazem compared with diuretics or β blockers, and a higher rate of withdrawal from treatment because of adverse effects with atenolol compared with losartan.

▶

# Prevention of cardiovascular events in diabetes

## What are the effects of treating dyslipidaemia in people with diabetes?

**BENEFICIAL**

### Statins

One systematic review and RCTs have found that statins reduce cardiovascular morbidity and mortality compared with placebo.

**LIKELY TO BE BENEFICIAL**

### Aggressive versus moderate lipid lowering with statins

One RCT found that, compared with usual care, treatment with atorvastatin to achieve a target low density lipoprotein below 2.6 mmol/L (< 100 mg/dL) reduces cardiovascular morbidity and mortality. Another RCT found no significant difference between a lower target low density lipoprotein (1.55–2.20 mmol/L) using lovastatin, along with cholestyramine if necessary, and a moderate target low density lipoprotein (3.36–3.62 mmol/L) in 4 year event rate for myocardial infarction and death.

### Fibrates

One RCT found that gemfibrozil reduced cardiovascular events over 5 years compared with placebo whereas another smaller RCT found no significant difference. One RCT found that bezafibrate reduced cardiovascular events compared with placebo.

### Low versus standard statin dose in older people

One RCT found no significant difference in cardiovascular events between low dose pravastatin (5 mg/day) and standard dose pravastatin (10–20 mg/day) over 4 years.

## What are the effects of antiplatelet drugs in people with diabetes?

**LIKELY TO BE BENEFICIAL**

### Adding glycoprotein IIb/IIIa inhibitors to heparin in acute coronary syndromes

We found no RCTs comparing glycoprotein IIb/IIIa inhibitors versus no antiplatelet treatment. One RCT in people presenting with unstable angina or acute myocardial infarction❻ without ST segment elevation found that addition of tirofiban (a glycoprotein IIb/IIIa inhibitor) to heparin reduced the composite outcome of death, myocardial infarction, or refractory ischaemia at 180 days compared with heparin alone. This RCT found no significant difference between tirofiban plus heparin and heparin alone in risk of bleeding in people already taking aspirin.

### Clopidogrel

We found no RCTs comparing only clopidogrel versus placebo. One RCT in people with diabetes and with recent ischaemic stroke, myocardial infarction, or established peripheral arterial disease found no significant difference between clopidogrel and aspirin at 28 days in cardiovascular events. This RCT also found a lower proportion of people hospitalised for a bleeding event with clopidogrel than with aspirin.

◀ TRADE OFF BETWEEN BENEFITS AND HARMS

## Prophylactic aspirin

One systematic review found that, compared with controls, antiplatelet treatment mainly with aspirin did not significantly reduce the combined risk of non-fatal myocardial infarction, non-fatal stroke, death from a vascular cause, or death from an unknown cause in people with diabetes and cardiovascular disease diagnosis. The review found that antiplatelet treatment was associated with an increase in the risk of major extracranial haemorrhage and haemorrhagic stroke, but the results for people with diabetes were not reported separately.

UNLIKELY TO BE BENEFICIAL

## Adding clopidogrel to aspirin in acute coronary syndromes

One RCT in people presenting with unstable angina or non-Q-wave myocardial infarction and also taking aspirin found no significant reduction in cardiovascular events after 12 months with addition of clopidogrel compared with placebo. This RCT also found a higher proportion of major bleeds with addition of clopidogrel than with placebo.

## *What are the effects of blood glucose control for prevention of cardiovascular disease in diabetes?*

LIKELY TO BE BENEFICIAL

## Intensive versus conventional glycaemic control

One systematic review found that, compared with conventional glycaemic control, intensive glycaemic control for more than 2 years reduced the occurrence of first major cardiovascular event in people with type 1 diabetes. Two RCTs found no significant difference in cardiovascular morbidity and mortality with intensive compared with conventional glycaemic control in people with type 2 diabetes. These RCTs also found an increase in weight gain and hypoglycaemic episodes with intensive compared with conventional treatment.

## Metformin versus diet alone as initial treatment in overweight or obese people with type 2 diabetes

One RCT in overweight or obese people with type 2 diabetes found that intensive treatment with metformin compared with conventional treatment with diet alone reduced myocardial infarction but not stroke over 5 years. This RCT found no significant increase in major hypoglycaemic episodes in the metformin group compared with the diet only group.

## *What are the effects of treating multiple risk factors in prevention of cardiovascular disease in people with diabetes?*
*New*

BENEFICIAL

## Intensive multiple risk factor treatment

One RCT found that, compared with conventional treatment according to clinical guidelines, intensive treatment of multiple risk factors with strict treatment goals in people with type 2 diabetes and microalbuminuria reduced cardiovascular disease over 8 years. Multiple risk factor treatment included simultaneously targeting diet, exercise, glycaemic control, blood pressure, treatment of microalbuminuria, and ▶

# Prevention of cardiovascular events in diabetes

antiplatelet treatment. We found no systematic review or RCTs comparing treatment of multiple risk factors with treatment of a single risk factor for cardiovascular outcomes.

## What are the effects of revascularisation procedures in people with diabetes?

**BENEFICIAL**

### Coronary artery bypass graft (CABG) compared with percutaneous transluminal coronary angioplasty (PTCA)

One systematic review found that, in people with diabetes, CABG reduces all cause mortality at 4 years after initial revascularisation compared with PTCA, but it found no significant difference at 6.5 years. One large RCT in people with diabetes and multivessel coronary artery disease found that CABG reduces mortality or myocardial infarction within 8 years compared with PTCA. Another smaller RCT found a non-significant reduction in mortality with CABG compared with PTCA at 4 years.

### Stent plus glycoprotein IIb/IIIa inhibitors in people undergoing PTCA

RCTs in people with diabetes undergoing PTCA have found that the combination of stent and a glycoprotein IIb/IIIa inhibitor reduces cardiovascular morbidity and mortality compared with stent plus placebo.

**TRADE OFF BETWEEN BENEFITS AND HARMS**

### CABG compared with PTCA plus stent

One RCT in people with diabetes and multivessel coronary artery disease found no significant difference, at time of discharge, between CABG and PTCA plus stent in cardiovascular morbidity or mortality, but found an increase in risk of stroke. However, the same RCT found that, compared with PTCA plus stent, CABG reduced cardiovascular risk at 1 year.

**UNKNOWN EFFECTIVENESS**

### PTCA compared with thrombolysis

We found no systematic review or RCTs comparing PTCA versus thrombolysis for prevention of cardiovascular events in people with diabetes. One RCT, in people with diabetes presenting with an acute myocardial infarction, found no significant difference between PTCA and thrombolysis with alteplase in simple outcome of death or composite outcome of death, reinfarction, or disabling stroke at 30 days.

DEFINITION    **Diabetes mellitus:** See definition under glycaemic control in diabetes, p 138. **Cardiovascular disease (CVD):** Atherosclerotic disease of the heart and/or the coronary, cerebral, or peripheral vessels leading to clinical events such as acute myocardial infarction⊕, congestive heart failure, sudden cardiac death, stroke, gangrene, and/or need for revascularisation procedures. **Population:** In previous versions of *Clinical Evidence* we attempted to differentiate between primary and secondary prevention in this topic. However, in middle aged and older people with type 2 diabetes this distinction may not be clinically important. We are not aware of any intervention that has been shown to be effective in secondary prevention but ineffective in primary prevention, or vice versa, in people with diabetes. In most cases a large proportion of people with diabetes entered into CVD prevention trials are middle aged and older with additional CVD risk factors, and a large portion of these actually have undiagnosed CVD.

◄ **INCIDENCE/ PREVALENCE**  Diabetes mellitus is a major risk factor for CVD. In the USA, a survey of deaths in 1986 suggested that 60–75% of people with diabetes die from cardiovascular causes.[1] The annual incidence of CVD is increased in people with diabetes (men: RR 2–3; women: RR 3–4, adjusted for age and other cardiovascular risk factors).[2] About 45% of middle aged and older white people with diabetes have evidence of coronary artery disease compared with about 25% of people without diabetes in the same populations. In a Finnish population based cohort study (1059 people with diabetes and 1373 people without diabetes, aged 45–64 years), the 7 year risk of acute myocardial infarction was as high in adults with diabetes without previous cardiac disease (20.2/100 person years) as it was in people without diabetes with previous cardiac disease (18.8/100 person years).[3]

**AETIOLOGY/ RISK FACTORS**  Diabetes mellitus increases the risk of CVD. Cardiovascular risk factors in people with diabetes include conventional risk factors (age, prior CVD, cigarette smoking, hypertension, dyslipidaemia, sedentary lifestyle, family history of premature CVD) and more diabetes specific risk factors (elevated urinary protein excretion, poor glycaemic control). Conventional risk factors for CVD contribute to an increase in the relative risk of CVD in people with diabetes to about the same extent as in those without diabetes (see aetiology under primary prevention, p 28). One prospective cohort study (164 women and 235 men with diabetes [mean age 65 years] and 437 women and 1099 men without diabetes [mean age 61 years] followed for mortality for a mean of 3.7 years after acute myocardial infarction) found that significantly more people with diabetes died compared with people without diabetes (116/399 [29%] with diabetes v 204/1536 [13%] without diabetes; RR 2.2, 95% CI 1.8 to 2.7).[4] It also found that the mortality risk after myocardial infarction associated with diabetes was higher for women than for men (adjusted HR 2.7, 95% CI 1.8 to 4.2 for women v 1.3, 95% CI 1.0 to 1.8 for men). Physical inactivity is a significant risk factor for cardiovascular events in both men and women. Another cohort study (5125 women with diabetes) found that participation in little (< 1 hour/week) or no physical activity compared with physical activity for at least 7 hours a week was associated with doubling of the risk of a cardiovascular event.[5] A third cohort study (1263 men with diabetes, mean follow up 12 years) found that low baseline cardiorespiratory fitness increased overall mortality compared with moderate or high fitness (RR 2.9, 95% CI 2.1 to 3.6), and overall mortality was higher in those reporting no recreational exercise in the previous 3 months than in those reporting any recreational physical activity in the same period (RR 1.8, 95% CI 1.3 to 2.5).[6] The absolute risk of CVD is almost the same in women as in men with diabetes. Diabetes specific cardiovascular risk factors include the duration of diabetes during adulthood (the years of exposure to diabetes before age 20 years add little to the risk of CVD); raised blood glucose concentrations (reflected in fasting blood glucose or HbA1c🄖); and any degree of microalbuminuria (albuminuria 30–299 mg/24 hours).[7] People with diabetes and microalbuminuria have a higher risk of coronary morbidity and mortality than do people with normal levels of urinary albumin and a similar duration of diabetes (RR 2–3).[8,9] Clinical proteinuria increases the risk of mortality from cardiac events in people with type 2 diabetes (RR 2.61, 95% CI 1.99 to 3.43)[10] and type 1 diabetes (RR 9)[7,11,12] compared with people with the same type of diabetes who have normal albumin excretion. An epidemiological analysis of people with diabetes enrolled in the Heart Outcomes Prevention Evaluation cohort study (3498 people with diabetes and at least 1 other cardiovascular risk factor, age > 55 years, of whom 1140 [32%] had microalbuminuria at baseline; 5 years' follow up) found higher risk for major cardiovascular events in those with microalbuminuria (albumin : creatinine ratio [ACR] ≥ 2.0 mg/mmol) than in those without microalbuminuria (adjusted RR 1.97, 95% CI 1.68 to 2.31), and for all ►

# Prevention of cardiovascular events in diabetes

cause mortality (RR 2.15, 95% CI 1.78 to 2.60).[13] It also found an association between ACR and the risk of major cardiovascular events (ACR 0.22–0.57 mg/mmol: RR 0.85, 95% CI 0.63 to 1.14; ACR 0.58–1.62 mg/mmol: RR 1.11, 95% CI 0.86 to 1.43; ACR 1.62–1.99 mg/mmol: RR 1.89, 95% CI 1.52 to 2.36).

**PROGNOSIS**  Diabetes mellitus increases the risk of mortality or serious morbidity after a coronary event (RR 1.5–3.0).[2,3,14,15] This excess risk is partly accounted for by increased prevalence of other cardiovascular risk factors in people with diabetes. A systematic review (search date 1998, 15 prospective cohort studies) found that, in people with diabetes admitted to hospital for acute myocardial infarction, "stress hyperglycaemia" was associated with significantly higher mortality in hospital compared with lower blood glucose levels (RR 1.7, 95% CI 1.2 to 2.4).[16] One large prospective cohort study (91 285 men aged 40–84 years) found higher all cause and coronary heart disease (CHD) mortality at 5 years' follow up in men with diabetes than in men without coronary artery disease or diabetes (age adjusted RR 3.3, 95% CI 2.6 to 4.1 in men with diabetes and without coronary artery disease v RR 2.3, 95% CI 2.0 to 2.6 in healthy people; RR 5.6, 95% CI 4.9 to 6.3 in men with coronary artery disease but without diabetes v RR 2.2, 95% CI 2.0 to 2.4 in healthy people; RR 12.0, 95% CI 9.9 to 14.6 in men with both risk factors v RR 4.7, 95% CI 4.0 to 5.4 in healthy people).[17] Multivariate analysis did not materially alter these associations. Diabetes mellitus alone is associated with a twofold increase in risk for all cause death, with a threefold increase in risk of death from CHD, and, in people with pre-existing CHD, with a 12-fold increase in risk of death from CHD compared with people with neither risk factor.[17]

Please refer to CD-ROM for full text and references.

Search date April 2003

*Birte Nygaard*

## What are the effects of treatments for clinical (overt) hypothyroidism?

### BENEFICIAL

**Levothyroxine (L-thyroxine)**

We found no RCTs comparing levothyroxine (L-thyroxine) versus placebo, although there is consensus that treatment is beneficial. Treating clinical (overt) hypothyroidism with thyroid hormone (levothyroxine; L-thyroxine) can induce hyperthyroidism and reduce bone mass in postmenopausal women and increase the risk of atrial fibrillation.

### UNKNOWN EFFECTIVENESS

**Levothyroxine (L-thyroxine) plus liothyronine**

We found insufficient evidence about the effects of levothyroxine (L-thyroxine) plus liothyronine versus levothyroxine alone in people with clinical (overt) hypothyroidism. Thyroid hormone treatment can induce hyperthyroidism and reduce bone mass in postmenopausal women and increase the risk of atrial fibrillation.

## What are the effects of treatments for subclinical hypothyroidism?

### UNKNOWN EFFECTIVENESS

**Levothyroxine (L-thyroxine)**

One RCT in women with biochemically defined subclinical hypothyroidism found no significant difference between levothyroxine (L-thyroxine) and placebo for dry skin, cold intolerance, and constipation at 1 year. The RCT may, however, have lacked power to exclude a clinically important difference between treatments. Another RCT found no significant difference in health related quality of life scores between levothyroxine and placebo. One RCT found inconclusive results about the effect of levothyroxine versus placebo on cognitive function in people with subclinical hypothyroidism. One RCT found that levothyroxine improved left ventricular function at 6 months compared with placebo. Treating subclinical hypothyroidism with thyroid hormone can induce hyperthyroidism and reduce bone mass in postmenopausal women and increase the risk of atrial fibrillation.

**DEFINITION**   Hypothyroidism is characterised by low levels of blood thyroid hormone. **Clinical (overt) hypothyroidism** is diagnosed on the basis of characteristic clinical features consisting of mental slowing, depression, dementia, weight gain, constipation, dry skin, hair loss, cold intolerance, hoarse voice, irregular menstruation, infertility, muscle stiffness and pain, bradycardia, hypercholesterolaemia, combined with a raised blood level of thyroid stimulating hormone (TSH) (serum TSH levels > 12 mU/L), and a low serum thyroxine ($T_4$ ⊕) level (serum $T_4$ < 60 nmol/L). **Subclinical hypothyroidism** is diagnosed when serum TSH is raised (serum TSH levels > 4 mU/L) but serum thyroxine is normal and there are no symptoms or signs, or only minor symptoms or signs, of thyroid dysfunction. **Primary hypothyroidism** is seen after destruction of the thyroid gland because of autoimmunity (the most common cause), or medical intervention such as surgery, radioiodine, and radiation. **Secondary** ▶

# Primary hypothyroidism

**hypothyroidism** is seen after pituitary or hypothalamic damage, and results in insufficient production of TSH. Secondary hypothyroidism is not covered in this review. **Euthyroid sick syndrome** is diagnosed when levels of tri-iodothyronine ($T_3$Ⓖ) are low, serum thyroxine is low, and TSH levels are normal or low. Euthyroid sick syndrome is not covered in this review.

**INCIDENCE/ PREVALENCE**
Hypothyroidism is more common in women than in men (the female : male ratio in the UK is 6 : 1). One study (2779 people in the UK with a median age of 58 years) found the incidence of clinical (overt) hypothyroidism was 40/10 000 women per year and 6/10 000 men per year. The prevalence was 9.3% in women and 1.3% in men.[1] In areas with high iodine intake, the incidence of hypothyroidism can be higher than in areas with normal or low iodine intake. In Denmark, where there is moderate iodine insufficiency, the overall incidence of hypothyroidism is 1.4/10 000 per year increasing to 8/10 000 per year in people older than 70 years.[2] The incidence of subclinical hypothyroidism increases with age. Up to 10% of women over the age of 60 years have subclinical hypothyroidism (evaluated from data from the Netherlands and USA).[3,4]

**AETIOLOGY/ RISK FACTORS**
Primary thyroid gland failure can occur as a result of chronic autoimmune thyroiditis, postradioactive iodine treatment, or thyroidectomy. Other causes include drug adverse effects (e.g. amiodarone and lithium), transient hypothyroidism due to silent thyroiditis, subacute thyroiditis, or postpartum thyroiditis.

**PROGNOSIS**
Hypothyroidism results in mental slowing, depression, dementia, weight gain, constipation, dry skin, hair loss, cold intolerance, hoarse voice, irregular menstruation, infertility, muscle stiffness and pain, bradycardia, and hypercholesterolaemia. In people with subclinical hypothyroidism, the risk of developing overt hypothyroidism is described in the UK Whickham Survey (25 years' follow up; for women: OR 8, 95% CI 3 to 20; for men: OR 44, 95% CI 19 to 104; if both a raised TSH and positive antithyroid antibodies were present; for women: OR 38, 95% CI 22 to 65; for men: OR 173, 95% CI 81 to 370). For women, the survey found an annual risk of 4.3%/year (if both raised serum TSH and antithyroid antibodies were present), 2.6%/year (if raised serum TSH was present alone); the minimum number of people with raised TSH and antithyroid antibodies who would need treating to prevent this progression to clinical (overt) hypothyroidism in one person over 5 years is 5–8.[1] **Cardiovascular disease:** A large cross-sectional study (25 862 people with serum TSH between 5.1–10 mU/L) found significantly higher mean total cholesterol concentrations in hypothyroid people compared with euthyroid people (5.8 v 5.6 mmol/L).[3] Another study (124 elderly women with subclinical hypothyroidism, 931 euthyroid women) found a significantly increased risk of myocardial infarction in women with subclinical hypothyroidism (OR 2.3, 95% CI 1.3 to 4.0) and for aortic atherosclerosis (OR 1.7, 95% CI 1.1 to 2.6).[4] **Mental health:** Subclinical hypothyroidism is associated with depression.[5] People with subclinical hypothyroidism may have depression that is refractory to both antidepressant drugs and thyroid hormone alone. Memory impairment, hysteria, anxiety, somatic complaints, and depressive features without depression have been described in people with subclinical hypothyroidism.[6]

Please refer to CD-ROM for full text and references.

## What are the effects of topical anti-inflammatory eye drops?

### UNKNOWN EFFECTIVENESS

**Topical non-steroidal anti-inflammatory drug eye drops**

One RCT found no significant difference between non-steroidal anti-inflammatory drug and placebo eye drops in clinical cure rate after 21 days. Three RCTs found no significant difference between non-steroidal anti-inflammatory drug and steroid eye drops in clinical cure rate.

**Topical steroid eye drops**

One small RCT found no significant difference with steroid (betamethasone phosphate/clobetasone butyrate) eye drops compared with placebo eye drops in symptom severity after 14 or 21 days. Two RCTs found no significant difference between prednisolone and rimexolone, in the anterior chamber cell count (a marker of disease severity). One RCT found that prednisolone increased the proportion of people with fewer than five anterior chamber cells per examination field compared with loteprednol after 28 days. The results of a second RCT comparing prednisolone with loteprednol were difficult to interpret. RCTs found that rimexolone and loteprednol were less likely than prednisolone to be associated with increased intraocular pressure, although differences were not statistically significant. Three RCTs found no significant difference between steroid and non-steroidal anti-inflammatory drug eye drops in clinical cure rate after 14 or 21 days.

**DEFINITION**    Anterior uveitis is inflammation of the uveal tract, and includes iritis🅖 and iridocyclitis🅖. It can be classified according to its clinical course into acute or chronic anterior uveitis, or according to its clinical appearance into granulomatous or non-granulomatous anterior uveitis. Acute anterior uveitis is characterised by an extremely painful red eye, often associated with photophobia and occasionally with decreased visual acuity. Chronic anterior uveitis is defined as inflammation lasting over 6 weeks. It is usually asymptomatic, but many people have mild symptoms during exacerbations.

**INCIDENCE/**    Acute anterior uveitis is rare, with an annual incidence of 12/100 000
**PREVALENCE**    population.[1] It is particularly common in Finland (annual incidence 22.6/ 100 000 population, prevalence 68.7/100 000 population), probably because of genetic factors such as the high frequency of HLA-B27 in the Finnish population.[2] It is equally common in men and women and more than 90% of cases occur in people older than 20 years of age.[2,3]

**AETIOLOGY/**    No cause is identified in 60–80% of people with acute anterior uveitis. Systemic
**RISK FACTORS** disorders that may be associated with acute anterior uveitis include ankylosing spondylitis; Reiter's syndrome; juvenile chronic arthritis; Kawasaki syndrome; infectious uveitis; Behçet's syndrome; inflammatory bowel disease; interstitial nephritis; sarcoidosis; multiple sclerosis; Wegener's granulomatosis; Vogt-Koyanagi-Harada syndrome; and masquerade syndromes🅖. Acute anterior uveitis also occurs in association with HLA-B27 expression not linked to any systemic disease, and it may also be the manifestation of an isolated eye disorder such as Fuchs' iridocyclitis, Posner-Schlossman syndrome, or Schwartz syndrome. Acute anterior uveitis may also occur following surgery or as an adverse drug or hypersensitivity reaction.[2,3]

# Acute anterior uveitis

**PROGNOSIS**   Acute anterior uveitis is often self limiting, but we found no evidence about how often it resolves spontaneously, in which people, or over what time period. Complications include posterior synechiae🄖, cataract, glaucoma, and chronic uveitis. In a study of 154 people (232 eyes) with acute anterior uveitis (119 people HLA-B27 positive), visual acuity was better than 20/60 in 209/232 (90%) eyes, 20/60 or worse in 23/232 (10%) eyes, and worse than 20/200 (classified as legally blind) in 11/232 (5%) eyes.[4]

Please refer to CD-ROM for full text and references.

# Age related macular degeneration

## Search date July 2003

*Jennifer Arnold and Shirley Sarks*

## What are the effects of interventions to prevent progression?

### LIKELY TO BE BENEFICIAL

### Antioxidant vitamin and zinc supplementation

One systematic review has found modest evidence from one large RCT that, in people with early to late age related macular degeneration, antioxidant vitamins plus zinc supplements reduce the risk of progression and vision loss over 6 years compared with placebo.

### UNKNOWN EFFECTIVENESS

### Laser to drusen

Two RCTs provided insufficient evidence that laser to drusen decreased incidence of late age related macular degeneration, choroidal neovascularisation, or geographic atrophy. One RCT found that laser improved visual acuity after 2 years compared with no treatment, but not compared with subthreshold treatment. The second, larger RCT found no significant difference between laser and no treatment in visual acuity after 1 year. However, subgroup analysis found improved visual acuity where laser treatment had reduced the number of drusen by 50% or more. The RCT also found that, in people with unilateral (but not bilateral) drusen, laser increased the short term incidence of choroidal neovascularisation compared with no treatment.

## What are the effects of treatments for exudative age related macular degeneration?

### BENEFICIAL

### Photodynamic treatment with verteporfin

Two systematic reviews in people with age related macular degeneration have found that photodynamic treatment❻ with verteporfin❻ reduces the risk of moderate❻ or severe loss of visual acuity and of legal blindness❻ after 1–2 years in selected people compared with placebo. Photodynamic treatment with verteporfin was associated with an initial loss of vision and photosensitive reactions in a small proportion of people.

### TRADE OFF BETWEEN BENEFITS AND HARMS

### Thermal laser photocoagulation

Four large RCTs have found that, in people with well demarcated exudative age related macular degeneration, thermal laser photocoagulation reduces severe visual loss❻ after 2–5 years compared with no treatment, but may be associated with an immediate and permanent reduction in visual acuity. RCTs found no significant difference in visual acuity between different laser wavelengths. Choroidal neovascularisation recurs within 2 years in about half of those treated.

### UNKNOWN EFFECTIVENESS

### Submacular surgery

Two small RCTs provided insufficient evidence on the effects of submacular surgery❻.

▶

# Age related macular degeneration

## UNLIKELY TO BE BENEFICIAL

### External beam radiation

Five RCTs found conflicting evidence of the effect of low dose external beam radiation compared with placebo or no treatment in people with exudative age related macular degeneration. However, the two largest, highest quality RCTs found no significant effect in the proportion of people with moderate vision loss, suggesting the treatment is unlikely to be beneficial. We found insufficient evidence on long term safety, although RCTs found no evidence of toxicity to the optic nerve or retina after 12–24 months.

## LIKELY TO BE INEFFECTIVE OR HARMFUL

### Subcutaneous interferon alfa-2a

One large RCT found that, compared with placebo, subcutaneous interferon alfa-2a (an antiangiogenesis drug) increased visual loss after 1 year, although the difference was not significant. The RCT also found evidence of serious ocular and systemic adverse effects.

**DEFINITION**   Age related macular degeneration (AMD) has three clinical stages: **early AMD** marked by drusen🇬 and pigmentary change, and usually associated with normal vision; **late or sight threatening AMD** associated with a decrease in central vision; and **end stage or blinding AMD**. Late stage AMD has two forms: atrophic (or dry) AMD, characterised by geographic atrophy🇬; and exudative (or wet) AMD, characterised by choroidal neovascularisation🇬, which eventually causes a disciform scar.

**INCIDENCE/**   AMD is a common cause of blindness registration in industrialised countries.
**PREVALENCE**   Atrophic AMD is more common than the more sight threatening exudative AMD, affecting about 85% of people with AMD.[1] End stage (blinding) AMD is found in about 2% of all people aged over 50 years, and incidence rises with age (0.7–1.4% of people aged 65–75 years; 11–19% of people aged > 85 years).[2–4]

**AETIOLOGY/**   Proposed hypotheses for the cause of AMD involve vascular factors and
**RISK FACTORS**   oxidative damage coupled with genetic predisposition.[5] Age is the strongest risk factor. Ocular risk factors for the development of exudative AMD include the presence of soft drusen🇬, macular pigmentary change, and choroidal neovas-cularisation in the other eye. Systemic risk factors include hypertension, smoking, and a family history of AMD.[5–7] Hypertension, diet (especially intake of antioxidant micronutrients), and oestrogen use are suspected as causal agents, but the effects of these factors remain unproved.[5]

**PROGNOSIS**   AMD impairs central vision, which is required for reading, driving, face recognition, and all fine visual tasks. **Atrophic AMD** progresses slowly over many years, and time to legal blindness🇬 is highly variable (usually about 5–10 years).[8,9] **Exudative AMD** is more often threatening to vision; 90% of people with severe visual loss🇬 due to AMD have the exudative type. This condition usually manifests with a sudden worsening and distortion of central vision. One study estimated (based on data derived primarily from cohort studies) that the risk of developing exudative AMD in people with bilateral soft drusen was 1–5% at 1 year and 13–18% at 3 years.[10] The observed 5 year rate in a population survey was 7%.[11] Most eyes (estimates vary from 60–90%) with exudative AMD progress to legal blindness and develop a central defect (scotoma) in the visual field.[12–15] Peripheral vision is preserved, allowing the person to be mobile and independent. The ability to read with visual aids depends on the size and density ▶

of the central scotoma and the degree to which the person retains sensitivity to contrast. Once exudative AMD has developed in one eye, the other eye is at high risk (cumulative estimated incidence: 10% at 1 year, 28% at 3 years, and 42% at 5 years).[16]

---

Please refer to CD-ROM for full text and references.

# Bacterial conjunctivitis

Search date June 2003

*Justine Smith*

Eye disorders

## What are the effects of antibiotic treatment?

### BENEFICIAL

**Antibiotic treatment in culture positive bacterial conjunctivitis**

One systematic review has found that antibiotics (polymyxin–bacitracin, ciprofloxacin, or ofloxacin) increase rates of clinical and microbiological cure compared with placebo. Four RCTs found no significant difference among antibiotics in clinical or microbiological cure. One RCT found that fusidic acid increased clinical cure rate compared with chloramphenicol. One RCT found that topical netilmicin increased clinical cure rate compared with topical gentamicin. One RCT found that topical levofloxacin increased microbiological cure rate, but not clinical cure rate, compared with topical ofloxacin.

### LIKELY TO BE BENEFICIAL

**Empirical antibiotic treatment of suspected bacterial conjunctivitis**

One systematic review found limited evidence from one RCT that topical norfloxacin increased rates of clinical and microbiological improvement or cure after 5 days compared with placebo. RCTs comparing different topical antibiotics versus each other found no significant difference in rates of clinical or microbiological cure. One RCT found no significant difference between topical polymyxin–bacitracin ointment and oral cefixime for clinical or microbiological improvement or cure.

**DEFINITION**
Conjunctivitis is any inflammation of the conjunctiva, generally characterised by irritation, itching, foreign body sensation, and watering or discharge. Bacterial conjunctivitis may often be distinguished from other types of conjunctivitis by the presence of a yellow–white mucopurulent discharge. There is also usually a papillary reaction (small bumps with fibrovascular cores on the palpebral conjunctiva, appearing grossly as a fine velvety surface). Bacterial conjunctivitis is usually bilateral. This review covers non-gonococcal bacterial conjunctivitis.

**INCIDENCE/ PREVALENCE**
We found no good evidence on the incidence or prevalence of bacterial conjunctivitis.

**AETIOLOGY/ RISK FACTORS**
Conjunctivitis may be infectious (caused by bacteria or viruses) or allergic. In adults, bacterial conjunctivitis is less common than viral conjunctivitis, although estimates vary widely (viral conjunctivitis has been reported to account for 8–75% of acute conjunctivitis).[1-3] *Staphylococcus* species are the most common pathogens for bacterial conjunctivitis in adults, followed by *Streptococcus pneumoniae* and *Haemophilus influenzae*.[4,5] In children, bacterial conjunctivitis is more common than viral, and is mainly caused by *H influenzae*, *S pneumoniae*, and *Moraxella catarrhalis*.[6,7]

**PROGNOSIS**
Most bacterial conjunctivitis is self limiting. One systematic review (search date 2001) found clinical cure or significant improvement with placebo within 2–5 days in 64% of people (99% CI 54% to 73%).[8] Some organisms cause corneal or systemic complications, or both. Otitis media may develop in 25% of children with *H influenzae* conjunctivitis,[9] and systemic meningitis may complicate primary meningococcal conjunctivitis in 18% of people.[10]

Please refer to CD-ROM for full text and references.

## What are the effects of surgery for age related cataract without other ocular co-morbidity? New

### BENEFICIAL

**Manual extracapsular extraction (better than intracapsular extraction)**

One RCT found that manual extracapsular extraction plus intraocular lens implant improved visual acuity and quality of life compared with intracapsular extraction⊙ plus aphakic glasses. The RCT also found a higher rate of complications with intracapsular extraction plus aphakic glasses.

**Phaco extracapsular extraction (better than manual extracapsular extraction)**

One RCT identified by a systematic review found improved vision up to 1 year after phaco extracapsular extraction plus foldable posterior chamber intraocular lens implant compared with manual extracapsular extraction⊙ plus rigid posterior chamber intraocular lens implant. The RCT and a systematic review of observational studies found that a higher proportion of people had complications with manual extracapsular extraction than with phaco extracapsular extraction.

**DEFINITION**       **Cataracts** are cloudy or opaque areas in the lens of the eye (which should usually be completely clear). This results in changes that can impair vision. **Age related (or senile) cataract** is defined as cataract occurring in people over 16 years of age in the absence of known mechanical, chemical, or radiation trauma. **Cataract surgery** is indicated when the chances of significant improvement of visual function outweigh the risks of a poor outcome from such surgery. It is not dependent on reaching a specific visual acuity standard. Other indications for cataract surgery include facilitation of treatment or monitoring of concurrent posterior segment disease such as laser treatment for proliferative diabetic retinopathy or to correct a difference in the refractive power of the two eyes or treat lens induced ocular disease.[1] Cataract extraction and intraocular lens implantation can be performed using a variety of techniques including manual extracapsular cataract extraction, phaco extracapsular extraction (phacoemulsification), and intracapsular cataract extraction. **Population:** This chapter covers surgery for age related cataract. It does not cover cataract in people with diabetes mellitus or recurrent uveitis — conditions that can affect the surgical outcome.

**INCIDENCE/**       Cataract accounts for over 40% of world blindness — around 38 million
**PREVALENCE**       people.[2] In a rural setting in the USA, the prevalence of visually significant cataract ranged from approximately 5% at the age of 65 years to around 50% in people older than 75 years.[3] The relative incidence of non-senile cataract within this population is so small that this can be taken as the effective incidence of senile cataract.

**AETIOLOGY/**       Diet, smoking,[4] and exposure to ultraviolet light[5] are thought to be risk factors
**RISK FACTORS**     in the development of age related cataract. In addition, there may be a genetic predisposition to development of age related cataract in a proportion of the population.[6]

# Cataract

**PROGNOSIS**   Age related cataract progresses with age, the rate of progression being unpredictable. We found no evidence for spontaneous regression or for the effectiveness of any non-invasive intervention.

---

Please refer to CD-ROM for full text and references.

## What are the effects of treatments for diabetic retinopathy?

### BENEFICIAL

**Control of diabetes (see glycaemic control in diabetes, p 138)**

**Control of hypertension (see primary prevention, p 25)**

**Macular photocoagulation to macular microaneurysus in people with clinically significant macular oedema**

One large RCT has found that laser photocoagulation to the macula reduces visual loss at 3 years in eyes with macular oedema plus mild to moderate diabetic retinopathy compared with no treatment. There was some evidence of greater benefit in eyes with better vision. Subgroup analysis found that focal laser treatment❻ reduced visual loss in eyes with clinically significant macular oedema❻ particularly in people in whom the centre of the macula was involved or imminently threatened.

**Peripheral retinal laser photocoagulation in people with preproliferative (*moderate/severe non-proliferative*\*) retinopathy and maculopathy**

RCTs in eyes with preproliferative retinopathy❻and maculopathy have found that peripheral retinal photocoagulation reduces the risk of severe visual loss at 5 years compared with no treatment.

**Peripheral retinal laser photocoagulation in people with proliferative retinopathy**

RCTs have found that peripheral retinal photocoagulation reduces the risk of severe visual loss at 2–3 years compared with no treatment. One RCT in eyes with high risk proliferative❻ diabetic retinopathy found that low intensity argon laser reduced vitreous haemorrhage❻ and macular oedema compared with standard intensity argon laser. It found no significant difference between treatments for visual acuity, although it may have lacked power to detect clinically important effects.

### LIKELY TO BE BENEFICIAL

**Grid photocoagulation to zones of retinal thickening in people with diabetic maculopathy**

One RCT found that grid photocoagulation❻ improved visual acuity in treated eyes at 12 months and at 24 months compared with no treatment. Photocoagulation reduced the risk of moderate visual loss by 50–70% compared with no treatment.

### UNKNOWN EFFECTIVENESS

**Macular photocoagulation in people with maculopathy but without clinically significant macular oedema**

We found no RCTs of macular photocoagulation in this population.

**Peripheral retinal laser photocoagulation in people with background or preproliferative (*non-proliferative*\*) retinopathy without maculopathy**

We found no RCTs in people with background or preproliferative❻ retinopathy without maculopathy.

▶

# Diabetic retinopathy

## What are the effects of treatments for vitreous haemorrhage?

### LIKELY TO BE BENEFICIAL

**Vitrectomy in people with severe vitreous haemorrhage and proliferative retinopathy (if performed early)**

One RCT found that early vitrectomy🌀 reduced visual loss at 1, 2, and 3 years in eyes with severe vitreous haemorrhage🌀 and proliferative retinopathy compared with deferred (for 1 year) vitrectomy.

### UNKNOWN EFFECTIVENESS

**Vitrectomy in people with maculopathy**

The role of vitrectomy in this population remains unclear.

| | |
|---|---|
| **DEFINITION** | Diabetic retinopathy is characterised by varying degrees of microaneurysms, haemorrhages, exudates *(hard exudates)*, venous changes, new vessel formation, and retinal thickening. It can involve the peripheral retina, the macula, or both. The range of severity of retinopathy includes background🌀 *(mild non-proliferative)*, preproliferative *(moderate/severe non-proliferative)*, proliferative🌀, and advanced retinopathy🌀. Involvement of the macula can be focal🌀, diffuse🌀, ischaemic🌀, or mixed. |
| **INCIDENCE/ PREVALENCE** | Diabetic eye disease is the most common cause of blindness in the UK, responsible for 12% of registrable blindness in people aged 16–64 years.[1] |
| **AETIOLOGY/ RISK FACTORS** | Risk factors include age, duration and control of diabetes, raised blood pressure, and raised serum lipids.[2] |
| **PROGNOSIS** | Natural history studies from the 1960s found that at least half of people with proliferative diabetic retinopathy progressed to Snellen visual acuity🌀 of less than 6/60 *(20/200)* within 3-5 years.[3–5] After 4 years' follow up, the rate of progression to less than 6/60 *(20/200)* visual acuity in the better eye was 1.5% in people with type 1 diabetes, 2.7% in people with non-insulin requiring type 2 diabetes, and 3.2% in people with insulin requiring type 2 diabetes.[6] |

*Terms in italics indicate US definitions.🌀

Please refer to CD-ROM for full text and references.

Search date April 2003

*Rajiv Shah and Richard Wormald*

## What are the effects of treatments for established primary open angle glaucoma?

### LIKELY TO BE BENEFICIAL

#### Laser trabeculoplasty (versus control or medical treatment)

One RCT in people with newly diagnosed glaucoma found that treatment with laser trabeculoplasty⊙ plus topical medical treatment to lower intraocular pressure reduced progression of glaucoma compared with control. One RCT found that, compared with medical treatment alone, combined treatment with initial laser trabeculoplasty followed by medical treatment reduced intraocular pressure and deterioration in optic disc appearance, and improved visual fields after a mean of 7 years.

#### Topical medical treatment (some RCTs included people with primary open angle glaucoma, primary open angle glaucoma or ocular hypertension, or ocular hypertension alone)

One systematic review that included RCTs of people with primary open angle glaucoma or ocular hypertension alone found limited evidence that topical medical treatments reduced intraocular pressure after a minimum follow up of 3 months or longer compared with placebo, but found no significant difference between treatments in visual field loss on follow up of 1 year or longer. The systematic review did not clearly define the medical treatments involved. One subsequent large RCT in people with ocular hypertension but no evidence of glaucomatous damage found that topical treatment lowering intraocular pressure reduced the probability of developing primary open angle glaucoma after 5 years compared with control. One RCT found that, compared with medical treatment alone, combined treatment with initial laser trabeculoplasty followed by medical treatment reduced intraocular pressure and deterioration in optic disc appearance, and improved visual fields after a mean of 7 years. Two RCTs found that surgical trabeculectomy⊙ reduced both visual field loss and intraocular pressures compared with medical treatment, but found no significant difference between treatments in visual acuity after about 5 years.

### TRADE OFF BETWEEN BENEFITS AND HARMS

#### Surgical trabeculectomy

Two RCTs found that surgical trabeculectomy reduced both visual field loss and intraocular pressures compared with medical treatment, but found no significant difference between treatments in visual acuity after about 5 years. Two RCTs found that surgical trabeculectomy reduced intraocular pressure compared with laser trabeculoplasty, but found mixed effects for changes in visual acuity after 5–7 years. Observational studies have found limited evidence that surgical trabeculectomy may reduce central vision.

### UNKNOWN EFFECTIVENESS

#### Laser trabeculoplasty (versus surgical treatment)

Two RCTs found that laser trabeculoplasty reduced intraocular pressures less than surgical trabeculectomy, but found mixed effects for changes in visual acuity after 5–7 years.

# Glaucoma

## What are the effects of lowering intraocular pressure in normal tension glaucoma?

**LIKELY TO BE BENEFICIAL**

### Medical treatments for lowering intraocular pressure in normal pressure glaucoma

One RCT found that surgical or medical treatment reduced progression of visual field loss after 8 years compared with no treatment.

**TRADE OFF BETWEEN BENEFITS AND HARMS**

### Surgical treatments for lowering intraocular pressure in normal pressure glaucoma

One RCT found that surgical or medical treatment reduced progression of visual field loss after 8 years compared with no treatment, but found that surgery increased cataract formation after 8 years.

## What are the effects of treatments for acute angle closure glaucoma?

**UNKNOWN EFFECTIVENESS**

### Medical treatments of acute angle closure glaucoma

We found no placebo controlled RCTs, but strong consensus suggests that medical treatments are effective. One RCT found no significant difference in intraocular pressure after 2 hours with low dose pilocarpine versus an intensive pilocarpine regimen versus pilocarpine ocular inserts. We found no RCTs of other medical treatments.

### Surgical treatments of acute angle closure glaucoma

We found no placebo controlled RCTs, but strong consensus suggests that surgical treatments are effective. One RCT found no significant difference between surgical iridectomy⊙ and laser iridotomy⊙ in visual acuity or intraocular pressure after 3 years.

DEFINITION    Glaucoma is a group of diseases characterised by progressive optic neuropathy. It is usually bilateral but asymmetric and may occur at any point within a wide range of intraocular pressures. All forms of glaucoma show optic nerve damage (cupping and/or pallor) associated with peripheral visual field loss. **Primary open angle glaucoma** occurs in people with an open drainage angle and no secondary identifiable cause. Although the understanding of the natural history of these conditions is not complete, it is thought that the problem starts with an intraocular pressure that is too high for the optic nerve even though, in a significant proportion (about 40%), this may be within statistically defined normal range. The term ocular hypertension generally applies to eyes with an intraocular pressure greater than the statistical upper limit of normal (about 21 mm Hg). However, only a relatively small proportion of eyes with raised intraocular pressure have an optic nerve that is vulnerable to its effects (about 10%). But because intraocular pressure is the main and only modifiable risk factor for the disease, studies on the effectiveness of reducing intraocular pressure often include people with both ocular hypertension and primary open angle glaucoma. Previously, trialists were anxious about withholding active treatment in overt primary open angle glaucoma so many placebo or no treatment trials selected people just with ocular hypertension. Trials comparing treatments often include both, but in these, the ▶

outcome is usually intraocular pressure alone. **Normal tension glaucoma** occurs in people with intraocular pressures that are consistently below 21 mm Hg (2 standard deviations above the population mean). **Acute angle closure glaucoma** is a rapid and severe rise in intraocular pressure caused by physical obstruction of the anterior chamber drainage angle.

**INCIDENCE/ PREVALENCE**    Glaucoma occurs in 1–2% of white people aged over 40 years, rising to 5% at 70 years. Primary open angle glaucoma accounts for two thirds of those affected, and normal tension glaucoma for about a quarter.[1,2] In black people glaucoma is more prevalent, presents at a younger age with higher intraocular pressures, is more difficult to control, and is the main irreversible cause of blindness in black populations of African origin.[1,3] Glaucoma related blindness is responsible for 8% of new blind registrations in the UK.[4]

**AETIOLOGY/ RISK FACTORS**    The major risk factor for developing primary open angle glaucoma is raised intraocular pressure. Lesser risk factors include family history and ethnic origin. The relationship between systemic blood pressure and intraocular pressure may be an important determinant of blood flow to the optic nerve head and, as a consequence, may represent a risk factor for glaucoma.[5] Systemic hypotension, vasospasm (including Raynaud's disease and migraine), and a history of major blood loss have been reported as risk factors for normal tension glaucoma in hospital based studies. Risk factors for acute angle closure glaucoma include family history, female sex, being long sighted, and cataract. A recent systematic review did not find any evidence supporting the theory that routine pupillary dilatation with short acting mydriatics was a risk factor for acute angle closure glaucoma.[6]

**PROGNOSIS**    Advanced visual field loss is found in about 20% of people with primary open angle glaucoma at diagnosis,[7] and is an important risk factor for glaucoma related blindness.[8] Blindness results from gross loss of visual field or loss of central vision. Once early field defects have appeared, and where the intraocular pressure is greater than 30 mm Hg, untreated people may lose the remainder of the visual field in 3 years or less.[9] As the disease progresses, people with glaucoma have difficulty moving from a bright room to a darker room, and judging steps and kerbs. Progression of visual field loss is often slower in normal tension glaucoma. Acute angle glaucoma leads to rapid loss of vision, initially from corneal oedema and subsequently from ischaemic optic neuropathy.

Please refer to CD-ROM for full text and references.

# Ocular herpes simplex

Search date August 2003

*Nigel H Barker*

---

## What are the effects of treatments for epithelial keratitis?

### BENEFICIAL

**Interferons**

One systematic review found that topical interferons (alpha or beta) increase healing after 7 and 14 days compared with placebo. The review found no significant difference between a topical interferon and a topical antiviral agent in healing after 7 days, but found that a topical interferon increased healing after 14 days. The review also found that topical interferon plus a topical antiviral agent increased healing compared with a topical antiviral agent alone after 14 days. "Healing" was not clearly defined.

**Topical antiviral agents**

One systematic review has found that topical antivirals (idoxuridine or vidarabine) increase healing after 14 days compared with placebo, and that trifluridine or aciclovir increase healing compared with idoxuridine after 7 and 14 days. The review has also found that antiviral treatment plus debridement increases healing after 7 days compared with either treatment alone. It found no significant difference in healing at 14 days between antiviral treatment plus debridement and antiviral treatment alone. It also found no significant difference between topical antiviral agents and topical interferon in healing after 7 days, but found that topical interferon increased healing after 14 days. The review also found that adding topical interferon to a topical antiviral agent increased healing compared with the antiviral agent alone. "Healing" was not clearly defined.

### UNKNOWN EFFECTIVENESS

**Debridement**

One systematic review has found no significant difference between debridement and no treatment. The review has also found that debridement plus antiviral treatment improves healing at 7 days compared with either treatment alone. This difference remained significant at 14 days for combined treatment compared with debridement alone.

---

## What are the effects of treatments for stromal keratitis?

### BENEFICIAL

**Topical corticosteroids**

One RCT in people receiving topical antiviral treatment found that topical corticosteroids reduced progression and shortened the duration of stromal keratitis❻ compared with placebo.

### UNLIKELY TO BE BENEFICIAL

**Oral aciclovir**

One RCT in people receiving topical corticosteroids plus topical antiviral treatment found no significant difference between oral aciclovir and placebo in rates of treatment failure at 16 weeks.

◄ *What are the effects of treatments to prevent recurrence of ocular herpes simplex?*

**BENEFICIAL**

**Long term (1 year) oral aciclovir**
One large RCT in people with at least one previous episode of epithelial🛈 or stromal keratitis🛈 found that long term oral aciclovir reduced recurrence after 1 year compared with placebo.

**UNLIKELY TO BE BENEFICIAL**

**Short term (3 weeks) oral aciclovir**
One RCT in people with epithelial keratitis receiving a topical antiviral agent (trifluridine) found no significant difference between short term prophylaxis with oral aciclovir and placebo in the rate of stromal keratitis or iritis at 1 year.

*What are the effects of treatments to prevent recurrence of ocular herpes simplex in people with corneal grafts?*

**LIKELY TO BE BENEFICIAL**

**Oral aciclovir**
One small RCT found limited evidence that prophylactic use of oral aciclovir reduced recurrence and improved graft survival compared with placebo.

**DEFINITION**     Ocular herpes simplex is usually caused by herpes simplex virus type 1 (HSV-1), but also occasionally by type 2 virus (HSV-2). Ocular manifestations of HSV are varied and include blepharitis (inflammation of the eyelids), canalicular obstruction, conjunctivitis, epithelial keratitis, stromal keratitis, iritis, and retinitis. HSV infections are classified as neonatal, primary (HSV in a person with no previous viral exposure), and recurrent (previous viral exposure with humoral and cellular immunity present).

**INCIDENCE/**     Infections with HSV are usually acquired in early life. A US study found
**PREVALENCE**     antibodies against HSV-1 in about 50% of people with high socioeconomic status and 80% of people with low socioeconomic status by the age of 30 years.[1] However, only about 20–25% of people with HSV antibodies had any history of clinical manifestations of ocular or cutaneous herpetic disease.[2] Ocular HSV is the most common cause of corneal blindness in high income countries and the most common cause of unilateral corneal blindness in the world.[3] A 33 year study of the population of Rochester, Minnesota, found the annual incidence of new cases of ocular herpes simplex was 8.4/100 000 (95% CI 6.9 to 9.9) and the annual incidence of all episodes (new and recurrent) was 20.7/100 000 (95% CI 18.3 to 23.1).[4] The prevalence of ocular herpes was 149 cases/100 000 population (95% CI 115 to 183). Twelve per cent of people had bilateral disease.

**AETIOLOGY/**     Epithelial keratitis results from productive, lytic viral infection of the corneal
**RISK FACTORS** epithelial cells. Stromal keratitis and iritis are thought to result from a combination of viral infection and compromised immune mechanisms. Observational evidence (346 people with ocular HSV in the placebo arm of an RCT) has found that the risk of developing stromal keratitis was 4% in people with no previous history of stromal keratitis (RR 1.0) as compared with 32% (RR 10, 95% CI 4.32 to 23.38) with previous stromal keratitis, but that a history of epithelial keratitis was not a risk factor for recurrent epithelial keratitis.[5] Age, sex, ethnicity, and previous experience of non-ocular HSV disease were not associated with an increased risk of recurrence.[5]

# Ocular herpes simplex

**PROGNOSIS**   HSV epithelial keratitis tends to resolve within 1–2 weeks. In a trial of 271 people treated with topical trifluorothymidine and randomly assigned to receive either oral aciclovir or placebo, the epithelial lesion had resolved completely or was at least less than 1 mm after 1 week of treatment with placebo in 89% of people and after 2 weeks in 99% of people.[6] Stromal keratitis or iritis occurs in about 25% of people following epithelial keratitis.[7] The effects of HSV stromal keratitis include scarring, tissue destruction, neovascularisation, glaucoma, and persistent epithelial defects. Rate of recurrence of ocular herpes for people with one episode is 10% at 1 year, 23% at 2 years, and 50% at 10 years.[8] The risk of recurrent ocular HSV infection (epithelial or stromal) has also been found to increase with the number of previous episodes reported (2 or 3 previous episodes: RR 1.41, 95% CI 0.82 to 2.42; 4 or more previous episodes: RR 2.09, 95% CI 1.24 to 3.50).[5] Of corneal grafts performed in Australia over a 10 year period, 5% were in people with visual disability or with actual or impending corneal perforation following stromal ocular herpes simplex. The recurrence of HSV in a corneal graft has a major effect on graft survival. The Australian Corneal Graft Registry has found that, in corneal grafts performed for HSV keratitis, there was at least one HSV recurrence in 58% of corneal grafts that failed over a follow up period of 9 years.[9]

---

Please refer to CD-ROM for full text and references.

## What are the effects of interventions to prevent scarring trachoma by reducing active trachoma?

### LIKELY TO BE BENEFICIAL

**Promotion of face washing plus topical tetracycline (better that tetracycline alone)**

One RCT found that promotion of face washing plus topical tetracycline reduced the rate of severe trachoma after 1 year compared with topical tetracycline alone. It found no significant difference in the overall rate of trachoma. However, the RCT may lack power to rule out a clinically important effect. One RCT found that face washing (performed by a teacher) plus topical tetracycline reduced the proportion of children with trachoma after 3 months compared with no intervention.

### UNKNOWN EFFECTIVENESS

**Antibiotics**

One systemic review provided insufficient evidence to compare antibiotics with placebo or each other in people with active trachoma. The same review found insufficient evidence on oral azithromycin versus topical tetracycline in active trachoma, and also on oral antibiotics other than azithromycin versus topical antibiotics in active trachoma. However, trials were heterogeneous and the review may not exclude clinically important effects.

**Face washing alone**

One RCT found no significant difference between face washing alone (performed by a teacher) and no intervention in the rate of trachoma in children after 3 months.

**Fly control using insecticide**

A small pilot study for an RCT found that fly control using deltamethrin reduced the incidence of trachoma after 3 months compared with no intervention.

## What are the effects of surgical treatments for scarring trachoma (entropion and trichiasis)?

### LIKELY TO BE BENEFICIAL

**Bilamellar tarsal rotation or tarsal advance and rotation (better than other types of eyelid surgery)**

In people with major trichiasis**G**, one RCT found limited evidence that bilamellar tarsal rotation**G** increased operative success and reduced adverse effects after 2 weeks compared with eversion splinting**G**, tarsal advance**G**, or tarsal grooving**G**. However, it found no significant difference between bilamellar tarsal rotation and tarsal advance and rotation**G** in operative success after 2 weeks. A second RCT found that bilamellar tarsal rotation increased operative success after 25 months compared with tarsal advance and rotation. In both RCTs, one experienced surgeon performed most of the operations. In people with minor trichiasis**G**, one of the RCTs found that tarsal rotation increased operative success after 25 months compared with cryoablation or electrolysis. One further RCT reporting combined results for major and minor trichiasis found no significant difference in recurrence between bilamellar tarsal rotation and tarsal advance and lid margin rotation after ▶

# Trachoma

3 months, although there were more minor complications (lid notching and pyogenic granuloma) with the bilamellar procedure. In this RCT, the operations were undertaken by less experienced surgeons under supervision.

**DEFINITION**  **Active trachoma** is chronic inflammation of the conjunctiva caused by infection with *Chlamydia trachomatis*. The World Health Organization classification for active trachoma defines mild trachoma (grade TF — trachomatis inflammation [follicular]) as the presence of five or more follicles in the upper tarsal conjunctiva of at least 0.5 mm in diameter. Severe trachoma (grade TI — trachomatis inflammation [intense]) is defined as pronounced inflammatory thickening of the upper tarsal conjunctiva that obscures more than half of the normal deep vessels.[1] **Scarring trachoma** is caused by repeated active infection by *C trachomatis* in which the upper eyelid is shortened and distorted (entropion) and the lashes abrade the eye (trichiasis❻). Scarring trachoma can exist without entropion/trichiasis but if entropion/trichiasis is present, there will be scarring. Blindness results from corneal opacification, which is related to the degree of entropion/trichiasis.

**INCIDENCE/**  Trachoma is the world's leading cause of preventable blindness and is second
**PREVALENCE**  only to cataract as an overall cause of blindness.[2] Globally, active trachoma affects an estimated 150 million people, most of them children. About 5.5 million people are blind or at risk of blindness as a consequence. Trachoma is a disease of poverty regardless of geographical region. Scarring trachoma is prevalent in large regions of Africa, the Middle East, south west Asia, the Indian subcontinent, and Aboriginal communities in Australia, and there are also small foci in Central and South America.[2] In areas where trachoma is constantly present at high prevalence, active disease is found in more than 50% of preschool children and may have a prevalence as high as 60–90%.[3] As many as 75% of women and 50% of men over the age of 45 years may show signs of scarring disease.[4] The prevalence of active trachoma decreases with increasing age, with fewer than 5% of adults showing signs of active disease.[3] Although similar rates of active disease are observed in boys and girls, the later sequelae of trichiasis, entropion, and corneal opacification are more common in women than men.[3]

**AETIOLOGY/**  Active trachoma is associated with youth and close contact between people.
**RISK FACTORS**  Discharge from the eyes and nose may be a source of further reinfection.[5] Sharing a bedroom with someone who has active trachoma is a risk factor for infection.[6] Facial contact with flies is held to be associated with active trachoma, but studies reporting this relationship used weak methods.[7]

**PROGNOSIS**  Corneal damage from trachoma is caused by multiple processes. Scarring trachoma may cause an inadequate tear film and a dry eye may be more susceptible to damage from inturned lashes, leading to corneal opacification. The prevalence of scarring trachoma and consequent blindness increases with age, and therefore, is most commonly seen in older adults.[8]

---

Please refer to CD-ROM for full text and references.

## What are the effects of preventive interventions?

**BENEFICIAL**

### Early diagnosis and treatment of sexually transmitted diseases

One RCT has found that early diagnosis and treatment of sexually transmitted diseases reduces the risk of acquiring HIV infection over 2 years.

**LIKELY TO BE BENEFICIAL**

### Postexposure prophylaxis in healthcare workers*

One case control study found limited evidence suggesting that postexposure prophylaxis with zidovudine may reduce the risk of HIV infection over 6 months. Evidence from other settings suggests that combining several antiretroviral drugs is likely to be more effective than zidovudine alone.

*Based on observational studies and indirectly from RCTs in other settings.

**UNKNOWN EFFECTIVENESS**

### Presumptive mass treatment of sexually transmitted diseases

One RCT found no significant difference in the incidence of HIV over 20 months between presumptive mass treatment for sexually transmitted diseases and no treatment.

## What are the effects of treatments?

**BENEFICIAL**

### Three antiretroviral drugs regimens (compared with two antiretroviral drugs regimens)

One systematic review has found that, compared with two antiretroviral drug regimens, three drug regimens reduce disease progression or death. Some of the reviewed trials included a non-nucleoside reverse transcriptase inhibitor as a third drug, and some a protease inhibitor.

### Two antiretroviral drugs regimens (compared with single antiretroviral drug regimens

Large RCTs, with a follow up of 1–3 years, have found that two drug regimens (zidovudine plus another nucleoside analogue or protease inhibitor drug) reduce the risk of new AIDS defining illnesses and death compared with zidovudine alone. Adverse events were common in all treatment groups.

**UNKNOWN EFFECTIVENESS**

### Early versus delayed antiretroviral treatment with multidrug regimens

One systematic review compared early versus delayed antiretroviral treatment, but the RCTs were all started when zidovudine was the only drug available. Overall, the systematic review found no significant difference in the risk of AIDS free survival or overall survival with extended follow up. We found no RCTs exploring this question with two or three drug regimens.

# HIV infection

◀ **Four antiretroviral drugs regimens (compared with three antiretroviral drugs regimens)** *New*

We found no systematic review or RCTs comparing four antiretroviral drugs regimens with three antiretroviral drugs regimens for clinical outcomes.

**DEFINITION** HIV infection refers to infection with the human immunodeficiency virus type 1 or type 2. Clinically, this is characterised by a variable period (average around 8–10 years) of asymptomatic infection, followed by repeated episodes of illness of varying and increasing severity as immune function deteriorates. The type of illness varies greatly by country, availability of specific treatment for HIV, and prophylaxis for opportunistic infections.

**INCIDENCE/ PREVALENCE** Worldwide estimates suggest that, by June 2001, about 51 million people had been infected with HIV, about 16 million people had died as a result, and about 16 000 new HIV infections were occurring each day.[1] About 90% of HIV infections occur in the developing world.[1] Occupationally acquired HIV infection in healthcare workers has been documented in 95 definite and 191 possible cases, although this is likely to be an underestimate.[2]

**AETIOLOGY/ RISK FACTORS** The major risk factor for transmission of HIV is unprotected heterosexual or homosexual intercourse. Other risk factors include needlestick injury, sharing drug injecting equipment, and blood transfusion. An HIV infected woman may also transmit the virus to her baby. This has been reported in 15–30% of pregnant women with HIV infection. Not everyone who is exposed to HIV will become infected, although risk increases if exposure is repeated, at high dose, or through blood. There is at least a two to five times greater risk of HIV infection among people with sexually transmitted diseases.[3]

**PROGNOSIS** Without treatment, about half of people infected with HIV will become ill and die from AIDS over about 10 years. A meta-analysis of 13 cohort studies from Europe and the USA looked at 12 574 treatment naïve people starting highly active antiretroviral therapy with a combination of at least three drugs.[4] During 24 310 person years of follow up, 1094 people developed AIDS or died. Baseline CD4 cell count and baseline HIV-1 viral load were associated with the probability of progression to AIDS or death. Other independent predictors of poorer outcome were advanced age, infection through injection drug use, and a previous diagnosis of AIDS. The CD4 cell count at initiation was the dominant prognostic factor in people starting highly active antiretroviral therapy. Genetic factors have been shown to affect response to antiretroviral treatment, but were not considered in the meta-analysis.[4]

---

Please refer to CD-ROM for full text and references.

*Jimmy Volmink*

## What are the effects of measures to reduce mother to child transmission of HIV?

### BENEFICIAL

#### Antiretroviral drugs

One systematic review has found that zidovudine reduces the incidence of HIV infection in infants compared with placebo. One RCT has found that the longer versus shorter courses of zidovudine ("long–long" versus "short–short" courses) given to mother and infant reduces the incidence of HIV in infants. One RCT has found that nevirapine given to the mother and to her newborn reduces the risk of HIV transmission compared with zidovudine. One RCT found no additional advantage in giving nevirapine to the mother and baby when transmission rates are already reduced by mothers receiving standard antiretroviral treatment. One RCT has found that zidovudine plus lamivudine given in the antenatal, intrapartum, and postpartum periods, or in the intrapartum and postpartum periods, reduces the risk of transmission of HIV compared with placebo. One RCT found no difference in newborn HIV infection rates between nevirapine versus zidovudine plus lamivudine given to the mother during labour and to the mother and baby after delivery.

### LIKELY TO BE BENEFICIAL

#### Avoiding breast feeding

One RCT in women with HIV who had access to clean water and health education has found that formula feeding reduces the incidence of HIV in infants after 24 months without increasing infant mortality compared with breast feeding.

#### Elective caesarean section

One RCT provided limited evidence that elective caesarean section compared with vaginal delivery reduced the incidence of HIV in infants at 18 months.

### UNKNOWN EFFECTIVENESS

#### Immunotherapy

One RCT found no significant difference in HIV transmission to infants from mothers taking zidovudine and either HIV hyperimmune globulin or immunoglobulin without HIV antibody. However, the study may have been too small to exclude a clinically important difference.

#### Vaginal microbicides

We found insufficient evidence about the effects of vaginal microbicides on the transmission of HIV to infants.

### LIKELY TO BE INEFFECTIVE OR HARMFUL

#### Vitamin supplements

Three RCTs found that vitamin A supplements given to HIV positive pregnant women had no significant effect on the risk of HIV infection in their infants compared with either placebo or no vitamin A. One RCT found that multivitamins given during pregnancy had no significant effect on HIV infection in their infants. ▶

# HIV: mother to child transmission

**DEFINITION**  Mother to child transmission of HIV-1ⓖ infection can occur during pregnancy, in the intrapartum period, or postnatally through breast feeding.[1] By contrast, HIV-2ⓖ is rarely transmitted from mother to child.[2] Infected children usually have no symptoms or signs of HIV at birth, but develop them over subsequent months or years.[3]

**INCIDENCE/ PREVALENCE**  A review of 13 cohorts found that the risk of mother to child transmission of HIV without antiviral treatment is on average about 15–20% in Europe, 15–30% in the USA, and 25–35% in Africa.[4] The risk of transmission is estimated to be 15–30% during pregnancy, with an additional risk of about 10–20% postpartum through breast feeding.[5] It has been estimated that 800 000 children below the age of 15 years were newly infected with HIV during 2001, bringing the total number of children with HIV/AIDS to 3 million worldwide.[6] Most of these children were infected from their mother and 90% live in sub-Saharan Africa.

**AETIOLOGY/ RISK FACTORS**  Transmission of HIV to children is more likely if the mother has a high viral load.[1,7,8] Women with detectable viraemia (by p24 antigen or culture) have double the risk of transmitting HIV-1 to their infants than those who do not.[1] Breast feeding has also been shown in prospective studies to be a risk factor.[9,10] Other risk factors include sexually transmitted diseases, chorioamnionitis, prolonged rupture of membranes, and vaginal mode of delivery.[6,11–14]

**PROGNOSIS**  About 25% of infants infected with HIV progress rapidly to AIDS or death in the first year. Some survive beyond 12 years of age.[3] One European study found a mortality of 15% in the first year of life and a mortality of 28% by the age of 5 years.[15] A recent study reported that, in children under 5 years of age in sub-Saharan Africa, HIV accounted for 2% of deaths in 1990 and almost 8% in 1999.[16] Five countries (Botswana, Namibia, Swaziland, Zambia, and Zimbabwe) had rates of HIV attributable mortality in excess of 30/1000 in children under the age of 5 years.

Please refer to CD-ROM for full text and references.

Search date April 2003

*John Ioannidis and David Wilkinson*

## What are the effects of prophylaxis for Pneumocystis carinii pneumonia (PCP) and toxoplasmosis?

### BENEFICIAL

### Trimethoprin/sulfamethoxazole (TMP/SMX — co-trimoxazole) for PCP

Systematic reviews have found that TMP/SMX reduces the incidence of PCP compared with placebo or pentamidine. Two systematic reviews have found that TMP/SMX reduced incidence of PCP compared with dapsone (with or without pyrimethamine), although only one of these reviews found that the reduction was significant. One systematic review and one subsequent RCT found no significant difference between high and low dose TMP/SMX for PCP prophylaxis, although adverse effects were more common with the higher dose.

### LIKELY TO BE BENEFICIAL

### Atovaquone (no difference compared with dapsone or aerosolised pentamidine for PCP in people intolerant of TMP/SMX)

We found no RCTs of atovaquone versus placebo. RCTs found no significant difference in the incidence of PCP with atovaquone versus dapsone or versus aerosolised pentamidine, both of which are regarded as effective in people intolerant of TMP/SMX.

### Azithromycin (for PCP)

One RCT has found that azithromycin, either alone or in combination with rifabutin reduces the risk of PCP in people receiving standard PCP prophylaxis compared with rifabutin alone.

### UNKNOWN EFFECTIVENESS

### TMP/SMX (for toxoplasmosis)

One RCT found no significant difference between TMP/SMX and placebo for preventing toxoplasmosis. One systematic review has found no significant difference between TMP/SMX and dapsone (with or without pyrimethamine) for preventing toxoplasmosis.

## What are the effects of antituberculosis prophylaxis in people with HIV infection?

### BENEFICIAL

### Tuberculosis prophylaxis versus placebo (in people with positive tuberculin test)

Systematic reviews have found that in people who are HIV and tuberculin skin test positive, antituberculosis prophylaxis reduces the frequency of tuberculosis compared with placebo over 2–3 years. The reviews found no evidence of benefit in people who are HIV positive but tuberculin skin test negative. One RCT found that the benefit of prophylaxis diminished with time after treatment was stopped. ▶

# HIV: prevention of opportunistic infections

## TRADE OFF BETWEEN BENEFITS AND HARMS

### Isoniazid for 6–12 months (v combination treatment for 2 months — similar benefits, fewer harms)

RCTs found no evidence of a difference in effectiveness between regimens using combinations of tuberculosis drugs for 2–3 months and those using isoniazid alone for 6–12 months. One RCT found that multidrug regimens increased the number of people with adverse reactions resulting in cessation of treatment.

## What are the effects of prophylaxis for disseminated Mycobacterium avium complex (MAC) disease for people without previous MAC disease?

## LIKELY TO BE BENEFICIAL

### Azithromycin

One RCT has found that azithromycin reduces the incidence of MAC compared with placebo.

### Clarithromycin

One RCT has found that clarithromycin reduces the incidence of MAC compared with placebo.

## TRADE OFF BETWEEN BENEFITS AND HARMS

### Combination treatment (rifabutin plus either clarithromycin or azithromycin)

One RCT has found that rifabutin plus clarithromycin or clarithromycin alone reduces the incidence of MAC compared with rifabutin alone. One RCT has found that rifabutin plus azithromycin reduces the incidence of MAC compared with azithromycin alone or rifabutin alone at 1 year. One systematic review and two subsequent RCTs found that toxicity, including uveitis, was more common with combination therapy that with clarithromycin or rifabutin alone.

## What are the effects of prophylaxis for disseminated MAC disease for people with previous MAC disease?

## LIKELY TO BE BENEFICIAL

### Clarithromycin, rifabutin, and ethambutol (v clarithromycin plus clofazimine)

One RCT found that clarithromycin, rifabutin, and ethambutol reduced MAC relapse compared with clarithromycin plus clofazimine.

### Ethambutol added to clarithromycin plus clofazimine

One RCT found that adding ethambutol to clarithromycin and clofazimine reduced MAC relapse compared with clarithromycin plus clofazimine.

## UNKNOWN EFFECTIVENESS

### Rifabutin added to clarithromycin plus ethambutol

One RCT found no significant difference in survival by adding rifabutin to clarithromycin plus ethambutol in people with previous MAC.

◄ **LIKELY TO BE INEFFECTIVE OR HARMFUL**

### Clofazimine added to ethambutol plus clarithromycin (v clofazimine plus ethambutol)

One RCT found that adding clarithromycin to clofazimine and ethambutol was associated with higher mortality compared with clofazimine plus ethambutol.

## What are the effects of prophylaxis for cytomegalovirus (CMV), herpes simplex virus (HSV), and varicella zoster virus (VZV)?

**BENEFICIAL**

### Aciclovir (for HSV and VZV)

One systematic review has found that aciclovir reduces HSV and VZV infection, and reduces overall mortality in people at different clinical stages of HIV infection compared with placebo. It found no reduction in CMV.

**TRADE OFF BETWEEN BENEFITS AND HARMS**

### Oral ganciclovir (in people with severe CD4 depletion)

One RCT has found that oral ganciclovir reduces the incidence of CMV in people with severe CD4 depletion compared with placebo. It found that 25% of people taking ganciclovir developed severe neutropenia. A second RCT found no significant differences between treatments.

**UNKNOWN EFFECTIVENESS**

### Famciclovir (for recurrent HSV)

One small RCT found that famciclovir reduced the rate of viral shedding compared with placebo, but provided insufficient evidence on the effect of famciclovir on HSV recurrence.

**LIKELY TO BE INEFFECTIVE OR HARMFUL**

### Valaciclovir (v aciclovir for CMV)

One RCT has found that valaciclovir compared with aciclovir reduces the incidence of CMV, but may be associated with increased mortality.

## What are the effects of prophylaxis for invasive fungal disease in people without previous fungal disease?

**TRADE OFF BETWEEN BENEFITS AND HARMS**

### Fluconazole or itraconazole

RCTs in people with advanced HIV disease have found that both fluconazole and itraconazole reduce the incidence of invasive fungal infections compared with placebo. One RCT found that fluconazole reduced the incidence of invasive fungal disease and mucocutaneous candidiasis compared with clotrimazole. One RCT found no difference between high and low dose fluconazole.

# HIV: prevention of opportunistic infections

## What are the effects of prophylaxis for invasive fungal disease in people with previous fungal disease?

### LIKELY TO BE BENEFICIAL

**Itraconazole (for *Penicillium marneffei*)**
Two RCTs have found that itraconazole reduces the incidence of relapse of *P marneffei* infection⊙ and candidiasis compared with placebo.

### UNKNOWN EFFECTIVENESS

**Itraconazole (for histoplasmosis)**
We found no RCTs.

### LIKELY TO BE INEFFECTIVE OR HARMFUL

**Itraconazole (v fluconazole for maintenance treatment of cryptococcal meningitis)**
One RCT found that itraconazole increased the risk of relapse of cryptococcal meningitis compared with fluconazole.

## What are the effects of discontinuing prophylaxis against opportunistic pathogens in people on highly active antiretroviral treatment (HAART)?

### LIKELY TO BE BENEFICIAL

**Discontinuing prophylaxis for MAC in people with CD4 > 100/mm³ on highly active antiretroviral treatment (HAART)**
Two RCTs in people taking HAART found that discontinuation of prophylaxis for MAC disease did not increase the incidence of MAC disease.

**Discontinuing prophylaxis for PCP and toxoplasmosis in people with CD4 > 200/mm³ on HAART**
One systematic review of two unblinded RCTs in people taking HAART found that discontinuation of prophylaxis did not increase the incidence of PCP. Two unblinded RCTs found that discontinuation of prophylaxis did not increase the incidence of toxoplasmosis.

### UNKNOWN EFFECTIVENESS

**Discontinuing prophylaxis for CMV in people with CD4 > 100/mm³ on HAART**
We found insufficient evidence on the effects of discontinuation of maintenance treatment for CMV retinitis or other end organ disease in people taking HAART.

**DEFINITION**     Opportunistic infections are intercurrent infections that occur in people infected with HIV. Prophylaxis aims to avoid either the first occurrence of these infections (primary prophylaxis) or their recurrence (secondary prophylaxis, maintenance treatment). This review includes PCP, *Toxoplasma gondii* encephalitis, *Mycobacterium tuberculosis*, MAC disease, CMV disease (most often retinitis), infections from other herpesviruses (HSV and VZV), and invasive fungal disease (*Cryptococcus neoformans*, *Histoplasma capsulatum*, and *P marneffei*).

**INCIDENCE/**     The incidence of opportunistic infections is high in people with immune
**PREVALENCE**    impairment. Data available before the introduction of HAART suggest that, with a CD4 < 250/mm³, the 2 year probability of developing an opportunistic ▶

infection is 40% for PCP, 22% for CMV, 18% for MAC, 6% for toxoplasmosis, and 5% for cryptococcal meningitis.[1] The introduction of HAART has reduced the rate of opportunistic infections. A recent cohort study found that the introduction of HAART decreased the incidence of PCP by 94%, CMV by 82%, and MAC by 64%, as presenting AIDS events. HAART decreased the incidence of events subsequent to the diagnosis of AIDS by 84% for PCP, 82% for CMV, and 97% for MAC.[2]

**AETIOLOGY/ RISK FACTORS**  Opportunistic infections are caused by a wide array of pathogens and result from immune defects induced by HIV. The risk of developing opportunistic infections increases dramatically with progressive impairment of the immune system. Each opportunistic infection has a different threshold of immune impairment, beyond which the risk increases substantially.[1] Opportunistic pathogens may infect the immunocompromised host *de novo*, but usually they are simply reactivations of latent pathogens in such hosts.

**PROGNOSIS**  Prognosis depends on the type of opportunistic infection. Even with treatment they may cause serious morbidity and mortality. Most deaths owing to HIV infection are caused by opportunistic infections.

Please refer to CD-ROM for full text and references.

# *Pneumocystis carinii* pneumonia in people with HIV

Search date November 2003

*Richard Bellamy*

## *What are the effects of treatments for Pneumocystis carinii pneumonia in people infected with HIV? New*

**BENEFICIAL**

**Adjuvant corticosteroids for moderate to severe *Pneumocystis carinii* pneumonia**

One systematic review has found that adjuvant corticosteroids reduce mortality when used early in the treatment of moderate to severe *Pneumocystis carinii* pneumonia (see definition, p 179).

**Atovaquone**

We found no RCTs comparing atovaquone versus placebo or no treatment as the first line treatment for *Pneumocystis carinii* pneumonia in people infected with HIV. One RCT found that atovaquone was less effective than TMP–SMX. One RCT found that atovaquone was equally effective as intravenous pentamidine. Adverse effects requiring termination of treatment occurred less frequently with atovaquone than with TMP–SMX or intravenous pentamidine.

**Clindamycin–primaquine**

RCTs found clindamycin–primaquine to be as effective as TMP–SMX as first line treatment for *Pneumocystis carinii* pneumonia in people effected with HIV, with no significant difference in rates of serious adverse effects.

**Pentamidine (aerosolised)**

We found no RCTs comparing aerosolised pentamidine versus placebo or no treatment as first line treatment for *Pneumocystis carinii* pneumonia in people infected with HIV. Two RCTs found no significant difference in mortality between aerosolised pentamidine and TMP–SMX, but found lower rates of serious adverse effects with aerosolised pentamidine. One RCT found no significant difference in mortality or treatment failure between aerosolised and intravenous pentamidine.

**Pentamidine (intravenous)**

We found no RCTs comparing intravenous pentamidine versus placebo or no treatment as first line treatment for *Pneumocystis carinii* pneumonia in people infected with HIV. Three RCTs found that intravenous pentamidine was as effective as TMP–SMX and found no difference in rates of serious adverse effects. One RCT found no significant difference between intravenous pentemidine and atovqquone caused fewer adverse effects requiring termination of treatment.

**TMP–dapsone (trimethoprim–dapsone)**

We found no RCTs comparing TMP–dapsone versus placebo or no treatment as first line treatment for *Pneumocystis carinii* pneumonia in people infected with HIV. RCTs have found that TMP–dapsone is as effective as TMP–SMX, with similar rates of adverse effects. One RCT found that TMP–dapsone was as effective as clindamycin-primaquine.

**TMP–SMX (trimethoprim–sulfamethoxazole; co–trimoxazole)**

We found no RCTs comparing TMP–SMX versus placebo or no treatment as first line treatment for PCP in people infected with HIV. RCTs have found that TMP–SMX is more effective than atovaquone or aerosolised pentamidine. RCTs have found that TMP–SMX is as effective as clindamycin–primaquine, TMP–dapsone, and intravenous pentamidine. RCTs have found that adverse events requiring termination of treatment are more frequent with TMP–SMX than atovaquone or aerosolised pentamidine.

## UNKNOWN EFFECTIVENESS

### Adjuvant corticosteroids for mild *Pneumocystis carinii* pneumonia
We found insufficient evidence on the effects of adjuvant corticosteroids in the early treatment of mild *Pneumocystis carinii* pneumonia (see definition, below).

### Treatment after failure of first line therapy
We found no systematic review and no RCTs comparing the effectiveness or adverse effects of different treatments following failure of first line therapy for PCP in people infected with HIV. One systematic review of cohort studies suggests that clindamycin–primaquine may be more effective than alternative treatments in this situation.

**DEFINITION**  *Pneumocystis carinii* pneumonia (PCP) is caused by an opportunistic fungal infection in people with impaired immune function. Most cases occur in people infected with HIV, in whom PCP is an AIDS defining illness. The pneumonia is generally classified as **mild** if $P_aO_2$ is greater than 70 mm Hg on room air and the alveolar–arterial oxygen gradient is less than 35 mm Hg. It is generally classified as **moderate/severe** if the $P_aO_2$ is less than 70 mm Hg and/or the alveolar–arterial oxygen gradient is greater than 35 mm Hg. This chapter focuses on the treatment of PCP in adults infected with HIV. Prevention of PCP is covered under HIV: prevention of opportunistic infections, p 173.

**INCIDENCE/ PREVALENCE**  PCP is the commonest AIDS defining illness in developed nations.[1] It is probably also common throughout the developing world, although the prevalence is harder to assess here because of difficulties in making the diagnosis. Prior to the widespread use of prophylaxis it was estimated that up to 80% of people with AIDS would eventually develop PCP.[2] Widespread use of prophylaxis against PCP and of highly active anti-retroviral therapy has dramatically reduced the incidence of this infection (see HIV: prevention of opportunistic infections, p 173).

**AETIOLOGY/ RISK FACTORS**  Risk factors for PCP include HIV infection, primary immune deficiencies, prematurity, cancer, use of immune suppressants following organ transplantation, and prolonged use of high dose corticosteroids. HIV infection is now responsible for the vast majority of cases of PCP. Among adults with HIV infection, those with a CD4 count below 200/mm$^3$ are at highest risk, and the median CD4 count at diagnosis of PCP is around 50 cells/mm$^3$.[3]

**PROGNOSIS**  It is generally believed that without treatment PCP would almost certainly be fatal in a person with AIDS. For ethical reasons, no studies have examined short term prognosis without treatment. People with AIDS and PCP frequently have other serious opportunistic infections, which can adversely affect their prognosis.

Please refer to CD-ROM for full text and references.

# Chickenpox

Search date July 2003

*George Swingler*

## What are the effects of preventive interventions?

### BENEFICIAL

**High dose aciclovir (> 3200 mg/day) in people with HIV infection**

One systematic review has found that high dose aciclovir (at least 3200 mg/day) reduces the risk of clinical chickenpox and reduces all cause mortality over 22 months' treatment compared with placebo.

**Live attenuated vaccine in healthy children**

Two RCTs have found that live attenuated varicella vaccine reduces clinical chickenpox compared with placebo, with no significant increase in adverse effects.

### LIKELY TO BE BENEFICIAL

**Zoster immune globulin versus human serum globulin in healthy children**

One small RCT in children exposed to a sibling with chickenpox found that zoster immune globulin❻ reduced the proportion of exposed children with clinical chickenpox at 20 days compared with human immune serum globulin❻.

### UNKNOWN EFFECTIVENESS

**Aciclovir in people with immunocompromise other than HIV**

We found no RCTs on the effects of aciclovir in people with immunocompromise other than HIV.

**Live attenuated vaccine in healthy adults**

We found no RCTs in healthy adults on the effects of live attenuated varicella vaccine.

**Live attenuated vaccine in immunocompromised people**

We found no RCTs in immunocompromised people on the effects of live attenuated varicella vaccine.

**Zoster immune globulin in immunocompromised adults**

We found no RCTs on the effects of zoster immune globulin in immuno-compromised adults.

**Zoster immune globulin versus varicella zoster immune globulin in immunocompromised children**

One RCT in immunocompromised children exposed to a sibling with chickenpox found no significant difference in clinical chickenpox with zoster immune globulin compared with varicella zoster immune globulin❻ at 12 weeks.

## What are the effects of treatments?

### BENEFICIAL

**Oral aciclovir in healthy people (given < 24 hours of onset of rash)**

Two systematic reviews have found that oral aciclovir compared with placebo reduces the symptoms of chickenpox in healthy people.

▶

Infectious diseases

◀ LIKELY TO BE BENEFICIAL

### Intravenous aciclovir for treatment of chickenpox in children with malignancy

Two RCTs compared intravenous aciclovir versus placebo. One large RCT has found that aciclovir reduces clinical deterioration. The other smaller RCT found no significant difference in clinical deterioration.

UNKNOWN EFFECTIVENESS

### Aciclovir in immunocompromised adults

We found no RCTs on the effects of aciclovir in immunocompromised adults.

### Oral aciclovir in healthy people (given > 24 hours after onset of rash)

One systematic review and one additional RCT have found that oral aciclovir given beyond 24 hours after onset of rash does not significantly reduce the symptoms of chickenpox compared with placebo.

**DEFINITION**   Chickenpox is due to primary infection with varicella zoster virus. In healthy people, it is usually a mild self limiting illness, characterised by low grade fever, malaise, and a generalised, itchy vesicular rash.

**INCIDENCE/**   Chickenpox is extremely contagious. Over 90% of unvaccinated people
**PREVALENCE**   become infected, but infection occurs at different ages in different parts of the world: over 80% of people have been infected by the age of 10 years in the USA, the UK, and Japan, but by 30 years of age in India, South East Asia, and the West Indies.[1,2]

**AETIOLOGY/**   Chickenpox is caused by exposure to varicella zoster virus.
**RISK FACTORS**

**PROGNOSIS**   **Infants and children:** In healthy children the illness is usually mild and self limiting. In the USA, death rates in infants and children (aged 1–14 years) with chickenpox are about 7/100 000 in infants and 1.4/100 000 in children.[3] In Australia, mortality in children aged between 1 and 11 years with chickenpox is about 0.5–0.6/100 000, and in infants with chickenpox it is about 1.2/100 000.[4] Bacterial skin sepsis is the most common complication in children under 5 years of age, and acute cerebellar ataxia is the most common complication in older children; both cause hospital admission in 2–3/10 000 children.[5] **Adults:** Mortality in adults is higher, at about 31/100 000.[3] Varicella pneumonia is the most common complication, causing 20–30 hospital admissions/10 000 adults.[5] Activation of latent varicella zoster virus infection can cause herpes zoster, also known as shingles (see postherpetic neuralgia, p 208). **Cancer chemotherapy:** One case series (77 children with cancer and chickenpox) found that more children receiving chemotherapy versus those in remission developed progressive chickenpox with multiple organ involvement (19/60 [32%] with children receiving chemotherapy v 0/17 [0%] with children in remission) and more children died (4/60 [7%] with children receiving chemotherapy v 0/17 [0%] with children in remission).[6] **HIV infection:** One retrospective case series (45 children with AIDS) found that one in four children with AIDS who acquired chickenpox in hospital developed pneumonia and 5% died.[7] In a retrospective cohort study (73 children with HIV and chickenpox; 83% with symptomatic HIV), infection beyond 2 months occurred in 10 children (14%) and recurrent varicella zoster virus infections occurred in 38 children (55%). There was a strong association between an increasing number of recurrences and low CD4 cell counts.[8] Half of recurrent infections involved generalised rashes and the other half had zoster. **Newborns:** We found no cohort studies of untreated children with perinatal exposure to chickenpox. One cohort study (281 neonates receiving varicella zoster immune globulin ⊙ ▶

# Chickenpox

because their mothers had developed a chickenpox rash during the month before or after delivery) found that 134 (48%) developed a chickenpox rash and 19 (14%) developed severe chickenpox.[9] Severe chickenpox occurred in neonates of mothers whose rash had started during the 7 days before delivery.

Please refer to CD-ROM for full text and references.

Search date November 2002

*Piero Olliaro*

## What are the effects of treating toxoplasmosis in pregnancy?

### UNKNOWN EFFECTIVENESS

### Spiramycin and other antiparasitic drugs

Two systematic reviews of cohort studies in women who seroconvert during pregnancy found insufficient evidence on the effects of current antiparasitic treatment compared with no treatment on mother or baby.

**DEFINITION** Toxoplasmosis is caused by the parasite *Toxoplasma gondii*. Infection is asymptomatic or unremarkable in immunocompetent individuals, but leads to a lifelong antibody response. During pregnancy, toxoplasmosis can be transmitted across the placenta and may cause intrauterine death, neonatal growth retardation, mental retardation, ocular defects, and blindness in later life. Congenital toxoplasmosis (confirmed infection of the fetus or newborn) can present at birth, either as subclinical disease, which may evolve with neurological or ophthalmological disease later in life, or as a disease of varying severity, ranging from mild ocular damage to severe mental retardation.

**INCIDENCE/ PREVALENCE** Reported rates of toxoplasma seroprevalence vary across and within countries, as well as over time. The risk of primary infection is highest in young people, including young women during pregnancy. We found no cohort studies describing annual seroconversion rates in women of childbearing age nor incidence of primary infection. One systematic review (search date 1996) identified 15 studies that reported rates of seroconversion in non-immune pregnant women ranging from 2.4–16/1000 in Europe and from 2–6/1000 in the USA.[1] France began screening for congenital toxoplasmosis in 1978, and during the period 1980–1995 the seroconversion rate during pregnancy in non-immune women was 4–5/1000.[2]

**AETIOLOGY/ RISK FACTORS** Toxoplasma infection is usually acquired by ingesting either sporocysts (from unwashed fruit or vegetables contaminated with cat faeces) or tissue cysts (from raw or undercooked meat). The risk of contracting toxoplasma infection varies with eating habits, contact with cats and other pets, and occupational exposure.

**PROGNOSIS** One systematic review of studies conducted from 1983–1996 found no population based prospective studies of the natural history of toxoplasma infection during pregnancy.[1] One systematic review (search date 1997) reported nine controlled, non-randomised studies, and found that untreated toxoplasmosis acquired during pregnancy was associated with infection rates in children of between 10–100%.[3] We found two European studies that correlated gestation at time of seroconversion with risk of transmission and severity of disease at birth.[4,5] Risk of transmission increased with gestational age at maternal seroconversion, reaching 70–90% for infections acquired after 30 weeks' gestation. In contrast, the risk of the infected infant developing clinical disease was highest when infection occurred early in pregnancy. The highest risk of early signs of disease (including chorioretinitis and hydrocephaly) was about 10%, and occurred with infection between 24 and 30 weeks' gestation.[5] Infants with untreated congenital toxoplasmosis and generalised neurological abnormalities at birth develop mental retardation, growth retardation, blindness ▶

# Congenital toxoplasmosis

or visual defects, seizures, and spasticity. Children with untreated subclinical infection at birth may have cognitive and motor deficits and visual defects or blindness, which may go undiagnosed for many years. One case control study (845 school children in Brazil) found mental retardation and retinochoroiditis to be significantly associated with positive toxoplasma serology (population attributable risk 6–9%).[6]

Please refer to CD-ROM for full text and references.

## What are the effects of supportive treatments for dengue haemorrhagic fever or dengue shock syndrome in children?
New

### LIKELY TO BE BENEFICIAL

**Intravenous fluids**

We found no RCTs comparing intravenous fluids versus placebo or no treatment. It is widely accepted that immediate fluid replacement should be undertaken in a child who has dengue haemorrhagic fever or dengue shock syndrome; it would be considered unethical to test its role in a placebo controlled trial.

### UNKNOWN EFFECTIVENESS

**Colloids**

Two RCTs found no significant difference in mortality between crystalloids and colloids for acute resuscitation in Vietnamese children with dengue shock syndrome, but they are likely to have been underpowered to detect a clinically important difference.

**Adding corticosteroids to standard intravenous fluids**

Two RCTs in Thai and Indonesian children with dengue shock syndrome found no significant difference in mortality between adding corticosteroids to standard fluid replacement and placebo. One open label RCT in Burmese children with dengue shock syndrome found that hydrocorticosone reduced mortality compared with other fluid replacements. An unpublished review of these RCTs and two uncontrolled studies found no significant difference between adding corticosteroids to standard intravenous fluids and standard intravenous fluids alone.

**Adding intravenous immune globulin to standard intravenous fluids**

We found no published RCTs on the effects of intravenous immune globulin in people with dengue haemorrhagic fever or dengue shock syndrome. One unpublished RCT in Filipino children with dengue shock syndrome found that intravenous immunoglobulin reduced mortality compared with placebo.

**DEFINITION**     Dengue infection is a mosquito borne arboviral infection. The spectrum of dengue virus infection ranges from asymptomatic or undifferentiated febrile illness to dengue fever and dengue haemorrhagic fever or dengue shock syndrome. An important epidemiologic criterion to consider in the diagnosis of dengue infection is history of travel or residence in a dengue endemic area within 2 weeks of onset of fever. Dengue fever is an acute febrile illness whose clinical presentation varies with age. Infants and young children may have an undifferentiated febrile disease with maculopapular rash. Children aged 15 years and older and adults may have either a mild febrile illness or the classic incapacitating disease also called "breakbone fever" presenting with high fever of sudden onset and non-specific signs and symptoms of severe headache; pain behind the eyes; muscle, bone, or joint pains; nausea; vomiting; and rash. Dengue haemorrhagic fever is characterised by four criteria: acute onset of high fever; haemorrhagic manifestations evidenced by positive tourniquet**ⓖ** test, skin haemorrhages, mucosal, and gastrointestinal tract bleeding; thrombocytopenia; and evidence of plasma leakage manifested by a rise or drop in haematocrit, fluid in the lungs or abdomen, or ▶

# Dengue fever

hypoproteinaemia. Dengue haemorrhagic fever is classified into four grades of severity❶.[1] Presence of thrombocytopenia and haemoconcentration differentiates dengue haemorrhagic fever grades I and II from dengue fever. Grades III and IV dengue haemorrhagic fever are considered dengue shock syndrome.[1] Plasma leakage is the major pathophysiological feature observed in dengue haemorrhagic fever.

**INCIDENCE/ PREVALENCE**
Dengue fever and dengue haemorrhagic fever are public health problems worldwide, particularly in low lying areas where *Aedes aegypti*, a domestic mosquito, is present. Cities near to the equator but high in the Andes are free of dengue because the *Aedes* mosquitoes do not survive at high altitudes. Worldwide an estimated 50–100 million cases of dengue fever and hundreds of thousands of dengue haemorrhagic fever occur yearly.[2] Endemic regions are the Americas, South East Asia, western Pacific, Africa, and the eastern Mediterranean. Major global demographic changes, particularly increases in the density and geographic distribution of the vector, with declining vector control; unreliable water supply systems; increasing non-biodegradable container and poor solid waste disposal; increased geographic range of virus transmission owing to increased air travel; and increased population density in urban areas are responsible for the resurgence of dengue in the last century.[3,4] The World Health Organization estimates that global temperature rises of 1.0–3.5 °C can increase transmission by shortening the extrinsic incubation period of viruses within the mosquito, adding 20 000–30 000 more fatal cases annually.[5]

**AETIOLOGY/ RISK FACTORS**
Dengue virus serotypes 1–4 (DEN 1, 2, 3, 4) belonging to the flavivirus genus are the main aetiologic agents. These serotypes are closely related but antigenically distinct and they provide specific lifetime immunity. *A aegypti*, the principal vector, transmits the virus to man. Dengue haemorrhagic fever and dengue shock syndrome typically occur in children under the age of 15 years, although dengue fever primarily occurs in adults and older children. Important risk factors influencing the proportion of people who will develop dengue haemorrhagic fever or severe disease during epidemics include the virus strain and serotype, immune status of the host, and age and genetic predisposition. There is evidence that sequential infection or pre-existing antidengue antibodies increases the risk of dengue haemorrhagic fever through antibody dependent enhancement.[3,4,6–8]

**PROGNOSIS**
Dengue fever is an incapacitating disease but prognosis is favourable in previously healthy adults, although dengue haemorrhagic fever and dengue shock syndrome are major causes of hospital admission and mortality in children. Dengue fever is generally self limiting, with less than 1% case fatality. The acute phase of the illness lasts for 2–7 days but the convalescent phase may be prolonged for weeks associated with fatigue and depression, especially in adults. Prognosis in dengue haemorrhagic fever and dengue shock syndrome depends on prevention or early recognition and treatment of shock. Case fatality ranges from 2.5% to 5.0%. Once shock sets in, fatality may be as high as 12–44%.[9] In centres with appropriate intensive supportive treatment, fatality can be less than 1%. There is no specific antiviral treatment. The standard of treatment is to give intravenous fluids to expand the plasma volume. People usually recover after prompt and adequate fluid and electrolyte supportive treatment. The optimal fluid regimen, however, remains unsettled. This is particularly important in dengue, wherein one of the management difficulties is to correct hypovolaemia rapidly without precipitating fluid overload.

Please refer to CD-ROM for full text and references.

## What are the effects of treatments?

### BENEFICIAL

**Amino acid oral rehydration solution (ORS) in severe diarrhoea**

One small RCT found that amino acid ORS reduced the total volume and duration of diarrhoea compared with ORS🅖.

**ORS in severe diarrhoea\***

ORS has not been compared in RCTs versus no treatment or intravenous rehydration. One small RCT found no difference in duration or volume of diarrhoea between intravenous rehydration and rehydration through a nasogastric tube, after both groups had received initial intravenous fluids.

**Rice based ORS in severe diarrhoea**

One systematic review has found that rice based ORS reduces the 24 hour stool volume compared with standard ORS.

\*Categorisation based on medical consensus.

### UNKNOWN EFFECTIVENESS

**Bicarbonate ORS in severe diarrhoea**

Two RCTs found no significant difference in the duration or volume of diarrhoea with bicarbonate ORS compared with standard ORS. One RCT found no significant difference in total stool output or duration of diarrhoea with bicarbonate ORS compared with an otherwise identical ORS in which the bicarbonate was replaced with chloride.

**Reduced osmolarity ORS in severe diarrhoea**

Three RCTs comparing reduced osmolarity ORS versus standard ORS found a small and inconsistent effect on total volume of stool and duration of diarrhoea.

### TRADE OFF BETWEEN BENEFITS AND HARMS

**Antibiotics used empirically in community acquired diarrhoea**

RCTs have found that ciprofloxacin reduces the duration of community acquired diarrhoea by 1–2 days compared with placebo. RCTs found limited evidence that other antibiotics reduced duration of diarrhoea compared with placebo. Adverse effects varied by agent.

**Antibiotics used empirically in travellers' diarrhoea**

One systematic review and one additional RCT have found that empirical use of antibiotics increases cure rate at 3 and 6 days compared with placebo. Gastrointestinal symptoms (cramps, nausea, and anorexia), dermatological symptoms (rash), and respiratory symptoms (cough and sore throat) were reported with all antibiotics. Antibiotic treatment is associated in some people with prolonged presence of bacterial pathogens in the stool and development of resistant strains.

**Antimotility agents in acute diarrhoea**

RCTs have found that, in people with acute diarrhoea, loperamide hydrochloride and loperamide oxide reduce the time to relief of symptoms, but frequently cause constipation compared with placebo. We found insufficient evidence about the effects of other antimotility agents.

▶

# Diarrhoea in adults (acute)

**DEFINITION**   Diarrhoea is watery or liquid stools, usually with an increase in stool weight above 200 g daily and an increase in daily stool frequency. This chapter covers empirical treatment of suspected infectious diarrhoea in adults.

**INCIDENCE/**   An estimated 4000 million cases of diarrhoea occurred worldwide in 1996,
**PREVALENCE**   resulting in 2.5 million deaths.[1] In the USA, the estimated incidence for infectious intestinal disease is 0.44 episodes per person a year (1 episode per person every 2.3 years), resulting in about one consultation with a doctor per person every 28 years.[2] A recent community study in the UK reported an incidence of 19 cases per 100 person years, of which 3.3 cases per 100 person years resulted in consultation with a general practitioner.[3] Both estimates derive from population based studies including both adults and children. The epidemiology of travellers' diarrhoea (in people who have crossed a national boundary) is not well understood. Incidence is higher in travellers visiting developing countries, but it varies widely by location and season of travel.[4]

**AETIOLOGY/**   The cause of diarrhoea depends on geographical location, standards of food
**RISK FACTORS**  hygiene, sanitation, water supply, and season. Commonly identified causes of sporadic diarrhoea in adults in developed countries include *Campylobacter*, *Salmonella*, *Shigella*, *Escherichia coli*, *Yersinia*, protozoa, and viruses. No pathogens are identified in more than half of people with diarrhoea. In returning travellers, about 50% of episodes are caused by bacteria such as enterotoxigenic *E coli*, *Salmonella*, *Shigella*, *Campylobacter*, *Vibrio*, enteroadherent *E coli*, *Yersinia*, and *Aeromonas*.[5]

**PROGNOSIS**   In developing countries, diarrhoea is reported to cause more deaths in children under 5 years of age than any other condition.[1] Few studies have examined which factors predict poor outcome in adults. In developed countries, death from infectious diarrhoea is rare, although serious complications, including severe dehydration and renal failure, can occur and may necessitate admission to hospital. Elderly people and those in long term care have an increased risk of death.[6]

---

Please refer to CD-ROM for full text and references.

## What are the effects of immunisation in countries with high endemicity?

### BENEFICIAL

**Selective immunisation of high risk individuals (evidence only for children born to HBsAg positive mothers)**

One non-systematic review of mainly observational studies with both plasma derived and recombinant vaccine, and three RCTs of plasma derived hepatitis B immunisation all found that immunisation prevented chronic carrier state compared with placebo or no treatment in children born to HBsAg⊖ positive mothers. One RCT found minor adverse events with immunisation; the other RCTs did not report on adverse events. We found no good evidence in other high risk groups. One cluster RCT found that selective immunisation in high risk individuals was less effective than universal immunisation of infants in preventing chronic carrier state and acute hepatitis events.

**Universal immunisation of infants (limited evidence that it may be better than selective immunisation of high risk individuals)**

One non-systematic review and four additional and subsequent RCTs provided evidence that universal (both recombinant and plasma derived) hepatitis B immunisation in infants in countries with high endemicity⊖, compared with placebo, reduces acute hepatitis and development of a chronic carrier state⊖ for at least 15 years. Observational studies and one RCT found only minor adverse reactions after recombinant hepatitis B immunisation. One cluster RCT found universal immunisation with first plasma and then recombinant vaccine⊖ reduced the development of chronic carrier state and acute hepatitis events compared with immunisation of high risk groups.

## What are the effects of immunisation in countries with low endemicity?

### LIKELY TO BE BENEFICIAL

**Selective immunisation of high risk individuals**

One systematic review found that, in countries with low endemicity⊖, plasma derived hepatitis B immunisation prevented acute hepatitis B and development of chronic carrier state in healthcare workers at high risk of exposure to bodily fluids. Three RCTs found that plasma derived hepatitis B immunisation prevented acute hepatitis B in homosexual men. One small RCT found no significant difference in hepatitis B events in heterosexual partners of infected people. Three RCTs of plasma derived immunisation in people on regular haemodialysis found potentially conflicting results. Two RCTs from France and Belgium found good protective efficacy⊖ against chronic carrier state. However, one large US based RCT found no good evidence of benefit. The systematic review of plasma derived vaccination found no significant difference between immunisation and placebo in the rate and severity of adverse events. One observational study showed a high prevalence of hepatitis B carrier state and low immunisation uptake in young homosexuals despite a national strategy to immunise high risk groups. Surveillance data from a national programme in Japan found that immunisation of neonates (with recombinant hepatitis B vaccine plus hepatitis B immunoglobulin [HBIG]) born to HBsAg ▶

# Hepatitis B (prevention)

positive mothers provided 95% protection against the development of a chronic carrier state. We found insufficient evidence to compare the effectiveness of selective immunisation in high risk individuals with other strategies.

## Universal immunisation of infants

One historical cohort study found a reduction in the prevalence of hepatitis B chronic carrier state after universal immunisation. We found insufficient evidence to compare its effectiveness with other strategies. Two cohort studies and surveillance data did not report any links between hepatitis B immunisation and serious adverse events.

### UNKNOWN EFFECTIVENESS

## Comparative effectiveness of different strategies

We found no systematic reviews, RCTs, or observational studies comparing the effectiveness of different immunisation strategies in countries with low endemicity.

## Universal immunisation of adolescents

We found insufficient evidence to assess the effects of universal adolescent immunisation, or to compare its effectiveness with other strategies. One observational study suggests minor adverse effects after hepatitis B immunisation in this group.

**DEFINITION** Hepatitis B is a viral infectious disease with an incubation period of 40–160 days. Acute hepatitis B infection is characterised by anorexia, vague abdominal discomfort, nausea and vomiting, jaundice, and occasional fever. Illness is associated with deranged liver function tests (especially raised alanine transaminases) and presence of serological markers of acute hepatitis B infection (e.g. hepatitis B surface antigen [HBsAg], antiHBc IgM).[1]

**INCIDENCE/ PREVALENCE** The incidence of acute hepatitis B and prevalence of its chronic carrier state varies widely across the globe. In areas with high endemicity (HBsAg prevalence ≥ 8%, e.g. South East Asia and Africa), more than half of the population becomes infected at some point in their lives.[2] In countries with low endemicity (HBsAg prevalence < 2%, e.g. North America, western Europe, Australia), most of the population do not become infected.[2] Nearly a third of the world population has been infected by hepatitis B at some point, and at least 350 million people (5–6% of world population) are currently chronic carriers of hepatitis B infection.[3]

**AETIOLOGY/ RISK FACTORS** In countries with high endemicity, most infections occur during childhood from an infected mother to her baby (vertical transmission) or from one family member to another (horizontal transmission).[4] Horizontal transmission is thought to be an important route of hepatitis B infection during early childhood, and probably occurs mainly through unnoticed contact with blood from infected family members.[5] In countries with high endemicity, the proportion of chronic HBsAg carriage attributable to vertical transmission has been estimated at 5–50%.[6–8] The proportion of chronic HBsAg carriage attributable to horizontal transmission is not known, although one survey in China found that 27.2% of families had one or more HBsAg positive members.[8] In developed countries, most hepatitis B infection occurs later, from sexual activity, injection drug use, or occupational exposure. Less frequent causes of infection include household contact, regular haemodialysis, transmission from a healthcare professional, and receipt of organs or blood products.[9] The vaccination policy of a country is a large determinant of the risk of developing hepatitis B. Since the development of plasma derived hepatitis B vaccine in the early 1980s, subsequently replaced by recombinant vaccine, many countries have adopted a policy of universal immunisation of all infants. On the basis of disease burden, the World Health Organization recommended that hepatitis B vaccine be incorporated into routine infant and childhood immunisation programmes in countries with ▶

high endemicity by 1995 and in all countries by 1997.[10] However, in many countries with low endemicity, universal immunisation policy remains controversial and has still not been adopted.[11] Some of these countries have adopted a policy of selective immunisation of high risk individuals. Others have adopted a universal adolescent immunisation policy.

**PROGNOSIS**  Hepatitis B infection resolves after the acute infection in 90–95% of cases. In the remainder (5–10%), it may result in several serious sequelae. Massive hepatic necrosis occurs in 1% of people with acute viral hepatitis, leading to a serious and often fatal condition called acute fulminant hepatitis. Between 2% and 10% of those infected as adults become chronic carriers, indicated by HBsAg persistence for more than 6 months. Chronic carriage is more frequent in those infected as children, and reaches up to 90% in those infected during the perinatal period.[1] Between 20% and 25% of chronic carriers develop a progressive chronic liver disease. In about one quarter to one third of cases, this progresses to cirrhosis and hepatocellular carcinoma.[12] These complications usually arise in older adults and are major causes of mortality in populations with high hepatitis B endemicity.[4] Observational studies suggest that in these countries almost 80% of chronic liver disease and cirrhosis is attributed to hepatitis B, and these complications lead to at least 1 million deaths every year worldwide.

Please refer to CD-ROM for full text and references.

# Influenza

Search date November 2002

*Lucy Hansen*

## What are the effects of antiviral treatment of influenza in adults?

### LIKELY TO BE BENEFICIAL

**Oral amantadine for early treatment of influenza A in adults (duration of symptoms reduced)**

One systematic review and three additional RCTs have found that oral amantadine reduces the duration of influenza A symptoms by about 1 day compared with placebo. We found insufficient evidence about adverse effects in this setting. We found no good evidence of benefit if amantadine is started more than 2 days after symptom onset.

**Orally inhaled zanamivir for early treatment of influenza A and B in adults (duration of symptoms reduced)**

One systematic review has found that orally inhaled zanamivir reduces the duration of influenza symptoms by about 1 day compared with placebo. Adverse effects were similar in people taking zanamivir and in people taking placebo. We found no good evidence of benefit if zanamivir is started more than 2 days after symptom onset.

**Oral oseltamivir for early treatment of influenza A and B in adults (duration of symptoms reduced)**

Two RCTs have found that oral oseltamivir reduces the duration of influenza symptoms by about 1 day compared with placebo. Oral oseltamivir increases the incidence of nausea and vomiting compared with placebo. We found no good evidence of benefit if oseltamivir is started more than 1.5 days after symptom onset.

**Oral rimantadine for early treatment of influenza A in adults (duration of symptoms reduced)**

One systematic review has found that oral rimantadine reduces the duration of influenza A symptoms by about 1 day compared with placebo. We found insufficient evidence about adverse effects in this setting. We found no good evidence of benefit if rimantadine is started more than 2 days after symptom onset.

### UNKNOWN EFFECTIVENESS

**All antivirals (reduction of serious influenza complications)**

We found insufficient evidence about the effects of antiviral agents on reducing serious complications of influenza.

**DEFINITION** Influenza is caused by infection with influenza viruses. Uncomplicated influenza is characterised by the abrupt onset of fever, chills, non-productive cough, myalgias, headache, nasal congestion, sore throat, and fatigue.[1] Influenza is usually diagnosed clinically. Not all people infected with influenza viruses become symptomatic. People infected with other pathogens may have symptoms identical to those of influenza.[2] The percentage of infections resulting in clinical illness can vary from about 40–85%, depending on age ▶

and pre-existing immunity to the virus.[3] Influenza can be confirmed by viral culture, immunofluorescence staining, enzyme immunoassay, or rapid diagnostic testing of nasopharyngeal, nasal or throat swab specimens, or by serological testing of paired sera. Some rapid tests detect influenza A only, some detect and distinguish between influenza A and B, whereas others detect but do not distinguish between influenza A and B.

**INCIDENCE/** In temperate areas of the northern hemisphere, influenza activity typically
**PREVALENCE** peaks between late December and early March, whereas in temperate areas of the southern hemisphere influenza activity typically peaks between May and September. In tropical areas, influenza can occur throughout the year.[2] The annual incidence of influenza varies yearly, and depends partly on the underlying level of population immunity to circulating influenza viruses.[1] One localised study in the USA found that serological conversion with or without symptoms occurred in 10–20% a year, with the highest infection rates in people aged under 20 years.[4] Attack rates are higher in institutions and in areas of overcrowding.[5]

**AETIOLOGY/** Influenza viruses are transmitted primarily from person to person through
**RISK FACTORS** respiratory droplets disseminated during sneezing, coughing, and talking.[1,6]

**PROGNOSIS** The incubation period of influenza is 1–4 days and infected adults are usually contagious from the day before symptom onset until 5 days after symptom onset. The signs and symptoms of uncomplicated influenza usually resolve within a week, although cough and fatigue may persist.[1] Complications include otitis media, bacterial sinusitis, secondary bacterial pneumonia, and, less commonly, viral pneumonia and respiratory failure. Complications are also caused by exacerbation of underlying disease.[1,2] In the USA each year, over 110 000 admissions to hospital and about 20 000 deaths are related to influenza.[2] The risk of hospitalisation is highest in people 65 years or older, in very young children, and in those with chronic medical conditions.[1,7,8] Over 90% of influenza related deaths during recent seasonal epidemics in the USA have been in people 65 years or older.[1] During influenza pandemics, morbidity and mortality may be high in younger age groups.[1] Severe illness is more common with influenza A infections than with influenza B infections.[1]

Please refer to CD-ROM for full text and references.

# Leprosy

Search date March 2003

*Diana Lockwood*

## What are the effects of preventive interventions?

### Bacillus Calmette Guerin (BCG) vaccine

One RCT evaluated four different vaccines and found that the largest effect was with ICRC vaccine and BCG plus killed *M leprae*, followed by BCG alone. The effectiveness of *Mycobacterium w* was only marginal. However, only for the BCG vaccine alone were the findings corroborated by large controlled clinical trials with long term follow up. Only one RCT reported on harms of vaccination; it found these to be minimal.

### BCG plus killed *Mycobacterium leprae*

One RCT evaluated four different vaccines and found that the largest effect was with ICRC vaccine and BCG plus killed *M leprae*, followed by BCG alone. The effectiveness of *Mycobacterium w* was only marginal. However, only for the BCG vaccine alone were the findings corroborated by large controlled clinical trials with long term follow up. Only one RCT reported on harms of vaccination; it found these to be minimal.

### ICRC vaccine

One RCT evaluated four different vaccines and found that the largest effect was with ICRC vaccine and BCG plus killed *M leprae*, followed by BCG alone. The effectiveness of *Mycobacterium w* was only marginal. However, only for the BCG vaccine alone were the findings corroborated by large controlled clinical trials with long term follow up. Only one RCT reported on harms of vaccination; it found these to be minimal.

### *Mycobacterium w* vaccine

One RCT evaluated four different vaccines and found that the largest effect was with ICRC vaccine and BCG plus killed *M leprae*, followed by BCG alone. The effectiveness of *Mycobacterium w* was only marginal. Only one RCT reported on harms of vaccination; it found these to be minimal.

## What are the effects of treatments?

### Multidrug treatment for multibacillary leprosy*

We found no reliable comparisons between multidrug treatment with rifampicin plus clofazimine plus dapsone versus dapsone alone, or versus dapsone plus rifampicin, in people with multibacillary leprosy. Observational studies found that multidrug treatment improved skin lesions and was associated with a low relapse rate. The evidence on the incidence of adverse effects is poor. Multidrug treatment was not compared with dapsone alone because rising dapsone resistance rates meant that it would have been unethical to do such a study. The same applies for multidrug treatment for paucibacillary leprosy below.

◀ **Multidrug treatment for paucibacillary leprosy***

We found no reliable comparison between multidrug treatment with rifampicin plus clofazimine plus dapsone versus dapsone alone, or against dapsone plus rifampicin, in people with multibacillary leprosy🄶. Observational studies found that multidrug treatment improved skin lesions and was associated with a low relapse rate. We found poor evidence on the incidence of adverse effects.

**Multiple dose versus single dose treatment for single lesion leprosy (both increase cure rates but multiple more than single dose)**

One RCT found that multiple dose treatment with rifampicin monthly plus dapsone daily for 6 months achieved higher cure rates at 18 months than single dose treatment with rifampicin plus minocycline plus ofloxacin. Some improvement occurred in 99% of people in both groups. Adverse effects were similar with both regimens.

*Observational evidence only, RCTs unlikely to be conducted.

**DEFINITION**  Leprosy is a chronic granulomatous disease caused by *Mycobacterium leprae*, primarily affecting the peripheral nerves and skin. The clinical outcome of infection is determined by the individual's immune response to *M leprae*. At the tuberculoid end of the Ridley–Jopling scale, individuals have good cell mediated immunity and few skin lesions. At the lepromatous end of the scale, individuals have good cell mediated immunity, causing uncontrolled bacterial spread and skin and mucosal infiltration. Peripheral nerve damage occurs across the spectrum. Nerve damage may occur before, during or, after treatment. Some patients have no nerve damage, others develop anaesthesia of the hands and feet, which puts them at risk of developing neuropathic injury. Weakness and paralysis of the small muscles of the hands, feet, and eyes puts patients at risk of developing deformity and contractures. Loss of the fingers and toes is due to repeated injury in a weak, anaesthetic limb. These visible deformities cause stigmatisation the world over. Classification is based on the clinical appearance and bacterial index of lesions🄶. The World Health Organization field classification🄶 is based on the number of skin lesions: single lesion leprosy🄶 (1 lesion), paucibacillary leprosy🄶 (2–5 skin lesions), and multibacillary leprosy🄶 (> 5 skin lesions).[1]

**INCIDENCE/**  Worldwide, about 720 000 new cases of leprosy are reported each year,[2] and
**PREVALENCE**  about 2 million people have leprosy related disabilities. Six major endemic countries (India, Brazil, Myanmar, Madagascar, Nepal, and Mozambique) account for 88% of all new cases. Cohort studies show a peak of disease presentation between 10–20 years of age.[3] After puberty there are twice as many male as female cases.

**AETIOLOGY/**  *M leprae* is discharged from the nasal mucosa of people with untreated
**RISK FACTORS**  lepromatous leprosy, and transmitted through the nasal mucosa with subsequent spread of mycobacteria to skin and nerves. It is a hardy organism and has been shown to survive in the Indian environment for many months.[4] Risk factors include household contact with a person with leprosy. We found no good evidence of a relationship between HIV infection, nutrition, and socioeconomic status.[5]

**PROGNOSIS**  Complications of leprosy include nerve damage, immunological reactions, and bacillary infiltration. Without treatment, tuberculoid infection eventually resolves spontaneously. Most people with borderline tuberculoid and borderline lepromatous leprosy gradually develop lepromatous infection. Many people have peripheral nerve damage at the time of diagnosis, ranging from 15% in Bangladesh to 55% in Ethiopia. Immunological reactions can occur with or without antibiotic treatment. Further nerve damage occurs through immune ▶

mediated reactions and neuritis🕒. Erythema nodosum leprosum🕒 is an immune complex mediated reaction causing fever, malaise, and neuritis, which is reported to occur in 20% of people with lepromatous leprosy and 15% with borderline lepromatous leprosy.[8] Secondary impairments (wounds, contractures, and digit resorption) occur in 33–56% of people with established nerve damage.[9] We found no recent information on mortality.

Please refer to CD-ROM for full text and references.

## What are the effects of preventive interventions and treatments?

### BENEFICIAL

**Lyme disease vaccine in people exposed to North American strains of *Borrelia burgdorferi***

One RCT has found that, compared with placebo, three doses of a vaccine (consisting of recombinant outer surface protein A [Osp–A] of *B burgdorferi* combined with adjuvant⊙) reduces the incidence of Lyme disease in immunocompetent people aged 15–70 years in Lyme disease endemic areas of North America.

**Prophylactic antibiotics after *Ixodes scapularis* tick bites in Lyme disease endemic areas in North America**

One systematic review in people with recognised *I scapularis* tick bites in the preceding 72 hours found that antibiotics reduced the risk of developing clinical Lyme disease compared with placebo, but the difference was not significant. One subsequent large RCT in people who had removed an attached *I scapularis* tick in the preceding 72 hours found that doxycycline reduced the proportion of people with erythema migrans at the site of the tick bite compared with placebo.

### LIKELY TO BE BENEFICIAL

**\*Cefotaxime (more effective than penicillin for late neurological Lyme disease)**

One RCT found weak evidence from a small subgroup analysis of people with late Lyme disease that cefotaxime improved symptoms of neuropathy compared with penicillin.

**\*Cefotaxime (more effective than penicillin for Lyme arthritis)**

One RCT found weak evidence from a small subgroup analysis of people with Lyme arthritis that cefotaxime increased the proportion of people with full recovery compared with penicillin.

**\*Ceftriaxone (more effective than penicillin for Lyme arthritis)**

One RCT found weak evidence from a small subgroup analysis of people with Lyme arthritis that ceftriaxone improved symptoms compared with penicillin.

**Doxycycline (as effective as amoxicillin plus probenecid for Lyme arthritis)**

One RCT in people with Lyme arthritis found no significant difference between doxycycline and amoxicillin plus probenecid in resolution of Lyme arthritis.

**Penicillin (better than placebo for Lyme arthritis)**

One RCT in people with Lyme arthritis has found that penicillin increases resolution of Lyme arthritis compared with placebo.

\*Based on subgroup analysis of RCTs.

### UNKNOWN EFFECTIVENESS

**Ceftriaxone (in late neurological Lyme disease)**

One RCT found insufficient evidence from a small subgroup analysis in people with late neurological Lyme disease about effects of ceftriaxone and cefotaxime.

# Lyme disease

### ◄ Lyme disease vaccine in Europe or Asia

We found no RCTs about the effects of recombinant outer surface protein A (Osp–A) vaccine in European or Asian populations. There is heterogeneity of the species that cause Lyme disease in Europe and Asia. The vaccine may not be as effective in European or Asian populations as it is in North American populations.

## LIKELY TO BE INEFFECTIVE OR HARMFUL

### Ceftriaxone plus doxycycline (in people with late neurological Lyme disease who had been previously treated)

One RCT comparing ceftriaxone plus doxycycline versus placebo in people with previously treated Lyme disease and persistent neurological symptoms found no significant difference in health related quality of life at interim analysis at 180 days; therefore the RCT was terminated.

**DEFINITION**  Lyme disease is an inflammatory illness resulting from infection with spirochetes of the *B burgdorferi* genospecies transmitted to humans by ticks. Some infected people have no symptoms. The characteristic manifestation of early Lyme disease is erythema migrans: a circular rash at the site of the infectious tick attachment that expands over a period of days to weeks in 80–90% of people with Lyme disease. Early disseminated infection may cause secondary erythema migrans, disease of the nervous system (facial palsy or other cranial neuropathies, meningitis, and radiculoneuritis), musculoskeletal disease (arthralgia), and, rarely, cardiac disease (myocarditis or transient atrioventricular block). Untreated or inadequately treated Lyme disease can cause late disseminated manifestations weeks to months after infection. These late manifestations include arthritis, polyneuropathy, and encephalopathy. Diagnosis of Lyme disease is based primarily on clinical findings and a high likelihood of exposure to infected ticks. Serological testing may be helpful in people with endemic exposure who have clinical findings consistent with later stage disseminated Lyme disease.

**INCIDENCE/ PREVALENCE**  Lyme disease occurs in temperate regions of North America, Europe, and Asia. It is the most commonly reported vector borne disease in the USA, with over 16 000 cases reported a year.[1] Most cases occur in the north-eastern and north-central states, with a reported annual incidence in endemic states as high as 67.9/100 000 people.[1] In highly endemic communities, the incidence of Lyme disease may exceed 1000/100 000 people a year.[2] In some countries of Europe, the incidence of Lyme disease has been estimated to be over 100/100 000 people a year.[3] Foci of Lyme disease have been described in northern forested regions of Russia, in China, and in Japan.[4] Transmission cycles of *B burgdorferi* have not been described in tropical areas or in the southern hemisphere.[4]

**AETIOLOGY/ RISK FACTORS**  Lyme disease is caused by infection with any of the *B burgdorferi* sensu lato genospecies. Virtually all cases of Lyme disease in North America are the result of infection with *B burgdorferi*. In Europe, Lyme disease may be caused by *B burgdorferi*, *B garinii*, or *B afzelii*. The infectious spirochetes are transmitted to humans through the bite of certain *Ixodes* ticks.[4] Humans who have frequent or prolonged exposure to the habitats of infected *Ixodes* ticks are at highest risk of acquiring Lyme disease. Individual risk depends on the likelihood of being bitten by infected tick vectors, which varies with the density of vector ticks in the environment, the prevalence of infection in ticks, and the extent of a person's contact with infected ticks. The risk of Lyme disease is often concentrated in focal areas. In the USA, risk is highest in certain counties within north-eastern and north-central states during the months of April to July.[2] People become infected when they engage in activities in wooded or bushy areas that are favourable habitats for ticks, and deer and rodent hosts.

▶

◀ **PROGNOSIS**   Lyme disease is rarely fatal. Untreated Lyme arthritis resolves at a rate of 10–20% a year; over 90% of facial palsies due to Lyme disease resolve spontaneously, and most cases of Lyme carditis resolve without sequelae.[5] However, untreated Lyme disease can result in arthritis (50% of untreated people), meningitis or neuropathies (15% of untreated people), carditis (5–10% of untreated people with erythema migrans), and, rarely, encephalopathy.

Please refer to CD-ROM for full text and references.

# Malaria: prevention in travellers

**Search date September 2003**

*Ashley M Croft*

---

## What are the effects of treatments?

### BENEFICIAL

**Insecticide treated nets**

We found no RCTs in travellers. One systematic review in adult and child residents of malaria endemic settings found that insecticide treated nets reduced the number of mild episodes of malaria and reduce child mortality.

### LIKELY TO BE BENEFICIAL

**Atovaquone plus proguanil in adults**

One RCT in migrants with limited immunity found that atovaquone plus proguanil reduced the proportion of people with malaria compared with placebo. One RCT found no significant difference between atovaquone plus proguanil and chloroquine plus proguanil in preventing malaria. One RCT of atovaquone plus proguanil versus mefloquine found no cases of clinical malaria throughout the trial, but found a higher rate of neuropsychiatric harm with mefloquine compared with atovaquone plus proguanil.

**Doxycycline in adults**

One RCT in soldiers and one RCT in migrants with limited immunity found that doxycycline reduced the risk of malaria compared with placebo. One of the RCTs found that doxycycline was associated with nausea and vomiting, diarrhoea, cough, headache, and unspecified dermatological symptoms over 13 weeks. We found no evidence on long term safety.

**Insecticide treated clothing in adults**

Two RCTs in soldiers and refugee householders found that permethrin treated fabric (clothing or sheets) reduced the incidence of malaria.

### TRADE OFF BETWEEN BENEFITS AND HARMS

**Mefloquine in adults**

One systematic review of one RCT in soldiers found that, compared with placebo, mefloquine had 100% protective efficacy. One RCT of mefloquine versus atovaquone plus proguanil found no cases of clinical malaria throughout the trial, but found a higher rate of neuropsychiatric harm with mefloquine compared with atovaquone plus proguanil.

### UNKNOWN EFFECTIVENESS

**Aerosol insecticides in adults**

We found no RCTs on the effects of aerosol insecticides in preventing malaria in travellers. One large questionnaire survey in travellers found insufficient evidence on the effects of aerosol insecticides in preventing malaria. Two community RCTs in residents of malaria endemic areas found that indoor spraying of aerosol insecticides reduced clinical malaria.

**Air conditioning and electric fans in adults**

We found no RCTs on the effects of air conditioning or electric fans in preventing malaria in travellers. One large questionnaire survey found that air conditioning reduced the incidence of malaria. One small observational study found that electric ceiling fans reduced total catches of culicine mosquitos in indoor spaces but did not significantly reduce total catches of anopheline mosquitoes.

▶

### Chloroquine in adults

We found no RCTs on the effects of chloroquine in travellers. One RCT in Austrian workers residing in Nigeria found no significant difference between chloroquine and sulfadoxine plus pyrimethamine in the incidence of malaria after 6–22 months. *Plasmodium falciparum* resistance to chloroquine is now established in most malaria endemic regions of the world.

### Chloroquine plus proguanil in adults

One RCT found no significant difference between chloroquine plus proguanil and chloroquine plus sulfadoxine plus pyrimethamine in the incidence of *P falciparum* malaria. One RCT found no significant difference between chloroquine plus proguanil and proguanil alone in the incidence of *P falciparum* malaria. One RCT found no significant difference between chloroquine plus proguanil and atovaquone plus proguanil in preventing malaria.

### Full length clothing in adults

We found no RCTs on the effects of full length clothing in preventing malaria in travellers. One large questionnaire survey in travellers found that wearing trousers and long sleeved shirts reduced the incidence of malaria.

### Insecticide treated nets in pregnant travellers

We found no RCTs on the effects of insecticide treated nets in preventing malaria in pregnant travellers. One RCT of pregnant long term residents of a malaria endemic area found insufficient evidence on the effects of permethrin treated nets in preventing malaria.

### Mosquito coils and vaporising mats in adults

We found no RCTs on the effects of coils and vaporising mats in preventing malaria in travellers. One RCT of coils and one observational study of pyrethroid vaporising mats found that these devices reduced numbers of culicine mosquitoes in indoor spaces.

### Pyrimethamine plus dapsone in adults

We found no RCTs in travellers. One RCT in Thai soldiers found insufficient evidence to compare pyrimethamine plus dapsone versus proguanil plus dapsone. We found limited observational evidence that pyrimethamine plus dapsone may cause agranulocytosis.

### Smoke

We found no RCTs on the effects of smoke in preventing malaria. One controlled clinical trial found that smoke repelled mosquitoes during the evening.

### Topical (skin applied) insect repellents in adults

We found no RCTs on the effects of topical (skin applied) insect repellents in preventing malaria in travellers. One small crossover RCT found that diethyltoluamide (DEET) preparations protected against mosquito bites. DEET has been reported to cause systemic and skin adverse reactions, particularly with prolonged use.

### Vaccines

We found no RCTs in travellers. One systematic review of antimalaria vaccines in residents of malaria endemic areas has found that the SPf66 vaccine reduces first attacks of malaria compared with placebo.

# Malaria: prevention in travellers

**Antimalaria drugs in airline pilots and aircrew; antimalaria drugs in pregnant travellers; biological control measures; insect electrocuters and ultrasonic buzzers; insecticide treated clothing in pregnant travellers; mefloquine in children; topical (skin applied) insect repellents in pregnant travellers**

We found no RCTs on the effects of these interventions.

## LIKELY TO BE INEFFECTIVE OR HARMFUL

### Amodiaquine in adults

We found no RCTs on the effects of amodiaquine in preventing malaria in travellers. We found limited observational evidence that amodiaquine may cause neutropenia, liver damage, and hepatitis.

### Sulfadoxine plus pyrimethamine in adults

One RCT found no significant difference between chloroquine plus proguanil and chloroquine plus sulfadoxine plus pyrimethamine in the incidence of *P falciparum* malaria. One retrospective observational study suggested that sulfadoxine plus pyrimethamine was associated with severe cutaneous reactions.

### Topical (skin applied) insect repellents containing DEET in children

We found no RCTs on the effects of DEET in preventing malaria in child travellers. Case reports in young children found serious adverse effects with DEET.

**DEFINITION**    Malaria is caused by a protozoan infection of red blood cells with one of four species of the genus *Plasmodium*: *P falciparum*, *P vivax*, *P ovale*, and *P malariae*.[1] Clinically, malaria may present in different ways but it is usually characterised by fever (which may be swinging), tachycardia, rigors, and sweating. Anaemia, hepatosplenomegaly, cerebral involvement, renal failure, and shock may occur; see chapter on malaria: severe, life treatening, p 204.[2,3] Travellers are defined here as visitors from a malaria free area to a malaria endemic area, and who stay in the endemic area for less than 1 year. This definition includes refugees and migrants.

**INCIDENCE/**    Each year there are 300–500 million clinical cases of malaria. About 40% of
**PREVALENCE**    the world's population is at risk of acquiring the disease.[2,3] Each year 25–30 million people from non-tropical countries visit malaria endemic areas, of whom 10 000–30 000 contract malaria.[4,5] Most RCTs of malaria prevention in travellers have been conducted in soldiers and travellers. The results of these trials may not be applicable to people such as refugees and migrants, who are likely to differ in their health status and in their susceptibility to disease and adverse drug effects.

**AETIOLOGY/**    Malaria is mainly a rural disease, requiring nearby standing water. It is trans-
**RISK FACTORS**    mitted by bites of infected female anopheline mosquitoes, mainly at dusk and during the night.[1,6–8] In cities, mosquito bites are usually from female culicine mosquitoes, which are not vectors of malaria.[9] Malaria is resurgent in most tropical countries and risk to travellers is increasing.[10] The sickle cell trait has been shown to convey some protection against malaria in non-immune carriers of that trait. Non-immune adults with the sickle cell trait who develop severe malaria have lower parasite densities, fewer complications (e.g. cerebral malaria), and a reduced mortality compared with adults without the trait.[11] There is little good evidence on the degree of protection afforded by the sickle cell trait.[12]

**PROGNOSIS**   Ninety per cent of tourists and business travellers who contract malaria do not become ill until after they return home.[5] "Imported malaria" is easily treated if diagnosed promptly, and follows a serious course in only about 12% of people.[13,14] The most severe form is cerebral malaria, with a case fatality rate in adult travellers of 2–6%, mainly because of delays in diagnosis.[3,15]

Please refer to CD-ROM for full text and references.

Infectious diseases

# Malaria: severe, life threatening

**Search date June 2003**

*Aika Omari and Paul Garner*

## What are the effects of antimalarial treatments for complicated falciparum malaria in non-pregnant people?

### LIKELY TO BE BENEFICIAL

**Artemether (as effective as quinine)**

Two systematic reviews and three subsequent RCTs found no significant difference in death rates between artemether and quinine in people with severe malaria.

**High initial dose quinine**

One systematic review (3 small RCTs) and one additional RCT found no significant difference in mortality between quinine regimens with high initial quinine dose and those with no loading dose. The systematic review found that high initial dose quinine reduced parasite and fever clearance times❻ compared with no loading dose.

**Quinine***

We found no RCTs comparing quinine versus either placebo or no treatment, but international consensus recommends quinine for the treatment of severe falciparum malaria.

**Rectal artemisinin**

One systematic review found no significant difference in mortality between rectal artemisinin and quinine in people with severe malaria.

*Based on consensus. RCTs would be considered unethical.

### UNKNOWN EFFECTIVENESS

**Intramuscular versus intravenous quinine**

One RCT in children found no significant difference between intramuscular and intravenous quinine in recovery times or death. However, the study may have lacked power to detect clinically important differences between treatments.

## What are the effects of adjunctive treatment for complicated falciparum malaria in non-pregnant people?

### UNKNOWN EFFECTIVENESS

**Desferrioxamine mesylate**

One systematic review found weak evidence that the risk of persistent seizures in children with cerebral malaria was reduced with desferrioxamine mesylate compared with placebo.

**Exchange blood transfusion**

One systematic review found no suitable RCTs. A systematic review of case control studies found no significant difference in mortality between exchange transfusion plus antimalarial drugs and antimalarial drugs alone.

**Initial blood transfusion**

One systematic review found no significant difference in mortality between initial and expectant blood transfusion among clinically stable children with malarial ▶

Infectious diseases

anaemia, but found that adverse events were more common with initial blood transfusion. We found no RCTs examining the effects of transfusion in adults with malaria.

## LIKELY TO BE INEFFECTIVE OR HARMFUL

**Dexamethasone**

One systematic review found no significant difference in mortality between dexamethasone and placebo, but gastrointestinal bleeding and seizures were more common with dexamethasone.

**DEFINITION**
Severe malaria is caused by protozoan infection of red blood cells with *Plasmodium falciparum* and comprises a variety of syndromes, which require hospitalisation. Clinically complicated malaria presents with life threatening conditions, which include coma, severe anaemia, renal failure, respiratory distress syndrome, hypoglycaemia, shock, spontaneous haemorrhage, and convulsions. The diagnosis of cerebral malaria should be considered where there is encephalopathy in the presence of malaria parasites. A strict definition of cerebral malaria requires the presence of unrousable coma, and no other cause of encephalopathy (e.g. hypoglycaemia, sedative drugs), in the presence of *P. falciparum* infection.[1] This review does not currently cover the treatment of malaria in pregnancy.

**INCIDENCE/ PREVALENCE**
Malaria is a major health problem in the tropics with 300–500 million clinical cases occurring annually, and an estimated 1.1–2.7 million deaths each year as a result of severe malaria.[2] Over 90% of deaths occur in children under 5 years of age, mainly from cerebral malaria and anaemia.[2] In areas where the rate of malaria transmission is stable (endemic), those most at risk of acquiring severe malaria are children under 5 years old, because adults and older children have partial immunity that offers some protection. In areas where the rate of malaria transmission is unstable (non-endemic), severe malaria affects both adults and children. Non-immune travellers and migrants are also at risk of developing severe malaria.

**AETIOLOGY/ RISK FACTORS**
Malaria is transmitted by the bite of infected female anopheline mosquitoes. Certain genes are associated with resistance to severe malaria. The human leukocyte antigens HLA-Bw53 and HLA-DRB1*1302 protect against severe malaria. However, the associations of HLA antigens with severe malaria are limited to specific populations.[3,4] Haemoglobin S[3] and haemoglobin C[5] are also protective against severe malaria. Genes, such as the tumour necrosis factor gene have also been associated with increased susceptibility to severe malaria (see aetiology under malaria: prevention in travellers, p 204).[6]

**PROGNOSIS**
In children under 5 years of age with cerebral malaria, the estimated case fatality of treated malaria is 19%, although reported hospital case fatality may be as high as 40%.[1,7] Neurological sequelae persisting for more than 6 months occur in more than 2% of survivors, and include ataxia, hemiplegia, speech disorders, behavioural disorders, epilepsy, and blindness. Severe malarial anaemia has a case fatality rate higher than 13%.[7] In adults the mortality of cerebral malaria is 20%; this rises to 50% in pregnancy, and neurological sequelae occur in about 3% of survivors.[8]

Please refer to CD-ROM for full text and references.

# Meningococcal disease

**Search date March 2003**

*Jailson B Correia and C A Hart*

*Infectious diseases*

---

## What are the effects of treatments?

### Antibiotics for throat carriage (reduce carriage but unknown effect on risk of disease)

RCTs have found that antibiotics reduce throat carriage of meningococci compared with placebo. We found no evidence that eradicating throat carriage reduces the risk of meningococcal disease.

### Pre-admission parenteral penicillin in suspected cases

We found no RCTs on the effects of pre-admission antibiotics in suspected cases❻. It is unlikely that RCTs will be performed because of the unpredictably rapid course of meningococcal disease in some people, the likely risks involved in delaying treatment, and the low risk of causing harm. Most observational studies suggest benefit with antibiotics, but at least one did not.

### Prophylactic antibiotics in contacts

We found no RCTs on the effects of prophylactic antibiotics on the incidence of meningococcal disease among contacts❻. RCTs are unlikely to be performed because the intervention has few associated risks whereas meningococcal disease has high associated risks. Observational evidence suggests that antibiotics reduce the risk of meningococcal disease. We found no evidence regarding which contacts should be treated.

**DEFINITION**  Meningococcal disease is any clinical condition caused by *Neisseria meningitidis* (the meningococcus) groups A, B, C, W135, or other serogroups. These conditions include purulent conjunctivitis, septic arthritis, meningitis❻, and septicaemia❻ with or without meningitis.

**INCIDENCE/ PREVALENCE**  Meningococcal disease is sporadic in temperate countries, and is most commonly caused by group B or C meningococci. Annual incidence in Europe varies from fewer than 1 case/100 000 people in France, up to 4–5 cases/100 000 people in the UK and Spain, and in the USA it is 0.6–1.5/ 100 000 people.[1,2] Occasional outbreaks occur among close family contacts❻, secondary school pupils, military recruits, and students living in halls of residence. Sub-Saharan Africa has regular epidemics in countries lying in the expanded "meningitis belt", reaching 500/100 000 people during epidemics, which are usually due to serogroup A, although recent outbreaks of serogroup W135 cause concern.[3–5]

**AETIOLOGY/ RISK FACTORS**  The meningococcus colonises and infects healthy people and is transmitted by close contact, probably by exchange of upper respiratory tract secretions❶.[6–14] Risk of transmission is greatest during the first week of contact.[9] Risk factors include crowding and exposure to cigarette smoke.[15] In the UK, children younger than 2 years have the highest incidence, with a second peak between ages 15–24 years. There is currently an increased incidence of meningococcal disease among university students, especially among those in their first term and living in catered accommodation,[16] although we found no accurate numerical estimate of risk from close contact in, for example, halls of residence. Close contacts of an index case have a much higher risk of infection than do people in the general population.[9,12,13] The risk of epidemic spread is higher with groups A and C meningococci than with group B ▶

meningococci.[6-8,10] It is not known what makes a meningococcus virulent. Certain clones tend to predominate at different times and in different groups. Carriage of meningococcus in the throat has been reported in 10–15% of people; recent acquisition of a virulent meningococcus is more likely to be associated with invasive disease.

**PROGNOSIS**  Mortality is highest in infants and adolescents, and is related to disease presentation and availability of therapeutic resources. In developed countries case fatality rates have been around 19–25% for septicaemia, 10–12% for meningitis plus septicaemia, and less than 1% in meningitis alone, but an overall reduction in mortality was observed in recent years in people admitted to paediatric intensive care units.[17-21]

Please refer to CD-ROM for full text and references.

# Postherpetic neuralgia

Search date May 2003

David Wareham

*Infectious diseases*

## What are the effects of interventions to prevent postherpetic neuralgia?

### LIKELY TO BE BENEFICIAL

**Aciclovir, famciclovir, valaciclovir, netivudine**
One systematic review has found limited evidence from RCTs that aciclovir given for 7–10 days reduced pain at 1–3 months. One systematic review has found that famciclovir reduces mean pain duration after acute herpes zoster compared with placebo. One RCT found that valaciclovir reduced the prevalence of postherpetic neuralgia at 6 months compared with aciclovir. One RCT found no significant difference in effectiveness between netivudine and aciclovir. One RCT found no significant difference between valaciclovir and famciclovir in the resolution of postherpetic neuralgia or in adverse effects over 7 days.

### UNKNOWN EFFECTIVENESS

**Amitriptyline**
One small RCT found no significant difference between amitriptyline and placebo started within 48 hours of rash onset in the prevalence of postherpetic neuralgia at 6 months. The RCT may have lacked power to detect a clinically important difference.

**Adenosine phosphate; amantadine; cimetidine; inosine pranobex; levodopa**
RCTs found insufficient evidence on the effects of these interventions.

### UNLIKELY TO BE BENEFICIAL

**Topical antiviral agents (idoxuridine) for pain at 6 months**
One systematic review has found that idoxuridine increases short term pain relief in acute herpes zoster compared with placebo or oral aciclovir, but found no significant difference at 6 months.

### LIKELY TO BE INEFFECTIVE OR HARMFUL

**Corticosteroids**
Systematic reviews found conflicting evidence from RCTs about the effects of corticosteroids alone on postherpetic neuralgia. We found insufficient evidence from two RCTs about effects of high dose steroids plus antiviral agents. There is concern that corticosteroids may cause dissemination of herpes zoster.

## What are the effects of treatments in established postherpetic neuralgia?

### BENEFICIAL

**Gabapentin**
One systematic review has found that gabapentin reduces pain at 8 weeks compared with placebo.

**Tricyclic antidepressants**
One systematic review has found that tricyclic antidepressants increase pain relief in postherpetic neuralgia after 2–6 weeks compared with placebo.

## TRADE OFF BETWEEN BENEFITS AND HARMS

### Oral opioids (oxycodone, morphine, methadone)

We found no RCTs examining effects of morphine or methadone in people with postherpetic neuralgia. One small RCT found that oral oxycodone reduced pain after 4 weeks compared with placebo, but was associated with more adverse effects.

### Topical counterirritants

Two systematic reviews and one small subsequent RCT found limited evidence that the topical counterirritant, capsaicin, improved pain relief in postherpetic neuralgia compared with placebo, but found that capsaicin may cause painful skin reactions.

## UNKNOWN EFFECTIVENESS

### Topical anaesthesia

We found insufficient evidence from three RCTs about the effects of lidocaine (lignocaine).

### Tramadol

One small RCT found that tramadol reduced pain more than clomipramine after 6 weeks. However, we were unable to draw reliable conclusions from this small study.

## LIKELY TO BE INEFFECTIVE OR HARMFUL

### Dextromethorphan

One systematic review and one subsequent RCT found no evidence that dextromethorphan was more effective than placebo or lorazepam after 3–6 weeks, but found that dextromethorphan was associated with sedation and ataxia at high doses.

### Epidural morphine

One small RCT found that epidural morphine reduced pain by more than 50% compared with placebo but the reduction was not maintained beyond 36 hours. Epidural morphine caused intolerable opioid effects in 75% of people.

**DEFINITION**     Postherpetic neuralgia is pain that sometimes follows resolution of acute herpes zoster and healing of the zoster rash. It can be severe, accompanied by itching, and follows the distribution of the original infection. Herpes zoster is an acute infection caused by activation of latent varicella zoster virus (human herpes virus 3) in people who have been rendered partially immune by a previous attack of chickenpox. Herpes zoster infects the sensory ganglia and their areas of innervation. It is characterised by pain along the distribution of the affected nerve, and crops of clustered vesicles over the area.

**INCIDENCE/**     In a UK general practice survey of 3600–3800 people, the annual incidence
**PREVALENCE**     of herpes zoster was 3.4/1000.[1] Incidence varied with age. Herpes zoster was relatively uncommon in people under the age of 50 years (< 2/1000 a year), but rose to 5–7/1000 a year in people aged 50–79 years, and 11/1000 in people aged 80 years or older. In a population based study of 590 cases in Rochester, Minnesota, USA, the overall incidence was lower (1.5/1000) but there were similar increases in incidence with age.[2] Prevalence of postherpetic neuralgia depends on when it is measured after acute infection. There is no agreed time point for diagnosis.

**AETIOLOGY/**     The main risk factor for postherpetic neuralgia is increasing age. In a UK general
**RISK FACTORS** practice study (involving 3600–3800 people, 321 cases of acute herpes zoster) there was little risk in those under the age of 50 years, but postherpetic ▶

# Postherpetic neuralgia

neuralgia developed in over 20% of people who had had acute herpes zoster aged 60–65 years and in 34% aged over 80 years.[1] No other risk factor has been found to predict consistently which people with herpes zoster will experience continued pain. In a general practice study in Iceland (421 people followed for up to 7 years after an initial episode of herpes zoster), the risk of postherpetic neuralgia was 1.8% (95% CI 0.6% to 4.2%) for people under 60 years of age and the pain was mild in all cases.[2] The risk of severe pain after 3 months in people aged over 60 years was 1.7% (95% CI 0% to 6.2%).

**PROGNOSIS** About 2% of people with acute herpes zoster in the UK general practice survey had pain for more than 5 years.[1] Prevalence of pain falls as time elapses after the initial episode. Among 183 people aged over 60 years in the placebo arm of a UK trial, the prevalence of pain was 61% at 1 month, 24% at 3 months, and 13% at 6 months after acute infection.[3] In a more recent RCT, the prevalence of postherpetic pain in the placebo arm at 6 months was 35% in 72 people over 60 years of age.[4]

Please refer to CD-ROM for full text and references.

Search date August 2003

*Paul Garner, Alison Holmes, and Lilia Ziganshina*

## What are the effects of interventions to prevent tuberculosis in high risk people without HIV infection? New

### TRADE OFF BETWEEN BENEFITS AND HARMS

**Isoniazid**
One systematic review, in people without HIV infection at high risk of tuberculosis, found that, without isoniazid prophylaxis for 6–12 months reduced the risk of active tuberculosis or extra-pulmonary tuberculosis compared with placebo. It also found that a short 6 month course was as effective as a 12 month course. One large RCT found that treatment with isoniazid significantly increased the risk of hepatotoxicity compared with placebo.

## What are the effects of different drug regimens in newly diagnosed pulmonary tuberculosis?

### BENEFICIAL

**Short course chemotherapy (as good as longer courses)**
One RCT found that a 6 month regimen of rifampicin plus isoniazid improved relapse rate compared with isoniazid alone. One RCT found no evidence of a difference in relapse rates between short course regimens containing isoniazid (6 months) and longer term (8–9 months) chemotherapy in people with pulmonary tuberculosis. Three RCTs suggested that treatment with pyrazinamide speeds up sputum clearance after 2 months and improves risk of relapse compared with treatment without pyrazinamide.

### LIKELY TO BE BENEFICIAL

**Intermittent short course chemotherapy (as good as daily treatment)**
Two RCTs in people with newly diagnosed tuberculosis found no significant difference in cure rates between daily and two or three times weekly short course chemotherapy regimens. However, the RCTs may have lacked power to exclude a clinically important difference.

**Pyrazinamide**
RCTs found that, in people with newly diagnosed tuberculosis, chemotherapy regimens containing pyrazinamide speed up sputum clearance in the first 2 months compared with other regimens, but have found limited evidence about effects on relapse rates.

### UNKNOWN EFFECTIVENESS

**Regimens containing quinolones**
We found insufficient evidence about effects of chemotherapy regimens containing quinolones.

### LIKELY TO BE INEFFECTIVE OR HARMFUL

**Chemotherapy for less than 6 months**
One systematic review found limited evidence that reducing duration of treatment to less than 6 months significantly increased relapse rates compared with 12 months treatment.

▶

### What are the effects of different drug regimens in multidrug resistant tuberculosis?

UNKNOWN EFFECTIVENESS

**Comparative benefits of different regimens in multidrug resistant tuberculosis**

We found no RCTs comparing different drug regimens for multidrug resistant tuberculosis in people with newly diagnosed tuberculosis.

### What are the effects of low level laser therapy in people with tuberculosis? New

UNKNOWN EFFECTIVENESS

**Laser therapy**

One systematic review found insufficient evidence about effects of low level laser therapy in people with tuberculosis.

### What are the effects of interventions to improve adherence and screening attendance?

LIKELY TO BE BENEFICIAL

**Cash incentives**

One systematic review has found that cash incentives improve attendance among people living in deprived circumstances compared with usual care. One subsequent RCT found that cash incentives improved treatment completion in intravenous drug users. Another subsequent RCT found no significant difference in treatment completion with immediate compared with deferred cash incentives.

**Community health advisors**

One RCT found that consultation with health advisors recruited from the community significantly increased the rate of treatment attendance compared with no consultation.

**Defaulter actions**

RCTs have found that intensive action (repeated home visits and reminder letters) significantly improves completion of treatment compared with routine action (single reminder letter and home visit) for defaulters⊙.

**Health education by a nurse**

One RCT found that health education by a nurse improved treatment completion compared with provision of an educational leaflet.

UNKNOWN EFFECTIVENESS

**Direct observation treatment**

One systematic review found no significant difference in cure rates between any direct observation treatment compared with self treatment. One large RCT, which allowed participants to choose their therapy supervisor, found that direct observation therapy significantly improved both cure rates and cure plus treatment completion rate combined, compared with self treatment. However co-intervention factors may have contributed to better treatment adherence in this study.

◀ **Prompts and contracts to improve reattendance for Mantoux test reading**

One RCT in healthy people found that telephone prompts to return for Mantoux test reading slightly increased the number of people who reattended compared with no prompts, but the difference was not significant. One RCT found that healthy people were more likely to reattend for Mantoux test reading after providing either a verbal or written commitment compared with no such commitment.

**Health education by a doctor; prompts to adhere to treatment; sanctions for non-adherence; staff training**

We found insufficient evidence on the effects of these interventions.

**DEFINITION**   Tuberculosis is caused by *Mycobacterium tuberculosis* and can affect many organs. Specific symptoms relate to site of infection and are generally accompanied by fever, sweats, and weight loss.

**INCIDENCE/**   About a third of the world's population is infected with *M tuberculosis*. The
**PREVALENCE**   organism kills more people than any other infectious agent. The World Health Organization estimates that 95% of cases are in developing countries, and that 25% of avoidable deaths in developing countries are caused by tuberculosis.[1]

**AETIOLOGY/**   Social factors include poverty, overcrowding, homelessness, and inadequate
**RISK FACTORS** health services. Medical factors include HIV and immunosuppression.

**PROGNOSIS**   Prognosis varies widely and depends on treatment.[2]

---

Please refer to CD-ROM for full text and references.

# Acute renal failure

Search date August 2003

*John A Kellum, Martine Leblanc, and Ramesh Venkataraman*

---

## *What are the effects of interventions to prevent acute renal failure in people at high risk?*

### Low osmolality contrast media (better than standard)

One systematic review found that low osmolality contrast media⊙ reduced nephrotoxicity in people with underlying renal failure needing contrast investigation compared with standard osmolality contrast media. One subsequent RCT found that non-ionic iso-osmolar contrast medium⊙ (iodixanol) reduced contrast media induced nephropathy compared with low osmolar non-ionic contrast medium (iohexol) in people with diabetes.

### Acetylcysteine

One systematic review found that N-acetylcysteine plus hydration reduced contrast induced renal failure compared with hydration alone in people with chronic renal insufficiency who were undergoing contrast nephrography.

### Fluids

One RCT of people undergoing non-emergency cardiac catheterisation found that intravenous saline hydration reduced acute renal failure compared with unrestricted fluids 48 hours after catheterisation. One RCT found that hydration with 0.9% sodium chloride infusion reduced radiocontrast induced nephropathy compared with 0.45% sodium chloride. This effect was greater in women, people with diabetes, and individuals who received more than 250 mL of contrast. One RCT found inconclusive evidence on the effects of inpatient hydration regimens compared with outpatient hydration regimens.

### Single dose aminoglycosides (as effective as multiple doses for treating infection, but with reduced nephrotoxicity)

One systematic review and one additional RCT compared single and multiple doses of aminoglycosides and found different results for nephrotoxicity. The systematic review, in people with fever and neutropenia receiving antibiotic therapy including aminoglycosides, found no significant differences in cure rates or nephrotoxicity between once daily compared with three times daily administration of the aminoglycoside. The RCT however, found that single doses of aminoglycosides significantly reduced nephrotoxicity compared with multiple doses in people with fever and receiving antibiotic therapy including an aminoglycoside.

### Lipid formulations of amphotericin B (better than standard formulations)

We found no RCTs. Lipid formulations⊙ of amphotericin B seem to cause less nephrotoxicity compared with standard formulations, but direct comparisons of long term safety are lacking.

### Fenoldopam

We found limited evidence from three small RCTs suggesting that fenoldopam may be of some benefit in maintaining renal perfusion and creatinine clearance, but found no evidence that it is effective in the prevention of acute renal failure. Fenoldopam may induce hypotension.

▶

◀ **Mannitol**

Small RCTs in people with traumatic rhabdomyolysis, or in people who had undergone coronary artery bypass, vascular, or biliary tract surgery, found that mannitol plus hydration did not reduce acute renal failure compared with hydration alone. One RCT found that mannitol increased the risk of acute renal failure compared with 0.45% sodium chloride infusion, but the difference was not significant.

**Theophylline in acute renal failure induced by contrast media**

One RCT found that in people with adequate intravenous hydration who required radiocontrast investigations, theophylline did not prevent radiocontrast induced nephropathy compared with placebo. One RCT also found that theophylline did not prevent acute renal failure after coronary artery bypass surgery compared with hydration alone.

## LIKELY TO BE INEFFECTIVE OR HARMFUL

**Calcium channel blockers for early allograft dysfunction**

One RCT found no significant difference between isradipine and placebo in preventing early allograft dysfunction❻ in renal transplantation. We found no RCTs assessing the effects of calcium channel blockers in preventing other forms of acute renal failure. Calcium channel blockers are associated with hypotension and bradycardia.

**Dopamine**

Two systematic reviews and one subsequent RCT found no significant difference between dopamine and placebo in the development of acute renal failure, the need for dialysis, or death. One RCT found insufficient evidence on the effects of combined dopamine and diltiazem in people undergoing cardiac surgery. Dopamine is associated with serious adverse effects, such as extravasation necrosis, gangrene, and conduction abnormalities.

**Loop diuretics**

One systematic review has found that loop diuretics plus fluids are not effective and may be harmful in preventing acute renal failure compared with fluids alone in people at high risk of acute renal failure. Two RCTs found that diuretics seem to worsen outcome in acute tubular necrosis induced by contrast media and after cardiac surgery compared with 0.9% sodium chloride infusion.

**Natriuretic peptides**

One large RCT found no significant difference in the prevention of acute renal failure induced by contrast media between natriuretic peptides and placebo. Subgroup analysis in another RCT found that atrial natriuretic peptide reduced dialysis free survival in non-oliguric people compared with placebo.

---

## *What are the effects of treatments in critically ill people with acute renal failure?*

## LIKELY TO BE BENEFICIAL

**High dose continuous renal replacement therapy (better than low dose)**

One RCT has found that high dose continuous renal replacement therapy (haemo-filtration) significantly reduces mortality compared with standard dose continuous therapy. A small prospective study found that intensive (daily) intermittent haemo-dialysis reduced mortality in people with acute renal failure compared with conventional alternate day haemodialysis. A subsequent small three arm RCT ▶

# Acute renal failure

found no significant difference in survival at 28 days between early, low dose haemofiltration; early, high dose haemofiltration; and late, low dose haemofiltration.

## UNKNOWN EFFECTIVENESS

### Continuous renal replacement therapy (compared with intermittent renal replacement therapy)

One systematic review found insufficient evidence to compare continuous versus intermittent renal replacement therapy in mortality, renal death, or dialysis dependence in critically ill adults with acute renal failure.

### Synthetic dialysis membranes (compared with cellulose based membranes)

Two systematic reviews found insufficient evidence on the effects of synthetic based membranes on mortality in critically ill people with acute renal failure compared with cellulose based Ⓖ membranes.

### Combined diuretics and albumin; continuous infusion of loop diuretics (compared with bolus injection)

We found insufficient evidence on the effects of these interventions.

## UNLIKELY TO BE BENEFICIAL

### Loop diuretics

One systematic review has found that loop diuretics plus fluids are not effective and may be harmful in preventing acute renal failure compared with fluids alone in people at high risk of acute renal failure. Two RCTs found that diuretics seem to worsen outcome in acute tubular necrosis induced by contrast media and after cardiac surgery compared with 0.9% sodium chloride infusion.

## LIKELY TO BE INEFFECTIVE OR HARMFUL

### Dopamine

One systematic review found no significant difference in mortality or need for dialysis between dopamine and control. One additional RCT found that low dose dopamine did not reduce renal dysfunction compared with placebo. Dopamine has been associated with important adverse effects, including extravasation necrosis, gangrene, tachycardia, and conduction abnormalities.

### Natriuretic peptides

RCTs found no significant difference between atrial natriuretic peptide, ularitide (urodilatin), and placebo in dialysis free survival in oliguric and non-oliguric people with acute renal failure. One of the RCTs found that atrial natriuretic peptide may reduce survival in non-oliguric people.

**DEFINITION**  Acute renal failure is characterised by abrupt and sustained decline in glomerular filtration rate Ⓖ,[1] which leads to accumulation of urea and other chemicals in the blood. There is no clear consensus on a biochemical definition,[2] but most studies define it as a serum creatinine of 2–3 mg/dL (200–250 µmol/L), an elevation of more than 0.5 mg/dL (45 µmol/L) over a baseline creatinine below 2 mg/dL (170 µmol/L), or a twofold increase of baseline creatinine. A recent international, interdisciplinary, consensus panel has classified acute renal failure according to a change from baseline serum creatinine or urine output. The three level classification begins with "Risk", defined by either a 50% increase in serum creatinine or a urine output of less than 0.5 mL/kg/hour for at least 6 hours, and concludes with "Failure", ▶

defined by a threefold increase in serum creatinine or a urine output of less than 0.3 mL/kg/hour for 24 hours.[3] Acute renal failure is usually additionally classified according to the location of the predominant primary pathology (prerenal, intrarenal, and postrenal failure). Critically ill people are unstable and at imminent risk of death, which usually implies that they need to be in, or have been admitted to, the intensive care unit.

**INCIDENCE/**
**PREVALENCE**
Two prospective observational studies (2576 people) have found that established acute renal failure affects nearly 5% of people in hospital and as many as 15% of critically ill people, depending on the definitions used.[4,5]

**AETIOLOGY/**
**RISK FACTORS**
**General risk factors:** Risk factors for acute renal failure that are consistent across multiple causes include hypovolaemia; hypotension; sepsis; pre-existing renal, hepatic, or cardiac dysfunction; diabetes mellitus; and exposure to nephrotoxins (e.g. aminoglycosides, amphotericin, immunosuppressive agents, non-steroidal anti-inflammatory drugs, angiotensin converting enzyme inhibitors, iv contrast media)❶. **Risk factors/aetiology in critically ill people:** Isolated episodes of acute renal failure are rarely seen in critically ill people, but are usually part of multiple organ dysfunction syndromes❻. Acute renal failure requiring dialysis is rarely seen in isolation (< 5% of people). The kidneys are often the first organs to fail.[6] In the perioperative setting, acute renal failure risk factors include prolonged aortic clamping, emergency rather than elective surgery, and use of higher volumes (> 100 mL) of intravenous contrast media. One study (3695 people) using multiple logistic regression identified the following independent risk factors: baseline creatinine clearance below 47 mL/minute (OR 1.20, 95% CI 1.12 to 1.30); diabetes (OR 5.5, 95% CI 1.4 to 21.0), and a marginal effect for doses of contrast media above 100 mL (OR 1.01, 95% CI 1.00 to 1.01). Mortality of people with acute renal failure requiring dialysis was 36% during hospitalisation.[7] Prerenal acute renal failure is caused by reduced blood flow to the kidney from renal artery disease, systematic hypotension, or maldistribution of blood flow. Intrarenal acute renal failure is caused by parenchymal injury (acute tubular necrosis, interstitial nephritis, embolic disease, glomerulonephritis, vasculitis, or small vessel disease). Postrenal acute renal failure is caused by urinary tract obstruction. Observational studies (in several hundred people from Europe, North America, and west Africa with acute renal failure) found a prerenal cause in 40–80%, an intrarenal cause in 10–50%, and a postrenal cause in the remaining 10%.[8-13] Prerenal acute renal failure is the most common type of acute renal failure in people who are critically ill,[8,14] but acute renal failure in this context is usually part of multisystem failure, and most frequently because of acute tubular necrosis resulting from ischaemic or nephrotoxic injury, or both.[15,16]

**PROGNOSIS**
One retrospective study (1347 people with acute renal failure) found that mortality was less than 15% in people with isolated acute renal failure.[17] One recent prospective study (> 700 people) found that, in people with acute renal failure, overall mortality and the need for dialysis were higher in an intensive care unit (ICU) than in a non-ICU setting, despite no significant difference between the groups in mean maximal serum creatinine (need for dialysis 71% in ICU v 18% in non-ICU; P < 0.001; mortality 72% in the ICU v 32% in non-ICU settings; P = 0.001).[18] One large study (> 17 000 people admitted to Austrian ICUs) found that acute renal failure was associated with a greater than fourfold increase in mortality.[19] Even after controlling for underlying severity of illness, mortality was still significantly higher in people with acute renal failure (62.8% v 38.5%), suggesting that acute renal failure is independently responsible for increased mortality, even if dialysis is used. However, the exact mechanism that leads to increased risk of death is uncertain.

Please refer to CD-ROM for full text and references.

# Benign prostatic hyperplasia

Search date July 2003

*Robyn Webber*

## What are the effects of treatments?

### BENEFICIAL

#### α Blockers

Systematic reviews have found that α blockers improve lower urinary tract symptom scores compared with placebo. Systematic reviews found limited evidence that different α blockers have similar effects. RCTs found limited evidence that α blockers improved symptom scores compared with the 5α reductase inhibitor finasteride. One RCT found no significant difference between tamsulosin and saw palmetto plant extracts in symptom scores or maximum flow rate after 1 year. Another RCT found limited evidence suggesting that α blockers were less effective than transurethral microwave thermotherapy in improving symptoms over 18 months. We found no RCTs comparing α blockers versus surgical treatment.

#### 5α Reductase inhibitors

One systematic review and additional RCTs have found that 5α reductase inhibitors improve symptom scores and reduce complications compared with placebo. The review found that 5α reductase inhibitors were associated with more adverse events than placebo, including decreased libido, impotence, and ejaculatory dysfunction. RCTs found limited evidence that the 5α reductase inhibitor finasteride was less effective at improving symptom scores than α blockers. One systematic review found no significant difference in symptom scores between finasteride and saw palmetto plant extracts. We found no RCTs comparing 5α reductase inhibitors versus surgical treatment.

#### Saw palmetto plant extracts

One systematic review has found that saw palmetto plant extracts improve symptom scores compared with placebo. It found no significant difference in symptom scores between saw palmetto plant extracts and the α blocker tamsulosin or the 5α reductase inhibitor finasteride. One RCT found no significant difference in symptom scores between tamsulosin and tamsulosin plus saw palmetto plant extracts.

#### Transurethral microwave thermotherapy

RCTs found that transurethral microwave thermotherapy reduced symptom scores compared with sham treatment. We found limited evidence that thermotherapy was less effective in relieving short term symptoms than transurethral resection. One RCT found that transurethral microwave thermotherapy improved symptom scores over 18 months compared with α blockers.

#### Transurethral resection versus no surgery

RCTs found that transurethral resection reduced symptom scores more than watchful waiting, and did not increase the risk of erectile dysfunction or incontinence.

### LIKELY TO BE BENEFICIAL

#### β-Sitosterol plant extract

One systematic review has found that β-sitosterol plant extract improves lower urinary tract symptom scores compared with placebo in the short term. We found no RCTs comparing β-sitosterol plant extract versus other treatments.

### *Pygeum africanum* New

One systematic review found limited evidence that *Pygeum africanum* increased peak urinary flow and reduced residual urine volume at 4–16 weeks compared with placebo. We found no RCTs comparing *Pygeum africanum* versus other treatments.

### Rye grass pollen extract

One systematic review found limited evidence that rye grass pollen extract increased self rated improvement and reduced nocturia at 12–24 weeks compared with placebo. However, the review identified only two small RCTs, from which we were unable to draw reliable conclusions. We found no RCTs comparing rye grass pollen extract versus other treatments.

### Transurethral resection versus less invasive surgical techniques

RCTs found no significant difference in symptom scores between transurethral resection and transurethral incision or between transurethral resection and electrical vaporisation. RCTs found limited evidence that transurethral resection improved symptom scores more than visual laser ablation but that transurethral resection may be associated with a higher risk of blood transfusion.

### Transurethral resection versus transurethral needle ablation

One RCT found that transurethral resection reduced symptom scores compared with transurethral needle ablation after 1 year, although transurethral needle ablation caused fewer adverse effects.

**DEFINITION**  Benign prostatic hyperplasia is defined histologically. Clinically, it is characterised by lower urinary tract symptoms (urinary frequency, urgency, a weak and intermittent stream, needing to strain, a sense of incomplete emptying, and nocturia) and can lead to complications, including acute urinary retention.

**INCIDENCE/ PREVALENCE**  Estimates of the prevalence of symptomatic benign prostatic hyperplasia range from 10–30% for men in their early 70s, depending on how benign prostatic hyperplasia is defined.[1]

**AETIOLOGY/ RISK FACTORS**  The mechanisms by which benign prostatic hyperplasia causes symptoms and complications are unclear, although bladder outlet obstruction is an important factor.[2] The best documented risk factors are increasing age and normal testicular function.[3]

**PROGNOSIS**  Community and practice based studies suggest that men with lower urinary tract symptoms can expect slow progression of the symptoms.[4,5] However, symptoms can wax and wane without treatment. In men with symptoms of benign prostatic hyperplasia, rates of acute urinary retention range from 1–2% a year.[5–7]

Please refer to CD-ROM for full text and references.

# Chronic prostatitis

Search date February 2003

*Jeffrey Stern and Anthony Schaeffer*

## What are the effects of treatments for chronic bacterial prostatitis?

### LIKELY TO BE BENEFICIAL

#### α Blockers (when added to antimicrobials)

We found no RCTs comparing α blockers versus placebo or no treatment. We found limited evidence from one RCT suggesting that adding α blockers to antimicrobials may improve symptoms and reduce recurrence compared with antimicrobials alone.

### UNKNOWN EFFECTIVENESS

#### Local injection of antimicrobials

We found no RCTs comparing local injection of antimicrobials with placebo or no treatment. One small RCT found that anal submucosal injection of amikacin improved symptom scores and bacterial eradication rates at 3 months compared with intramuscular amikacin.

#### Oral antimicrobial drugs

We found no placebo controlled RCTs. One RCT found no significant difference between lomefloxacin and ciprofloxacin in rates of clinical success or bacteriological cure at 6 months. We found no other RCTs of the effects of oral antimicrobial drugs. Retrospective observational studies reported cure rates of 0–88% depending on the drug used and the duration of treatment.

#### Radical prostatectomy; transurethral resection

We found no RCTs on the effects of these interventions.

## What are the effects of treatments for chronic abacterial prostatitis?

### UNKNOWN EFFECTIVENESS

#### α Blockers

One systematic review found limited evidence from two small RCTs that α blockers may improve maximal flow time and pain compared with placebo. However, we were unable to draw reliable conclusions from these small studies.

#### 5α Reductase inhibitors

One systematic review of one small RCT found insufficient evidence about the effects of 5α reductase inhibitors compared with placebo in men with chronic abacterial prostatitis.

#### Allopurinol

We found insufficient evidence from one small RCT about the effects of allopurinol compared with placebo in men with chronic abacterial prostatitis.

#### Anti-inflammatory medications

We found insufficient evidence about the effects of anti-inflammatory medications compared with placebo or no treatment in men with chronic abacterial prostatitis. ▶

◀ **Transurethral microwave thermotherapy**

One systematic review found limited evidence from one small RCT suggesting that transurethral microwave thermotherapy may significantly improve quality of life at 3 months, and symptoms over 21 months, compared with sham treatment. However, we were unable to draw reliable conclusions from this one small study.

### Biofeedback; prostatic massage; Sitz bath

We found no good evidence on these interventions.

| | |
|---|---|
| **DEFINITION** | **Chronic bacterial prostatitis** is characterised by a positive culture of expressed prostatic secretions. It can be symptomatic (recurrent urinary tract infection, or suprapubic, lower back, or perineal pain), asymptomatic, or associated with minimal urgency, frequency, and dysuria. **Chronic abacterial prostatitis** is characterised by pelvic or perineal pain, often associated with urinary urgency, nocturia, weak urinary stream, frequency, dysuria, hesitancy, dribbling after micturition, interrupted flow, and inflammation (white cells) in prostatic secretions. Symptoms can also include suprapubic, scrotal, testicular, penile, or lower back pain or discomfort, known as prostodynia, in the absence of bacteria in prostatic secretions. |
| **INCIDENCE/ PREVALENCE** | One US community based study (58 955 visits by men ≥ 18 years to office based physicians) estimated that 9% of men have a diagnosis of chronic prostatitis at any one time.[1] Another study found that, of men with genitourinary symptoms, 8% presenting to urologists and 1% presenting to primary care physicians are diagnosed with chronic prostatitis.[2] Most cases of chronic prostatitis are abacterial. Acute bacterial prostatitis, although easy to diagnose, is rare. |
| **AETIOLOGY/ RISK FACTORS** | Organisms commonly implicated in bacterial prostatitis include *Escherichia coli*, other Gram negative Enterobacteriaceae, occasionally *Pseudomonas* species, and rarely Gram positive enterococci. The cause of abacterial prostatitis is unclear, but autoimmunity could be involved.[3] |
| **PROGNOSIS** | One recent study found that chronic abacterial prostatitis had an impact on quality of life similar to that from angina, Crohn's disease, or a previous myocardial infarction.[4] |

Please refer to CD-ROM for full text and references.

# Erectile dysfunction

**Search date August 2003**

*Robyn Webber*

## *What are the effects of treatments?*

**BENEFICIAL**

### Intracavernosal alprostadil

One large RCT found that intracavernosal alprostadil increased the chances of a satisfactory erection compared with placebo. One small RCT found limited evidence that vacuum devices were as effective as intracavernosal alprostadil injections for rigidity but not for orgasm.

### Intraurethral alprostadil

One large RCT (in men who had previously responded to alprostadil) found limited evidence that intraurethral alprostadil (prostaglandin E1) increased the chances of successful sexual intercourse and at least one orgasm over 3 months compared with placebo. About a third of men suffered penile ache. We found no direct comparisons of intraurethral alprostadil versus either intracavernosal alprostadil or oral drug treatments.

### Sildenafil

One systematic review and 15 subsequent RCTs have found that sildenafil improves erections and increases rates of successful intercourse compared with placebo. Adverse effects, including headaches, flushing, and dyspepsia, are reported in up to a quarter of men. Deaths have been reported in men on concomitant treatment with oral nitrates.

### Yohimbine

One systematic review has found that yohimbine improves self reported sexual function and penile rigidity at 2–10 weeks compared with placebo. Transient adverse effects are reported in up to a third of men.

**TRADE OFF BETWEEN BENEFITS AND HARMS**

### Topical alprostadil

Two quasi randomised trials found limited evidence that topical alprostadil increased the number of men with erections sufficient for intercourse compared with placebo but was commonly associated with skin irritation.

**UNKNOWN EFFECTIVENESS**

### L-arginine

One small RCT found no significant difference in sexual function between L-arginine and placebo, but it may have been too small to exclude a clinically important difference.

### Penile prostheses

We found no RCTs of penile prostheses in men with erectile dysfunction.

### Trazodone

One small RCT found no significant difference in erections or libido with trazodone compared with placebo, but it may have been too small to exclude a clinically important difference.

◀ **Vacuum devices**

Vacuum devices have not been adequately assessed in RCTs. One small RCT found limited evidence that they were as effective as intracavernosal alprostadil (prostaglandin E1) injections for rigidity but not for orgasm.

**DEFINITION**
Erectile dysfunction has largely replaced the term "impotence". It is defined as the persistent inability to obtain or maintain sufficient rigidity of the penis to allow satisfactory sexual performance.

**INCIDENCE/ PREVALENCE**
We found little good epidemiological information, but one cross sectional study found that age is the variable most strongly associated with erectile dysfunction and that up to 30 million men in the USA may be affected.[1] Even among men in their 40s, nearly 40% report at least occasional difficulty obtaining or maintaining erection, whereas this approaches 70% in 70 year olds.

**AETIOLOGY/ RISK FACTORS**
About 80% of cases of erectile dysfunction now are believed to have an organic cause, the rest being psychogenic in origin. Risk factors include increasing age, smoking, and obesity. Erectile problems fall into three categories: failure to initiate; failure to fill, caused by insufficient arterial inflow into the penis to allow engorgement and tumescence because of vascular insufficiency; and failure to store because of veno-occlusive dysfunction. Erectile dysfunction is a recognised adverse effect of a wide variety of pharmaceutical agents.

**PROGNOSIS**
We found no good evidence on prognosis in untreated organic erectile dysfunction.

Please refer to CD-ROM for full text and references.

# Prostate cancer (metastatic)

Search date September 2002

*M Dror Michaelson, Matthew R Smith, and James A Talcott*

## What are the effects of treatments in men with metastatic prostate cancer?

### LIKELY TO BE BENEFICIAL

**Androgen deprivation**

We found limited evidence from RCTs suggesting that androgen deprivation⊕ reduced mortality compared with no initial treatment. One non-systematic review of RCTs found that orchidectomy⊕, diethylstilbestrol, and gonadorelin analogues initially improved symptoms and objective signs of disease in most men, but found no evidence of a difference between different types of androgen deprivation.

**Combined androgen blockade (androgen deprivation and antiandrogen) versus androgen deprivation alone**

Systematic reviews found limited evidence of a 2–5% improvement in 5 year survival associated with combined androgen blockade⊕ (androgen deprivation plus a non-steroidal antiandrogen) compared with androgen deprivation alone.

### UNKNOWN EFFECTIVENESS

**Intermittent androgen deprivation**

We found no RCTs comparing long term effects of intermittent androgen deprivation versus those of continuous androgen deprivation on mortality, morbidity, or quality of life.

### LIKELY TO BE INEFFECTIVE OR HARMFUL

**Deferred androgen deprivation without surveillance**

One systematic review found limited evidence of a small survival advantage at 10 years for immediate androgen deprivation therapy with gonadorelin analogues or orchidectomy in men with advanced, asymptomatic prostate cancer. There was no significant change in overall survival at 1, 2, or 5 years. The risk of major complications is increased in men whose treatment is deferred until disease progression.

## What are the effects of treatments in men with symptomatic androgen independent metastatic disease?

### LIKELY TO BE BENEFICIAL

**Chemotherapy (palliation but no evidence of an effect on survival)**

RCTs found limited evidence that chemotherapy with some new agents plus corticosteroids reduced pain, lengthened palliation, and improved quality of life, but found no improvement in overall survival compared with corticosteroids alone. Earlier RCTs failed to demonstrate any benefit of chemotherapy in men with metastatic prostate cancer.

**External beam radiation (palliation but no evidence of an effect on survival)***

We found no RCTs comparing external beam radiation with palliative treatments other than radionuclides. Observational evidence suggests that complete pain relief is achieved in about a quarter of people, and placebo controlled RCTs would probably be considered unethical.

▶

◀ **Radionuclides (palliation but no clear evidence of an effect on survival)**

One systematic review found one small RCT in men with symptomatic bone metastases, which found no significant difference in survival between external beam radiation plus placebo and external beam radiation plus strontium-89. However, strontium-89 significantly reduced the number of new sites of pain. One small subsequent RCT in men with painful bone metastases found that samarium-153 significantly reduced pain scores compared with placebo. A second small subsequent RCT, in a selected population, found an improvement in survival with strontium-89 compared with placebo, but the results are difficult to generalise.

## UNKNOWN EFFECTIVENESS

### Bisphosphonates

One systematic review of two RCTs found insufficient evidence about the effects of bisphosphonates.

*Categorisation based on observational evidence; RCTs unlikely to be conducted.

**DEFINITION** See prostate cancer (non-metastatic), p 227. Androgen independent meta-static disease is defined as disease that progresses despite androgen deprivation.

**INCIDENCE/ PREVALENCE** See prostate cancer (non-metastatic), p 227.

**AETIOLOGY/ RISK FACTORS** See prostate cancer (non-metastatic), p 228.

**PROGNOSIS** Prostate cancer metastasises predominantly to bone. Metastatic prostate cancer can result in pain, weakness, paralysis, and death.

Please refer to CD-ROM for full text and references.

# Prostate cancer (non-metastatic)

**Search date February 2003**

*Timothy Wilt*

## What are the effects of treatments for clinically localised prostate cancer?

### TRADE OFF BETWEEN BENEFITS AND HARMS

**Radical prostatectomy**

Two RCTs found no significant difference in death from any cause between radical prostatectomy🟢 and watchful waiting in men with clinically detected disease after median follow up of 6.2 and 23 years. The larger of the RCTs found that radical prostatectomy reduced death due to prostate cancer and metastases at 6 years compared with watchful waiting. Two small RCTs found that radical prostatectomy reduced the risk of treatment failure compared with external beam radiation. Radical prostatectomy carries the risks of major surgery and of sexual and urinary dysfunction.

**Watchful waiting**

Two RCTs found no significant difference in overall survival between watchful waiting and radical prostatectomy in men with clinically detected disease after median follow up of 6 and 23 years. The larger RCT found that radical prostatectomy reduced death rates due to prostate cancer and metastases at 6 years compared with watchful waiting. One RCT found that radical prostatectomy increased erectile dysfunction compared with watchful waiting but found no significant difference in quality of life after 12 months.

### UNKNOWN EFFECTIVENESS

**Androgen suppression**

We found no RCTs of early androgen suppression🟢 on length or quality of life in men with asymptomatic, clinically localised prostate cancer. One RCT identified by a systematic review found limited evidence that oestrogen decreased prostate cancer related deaths compared with watchful waiting. It found no significant difference in overall survival. One preliminary report of three large ongoing RCTs in men with localised or locally advanced prostate cancer found that bicalutamide plus standard care reduced rates of radiological progression and bone metastases at 2–3 years compared with standard care alone. There was no significant difference between treatments in overall survival.

**External beam radiation**

We found no RCTs comparing external beam radiation versus watchful waiting. Two RCTs found that external beam radiation increased the risk of treatment failure compared with radical prostatectomy. Two small RCTs found no significant difference between conformal radiotherapy🟢 and conventional radiotherapy in overall survival or tumour control at 3–5 years. One systematic review found limited evidence that conformal radiotherapy with dose escalation reduced acute and late treatment related morbidity compared with conventional radiotherapy for men with T1 or T2 low or intermediate risk prostate cancer.

**Androgen suppression in asymptomatic men with raised prostate specific antigen concentrations after early treatment; brachytherapy🟢; cryosurgery**

We found no RCTs on the effects of these interventions.

▶

◄ *What are the effects of treatments for locally advanced*
*prostate cancer?*

**Immediate androgen suppression after radical prostatectomy and pelvic
lymphadenectomy in men with node positive prostate cancer (compared
with radical prostatectomy and deferred androgen suppression)**

One small RCT in men with node positive prostate cancer found that immediate
androgen suppression compared with deferred androgen suppression after radical
prostatectomy❻ and pelvic lymphadenectomy reduced mortality over a median of
7 years' follow up.

**Androgen suppression initiated at diagnosis**

RCTs found no significant difference in overall survival between androgen suppression with bicalutamide and no androgen suppression in men with localised or
locally advanced prostate cancer at 2–10 years. The RCTs found that bicalutamide
reduced objective progression compared with no bicalutamide. One systematic
review found that early androgen suppression increased survival at 10 years
compared with deferred treatment in men with locally advanced prostate cancer
but found no significant difference in survival at 5 years. One RCT found limited
evidence that immediate androgen suppression reduced complications compared
with deferred androgen suppression.

**Early androgen suppression in addition to external beam radiation
(improves survival compared with radiation and deferred androgen
suppression)**

RCTs found limited evidence that androgen suppression initiated at diagnosis plus
external beam radiation improved long term survival compared with radiation alone
or radiation plus deferred androgen suppression. One RCT found limited evidence
that immediate androgen suppression reduced complications compared with
deferred androgen suppression.

**DEFINITION**    Prostatic cancer is staged according to two systems: the tumour, node,
metastasis (TNM) classification system and the American urologic staging
system❶. Non-metastatic prostate cancer can be divided into clinically
localised disease and locally advanced disease. Clinically localised disease is
prostate cancer thought, after clinical examination, to be confined to the
prostate gland. Locally advanced disease is prostate cancer that has spread
outside the capsule of the prostate gland but has not yet spread to other
organs. Metastatic disease is prostate cancer that has spread outside the
prostate gland to either local, regional, or systemic lymph nodes, seminal
vesicles, or to other body organs (e.g. bone, liver, brain) and is not connected
to the prostate gland. We consider clinically localised and locally advanced
disease here. Metastatic disease is covered in a separate chapter (see
prostate cancer [metastatic], p 224).

**INCIDENCE/**    Prostate cancer is the sixth most common cancer in the world and the third
**PREVALENCE**    most common cancer in men. In 2000, an estimated 513 000 new cases of
prostate caner were diagnosed and about 250 000 deaths were attributed to
prostate cancers worldwide. Prostate cancer is uncommon under the age of
50 years. About 85% of men with prostate cancer are diagnosed after the age
of 65 years. Autopsy studies suggest that the prevalence of subclinical ►

# Prostate cancer (non-metastatic)

prostate cancer is high at all ages: 30% for men aged 30–39 years, 50% for men aged 50–59 years, and more than 75% for men older than 85 years. Incidence varies widely by ethnic group and around the world. The highest rates occur in men of black ethnic group living in the USA and the lowest among men living in China.[1]

**AETIOLOGY/ RISK FACTORS**
Risk factors for prostate cancer include increasing age, family history of prostate cancer, black race, and possibly higher dietary consumption of fat and meat, low intake of lycopene (from tomato products), low intake of fruit, and high dietary calcium. In the USA, black men have about a 60% higher incidence than white men.[2] The prostate cancer incidence for black men living in the USA is about 90/100 000 in men aged less than 65 years and about 1300/ 100 000 in men aged 65–74 years. For white men, incidence is about 44/100 000 in men aged less than 65 years and 900/100 000 in men aged 65–74 years.[2]

**PROGNOSIS**
The chance that men with well to moderately differentiated, palpable, clinically localised prostate cancer will remain free of symptomatic progression is 70% at 5 years and 40% at 10 years.[3] The risk of symptomatic disease progression is higher in men with poorly differentiated prostate cancer.[4] One retrospective analysis of a large surgical series in men with clinically localised prostate cancer found that the median time from the increase in prostate specific antigen (PSA) concentration to the development of metastatic disease was 8 years.[5] Time to PSA progression, PSA doubling time, and Gleason score**ⓖ** were predictive of the probability and time to development of metastatic disease. Once men developed metastatic disease, the median actuarial time to death was less than 5 years.[5] Morbidity from local or regional disease progression includes haematuria, bladder obstruction, and lower extremity oedema. The age adjusted prostate cancer specific mortality in the USA for all men aged 65 years and older has decreased by about 15% (244 deaths/100 000 to 207 deaths/ 100 000) from 1991–1997. The reasons for this are unclear, although inaccurate death certification, PSA screening, and earlier, more intensive treatment, including radical prostatectomy**ⓖ**, radiotherapy, and androgen suppression**ⓖ**, have been suggested. However, regions of the USA and Canada where PSA testing and early treatment are more common have similar prostate cancer mortality to regions with lower testing and early treatment rates.[6] Similarly, countries with low rates of PSA testing and treatment, such as the UK, have similar age adjusted prostate cancer mortality to countries with high rates of testing and treatment, such as the USA.[7]

Please refer to CD-ROM for full text and references.

Search date April 2003

*Bazian Ltd*

## What are the effects of treatments in men with varicocele?
*New*

### UNKNOWN EFFECTIVENESS

#### Effects of treatments on pain or discomfort due to varicocele

We found no evidence examining the effects of expectant management, surgical ligation, sclerotherapy, or transcatheter embolisation on pain or discomfort due to varicocele.

#### Expectant management

One systematic review and subsequent RCTs in couples with male factor subfertility found no significant difference in pregnancy rate between expectant management and occlusive treatments (surgery or sclerotherapy). However, the studies were heterogeneous and of poor methodological quality.

#### Sclerotherapy

One RCT found no significant difference in pregnancy rate between sclerotherapy and no treatment.

#### Surgical ligation

We found insufficient evidence on the effects of surgical ligation in improving pregnancy rate compared with, no treatment, sclerotherapy, or embolisation in men with varicocele. We also found insufficient evidence comparing the effects of different ligation techniques.

#### Embolisation

We found no RCTs comparing embolisation versus no treatment. We found insufficient evidence on the effects of embolisation for improving fertility in men with varicocele compared with ligation techniques.

**DEFINITION** Varicocele is a dilation of the pampiniform plexus of the spermatic cord. Severity is commonly graded as follows: grade 0, only demonstrable by technical investigation; grade 1, palpable or visible only on Valsalva manoeuvre (straining); grade 2, palpable but not visible when standing upright at room temperature; and grade 3, visible when standing upright at room temperature. Varicocele is unilateral and left sided in at least 85% of cases. In most of the remaining cases, the condition is bilateral. Unilateral right sided varicocele is rare. Many men who have a varicocele have no symptoms. Symptoms may include testicular ache or discomfort and distress about cosmetic appearance. The condition is widely believed to be associated with male factor infertility, which is the commonest reason for referral for treatment. However, evidence for a causal relationship is sparse (see incidence/prevalence, below).[1]

**INCIDENCE/ PREVALENCE** We found few data on the prevalence of varicocele. Anecdotally, it has been estimated that about 10–15% of both men and adolescent boys in the general population have varicocele.[1] One multicentre study found that, in couples with subfertility, the prevalence of varicocele in male partners was about 12%.[2] In men with abnormal semen analysis, the prevalence of varicocele was about 25%.

# Varicocele

**AETIOLOGY/ RISK FACTORS** We found no reliable data on epidemiological risk factors for varicocele, such as a family history or environmental exposures. Anatomically, varicoceles are caused by dysfunction of the valves in the spermatic vein, which allows pooling of blood in the pampiniform plexus. This is more likely to occur in the left spermatic vein than in the right because of normal anatomical asymmetry.

**PROGNOSIS** Varicocele is believed to be associated with subfertility, although reliable evidence is sparse (see incidence/prevalence, above). The natural history of varicocele is unclear.

Please refer to CD-ROM for full text and references.

Search date April 2003

*Janet Treasure and Ulrike Schmidt*

## What are the effects of treatments?

### UNKNOWN EFFECTIVENESS

### Inpatient versus outpatient treatment setting (in people not requiring emergency intervention)

One small RCT found no significant difference between outpatient treatment and inpatient treatment☉ for increasing weight and improving Morgan Russell scale☉ global scores at 1, 2, and 5 years in people who did not need emergency intervention.

### Oestrogen treatment (for prevention of fractures)

We found no good evidence about the effects of oestrogen treatment on fracture rates in people with anorexia. Two small RCTs found no significant difference between oestrogen and placebo or no treatment in bone mineral density in people with anorexia.

### Psychotherapies

We found insufficient evidence from small RCTs to compare psychotherapies versus dietary counselling☉ or versus each other.

### Selective serotonin reuptake inhibitors

We found insufficient evidence from three small RCTs about effects of selective serotonin reuptake inhibitors compared with placebo or no treatment in people with anorexia.

### Zinc

One small RCT found limited evidence that zinc may improve daily body mass index☉ gain compared with placebo in people managed in an inpatient setting. However, we were unable to draw reliable conclusions from this small study.

### LIKELY TO BE INEFFECTIVE OR HARMFUL

### Cisapride

One small RCT found no significant difference between cisapride and placebo in weight gain at 8 weeks. Use of cisapride has been restricted in many countries because of concern about cardiac irregularities, including ventricular tachycardia, torsades de pointes, and sudden death.

### Cyproheptadine

One small RCT in an outpatient setting and two RCTs in inpatient settings found no significant difference between cyproheptadine and placebo for weight gain.

### Neuroleptic drugs

We found no RCTs. The QT interval may be prolonged in people with anorexia nervosa, and many neuroleptic drugs (haloperidol, pimozide, sertindole, thioridazine, chlorpromazine, and others) also increase the QT interval. Prolongation of the QT interval may be associated with increased risk of ventricular tachycardia, torsades de pointes, and sudden death.

▶

# Anorexia nervosa

◀ **Tricyclic antidepressants**

Two small RCTs found no evidence of benefit with amitriptyline compared with placebo. They found that amitriptyline was associated with more adverse effects, such as palpitations, dry mouth, and blurred vision.

**DEFINITION**  Anorexia nervosa is characterised by a refusal to maintain weight at or above a minimally normal weight (< 85% of expected weight for age and height, or body mass index < 17.5 kg/m$^2$), or a failure to show the expected weight gain during growth. In association with this, there is often an intense fear of gaining weight, preoccupation with weight, denial of the current low weight and its adverse impact on health, and amenorrhoea. Two subtypes of anorexia nervosa, binge–purge and restricting, have been defined.[1]

**INCIDENCE/**  A mean incidence in the general population of 19/100 000 a year in females
**PREVALENCE**  and 2/100 000 a year in males has been estimated from 12 cumulative studies.[2] The highest rate was in female teenagers (age 13–19 years), where there were 50.8 cases/100 000 a year. A large cohort study screened 4291 Swedish school children, aged 16 years, by weighing and subsequent interview, and found the prevalence of anorexia nervosa (defined using DSM-III and DSM-III-R criteria) to be 7/1000 for girls and 1/1000 for boys.[3] Little is known of the incidence or prevalence in Asia, South America, or Africa.

**AETIOLOGY/**  Anorexia nervosa has been related to family, biological, social, and cultural
**RISK FACTORS**  factors. Studies have found that anorexia nervosa is associated with a family history of anorexia nervosa (adjusted HR 11.4, 95% CI 1.1 to 89.0), of bulimia nervosa (adjusted HR 3.5, 95% CI 1.1 to 14.0),[4] depression, generalised anxiety disorder, obsessive compulsive disorder, or obsessive compulsive personality disorder (adjusted RR 3.6, 95% CI 1.6 to 8.0).[5] A twin study suggested that anorexia nervosa may be related to genetic factors but it was unable to estimate reliably the contribution of non-shared environmental factors.[6] Specific aspects of childhood temperament thought to be related include perfectionism, negative self evaluation, and extreme compliance.[7] Perinatal factors include prematurity, particularly if the baby was small for gestational age (prematurity: OR 3.2, 95% CI 1.6 to 6.2; small for gestational age: OR 5.7, 95% CI 1.1 to 28.7).[8]

**PROGNOSIS**  One prospective study followed up 51 people with teenage-onset anorexia nervosa, about half of whom received no or minimal treatment (< 8 sessions). After 10 years, 14/51 people (27%) had a persistent eating disorder, three (6%) had ongoing anorexia nervosa, and six (12%) had experienced a period of bulimia nervosa. People with anorexia nervosa were significantly more likely to have an affective disorder than controls matched for sex, age, and school (lifetime risk of affective disorder 96% in people with anorexia v 23% with controls, ARI 73%, 95% CI 60% to 85%). Obsessive compulsive disorder was, similarly, significantly more likely in people with anorexia nervosa compared with controls) (30% v 10%; ARI 20%, 95% CI 10% to 41%). However, in 35% of people with obsessive compulsive disorder and anorexia nervosa, obsessive compulsive disorder preceded the anorexia. About half of all participants continued to have poor psychosocial functioning at 10 years (assessed using the Morgan Russell scale and Global Assessment of Functioning Scale).[9] A summary of treatment studies (68 studies published between 1953 and 1989, 3104 people, length of follow up 1–33 years) found that 43% of people recover completely (range 7–86%), 36% improve (range 1–69%), 20% develop a chronic eating disorder (range 0–3%), and 5% die from anorexia nervosa (range 0–21%).[10] Favourable prognostic factors include an early age at onset and a short interval between onset of symptoms and the beginning of treatment. Unfavourable prognostic factors include vomiting, bulimia, profound weight loss, chronicity, and a history of premorbid developmental or clinical abnormalities. The all cause standardised mortality ratio of eating disorders (anorexia ▶

nervosa and bulimia nervosa) has been estimated at 538, about three times higher than other psychiatric illnesses.[11] The average annual mortality was 0.59% a year in females in 10 eating disorder populations (1322 people) with a minimum follow up of 6 years.[12] The mortality was higher for people with lower weight and with older age at presentation. Young women with anorexia nervosa are at an increased risk of fractures later in life.[13]

---

**Please refer to CD-ROM for full text and references.**

# Bipolar disorder

Search date April 2002

*John Geddes*

## *What are the effects of treatments in mania?*

**BENEFICIAL**

### Lithium

One RCT in people with bipolar type I disorder experiencing a manic episode found that lithium increased the proportion of people who responded after 3–4 weeks compared with placebo. One systematic review found that lithium increased the proportion of people who had remission of manic symptoms at 3 weeks compared with chlorpromazine, and found no significant difference in symptoms at 3–6 weeks between lithium and haloperidol, olanzapine, valproate, lamotrigine, or clonazepam. One RCT found that lithium was less effective than risperidone in reducing manic symptoms at 4 weeks. Lithium can cause a range of adverse effects. The RCTs provided insufficient evidence about how the adverse effects of lithium compared with those of other antipsychotic drugs.

### Olanzapine

One systematic review in people with bipolar type I disorder found that olanzapine increased the proportion of people who responded at 3–6 weeks compared with placebo, both as monotherapy and as add on therapy to lithium or valproate, and found no significant difference in symptoms at 28 days between olanzapine and lithium. RCTs found that olanzapine was more effective in reducing symptoms than valproate, but was also more likely to cause adverse effects such as sedation and weight gain. The acceptability of olanzapine may be limited by weight gain.

### Valproate

One systematic review in people with bipolar type I disorder experiencing a manic episode found that valproate increased the proportion of people who responded over 3 weeks compared with placebo. It found no significant difference in response at 1–6 weeks between valproate and lithium, haloperidol, or carbamazepine. It found that valproate was less effective in reducing manic symptoms than olanzapine, but was also less likely to cause adverse effects such as sedation and weight gain.

**LIKELY TO BE BENEFICIAL**

### Carbamazepine

RCTs in people with bipolar type I disorder experiencing a manic episode found no significant difference in manic symptoms at 4–6 weeks between carbamazepine and lithium or valproate.

### Clonazepam

We found no RCTs comparing clonazepam versus placebo in people with bipolar mania. RCTs in people with bipolar type I disorder experiencing a manic episode suggest that clonazepam may be as effective as lithium in improving manic symptoms at 1–4 weeks.

### Haloperidol

We found no RCTs comparing haloperidol versus placebo in people with bipolar mania. RCTs in people with bipolar type I disorder experiencing a manic episode found no significant difference in manic symptoms at 1–3 weeks between haloperidol and lithium or valproate, although haloperidol was associated with more extrapyramidal adverse effects and sedation than valproate.

◀ **Risperidone**

We found no RCTs comparing risperidone versus placebo in people with bipolar mania. One RCT in people with bipolar type I disorder experiencing a manic episode found that risperidone reduced manic symptoms at 4 weeks compared with lithium. It gave no information on adverse effects.

**UNKNOWN EFFECTIVENESS**

**Chlorpromazine**

One very small RCT in people with mania found limited evidence that chlorpromazine may improve manic symptoms over 7 weeks more than placebo or imipramine. One systematic review found that fewer people had remission of symptoms at 3 weeks with chlorpromazine than with lithium.

**Lamotrigine**

We found no RCTs comparing lamotrigine versus placebo in people with bipolar mania. One RCT in people with bipolar type I disorder experiencing a manic episode found no significant difference in manic symptoms at 4 weeks between lamotrigine and lithium.

---

## What are the effects of treatments in bipolar depression?

**LIKELY TO BE BENEFICIAL**

**Lamotrigine**

One RCT in people with bipolar type I disorder experiencing a major depressive episode found that lamotrigine increased the proportion of people who responded over 7 weeks compared with placebo.

**TRADE OFF BETWEEN BENEFITS AND HARMS**

**Antidepressants**

Systematic reviews found that antidepressants improved depressive symptoms at the end of the trial (unspecified) compared with placebo. They found limited evidence that selective serotonin reuptake inhibitors were more effective than tricyclic antidepressants, and found no significant difference in symptoms between monoamine oxidase inhibitors and tricyclic antidepressants or between selective serotonin reuptake inhibitors and serotonin noradrenaline reuptake inhibitors. The reviews provided insufficient evidence to assess whether antidepressants induce bipolar mania.

**UNKNOWN EFFECTIVENESS**

**Carbamazepine; lithium**

One systematic review identified no RCTs of sufficient quality to assess these treatments in people with bipolar depression.

**Psychological treatments; valproate**

We found no RCTs of these treatments in people with bipolar depression. ▶

# Bipolar disorder

## What are the effects of interventions to prevent relapse of mania or bipolar depression?

### BENEFICIAL

**Lithium**

RCTs have found that lithium reduces relapse⊕ over 2 years compared with placebo, and have found no significant difference in relapse between lithium and valproate, carbamazepine, or lamotrigine.

### LIKELY TO BE BENEFICIAL

**Carbamazepine**

We found no RCTs comparing carbamazepine versus placebo in preventing relapse. One systematic review found no significant difference between carbamazepine and lithium in the proportion of people who relapsed over 1–3 years.

**Education to recognise symptoms of relapse**

One RCT found limited evidence that an educational programme to recognise symptoms of relapse reduced manic relapse over 18 months, but that it may increase depressive episodes.

**Lamotrigine (bipolar depressive episodes)**

Three RCTs have found that lamotrigine reduces relapse compared with placebo. However, secondary analyses in two of the RCT suggested that lamotrigine protected against depressive relapse, but not manic relapse. RCTs have found no significant difference between lamotrigine and lithium in the proportion of people who relapse.

**Valproate**

One RCT found that valproate reduced relapse over 12 months compared with placebo. One systematic review found no significant difference between lithium and valproate in relapse over 12 months.

### UNKNOWN EFFECTIVENESS

**Antidepressant drugs**

One systematic review provided insufficient evidence to assess antidepressants in preventing relapse of bipolar disorder.

**Family focused psychoeducation**

One RCT found that 21 sessions of family focused psychoeducation reduced relapse over 12 months compared with two family sessions plus crisis management.

**DEFINITION** Bipolar disorder (bipolar affective disorder, manic depressive disorder) is characterised by marked mood swings between mania (mood elevation) and bipolar depression that cause significant personal distress or social dysfunction, and are not caused by drugs or known physical disorder. **Bipolar type I disorder** is diagnosed when episodes of depression are interspersed with mania or mixed episodes. **Bipolar type II disorder** is diagnosed when depression is interspersed with less severe episodes of elevated mood that do not lead to dysfunction or disability (hypomania). Bipolar disorder has been subdivided in several further ways❶.[1]

**INCIDENCE/ PREVALENCE**

One 1996 cross-national community based study (38 000 people) found lifetime prevalence rates of bipolar disorder ranging from 0.3% in Taiwan to 1.5% in New Zealand.[2] It found that men and women were at similar risk, and that the age at first onset ranged from 19–29 years (average of 6 years earlier than first onset of major depression).

**AETIOLOGY/ RISK FACTORS**

The cause of bipolar disorder is uncertain, although family and twin studies suggest a genetic basis.[3] The lifetime risk of bipolar disorder is increased in first degree relatives of a person with bipolar disorder (40–70% for a monozygotic twin; 5–10% for other first degree relatives). If the first episode of mania occurs in an older adult, it may be secondary mania due to underlying medical or substance induced factors.[4]

**PROGNOSIS**

Bipolar disorder is a recurring illness and is one of the leading causes of worldwide disability, especially in the 15–44 year age group.[5] One 4 year inception cohort study (173 people treated for a first episode of mania or mixed affective disorder) found that 93% of people no longer met criteria for mania at 2 years (median time to recover from a syndrome 4.6 weeks), but that only 36% had recovered to premorbid function.[6] It found that 40% of people had a recurrent manic (20%) or depressive (20%) episode within 2 years of recovering from the first episode. A meta-analysis, comparing observed suicide versus expected rates of suicide in an age and sex matched sample of the general population, found that the lifetime prevalence of suicide was about 2%, or 15 times greater than expected, in people with bipolar disorder.[7]

Please refer to CD-ROM for full text and references.

# Bulimia nervosa

Search date December 2002

*Phillipa Hay and Josue Bacaltchuk*

## What are the effects of treatments?

### LIKELY TO BE BENEFICIAL

### Antidepressant medication (tricyclic antidepressants, monoamine oxidase inhibitors, and fluoxetine)

Systematic reviews and one subsequent RCT have found short term reduction in bulimic symptoms with tricyclic antidepressants, monoamine oxidase inhibitors, and fluoxetine. A further subsequent RCT found no significant difference in symptoms between moclobemide and placebo. One systematic review and one subsequent RCT found no significant difference in symptoms with antidepressants versus cognitive behavioural therapy.

### Cognitive behavioural therapy

One systematic review has found that cognitive behavioural therapy⊕ compared with remaining on a waiting list reduces specific symptoms of bulimia nervosa and improves non-specific symptoms such as depression. One systematic review found cognitive behavioural therapy compared with other psychotherapies improved abstinence from binge eating and depression scores at the end of treatment. One RCT in the review found that cognitive behavioural therapy compared with interpersonal psychotherapy reduced binge eating in the short term, but there was no significant difference in the longer term. One systematic review and one RCT found no significant difference in symptoms with cognitive behavioural therapy compared with antidepressants.

### Other psychotherapies

One systematic review has found that non-cognitive behavioural psychotherapy increases abstinence from binge eating compared with waiting list controls. The systematic review found that the combined result for four specific psychotherapies, other than cognitive behavioural therapy, reduced bulimic symptoms compared with specified control psychotherapies, but the review included RCTs with weak methods, and the result was significant in only one of the four individual results. One systematic review found cognitive behavioural therapy compared with other psychotherapies improved abstinence from binge eating and depression scores at the end of treatment. One RCT in the review found that cognitive behavioural therapy compared with interpersonal psychotherapy⊕ reduced binge eating in the short term, but there was no significant difference in the longer term.

### Combination treatment (antidepressants plus psychotherapy)

One systematic review and one subsequent RCT found no significant difference between combination treatment (antidepressants plus psychotherapy) and antidepressants alone in binge frequency, depressive symptoms, and remission rates. The systematic review found that, compared with psychotherapy alone, combination treatment improved short term remission, but there was no significant difference in binge frequency and depressive symptoms. The systematic review found that combination treatment was with psychotherapy were associated with higher withdrawal rates compared with psychotherapy alone. One subsequent RCT of cognitive behavioural therapy in a self help form plus fluoxetine found limited evidence that combined treatment reduced bulimic symptoms compared with cognitive behavioural therapy alone. A second subsequent RCT found no significant difference in symptoms between group based CBT, fluoxetine, and their combination.

◀ **UNKNOWN EFFECTIVENESS**

### Antidepressants as maintenance
We found insufficient evidence to assess the effects of antidepresssants for maintenance.

### Other antidepressants (venlafaxine, mirtazapine, and reboxetine)
We found no RCTs on the effects of venlafaxine, mirtazapine, and reboxetine.

### Selective serotonin reuptake inhibitors (other than fluoxetine)
We found no good evidence on selective serotonin reuptake inhibitors other than fluoxetine.

**DEFINITION**
Bulimia nervosa🅖 is an intense preoccupation with body weight and shape, with regular episodes of uncontrolled overeating of large amounts of food (binge eating🅖) associated with use of extreme methods to counteract the feared effects of overeating. If a person also meets the diagnostic criteria for anorexia nervosa, then the diagnosis of anorexia nervosa takes precedence.[1] Bulimia nervosa can be difficult to identify because of extreme secrecy about binge eating and purgative behaviour. Weight may be normal but there is often a history of anorexia nervosa or restrictive dieting. Some people alternate between anorexia nervosa and bulimia nervosa. Some RCTs included participants with subthreshold bulimia nervosa or a related eating disorder, binge eating disorder. Where possible, only results relevant to bulimia nervosa are reported in the review.

**INCIDENCE/ PREVALENCE**
In community based studies, the prevalence of bulimia nervosa is between 0.5% and 1.0% in young women, with an even social class distribution.[2–4] About 90% of people diagnosed with bulimia nervosa are women. The numbers presenting with bulimia nervosa in industrialised countries increased during the decade that followed its recognition in the late 1970s and "a cohort effect" is reported in community surveys,[2,5,6] implying an increase in incidence. The prevalence of eating disorders such as bulimia nervosa is lower in non-industrialised populations[7] and varies across ethnic groups. African-American women have a lower rate of restrictive dieting than white American women, but have a similar rate of recurrent binge eating.[8]

**AETIOLOGY/ RISK FACTORS**
Young women from the developed world who restrict their dietary intake are at greatest risk of developing bulimia nervosa and other eating disorders. One community based case control study compared 102 people with bulimia nervosa with 204 healthy controls and found higher rates of the following in people with the eating disorder: obesity, mood disorder, sexual and physical abuse, parental obesity, substance misuse, low self esteem, perfectionism, disturbed family dynamics, parental weight/shape concern, and early menarche.[9] Compared with a control group of 102 women who had other psychiatric disorders, women with bulimia nervosa had higher rates of parental problems and obesity.

**PROGNOSIS**
A 10 year follow up study (50 people with bulimia nervosa from a former trial of mianserin treatment) found that 52% had fully recovered, and only 9% continued to experience full symptoms of bulimia nervosa.[10] A larger study (222 people from a trial of antidepressants and structured, intensive group psychotherapy) found that, after a mean follow up of 11.5 years, 11% still met criteria for bulimia nervosa, whereas 70% were in full or partial remission.[11] Short term studies found similar results: about 50% of people made a full recovery, 30% made a partial recovery, and 20% continued to be symptomatic.[12] There are few consistent predictors of longer term outcome. Good prognosis has been associated with shorter illness duration, a younger age of onset, higher social class, and a family history of alcohol abuse.[10] Poor prognosis has been associated with a history of substance misuse,[13] premorbid ▶

# Bulimia nervosa

and paternal obesity,[14] and, in some studies, personality disorder.[15–18] One study (102 people) of the natural course of bulimia nervosa found that 31% still had the disorder at 15 months and 15% at 5 years.[19] Only 28% received treatment during the follow up period. In an evaluation of response to cognitive behavioural therapy, early progress (by session 6) best predicted outcome.[20] A subsequent systematic review of the outcome literature found no consistent evidence to support early intervention and a better prognosis.[21]

Please refer to CD-ROM for full text and references.

Search date April 2003

*G Mustafa Soomro*

*Mental health*

## What are the effects of treatments for deliberate self harm in adults?

We found little RCT evidence for any intervention in people with deliberate self harm. Most RCTs and meta-analyses of small RCTs are likely to have been underpowered to detect clinically important outcomes of interventions.

### UNKNOWN EFFECTIVENESS

### Continuity of care

One systematic review of one RCT found limited evidence that follow up after hospital treatment with the same compared with a different therapist may increase repetition of deliberate self harm over 3 months, although this may be explained by a higher level of risk factors for repetition in the group receiving same therapist follow up, despite randomisation.

### Dialectal behaviour therapy

One RCT found limited and equivocal evidence that dialectical behaviour therapy⑥ may reduce the proportion of people with repetition of self harm over 12 months compared with usual care.

### Emergency card

One systematic review found no significant difference in the proportion of people who repeated deliberate self harm over 12 months between emergency card (allowing emergency admission or contact with a doctor) and usual care.

### Flupentixol depot injection

One small RCT found that flupentixol depot injection reduced the proportion of people who repeated deliberate self harm over 6 months compared with placebo. However, we were unable to draw reliable conclusions from this small study. Typical antipsychotics such as flupentixol are associated with a wide range of adverse effects.

### Hospital admission

One RCT found no significant difference between hospital admission and immediate discharge in the proportion of people who repeated deliberate self harm over 16 weeks, but it is likely to have been too small to exclude a clinically important difference.

### Intensive outpatient follow up plus outreach

One systematic review found no significant difference in the proportion of people who repeated deliberate self harm over 4–12 months between intensive intervention plus outreach and usual care.

### Mianserin

RCTs provided insufficient evidence to assess mianserin.

### Nurse led case management

One RCT found no significant difference between nurse led case management⑥ and usual care in the proportion of people who were admitted to emergency departments for episodes of deliberate self harm over 12 months.

►

# Deliberate self harm

## Paroxetine

One RCT in people with deliberate self harm receiving psychotherapy found no significant difference between paroxetine and placebo in the proportion of people who repeated self harm over 12 months. It found that paroxetine increased diarrhoea and tremor compared with placebo.

## Problem solving therapy

One systematic review of small RCTs found no significant difference between problem solving therapy⊖ and usual care in the proportion of people who repeated deliberate self harm over 6-12 months. Another systematic review found that problem solving therapy reduced depression, anxiety, and hopelessness, and improved problems compared with usual care.

## Psychodynamic interpersonal therapy

One RCT found that psychodynamic interpersonal therapy⊖ for 4 weeks reduced repetition of deliberate self harm, depression, and suicidal ideation over 6 months compared with usual care. However, we were unable to draw reliable conclusions from one RCT.

## Same number of therapy sessions given over long term versus over short term

One systematic review of one RCT found no significant difference in the proportion of people who repeated deliberate self harm at 12 months with therapy given over 3 months compared with 12 months.

## Telephone contact

One RCT found no significant difference between telephone contact at 4 and 8 months and usual care in repetition of deliberate self harm, global functioning, and suicidal ideation over 12 months.

### UNLIKELY TO BE BENEFICIAL

## General practice based guidelines

One large cluster randomised trial comparing the use of general practitioner guidelines for management of deliberate self harm versus usual care found no significant difference in the proportion of people who repeated self harm over 12 months or in the time to repetition of self harm.

DEFINITION   Deliberate self harm is an acute non-fatal act of self harm carried out deliberately in the form of an acute episode of behaviour by an individual with variable motivation.[1] The intention to end life may be absent or present to a variable degree. Other terms used to describe this phenomenon are "attempted suicide" and "parasuicide". The terms are not entirely satisfactory. Common methods of deliberate self harm include self cutting and self poisoning, such as overdosing on medicines. Some acts of deliberate self harm are characterised by high suicidal intent, meticulous planning (including precautions against being found out), and severe lethality. Other acts of deliberate self harm are characterised by no or low intention of suicide, lack of planning and concealing of the act, and low lethality of the method used. The related term of "suicide" is defined as an act with a fatal outcome that is deliberately initiated and performed by the person with the knowledge or expectation of its fatal outcome.[1] This review focuses on recent deliberate self harm as the main presenting problem and excludes RCTs in which deliberate self harm is assessed as an outcome associated with other disorders, such as depression or borderline personality disorder. Deliberate self harm is not defined in the *Diagnostic and statistical manual of mental disorders* (DSM IV)[2] or the *International classification of mental and behavioural disorders* (ICD-10).[3]

Based on data from 16 European countries between 1989–1992, the lifetime prevalence of deliberate self harm in people treated in hospital and other medical facilities, including general practice settings, is estimated at about 3% for women and 2% for men.[4] Over the last 50 years there has been a rise in the incidence of deliberate self harm in the UK.[4] A reasonable current estimate is about 400/100 000 population a year.[5] In two community studies in the USA, 3–5% of responders said that they had made an attempt at deliberate self harm at some time.[6] Self poisoning using organophosphates is particularly common in developing countries.[7] A large hospital (catering for 900 000 people) in Sri Lanka, reported 2559 adult hospital admissions and 41% occupancy of medical intensive care beds for deliberate self harm with organophosphates over 2 years.[8] An international survey using representative community samples of adults (aged 18–64 years) reported lifetime prevalence of self reported suicide attempts of 3.82% in Canada, 5.93% in Puerto Rico, 4.95% in France, 3.44% in West Germany, 0.72% in Lebanon, 0.75% in Taiwan, 3.2% in Korea, and 4.43% in New Zealand.[6]

**AETIOLOGY/**
**RISK FACTORS** Familial, biological, and psychosocial factors may contribute to deliberate self harm. Evidence for genetic factors includes a higher risk of familial suicide and greater concordance in monozygotic than dizygotic twins for deliberate self harm and suicide.[9] Evidence for biological factors includes reduced cerebrospinal fluid 5-hydroxyindole acetic acid (5-HIAA) levels and blunted prolactin response to fenfluramine challenge test, indicating a reduction in the function of serotonin in the central nervous system.[10] People who deliberately self harm also show traits of impulsiveness and aggression, inflexible and impulsive cognitive style, and impaired decision making and problem solving**ⓖ**.[11] Deliberate self harm is more likely in women, young adults, and people who are single or divorced, of low education level, unemployed, disabled, or suffering from a psychiatric disorder[12] particularly depression,[13] substance misuse,[14] borderline and antisocial personality disorders,[15] severe anxiety disorders,[16] and physical illness.[17]

**PROGNOSIS** Suicide is highest during the first year after deliberate self harm.[18] One systematic review found median rates of repetition of deliberate self harm of 16.0% (interquartile range [IQR] 12.0% to 25.0%) within the first year, 21.0% (IQR 12.0% to 30.0%) within 1–4 years, and 23% (IQR 11% to 32%) within 4 years or longer. It found median mortality from suicide after deliberate self harm of 1.8% (IQR 0.8% to 2.6%) within the first year, 3.0% (IQR 2.0% to 4.4%) within 1–4 years, 3.4% (IQR 2.5% to 6.0%) within 5–10 years, and 6.7% (IQR 5.0% to 11.0%) within 9 years or longer.[18] Repetition of deliberate self harm is more likely in people aged 25–49 years, who are unemployed, divorced, from lower social class, or who suffer from substance misuse, depression, hopelessness, powerlessness, personality disorders, have unstable living conditions or live alone, have a criminal record, previous psychiatric treatment, a history of stressful traumatic life events, or a history of coming from broken home or of family violence.[12] Factor associated with risk of suicide after deliberate self harm are age over 45 years, male gender, unemployed or retired, separated, divorced, widowed, living alone, poor physical health, psychiatric disorder (particularly depression, alcoholism, schizophrenia, and sociopathic personality disorder), high suicidal intent in current episode including leaving a written note, violent method used in current attempt, and previous history of deliberate self harm.[19]

Please refer to CD-ROM for full text and references.

# Dementia

## Search date June 2003

*James Warner, Rob Butler, and Pradeep Arya*

People in RCTs of treatments for dementia are often not representative of people with dementia. Few RCTs are conducted in primary care and few are conducted in people with types of dementia other than Alzheimer's disease.

## What are the effects of treatments on cognitive symptoms of dementia?

### BENEFICIAL

### Donepezil

One systematic review has found that donepezil improves cognitive function and global clinical state at up to 52 weeks compared with placebo in people with mild to moderate Alzheimer's disease. The review found no significant difference in patient rated quality of life at 12 or 24 weeks between donepezil and placebo. One large RCT identified by the review found that donepezil delayed the median time to "clinically evident functional decline" by 5 months compared with placebo. One open label RCT in people with mild to moderate Alzheimer's disease found no significant difference in cognitive function at 12 weeks between donepezil and rivastigmine, although fewer people taking donepezil withdrew from the trial for any cause.

### Galantamine

RCTs have found that galantamine improves cognitive function and global clinical state over 6 months compared with placebo in people with Alzheimer's disease or vascular dementia.

### LIKELY TO BE BENEFICIAL

### Ginkgo biloba

RCTs found limited evidence that ginkgo biloba improved cognitive function over 24–26 weeks compared with placebo in people with Alzheimer's disease or vascular dementia.

### Memantine *New*

One systematic review has found that memantine improves cognitive function at 12–28 weeks compared with placebo in people with mild to moderate vascular dementia. Subsequent RCTs have found that memantine improves global clinical outcome and reduces care dependence at 12–28 weeks in people with more severe Alzheimer's disease or vascular dementia.

### Reality orientation

One systematic review of small RCTs found that reality orientation➌ improved cognitive function compared with no treatment in people with various types of dementia.

### TRADE OFF BETWEEN BENEFITS AND HARMS

### Oestrogen (in postmenopausal women)

One systematic review has found that, in postmenopausal women with mild to moderate Alzheimer's disease, oestrogen improves cognition over 7 weeks to 12 ▶

months' treatment compared with placebo or no treatment but there is concern that oestrogen treatment may increase the risk of developing breast cancer and cardiovascular events.

## Physostigmine

One RCT in people with Alzheimer's disease found limited evidence that slow release physostigmine improved cognitive function over 12 weeks compared with placebo, but adverse effects, including nausea, vomiting, diarrhoea, dizziness, and stomach pain, were common.

## Rivastigmine

One systematic review and one additional RCT have found that rivastigmine improves cognitive function compared with placebo in people with Alzheimer's disease or Lewy body dementia, but adverse effects such as nausea, vomiting, and anorexia are common. Subgroup analysis from one RCT in people with Alzheimer's disease suggests that people with vascular risk factors may respond better to rivastigmine than those without. One open label RCT in people with mild to moderate Alzheimer's disease found no significant difference in cognitive function at 12 weeks between rivastigmine and donepezil, although more people taking rivastigmine withdrew from the trial for any cause.

## Tacrine

Two systematic reviews found limited evidence that tacrine improved cognitive function and global state at at 3–36 weeks weeks compared with placebo in people with Alzheimer's disease, but adverse effects, including nausea and vomiting, diarrhoea, anorexia, and abdominal pain, were common.

### UNKNOWN EFFECTIVENESS

## Lecithin

Small, poor RCTs identified by a systematic review provided insufficient evidence to assess lecithin in people with Alzheimer's disease.

## Music therapy

Poor studies identified by a systematic review provided insufficient evidence to assess music therapy in people with dementia.

## Nicotine

One systematic review found no RCTs of sufficient quality on the effects of nicotine in people with dementia.

## Non-steroidal anti-inflammatory drugs

One RCT in people with Alzheimer's disease found no significant difference in cognitive function after 25 weeks' treatment with diclofenac plus misoprostol compared with placebo. Another RCT in people with Alzheimer's disease provided insufficient evidence to compare indometacin versus placebo in people with Alzheimer's disease.

## Reminiscence therapy

One systematic review provided insufficient evidence to assess reminiscence therapy❻ in people with dementia.

## Selegiline

One systematic review found that, in people with mild to moderate Alzheimer's disease, selegiline for 2–4 months improved cognitive function compared with placebo. It found no significant difference in global clinical state or activities of daily living. RCTs assessing outcomes beyond 4 months found no significant difference between selegiline and placebo.

**Vitamin E**

One RCT in people with moderate to severe Alzheimer's disease found no significant difference in cognitive function after 2 years' treatment with vitamin E compared with placebo. However, it found that vitamin E reduced mortality, institutionalisation, loss of ability to perform activities of daily living, and the proportion of people who developed severe dementia.

## What are the effects of treatments on behavioural and psychological symptoms of dementia?

### LIKELY TO BE BENEFICIAL

**Carbamazepine**

One RCT found that carbamazepine reduced agitation and aggression over 6 weeks compared with placebo in people with various types of dementia and behavioural and psychological symptoms.

**Reality orientation**

One systematic review of small RCTs found that reality orientation◉ improved behaviour compared with no treatment in people with various types of dementia.

### TRADE OFF BETWEEN BENEFITS AND HARMS

**Haloperidol**

One systematic review in people with various types of dementia plus behavioural and psychological symptoms found no significant difference in agitation at 6–16 weeks between haloperidol and placebo. However, it found that haloperidol may reduce aggression. It found that haloperidol increased the frequency and severity of extrapyramidal symptoms compared with placebo. Another systematic review in people with various types of dementia plus behavioural and psychological symptoms found limited evidence that haloperidol and risperidone were similarly effective in reducing agitation over 12 weeks but that haloperidol caused more frequent and more severe extrapyramidal symptoms. Two RCTs in people with agitated behaviour associated with dementia found no significant difference in agitation between trazodone and haloperidol, but may have been too small to exclude a clinically important difference.

**Olanzapine**

One RCT identified by a systematic review in nursing home residents with Alzheimer's disease or Lewy body dementia plus behavioural and psychological symptoms found that olanzapine reduced agitation, hallucinations, and delusions over 6 weeks compared with placebo. Olanzapine has been associated with cerebrovascular adverse effects.

**Risperidone**

One systematic review and one subsequent RCT in people with various types of dementia, primarily Alzheimer's disease, all with behavioural and psychological symptoms, found that risperidone improved symptoms over 12 weeks compared with placebo. Another systematic review in people with various types of dementia plus aggressive behaviours found limited evidence that risperidone and haloperidol were similarly effective in reducing agitation over 12 weeks but that risperidone caused fewer and less severe extrapyramidal symptoms. Risperidone has been associated with cerebrovascular adverse events.

▶

◀ UNKNOWN EFFECTIVENESS

### Sodium valproate

One RCT found that sodium valproate reduced agitation over 6 weeks compared with placebo in people with dementia plus behavioural and psychological problems. Another RCT found no significant difference in aggressive behaviour over 8 weeks between sodium valproate and placebo.

### Trazodone

We found no RCTs comparing trazodone versus placebo. One small RCT in people with agitated behaviour associated with dementia found no significant difference in agitation over 9 weeks between trazodone and haloperidol. Another small RCT in people with Alzheimer's disease and agitated behaviour found no significant difference in outcomes over 16 weeks among trazodone, haloperidol, behaviour management techniques, and placebo. The RCTs may have been underpowered to detect a clinically important difference.

### Donepezil; galantamine

RCTs provided inconclusive evidence about the effects of donepezil or galantamine compared with placebo on behavioural and psychiatric symptoms in people with mild to moderate Alzheimer's disease.

DEFINITION    **Dementia** is characterised by chronic, global, non-reversible impairment of cerebral function. It usually results in loss of memory (initially of recent events), loss of executive function (such as the ability to make decisions or sequence complex tasks), and changes in personality. **Alzheimer's disease** is a type of dementia characterised by an insidious onset and slow deterioration, and involves speech, motor, personality, and executive function impairment. It should be diagnosed after other systemic, psychiatric, and neurological causes of dementia have been excluded clinically and by laboratory investigation. **Vascular dementia** is multi-infarct dementia involving a stepwise deterioration of executive function with or without language and motor dysfunction occurring as a result of cerebral arterial occlusion. It usually occurs in the presence of vascular risk factors (diabetes, hypertension, and smoking). Characteristically, it has a more sudden onset and stepwise progression than Alzheimer's disease. **Lewy body dementia** is a type of dementia involving insidious impairment of executive function with (1) Parkinsonism, (2) visual hallucinations, and (3) fluctuating cognitive abilities and increased risk of falls or autonomic failure.[1,2] Careful clinical examination of people with mild to moderate dementia and the use of established diagnostic criteria accurately identifies 70–90% of cases confirmed at postmortem.[3,4]

INCIDENCE/    About 6% of people aged over 65 years and 30% of people aged over 90 years
PREVALENCE    have some form of dementia.[5] Dementia is rare before the age of 60 years. Alzheimer's disease and vascular dementia (including mixed dementia) are each estimated to account for 35–50% of dementia, and Lewy body dementia is estimated to account for up to 20% of dementia in the elderly, varying with geographical, cultural, and racial factors.[1,5–10]

AETIOLOGY/    **Alzheimer's disease:** The cause of Alzheimer's disease is unclear. A key
RISK FACTORS  pathological process is deposition of abnormal amyloid in the central nervous system.[11] Most people with the relatively rare condition of early onset Alzheimer's disease (before age 60 years) show an autosomal dominant inheritance owing to mutations on presenelin or amyloid precursor protein genes. Several genes (*APP*, *PS-1*, and *PS-2*) have been identified. Later onset dementia is sometimes clustered in families, but specific gene mutations have not been identified. Head injury, Down's syndrome, and lower premorbid intellect may be risk factors for Alzheimer's disease. **Vascular dementia** is related to cardiovascular risk factors, such as smoking, hypertension, and ▶

diabetes. **Lewy body dementia:** The cause of Lewy body dementia is unknown. Brain acetylcholine activity is reduced in many forms of dementia, and the level of reduction correlates with cognitive impairment. Many treatments for Alzheimer's disease enhance cholinergic activity.[1,6]

**PROGNOSIS**    **Alzheimer's disease:** Alzheimer's disease usually has an insidious onset with progressive reduction in cerebral function. Diagnosis is difficult in the early stages. Average life expectancy after diagnosis is 7–10 years.[10] **Lewy body dementia:** People with Lewy body dementia have an average life expectancy of about 6 years after diagnosis.[5] Behavioural problems, depression, and psychotic symptoms are common in all types of dementia.[12,13] Eventually, most people with dementia find it difficult to perform simple tasks without help.

Please refer to CD-ROM for full text and references.

## What are the effects of treatments?

We found no reliable direct evidence that one type of treatment (drug or non-drug) is superior to another in improving symptoms of depression. However, we found strong evidence that some treatments are effective, whereas the effectiveness of others remains uncertain. Of the interventions examined, prescription antidepressant drugs and electroconvulsive therapy are the only treatments for which there is good evidence of effectiveness in severe and psychotic depressive disorders. We found no RCTs comparing drug and non-drug treatments in severe depressive disorders.

### BENEFICIAL

### Cognitive therapy (in mild to moderate depression)

One systematic review in younger and older adults has found that cognitive therapy⊙ significantly improves the symptoms of depression compared with no treatment.

### Continuation drug treatment in mild to moderate depression (reduces risk of relapse in mild to moderate depression)

One systematic review and subsequent RCTs in younger and older adults have found that continuation treatment⊙ with antidepressant drugs compared with placebo for 4–6 months after recovery significantly reduces the risk of relapse. One RCT in people aged over 60 years has found that continuation treatment with dosulepin (dothiepin) significantly reduces the risk of relapse over 2 years compared with placebo.

### Electroconvulsive therapy (in severe depression)

Two systematic reviews and additional RCTs in people aged over 16 years have found that electroconvulsive therapy significantly improves symptoms in severe depression compared with simulated electroconvulsive therapy.

### Interpersonal psychotherapy (in mild to moderate depression)

One large RCT has found that interpersonal psychotherapy⊙ significantly improves rates of recovery from depression after 16 weeks compared with antidepressants or standard care.

### Prescription antidepressant drugs (in mild to moderate and severe depression)

Systematic reviews in people aged 16 years or over have found that antidepressant drugs are effective in acute treatment of all grades of depressive disorders compared with placebo. Systematic reviews have found no significant difference in outcomes with different kinds of antidepressant drug. One systematic review in people aged 55 years or over with all grades of depressive disorder has found that tricyclic antidepressants, selective serotonin reuptake inhibitors, or monoamine oxidase inhibitors significantly reduce the proportion of people who fail to recover over 26–49 days compared with placebo. We found no specific evidence on adverse effects in older adults. However, the drugs differ in their adverse event profiles.

One systematic review found that monoamine oxidase inhibitors were less effective than tricyclic antidepressants in people with severe depressive disorders, but may be more effective in atypical depressive disorders with biological features such as increased sleep, increased appetite, mood reactivity, and rejection sensitivity. ▶

# Depressive disorders

One systematic review found that selective serotonin reuptake inhibitors were associated with a lower rate of adverse effects compared with tricyclic antidepressants, but the difference was small. Another systematic review and one retrospective cohort study found no strong evidence that fluoxetine was associated with increased risk of suicide compared with tricyclic antidepressants or placebo. One RCT and observational data suggest that abrupt withdrawal of selective serotonin reuptake inhibitors is associated with symptoms including dizziness, nausea, paraesthesia, headache, and vertigo, and that these symptoms are more likely with drugs with a short half life, such as paroxetine.

### Tricyclic antidepressants

One systematic review found that tricyclic antidepressants were associated with higher rates of adverse effects compared with selective serotonin reuptake inhibitors, but the difference was small.

## LIKELY TO BE BENEFICIAL

### Care pathways (in mild to moderate depression)

Five RCTs in people aged over 18 years found limited evidence that the effectiveness of antidepressant treatment may be improved by several approaches, including collaborative working between primary care clinicians and psychiatrists plus intensive patient education, case management, telephone support, and relapse prevention programmes. One RCT found that a clinical practice guideline and practice based education did not improve either detection or outcome of depression compared with usual care.

### Combining prescription antidepressant drug and psychological treatment (in mild to moderate and severe depression)

One non-systematic review of RCTs in people aged 18–80 years has found that, in people with severe depression, adding drug treatment to interpersonal psychotherapy or to cognitive therapy compared with either psychological treatment alone improves symptoms, but found no significant difference in symptoms in people with mild to moderate depression. Subsequent RCTs in younger and older adults with mild to moderate depression have found that combining antidepressants plus psychotherapy improves symptoms significantly more than either antidepressants or psychotherapy alone. One RCT in older adults with mild to moderate depression found that cognitive behavioural therapy⊕ plus desipramine improved symptoms significantly more than desipramine alone.

### Non-directive counselling (in mild to moderate depression)

One systematic review in people aged over 18 years with recent onset psychological problems, including depression, found that brief, non-directive counselling⊕ significantly reduced symptom scores in the short term (< 6 months) compared with usual care, but found no significant difference in scores in the long term (> 6 months).

### Problem solving treatment (in mild to moderate depression)

RCTs have found that problem solving treatment⊕ significantly improves symptoms over 3–6 months compared with placebo or control, and have found no significant difference in symptoms between problem solving treatment and drug treatment.

### St John's Wort (in mild to moderate depression)

Systematic reviews in people with mild to moderate depressive disorders have found that St John's Wort (*Hypericum perforatum*) significantly improves depressive symptoms over 4–12 weeks compared with placebo, and have found no significant difference in symptoms with St John's Wort compared with prescription antidepressant drugs. The results of the reviews should be interpreted with caution ▶

because the RCTs did not use standardised preparations of St John's Wort, and doses of antidepressants varied. One large subsequent RCT in people aged over 18 with major depressive disorder found no significant difference in depressive symptoms at 8 weeks between a standardised preparation of St John's Wort and placebo or sertraline, but it is likely to have been underpowered to detect a clinically important difference.

## UNKNOWN EFFECTIVENESS

### Befriending (in mild to moderate depression)
One small RCT provided insufficient evidence to assess befriending🅖.

### Bibliotherapy (in mild to moderate depression)
One systematic review of RCTs in younger and older adults recruited by advertisement found limited evidence that bibliotherapy🅖 may reduce mild depressive symptoms compared with waiting list control or standard care. Another systematic review in people with combined anxiety and depression, anxiety, or chronic fatigue found that bibliotherapy may improve symptoms over 2–6 months compared with standard care. It is unclear whether people in the RCTs identified by the reviews are clinically representative of people with depressive disorders.

### Care pathways versus usual care for long term outcomes (in mild to moderate depression)
One RCT found that a multifaceted "quality improvement programme" significantly improved symptoms and increased the proportion of people who returned to work over 1 year compared with usual care, but found no significant difference in outcomes at 2 years.

### Cognitive therapy versus antidepressants for long term outcomes (in mild to moderate depression)
One systematic review and one additional RCT in younger and older adults found limited evidence by combining relapse rates across different RCTs that cognitive therapy may reduce the risk of relapse over 2 years compared with antidepressants.

### Exercise (in mild to moderate depression)
One systematic review found limited evidence from poor RCTs that exercise may improve symptoms compared with placebo, and may be as effective as cognitive therapy or anitdepressants.

### Psychological treatments (cognitive therapy, interpersonal psychotherapy, and problem solving treatment) in severe depression
RCTs provided insufficient evidence to assess psychological treatments in severe depression.

DEFINITION **Depressive disorders** are characterised by persistent low mood, loss of interest and enjoyment, and reduced energy. They often impair day to day functioning. Most of the RCTs assessed in this review classify depression using the *Diagnostic and statistical manual of mental disorders* (DSM IV)[1] or the *International classification of mental and behavioural disorders* (ICD-10).[2] DSM IV divides depression into major depressive disorder or dysthymic disorder. **Major depressive disorder** is characterised by one or more major depressive episodes (i.e. at least 2 wks of depressed mood or loss of interest accompanied by at least 4 additional symptoms of depression). **Dysthymic disorder** is characterised by at least 2 years of depressed mood for more days than not, accompanied by additional symptoms that do not reach the criteria for major depressive disorder.[1] ICD-10 divides depression into mild to moderate or severe depressive episodes.[2] **Mild to moderate depression** is characterised by depressive symptoms and some functional impairment. ▶

# Depressive disorders

**Severe depression** is characterised by additional agitation or psychomotor retardation with marked somatic symptoms.[2] In this review, we use both DSM IV and ICD-10 classifications, but treatments are considered to have been assessed in severe depression if the RCT included inpatients. **Older adults:** Older adults are generally defined as people aged 65 years or older. However, some of the RCTs of older people in this review included people aged 55 years or over. The presentation of depression in older adults may be atypical: low mood may be masked and anxiety or memory impairment may be the principal presenting symptoms. Dementia should be considered in the differential diagnosis of depression in older adults.[3]

**INCIDENCE/ PREVALENCE** Depressive disorders are common, with a prevalence of major depression between 5% and 10% of people seen in primary care settings.[4] Two to three times as many people may have depressive symptoms but do not meet DSM IV criteria for major depression. Women are affected twice as often as men. Depressive disorders are the fourth most important cause of disability worldwide and they are expected to become the second most important cause by the year 2020.[5,6] **Older adults:** Between 10% and 15% of older people have depressive symptoms, although major depression is relatively rare in older adults.[7]

**AETIOLOGY/ RISK FACTORS** The causes are uncertain but include both childhood events and current psychosocial adversity.

**PROGNOSIS** About half of people suffering a first episode of major depressive disorder experience further symptoms in the next 10 years.[8] **Older adults:** One systematic review (search date 1996, 12 prospective cohort studies, 1268 people, mean age 60 years) found that the prognosis may be especially poor in elderly people with a chronic or relapsing course of depression.[9] Another systematic review (search date 1999, 23 prospective cohort studies in people aged > 65 years, including 5 identified by the first review) found that depression in older people was associated with increased mortality (15 studies; pooled OR 1.73, 95% CI 1.53 to 1.95).[10]

Please refer to CD-ROM for full text and references.

## What are the effects of treatments?

### LIKELY TO BE BENEFICIAL

**Buspirone**

RCTs have found that buspirone improves symptoms over compared with placebo 4–9 weeks. RCTs found no significant difference in symptoms over 6–8 weeks between buspirone and antidepressants, diazepam, or hydroxyzine, but the studies may have lacked power to detect clinically important differences among treatments.

**Certain antidepressants (imipramine, opipramol, paroxetine, and venlafaxine)**

RCTs have found that antidepressants (imipramine, opipramol, paroxetine, and venlafaxine) improve symptoms over 4–28 weeks compared with placebo. RCTs found no significant difference among these antidepressants or between antidepressants and benzodiazepines or buspirone. RCTs and observational studies have found that antidepressants are associated with sedation, dizziness, nausea, falls, and sexual dysfunction.

**Cognitive behavioural therapy**

Two systematic reviews and two subsequent RCTs have found that cognitive behavioural therapy❻ (using a combination of interventions, such as exposure, relaxation, and cognitive restructuring) improves anxiety and depression over 4–12 weeks compared with waiting list control, anxiety management alone, relaxation alone, or non-directive psychotherapy. Three subsequent RCTs, two in people aged ≥ 60 years, found no significant difference in symptoms at 13 weeks, 6 months, or 24 months between cognitive therapy and applied relaxation.

**Hydroxyzine**

Three RCTs comparing hydroxyzine versus placebo found different results. Two RCTs found that, compared with placebo, hydroxyzine improved symptoms of anxiety at 4 or 12 weeks, but a third RCT found no significant difference in the proportion of people with improved symptoms of anxiety at 5 weeks. One of the RCTs found that hydroxyzine increased somnolence and headaches compared with placebo. One RCT found no significant difference between hydroxyzine and bromazepam in the proportion of people who responded after 6 weeks. Another RCT found no significant difference between hydroxyzine and buspirone in the proportion of people who responded after 4 weeks.

### TRADE OFF BETWEEN BENEFITS AND HARMS

**Benzodiazepines**

One systematic review and one subsequent RCT found that benzodiazepines reduced symptoms over 2–9 weeks compared with placebo. RCTs found no significant difference in symptoms over 3–8 weeks between alprazolam and bromazepam or mexazolam, or between benzodiazepines and buspirone, hydroxyzine, abecarnil, or antidepressants. RCTs and observational studies found that benzodiazepines increased the risk of dependence, sedation, industrial accidents, and road traffic accidents and that, if used in late pregnancy or while breast feeding, benzodiazepines may cause adverse effects in neonates. RCTs found no significant difference in symptoms over 3–8 weeks between alprazolam and ▶

# Generalised anxiety disorder

bromazepam or mexazolam, or between benzodiazepines and buspirone, hydroxyzine, abecarnil, or antidepressants. One systematic review of poor quality RCTs provided insufficient evidence to assess long term treatment with benzodiazepines.

## Kava

One systematic review in people with anxiety disorders, including generalised anxiety disorder, found that kava reduced symptoms of anxiety over 1–24 weeks compared with placebo. It is unclear whether results of the review are generalisable to people with generalised anxiety disorder. Observational evidence suggests that kava may be associated with hepatotoxicity.

## Trifluoperazine

One large RCT found that trifluoperazine reduced anxiety after 4 weeks compared with placebo, but caused more drowsiness, extrapyramidal reactions, and other movement disorders.

### UNKNOWN EFFECTIVENESS

## Abecarnil

One RCT found limited evidence that low dose abecarnil improved symptoms compared with placebo. Another RCT found no significant difference in symptoms at 6 weeks between abecarnil and placebo or diazepam. Both RCTs found that abecarnil increased drowsiness compared with placebo.

## Applied relaxation

We found no RCTs comparing applied relaxation versus placebo or no treatment. Three RCTs found no significant difference in symptoms at 13 weeks, 6 months, or 24 months between applied relaxation and cognitive behavioural therapy.

## β Blockers

We found no RCTs on the effects of β blockers in people with generalised anxiety disorder.

**DEFINITION**   Generalised anxiety disorder (GAD) is defined as excessive worry and tension about every day events and problems, on most days, for at least 6 months, to the point where the person experiences distress or has marked difficulty in performing day-to-day tasks.[1] It may be characterised by the following symptoms and signs: increased motor tension (fatigability, trembling, restlessness, and muscle tension); autonomic hyperactivity (shortness of breath, rapid heart rate, dry mouth, cold hands, and dizziness); and increased vigilance and scanning (feeling keyed up, increased startling, and impaired concentration), but not panic attacks.[1] One non-systematic review of epidemiological and clinical studies found marked reduction of quality of life and psychosocial functioning in people with anxiety disorders (including GAD).[2] It also found that people with GAD have low overall life satisfaction and some impairment in ability to fulfil roles, social tasks, or both.[2]

**INCIDENCE/ PREVALENCE**   One overview of observational studies published in English found that the prevalence of GAD among adults in the community is 1.5–3.0%.[3] It found that 3–5% of adults have had GAD in the past year and 4–7% have had GAD during their life. The US National Comorbidity Survey found that over 90% of people diagnosed with GAD had a co-morbid diagnosis, including dysthymia (22%), depression (39–69%), somatisation, other anxiety disorders, bipolar disorder, or substance abuse.[4] The Harvard Brown Anxiety Research Program also found that only 30/180 (17%) people had GAD alone.[5] Subgroup analysis suggested that 46/122 (38%) of people with GAD had co-morbid personality disorder.[6] A systematic review of the comorbidity of eating disorders and anxiety disorders (search date 2001, 2 observational studies, 55 people) found a lifetime prevalence of GAD among people with anorexia nervosa of ▶

24% in one study and 31% in the other.[7] The lifetime prevalence of GAD in the control group of one of the studies (44 people) was 2%. The reliability of the measures used to diagnose GAD in epidemiological studies is unsatisfactory.[8,9] One US study, with explicit diagnostic criteria (DSM-III-R), estimated that 5% of people will develop GAD at some time during their life.[9] A recent cohort study of people with depressive and anxiety disorders found that 49% of people initially diagnosed with GAD retained this diagnosis over 2 years.[10] The incidence of GAD in men is only half the incidence in women[11] and is lower in older people.[12] A non-systematic review (20 observational studies in younger and older adults) suggested that autonomic arousal to stressful tasks is decreased in older people, and that older people become accustomed to stressful tasks more quickly than younger people.[13]

**AETIOLOGY/ RISK FACTORS** GAD is believed to be associated with an increase in the number of minor stressors, independent of demographic factors,[14,15] but this finding is also common in people with other diagnoses in the clinical population.[10] One non-systematic review (5 case control studies) of psychological sequelae to civilian trauma found that rates of GAD reported in four of the five studies were significantly increased compared with a control population (rate ratio 3.3, 95% CI 2.0 to 5.5).[16] One systematic review (search date 1997) of cross-sectional studies found that bullying (or peer victimisation) was associated with a significant increase in the incidence of GAD (effect size 0.21).[17] Genetic factors are also implicated. One systematic review (search date not reported, 2 family studies, 45 index cases, 225 first degree relatives) found a significant association between GAD in the index cases and in their first degree relatives (OR 6.1, 95% CI 2.5 to 14.9).[18] The review also identified three twin studies (13 305 people), which estimated that 32% (95% CI 24% to 39%) of the variance to liability to GAD was explained by genetic factors.

**PROGNOSIS** One systematic review found that 25% of adults with GAD will be in full remission after 2 years, and 38% will have a remission after 5 years.[3] The Harvard-Brown anxiety research program reported 5 year follow up of 167 people with GAD.[19] In this period, the weighed probability for full remission was 38% and for at least partial remission was 47%: the probability of relapse from full remission was 27% and relapse from partial remission was 39%.

Please refer to CD-ROM for full text and references.

Search date September 2003

*G Mustafa Soomro*

## *What are the effects of initial treatments in adults?*

**BENEFICIAL**

### Behavioural therapy

We found no RCTs comparing behavioural therapy versus no treatment. One systematic review and subsequent RCTs have found that behavioural therapy⊕ improves symptoms compared with relaxation. The review and one subsequent RCT found no significant difference in symptoms over 4–16 weeks between behavioural therapy and cognitive therapy⊕. One subsequent RCT found limited evidence that group behavioural therapy improved symptoms after 12 weeks compared with group cognitive behavioural therapy.

### Cognitive or cognitive behavioural therapy

We found no RCTs comparing cognitive therapy versus no treatment. One RCT found that cognitive behavioural group therapy improved symptoms and quality of life compared with no treatment after 12 weeks. One systematic review and one subsequent RCT found no significant difference in symptoms over 4–16 weeks between behavioural therapy and cognitive therapy. Another subsequent RCT found limited evidence that group behavioural therapy improved symptoms over 12 weeks compared with group cognitive behavioural therapy.

### Serotonin reuptake inhibitors (citalopram, clomipramine, fluoxetine, fluvoxamine, paroxetine, sertraline)

RCTs have found that selective and non-selective serotonin reuptake inhibitors (citalopram, clomipramine, fluoxetine, fluvoxamine, paroxetine) improve symptoms compared with placebo. Two systematic reviews found inconsistent results about the effects of sertraline compared with placebo. RCTs have found that selective and non-selective serotonin reuptake inhibitors (citalopram, clomipramine, fluoxetine, fluvoxamine, paroxetine, sertraline) improve symptoms compared with tricyclic antidepressants or monoamine oxidase inhibitors. RCTs have found no consistent evidence of a difference in efficacy among serotonin reuptake inhibitors, but have found that the non-selective serotonin reuptake inhibitor clomipramine is associated with more adverse effects than selective serotonin reuptake inhibitors.

**UNKNOWN EFFECTIVENESS**

### Behavioural or cognitive therapy plus serotonin reuptake inhibitors (compared with behavioural or cognitive therapy alone)

RCTs provided insufficient evidence to assess the effects of adding serotonin reuptake inhibitors to behavioural or cognitive therapy.

### Electroconvulsive therapy

We found no RCTs of electroconvulsive therapy in people with obsessive compulsive disorder.

### Venlafaxine

One RCT provided insufficient evidence to compare vanlafaxine versus clomipramine.

◄ *What are the best forms of maintenance treatment in adults?*

UNKNOWN EFFECTIVENESS

### Optimum duration of treatment with serotonin reuptake inhibitors

RCTs provided insufficient evidence to define the optimum duration of treatment with serotonin reuptake inhibitors.

*What are the effects of treatments in adults who have not responded to initial treatment with serotonin reuptake inhibitors?*

LIKELY TO BE BENEFICIAL

### Addition of antipsychotics to serotonin reuptake inhibitors

Three small RCTs in people unresponsive to serotonin reuptake inhibitors found that the addition of antipsychotics improved symptoms compared with placebo.

**DEFINITION**   Obsessive compulsive disorder involves obsessions, compulsions, or both, that are not caused by drugs or a physical disorder, and which cause significant personal distress or social dysfunction.[1,2] The disorder may have a chronic🅖 or an episodic🅖 course. **Obsessions** are recurrent and persistent ideas, images, or impulses that cause pronounced anxiety and that the person perceives to be self produced. **Compulsions** are repetitive behaviours or mental acts performed in response to obsessions or according to certain rules, which are aimed at reducing distress or preventing certain imagined dreaded events. People with obsessive compulsive disorder may have insight into their condition, in that obsessions and compulsions are usually recognised and resisted. There are minor differences in the criteria for obsessive compulsive disorder between the third, revised third, and fourth editions of the *Diagnostic and Statistical Manual* (DSM-III, DSM-III-R, and DSM-IV)[1] and *The ICD-10 Classification of Mental and Behavioural Disorders.*[2]

**INCIDENCE/**   One national, community based survey of obsessive compulsive disorder in
**PREVALENCE**   the UK (1993, 10 000 people) found that 1% of men and 1.5% of women reported symptoms in the past month.[3] An epidemiological catchment area (ECA) survey carried out in the USA in 1984 (about 10 000 people) found age and sex standardised annual prevalence of obsessive compulsive disorder in people aged 26–64 years of 1.3%, and lifetime prevalence of 2.3%.[4] Subsequent cross national surveys using methodology comparable to ECA found age and sex standardised annual and lifetime prevalence in people aged 26–64 years as follows: Canada (survey size about 2200 people), annual prevalence 1.4% (SE 0.25), and lifetime prevalence 2.3% (SE 0.32); Puerto Rico (survey size about 1200 people), annual prevalence 1.8% (SE 0.39), and lifetime prevalence 2.5% (SE 0.46); Germany (survey size 4811 people), annual prevalence 1.6% (SE 0.57), and lifetime prevalence 2.1% (SE 0.66); Taiwan (survey size about 7400 people), annual prevalence 0.4% (SE 0.07), and lifetime prevalence 0.7% (SE 0.10); Korea (survey size about 4000 people), annual prevalence 1.1% (SE 0.10), and lifetime prevalence 1.9% (SE 0.20); and New Zealand (survey size about 1200 people), annual prevalence 1.1% (SE 0.31), and lifetime prevalence 2.2% (SE 0.42).[4]

**AETIOLOGY/**   The cause of obsessive compulsive disorder is uncertain. Behavioural, cogni-
**RISK FACTORS**   tive, genetic, and neurobiological factors have been implicated.[5–11] Risk factors include a family history of obsessive compulsive disorder, being single (which ▶

could be a consequence of the disorder), and belonging to a higher socioeconomic class.[12] Other risk factors include cocaine abuse, female sex, not being in paid employment, past history of alcohol dependence, affective disorder, and phobic disorder.[4]

**PROGNOSIS** One study (144 people followed for a mean of 47 years) found that an episodic course of obsessive compulsive disorder was more common during the initial years (about 1–9 years), but a chronic course was more common afterwards.[13] Over time, the study found that 39–48% of people had symptomatic improvement. A 1 year prospective cohort study found 46% of people had an episodic course and 54% had a chronic course.[14]

Please refer to CD-ROM for full text and references.

### Search date September 2003

*Shailesh Kumar and Mark Oakley-Browne*

## What are the effects of drug treatments?

### BENEFICIAL

#### Selective serotonin reuptake inhibitors

Systematic reviews and one additional RCT have found that selective serotonin reuptake inhibitors improve symptoms in panic disorder compared with placebo. One subsequent RCT found that discontinuation of sertraline in people with a good response increased exacerbation of symptoms. A second subsequent RCT found that paroxetine plus cognitive behavioural therapy☉ improved symptoms compared with placebo plus cognitive behavioural therapy.

#### Tricyclic antidepressants (imipramine)

One systematic review, one subsequent RCT, and one additional RCT have found that imipramine improves symptoms compared with placebo. One subsequent RCT found that imipramine reduced relapse rates over 12 months.

### TRADE OFF BETWEEN BENEFITS AND HARMS

#### Benzodiazepines

One systematic review and one additional RCT have found that alprazolam reduces the number of panic attacks and improves symptoms compared with placebo. However, benzodiazepines are associated with a wide range of adverse effects, both during and after treatment.

### UNKNOWN EFFECTIVENESS

#### Buspirone

We found insufficient evidence to assess the effects of buspirone compared with placebo.

#### Monoamine oxidase inhibitors

We found no RCTs on the effects of monoamine oxidase inhibitors.

**DEFINITION**     A panic attack is a period in which there is sudden onset of intense apprehension, fearfulness, or terror often associated with feelings of impending doom. Panic disorder occurs when there are recurrent, unpredictable attacks followed by at least 1 month of persistent concern about having another panic attack, worry about the possible implications or consequences of the panic attacks, or a significant behavioural change related to the attacks.[1] The term panic disorder excludes panic attacks attributable to the direct physiological effects of a general medical condition, a substance, or another mental disorder. Panic disorder is sometimes categorised as being with or without agoraphobia.[1] Alternative categorisations focus on phobic anxiety disorders and specify agoraphobia with or without panic disorder.[2]

**INCIDENCE/**     Panic disorder often starts at around 20 years of age (between late adoles-
**PREVALENCE**     cence and the mid 30s).[3] Lifetime prevalence is 1–3%, and panic disorder is more common in women than in men.[4] An Australian community study found 1 month prevalence rates for panic disorder (with or without agoraphobia) of 0.4% using International Classification of Diseases (ICD)-10 diagnostic criteria, and of 0.5% using Diagnostic and Statistical Manual (DSM)-IV diagnostic criteria.[5]

# Panic disorder

**AETIOLOGY/ RISK FACTORS**  Stressful life events tend to precede the onset of panic disorder,[6,7] although a negative interpretation of these events in addition to their occurrence has been suggested as an important casual factor.[8] Panic disorder is associated with major depression,[9] social phobia, generalised anxiety disorder, obsessive compulsive disorder,[10] and a substantial risk of drug and alcohol abuse.[11] It is also associated with avoidant, histrionic, and dependent personality disorders.[10]

**PROGNOSIS**  The severity of symptoms in people with panic disorder fluctuates considerably, and patients commonly experience periods of no attacks, or only mild attacks with few symptoms. There is often a long delay between the initial onset of symptoms and presentation for treatment. Recurrent attacks may continue for several years, especially if associated with agoraphobia. Reduced social or occupational functioning varies among people with panic disorder and is worse in people with associated agoraphobia. Panic disorder is also associated with an increased rate of attempted, but unsuccessful, suicide.[12] One study analysing data from RCTs and systematic reviews found that co-existence of anxiety and depressive features adversely affected treatment response at 12 years compared with treatment of panic disorder alone.[13]

Please refer to CD-ROM for full text and references.

## What are the effects of preventive interventions?

### LIKELY TO BE BENEFICIAL

**Multiple session cognitive behavioural therapy in people with acute stress disorder**

Two small RCTs in people with acute stress disorder after a traumatic event (accident or non-sexual assault) found that five sessions of cognitive behavioural therapy❻ reduces the proportion of people with post-traumatic stress disorder after 6 months compared with supportive counselling❻.

### UNKNOWN EFFECTIVENESS

**Hydrocortisone** *New*

One small RCT in people in intensive care with septic shock provided insufficient evidence to assess hydrocortisone in preventing post-traumatic stress disorder.

**Multiple session cognitive behavioural therapy in all people exposed to a traumatic event**

One RCT in bus drivers who had been attacked in the past 5 months found that cognitive behavioural therapy improved measures of anxiety and intrusive symptoms at 6 months compared with standard care. It found no significant difference in measures of depression or avoidance symptoms. Another RCT provided insufficient evidence to assess cognitive behavioural therapy plus educational techniques in preventing post-traumatic stress disorder in road traffic accident survivors. A third small RCT provided insufficient evidence to compare memory structuring versus supportive listening in road traffic accident survivors.

**Multiple session education**

One RCT provided insufficient evidence to assess educational techniques plus cognitive behavioural therapy in preventing post-traumatic stress disorder in road traffic accident survivors.

**Multiple session trauma support**

Two RCTs provided insufficient evidence to assess collaborative care❻ interventions involving emotional, social, and practical support in people exposed to a traumatic event in the past 1 day to 1 week.

**Propranolol** *New*

One small RCT provided insufficient evidence to assess propranolol in preventing post-traumatic stress disorder in people with early symptoms of post-traumatic stress disorder after a traumatic event.

**Temazepam** *New*

One small RCT provided insufficient evidence to assess temazepam in preventing post-traumatic stress disorder in people with acute stress disorder or early symptoms of post-traumatic stress disorder after road traffic accident, industrial accident, or non-sexual assault.

# Post-traumatic stress disorder

## UNLIKELY TO BE BENEFICIAL

### Single session psychological interventions ("debriefing") in all people exposed to a traumatic event

RCTs in people who had been exposed to a traumatic event in the previous month found no significant difference between a single session of psychological debriefing⊕ and no debriefing in the incidence of post-traumatic stress disorder at 3 months or 1 year. One RCT found that debriefing within 10 hours reduced post-traumatic stress disorder compared with debriefing after 48 hours.

## *What are the effects of treatments?*

### BENEFICIAL

### Cognitive behavioural therapy

RCTs have found that cognitive behavioural therapy⊕ improves post-traumatic stress disorder symptoms, anxiety, and depression immediately after treatment and at up to 1 year compared with no treatment or supportive counselling⊕.

### Eye movement desensitisation and reprocessing

RCTs have found that eye movement desensitisation and reprocessing⊕ improves symptoms compared with no treatment. RCTs have found no significant difference in symptoms between eye movement desensitisation and reprocessing and cognitive behavioural therapy.

### Paroxetine

One systematic review and subsequent RCTs found that paroxetine reduced symptoms at 3 months compared with placebo.

### Sertraline

RCTs found that sertraline reduced symptoms at 3–7 months compared with placebo.

### LIKELY TO BE BENEFICIAL

### Fluoxetine

Two RCTs found that fluoxetine may reduce symptoms at 3 months compared with placebo.

### UNKNOWN EFFECTIVENESS

**Affect management⊕; benzodiazepines; carbamazepine, drama therapy⊕; eclectic psychotherapy; group therapy; hypnotherapy⊕; inpatient programmes; interapy⊕; lamotrigine; mirtazapine; monoamine oxidase inhibitors (brofaromine, phenelzine); nefazodone; propranolol; psychodynamic psychotherapy⊕; risperidone *New*; supportive counselling; tricyclic antidepressants (amitriptyline, imipramine)**

We found insufficient evidence about the effects of these interventions in improving symptoms.

DEFINITION    **Post-traumatic stress disorder (PTSD)** can occur after any major traumatic event. Symptoms include upsetting thoughts and nightmares about the traumatic event, avoidance behaviour, numbing of general responsiveness, increased irritability, and hypervigilance.[1] To fulfil the *Diagnostic and statistical manual of mental disorders* (DSM IV) criteria for PTSD, an individual must have been exposed to a traumatic event, have at least one re-experiencing, three avoidance and two hyperarousal phenomena, have had the symptoms for at least 1 month, and the symptoms must cause clinically important ▶

distress or reduced day to day functioning.[1] People with **sub-syndromal PTSD** have all the criteria for PTSD except one of the re-experiencing, avoidance, or hyperarousal phenomena. **Acute stress disorder** occurs within the first month after a major traumatic event and requires the presence of symptoms for at least 2 days. It is similar to PTSD but dissociative symptoms🅖 are required to make the diagnosis.

**INCIDENCE/ PREVALENCE**
One large cross-sectional study in the USA found that 1/10 women and 1/20 men experience PTSD at some stage in their lives.[2]

**AETIOLOGY/ RISK FACTORS**
Risk factors include major trauma, such as rape, a history of psychiatric disorders, acute distress and depression after the trauma, lack of social support, and personality factors.[3]

**PROGNOSIS**
One large cross-sectional study in the USA found that over a third of sufferers continued to satisfy the criteria for a diagnosis of PTSD 6 years after diagnosis.[2] However, cross-sectional studies provide weak evidence about prognosis.

---

Please refer to CD-ROM for full text and references.

# Schizophrenia

**Search date December 2002**

*Zia Nadeem, Andrew McIntosh, and Stephen Lawrie*

---

## What are the effects of treatments?

Most evidence is from systematic reviews of RCTs that report disparate outcomes. There is a need for larger RCTs, over longer periods, with well designed end points, including standardised, validated symptom scales. No intervention has been found to consistently reduce negative symptoms.

### BENEFICIAL

#### Continuation of antipsychotic drugs for 6–9 months after an acute episode to reduce relapse rates

Systematic reviews have found that continuing antipsychotic drugs for at least 6 months after an acute episode reduces relapse rates compared with no treatment or placebo, and that some benefit of continuing antipsychotics is apparent for up to 2 years.

#### Multiple session family interventions to reduce relapse rates

One systematic review found that multiple session family interventions reduced relapse rates at 12 months compared with usual care, single session family interventions, or psychoeducational interventions.

#### Psychoeducational interventions to reduce relapse rates

One systematic review has found that psychoeducation reduces relapse rates at 9–18 months compared with a control intervention.

### LIKELY TO BE BENEFICIAL

#### Behavioural therapy to improve adherence

One RCT found that behavioural interventions improved adherence to antipsychotic medication over 3 months compared with usual treatment. Two RCTs found limited evidence that behavioural interventions may improve adherence more than psychoeducational therapy.

#### Compliance therapy to improve adherence

Two RCTs found limited evidence that compliance therapy⊙ may increase adherence to antipsychotic drugs at 6 and 18 months compared with non-specific counselling.

#### Psychoeducational interventions to improve adherence

One systematic review found limited evidence that psychoeducation improved adherence to antipsychotic medication compared with usual care. Two RCTs found limited evidence that psychoeducational therapy may improve adherence less than behavioural therapy.

### TRADE OFF BETWEEN BENEFITS AND HARMS

#### Chlorpromazine

One systematic review has found that, compared with placebo, chlorpromazine reduces the proportion of people who have no improvement, or have marked or worse severity of illness at 6 months on a psychiatrist rated scale. The review found that chlorpromazine caused more adverse effects, such as sedation, acute dystonia, and parkinsonism, than placebo.

▶

### ◀ Clozapine

Two systematic reviews found that clozapine improved symptoms over 4–10 weeks compared with standard antipsychotic drugs. However, RCTs found that clozapine may be associated with blood dyscrasias. Three systematic reviews of small RCTs provided insufficient evidence to compare clozapine versus other new antipsychotic drugs. One systematic review in people resistant to standard treatment found that clozapine improved symptoms after 12 weeks and after 2 years compared with standard antipsychotic drugs. RCTs provided insufficient evidence to compare clozapine versus other newer antipsychotics in people resistant to standard antipsychotic drugs.

### Depot bromperidol decanoate

RCTs found no significant difference in the proportion of people who needed additional medication, left the trial early, or had movement disorders over 6–12 months between depot bromperidol decanoate and haloperidol or fluphenazine decanoate.

### Depot haloperidol decanoate

One systematic review of one small RCT found no significant difference in global clinical state at 4 months between depot haloperidol decanoate and oral haloperidol, but it may have been too small to exclude a clinically important difference. Haloperidol is associated with acute dystonia, akathisia, and parkinsonism.

### Haloperidol

One systematic review has found that haloperidol increases physician rated global improvement at 6 and 24 weeks compared with placebo but is associated with acute dystonia, akathisia, and parkinsonism.

### Thioridazine

One systematic review has found that thioridazine improves global mental state over 3–12 months compared with placebo.

### Amisulpride; loxapine; molindone; olanzapine; pimozide; quetiapine; risperidone; sulpiride; ziprasidone; zotepine

Systematic reviews have found that these newer antipsychotic drugs are as effective in improving symptoms as standard antipsychotic drugs, and have different profiles of adverse effects.

### UNKNOWN EFFECTIVENESS

### Cognitive behavioural therapy to reduce relapse rates

Limited evidence from a systematic review of two RCTs found no significant difference in relapse rates between cognitive behavioural therapy plus standard care and standard care alone.

### Multiple session family interventions to improve adherence

One systematic review found that "compliance with medication" over 9–24 months was higher in people who received multiple family interventions compared with usual care, single family interventions, or psychoeducational interventions, but the difference did not quite reach significance.

### Perazine

RCTs provided insufficient evidence to assess perazine.

### Social skills training to reduce relapse rates

One systematic review of small RCTs provided insufficient evidence to assess social skills training.

# Schizophrenia

**DEFINITION**   Schizophrenia is characterised by the positive symptoms❿ of auditory hallu-cinations, delusions, and thought disorder, and by the negative symptoms❿ of demotivation, self neglect, and reduced emotion.[1] People are defined as being resistant to standard antipsychotic drugs if, over the preceding 5 years, they have not had a clinically important improvement in symptoms after 2–3 regimens of treatment with standard antipsychotic drugs for at least 6 weeks (from at least 2 classes at doses equivalent to or greater than 1000 mg/day chlorpromazine) and they have had no period of good functioning.[2,3] Approxi-mately 30% (10–45%) of people with schizophrenia meet these criteria.[3]

**INCIDENCE/**   Onset of symptoms typically occurs in early adult life (average age 25 years)
**PREVALENCE**   and is earlier in men than women.[4,5] Prevalence worldwide is 2–4/1000. One in 100 people will develop schizophrenia in their lifetime.

**AETIOLOGY/**   Risk factors include a family history (although no major genes have been
**RISK FACTORS** identified); obstetric complications; developmental difficulties; central nervous system infections in childhood; cannabis use; and acute life events.[4] The precise contributions of these factors and ways in which they may interact are unclear.

**PROGNOSIS**   About three quarters of people suffer recurrent relapse and continued disability, although the proportion of people who improved significantly increased after the mid-1950s (mean 48.5% from 1956–1985 v 35.4% from 1895–1956).[6] Outcome may be worse in people with insidious onset and delayed initial treatment, social isolation, or a strong family history; in people living in industrialised countries; in men; and in people who misuse drugs.[5] Drug treatment is generally successful in treating positive symptoms, but up to a third of people derive little benefit and negative symptoms are notoriously difficult to treat. About half of people with schizophrenia do not adhere to treatment in the short term. The figure is even higher in the longer term.[7]

Please refer to CD-ROM for full text and references.

Search date July 2003

*Peter Struijs and Gino Kerkhoffs*

## What are the effects of treatment strategies for acute ankle ligament ruptures?

### BENEFICIAL

#### Functional treatment

One systematic review and one subsequent RCT found limited evidence that functional treatment⊕ reduced the risk of the ankle giving way compared with minimal treatment. One systematic review and one subsequent RCT found that, compared with immobilisation⊕, functional treatment improved symptoms and functional outcomes at short (< 6 weeks), intermediate (6 weeks to 1 year), or long term (> 1 year) follow up. However, effects were to be less marked at long term follow up, or if only results from high quality trials were analysed. One systematic review and one subsequent RCT provided insufficient evidence to compare functional treatment versus surgery. One systematic review and three additional RCTs provided insufficient evidence to compare different functional treatments.

### LIKELY TO BE BENEFICIAL

#### Immobilisation

There is consensus that immobilisation is more effective than no treatment, however one systematic review and one subsequent RCT found that, compared with functional treatment, immobilisation was associated with less improvement in symptoms and functional outcomes at either short (< 6 weeks), intermediate (6 weeks to 1 year), or long term (> 1 year) follow up. However, effects were less marked at long term follow up, or if only results from high quality trials were analysed. One systematic review found no significant difference between immobilisation and surgery in pain or subjective instability. One systematic review found insufficient evidence to compare immobilisation versus physiotherapy.

#### Surgery

One systematic review found no significant difference between surgery and immobilisation in pain or subjective instability. Other systematic reviews and one subsequent RCT provided insufficient evidence to compare surgery versus functional treatment or versus conservative treatment (including both immobilisation and functional treatment).

### UNKNOWN EFFECTIVENESS

#### Diathermy

One systematic review found insufficient evidence on the effects of diathermy versus placebo on walking ability and reduction in swelling.

#### Homeopathic ointment

One systematic review of one small RCT found limited evidence that homeopathic ointment improved outcome on a "composite criteria of treatment success" compared with placebo.

▶

# Ankle sprain

## UNLIKELY TO BE BENEFICIAL

### Cold pack compression

Two RCTs found no significant difference in symptoms between cold pack placement and placebo or control. One RCT found less oedema with cold pack placement compared with heat or a contrast bath at 3–5 days after injury.

### Ultrasound

One systematic review found no significant difference between ultrasound and sham ultrasound in the general improvement of symptoms or the ability to walk or bear weight at 7 days. Three RCTs provided insufficient evidence to compare ultrasound versus other treatments.

**DEFINITION**      Ankle sprain is an injury of the lateral ligament complex of the ankle joint. Such injury can range from mild to severe and is graded on the basis of severity.[1–5] Grade I is a mild stretching of the ligament complex without joint instability; grade II is a partial rupture of the ligament complex with mild instability of the joint (such as isolated rupture of the anterior talofibular ligament); and grade III involves complete rupture of the ligament complex with instability of the joint. Practically, this gradation may be considered as purely theoretical, because it has no therapeutic or prognostic consequences. Unless otherwise stated, studies included in this topic did not specify the grades of injury included, or included a wide range of grades.

**INCIDENCE/**      Ankle sprain is a common problem in acute medical care, occurring at a rate
**PREVALENCE**   of about one injury/10 000 population a day.[6] Injuries of the lateral ligament complex of the ankle form a quarter of all sports injuries.[6]

**AETIOLOGY/**      The usual mechanism of injury is inversion and adduction (usually referred to as
**RISK FACTORS** supination) of the plantar flexed foot. Predisposing factors are a history of ankle sprains and specific malalignment, like crus varum🌀 and pes cavo-varus🌀.

**PROGNOSIS**      Some sports (e.g. basketball, football/soccer, and volleyball) are associated with a particularly high incidence of ankle injuries. Pain is the most frequent residual problem, often localised on the medial side of the ankle.[4] Other residual complaints include mechanical instability, intermittent swelling, and stiffness. People with more extensive cartilage damage have a higher incidence of residual complaints.[4] Long term cartilage damage can lead to degenerative changes, especially if there is persistent or recurrent instability. Every further sprain has the potential to add new damage.

Please refer to CD-ROM for full text and references.

Search date September 2003

*Jill Ferrari*

## What are the effects of conservative treatments?

### UNKNOWN EFFECTIVENESS

**Night splints**
We found no RCTs about the effects of night splints compared with other treatments or no treatmnt.

**Orthoses to treat hallux valgus in adults**
One RCT found that, in adults, orthoses reduced pain compared with no treatment at 6 months but not at 1 year.

### LIKELY TO BE INEFFECTIVE OR HARMFUL

**Antipronatory orthoses in children**
One RCT in children found limited evidence that antipronatory orthoses increased deterioration in metatarsophalangeal joint angles after 3 years compared with no treatment, although the difference was not statistically significant.

## What are the effects of surgery?

### LIKELY TO BE BENEFICIAL

**Chevron osteotomy (more effective than no treatment or orthoses, but insufficient evidence to compare with other metatarsal osteotomies)**
One RCT found that chevron osteotomy improved outcomes compared with orthoses or no treatment after 1 year. A systematic review found conflicting evidence on the effects of chevron osteotomy compared with other metatarsal osteotomies.

### UNKNOWN EFFECTIVENESS

**Chevron osteotomy plus adductor tenotomy**
A systematic review found no evidence that adductor tenotomy plus chevron osteotomy improved outcomes compared with chevron osteotomy alone.

**Chevron osteotomy plus Akin osteotomy**
One small RCT found no significant difference in outcomes between chevron osteotomy plus Akin osteotomy and Akin osteotomy plus distal soft tissue reconstruction at 1 year. However, this trial may have lacked power to detect a clinically significant difference.

**Different methods of bone fixation**
One small RCT found no significant difference between absorbable pin fixation and standard fixation in clinical or radiological outcomes; however, it may have lacked power to detect a clinically significant difference. One small RCT found that screw fixation plus early weight bearing reduced time to return to work and social activity compared with suture fixation and later weight bearing, but found no significant difference in radiological outcomes.

**Keller's arthroplasty**
One systematic review provided insufficient evidence on the effects of Keller's arthroplasty compared with other types of operation.

# Bunions

Musculoskeletal disorders

## What are the effects of postoperative care?

### Continuous passive motion
One systematic review provided insufficient evidence on the effects of continuous passive motion.

### Early weight bearing
One systematic review provided insufficient evidence on the effects of early weight bearing.

### Slipper casts
Two RCTs provided insufficient evidence on the effects of plaster slipper casts.

**DEFINITION**    **Hallux valgus** is a deformity of the great toe, whereby the hallux (great toe) moves towards the second toe, overlying it in severe cases. This movement of the hallux is described as abduction (movement away from the midline of the body) and it is usually accompanied by some rotation of the toe so that the nail is facing the midline of the body (valgus rotation). With the deformity, the metatarsal head becomes more prominent and the metatarsal is said to be in an adducted position as it moves towards the midline of the body.[1] Radio-logical criteria for hallux valgus vary, but a commonly accepted criterion is to measure the angle formed between the metatarsal and the abducted hallux. This is called the metatarsophalangeal joint angle or hallux abductus angle and it is considered abnormal when it is greater than $14.5°$.[2] **Bunion** is the lay term used to describe a prominent and often inflamed metatarsal head and overlying bursa. Symptoms include pain, limitation in walking, and problems with wearing normal shoes.

**INCIDENCE/**    The prevalence of hallux valgus varies in different populations. In a recent
**PREVALENCE**    study of 6000 UK school children aged 9–10 years, 2.5% had clinical evidence of hallux valgus, and 2% met both clinical and radiological criteria for hallux valgus. An earlier study found hallux valgus in 48% of adults.[2] Differences in prevalence may result from different methods of measurement, varying age groups, or different diagnostic criteria (e.g. metatarsal joint angle $> 10°$ or $> 15°$).[3]

**AETIOLOGY/**    Nearly all population studies have found that hallux valgus is more common in
**RISK FACTORS**   women. Footwear may contribute to the deformity, but studies comparing people who wear shoes with those who do not have found contradictory results. Hypermobility of the first ray🝆 and excessive foot pronation are associated with hallux valgus.[4]

**PROGNOSIS**    We found no studies that looked at the progression of hallux valgus. While progression of deformity and symptoms is rapid in some people, others remain asymptomatic. One study found that hallux valgus is often unilateral initially, but usually progresses to bilateral deformity.[2]

Please refer to CD-ROM for full text and references.

## Search date September 2002

*Shawn Marshall*

## *What are the effects of treatments?*

### BENEFICIAL

#### Local corticosteroid injection (short term)

Two RCTs found local corticosteroid injection (methylprednisolone, hydrocortisone) versus placebo or no treatment significantly improved symptoms after 4–6 weeks. One small RCT found that local betamethasone injection versus betamethasone injection into the deltoid significantly improved symptoms after 1 month. One RCT found no significant difference with local methylprednisolone injection versus oral prednisolone in symptoms after 2 weeks, but found that local methylprednisolone injection versus oral prednisolone significantly improved symptoms after 8 and 12 weeks. One small RCT found that local methylprednisolone injection versus helium neon laser significantly improved symptoms after 20 days, but found no significant difference in symptoms between the two groups after 6 months. One small RCT found no significant difference with local methylprednisolone injection versus non-steroidal anti-inflammatory plus nocturnal neutral angle wrist splints in symptoms after 2 or 8 weeks.

#### Oral corticosteroids (short term)

One small RCT found that oral prednisone versus placebo significantly improved the mean global symptom score after 2 weeks, but not after 4 or 8 weeks. One small RCT found that oral prednisolone versus placebo significantly improved the mean global symptom score after 2 and 4 weeks. One small RCT found that oral prednisolone versus placebo significantly improved the median global symptom score after 2 and 8 weeks. One RCT found no significant difference with local methylprednisolone injection versus oral prednisolone in symptoms after 2 weeks, but found that local methylprednisolone injection versus oral prednisolone significantly improved symptoms after 8 and 12 weeks.

### TRADE OFF BETWEEN BENEFITS AND HARMS

#### Endoscopic carpal tunnel release versus open carpal tunnel release

We found no RCTs comparing surgery versus placebo. One systematic review and subsequent RCTs found no clear evidence of a difference in symptoms with endoscopic carpal tunnel release versus open carpal tunnel release up to 12 months after the operation. RCTs found conflicting evidence on differences in the time taken to return to work between endoscopic carpal tunnel release versus open carpal tunnel release. Harms resulting from endoscopic carpal tunnel release and open carpal tunnel release vary between RCTs. One systematic review comparing the interventions suggests that endoscopic carpal tunnel release may cause more transient nerve problems whereas open carpal tunnel release may cause more wound problems.

### UNKNOWN EFFECTIVENESS

#### Nerve and tendon gliding exercises

One small RCT found no significant difference with nerve and tendon gliding exercises⊕ plus neutral angle wrist splint versus neutral angle wrist splint alone in mean symptom severity score or mean functional status score assessed 8 weeks after the end of the treatment.

# Carpal tunnel syndrome

### Pyridoxine

One very small RCT found a similar improvement in symptoms with pyridoxine versus placebo or no treatment after 10 weeks. The RCT may have been too small to detect a clinically important difference between treatments. One small RCT found no significant difference with pyridoxine versus placebo in nocturnal pain, numbness, or tingling after 12 weeks.

### Surgery versus placebo or non-surgical intervention

We found no RCTs comparing surgery versus placebo. One very small RCT found limited evidence that surgical section of the anterior carpal ligament versus splinting of the hand, wrist, and arm for 1 month increased the proportion of people with clinical improvement after 1 year.

### Therapeutic ultrasound

One RCT found ultrasound versus placebo significantly increased the proportion of wrists with satisfactory improvement or complete remission of symptoms after 6 months. One RCT found no significant difference in mean symptom severity with high intensity or low intensity ultrasound versus placebo after 2 weeks. One RCT found no significant difference in symptom severity scores with ibuprofen plus nocturnal wrist splint versus chiropractic manipulation plus ultrasound plus nocturnal wrist splint after 9 weeks.

### Wrist splints

One RCT found a significant improvement in symptoms after 2 and 4 weeks with a nocturnal hand brace versus no treatment. RCTs found no significant difference in symptoms with neutral angle versus 20° extension wrist splinting, or with full time versus night time only neutral angle wrist splinting.

### Local corticosteroid injection (long term); oral corticosteroids (long term)

We found no RCTs on the effects of these interventions.

## UNLIKELY TO BE BENEFICIAL

### Diuretics

One small RCT found no significant difference with trichlormethiazide versus placebo in mean global symptom score after 2 or 4 weeks. One RCT found no significant difference with bendrofluazide versus placebo in the proportion of people with no improvement in symptoms after 4 weeks.

### Internal neurolysis in conjunction with open carpal tunnel release

Three RCTs found no significant difference with open carpal tunnel release alone versus open carpal tunnel release plus internal neurolysis in symptoms.

### Non-steroidal anti-inflammatory drugs

One small RCT found no significant difference with tenoxicam versus placebo in mean global symptom score after 2 or 4 weeks. One RCT found no significant difference in symptom severity scores with ibuprofen plus nocturnal wrist splint versus chiropractic manipulation plus ultrasound plus nocturnal wrist splint after 9 weeks.

## LIKELY TO BE INEFFECTIVE OR HARMFUL

### Wrist splinting after carpal tunnel release surgery

Two RCTs in people after carpal tunnel release surgery found no significant difference with wrist splinting versus no splinting in median grip strength or in the number of people who considered themselves "cured". Another RCT found that splinting versus no splinting significantly increased pain at 1 month and the number of days taken to return to work.

◀ **DEFINITION**  Carpal tunnel syndrome is a neuropathy caused by compression of the median nerve within the carpal tunnel.[1] Classical symptoms of carpal tunnel syndrome include numbness, tingling, burning, or pain in at least two of the three digits supplied by the median nerve (i.e. the thumb, index, and middle fingers).[2] The American Academy of Neurology has described diagnostic criteria❸ that rely on a combination of symptoms and physical examination findings.[3] Other diagnostic criteria include results from electrophysiological studies.[2]

**INCIDENCE/ PREVALENCE**  A general population survey in Rochester, Minnesota, found the age adjusted incidence of carpal tunnel syndrome to be 105 (95% CI 99 to 112) cases per 100 000 person years.[4,5] Age adjusted incidence rates were 52 (95% CI 45 to 59) cases for men and 149 (95% CI 138 to 159) cases for women per 100 000 person years. The study found incidence rates increased from 88 (95% CI 75 to 101) cases per 100 000 person years in 1961–1965 to 125 (95% CI 112 to 138) cases per 100 000 person years in 1976–1980. Incidence rates of carpal tunnel syndrome increased with age for men, whereas for women they peaked between the ages of 45–54 years. A general population survey in the Netherlands found prevalence to be 1% for men and 7% for women.[6] A more comprehensive study in southern Sweden found the general population prevalence for carpal tunnel syndrome was 3% (95% CI 2% to 3%).[7] As in other studies, the overall prevalence in women was higher than in men (male to female ratio 1 : 1.4); however, among older people, the prevalence in women was almost four times that in men (age group 65–74 years: men 1%, 95% CI 0% to 4%; women 5%, 95% CI 3% to 8%).

**AETIOLOGY/ RISK FACTORS**  Most cases of carpal tunnel syndrome have no easily identifiable cause (idiopathic).[4] Secondary causes of carpal tunnel syndrome include the following: space occupying lesions (tumours, hypertrophic synovial tissue, fracture callus, and osteophytes); metabolic and physiological (pregnancy, hypothyroidism, rheumatoid arthritis); infections; neuropathies (associated with diabetes mellitus or alcoholism); and familial disorders.[4] One case control study found that risk factors in the general population included repetitive activities requiring wrist extension or flexion, obesity, very rapid dieting, shorter height, hysterectomy without oopherectomy, and recent menopause.[8]

**PROGNOSIS**  One observational study (carpal tunnel syndrome defined by symptoms and electrophysiological study results) found that 34% of people with idiopathic carpal tunnel syndrome without treatment had complete resolution of symptoms (remission) within 6 months of diagnosis.[9] Remission rates were higher for younger age groups, for women versus men, and for pregnant versus non-pregnant women. A more recent observational study of untreated idiopathic carpal tunnel syndrome also demonstrated that symptoms may spontaneously resolve in some people. The main positive prognostic indicators were short duration of symptoms and young age, whereas bilateral symptoms and a positive Phalen's test were indicators of a poorer prognosis.[10]

Please refer to CD-ROM for full text and references.

**Chronic fatigue syndrome**

Search date March 2003

*Steven Reid, Trudie Chalder, Anthony Cleare, Matthew Hotopf, and Simon Wessely*

## What are the effects of treatments?

### BENEFICIAL

**Cognitive behavioural therapy**

One systematic review found that cognitive behavioural therapy administered by highly skilled therapists in specialist centres improved quality of life and physical functioning compared with standard medical care or relaxation therapy. One additional multicentre RCT found that cognitive behavioural therapy administered by less experienced therapists may also be effective compared with guided support groups or no interventions.

**Graded aerobic exercise**

RCTs have found that a graded aerobic exercise programme improves measures of fatigue and physical functioning compared with flexibility and relaxation training or general advice. One RCT has found that an educational package to encourage graded exercise improved measures of physical functioning, fatigue, mood, and sleep at 1 year compared with written information alone.

### UNKNOWN EFFECTIVENESS

**Dietary supplements**

One small RCT found no significant difference between a nutritional supplement (containing multivitamins, minerals, and coenzymes) and placebo in fatigue severity or functional impairment at 10 weeks.

**Evening primrose oil**

One small RCT found no significant difference between evening primrose oil and placebo in depression scores at 3 months.

**Magnesium (intramuscular)**

One small RCT found that intramuscular magnesium injections improved symptoms at 6 weeks compared with placebo. However, we were unable to draw reliable conclusions from this small study.

**Antidepressants; corticosteroids; oral nicotinamide adenine dinucleotide**

RCTs found insufficient evidence about the effects of these interventions in people with chronic fatigue syndrome.

### UNLIKELY TO BE BENEFICIAL

**Immunotherapy**

Small RCTs found limited evidence that immunoglobulin G modestly improved physical functioning and fatigue at 3–6 months compared with placebo, but it was associated with considerable adverse effects. Small RCTs found insufficient evidence on the effects of interferon alfa or aciclovir compared with placebo. One RCT found that staphylococcus toxoid improved symptoms at six months compared with placebo, although it is associated with local reaction and could cause anaphylaxis.

**Prolonged rest**

We found no RCTs on the effects of prolonged rest. Indirect observational evidence in healthy volunteers and in people recovering from a viral illness suggests that prolonged rest may perpetuate or worsen fatigue and symptoms.

**Musculoskeletal disorders**

**DEFINITION** ◀ Chronic fatigue syndrome (CFS) is characterised by severe, disabling fatigue and other symptoms, including musculoskeletal pain, sleep disturbance, impaired concentration, and headaches. Two widely used definitions of CFS, from the US Centers for Disease Control and Prevention[1] and from Oxford, UK,[2] were developed as operational criteria for research❶. There are important differences between these definitions. The UK criteria insist upon the presence of mental fatigue, whereas the US criteria include a requirement for several physical symptoms, reflecting the belief that CFS has an underlying immunological or infective pathology.

**INCIDENCE/** Community and primary care based studies have reported the prevalence of
**PREVALENCE** CFS to be 0–3%, depending on the criteria used.[3,4] Systematic population surveys have found similar prevalences of CFS in people of different socio-economic status and in all ethnic groups.[4,5]

**AETIOLOGY/** The cause of CFS is poorly understood. Women are at higher risk than men (RR
**RISK FACTORS** 1.3–1.7 depending on diagnostic criteria used).[6]

**PROGNOSIS** Studies have focused on people attending specialist clinics. A systematic review of studies of prognosis (search date 1996) found that children with CFS had better outcomes than adults: 54–94% of children showed definite improvement (after up to 6 years' follow up), whereas 20–50% of adults showed some improvement in the medium term and only 6% returned to premorbid levels of functioning.[7] Despite the considerable burden of morbidity associated with CFS, we found no evidence of increased mortality. The systematic review found that outcome was influenced by the presence of psychiatric disorders (depression and anxiety) and beliefs about causation and treatment.[7]

Please refer to CD-ROM for full text and references.

Musculoskeletal disorders

# Fracture prevention in postmenopausal women

## Search date May 2003

*Olivier Bruyère, John Edwards, and Jean-Yves Reginster*

## What are the effects of treatments to prevent fractures in postmenopausal women?

### BENEFICIAL

**Alendronate**

Two systematic reviews in postmenopausal women have found that alendronate reduces vertebral and non-vertebral fractures compared with placebo.

**Risedronate**

One systematic review in postmenopausal women has found that risedronate reduces vertebral and non-vertebral fractures compared with placebo.

### LIKELY TO BE BENEFICIAL

**Calcitonin**

One systematic review in postmenopausal women found that calcitonin reduced vertebral fractures compared with placebo, but found no significant difference between calcitonin and placebo in non-vertebral fractures.

**Calcium plus vitamin D**

One large RCT in women aged 69–106 years living in nursing homes found that calcium plus vitamin D3 reduced hip fractures and non-vertebral fractures over 18 months to 3 years compared with placebo. One smaller RCT in women and men aged 65 years or older found that calcium plus vitamin D3 reduced non-vertebral fractures compared with placebo, but found no significant difference in hip fractures. One smaller RCT in postmenopausal women found no significant difference between calcium plus vitamin D3 and placebo in hip fracture after 2 years. The two smaller RCTs may have lacked power to exclude a clinically important difference. One systematic review in postmenopausal women reporting a combined analysis (for vitamin D alone and vitamin D plus calcium) found that standard or hydroxylated vitamin D with or without calcium reduced vertebral fractures compared with control, but found no significant difference between groups in non-vertebral fractures.

**Etidronate**

One systematic review in postmenopausal women found that etidronate reduced vertebral fractures over 2 years compared with control (placebo, calcium, or calcium plus vitamin D), but found no significant difference in non-vertebral fractures.

**Hip protectors**

One systematic review in elderly residents of nursing homes and one subsequent RCT found that hip protectors reduced hip fractures over 9–19 months compared with no hip protectors, whereas four other subsequent RCTs found no significant difference in hip fractures between groups. One other subsequent RCT in men and women aged over 65 years in institutional care found that a multifactorial intervention (including staff education, environmental manipulation, exercise, walking aids, drug regimen reviews, and hip protectors for those considered at higher risk) reduced hip fractures over 34 weeks compared with usual care. RCTs found no significant difference between hip protectors and no hip protectors in the occurrence of pelvic fractures.

### Pamidronate

One RCT in men and postmenopausal women found that pamidronate reduced new vertebral fractures after 3 years compared with placebo. One small RCT in postmenopausal women found no significant difference between pamidronate and placebo in vertebral fracture rate, but it was too small to exclude a clinically important difference.

### UNKNOWN EFFECTIVENESS

### Environmental manipulation

We found no RCTs assessing environmental manipulation⊙ alone. One RCT in men and women aged over 70 years found no significant difference in new fractures over 4 years between health visitor care (aimed at assessing nutritional deficiencies, reducing smoking and alcohol intake, improving muscle tone and fitness, assessing medical conditions, use of medication, improving home environment such as lighting) and control. Another RCT in men and women aged over 65 years in institutional care found that a multifactorial intervention (including staff education, environmental manipulation, exercise, walking aids, drug regimen reviews, and hip protectors for those considered at higher risk) reduced hip fractures over 34 weeks compared with usual care.

### Exercise

Three RCTs found no significant difference in falls resulting in fracture over 1 year between exercise (advice to walk briskly three times weekly or balance and strength exercises plus walking) and control. One small RCT in postmenopausal women found no significant difference between a 2 year back strengthening exercise programme and usual care in vertebral fractures over 10 years. Another RCT in men and women aged over 65 years in institutional care found that a multifactorial intervention (including staff education, environmental manipulation, exercise, walking aids, drug regimen reviews, and hip protectors for those considered at higher risk) reduced hip fractures over 34 weeks compared with usual care.

### UNLIKELY TO BE BENEFICIAL

### Calcium alone

One systematic review in postmenopausal women found no significant difference between calcium supplementation and placebo in vertebral or non-vertebral fractures.

### Vitamin D alone

One large RCT in postmenopausal women and two large RCTs in postmenopausal women and men found no significant difference between vitamin D3 and placebo in hip fractures or non-vertebral fractures. However, one systematic review found limited evidence from two small RCTs in postmenopausal women that calcitriol reduced vertebral fractures over 3 years compared with placebo.

### LIKELY TO BE INEFFECTIVE OR HARMFUL

### Hormone replacement therapy

We found insufficient evidence of benefit, but reliable evidence of harm. One systematic review in postmenopausal women found that hormone replacement therapy reduced vertebral fractures compared with control. However, another systematic review and one subsequent RCT in postmenopausal women found no significant difference in vertebral fractures. Two systematic reviews and two subsequent RCTs provided insufficient evidence on the effects of hormone ▶

# Fracture prevention in postmenopausal women

replacement therapy on non-vertebral fractures. One large RCT of oestrogen plus progestin versus placebo for primary prevention of coronary heart disease in healthy postmenopausal women was stopped because hormonal treatment increased risks of invasive breast cancer, coronary events, stroke, and pulmonary embolism.

**DEFINITION**   This topic covers interventions to prevent fractures in postmenopausal women. Fractures may be symptomatic or asymptomatic. A fracture is a break or disruption of bone or cartilage. Symptoms and signs may include immobility, pain, tenderness, numbness, bruising, joint deformity, joint swelling, limb deformity, and limb shortening.[1] Diagnosis is usually based on a typical clinical picture combined with results from an appropriate imaging technique. Usually in trials dealing with osteoporosis, menopause is considered to be present 12 months after the last menstruation.

**INCIDENCE/**   The lifetime risk of fracture in white women is 20% for the spine, 15% for the
**PREVALENCE**   wrist, and 18% for the hip.[2] The incidence of postmenopausal fracture increases with age.[3] One observational study found that age specific incidence rates for postmenopausal fracture of the hip increased exponentially beyond the age of 50 years.[4]

**AETIOLOGY/**   Fractures usually arise from trauma. General risk factors include those associ-
**RISK FACTORS** ated with an increased risks of falling (such as ataxia, drug and alcohol intake, loose carpets), age, osteoporosis, bony metastases, and other bone disorders. Postmenopausal women are at increased risk of fracture because of hormonal bone loss. Risk factors for fractures in postmenopausal women include increasing age, low body mass index, time since menopause, alcohol consumption, smoking, some endocrine diseases, such as hyperparathyroidism or thyroid disease, and steroid use, among others.

**PROGNOSIS**   Fractures may result in pain, short or long term disability, haemorrhage, thromboembolic disease (see thromboembolism, p 40), shock, and death. Vertebral fractures are associated with pain, physical impairment, muscular atrophy, changes in body shape, loss of physical function, and lower quality of life.[5] About 20% of women die in the first year after a hip fracture, representing an increase in mortality of 12–20% compared with women of similar age and no hip fracture. Half of elderly women who had been independent become partly dependent after hip fracture. A third become totally dependent.

Please refer to CD-ROM for full text and references.

Search date August 2003

*Martin Underwood*

## What are the effects of treatments for acute gout?

**UNKNOWN EFFECTIVENESS**

### Corticosteroids

We found no RCTs on the effects of intra-articular, parenteral, or oral corticosteroids in people with gout.

### Non-steroidal anti-inflammatory drugs

One RCT provided limited evidence that tenoxicam reduced short term pain and tenderness in people with gout compared with placebo. However, this study was too small to provide reliable conclusions. We found no RCTs comparing other non-steroidal anti-inflammatory drugs with placebo in people with gout. Five RCTs found no significant difference in efficacy between different non-steroidal anti-inflammatory drugs in people with acute gout; however, these RCTs may have lacked power to detect clinically relevant differences. One equivalence study found that etoricoxib and indometacin had equivalent effects on pain, but that indometacin was associated with more adverse effects.

### Oral colchicine

One small RCT provided limited evidence that colchicine improved pain in people with gout. However, we were unable to draw reliable conclusions from this small RCT. The high incidence of adverse effects in people taking colchicine precludes its use as routine treatment.

## What are the effects of treatments to prevent recurrent gout in people with prior episodes?

**UNKNOWN EFFECTIVENESS**

### Advice to lose weight, reduce alcohol intake, or reduce dietary intake of purines; allopurinol; benzbromarone; colchicine; probenecid; sulphinpyrazone

We found no RCTs on the effects of these treatments to prevent recurrent gout.

**DEFINITION**   Gout is a syndrome caused by deposition of urate crystals.[1] It typically presents as an acute monoarthritis of rapid onset. The first metatarsophalangeal joint is the most commonly affected joint (podagra). Gout also affects other joints: joints in the foot, ankle, knee, wrist, finger, and elbow are the most frequently affected. Crystal deposits (tophi) may develop around hands, feet, elbows, and ears. Diagnosis is usually made clinically. The American College of Rheumatology (ACR) criteria for diagnosing gout are as follows: (1) characteristic urate crystals in joint fluid; (2) a tophus proved to contain urate crystals; or (3) the presence of six or more defined clinical laboratory and x ray phenomena❶.[2] We have included studies of people meeting the ACR criteria, studies in which the diagnosis was made clinically, and studies that used other criteria.

**INCIDENCE/**   Gout is more common in older people and men.[3] In people aged 65–74 years
**PREVALENCE**   in the UK, the prevalence is about 50/1000 in men and about 9/1000 in women.[4] The annual incidence of gout in people aged over 50 years in the USA is 1.6/1000 for men and 0.3/1000 for women.[5] Gout may be more common in some non-white ethnic groups.[3] Cohort studies of former medical students found the annual incidence of gout to be 3.1/1000 in black men and ▶

1.8/1000 in white men.[6] After correcting for the higher prevalence of hypertension among black men, which is a risk factor for gout, the relative risk of gout in black men compared with white men was 1.3 (95% CI 0.77 to 2.19).

**AETIOLOGY/ RISK FACTORS**  Urate crystals form when serum urate concentration exceeds 0.42 mmol/L.[7] Serum urate concentration is the principal risk factor for a first attack of gout,[8] although 40% of people have normal serum urate concentration during an attack of gout.[7,9–11] A cohort study of 2046 men followed for about 15 years found that the annual incidence is about 0.4% in men with a urate concentration of 0.42–0.47 mmol/L, rising to 4.3% when serum urate concentration is 0.45–0.59 mmol/L.[12] A 5 year longitudinal study of 223 asymptomatic men with hyperuricaemia estimated 5 year cumulative incidence of gout to be 10.8% for those with baseline serum urate of 0.42–0.47 mmol/L, 27.7% for baseline urate 0.48–0.53 mmol/L, and 61.1% for baseline urate levels of 0.54 mmol/L or more.[8] The study found that a 0.6 mmol/L difference in baseline serum urate increased the odds of an attack of gout by a factor of 1.8 (OR adjusted for other risk factors for gout: 1.84, 95% CI 1.24 to 2.72). It also found that alcohol and diuretics were risk factors for gout (adjusted OR for any alcohol intake v no alcohol intake: 3.45, 95% CI 1.58 to 7.56; adjusted OR for diuretics v no diuretics: OR 6.55, 95% CI 2.98 to 14.35). Other suggested risk factors for gout include obesity, insulin resistance, dyslipidaemia, hypertension, and cardiovascular disorders.[13,14]

**PROGNOSIS**  We found few reliable data about prognosis or complications of gout. One study found that 3/11 (27%) people with untreated gout of the first metatarsophalangeal joint experienced spontaneous resolution after 7 days.[15] A case series of 614 people with gout who had not had treatment to reduce urate levels, and could recall the interval between first and second attacks, reported recurrence rates of 62% after 1 year, 78% after 2 years, and 84% after 3 years.[16] An analysis of two prospective cohort studies of 371 black and 1181 white male former medical students followed up for about 30 years found no significant difference in risk of coronary heart disease in men who had developed gout compared with men who had not (RR 0.85, 95% CI 0.40 to 1.81).[17]

Please refer to CD-ROM for full text and references.

### Search date August 2003

*Jo Jordan, Tamara Shawver Morgan, and James Weinstein*

## What are the effects of treatments?

### LIKELY TO BE BENEFICIAL

#### Microdiscectomy (as effective as standard discectomy)

We found no RCTs comparing microdiscectomy❻ versus conservative treatment. Three RCTs found no significant difference in clinical outcomes between microdiscectomy and standard discectomy❻. One RCT found no significant difference in satisfaction or pain between video assisted arthroscopic microdiscectomy and standard discectomy at about 30 months, although postoperative recovery was slower with standard discectomy. We found insufficient evidence on the effects of automated percutaneous discectomy❻ compared with microdiscectomy.

#### Spinal manipulation

One RCT in people with sciatica caused by disc herniation found that spinal manipulation increased self perceived improvement after 2 weeks compared with a placebo of infrequent infrared heat. One RCT comparing spinal manipulation, manual traction, exercise, and corsets found no significant difference among groups in self perceived improvement after 1 month. One RCT found that spinal manipulation increased the proportion of people with improved symptoms compared with traction. Concerns exist regarding possible further herniation from spinal manipulation in people who are surgical candidates.

#### Standard discectomy (short term benefit)

One RCT found that standard discectomy increased self reported improvement at 1 year, but not at 4 and 10 years, compared with conservative treatment (physiotherapy). Three RCTs found no significant difference in clinical outcomes between standard discectomy and microdiscectomy. Adverse effects were similar with both procedures.

### UNKNOWN EFFECTIVENESS

#### Acupuncture *New*

One systematic review found insufficient evidence on the effects of acupuncture in people with herniated lumber discs.

#### Advice to stay active

One systematic review of conservative treatments for sciatica caused by lumbar disc herniation found no RCTs on advice to stay active.

#### Automated percutaneous discectomy

We found no RCTs comparing automated percutaneous discectomy versus either conservative treatment or standard discectomy. We found insufficient evidence on the clinical effects of automated percutaneous discectomy compared with microdiscectomy.

#### Exercise therapy *New*

One systematic review of one RCT found no significant difference in global improvement between isometric exercise and manual traction in people with sciatica caused by disc herniation.

#### Heat or ice

One systematic review identified no RCTs of heat or ice for sciatica caused by lumbar disc herniation.

▶

# Herniated lumbar disc

◀ **Massage**

One systematic review identified no RCTs of massage in people with symptomatic lumbar disc herniation.

**Analgesics; antidepressants; laser discectomy⊕; muscle relaxants**

We found no systematic review or RCTs on these interventions for treatment of people with symptomatic herniated lumbar discs.

| UNLIKELY TO BE BENEFICIAL |
|---|

**Bed rest**

One systematic review of conservative treatment found no RCTs on bed rest in people with symptomatic herniated discs. One subsequent RCT in people with sciatica found no significant difference between bed rest and watchful waiting for 2 weeks in people's perceived improvement, mean pain scores, mean disability scores, or mean satisfaction scores after 12 weeks.

**Epidural corticosteroid injections**

One systematic review found limited evidence that epidural steroid injections increased global improvement compared with placebo. However, one subsequent RCT found no significant difference between epidural steroid injections plus conservative treatment and conservative treatment alone in pain, mobility, or people returning to work at 6 months. Another subsequent RCT found no significant difference between epidural steroid injection and control injection in pain, disability, or self rated improvement after 35 days.

**Non-steroidal anti-inflammatory drugs**

One systematic review found no significant difference in overall improvement between non-steroidal anti-inflammatory drugs and placebo in people with sciatica caused by disc herniation.

**DEFINITION** Herniated lumbar disc is a displacement of disc material (nucleus pulposus or annulus fibrosis) beyond the intervertebral disc space.[1] The diagnosis can be confirmed by radiological examination; however, magnetic resonance imaging findings of herniated disc are not always accompanied by clinical symptoms.[2,3] This review covers treatment of people who have clinical symptoms relating to confirmed or suspected disc herniation. It does not include treatment of people with spinal cord compression or people with cauda equina syndrome⊕, which often requires emergency intervention. The management of non-specific acute low back pain (see p 286) and chronic low back pain (see p 289) are covered elsewhere in *Clinical Evidence*.

**INCIDENCE/ PREVALENCE** The prevalence of symptomatic herniated lumbar disc is about 1–3% in Finland and Italy, depending on age and sex.[4] The highest prevalence is among people aged 30–50 years,[5] with a male to female ratio of 2 : 1.[6] In people aged between 25 and 55 years, about 95% of herniated discs occur at the lower lumbar spine (L4–L5 level); in people over 55 years of age, disc herniation is more common above this level.[7,8]

**AETIOLOGY/ RISK FACTORS** Radiographical evidence of disc herniation does not reliably predict low back pain in the future or correlate with symptoms; 19–27% of people without symptoms have disc herniation on imaging.[2,9] Risk factors for disc herniation include smoking (OR 1.7, 95% CI 1.0 to 2.5), weight bearing sports (e.g. weight lifting, hammer throw etc), and certain work activities such as repeated lifting. Driving motor vehicles is also associated with increased risk (OR 1.7, 95% CI 0.2 to 2.7, depending on the vehicle model).[6,10,11] This may be because the resonant frequency of the spine is similar to that of certain vehicles. ▶

**◀ PROGNOSIS** The natural history of disc herniation is difficult to determine because most people take some form of treatment for their back pain, and a formal diagnosis is not always made.[6] Clinical improvement is usual in most people, and only about 10% of people still have sufficient pain after 6 weeks to consider surgery. Sequential magnetic resonance images have shown that the herniated portion of the disc tends to regress over time, with partial to complete resolution after 6 months in two thirds of people.[12]

Please refer to CD-ROM for full text and references.

Musculoskeletal disorders

# Leg cramps

**Search date June 2003**

*Gavin Young*

---

## What are the effects of treatments for idiopathic leg cramps?

### BENEFICIAL

**Quinine**

One systematic review has found that quinine reduces the frequency of nocturnal leg cramp attacks compared with placebo over 4 weeks. We found no evidence about the optimal dose of quinine or length of treatment.

### LIKELY TO BE BENEFICIAL

**Quinine plus theophylline**

One small RCT found limited evidence that quinine plus theophylline reduced the number of nights affected by leg cramps compared with quinine alone over 2 weeks.

### UNKNOWN EFFECTIVENESS

**Analgesics; antiepileptic drugs; compression hosiery**

We found no RCTs on the effects of these interventions on idiopathic leg cramps❻.

### UNLIKELY TO BE BENEFICIAL

**Vitamin E**

One small RCT found no significant difference between vitamin E and placebo in the number of nights disturbed by leg cramps.

---

## What are the effects of treatments for leg cramps in pregnancy?

### LIKELY TO BE BENEFICIAL

**Magnesium salts**

One systematic review identified one small RCT in pregnant women, which found that magnesium tablets (primarily magnesium lactate, magnesium citrate) reduced leg cramps compared with placebo after 3 weeks.

### UNKNOWN EFFECTIVENESS

**Calcium salts**

One systematic review identified two RCTs that compared calcium versus vitamin C or no treatment, which found different results.

**Multivitamins and mineral supplements**

One systematic review identified one small RCT in pregnant women, which found no significant difference between a multivitamin plus mineral tablet and placebo in leg cramps in the ninth month of pregnancy.

**Sodium chloride**

One systematic review found insufficient evidence about the effects of sodium chloride on leg cramps in pregnancy.

◀ **DEFINITION**   Leg cramps are involuntary, localised, and usually painful skeletal muscle contractions, which commonly affect calf muscles. Leg cramps typically occur at night and usually last only seconds to minutes. Leg cramps may be idiopathic☉ or related to a definable process or condition such as pregnancy, renal dialysis, or venous insufficiency.

**INCIDENCE/**
**PREVALENCE**   Leg cramps are common and their incidence increases with age. About half of the people attending a general medicine clinic have had leg cramps within 1 month of their visit, and over two thirds of people over 50 years of age have experienced leg cramps.[1]

**AETIOLOGY/**
**RISK FACTORS**   Very little is known about the causes of leg cramps. Risk factors include pregnancy, exercise, salt depletion, renal dialysis, electrolyte imbalances, peripheral vascular disease (both venous and arterial), peripheral nerve injury, polyneuropathies, motor neuron disease, muscle diseases, and certain drugs. Other causes of calf pain include trauma, deep venous thrombosis (see thromboembolism, p 40), and ruptured Baker's cyst☉.

**PROGNOSIS**   Leg cramps may cause severe pain and sleep disturbance, both of which are distressing.

---

Please refer to CD-ROM for full text and references.

# Low back pain and sciatica (acute)

Search date February 2003

*Maurits van Tulder and Bart Koes*

---

## What are the effects of treatments?

### BENEFICIAL

**Advice to stay active**

Two systematic reviews and one subsequent RCT found that advice to stay active increased the rate of recovery, reduced pain, reduced disability, and reduced time spent off work compared with advice to rest in bed or bed rest.

**Non-steroidal anti-inflammatory drugs**

One systematic review and one additional RCT have found that non-steroidal anti-inflammatory drugs increased overall improvement after 1 week and reduced the need for additional analgesics compared with placebo. One systematic review and additional RCTs have found no significant difference among non-steroidal anti-inflammatory drugs or between non-steroidal anti-inflammatory drugs and other treatments (paracetamol, opioids, muscle relaxants, and non-drug treatments) in pain relief.

### LIKELY TO BE BENEFICIAL

**Behavioural therapy**

One RCT found that cognitive behavioural therapy☉ reduced acute low back pain and disability compared with traditional care or electromyographic biofeedback☉.

**Multidisciplinary treatment programmes (for subacute low back pain)**

We found no RCTs in people with acute low back pain. One systematic review in people with subacute low back pain found limited evidence that multidisciplinary treatment☉, including a workplace visit, reduced sick leave compared with usual care.

### TRADE OFF BETWEEN BENEFITS AND HARMS

**Muscle relaxants**

Systematic reviews have found that muscle relaxants improve symptoms (including pain and muscle tension) and increase mobility compared with placebo, but found no significant difference in outcomes among muscle relaxants. Adverse effects in people using muscle relaxants were common and included dependency, drowsiness, and dizziness.

### UNKNOWN EFFECTIVENESS

**Acupuncture**

We found no RCTs of acupuncture☉ specifically in people with acute low back pain.

**Analgesics (paracatemol, opioids)**

We found no placebo controlled RCTs. Systematic reviews have found no consistent difference between analgesics and non-steroidal anti-inflammatory drugs in reducing pain.

**Back schools**

One systematic review found limited evidence that back schools increased rates of recovery and reduced sick leave compared with placebo in the short term. The ▶

review found no significant difference in outcomes between back school and physiotherapy, and found that back school increased pain and sick leave compared with McKenzie exercises⊙.

## Epidural steroid injections

One RCT found that epidural steroids increased the proportion of people who were pain free compared with subcutaneous lidocaine (lignocaine) injections after 3 months. A second RCT found no significant difference in the proportion of people cured or improved between epidural steroids and epidural saline, epidural bupivacaine, or dry needling.

## Lumbar supports

We found no RCTs on the effects of lumbar supports.

## Massage

One systematic review found insufficient evidence from one RCT about the effects of massage⊙ compared with spinal manipulation or electrical stimulation.

## Spinal manipulation

Systematic reviews found conflicting evidence on the effects of spinal manipulation.

## Traction

RCTs found conflicting evidence on the effects of traction.

## Colchicine; electromyographic biofeedback⊙; temperature treatments (short wave diathermy, ultrasound, ice, heat); transcutaneous electrical nerve stimulation

We found insufficient evidence on the effects of these interventions.

### UNLIKELY TO BE BENEFICIAL

## Back exercises

Systematic reviews and additional RCTs have found either no significant difference between back exercises and conservative or inactive treatments in pain or disability, or have found that back exercises increase pain or disability.

### LIKELY TO BE INEFFECTIVE OR HARMFUL

## Bed rest

Systematic reviews have found that bed rest could be worse than no treatment, advice to stay active, back exercises, physiotherapy, spinal manipulation, or non-steroidal anti-inflammatory drugs. One systematic review has found that adverse effects of bed rest include joint stiffness, muscle wasting, loss of bone mineral density, pressure sores, and venous thromboembolism.

**DEFINITION** Low back pain is pain, muscle tension, or stiffness localised below the costal margin and above the inferior gluteal folds, with or without leg pain (sciatica⊙),[1] and is designated as acute when it persists for less than 12 weeks.[2] Non-specific low back pain is low back pain not attributed to a recognisable pathology (such as infection, tumour, osteoporosis, rheumatoid arthritis, fracture, or inflammation).[1] This review excludes low back pain or sciatica with symptoms or signs at presentation that suggest a specific underlying condition.

**INCIDENCE/ PREVALENCE** Over 70% of people in developed countries will experience low back pain at some time in their lives.[3] Each year, 15–45% of adults suffer low back pain, and 1/20 (5%) people present to hospital with a new episode. Low back pain is most common between the ages of 35–55 years.[3]

# Low back pain and sciatica (acute)

**AETIOLOGY/ RISK FACTORS**  Symptoms, pathology, and radiological appearances are poorly correlated. Pain is non-specific in about 85% of people. About 4% of people with low back pain in primary care have compression fractures and about 1% have a tumour. The prevalence of prolapsed intervertebral disc is about 1–3%.[3] Ankylosing spondylitis and spinal infections are less common.[4] Risk factors for the development of back pain include heavy physical work, frequent bending, twisting, lifting, and prolonged static postures. Psychosocial risk factors include anxiety, depression, and mental stress at work.[3,5]

**PROGNOSIS**  Acute low back pain is usually self limiting (90% of people recover within 6 weeks), although 2–7% develop chronic pain. One study found recurrent pain accounted for 75–85% of absenteeism from work.[6]

Please refer to CD-ROM for full text and references.

### Search date February 2003

*Maurits van Tulder and Bart Koes*

## What are the effects of treatments?

**BENEFICIAL**

### Exercise

Systematic reviews and additional RCTs have found that exercise improves pain and functional status compared with usual care. RCTs found conflicting evidence on the effects of different types of exercise, or exercise compared with inactive treatments.

### Intensive multidisciplinary treatment programmes

One systematic review has found that intensive multidisciplinary biopsychosocial rehabilitation with functional restoration reduces pain and improves function compared with inpatient or outpatient non-multidisciplinary treatments or usual care. The review found no significant difference between less intensive multidisciplinary treatments and non-multidisciplinary treatment or usual care in pain or function.

**LIKELY TO BE BENEFICIAL**

### Analgesics

One RCT found that tramadol decreased pain and functional status compared with placebo. A second RCT found that paracetamol increased the proportion of people who rated the treatment as good or excellent compared with diflunisal.

### Back schools in occupational settings (versus no treatment)

One systematic review has found that, in occupational settings, back schools⊙ improve pain and reduce disability compared with no treatment. Systematic reviews and one subsequent RCT found conflicting evidence on the effects of back schools compared with other treatments.

### Behavioural therapy

Systematic reviews have found that behavioural therapy reduces pain and improves functional status and behavioural outcomes compared with no treatment, placebo, or waiting list control. Systematic reviews found no significant difference in functional status, pain, or behavioural outcomes between different types of behavioural therapy, and found conflicting results with behavioural therapy compared with other treatments.

### Massage (versus other treatments)

One systematic review found that massage⊙ combined with exercises and education is more effective than inert treatment. The review found conflicting evidence about the effects of massage compared with other treatments.

### Non-steroidal anti-inflammatory drugs

One RCT found that naproxen increased pain relief compared with placebo. One systematic review and additional RCTs found no significant difference with non-steroidal anti-inflammatory drugs compared with each other for symptom outcomes. Two RCTs found conflicting evidence on the effects of non-steroidal anti-inflammatory drugs compared with other analgesics.

# Low back pain and sciatica (chronic)

◄ **Trigger point and ligamentous injections**

One systematic review found limited evidence that steroid plus local anaesthetic injection of trigger points increased pain relief compared with local anaesthetic injection alone, and that phenol increased pain relief compared with saline injection of the lumbar interspinal ligament.

## UNKNOWN EFFECTIVENESS

### Acupuncture

We found conflicting evidence from two systematic reviews and two subsequent RCTs about the effects of acupuncture compared with placebo or no treatment. One systematic review and one subsequent RCT have found that acupuncture reduces pain intensity and increases overall improvement compared with transcutaneous electrical nerve stimulation.

### Antidepressants

One systematic review and additional RCTs have found that antidepressants significantly increase pain relief compared with placebo. However, they found no consistent difference in functioning or depression. Additional RCTs found conflicting results on pain relief with antidepressants compared with each other or analgesics.

### Electromyographic biofeedback

One systematic review found no difference in pain relief or functional status between electromyographic biofeedback and placebo or waiting list control, but found conflicting results on the effects of electromyographic biofeedback compared with other treatments.

### Epidural steroid injections

One systematic review found no significant difference between epidural steroid injections and placebo in pain relief after 6 weeks or 6 months.

### Lumbar supports

We found insufficient evidence on the effects of lumbar supports.

### Muscle relaxants

We found insufficient evidence about the benefits of muscle relaxants. One RCT found that adverse effects in people using muscle relaxants are common and include dependency, drowsiness, and dizziness.

### Physical conditioning programmes

One systematic review has found that physical conditioning programmes with a cognitive behavioural approach plus physical training for workers with back pain reduced sick days but not the risk of being off work at 12 months compared with general practitioner care.

### Spinal manipulation

We found five systematic reviews, which identified 13 RCTs. One of the reviews found that spinal manipulation improved outcomes compared with placebo; one concluded that improvements in pain and disability scores were too small to be clinically worthwhile, and the other three were conflicting.

### Transcutaneous electrical nerve stimulation

One systematic review found no significant difference in pain relief between transcutaneous electrical nerve stimulation and sham stimulation.

►

◀ LIKELY TO BE INEFFECTIVE OR HARMFUL

## Facet joint injections

One systematic review found no significant difference in pain relief between facet joint injections and placebo or facet joint nerve blocks.

## Traction

One systematic review and two additional RCTs found no significant difference between traction and placebo or between traction plus massage and interferential treatment in pain relief or functional status.

**DEFINITION**     Low back pain is pain, muscle tension, or stiffness localised below the costal margin and above the inferior gluteal folds, with or without leg pain (sciatica $\textbf{G}$),[1] and is defined as chronic when it persists for 12 weeks or more (see definition of low back pain and sciatica [acute], p 287).[2] Non-specific low back pain is low back pain not attributed to a recognisable pathology (such as infection, tumour, osteoporosis, rheumatoid arthritis, fracture, or inflammation).[1] This review excludes low back pain or leg pain with symptoms or signs at presentation that suggest a specific underlying condition.

**INCIDENCE/**     Over 70% of people in developed countries will experience low back pain at
**PREVALENCE**     some time in their lives.[3] Each year, 15–45% of adults suffer low back pain, and 1/20 people present to hospital with a new episode. About 2–7% of patients with acute low back pain will go on to become chronic. Low back pain is most common between the ages of 35–55 years.[3]

**AETIOLOGY/**     Symptoms, pathology, and radiological appearances are poorly correlated. Pain
**RISK FACTORS**     is non-specific in about 85% of people. About 4% of people with low back pain in primary care have compression fractures and about 1% have a tumour. The prevalence of prolapsed intervertebral disc is about 1–3%.[3] Ankylosing spondylitis and spinal infections are less common.[4] Risk factors for the development of back pain include heavy physical work, frequent bending, twisting, lifting, and prolonged static postures. Psychosocial risk factors include anxiety, depression, and mental stress at work.[3,5] Having a previous history of low back pain and a longer duration of the present episode are significant risk factors for chronicity. A recently published systematic review of prospective cohort studies found that some psychological factors (distress, depressive mood, and somatisation) are associated with an increased risk of chronic low back pain.[6] Individual and workplace factors have also been reported to be associated with the transition to chronic low back pain.[7]

**PROGNOSIS**     Generally, the clinical course of an episode of low back pain seems to be favourable, and most pain will resolve within 2 weeks. Back pain among primary care patients typically has a recurrent course characterised by variation and change, rather than an acute, self limiting course.[8] Most back pain patients will have experienced a previous episode, and acute attacks often occur as exacerbations of chronic low back pain. In general, recurrences will occur more frequently and be more severe if patients had frequent or long lasting low back pain complaints in the past. The course of sick leave due to low back pain is similarly favourable. One study reported that 67% of patients with sick leave due to low back pain will have returned to work within a week, and 90% within 2 months. However, the longer the period of sick leave the less likely the return to work becomes. Less than half of the low back pain patients who have been off work for 6 months will return to work. After 2 years of work absenteeism, the chance to return to work is virtually zero.[9]

Please refer to CD-ROM for full text and references.

# Neck pain

**Search date September 2003**

*Allan Binder*

---

## What are the effects of treatments for uncomplicated neck pain without severe neurological deficit?

### LIKELY TO BE BENEFICIAL

**Manual treatments (mobilisation and manipulation)**
Systematic reviews and RCTs found limited evidence that manipulation or mobilisation improved symptoms compared with other or no treatment in people with neck pain.

**Physical treatments (active physiotherapy, exercise, pulsed electromagnetic field treatment)**
Systematic reviews and RCTs have found that active physiotherapy reduces pain compared with passive treatment, and that exercise programmes reduce pain compared with management that does not include exercise programmes. One RCT provided limited evidence that pulsed electromagnetic field treatment reduced pain compared with sham treatment.

### UNKNOWN EFFECTIVENESS

**Drug treatments (analgesics, non-steroidal anti-inflammatory drugs, antidepressants, or muscle relaxants)**
We found insufficient evidence on the effects of analgesics, non-steroidal anti-inflammatory drugs, antidepressants, or muscle relaxants for neck pain, although they are widely used. Several drugs used to treat neck pain are associated with well documented adverse effects.

**Multidisciplinary (multimodal) treatment**
RCTs provided insufficient evidence to compare effects of multimodal treatment with other treatment in people with uncomplicated neck pain.

**Physical treatments (heat or cold, traction, biofeedback, spray and stretch, acupuncture, laser)**
Systematic reviews found insufficient evidence about the effects of these physical treatments.

**Soft collars and special pillows**
We found no RCTs of sufficient quality on the effects of soft collars or special pillows.

### UNLIKELY TO BE BENEFICIAL

**Patient education**
Three RCTs found no significant difference between patient education (advice or group instruction) with or without analgesics compared with no treatment, stress management, placebo, or usual care.

---

## What are the effects of treatments for acute whiplash injury?

### LIKELY TO BE BENEFICIAL

**Early mobilisation**
Systematic reviews and subsequent RCTs provided limited evidence that early mobilisation reduced pain compared with immobilisation or rest plus a collar. ▶

### Early return to normal activity
Systematic reviews and subsequent RCTs provided limited evidence that advice to "act as usual" plus anti-inflammatory drugs improved mild symptoms compared with immobilisation plus 14 days' sick leave.

### Electrotherapy
One small RCT provided limited evidence that electromagnetic field treatment reduced pain after 4 weeks but not after 3 months compared with sham treatment.

### Multimodal treatment
One RCT found that multimodal treatment reduced pain at the end of treatment and after 6 months compared with physical treatment.

**UNKNOWN EFFECTIVENESS**

### Drug treatments
We found no RCTs of drug treatments in acute whiplash injury.

### Home exercise programmes
One RCT found no significant difference between different home exercise programmes in pain or disability.

## What are the effects of treatments for chronic whiplash injury?

**LIKELY TO BE BENEFICIAL**

### Percutaneous radiofrequency neurotomy
One RCT provided limited evidence that percutaneous radiofrequency neurotomy reduced pain compared with sham treatment after 27 weeks.

**UNKNOWN EFFECTIVENESS**

### Multimodal treatment (physiotherapy plus cognitive behavioural treatment)
One RCT found no significant difference between multimodal treatment (physiotherapy plus cognitive behavioural treatment) in disability, pain, or range of movement at the end of treatment ot at 3 months.

### Physiotherapy
One RCT found no significant difference between physiotherapy alone and multimodal treatment (physiotherapy plus cognitive behavioural treatment) in disability, pain, or range of movement at the end of treatment or at 3 months.

## What are the effects of treatments for neck pain with radiculopathy?

**UNKNOWN EFFECTIVENESS**

### Drug treatments (epidural steroid injections, analgesics, non-steroidal anti-inflammatory drugs, or muscle relaxants)
We found no RCTs on the effects of epidural steroid injections, analgesics, non-steroidal anti-inflammatory drugs, or muscle relaxants.

### Surgery versus conservative treatment
One RCT found no significant difference between surgery and conservative treatment in symptoms after 1 year.

# Neck pain

**DEFINITION**  In this topic we have differentiated uncomplicated neck pain from whiplash, although many studies, particularly in people with chronic pain (duration more than 3 months), do not specify which types of people are included. Most studies of acute pain (duration less than 3 months) are confined to whiplash. We have included under radiculopathy those studies involving people with predominantly radicular symptoms arising in the cervical spine. Neck pain often occurs in combination with limited movement and poorly defined neurological symptoms affecting the upper limbs. The pain can be severe and intractable, and can occur with radiculopathy or myelopathy.

**INCIDENCE/ PREVALENCE**  About two thirds of people will experience neck pain at some time in their lives.[1,2] Prevalence is highest in middle age. In the UK about 15% of hospital based physiotherapy and in Canada 30% of chiropractic referrals are for neck pain.[3,4] In the Netherlands neck pain contributes up to 2% of general practitioner consultations.[5]

**AETIOLOGY/ RISK FACTORS**  Most uncomplicated neck pain is associated with poor posture, anxiety and depression, neck strain, occupational injuries, or sporting injuries. With chronic pain, mechanical and degenerative factors (often referred to as cervical spondylosis) are more likely. Some neck pain results from soft tissue trauma, most typically seen in whiplash injuries. Rarely, disc prolapse and inflammatory, infective, or malignant conditions affect the cervical spine and present with neck pain with or without neurological features.

**PROGNOSIS**  Neck pain usually resolves within days or weeks but can recur or become chronic. In some industries, neck related disorders account for as much time off work as low back pain (see low back pain and sciatica [acute], p 286).[6] The percentage of people in whom neck pain becomes chronic depends on the cause but is thought to be about 10%,[1] similar to low back pain. Neck pain causes severe disability in 5% of affected people.[2] **Whiplash:** Whiplash injuries were more likely to cause disability than neck pain due to other causes; up to 40% of sufferers reported symptoms even after 15 years' follow up.[7] Factors associated with a poorer outcome after whiplash are not well defined.[8] The incidence of chronic disability after whiplash varies among countries, although reasons for this variation are unclear.[9]

Please refer to CD-ROM for full text and references.

## Are there any important differences between available non-steroidal anti-inflammatory drugs (NSAIDs)?

**BENEFICIAL**

### Topical NSAIDs in acute and chronic pain conditions

One systematic review in people with acute and chronic pain conditions has found that topical NSAIDs reduce pain compared with placebo.

**UNKNOWN EFFECTIVENESS**

### Choice between different NSAIDs

Systematic reviews found no important differences in efficacy between different NSAIDs. Cyclo-oxygenase-2 (COX 2) inhibitors reduce gastroscopically diagnosed ulcers compared with other NSAIDs, but the clinical importance of this effect is not clear, and COX 2 inhibitors may increase the risk of myocardial infarction.

### Topical versus systemic NSAIDs or alternative analgesics

One systematic review found no high quality RCTs of topical NSAIDs compared with oral forms of the same NSAID, or with paracetamol.

**UNLIKELY TO BE BENEFICIAL**

### NSAIDs in increased doses

Systematic reviews have found that benefits of NSAIDs increase towards a maximum value at high doses. Recommended doses are close to creating the maximum benefit. In contrast, three systematic reviews found no ceiling for adverse effects, which increased in an approximately linear fashion with dose.

## What are the effects of co-treatments to reduce the risk of gastrointestinal adverse effects of NSAIDs?

**LIKELY TO BE BENEFICIAL**

### $H_2$ blockers in people who cannot avoid NSAIDs

One systematic review in people who had taken NSAIDs for 3 months has found that $H_2$ blockers reduce endoscopically diagnosed gastric and duodenal ulcers compared with placebo. We found limited evidence from one weak RCT that misoprostol reduced the number of people with NSAID induced gastric ulcers compared with 300 mg ranitidine daily.

### Omeprazole in people who cannot avoid NSAIDs

One systematic review in people who had taken NSAIDs for at least 3 months has found that omeprazole reduces endoscopically diagnosed gastric and duodenal ulcers compared with placebo.

**TRADE OFF BETWEEN BENEFITS AND HARMS**

### Misoprostol in people who cannot avoid NSAIDs

One systematic review in people who had taken NSAIDs for at least 3 months has found that misoprostol reduces gastric or duodenal ulcers compared with placebo. However, RCTs have found that misoprostol increases clinical gastrointestinal adverse events, such as diarrhoea and abdominal pain compared with placebo. ▶

# Non-steroidal anti-inflammatory drugs

One RCT found no significant difference in the number of people taking NSAIDS and with proven gastric ulceration or erosion in successful response to treatment with misoprostol compared with ameprazole.

**DEFINITION**      Non-steroidal anti-inflammatory drugs (NSAIDs) have anti-inflammatory, analgesic, and antipyretic effects, and inhibit platelet aggregation. The drugs have no documented effect on the course of musculoskeletal diseases, such as rheumatoid arthritis and osteoarthritis (p 297).

**INCIDENCE/**      NSAIDs are widely used. Almost 10% of people in the Netherlands used a
**PREVALENCE**  non-aspirin NSAID in 1987, and the overall use was 11 defined daily doses per 1000 population per day.[1] In Australia in 1994, overall use was 35 defined daily doses per 1000 population per day, with 36% of the people receiving NSAIDs for osteoarthritis, 42% for sprain and strain or low back pain, and 4% for rheumatoid arthritis; 35% were aged over 60 years.[2]

Please refer to CD-ROM for full text and references.

Search date November 2002

*David Scott, Claire Smith, Stefan Lohmander, and Jiri Chard*

## What are the effects of treatments?

### BENEFICIAL

**Hip replacement**

One systematic review of RCTs and observational studies has found that hip replacement is effective for at least 10 years.

**Knee replacement**

Systematic reviews of observational studies have found that knee replacement is effective in relieving pain and improving function. One RCT found limited evidence that unicompartmental knee replacement is more effective than tricompartmental replacement at 5 years' follow up. One systematic review of observational studies found better outcomes with unicompartmental knee operations compared with bicompartmental operations.

**Oral non-steroidal anti-inflammatory drugs (short term pain relief)**

Systematic reviews have found that non-steroidal anti-inflammatory drugs (NSAIDs) reduce short term pain in osteoarthritis compared with placebo. NSAIDs are associated with an increased risk of gastrointestinal haemorrhage. RCTs provided insufficient evidence to compare the effects of oral versus topical NSAIDs. RCTs found no good evidence that simple analgesics, such as paracetamol (acetaminophen), are significantly different from NSAIDs in pain relief. Concerns exist relating to trial quality and commercial bias.

**Simple oral analgesics (short term pain relief)**

Systematic reviews in people with osteoarthritis of the hip or knee found limited evidence that simple analgesics, such as paracetamol, reduced pain compared with placebo. RCTs found no good evidence that simple analgesics, such as paracetamol (acetaminophen), are significantly different from NSAIDs in pain relief.

**Topical agents (short term pain relief)**

One systematic review and RCTs have found that topical agents containing NSAIDs reduce pain compared with placebo. One systematic review found that systemic adverse events were no more common than with placebo. RCTs provided insufficient evidence to compare the effects of oral versus topical NSAIDs. We found no RCTs comparing topical agents versus other local treatments such as heat or cold packs. RCTs found limited evidence that capsaicin improved pain compared with placebo.

### LIKELY TO BE BENEFICIAL

**Exercise (pain relief and improved function)**

Systematic reviews and subsequent RCTs have found that exercise and physical therapy reduce pain and disability in people with hip or knee osteoarthritis, although many of the RCTs were limited by poor methods and reporting.

**Intra-articular glucocorticoid injections of the knee (short term pain relief)**

One systematic review and one subsequent RCT found limited evidence that intra-articular glucocorticoids reduced pain for 1–4 weeks compared with placebo. ▶

# Osteoarthritis

### Intra-articular hyaluronan injections of the knee

One systematic review and RCTs found limited evidence that hyaluronan reduced pain for 1–6 months compared with placebo.

### Osteotomy

We found no RCTs comparing osteotomy versus conservative treatment. Two RCTs found similar functional outcomes with osteotomy compared with knee replacement. Two RCTs provided insufficient evidence on the effects of different types of osteotomy

### Physical aids

RCTs in people with knee osteoarthritis found limited evidence that joint bracing or taping may improve disease specific quality of life and symptoms compared with control treatment. RCTs provided insufficient evidence to compare the effects of different insoles.

## UNKNOWN EFFECTIVENESS

### Chondroitin

One systematic review and RCTs provided insufficient evidence on the effects of chondroitin in people with osteoarthritis.

### Education

RCTs provided insufficient evidence to assess the effects of education and behavioural change in people with hip or knee osteoarthritis.

### Glucosamine

Systematic reviews and subsequent RCTs found limited evidence that glucosamine improved symptoms compared with placebo, but publication bias and poor trial quality makes the results difficult to interpret.

### Glucosamine plus chondroitin

We found no RCTs of glucosamine plus chondroitin alone. RCTs found limited evidence that glucosamine plus chondroitin plus manganese ascorbate improved disease severity scores compared with placebo.

### Hip replacement (who is most likely to benefit)

We found no RCTs. One systematic review of observational studies has suggested younger age (< 45 years), older age (> 75 years), and weight over 70 kg may be associated with worse outcomes in terms of pain relief and function after hip replacement. One cohort study found that younger people were at greater risk of revision, whereas another study found lower rates of implant survival in obese people.

### Intra-articular injection of the knee other than glucocorticoid or hyaluronan

We found insufficient evidence on the effects of other intra-articular treatments, such as radioactive isotopes, glycosaminoglycan polysulphuric acid, orgotein, and morphine.

### Knee replacement (who is most likely to benefit)

We found no RCTs. We found insufficient evidence from observational studies on the effects of obesity on knee replacement outcomes. We found limited evidence from observational studies that knee replacement is effective in elderly people.

◄ **LIKELY TO BE INEFFECTIVE OR HARMFUL**

### Oral NSAIDs in older people and people at risk of renal disease or peptic ulceration

Studies have found that NSAIDs increased the risk of renal or gastrointestinal damage in older people with osteoarthritis, particularly those with intercurrent disease.

### Simple oral analgesics in people with existing liver damage

Observational evidence suggests that lower doses of paracetamol may cause liver damage in people with liver disease.

**DEFINITION**   Osteoarthritis is a heterogeneous condition for which the prevalence, risk factors, clinical manifestations, and prognosis vary according to the joints affected. It most commonly affects hands, knees, hips, and spinal apophyseal joints. It is usually defined by pathological or radiological criteria rather than clinical features, and is characterised by focal areas of damage to the cartilage surfaces of synovial joints, associated with remodelling of the underlying bone and mild synovitis. When severe, there is characteristic joint space narrowing and osteophyte formation, with visible subchondral bone changes on radiography.

**INCIDENCE/**   Osteoarthritis is common and an important cause of pain and disability in
**PREVALENCE**  older adults.[1,2] Radiographic features are practically universal in at least some joints in people aged over 60 years, but significant clinical disease probably affects 10–20% of people. Knee disease is about twice as prevalent as hip disease in people aged over 60 years (about 10% v 5%).[3,4]

**AETIOLOGY/**   The main initiating factors are abnormalities in joint shape or injury. Genetic
**RISK FACTORS** factors are probably implicated.

**PROGNOSIS**   The natural history of osteoarthritis is poorly understood. Only a minority of people with clinical disease of the hip or knee joint progress to requiring surgery.

Please refer to CD-ROM for full text and references.

# Plantar heel pain and fasciitis

Search date September 2003

*Fay Crawford*

## What are the effects of treatments?

**UNKNOWN EFFECTIVENESS**

### Casted orthoses (custom made insoles)

One systematic review found no RCTs on the effects of orthoses❻ versus placebo or no treatment. The review found limited and conflicting evidence from RCTs about the effects of orthoses with or without heel pads of stretching exercises versus corticosteroids, corticosteroids plus local anaesthesia, stretching exercises, or other physical supports.

### Corticosteroid injection (in the short term)

One systematic review identified no RCTs comparing corticosteroid injections alone versus placebo.

### Corticosteroid injection plus local anaesthetic injection in the short term (with or without non-steroidal anti-inflammatory drugs or heel pads)

One systematic review identified no RCTs comparing corticosteroid injections plus local anaesthesia versus placebo. RCTs provided insufficient evidence about clinically important effects of corticosteroids plus local anaesthesia (alone or combined with non-steroidal anti-inflammatory drugs or heel pads) compared with other treatments.

### Extracorporeal shock wave therapy

We found one systematic review and four subsequent RCTs of extracorporeal shock wave therapy❻ (ESWT). Seven small RCTs provided insufficient evidence to assess extracorporeal shock wave therapy compared with placebo. Two RCTs found limited evidence that high dose extracorporeal shock wave therapy reduced pain and walking scores compared with low dose therapy. However, the clinical importance of these effects is not clear.

### Heel pads and heel cups

One systematic review found no RCTs on the effects of heel pads❻ and heel cups❻ compared with placebo or no treatment. The review found limited and conflicting evidence on the effects of heel pads and heel cups (alone or in combination with other treatments) compared with other treatment modalities.

### Lasers

One small RCT identified by a systematic review found no significant difference between laser treatment and placebo.

### Local anaesthetic injection

One systematic review identified no RCTs comparing local anaesthesia versus placebo or no treatment.

### Night splints plus non-steroidal anti-inflammatory drugs

One RCT found no significant difference in pain between a night splint plus non-steroidal anti-inflammatory drugs and non-steroidal anti-inflammatory drugs alone after 3 months.

### Stretching exercises

One systematic review identified no RCTs comparing stretching exercises versus no treatment in people with heel pain. One RCT found that plantar fascia stretching plus insole was more effective at reducing morning heel pain than Achilles tendon stretching plus insole. One RCT found no significant difference in pain after 8 ▶

weeks between stretching alone (Achilles tendon stretching❻ and plantar fascia stretching❻) and stretching plus orthoses. One RCT found no significant difference in pain between sustained and intermittent Achilles tendon stretching exercises.

## Surgery

One systematic review found no RCTs of surgery for heel pain.

## Ultrasound

One systematic review found one small RCT. It found no significant difference in pain between ultrasound and sham ultrasound.

### LIKELY TO BE INEFFECTIVE OR HARMFUL

## Corticosteroid injection in the medium to long term (with or without heel pad)

One systematic review identified no RCTs comparing corticosteroid injections versus placebo. One small RCT provided insufficient evidence about the long term clinical effects of corticosteroid injection plus heel pad compared with placebo plus heel pad. Observational studies have found a high rate of plantar fascia rupture and other complications associated with corticosteroid injections, which may lead to chronic disability in some people.

## Corticosteroid injection plus local anaesthesic injection in the medium to long term (with or without non-steroidal anti-inflammatory drugs or heel pads)

One systematic review identified no RCTs comparing corticosteroid injections plus local anaesthesia versus placebo. RCTs provided insufficient evidence about clinically important effects of corticosteroids plus local anaesthesia (alone or combined with non-steroidal anti-inflammatory drugs or heel pads) compared with other treatments. Observational studies have found a high rate of plantar fascia rupture and other complications associated with corticosteroid injections, which may lead to chronic disability in some people.

**DEFINITION**    Plantar heel pain is soreness or tenderness of the heel that is restricted to the sole of the foot. It often radiates from the central part of the heel pad or the medial tubercle of the calcaneum, but may extend along the plantar fascia into the medial longitudinal arch of the foot. Severity may range from an irritation at the origin of the plantar fascia, which is noticeable on rising after rest, to an incapacitating pain. This review excludes clinically evident underlying disorders, for example, infection, calcaneal fracture, and calcaneal nerve entrapment, which may be distinguished clinically — a calcaneal fracture may present after trauma, and calcaneal nerve entrapment gives rise to shooting pains and feelings of "pins and needles" on the medial aspect of the heel.

**INCIDENCE/**    The incidence and prevalence of plantar heel pain is uncertain. Plantar heel
**PREVALENCE**    pain primarily affects those in mid to late life.[1]

**AETIOLOGY/**    Unknown.
**RISK FACTORS**

**PROGNOSIS**    One systematic review (search date 2002) found that almost all of the included trials reported an improvement in discomfort regardless of the intervention received (including placebo), suggesting that the condition is at least partially self limiting.[1] A telephone survey of 100 people treated conservatively (average follow up 47 months) found that 82 people had resolution of symptoms, 15 ▶

had continued symptoms but no limitations of activity or work, and three had persistent bilateral symptoms that limited activity or changed work status.[2] Thirty one people said that they would have seriously considered surgical treatment at the time that medical attention was sought.

Please refer to CD-ROM for full text and references.

## What are the effects of treatments?

### TRADE OFF BETWEEN BENEFITS AND HARMS

**Nifedipine**

Six RCTs found that nifedipine reduced the frequency and severity of attacks over 4–12 weeks compared with placebo, and was rated by participants as more effective than placebo in improving overall symptoms. The RCTs found that nifedipine was associated with higher rates of adverse effects compared with placebo, including flushing, headache, oedema, and tachycardia.

### UNKNOWN EFFECTIVENESS

**Amlodopine; diltiazem; moxisylyte (thymoxamine)**

We found no good RCTs of these interventions.

**Inositol nicotinate; naftidrofuryl oxalate; nicardipine; prazosin**

RCTs provided insufficient evidence to assess these interventions.

**DEFINITION**  Raynaud's phenomenon is episodic vasospasm of the peripheral arteries, causing pallor followed by cyanosis and redness with pain and sometimes paraesthesia, and, rarely, ulceration of the fingers and toes (and in some cases of the ears or nose). Primary or idiopathic Raynaud's phenomenon (Raynaud's disease) occurs without an underlying disease. Secondary Raynaud's phenomenon (Raynaud's syndrome) occurs in association with an underlying disease — usually connective tissue disorders such as scleroderma, systemic lupus erythematosus, rheumatoid arthritis, or polymyositis. This review excludes secondary Raynaud's phenomenon.

**INCIDENCE/**  The prevalence of primary Raynaud's phenomenon varies by gender, country,
**PREVALENCE**  and exposure to workplace vibration. One large US cohort study (4182 people) found symptoms in 9.6% of women and 8.1% of men, of whom 81% had primary Raynaud's phenomenon.[1] Smaller cohort studies in Spain have estimated the prevalence of Raynaud's phenomenon to be 3.7–4.0%, of which 90% is primary Raynaud's phenomenon.[2,3] One cohort study in Japan (332 men, 731 women) found symptoms of primary Raynaud's phenomenon in 3.4% of women and 3.0% of men.[4]

**AETIOLOGY/**  The aetiology of primary Raynaud's phenomenon is unknown.[5] There is evi-
**RISK FACTORS**  dence for genetic predisposition,[6,7] most likely in those people with early onset Raynaud's phenomenon (aged < 40 years).[8] One prospective observational study (424 people with Raynaud's phenomenon) found that 73% of sufferers first developed symptoms before age 40 years.[8] Women are more at risk than men (OR 3.0, 95% CI 1.2 to 7.8, in 1 US case control study [235 people]).[9] The other known risk factor is occupational exposure to vibration from tools (symptoms developed in about 8% with exposure v 2.7% with no exposure in 2 cohorts from Japan).[10,11] People who are obese may be less at risk.[9] Symptoms are often worsened by cold or emotion.

**PROGNOSIS**  Attacks may last from several minutes to a few hours. One systematic review (search date 1996, 10 prospective observational studies, 639 people with primary Raynaud's phenomenon) found that only 13% of long term sufferers later manifested an underlying disorder such as scleroderma.[12]

Please refer to CD-ROM for full text and references.

# Shoulder pain

**Search date June 2003**

*Cathy Speed and Brian Hazleman*

---

## What are the effects of treatments?

Shoulder pain is not a specific diagnosis. Well designed, double blind RCTs of specific interventions in specific shoulder disorders are needed. Systematic reviews have found RCTs mostly with poor methods, and pronounced heterogeneity of study populations and outcome measures. We found insufficient evidence on the effects of most interventions in people with non-specific shoulder pain.

### LIKELY TO BE BENEFICIAL

#### Laser treatment

One systematic review found three small RCTs. Two of the RCTs found that laser improved pain after 2–3 weeks compared with placebo, and one RCT found no significant difference at 8 weeks between treatments, although it may have lacked power to detect a difference. One additional RCT found that laser significantly increased recovery rates at 1 month compared with placebo.

#### Physiotherapy (manual treatments and exercises)

One RCT in people with mixed shoulder disorders found that physiotherapy improved function at 4 weeks compared with no treatment. One RCT in people with rotator cuff disease found that a supervised exercise regimen plus advice on pain management improved pain and function compared with no exercise regimen at 6 months and 2.5 years. One RCT in people with adhesive capsulitis found that intra-articular steroids improved pain and function at 6 weeks compared with physiotherapy, although the magnitude of effect declined by 12 months.

#### Surgical arthroscopic decompression/forced manipulation

One RCT found that arthroscopic decompression by experienced surgeons followed by physiotherapy improved pain and function compared with sham laser but not compared with supervised exercises at 6 months and 2.5 years. One small RCT found that forced manipulation plus intra-articular hydrocortisone injection increased recovery rate at 3 months compared with intra-articular hydrocortisone injection alone.

### UNKNOWN EFFECTIVENESS

#### Arthroscopic laser subacromial decompression

One systematic review found no RCTs on arthroscopic laser subacromial decompression.

#### Electrical stimulation

Three small RCTs provided insufficient evidence about the effects of electrical stimulation in people with shoulder pain.

#### Extracorporeal shock wave therapy

Small and limited RCTs provided insufficient evidence about the effects of extracorporeal shock wave therapy compared with sham treatment or no treatment in people with non-calcifying rotator cuff tendinosis and chronic supraspinatus tendinosis. There was limited evidence of benefit in people with calcific tendinitis.

#### Ice

One small RCT provided insufficient evidence about the effects of ice.

◀ **Intra-articular corticosteroid injection**

We found inconclusive evidence about the effects of intra-articular steroids, with or without local anaesthetic or physiotherapy, compared with placebo or physiotherapy alone in people with shoulder pain.

**Intra-articular guanethidine**

We found no systematic review or RCTs of intra-articular guanethidine in people with non-arthritic shoulder pain.

**Multidisciplinary biopsychosocial rehabilitation**

One systematic review found no good quality RCTs of multidisciplinary biopsychosocial rehabilitation❻ in people with shoulder pain.

**Oral corticosteroids**

Two small RCTs found no evidence of reduced pain or improved abduction with oral corticosteroids compared with placebo or no treatment at 4–8 months. Adverse effects of corticosteroids are well documented (see asthma, p 371).

**Oral non-steroidal anti-inflammatory drugs**

One systematic review and one additional RCT provided insufficient evidence to draw reliable conclusions about the effects of oral non-steroidal anti-inflammatory drugs compared with placebo in people with non-specific shoulder pain.

**Phonophoresis❻**

We found no RCTs solely in people with shoulder pain.

**Subacromial corticosteroid injection**

We found no RCTs comparing subacromial injection of steroids versus placebo. Three small RCTs in people with rotator cuff tendinitis and one small RCT in people with subacromial impingement provided insufficient evidence to compare the clinical effects of corticosteroid plus lidocaine versus lidocaine alone. One RCT found no significant difference between subacromial steroid plus lidocaine and physiotherapyin terms of disability or successful outcome at 6 months in people attending their general practitioner because of a new episode of unilateral shoulder pain, but found that steroid injection increased the need for repeat consultation or other intervention.

**Transdermal glyceryl trinitrate**

We found no reliable RCTs.

**Paracetamol or opiates; topical or intra-articular non-steroidal anti-inflammatory drugs**

We found no RCTs about these interventions.

**UNLIKELY TO BE BENEFICIAL**

**Ultrasound**

One RCT identified by a systematic review found that ultrasound significantly improved pain and quality of life at the end of treatment (6 weeks) in people with calcific tendinitis, but found no significant difference at 9 months. Four other RCTs identified by the review found no significant difference between ultrasound and sham ultrasound, but may have been too small to detect a clinically important difference. ▶

**Musculoskeletal disorders**

# Shoulder pain

**DEFINITION**

Shoulder pain arises in or around the shoulder from the glenohumeral, acromioclavicular, sternoclavicular, "subacromial", and scapulothoracic articulations, and surrounding soft tissues. Regardless of the disorder, pain is the most common reason for consulting a practitioner. In adhesive capsulitis (frozen shoulder), pain is associated with pronounced restriction of movement. For most shoulder disorders, diagnosis is based on clinical features, with imaging studies playing a role in some people. Post-stroke shoulder pain is not addressed in this chapter.

**INCIDENCE/ PREVALENCE**

Each year in primary care in the UK, about 1% of adults aged over 45 years present with a new episode of shoulder pain.[1] Prevalence is uncertain, with estimates from 4–20%.[2–6] One community survey (392 people) found a 1 month prevalence of shoulder pain of 34%.[7] A second community survey (644 people aged ≥ 70 years) reported a point prevalence of 21%, with a higher frequency in women than men (25% v 17%).[8] Seventy per cent of cases involved the rotator cuff. One survey of 134 people in a community based rheumatology clinic found that 65% of cases were rotator cuff lesions; 11% were caused by localised tenderness in the pericapsular musculature; 10% acromioclavicular joint pain; 3% glenohumeral joint arthritis; and 5% were referred pain from the neck.[9] One survey found that, in adults, the annual incidence of frozen shoulder was about 2%, with those aged 40–70 years most commonly affected.[10] The age distribution of specific shoulder disorders in the community is unknown.

**AETIOLOGY/ RISK FACTORS**

Rotator cuff disorders are associated with excessive overloading, instability of the glenohumeral and acromioclavicular joints, muscle imbalance, adverse anatomical features (narrow coracoacromial arch and a hooked acromion), cuff degeneration with ageing, ischaemia, and musculoskeletal diseases that result in wasting of the cuff muscles.[11–14] Risk factors for frozen shoulder include female sex, older age, shoulder trauma, surgery, diabetes, cardiorespiratory disorders, cerebrovascular events, thyroid disease, and hemiplegia.[10,15,16] Arthritis of the glenohumeral joint can occur in numerous forms, including primary and secondary osteoarthritis, rheumatoid arthritis, and crystal arthritides.[11]

**PROGNOSIS**

One survey in an elderly community found that most people with shoulder pain were still affected 3 years after the initial survey.[17] One prospective cohort study of 122 people in primary care found that 25% of people with shoulder pain reported previous episodes and 49% reported full recovery at 18 months' follow up.[18]

Please refer to CD-ROM for full text and references.

Search date April 2003

*Willem Assendelft, Sally Green, Rachelle Buchbinder, Peter Struijs, and Nynke Smidt*

## What are the effects of treatments?

### BENEFICIAL

**Topical non-steroidal anti-inflammatory drugs for short term pain relief**

One systematic review has found that topical non-steroidal anti-inflammatory drugs improve pain in the short term compared with placebo. Minor adverse effects have been reported. We found no RCTs comparing oral versus topical non-steroidal anti-inflammatory drugs.

### LIKELY TO BE BENEFICIAL

**Oral non-steroidal anti-inflammatory drugs for short term pain relief**

One systematic review found limited evidence that an oral non-steroidal anti-inflammatory drug reduced pain and improved function compared with placebo in the short term, although we found limited evidence that it was less effective than corticosteroid injection in the short term.

### TRADE OFF BETWEEN BENEFITS AND HARMS

**Corticosteroid injections**

One systematic review and subsequent RCTs of corticosteroid injections found limited evidence of a short term improvement in symptoms with steroid injections compared with placebo, a local anaesthetic, orthoses (elbow strapping), physiotherapy, or oral non-steroidal anti-inflammatory drugs. We found no good evidence on long term effects of corticosteroids compared with placebo, local anaesthetic, physiotherapy (mobilisation plus massage) or elbow strapping, and found limited evidence that corticosteroid injection was less effective than physiotherapy or oral non-steroidal anti-inflammatory drugs in the long term.

### UNKNOWN EFFECTIVENESS

**Acupuncture**

We found insufficient evidence from small, methodologically weak RCTs about effects of needle acupuncture, laser acupuncture, or electro-acupuncture in people with tennis elbow.

**Exercise and mobilisation**

One small RCT identified by a systematic review found limited evidence that exercise reduced symptoms at 8 weeks compared with ultrasound plus friction massage. However, we were unable to draw reliable conclusions from this small study.

**Non-steroidal anti-inflammatory drugs for longer term pain relief**

We found insufficient evidence to assess the longer term effects of oral or topical non-steroidal anti-inflammatory drugs, although one RCT found that non-steroidal anti-inflammatory drugs were more effective than corticosteroid injections in the long term.

**Orthoses**

One systematic review found insufficient evidence about the effects of orthoses (braces) compared with placebo or physiotherapy. It found limited evidence of a short term improvement in symptoms compared with corticosteroid injections. ▶

# Tennis elbow

◀ **Surgery**
One systematic review found no RCTs of surgical treatment.

**UNLIKELY TO BE BENEFICIAL**

**Extracorporeal shock wave therapy**
One systematic review and one subsequent RCT found no significant difference in symptoms between extracorporeal shock wave therapy and sham treatment at 3 months.

**DEFINITION** Tennis elbow has many analogous terms, including lateral elbow pain, lateral epicondylitis, rowing elbow, tendonitis of the common extensor origin, and peritendinitis of the elbow. Tennis elbow is characterised by pain and tenderness over the lateral epicondyle of the humerus and pain on resisted dorsiflexion of the wrist, middle finger, or both. For the purposes of this review, tennis elbow is restricted to lateral elbow pain or lateral epicondylitis.

**INCIDENCE/ PREVALENCE** Lateral elbow pain is common (population prevalence 1–3%).[1] Peak incidence is at 40–50 years of age and for women of 42–46 years of age the incidence increases to 10%.[2,3] The incidence of lateral elbow pain in general practice is 4–7/1000 people a year.[3–5]

**AETIOLOGY/ RISK FACTORS** Tennis elbow is considered to be an overload injury, typically after minor and often unrecognised trauma of the extensor muscles of the forearm. Despite the title tennis elbow, tennis is a direct cause in only 5% of those with lateral epicondylitis.[6]

**PROGNOSIS** Although lateral elbow pain is generally self limiting, in a minority of people symptoms persist for 18 months to 2 years and in some cases for much longer.[7] The cost is therefore high, both in terms of lost productivity, and healthcare use. In a general practice trial of an expectant waiting policy, 80% of the people with elbow pain of already greater than 4 weeks' duration had recovered after 1 year.[8]

Please refer to CD-ROM for full text and references.

Neurological disorders

## What are the effects of interventions to prevent acute mountain sickness? *New*

### BENEFICIAL

**Acetazolamide**

One systematic review has found that acetazolamide reduces the incidence of acute mountain sickness compared with placebo. The review found that acetazolamide caused polyuria and/or paraesthesia in over a third of people. We found no good RCTs comparing acetazolamide versus dexamethasone.

**Dexamethasone**

One systematic review and further RCTs have found that dexamethasone is more effective than placebo for preventing acute mountain sickness. However, the review found that adverse effects (including depression) occurred in a quarter of people on withdrawal of dexamethasone. We found no good RCTs comparing dexamethasone versus acetazolamide.

**Slow ascent (or acclimatisation)\***

We found no RCTs evaluating different rates of ascent or acclimatisation. One non-randomised trial, observational studies, and consensus opinion suggest that slower ascent reduces the risk of acute mountain sickness compared with more rapid ascent.

## What are the effects of treatments for acute mountain sickness? *New*

### LIKELY TO BE BENEFICIAL

**Descent compared with resting at the same altitude\***

We found no RCTs on the effects of descent compared with resting at the same altitude in people with acute mountain sickness. Consensus opinion suggests that people with acute mountain sickness should descend if possible. However, we found no RCTs examining effects of different distances of descent, or about the balance of risks and benefits in people who might find it difficult to descend.

**Dexamethasone**

One small RCT in climbers with symptoms and signs of acute mountain sickness found that dexamethasone reduced mean acute mountain sickness scores compared with placebo.

### UNKNOWN EFFECTIVENESS

**Acetazolamide**

We found no good RCTs on the effects of acetazolamide compared with placebo for treating people with acute mountain sickness.

\*Although we found no RCTs on the effects of these interventions, there is a general consensus that they are effective.

**DEFINITION**   Altitude sickness (or high altitude illness) includes acute mountain sickness, high altitude pulmonary oedema, and high altitude cerebral oedema. Acute mountain sickness typically occurs at altitudes greater than 2500 metres (about 8000 feet) and is characterised by the development of some or all of ▶

# Altitude sickness

the symptoms of headache, weakness, fatigue, listlessness, nausea, insomnia, breathlessness on exertion, suppressed appetite, and peripheral oedema. Symptoms may take days to develop or may occur within hours, depending on the rate of ascent and the altitude attained. More severe forms of altitude sickness have been identified. High altitude pulmonary oedema is characterised by symptoms and signs typical of pulmonary oedema, such as shortness of breath, coughing, and production of frothy or blood stained sputum. High altitude cerebral oedema is characterised by confusion, ataxia, and decreasing level of consciousness. This review covers only acute mountain sickness.

**INCIDENCE/ PREVALENCE**  The incidence of acute mountain sickness increases with absolute height attained and with the rate of ascent. One survey in Taiwan (93 people ascending above 3000 metres) found that 27% of people experienced acute mountain sickness.[1] One survey in the Himalayas (278 unacclimatised hikers at 4243 metres) found that 53% of people developed acute mountain sickness.[2] One survey in the Swiss Alps (466 climbers at 4 altitudes between 2850 metres and 4559 metres) found the prevalence of two or more symptoms of acute mountain sickness to be 9% of people at 2850 metres; 13% of people at 3050 metres; 34% of people at 3650 metres; and 53% of people at 4559 metres.[3]

**AETIOLOGY/ RISK FACTORS**  The Himalayan study identified the rate of ascent and absolute height attained as the only risk factors.[2] It found no evidence of a difference in risk between men and women, or that previous episodes of altitude experience, load carried, or recent respiratory infections affected risk. However, the study was too small to exclude these as risk factors or to quantify risks reliably. One systematic review of RCTs (search date 1999) comparing prophylactic agents versus placebo found that, among people receiving placebo, the incidence of acute mountain sickness was higher with a faster rate of ascent (54% of people at a mean ascent rate of 91 metres/hour; 73% at a mean ascent rate of 1268 metres/hour; 89% at a simulated ascent rate in a hypobaric chamber of 1647 metres/hour).[4]

**PROGNOSIS**  We found no reliable data on prognosis. It is widely held that if no further ascent is attempted, the symptoms of acute mountain sickness tend to resolve over a few days. We found no reliable data about long term sequelae in people whose symptoms have completely resolved.

Please refer to CD-ROM for full text and references.

### Search date November 2002

*Rodrigo Salinas*

## What are the effects of treatments in adults and children?

### UNKNOWN EFFECTIVENESS

**Antiviral treatment**

Two systematic reviews found no RCTs of aciclovir versus placebo. One RCT found limited evidence that aciclovir plus prednisone improved facial function compared with prednisone alone after 4 months.

**Corticosteroids**

One systematic review found no clear evidence that corticosteroid improved the recovery of facial motor function or cosmetically disabling sequelae compared with placebo after 6 months.

**Facial nerve decompression surgery**

One systematic review identified no RCTs of facial nerve decompression.

**DEFINITION**    Bell's palsy is an acute, unilateral paresis or paralysis of the face in a pattern consistent with peripheral nerve dysfunction, without detectable causes.[1] Additional symptoms may include pain in or behind the ear, numbness in the affected side of the face, hyperacusis, and disturbed taste on the ipsilateral anterior part of the tongue.[2–5]

**INCIDENCE/**    The incidence is about 23/100 000 people a year, or about 1/60–70 people
**PREVALENCE**    in a lifetime.[6] Bell's palsy affects men and women more or less equally, with a peak incidence between the ages of 10 and 40 years. It occurs with equal frequency on the right and left sides of the face.[7]

**AETIOLOGY/**    The cause is unclear. Viral infection, vascular ischaemia, autoimmune inflam-
**RISK FACTORS**    matory disorders, and heredity have been proposed as underlying causes.[2,8,9] A viral cause has gained popularity since the isolation of the herpes simplex virus-1 genome from facial nerve endoneurial fluid in people with Bell's palsy.[10]

**PROGNOSIS**    More than two thirds of people with Bell's palsy achieve full spontaneous recovery. The largest series of people with Bell's palsy who received no specific treatment (1011 people) found the first signs of improvement within 3 weeks of onset in 85% of people.[11] For the other 15%, some improvement occurred 3–6 months later. The same series found that 71% of people recovered normal function of the face, 13% had insignificant sequelae, and the remaining 16% had permanently diminished function, with contracture and synkinesis**ⓖ**. These figures are roughly similar to those of other series of people receiving no specific treatment for Bell's palsy.[7,8,12]

Please refer to CD-ROM for full text and references.

Neurological disorders

# Epilepsy

Search date March 2003

*Anthony Marson and Sridharan Ramaratnam*

## What are the effects of treatments?

### BENEFICIAL

**Addition of second line drugs for drug resistant partial epilepsy**

Systematic reviews in people with drug resistant partial epilepsy have found that adding gabapentin, levetiracetam, lamotrigine, oxcarbazepine, tiagabine, topiramate, vigabatrin, or zonisamide to usual treatment reduces seizure frequency compared with adding placebo. The reviews have found that adding any of the drugs increases the frequency of adverse effects compared with adding placebo. We found no good evidence from RCTs on which to base a choice among drugs.

**Antiepileptic monotherapy in generalised epilepsy***

We found no placebo controlled trials of the main antiepileptic drugs (carbamazepine, phenobarbital, phenytoin, sodium valproate), but widespread consensus holds that these drugs are effective. Systematic reviews found no good evidence on which to base a choice among these drugs in terms of seizure control.

**Antiepileptic monotherapy in partial epilepsy***

We found no placebo controlled RCTs of the main antiepileptic drugs (carbamazepine, phenobarbital, phenytoin, sodium valproate) used as monotherapy in people with partial epilepsy, but widespread consensus holds that these drugs are effective. Systematic reviews found no reliable evidence on which to base a choice among drugs in terms of seizure control. Systematic reviews have found that phenobarbital is more likely to be withdrawn than phenytoin or carbamazepine and that phenytoin is more likely to be withdrawn than carbamazepine.

*We found no placebo controlled RCTs. However, widespread consensus holds that these drugs are effective.

### LIKELY TO BE BENEFICIAL

**Educational programmes**

One RCT found that a 2 day education programme reduced seizure frequency at 6 months compared with waiting list control, although it found no significant difference in health related quality of life. Two RCTs found that an educational package improved knowledge and understanding of epilepsy, adjustment to epilepsy, and psychosocial functioning compared with control.

### TRADE OFF BETWEEN BENEFITS AND HARMS

**Antiepileptic drug withdrawal for people in remission**

One systematic review of observational studies and one RCT have found that antiepileptic drug withdrawal for people in remission is associated with a higher risk of seizure recurrence than is continued treatment. Clinical predictors of relapse after drug withdrawal include age, seizure type, number of antiepileptic drugs being taken, whether seizures have occurred since antiepileptic drugs were started, and the period of remission before drug withdrawal.

**Antiepileptic drugs after a single seizure**

RCTs have found that immediate treatment of a single seizure with antiepileptic drugs reduces seizure recurrence at 2 years compared with no treatment. However, we found no evidence that treatment alters long term prognosis. Long term antiepileptic drug treatment is potentially harmful.

▶

◀ UNKNOWN EFFECTIVENESS

### Cognitive behavioural therapy
We found insufficient evidence about the effects of cognitive behavioural therapy⦿ in people with epilepsy from two small RCTs.

### Family counselling
We found insufficient evidence on family counselling from one small RCT that employed weak methods.

### Relaxation plus behavioural modification therapy
RCTs found insufficient evidence about the effects of combined relaxation and behavioural modification on seizures.

### Biofeedback; relaxation therapy⦿; yoga
Systematic reviews found insufficient evidence on the effects of these interventions.

| | |
|---|---|
| **DEFINITION** | Epilepsy is a group of disorders rather than a single disease. Seizures can be classified by type as partial (categorised as simple partial⦿, complex partial⦿, and secondary generalised tonic clonic seizures), or generalised (categorised as generalised tonic clonic, absence, myoclonic, tonic, and atonic seizures⦿).[1] |
| **INCIDENCE/ PREVALENCE** | Epilepsy is common, with an estimated prevalence in the developed world of 5–10/1000, and an annual incidence of 50/100 000 people.[2] About 3% of people will be given a diagnosis of epilepsy at some time in their lives.[3] |
| **AETIOLOGY/ RISK FACTORS** | Epilepsy can also be classified by cause.[1] Idiopathic generalised epilepsies (such as juvenile myoclonic epilepsy or childhood absence epilepsy) are largely genetic. Symptomatic epilepsies result from a known cerebral abnormality; for example, temporal lobe epilepsy may result from a congenital defect, mesial temporal sclerosis, or a tumour. Cryptogenic epilepsies are those that cannot be classified as idiopathic or symptomatic and in which no causative factor has been identified, but is suspected. |
| **PROGNOSIS** | For most people with epilepsy the prognosis is good. About 70% go into remission, defined as being seizure free for 5 years on or off treatment. This leaves 20–30% who develop chronic epilepsy, which is often treated with multiple antiepileptic drugs.[4] About 60% of untreated people have no further seizures in the 2 years after their first seizure.[5] |

Please refer to CD-ROM for full text and references.

# Essential tremor

Search date May 2003

*Joaquim Ferreira and Cristina Sampaio*

## What are the effects of drug treatments in people with essential tremor of the hand?

### LIKELY TO BE BENEFICIAL

**Propranolol (increases response rates at 6 weeks)**

Small RCTs have found that propranolol (60–240 mg) for 1 month improves clinical scores, tremor amplitude, and self evaluation of severity at up to 6 weeks compared with placebo. RCTs provided insufficient evidence to compare propranolol versus other β blockers.

### TRADE OFF BETWEEN BENEFITS AND HARMS

**Botulinum A toxin–haemagglutinin complex (improves clinical rating scales at 4–12 weeks but associated with hand weakness)**

Two RCTs in people with essential hand tremor found that botulinum A toxin–haemagglutinin complex improved clinical rating scales at 4–12 weeks but found no consistent improvement in motor tasks or functional disability. Hand weakness, which is dose dependent and transient, is a frequent adverse effect

**Phenobarbital (improves tremor at 5 weeks but associated with depression and cognitive adverse effects)**

One small RCT found that phenobarbital improved tremor scores at 5 weeks compared with placebo, but two RCTs found no significant difference in tremor scores at 4–5 weeks between phenobarbital and placebo. Phenobarbital is associated with depression and cognitive and behavioural adverse effects.

**Primidone (improves tremor and function at 5 weeks but associated with depression and cognitive adverse effects)**

Three small, short term RCTs found limited evidence that primidone improved tremor and functional ability over 4–5 weeks compared with placebo. Primidone is associated with depression and cognitive and behavioural adverse effects.

**Topiramate (improves tremor scores after 2 weeks' treatment but associated with appetite suppression, weight loss, and paraesthesias)**

One RCT found that topiramate improved observer rated tremor score after 2 weeks' treatment compared with placebo but was associated with adverse effects, including appetite suppression, weight loss, and paraesthesias. The clinical importance of the difference in tremor score is uncertain.

### UNKNOWN EFFECTIVENESS

**All treatment options in the long term**

We found no RCTs that reported the long term effects of drug treatments for essential tremor.

**β Blockers other than propranolol (atenolol, metoprolol, nadolol, pindolol, sotalol)**

Three small RCTs found weak evidence that atenolol or sotalol improved symptoms and self evaluated measures of tremor at 5 days to 4 weeks compared with placebo. One small RCT found no significant difference in symptoms between metoprolol and placebo and another small RCT found that people taking pindolol had worse tremor amplitude compared with people taking placebo. A third very ▶

◀ small RCT provided insufficient evidence to compare nadolol versus placebo. RCTs provided insufficient evidence to compare other β blockers versus propranolol.

## Benzodiazepines

Two small short term RCTs found weak evidence that alprazolam may improve tremor and function at 2–4 weeks compared with placebo. However, we were unable to draw reliable conclusions about effects. One very small RCT provided insufficient evidence to compare clonazepam versus placebo. Adverse effects with benzodiazepines, including dependency, sedation and cognitive and behavioural effects, have been well described for other conditions (see panic disorder, p 259).

## Calcium channel blockers (dihydropyridine)

Poor quality RCTs provided insufficient evidence to compare the dihydropyridine calcium channel blockers nicardipine and nimodipine versus placebo.

## Carbonic anhydrase inhibitors

Small RCTs provided insufficient evidence to assess methazolamide or acetazolamide in people with essential tremor.

## Clonidine

One RCT found no significant difference between clonidine and placebo in essential hand tremor. However, it lacked power to rule out a clinically important difference.

## Flunarizine

One small RCT found weak evidence that flunarizine may improve symptoms after 1 months' treatment compared with placebo.

## Gabapentin

Small crossover RCTs provided insufficient evidence to compare gabapentin versus placebo.

## Isoniazid

One RCT found no significant difference between isoniazid and placebo in essential hand tremor, but it may have lacked power to detect a clinically important difference.

**DEFINITION** Tremor is a rhythmic, mechanical oscillation of at least one body region. The term essential tremor is used when there is either a persistent bilateral tremor of hands and forearms, or an isolated tremor of the head without abnormal posturing, and when there is no evidence that the tremor arises from another identifiable cause. The diagnosis is not made if there are abnormal neurological signs, known causes of enhanced physiological tremor, a history or signs of psychogenic tremor, sudden change in severity, primary orthostatic tremor, isolated voice tremor, isolated position specific or task specific tremors, and isolated tongue, chin, or leg tremor.[1]

**INCIDENCE/** Essential tremor is one of the most common movement disorders throughout
**PREVALENCE** the world, with a prevalence of 0.4–3.9% in the general population.[2]

**AETIOLOGY/** Essential tremor is sometimes inherited with an autosomal dominant pattern.
**RISK FACTORS** About 40% of people with essential tremor have no family history. Alcohol ingestion provides symptomatic benefit in 50–70% of people.[3]

▶

# Essential tremor

**PROGNOSIS**   Essential tremor is a persistent and progressive condition. It usually begins during early adulthood and the severity of the tremor increases slowly. Only a small proportion of people with essential tremor seek medical advice, but the proportion in different surveys varies from 0.5–11%.[2] Most people with essential tremor are only mildly affected. However, most of the people who seek medical care are disabled to some extent, and most are socially handicapped by the tremor.[4] A quarter of people receiving medical care for the tremor change jobs or retire because of essential tremor induced disability.[3,5]

Please refer to CD-ROM for full text and references.

## What are the effects of treatments?

We found only limited evidence about the treatment of chronic tension-type headache.

### BENEFICIAL

**Amitriptyline (only short term evidence)**

One systematic review and three small, short duration RCTs have found that amitriptyline reduces duration and frequency of chronic tension-type headache compared with placebo.

### LIKELY TO BE BENEFICIAL

**Cognitive behavioural therapy**

One systematic review of three small RCTs and one subsequent RCT found limited evidence that cognitive behavioural therapy reduced symptoms at 6 months compared with no treatment.

### UNKNOWN EFFECTIVENESS

**Acupuncture**

We found insufficient evidence from heterogeneous RCTs about effects of acupuncture compared with placebo in people with episodic or chronic tension-type headache. Many of the RCTs were of poor quality. Some of the RCTs may have lacked power to exclude a clinically important effect.

**Botulinum toxin; relaxation☺ and electromyographic biofeedback therapy☺; serotonin reuptake inhibitors; tricyclic antidepressants other than amitriptyline**

We found insufficient evidence about the effects of these interventions.

### LIKELY TO BE INEFFECTIVE OR HARMFUL

**Benzodiazepines**

Two RCTs found insufficient evidence about the effects of benzodiazepines compared with placebo or other treatments. Benzodiazepines are commonly associated with adverse effects if taken regularly.

**Regular acute pain relief medication**

We found no RCTs. We found insufficient evidence from one non-systematic review of observational studies about benefits of common analgesics in people with chronic tension-type headache. It found that sustained and frequent use of some analgesics was associated with chronic headache and reduced the effectiveness of prophylactic treatment.

DEFINITION    The 1988 International Headache Society criteria for chronic tension-type headache (CTTH) are headaches on 15 or more days a month (180 days/ year) for at least 6 months; pain that is bilateral, pressing, or tightening in quality, of mild or moderate intensity, which does not prohibit activities and is not aggravated by routine physical activity; presence of no more than one additional clinical feature (nausea, photophobia, or phonophobia) and no vomiting.[1] CTTH is distinguished from chronic daily headache, which is simply a descriptive term for any headache type that occurs for 15 days or more a month that may be due to CTTH as well as migraine or analgesic associated headache.[2] In contrast to CTTH, episodic tension-type headache can last for ▶

# Headache (chronic tension-type)

30 minutes to 7 days and occurs for fewer than 180 days a year. Terms based on assumed mechanisms (muscle contraction headache, tension headache) are not operationally defined. Old studies that used these terms may have included people with many different types of headache. The greatest obstacle to studying tension-type headache is the lack of any single proved specific or reliable, clinical, or biological defining characteristic of the disorder.

**INCIDENCE/ PREVALENCE**
The prevalence of chronic daily headache from a survey of the general population in the USA was 4.1%. Half of sufferers met the International Headache Society criteria for CTTH.[3] In a survey of 2500 undergraduate students in the USA, the prevalence of CTTH was 2%.[4] The prevalence of CTTH was 2.5% in a Danish population based survey of 975 individuals.[5] One community based survey in Singapore (2096 people from the general population) found that prevalence was 1.8% in females and 0.9% males.[6]

**AETIOLOGY/ RISK FACTORS**
Tension type headache is more prevalent in women (65% of cases in one survey).[7] Symptoms begin before the age of 10 years in 15% of people with CTTH. Prevalence declines with age.[8] There is a family history of some form of headache in 40% of people with CTTH,[9] although a twin study found that risk of CTTH was similar for identical and non-identical twins.[10]

**PROGNOSIS**
The prevalence of CTTH declines with age.[8]

Please refer to CD-ROM for full text and references.

*Neurological disorders*

## What are the effects of drug treatment?

### BENEFICIAL

**Eletriptan**

One systematic review and subsequent RCTs have found that eletriptan increases headache relief⊕ at 2 hours compared with placebo. One systematic review and subsequent RCTs have found that eletriptan 40 and 80 mg increases headache relief at 2 hours compared with sumatriptan 50 and 100 mg. One RCT has found that eletriptan 40 and 80 mg increases headache relief at 2 hours compared with ergotamine plus caffeine.

**Ibuprofen**

Five RCTs have found that ibuprofen improves migraine symptoms compared with placebo.

**Naratriptan**

One systematic review and subsequent RCTs have found that naratriptan increases headache relief at 2 hours compared with placebo. One systematic review has found that sumatriptan 100 mg increases headache relief at 2 hours compared with naratriptan 2.5 mg. However, one subsequent RCT found no significant difference in headache recurrence⊕. One RCT found no significant difference between naratriptan 2.5 mg and zolmitriptan 2.5 mg in headache relief at 4 hours. One RCT identified by a systematic review found that naratriptal reduced headache relief at 2 hours compared with nizatriptan.

**Rizatriptan**

One systematic review and subsequent RCTs have found that rizatriptan improves headache relief compared with placebo. Two RCTs found no significant difference between rizatriptan and zolmitriptan in headache relief at 2 hours. One RCT identified by a systematic review has found that rizatriptan increases headache relief at 2 hours compared with naratriptan. One RCT has found that rizatriptan increases headache relief and reduces nausea and vomiting at 2 hours compared with ergotamine plus caffeine.

**Salicylates**

RCTs have found that oral or intravenous salicylates (alone or in combination with metoclopramide, paracetamol, or caffeine) increase headache relief compared with placebo. One RCT found no significant difference between aspirin and paracetamol plus codeine in headache relief. One RCT found no significant difference between aspirin plus metoclopramide and sumatriptan in headache relief. One RCT has found that oral lysine acetylsalicylate plus metoclopramide increases headache relief and reduces nausea and vomiting at 2 hours compared with ergotamine plus caffeine. One RCT found no significant difference in headache relief between aspirin plus metoclopramide and zolmitriptan.

**Sumatriptan**

Systematic reviews and subsequent RCTs have found that subcutaneous, oral, or intranasal sumatriptan increases headache relief compared with placebo. RCTs found no significant difference in headache relief between sumatriptan and aspirin plus metoclopramide, tolfenamic acid, or zolmitriptan. RCTs have found that oral or nasal sumatriptan increase headache relief compared with oral or nasal ergotamine. One systematic review has found that sumatriptan 100 mg increases ▶

headache relief at 2 hours compared with naratriptan 2.5 mg. However, one subsequent RCT found no significant difference in headache recurrence. One systematic review and subsequent RCTs have found that eletriptan 40 and 80 mg increases headache relief at 2 hours compared with sumatriptan 50 and 100 mg.

## Zolmitriptan

One systematic review and two subsequent RCTs have found that oral zolmitriptan increases headache relief compared with placebo. One systematic review and two subsequent RCTs found no significant difference between zolmitriptan and sumatriptan in headache relief. One RCT found no significant difference in headache relief between aspirin plus metoclopramide and zolmitriptan. One RCT found no significant difference between naratriptan 2.5 mg and zolmitriptan 2.5 mg in headache relief at 4 hours.

### LIKELY TO BE BENEFICIAL

## Diclofenac

RCTs have found that oral or intramuscular diclofenac improves headache symptoms compared with placebo. One RCT has found that intramuscular diclofenac improves migraine symptoms compared with intramuscular paracetamol.

## Ergotamine

One systematic review found limited evidence from four RCTs that ergotamine (with or without caffeine) improved headache relief compared with placebo. One overview of harms suggested that ergotamine increased nausea and vomiting compared with placebo. RCTs have found that ergotamine (or its derivatives, with or without caffeine and cyclizine) is less effective for migraine symptoms than sumatriptan. They found limited evidence that it was less effective than naproxen. RCTs found that ergotamine plus caffeine reduced headache relief and increased nausea and vomiting at 2 hours compared with oral lysine acetylsalicylate plus metoclopramide and rizatriptan.

## Naproxen

Three small RCTs have found that naproxen reduces migraine symptoms compared with placebo. Two RCTs have found that naproxen reduces symptoms compared with ergotamine (with or without caffeine plus cyclizine). However, one further RCT found no significant difference between naproxen and ergotamine in pain relief after 1 hour.

## Tolfenamic acid

RCTs found limited evidence that tolfenamic acid improved duration and severity of headache compared with placebo. RCTs found no significant difference in symptom relief between tolfenamic acid and sumatriptan or paracetamol.

**DEFINITION**    Migraine is a primary headache disorder manifesting as recurring attacks usually lasting for 4–72 hours and involving pain of moderate to severe intensity, often with nausea, sometimes vomiting, and/or sensitivity to light, sound, and other sensory stimuli. The 1988 International Headache Society criteria**G** include separate criteria for migraine with and migraine without associated aura.[1] Unless stated otherwise, RCTs used International Headache Society criteria for migraine with or without aura.

**INCIDENCE/**    Migraine is common worldwide. Prevalence has been reported to be 5–25%
**PREVALENCE**    in women and 2–10% in men. Overall, the highest incidence for migraine without aura has been reported between the ages of 10 and 11 years (10/1000 person years). The peak incidence of migraine without aura in males is between ages 10 and 11 years (10/1000 person years) and in females between ages 14 and 17 years (19/1000 person years).[2] The incidence of migraine with aura peaks in males at about age 5 years (7/1000

person years) and in females at about age 12–13 years (14/1000 person years).[2] Female prevalence of migraine with or without aura has a declining trend after age 45–50 years.

**AETIOLOGY/ RISK FACTORS** Data from independent representative samples from Canada,[3,4] the USA,[5,6] several countries in Latin America,[7] several countries in Europe,[8–11] Hong Kong,[12] and Japan[13] show a female to male predominance and a peak in middle aged women. Migraine has been reported to be 50% more likely in people with a family history of migraine.[14]

**PROGNOSIS** Acute migraine is self limiting and only rarely results in permanent neurological complications. Chronic recurrent migraine may cause disability through pain, and may affect daily functioning and quality of life.

Please refer to CD-ROM for full text and references.

# Multiple sclerosis

Search date March 2003

*Mike Boggild and Helen Ford*

## *What are the effects of interventions aimed at reducing relapse rates and disability?*

We found no evidence from RCTs that any treatment alters long term outcome in multiple sclerosis.

### LIKELY TO BE BENEFICIAL

#### Glatiramer acetate

One RCT in people with relapsing and remitting multiple sclerosis found that, compared with placebo, glatiramer acetate reduced relapse rates over 2 years, but had no effect on disability. We found no good quality RCTs in people with secondary progressive multiple sclerosis.

#### Interferon beta

Two RCTs in people experiencing a first demyelinating event found that interferon beta-1a decreased the risk of conversion to clinically definite multiple sclerosis over 2–3 years compared with placebo. One systematic review in people with active relapsing remitting multiple sclerosis found limited evidence that, compared with placebo, interferon beta-1a/b reduced exacerbations and disease progression over 2 years. One subsequent RCT in people with relapsing remitting multiple sclerosis found that interferon beta-1b reduced the proportion of people with relapse over 2 years compared with interferon beta-1a. We found conflicting evidence from three RCTs about the effects of interferon beta on disease progression in people with secondary progressive multiple sclerosis.

### UNKNOWN EFFECTIVENESS

#### Azathioprine

One systematic review in people with relapsing and remitting or progressive multiple sclerosis comparing azathioprine versus placebo or no treatment found a modest reduction in relapse rates over 2 years, but no evidence of a difference in disability. However, we were unable to draw reliable conclusions because of clinical heterogeneity among included RCTs.

#### Intravenous immunoglobulin

One RCT in people with relapsing and remitting multiple sclerosis found limited evidence from baseline comparisons that intravenous immunoglobulin may reduce disability over 2 years compared with placebo. However, the clinical importance of this difference is unclear. We found no good quality RCTs in people with secondary progressive multiple sclerosis.

#### Methotrexate

We found insufficient evidence from one small RCT about the effects of methotrexate in people with multiple sclerosis.

### TRADE OFF BETWEEN BENEFITS AND HARMS

#### Mitoxantrone

One RCT in people with worsening, relapsing, remitting, or progressive multiple sclerosis found that mitoxantrone reduced progression of disability compared with placebo. One small RCT in people with active multiple sclerosis found limited ▶

evidence that mitoxantrone plus methylprednisolone reduced relapse compared with methylprednisolone alone. However, mitoxantrone is associated with leukopenia, menstrual disorders, and arrhythmia.

## What are the effects of treatments for acute relapse?

**LIKELY TO BE BENEFICIAL**

### Corticosteroids (methylprednisolone or corticotrophin)

One systematic review in people with multiple sclerosis requiring treatment for acute exacerbations has found that corticosteroids (methylprednisolone or corticotrophin) improves symptoms compared with placebo within the first 5 weeks of treatment. The optimal dose, route, and duration of treatment are unclear.

**UNKNOWN EFFECTIVENESS**

### Plasma exchange

One small RCT provided insufficient evidence to assess plasma exchange in people with acute relapses of multiple sclerosis.

## What are the effects of treatments for fatigue?

**UNKNOWN EFFECTIVENESS**

### Amantadine

We found insufficient evidence from one systematic review of poor quality RCTs about the effects of amantadine on fatigue in people with multiple sclerosis.

### Behaviour modification

We found no RCTs on the effects of behavioural modification treatment in people with multiple sclerosis related fatigue.

### Exercise

We found insufficient evidence from two RCTs about the effects of exercise in people with multiple sclerosis related fatigue.

**UNLIKELY TO BE BENEFICIAL**

### Pemoline

One systematic review found no significant difference in the self reporting of fatigue with pemoline compared with placebo.

## What are the effects of treatments for spasticity?

**UNKNOWN EFFECTIVENESS**

### Botulinum toxin

We found insufficient evidence from one small RCT about the effects of botulinum toxin on functional outcomes in people with spasticity due to multiple sclerosis.

### Intrathecal baclofen

One small crossover RCT provided insufficient evidence to assess functional effects of intrathecal baclofen.

### Oral drug treatments

One systematic review found insufficient evidence about the effects of oral drugs on functional outcomes in people with spasticity due to multiple sclerosis. RCTs provided insufficient evidence to assess other oral drug treatments.

# Multiple sclerosis

◀ **Physiotherapy**

We found insufficient evidence from two small RCTs about the effects of physiotherapy. One of the RCTs found limited evidence that twice weekly hospital or home based physiotherapy for 8 weeks briefly improved mobility compared with no physiotherapy. The other, in people with progressive multiple sclerosis, found no significant difference between early versus delayed physiotherapy in mobility or activities of daily living.

## What are the effects of multidisciplinary care?

**UNKNOWN EFFECTIVENESS**

### Inpatient rehabilitation

Two small RCTs provided insufficient evidence to assess the effectiveness of inpatient rehabilitation. Both RCTs found short term benefit, but no reduction in neurological impairment. Longer term effects are uncertain.

### Outpatient rehabilitation

One small RCT provided insufficient evidence to assess the effectiveness of outpatient rehabilitation.

**DEFINITION**      Multiple sclerosis is a chronic inflammatory disease of the central nervous system. Diagnosis requires evidence of lesions that are separated in both time and space, and the exclusion of other inflammatory, structural, or hereditary conditions that might give a similar clinical picture. The disease takes three main forms: relapsing and remitting multiple sclerosis, characterised by episodes of neurological dysfunction interspersed with periods of stability; primary progressive multiple sclerosis, where progressive neurological disability occurs from the outset; and secondary progressive multiple sclerosis, where progressive neurological disability occurs later in the course of the disease.

**INCIDENCE/**      Prevalence varies with geography and racial group; it is highest in white
**PREVALENCE**   populations in temperate regions.[1] In Europe and North America, prevalence is 1/800 people, with an annual incidence of 2–10/100 000, making multiple sclerosis the most common cause of neurological disability in young adults. Age of onset is broad, peaking between 20 and 40 years.[2]

**AETIOLOGY/**      The cause remains unclear, although current evidence suggests that multiple
**RISK FACTORS** sclerosis is an autoimmune disorder of the central nervous system resulting from an environmental stimulus in genetically susceptible individuals. Multiple sclerosis is currently regarded as a single disorder with clinical variants, but there is some evidence that it may consist of several related disorders with distinct immunological, pathological, and genetic features.[1,3]

**PROGNOSIS**      In 90% of people, early disease is relapsing and remitting. Although some people follow a relatively benign course over many years, most develop secondary progressive disease, usually 6–10 years after onset. In 10% of people, initial disease is primary progressive. Apart from a minority of people with "aggressive" multiple sclerosis, life expectancy is not greatly affected and the disease course is often of more than 30 years' duration.

Please refer to CD-ROM for full text and references.

### Search date August 2003

*Carl Clarke and A Peter Moore*

## What are the effects of drug treatments in people with early stage Parkinson's disease?

### LIKELY TO BE BENEFICIAL

**Selegiline**

RCTs have found that selegiline improves the symptoms of Parkinson's disease and delays the need for levodopa compared with placebo. One of the RCTs found weak evidence of increased mortality in people treated with selegiline.

### TRADE OFF BETWEEN BENEFITS AND HARMS

**Dopamine agonists (reduce dyskinesia and motor fluctuations compared with levodopa\*, but are associated with increased treatment withdrawal and poorer motor scores)**

One systematic review and one subsequent RCT found that dopamine agonist monotherapy reduced the incidence of dyskinesias and fluctuations in motor response compared with levodopa monotherapy. However, the subsequent RCT found that dopamine agonist monotherapy was associated with poorer motor scores than was levodopa monotherapy, and with an increased the risk of treatment withdrawal.

**Dopamine agonists plus levodopa\* (reduce dyskinesia compared with levodopa alone, but increase disability)**

One systematic review and subsequent RCTs have found that dopamine agonist treatment plus levodopa reduces dyskinesia compared with levodopa alone. However, some RCTs found that levodopa alone improved motor impairments and disability compared with dopamine agonist plus levodopa.

**Levodopa\***

We found no placebo controlled RCTs, although experience suggests that levodopa improves motor function, but that dyskinesias❻ and fluctuations❻ in motor response are related to long term levodopa treatment and are irreversible.

### UNLIKELY TO BE BENEFICIAL

**Modified release levodopa (no more effective than immediate release levodopa)\***

RCTs found no significant difference with modified versus immediate release levodopa in motor complications or disease control after 5 years. One RCT found that modified release co-careldopa was better tolerated than immediate release co-careldopa.

## What are the effects of adding a dopamine agonist in people with a fluctuating response to levodopa\*?

### TRADE OFF BETWEEN BENEFITS AND HARMS

**Adding a dopamine agonist to levodopa\***

Systematic reviews have found that, in people with response fluctuations❻ to levodopa, adjuvant dopamine agonists reduce "off" time❻, improve motor impairment and activities of daily living, and reduce levodopa dose, but increase dopaminergic adverse effects❻ and dyskinesias.

# Parkinson's disease

## What are the effects of surgery in people with later Parkinson's disease?

### TRADE OFF BETWEEN BENEFITS AND HARMS

#### Pallidal surgery

One systematic review found evidence that unilateral pallidotomy🅖 improved motor examination and activities of daily living compared with medical treatment. There is a high incidence of adverse effects with pallidotomy. One RCT found insufficient evidence to assess the effects of pallidotomy compared with those of deep brain stimulation🅖. We found no systematic review or RCTs comparing pallidal deep brain stimulation versus medical treatment. One small RCT found insufficient evidence to assess the effects of pallidal deep brain stimulation compared with those of subthalamic deep brain stimulation.

### UNKNOWN EFFECTIVENESS

#### Subthalamic surgery

One systematic review found no RCTs comparing subthalamic surgery versus medical treatment. One small RCT comparing subthalamic deep brain stimulation versus pallidal deep brain stimulation found no significant difference in motor scores.

#### Thalamic surgery

Systematic reviews identified no RCTs comparing thalamic surgery versus medical treatment. One RCT found that thalamic deep brain stimulation improved functional status and caused fewer adverse effects compared with thalamotomy. Case series found that, in 14–23% of people, thalamotomy was associated with permanent complications, including speech disturbance, apraxia, and death.

## What are the effects of rehabilitation treatments in people with later Parkinson's disease?

### UNKNOWN EFFECTIVENESS

#### Occupational therapy; physiotherapy; speech and language therapy for speech disturbance; swallowing therapy for dysphagia

Systematic reviews of poor quality RCTs provided insufficient evidence about the effects of these interventions.

*We have used the term "levodopa" to refer to a combination of levodopa and a peripheral decarboxylase inhibitor.

DEFINITION    Idiopathic Parkinson's disease is an age related neurodegenerative disorder, which is associated with a combination of asymmetrical bradykinesia, hypokinesia, and rigidity, sometimes combined with rest tremor and postural changes. Clinical diagnostic criteria have a sensitivity of 80% and a specificity of 30% compared with the gold standard of diagnosis at autopsy.[1] The primary pathology is progressive loss of cells that produce the neurotransmitter dopamine from the substantia nigra in the brainstem. Treatment aims to replace or compensate for the lost dopamine. A good response to treatment supports, but does not confirm the diagnosis. Several other catecholaminergic neurotransmitter systems are also affected in Parkinson's disease. There ▶

is no consistent definition of early and late stage Parkinson's disease. In this chapter we consider people with early stage disease to be those who have not yet developed motor complications associated with long term levodopa treatment (such as dyskinesias and "on/off" fluctuations). Late stage Parkinson's disease is taken to mean that motor complications of long term levodopa treatment are present.

**INCIDENCE/ PREVALENCE**
Parkinson's disease occurs worldwide with equal incidence in both sexes. In 5–10% of people who develop Parkinson's disease the condition appears before the age of 40 years (young onset), and the mean age of onset is about 65 years. Overall age adjusted prevalence is 1% worldwide and 1.6% in Europe, rising from 0.6% at age 60–64 years to 3.5% at age 85–89 years.[2,3]

**AETIOLOGY/ RISK FACTORS**
The cause is unknown. Parkinson's disease may represent different conditions with a final common pathway. People may be affected differently by a combination of genetic and environmental factors (viruses, toxins, 1-methyl-4-phenyl-1,2,3,6-tetrahydropyridine, well water, vitamin E, and smoking).[4–7] First degree relatives of affected people may have twice the risk of developing Parkinson's disease (17% chance of developing the condition in their lifetime) compared with people in the general population.[8–10] However, purely genetic varieties probably affect a small minority of people with Parkinson's disease.[11,12] The parkin gene on chromosome 6 may be associated with Parkinson's disease in families with at least one member with young onset Parkinson's disease, and multiple genetic factors, including the tau gene on chromosome 17q21, may be involved in idiopathic late onset disease.[13,14]

**PROGNOSIS**
Parkinson's disease is currently incurable. Disability is progressive and associated with increased mortality (RR of death compared with matched control populations ranges from 1.6–3.0).[15] Treatment can reduce symptoms and slow progression but it rarely achieves complete control. The question of whether treatment reduces mortality remains controversial.[16] Levodopa seemed to reduce mortality in the UK for 5 years after its introduction, before a "catch up" effect was noted and overall mortality rose toward previous levels. This suggested a limited prolongation of life.[17] An Australian cohort study followed 130 people treated for 10 years.[18] The standardised mortality ratio was 1.58 (P < 0.001). At 10 years, 25% had been admitted to a nursing home and only four were still employed. The mean duration of disease until death was 9.1 years. In a similar Italian cohort study conducted over 8 years, the relative risk of death for affected people compared with healthy controls was 2.3 (95% CI 1.60 to 3.39).[19] Age at initial census date was the main predictor of outcome (for people aged < 75 years: RR of death 1.80, 95% CI 1.04 to 3.11; for people aged > 75 years: RR of death 5.61, 95% CI 2.13 to 14.80).

Please refer to CD-ROM for full text and references.

# Trigeminal neuralgia

Search date March 2003

*Joanna M Zakrzewska and Benjamin C Lopez*

## What are the effects of treatments?

### LIKELY TO BE BENEFICIAL

**Carbamazepine**

One systematic review of three crossover RCTs found that carbamazepine increased pain relief compared with placebo. The review found that carbamazepine increased adverse effects (drowsiness, dizziness, constipation, and ataxia) compared with placebo. One small RCT provided insufficient evidence to compare tizanidine versus carbamazepine. One RCT found that pimozide reduced pain over 8 weeks compared with carbamazepine, but increased adverse effects (including hand tremors, memory impairment, and involuntary movements). One systematic review found one RCT of tocainide versus carbamazepine that was of insufficient quality.

### TRADE OFF BETWEEN BENEFITS AND HARMS

**Pimozide**

One RCT found that pimozide reduced pain over 8 weeks compared with carbamazepine, but increased adverse effects (including hand tremors, memory impairment, and involuntary movements). Cardiac toxicity and sudden death have been reported with pimozide.

### UNKNOWN EFFECTIVENESS

**Baclofen**

We found insufficient evidence on the effects of baclofen versus placebo or versus other active drugs.

**Combined streptomycin and lidocaine nerve block**

Small RCTs provided insufficient evidence about the effects of nerve block with streptomycin plus lidocaine compared with nerve block with lidocaine alone.

**Lamotrigine**

One systematic review provided insufficient evidence to compare lamotrigine versus placebo in people with trigeminal neuralgia.

**Other drugs (phenytoin, clonazepam, sodium valproate, gabapentin, mexiletine, oxcarbazepine, topiramate)**

We found insufficient evidence about the effects of these drugs in people with trigeminal neuralgia.

**Peripheral laser treatment**

We found insufficient evidence on the effects of peripheral laser treatment⊕ in people with trigeminal neuralgia.

**Stereotactic radiosurgery**

We found insufficient evidence about the effects of stereotactic radiosurgery in people with trigeminal neuralgia.

**Tizanidine**

One small RCT provided insufficient evidence to compare tizanidine versus carbamazepine.

◄ **Cryotherapy©️ of peripheral nerves; peripheral acupuncture; peripheral alcohol injection; peripheral injection of phenol; peripheral neurectomy; peripheral radiofrequency thermocoagulation©️**

We found no RCTs about the effects of these interventions.

## UNLIKELY TO BE BENEFICIAL

### Proparacaine eye drops

One RCT found no significant difference in pain at 30 days between placebo and a single application of proparacaine hydrochloride eye drops to the eye on the same side as the pain.

## LIKELY TO BE INEFFECTIVE OR HARMFUL

### Tocainide

One systematic review found one RCT of tocainide versus carbamazepine which was of insufficient quality. The use of tocainide is limited by considerable harms (including serious haematological effects).

**DEFINITION**
Trigeminal neuralgia is a characteristic pain in the distribution of one or more branches of the fifth cranial nerve. The diagnosis is made on the history alone, based on characteristic features of the pain. It occurs in paroxysms that last a few seconds to 2 minutes. The frequency of paroxysms is highly variable: from hundreds of attacks a day to long periods of remission that can last years. The pain is severe and described as intense, sharp, superficial, stabbing, burning, or like an electric shock. In any individual, the pain has the same character in different attacks. It is often triggered by touch in a specific area or by eating, talking, washing the face, or cleaning the teeth. Between paroxysms the person is asymptomatic. Other causes of facial pain may need to be excluded.[1] In trigeminal neuralgia the neurological examination is usually normal.[2,3]

**INCIDENCE/ PREVALENCE**
Most evidence about the incidence and prevalence of trigeminal neuralgia is from the USA.[4] The annual incidence (when age adjusted to 1980 age distribution of the USA) is 5.9/100 000 women and 3.4/100 000 men. The incidence tends to be slightly higher in women at all ages. The incidence increases with age. In men aged over 80 years the incidence is 45.2/ 100 000.[5] Other published surveys are small. One questionnaire survey of neurological disease in a single French village found one person with trigeminal neuralgia among 993 people.[6]

**AETIOLOGY/ RISK FACTORS**
The cause of trigeminal neuralgia remains unclear.[7] It is more common in people with multiple sclerosis (RR 20.0, 95% CI 4.1 to 59.0).[5] Hypertension is a risk factor in women (RR 2.1, 95% CI 1.2 to 3.4) but the evidence is less clear for men (RR 1.53, 95% CI 0.30 to 4.50).[5] A study in the USA found that people with trigeminal neuralgia smoked less, consumed less alcohol, had fewer tonsillectomies, and were less likely than matched controls to be Jewish or an immigrant.[8]

**PROGNOSIS**
One study found no reduction of 10 year survival with trigeminal neuralgia.[9] We found no evidence about the natural history of trigeminal neuralgia. The illness is characterised by recurrences and remissions. Many people have periods of remission with no pain for months or years.[3] Anecdotal reports suggest that in many people it becomes more severe and less responsive to treatment with time.[10] Most people with trigeminal neuralgia are initially managed medically, and a proportion eventually have a surgical procedure.[5] We found no good evidence about the proportion of people who require surgical treatment for pain control.

Please refer to CD-ROM for full text and references.

**Oral health**

# Aphthous ulcers (recurrent)

**Search date August 2003**

*Stephen Porter and Crispian Scully CBE*

## What are the effects of treatments?

LIKELY TO BE BENEFICIAL

### Chlorhexidine

RCTs found that chlorhexidine gluconate mouth rinses reduced the severity of each episode of ulceration, but did not effect the incidence of ulceration. Limited evidence from one RCT suggests that 0.2% chlorhexidine gel may reduce the incidence and duration of ulceration compared with control preparation. RCTs found that chlorhexidine reduced the mean severity of pain compared with an inert preparation.

### UNKNOWN EFFECTIVENESS

### Topical corticosteroids

Small RCTs found that topical corticosteroids reduced the number of ulcer days compared with control. RCTs found no consistent effect of topical corticosteroids on the incidence of new ulcers compared with control preparations. They found weak evidence that topical corticosteroids may reduce the duration and pain of ulcers and hasten pain relief without causing notable local or systemic adverse effects.

### UNLIKELY TO BE BENEFICIAL

### Hexitidine

Limited evidence from single RCTs found no significant difference in any of the reported outcomes between hexitidine mouthwash or a proprietary antibacterial mouthwash and control mouthwashes.

**DEFINITION**       Recurrent aphthous ulcers are superficial and rounded, with painful mouth ulcers usually occurring in recurrent bouts at intervals of a few days to a few months.[1]

**INCIDENCE/**       The point prevalence of recurrent aphthous ulcers in Swedish adults has been
**PREVALENCE**       reported as 2%.[1] Prevalence may be 5–10% in some groups of children. Up to 66% of young adults give a history consistent with recurrent aphthous ulceration.[1]

**AETIOLOGY/**       The causes of aphthous ulcers remain unknown. Associations with haematinic
**RISK FACTORS** deficiency, infections, gluten sensitive enteropathy, food sensitivities, and psychological stress have rarely been confirmed. Similar ulcers are seen in Behçet's syndrome. Local physical trauma may initiate ulcers in susceptible people. Recurrent aphthous ulcers are uncommon on keratinised oral mucosal surfaces, and the frequency of recurrent aphthous ulcers may fall if patients cease any tobacco smoking habit.

**PROGNOSIS**       About 80% of people with recurrent aphthous ulcers develop a few ulcers smaller than 1 cm in diameter that heal within 5–14 days without scarring (the pattern known as minor aphthous ulceration). The episodes recur typically after an interval of 1–4 months. One in 10 people with recurrent ulceration may have multiple minute ulcers (herpetiform ulceration). Likewise, one in 10 sufferers ▶

has a more severe form (major aphthous ulceration), with lesions larger than 1 cm that may recur after a shorter interval and can cause scarring. The majority of trials in this review have focused upon the treatment of minor aphthous ulceration.

Please refer to CD-ROM for full text and references.

# Burning mouth syndrome

Search date June 2003

*John Buchanan and Joanna Zakrzewska*

## What are the effects of treatments?

### LIKELY TO BE BENEFICIAL

**Cognitive behavioural therapy**
One small RCT found that cognitive behavioural therapy reduced symptom intensity in people with resistant burning syndrome after 6 months compared with placebo treatment.

### UNKNOWN EFFECTIVENESS

**Dietary supplementation**
We found insufficient evidence from three small methodologically flawed RCTs to draw reliable conclusions about the effects of alphalipoic acid in people with burning mouth syndrome. We found no RCTs evaluating other vitamin or coenzyme supplements.

**Hormone replacement therapy in postmenopausal women**
We found limited evidence from one small methodologically flawed RCT that tibolone improved symptoms compared with oryzanol plus vitamin E at 6 months.

**Antidepressants; benzydamine hydrochloride**
We found insufficient evidence on the effects of these interventions.

**DEFINITION** Burning mouth syndrome is a psychogenic or idiopathic burning discomfort or pain affecting people with clinically normal oral mucosa in whom a medical or dental cause has been excluded.[1–3] Terms previously used to describe what is now called burning mouth syndrome include glossodynia, glossopyrosis, stomatodynia, stomatopyrosis, sore tongue, and oral dysaesthesia.[4] A survey of 669 men and 758 women randomly selected from 48 500 people aged between 20 and 69 years found that people with burning mouth also have subjective dryness (66%), take some form of medication (64%), report other systemic illnesses (57%), and have altered taste (11%).[5] Many studies of people with symptoms of burning mouth do not distinguish those with burning mouth syndrome (i.e. idiopathic disease) from those with other conditions (such as vitamin B deficiency), making results unreliable. Local and systemic factors (such as infections, allergies, ill fitting dentures,[6] hypersensitivity reactions,[7] and hormone and vitamin deficiencies[8–10]) may cause the symptom of burning mouth and should be excluded before diagnosing burning mouth syndrome.

**INCIDENCE/ PREVALENCE** Burning mouth syndrome mainly affects women,[11–13] particularly after the menopause when its prevalence may be 18–33%.[14] One recent study in Sweden found a prevalence of 4% for the symptom of burning mouth without clinical abnormality of the oral mucosa (11/669 [2%] men, mean age 59 years; 42/758 [6%] women, mean age 57 years), with the highest prevalence (12%) in women aged 60–69 years.[5] Reported prevalence in general populations varies from 1%[15] to 15%.[11] Incidence and prevalence vary according to diagnostic criteria,[4] and many studies included people with the symptom of burning mouth rather than with burning mouth syndrome as defined above.

**AETIOLOGY/ RISK FACTORS** The cause is unknown, and we found no good aetiological studies. Possible causal factors include hormonal disturbances associated with the menopause,[12–14] psychogenic factors (including anxiety, depression, stress, life events, personality disorders, and phobia of cancer),[6,16,17] and neuropathy in so-called supertasters🅖.[18]

▶

◄ **PROGNOSIS**    We found no prospective cohort studies or other reliable evidence describing the natural history of burning mouth syndrome.[19] We found anecdotal reports of at least partial spontaneous remission in about half of people with burning mouth syndrome within 6–7 years.[16]

Please refer to CD-ROM for full text and references.

# Candidiasis (oropharyngeal)

**Search date February 2003**

*Caroline Pankhurst*

## What are the effects of preventive interventions?

**BENEFICIAL**

### Antifungal prophylaxis in people undergoing cancer treatments

One systematic review in people undergoing treatment for cancer found that antifungal drugs reduced the risk of oropharyngeal candidiasis compared with placebo or no treatment. One review found that drugs that were absorbed or partially absorbed via the gastrointestinal tract were more effective than non-absorbed drugs in preventing oral candidiasis.

### Antifungal prophylaxis in people with advanced HIV disease

RCTs in people with HIV infection have found that daily or weekly antifungal prophylaxis with fluconazole, itraconazole, or nystatin reduces incidence and relapse of oropharyngeal candidiasis compared with placebo.

**LIKELY TO BE BENEFICIAL**

### Antifungal prophylaxis in immunocompromised infants and children

One large RCT in immunocompromised infants and children found that fluconazole reduced the incidence of oropharyngeal candidiasis compared with oral nystatin or amphotenicin B.

**UNKNOWN EFFECTIVENESS**

### Antifungal prophylaxis in people receiving tissue transplants

Two small RCTs in people with liver transplant found no significant difference in the risk of oropharyngeal candidiasis between nystatin and fluconazole or clotrimazole. However, the trials may have lacked power to exclude clinically important differences. We found insufficient evidence from two RCTs about the effects of prophylactic chlorhexidine mouth rinse with or without nystatin compared with placebo in people receiving bone marrow transplant.

### Continuous prophylaxis versus intermittent treatment in people with HIV infection and acute episodes of oropharyngeal candidiasis (in preventing antifungal resistance)

One RCT in people with HIV infection and acute episodes of oropharyngeal candidiasis found no significant difference in emergence of antifungal resistance between continuous antifungal prophylaxis with fluconazole and intermittent antifungal treatment with fluconazole.

### Preventive interventions in people with diabetes

We found no systematic review or RCTs.

## What are the effects of treatments?

**BENEFICIAL**

### Antifungal treatment in immunocompetent and immunocompromised infants and children

RCTs found that miconazole and fluconazole increased clinical cure of oropharyngeal candidiasis compared with nystatin in immunocompetent and immunocompromised infants and children.

◄ **Oral suspension of systemically absorbed azoles in people with HIV infection**

RCTs have found that topical preparations of itraconazole, fluconazole, and clotrimazole effectively treat oropharyngeal candidiasis in people with HIV infection. One RCT found that fluconazole significantly reduced symptoms and signs of oropharyngeal candidiasis compared with topical nystatin.

**UNKNOWN EFFECTIVENESS**

### Antifungal treatment for denture stomatitis

We found insufficient evidence from small RCTs to compare effects of antifungals versus placebo or versus each other for treating oropharyngeal candidiasis in people who wear dentures.

### Antifungal treatment in people undergoing chemotherapy, radiotherapy, or both treatments for cancer

One systematic review found insufficient evidence from RCTs about the clinical effects of antifungals compared with placebo for treating oropharyngeal candidiasis in people undergoing chemotherapy or radiotherapy. It also found insufficient evidence about the effects of different antifungal agents or doses in people with oropharyngeal candidiasis who are receiving radiotherapy or chemotherapy.

### Denture hygiene

We found insufficient evidence from RCTs to assess clinical effects on oropharyngeal candidiasis of mouth rinses, disinfectants, denture soaks, denture scrubbing, and microwave irradiation of dentures. Microwave treatment is not suitable for all dentures.

### Treatments in people with diabetes mellitus

We found no RCTs assessing treatments for oral candidiasis in people with diabetes mellitus.

**DEFINITION**
Oropharyngeal candidiasis is an opportunistic mucosal infection caused, in most cases, by *Candida albicans*. The four main types of oropharyngeal candidiasis are: (1) pseudomembranous (thrush), consisting of white discrete plaques on an erythematous background, located on the buccal mucosa, throat, tongue, or gingivae; (2) erythematous, consisting of smooth red patches on the hard or soft palate, dorsum of tongue, or buccal mucosa; (3) hyperplastic, consisting of white, firmly adherent patches or plaques, usually bilateral on the buccal mucosa; and (4) denture induced stomatitis, presenting as either a smooth or granular erythema confined to the denture bearing area of the hard palate and often associated with an angular cheilitis.[1] Symptoms vary, ranging from none to a sore and painful mouth with a burning tongue and altered taste. Oropharyngeal candidiasis can impair speech, nutritional intake, and quality of life.

**INCIDENCE/ PREVALENCE**
Candida species are commensals in the gastrointestinal tract. Transmission occurs directly between infected people or on fomites (objects that can harbour pathogenic organisms). Candida is found in the mouth of 31–60% of healthy people.[2] Denture stomatitis associated with Candida is prevalent in 65% of denture wearers.[2] Oropharyngeal candidiasis affects 15–60% of people with haematological or oncological malignancies during periods of immunosuppression.[3] Oropharyngeal candidiasis occurs in 7–48% of people with HIV infection and in over 90% of those with advanced disease. In severely immunosuppressed people, relapse rates are high (30–50%) and usually occur within 14 days of stopping treatment.[4]

▶

# Candidiasis (oropharyngeal)

**AETIOLOGY/ RISK FACTORS**  Risk factors associated with symptomatic oropharyngeal candidiasis include local or systemic immunosuppression, haematological disorders, broad spectrum antibiotic use, inhaled or systemic steroids, xerostomia, diabetes, and wearing dentures, obturators, or orthodontic appliances.[1,5] The same strain may persist for months or years in the absence of infection. In people with HIV infection, there is no direct correlation between the number of organisms and the presence of clinical disease. Symptomatic oropharyngeal candidiasis associated with *in vitro* resistance to fluconazole occurs in 5% of people with advanced HIV disease.[6] Resistance to azole antifungals is associated with severe immunosuppression ($\leq$ 50 CD4 cells/mm$^3$), more episodes treated with antifungal drugs, and longer median duration of systemic azole treatment.[7]

**PROGNOSIS**  Untreated candidiasis persists for months or years unless associated risk factors are treated or eliminated. In neonates, spontaneous cure of oropharyngeal candidiasis usually occurs after 3–8 weeks.

Please refer to CD-ROM for full text and references.

## What are the effects of treatments in people with physiological halitosis?

### LIKELY TO BE BENEFICIAL

#### Single-use mouthwash (short term benefit only)

Three small RCTs in people with confirmed halitosis found limited evidence that single-use mouthwash reduced odour unpleasantness and odour intensity between 1–8 hours after use compared with distilled water, saline rinse, or no treatment. One of these RCTs found no significant difference between single-use mouthwash and distilled water in odour unpleasantness or odour intensity after 24 hours.

### UNKNOWN EFFECTIVENESS

#### Regular-use mouthwash

We found no RCTs on the effects of the regular use of mouthwash.

#### Artificial saliva; sugar free chewing gums; tongue cleaning, brushing, or scraping; zinc toothpastes

We found no RCTs on the effects of these interventions.

| | |
|---|---|
| **DEFINITION** | Halitosis is an unpleasant odour emitted from the mouth. It can be because of oral conditions including poor oral hygiene and periodontal disease or extraoral conditions such as chronic sinusitis and bronchiectasis.[1,2] In this topic, we deal only with physiological halitosis, that is, confirmed persistent bad breath in the absence of systemic, periodontal, or gum disease. We have excluded halitosis due to underlying disease, which would require disease specific treatment, pseudo-halitosis (in people who believe they have bad breath but whose breath is not considered malodourous by others), and artificially induced halitosis (e.g. in studies requiring people to stop brushing their teeth). This topic is only applicable, therefore, to people in whom underlying causes have been ruled out, and in whom pseudo-halitosis has been excluded. There is no consensus regarding duration of bad breath for diagnosis of halitosis, although the standard organoleptic test❻ for bad breath involves smelling the breath on at least two or three different days.[1] |
| **INCIDENCE/ PREVALENCE** | We found no reliable estimate of prevalence, although several studies report population prevalence of halitosis (physiological or because of underlying disease) to be about 50%.[1,3–5] One cross-sectional study of 491 people found that about 5% of people with halitosis have pseudo-halitosis and about 40% of people with halitosis have physiological bad breath not due to underlying disease.[6] We found no reliable data about age or sex distribution of physiological halitosis. |
| **AETIOLOGY/ RISK FACTORS** | We found no reliable data about risk factors for physiological bad breath. Mass spectrometric and gas chromatographic analysis of expelled air from the mouth of people with any type of halitosis have shown that the main malodourants are volatile sulphur compounds including hydrogen sulphide, methyl mercaptan, and dimethyl suphide.[7,8] |
| **PROGNOSIS** | We found no evidence on the prognosis of halitosis. |

Please refer to CD-ROM for full text and references.

**Oral health**

# Impacted wisdom teeth

Search date October 2003

*Marco Esposito*

## What are the effects of prophylactic removal of impacted wisdom teeth?

**LIKELY TO BE INEFFECTIVE OR HARMFUL**

**Extraction of asymptomatic impacted wisdom teeth**
One systematic review of two RCTs found no evidence that prophylactic extraction improves outcomes compared with no extraction. Removal of lower wisdom teeth causes permanent numbness of the lower lip or tongue in about 1/200 people.

**DEFINITION**
Wisdom teeth are third molars that develop in almost all adults and generally erupt between the ages of 18 and 24 years, although there is a wide variation in the age of eruption. In some people, the teeth become partially or completely impacted below the gum line because of lack of space, obstruction, or abnormal position. Impacted wisdom teeth may be diagnosed because of pain and swelling or incidentally by routine dental radiography.

**INCIDENCE/ PREVALENCE**
Third molar impaction is common. Over 72% of Swedish people aged 20–30 years have at least one impacted lower third molar.[1] The surgical removal of impacted third molars (symptomatic and asymptomatic) is the most common procedure performed by oral and maxillofacial surgeons. It is performed on about 4/1000 people per year in England and Wales, making it one of the top 10 inpatient and day case procedures.[2–4] Up to 90% of people on oral and maxillofacial surgery hospital waiting lists are awaiting removal of wisdom teeth.[3]

**AETIOLOGY/ RISK FACTORS**
Impacted wisdom teeth might be caused by changes in diet. A softer diet in childhood might increase the likelihood of retaining wisdom teeth in adult life.[5]

**PROGNOSIS**
Impacted wisdom teeth can cause pain, swelling, and infection, as well as destroying adjacent teeth and bone. The removal of diseased and symptomatic wisdom teeth alleviates pain and suffering and improves oral health and function. We found no good evidence on what happens without treatment in people with asymptomatic impacted wisdom teeth.

Please refer to CD-ROM for full text and references.

## What are the effects of preventive interventions?

### BENEFICIAL

**Epidural anaesthesia**

Two systematic reviews have found that epidural anaesthesia with or without postoperative epidural or spinal analgesia reduces postoperative pulmonary infections compared with general anaesthesia with or without postoperative systemic analgesia. Neither review sought data on adverse effects. Subsequent and additional RCTs found inconsistent results.

**Postoperative chest physiotherapy (deep breathing exercises)**

One systematic review and one subsequent RCT have found that deep breathing exercises⊕ reduce postoperative pulmonary infections compared with control.

### LIKELY TO BE BENEFICIAL

**Postoperative chest physiotherapy (incentive spirometry and intermittent positive pressure breathing)**

Two RCTs found that incentive spirometry⊕ reduced pulmonary complications compared with control. One RCT found that intermittent positive pressure⊕ breathing reduced postoperative pulmonary complications compared with control.

### UNKNOWN EFFECTIVENESS

**Advice to stop smoking preoperatively**

We found no RCTs about the effects of preoperative advice to stop cigarette smoking on postoperative pulmonary infections. Two observational studies found that people who smoked were more likely to develop postoperative pulmonary complications of all kinds than those who did not. One study suggested that people who had stopped smoking for at least 2 months in the 6 months prior to surgery reverted to the risk of those who had never smoked.

**DEFINITION**    A working diagnosis of postoperative pulmonary infection may be based on three or more new findings from: cough, phlegm, shortness of breath, chest pain, temperature above 38 °C, and pulse rate above 100 a minute.[1] In this chapter, the diagnosis of pneumonia implies consolidation observed on a chest x ray.[2]

**INCIDENCE/**    Reported morbidity for chest complications depends on how carefully they are
**PREVALENCE**    investigated. One study found blood gas and chest radiograph abnormalities in about 50% of people after open cholecystectomy.[3] However, less than 20% of these had abnormal clinical signs and only 10% had a clinically significant chest infection. Another study estimated the incidence of pneumonia as 20%.[4] Another used a similarly strict definition and found the incidence was 23%.[5]

**AETIOLOGY/**    Risk factors include increasing age (> 50 years), cigarette smoking, obesity,
**RISK FACTORS**    thoracic or upper abdominal operations, and pre-existing lung disease.[6] One multivariate analysis did not confirm the association with cigarette smoking, but suggested that longer preoperative hospital stay and higher grading on the American Society of Anesthesiologists' physical status scale (> 2) increased the risk of postoperative pulmonary complications.[5] Depression of the immune system may also contribute.[7]

**Postoperative pulmonary infections**

**PROGNOSIS** In one large systematic review (search date 1997, 141 RCTs, 9559 people), 10% of people with postoperative pneumonia died.[8] If systemic sepsis ensues, mortality is likely to be substantial.[9] Pneumonia delays recovery from surgery and poor tissue oxygenation may contribute to delayed wound healing.

Please refer to CD-ROM for full text and references.

### Search date March 2003

*Michael Eddleston, Surjit Singh, and Nick Buckley*

## What are the effects of treatments for acute organophosphorus poisoning?

### LIKELY TO BE BENEFICIAL

#### Atropine*

Consensus supports atropine treatment. Many case series have found that it reverses the early muscarinic effects of acute organophosphorus poisoning. We found no RCTs comparing atropine versus placebo, but such an RCT would now be considered unethical.

#### Benzodiazepines to control organophosphorus induced seizures*

Consensus supports benzodiazepines for organophosphorus induced seizures. We found no RCTs comparing a benzodiazepine versus placebo or another anticonvulsant. It would now be unethical to conduct an RCT comparing benzodiazepines versus placebo.

#### Glycopyrronium bromide (glycopyrrolate)*

One small RCT found no significant difference in death or ventilation rates between glycopyrronium bromide and atropine, but it may have lacked power to detect clinically important differences. Glycopyrronium bromide (glycopyrrolate) has been used instead of atropine because it is thought to have fewer adverse effects on the central nervous system.

#### Washing the poisoned person and removing contaminated clothes*

Washing the poisoned person with warm water and soap and removing contaminated clothes after dermal and mucocutaneous exposure appears important and widely recommended, but this intervention has not been assessed in RCTs.

### UNKNOWN EFFECTIVENESS

#### Gastric lavage

We found no RCTs assessing the role of gastric lavage in acute organophosphorus poisoning. If the procedure cannot be performed in sedated and intubated patients, the risk of harm due to aspiration is likely to surpass its potential benefits.

#### Milk or other home remedy immediately after ingestion

We found no RCTs on the effect of giving a "home remedy" soon after the ingestion.

#### Oximes

One systematic review found insufficient evidence about the effects of oximes in acute organophosphorus poisoning.

#### Activated charcoal (single or multiple dose); $\alpha_2$ adrenergic receptor agonists (clonidine); N-methyl-D-aspartate receptor antagonists; organophophorus hydrolases; sodium bicarbonate

We found insufficient evidence about the effects of these interventions.

# Acute organophosphorus poisoning

## LIKELY TO BE INEFFECTIVE OR HARMFUL

### Ipecacuanha (ipecac)*

We found no RCTs on the effects of ipecacuanha in acute organophosphorus poisoning. The significant risk of harm, although not quantified, probably outweighs any potential benefits.

*Based on consensus, RCTs would be considered unethical.

**DEFINITION**  Acute organophosphorus poisoning occurs after dermal, respiratory, or oral exposure to either low volatility pesticides (e.g. chlorpyrifos, dimethoate) or high volatility nerve gases (e.g. sarin, tabun). Acetylcholinesterase🄖 inhibition at synapses results in accumulation of acetylcholine and over-activation of acetylcholine receptors at the neuromuscular junction and in the autonomic and central nervous systems.[1] Early clinical features mainly involve the parasympathetic system: bradycardia, bronchorrhoea, miosis, salivation, lachrymation, defecation, urination, and hypotension. Features of neuromuscular junction (muscle weakness and fasciculations) and central nervous system (seizures, coma) involvement are also common at this stage. An intermediate syndrome has been described (cranial nerve palsies and proximal muscle weakness with preserved distal muscle power after resolution of early cholinergic symptoms), but its definition, pathophysiology, and incidence are still unclear. A late motor or motor/sensory peripheral neuropathy may also develop after recovery from acute poisoning with some organophosphorus compounds.[1]

**INCIDENCE/**
**PREVALENCE**  Most cases occur in the developing world following occupational or deliberate exposure to organophosphorus pesticides.[2] Although data are sparse, organophosphates appear to be the most important cause of death from deliberate self poisoning worldwide.[3] In Sri Lanka, at least 17 000 cases of organophosphorus or carbamate poisoning occurred in 1999, resulting in 1700 deaths. More than 80% were intentional.[4] Case fatality rates across the developing world are commonly greater than 20%.[3] In Central America, occupational poisoning is more common than intentional poisoning and deaths are fewer.[5] Extrapolating from limited data, the World Health Organization has estimated that each year more than 200 000 people worldwide die from pesticide poisoning,[6] but these figures are old and widely contested.[2] Most deaths occur in Asia and organophosphorus pesticides probably cause at least 50% of cases.[3] Deaths from organophosphorus nerve gases occurred in Iran during the Iran–Iraq war.[7] Military or terrorist action with these chemical weapons remains possible. Twelve people died in a terrorist attack in Tokyo and thousands probably died in Iran after military or terrorist exposure.

**AETIOLOGY/**
**RISK FACTORS**  The widespread accessibility of pesticides in rural parts of the developing world makes them easy options for acts of self harm.[3] Occupational exposure is due to insufficient or inappropriate protective equipment in the use of toxic compounds.[2]

**PROGNOSIS**  There are no validated scoring systems for categorising severity or predicting outcome, although many have been proposed. The highly variable natural history and difficulty in determining ingested dose make predicting outcome for an individual inaccurate and potentially hazardous, because people admitted in good condition can deteriorate rapidly and require intubation and mechanical ventilation. Prognosis in acute self poisoning is likely to depend on dose and toxicity of the ingested organophosphorus (e.g. neurotoxicity potential, half life, rate of ageing🄖, whether activation to the toxic compound is required [propoison🄖], and whether dimethylated or diethylated).[8,9] Prognosis in occupational exposure is better because the dose is normally smaller and the route is dermal.

Please refer to CD-ROM for full text and references.

# Paracetamol (acetaminophen) poisoning

Search date July 2003

*Nick Buckley and Michael Eddleston*

## What are the effects of treatments?

### BENEFICIAL

**Acetylcysteine**

One systematic review found one RCT in people with established paracetamol induced liver failure. It found that acetylcysteine reduced mortality after 21 days compared with placebo. One observational study found that people given early treatment with acetylcysteine were less likely to develop liver damage than untreated historical controls.

### LIKELY TO BE BENEFICIAL

**Methionine**

One systematic review found insufficient evidence on the effects of methionine on mortality. It found limited evidence that methionine reduced hepatotoxicity compared with supportive care.

### UNKNOWN EFFECTIVENESS

**Activated charcoal (single or multiple dose)**

One systematic review found no evidence on the effects of activated charcoal, whether in single or multiple dose regimens, in people poisoned by paracetamol. One large case series found that clinically significant complications of multiple dose activated charcoal are rare.

**Gastric lavage**

One systematic review found no evidence of the effects of gastric lavage in paracetamol poisoning.

**Ipecacuanha**

One systematic review found no evidence on the clinical effects of ipecacuanha in paracetamol poisoning.

**DEFINITION** Paracetamol poisoning occurs as a result of either accidental or intentional overdose with paracetamol (acetaminophen).

**INCIDENCE/ PREVALENCE** Paracetamol is the most common drug used for self poisoning in the UK.[1] It is also a common means of self poisoning in the rest of Europe, North America, and Australasia. An estimated 41 200 cases of poisoning with products containing paracetamol occurred in 1989–1990 in England and Wales, with a mortality of 0.40% (95% CI 0.38% to 0.46%). Overdoses owing to paracetamol alone result in an estimated 150–200 deaths and 15–20 liver transplants each year in England and Wales.

**AETIOLOGY/ RISK FACTORS** Most cases in the UK are impulsive acts of self harm in young people.[1,2] In one study of 80 people who had overdosed with paracetamol, 42 had obtained the tablets for the specific purpose of taking an overdose and 33 had obtained them less than 1 hour before the act.[2]

**PROGNOSIS** People with blood paracetamol concentrations above the standard treatment line (defined in the UK as a line joining 200 mg/L at 4 hours and 30 mg/L at 15 hours on a semilogarithmic plot) have a poor prognosis without treatment **G**.[3–5] In one study of 57 untreated people with blood concentrations above this line, 33 developed severe liver damage and three died.[4] People with a history of ▶

# Paracetamol (acetaminophen) poisoning

chronic alcohol misuse, use of enzyme inducing drugs, eating disorders, or multiple paracetamol overdoses may be at risk of liver damage with blood concentrations below this line.[6] In the USA, a lower line is used as an indication for treatment but we found no data relating this line to prognostic outcomes.[7]

**Dose effect:** The dose ingested also indicates the risk of hepatotoxicity. People ingesting less than 125 mg/kg had no significant hepatotoxicity with a sharp dose dependent rise for higher doses.[8] The threshold for toxicity after acute ingestion may be higher in children, where a single dose of less than 200 mg/kg has not been reported to lead to death and rarely causes hepatotoxicity.[9] For people who present later than 24 hours or an unknown time after ingestion, several other prognostic indicators have been proposed, including prothrombin time and abnormal liver function tests.[10,11] These have not been validated prospectively.

Please refer to CD-ROM for full text and references.

## What are the effects of treatments for non-ruptured tubal pregnancy? New

### TRADE OFF BETWEEN BENEFITS AND HARMS

#### Choice between open and laparoscopic salpingostomy

One systematic review found that, compared with laparoscopic salpingostomy❻, open salpingostomy increased rates of elimination of tubal pregnancy. It found no significant difference in rates of subsequent intrauterine pregnancy or repeat ectopic pregnancy, but perioperative blood loss was higher with open salpingostomy.

### UNKNOWN EFFECTIVENESS

#### Methotrexate (oral)

One small RCT identified by a systematic review found no significant difference between oral methotrexate 2.5 mg daily for 5 days and expectant management❻ in the need for laparoscopy within 3 months.

#### Salpingostomy (open or laparoscopic)

One RCT identified by one systematic review found no significant difference in elimination of tubal pregnancy, tubal preservation, spontaneous intrauterine pregnancy, or repeat ectopic pregnancy at 18 months between multiple dose methotrexate (1 mg/kg on days 1, 2, 4, and 6) plus folic acid compared with laparoscopic salpingostomy. One systematic review found higher rates of persistent ectopic pregnancy❻ and lower rates of elimination of tubal pregnancy with single dose intramuscular methotrexate 1 mg/kg or 50 mg/m$^2$ compared with laparoscopic salpingostomy.

#### Fimbrial expression, salpingectomy, and salpingo-oophorectomy

We found no systematic review or RCTs that evaluated these interventions❻.

### UNLIKELY TO BE BENEFICIAL

#### Methotrexate (intramuscular, multiple or single dose)

One RCT identified by one systematic review found no significant difference in elimination of tubal pregnancy, tubal preservation, spontaneous intrauterine pregnancy, or repeat ectopic pregnancy at 18 months between multiple dose methotrexate (1 mg/kg on days 1, 2, 4, and 6) plus folic acid compared with laparoscopic salpingostomy. One systematic review found higher rates of persistent ectopic pregnancy❻ and lower rates of elimination of tubal pregnancy with single dose intramuscular methotrexate 1 mg/kg or 50 mg/m$^2$ compared with laparoscopic salpingostomy.

**DEFINITION**     In ectopic pregnancy, the fertilised ovum implants on a surface other than the uterine endometrium. Almost all ectopic pregnancies implant in the fallopian tubes. This topic covers management in women with non-ruptured, tubal ectopic pregnancy only. Ectopic pregnancies are detected by clinical suspicion and serial measurement of serum human chorionic gonadotrophin❻ (hCG) or ultrasound.[1] Spontaneous resolution occurs only in selected cases: in women ▶

# Ectopic pregnancy

with a small adnexal mass on transvaginal sonography, decreasing hCG levels, and only minor symptoms.[2,3] **Population:** In this topic, we have excluded women with an acute presentation of ectopic pregnancy (such as peritonism, or with evidence of rupture or bleeding). Typically, this group would consist of women with small tubal pregnancies confirmed ultrasonographically or based on serial hCG levels.

**INCIDENCE/ PREVALENCE**
Small studies suggest that 1–2% of reported pregnancies are ectopic.[4,5] A recent large study attempted to estimate the proportion of ectopic pregnancies in the USA using national data sets, but found that data were too flawed to provide an accurate estimate of the incidence.[6]

**AETIOLOGY/ RISK FACTORS**
A recent large case-control study suggested that the main risk factors for ectopic pregnancy were history of pelvic infection (OR 3.4, 95% CI 2.4 to 5.0) and smoking (OR 3.9, 95% CI 2.6 to 5.9).[7] Other risk factors were age, previous spontaneous abortion, history of infertility, and previous use of an intrauterine contraceptive device.[7] Earlier studies have found that previous ectopic pregnancy, previous tubal surgery including tubal sterilisation, documented tubal pathology, intrauterine contraceptive device, previous genital infections, smoking and *in utero* diethylstilbestrol exposure were associated with ectopic pregnancy.[8–10] The risk of ectopic pregnancy varies with method of tubal sterilisation. Women sterilised by bipolar tubal coagulation before the age of 30 years were found to have a risk of ectopic pregnancy 27 times greater than women who had postpartum partial salpingectomy.[9]

**PROGNOSIS**
Risks of ectopic pregnancy include tubal rupture, life-threatening bleeding, and subsequent infertility. The combination of transvaginal ultrasound and hCG measurements allow the condition to be diagnosed earlier now than previously. Consequently, mortality has fallen over time in the developed world from 35.5 deaths per 10 000 cases to 3.8 deaths per 10 000 cases between 1970 and 1989 in the USA and from 16 deaths per 10 000 cases to three deaths per 10 000 pregnancies between 1973 and 1993 in the UK.[3] However, mortality remains high in poorer countries: 100–300 deaths per 10 000 cases in one African survey.[11] Evaluating expectant management to assess prognosis is difficult because of ethical concerns about exposing women to undue risk of acute complications, which may have medico-legal implications.[12] However, expectant management has been suggested as a feasible option in women at low risk of acute complications (such as asymptomatic women and women with small adnexal masses and decreasing hCG levels), and in the presence of close monitoring. A recent non-systematic review found rates of spontaneous resolution with expectant management to range from 46–65%.[3] One prospective cohort study (118 women) found that rates of spontaneous resolution varied with hCG level from 98% where hCG concentrations were less than 200 mIU/mL to 25% for hCG concentration greater than 2000 mIU/mL.[2] However, no factors have yet been found that reliably predict tubal rupture or bleeding.[3]

Please refer to CD-ROM for full text and references.

Search date July 2003

*Richmal Oates-Whitehead*

## What are the effects of treatment for nausea and vomiting in early pregnancy?

### BENEFICIAL

#### Ginger

Three RCTs and one randomised crossover trial found that ginger reduced nausea and vomiting in early pregnancy. One further RCT found that ginger reduced nausea and dry retching, but had no effect on episodes of vomiting.

### LIKELY TO BE BENEFICIAL

#### Acupressure

One systematic review of small RCTs found limited evidence that P6 acupressure🅖 reduced self reported morning sickness compared with sham acupressure or no intervention. Three subsequent RCTs and two randomized trials found that P6 acupressure reduced the duration, but not necessarily the intensity, of nausea and vomiting.

#### Antihistamines (H1 antagonists)

Two systematic reviews found limited evidence that antihistamines reduced nausea and vomiting, with no evidence of teratogenicity.

#### Cyanocobalamin (vitamin $B_{12}$)

One systematic review has found that cyanocobalamin🅖 reduces vomiting episodes compared with placebo.

#### Pyridoxine (vitamin $B_6$)

Two systematic reviews found limited evidence that pyridoxine reduced nausea but found no evidence of an effect on vomiting.

### UNKNOWN EFFECTIVENESS

#### Acupuncture

One RCT found that acupuncture reduced nausea and retching compared with no acupuncture, with no evidence of adverse effects. However, an improvement was also found with sham acupuncture compared with no treatment. A second smaller RCT found no significant difference in nausea between acupuncture and sham acupuncture.

#### Dietary interventions (other than ginger)

We found no RCTS of dietary interventions (other than ginger).

#### Phenothiazines

One systematic review found limited evidence that phenothiazines reduced the proportion of women with nausea and vomiting. However, results were not conclusive. The review found no evidence of teratogenicity.

## What are the effects of treatments for hyperemesis gravidarum?

### UNKNOWN EFFECTIVENESS

#### Acupuncture

One small randomised, crossover RCT found a faster reduction in nausea, as measured on a visual analogue scale, after active PC6 acupuncture compared with sham acupuncture. Episodes of vomiting were also reduced. However, we were unable to draw reliable conclusions from this study.

#### Corticosteroids

One small RCT found no significant improvement in persistent vomiting or readmission to hospital after 1 week of treatment with prednisolone compared with placebo. One small RCT found no significant improvement in persistence of vomiting but found that prednisolone reduced admission to hospital compared with promethazine.

#### Corticotropins

One small RCT found no significant difference in nausea and vomiting between intramuscular corticotropin (adrenocorticotrophic hormone [ACTH]) and placebo.

#### Diazepam

One RCT provided insufficient evidence to assess the effects of diazepam in women with hyperemesis gravidarum.

#### Dietary interventions (other than ginger)

One small crossover RCT found no significant difference in nausea and vomiting after 3 weeks of dietary supplementation with carob seed flour compared with placebo.

#### Ginger

One small RCT provided insufficient evidence to assess the effects of ginger in hyperemesis gravidarum.

#### Ondansetron

One small RCT provided insufficient evidence to assess the effects of ondansetron in hyperemesis gravidarum.

DEFINITION  **Nausea and vomiting** are both common in early pregnancy. Although often called "morning sickness", nausea and vomiting can occur at any time of the day and may be constant.[1] Symptoms usually start between 4 and 7 weeks' gestation (one study found this to be the case in 70% of affected women)[2] and stop by 16 weeks in about 90% of women.[1-3] One study found that fewer than 10% of affected women suffer nausea and/or vomiting before the first missed period.[3] Most women do not require treatment. However, persistent vomiting and severe nausea can progress to hyperemesis if the woman is unable to maintain adequate hydration, fluid and electrolyte balance, and nutrition. **Hyperemesis gravidarum** is a diagnosis of exclusion, characterised by prolonged and severe nausea and vomiting, dehydration, and weight loss.[1] Laboratory investigation may show elevated plasma ketone levels in the absence of acidosis (ketosis), low serum levels of sodium (hyponatraemia), potassium (hypokalaemia), and urea (hypouricaemia), metabolic hypochloraemic alkalosis (excess base alkali in the body fluids caused by chloride loss), and excess ketones in the urine (ketonuria).

| | |
|---|---|
| **INCIDENCE/ PREVALENCE** | Nausea affects about 70% and vomiting about 60% of pregnant women.[1] The true incidence of hyperemesis gravidarum is not known. It has been documented to range from 3 to 20 per thousand pregnancies. However, most authors report an incidence of 1 in 200.[2] |
| **AETIOLOGY/ RISK FACTORS** | The causes of nausea and vomiting in pregnancy are unknown. One theory, that they are caused by the rise in human chorionic gonadotrophin concentration, is compatible with the natural history of the condition, its severity in pregnancies affected by hydatidiform mole⊕, and its good prognosis (see prognosis below).[4] The aetiology of hyperemesis gravidarum is also uncertain. Again, endocrine and psychological factors are suspected, but evidence is inconclusive.[4] |
| **PROGNOSIS** | One systematic review (search date 1988) found that nausea and vomiting were associated with a reduced risk of miscarriage (6 studies, 14 564 women; OR 0.36, 95% CI 0.32 to 0.42) but found no association with perinatal mortality.[5] Nausea and vomiting and hyperemesis usually improve over the course of pregnancy, but in one cross sectional observational study 13% of women reported that nausea and vomiting persisted beyond 20 weeks' gestation.[6] |

Please refer to CD-ROM for full text and references.

# Perineal care

Search date August 2003

*Chris Kettle*

## What are the effects of intrapartum interventions on rates of perineal trauma and of different methods and materials used for primary repair of perineal trauma?

### BENEFICIAL

**Absorbable synthetic sutures for perineal repair of first and second degree tears and episiotomies (reduces short term pain)**

One systematic review has found that absorbable synthetic sutures reduce pain at up to 10 days after birth compared with catgut sutures. One subsequent RCT, however, found no significant difference in perineal pain at 3 days, although it may have lacked power to detect a clinically important effect. The systematic review and the subsequent RCT found no significant difference between absorbable synthetic sutures and catgut sutures in pain or dyspareunia at 3 months, but one RCT with 12 months' follow up, which was included in the review, found lower rates of dyspareunia with absorbable synthetic sutures. RCTs found no significant difference between rapidly absorbed and standard synthetic sutures in overall perineal pain, pain on sitting, or dyspareunia. The RCTs found reduced perineal pain on walking with rapidly absorbed synthetic sutures.

**Continuous subcutaneous technique of perineal skin closure of first and second degree tears and episiotomies (reduces short term pain)**

One systematic review has found that continuous subcuticular sutures for perineal skin reduced short term pain compared with interrupted sutures, but there was no significant difference in perineal pain or dyspareunia at 3 months post partum. One RCT found that a loose continuous suture reduced short term perineal pain and suture removal compared with interrupted sutures for repair of all layers up to 3 months post partum.

**Continuous support during labour (reduces operative vaginal birth)**

One systematic review has found that providing continuous support@ for women during childbirth reduces the rate of operative vaginal birth (vacuum extraction or forceps) compared with usual care. It found no significant difference in the risk of episiotomy or perineal trauma (defined as episiotomy or laceration requiring suturing).

**Restrictive use of episiotomy (reduces risk of posterior trauma compared with routine use)**

One systematic review found that restricting episiotomy to specific fetal and maternal indications reduced rates of posterior perineal trauma, need for suturing, and healing complications compared with routine use, but increased the rates of anterior vaginal and labial trauma, which carries minimal morbidity.

### LIKELY TO BE BENEFICIAL

**Non-suturing of perineal skin in first and second degree tears and episiotomies (reduces dyspareunia)**

One large RCT has found no significant difference between leaving the perineal skin unsutured compared with conventional suturing in pain at 10 days after birth. A second RCT found that non-suturing reduced pain for up to 3 months following delivery. Both RCTs found that non-suturing of the perineal skin reduced dyspareunia at 3 months after birth.

▶

◀ TRADE OFF BETWEEN BENEFITS AND HARMS

**"Hands poised" versus "hands on" method of delivery (increases pain and need for manual delivery of placenta, no significant difference in rate of perinea trauma, and reduces episiotomy rate)**

One multicentre RCT and one quasi-randomised trial found that the "hands poised" method (not touching the baby's head or supporting the mother's perineum) reduced episiotomy rates compared with the conventional "hands on" method (applying pressure to the baby's head during delivery and supporting the mother's perineum). The RCT found no evidence of an effect on the risk of perineal trauma, but found that the "hands poised" group had an increased risk of requiring manual removal of the placenta and higher rates of short term perineal pain.

**Upright versus supine or lateral position during delivery (fewer episiotomies but more second degree tears than supine or lateral positions)**

One systematic review found that any upright position marginally reduced episiotomies compared with supine or lateral positions for delivery, but this was offset by an increase in second degree tears. Rates of assisted vaginal delivery were slightly reduced in the upright group.

**Vacuum extraction (less perineal trauma than with forceps but newborns have increased risk of cephalheamatoma)**

One systematic review and subsequent RCTs have found that vacuum extraction reduces the rate of severe perineal trauma compared with forceps delivery, but increases the incidence of neonatal cephalhaematoma and retinal haemorrhage.

UNKNOWN EFFECTIVENESS

**Different methods and materials for repair of third and fourth degree tears**

One small RCT comparing the overlap⊕ method versus the end-to-end⊕ method for primary repair of third degree obstetric tears found no significant difference in perineal discomfort and a non-significant reduction in the rate of reported faecal urgency and anal incontinence.

**Passive descent in the second stage of labour**

One RCT comparing passive fetal descent⊕ versus immediate active pushing found no significant difference in perineal trauma.

**Sustained breath holding (Valsalva) method of pushing**

One systematic review of two poor quality controlled clinical trials found no significant difference in the extent or rate of perineal trauma between sustained breath holding (Valsalva) and spontaneous exhalatory methods of pushing during the second stage of labour.

UNLIKELY TO BE BENEFICIAL

**Midline episiotomy incision (associated with higher risk of third or fourth degree tears compared with mediolateral incision)**

We found no evidence that midline episiotomy incision improved perineal pain or wound dehiscence compared with mediolateral incision. Limited evidence from one quasi-randomised trial suggests that midline incision may increase the risk of third and fourth degree tears compared with mediolateral incision.

LIKELY TO BE INEFFECTIVE OR HARMFUL

**Epidural anaesthesia (increases instrumental delivery, which is associated with increased rates of perineal trauma)**

One systematic review found no direct evidence about the effects of epidural compared with other forms of anaesthesia on rates of perineal trauma. However, ▶

# Perineal care

RCTs found that epidural anaesthesia maintained beyond the first stage of labour compared with epidural restricted to the first stage of labour significantly increased the risk of instrumental delivery, which in turn is associated with an increased risk of perineal trauma.

## Non-suturing of muscle and skin in first and second degree perineal tears (poorer wound healing than with suturing)

Two small RCTs found no significant difference in short term perineal pain between non-suturing and suturing of first and second degree tears. One of the RCTs found no significant difference in healing between groups but the second RCT found that a greater proportion of women in the non-sutured group had poorer wound healing at 6 weeks after birth.

**DEFINITION**    Perineal trauma is any damage to the genitalia during childbirth that occurs spontaneously or intentionally by surgical incision (episiotomy). Anterior perineal trauma is injury to the labia, anterior vagina, urethra, or clitoris, and is usually associated with little morbidity. Posterior perineal trauma is any injury to the posterior vaginal wall, perineal muscles, or anal sphincter. First degree spontaneous tears involve only skin; second degree tears involve perineal muscles; third degree tears partially or completely disrupt the anal sphincter; and fourth degree tears completely disrupt the external and internal anal sphincter and epithelium.[1]

**INCIDENCE/**    Over 85% of women having a vaginal birth sustain some form of perineal
**PREVALENCE**    trauma,[2] and 60–70% receive stitches — equivalent to 400 000 women a year in the UK in 1997.[2,3] There are wide variations in rates of episiotomy: 8% in the Netherlands, 13% in England, 43% in the USA, and 99% in east European countries.[4–6] Sutured spontaneous tears are reported in about a third of women in the USA[4] and the UK,[7] but this is probably an underestimate because of inconsistency of reporting and classification of perineal trauma. The incidence of anal sphincter tears varies between 0.5% in the UK, 2.5% in Denmark, and 7% in Canada.[8]

**AETIOLOGY/**    Perineal trauma occurs during spontaneous or assisted vaginal delivery and is
**RISK FACTORS**    usually more extensive after the first vaginal delivery.[1] Associated risk factors also include increased fetal size, mode of delivery, and malpresentation and malposition of the fetus. Other maternal factors that may increase the extent and degree of trauma are ethnicity (white people are probably at greater risk than black people), older age, abnormal collagen synthesis, and poor nutritional state.[10] Clinicians' practices or preferences in terms of intrapartum interventions may influence the severity and rate of perineal trauma (e.g. use of ventouse v forceps).

**PROGNOSIS**    Perineal trauma affects women's physical, psychological, and social wellbeing in the immediate postnatal period as well as the long term. It can also disrupt breast feeding, family life, and sexual relations. In the UK, about 23–42% of women will continue to have pain and discomfort for 10–12 days post partum, and 7–10% of women will continue to have long term pain (3–18 months after delivery);[2,3,10] 23% of women will experience superficial dyspareunia at 3 months; 3–10% will report faecal incontinence;[11,12] and up to 24% will have urinary problems.[2,3] Complications depend on the severity of perineal trauma and on the effectiveness of treatment.

Please refer to CD-ROM for full text and references.

## *What are the effects of treatments?* New

### LIKELY TO BE BENEFICIAL

### Antidepressants (fluoxetine)

Limited evidence from one small RCT suggests that fluoxetine may improve postnatal depression at 4 and 12 weeks compared with placebo. The RCT had problems with recruitment and a high drop out rate, and it excluded breastfeeding women. We found no RCTs that satisfactorily compared fluoxetine versus psychological treatment.

### Cognitive behavioural therapy (individual)

One RCT provided limited evidence that individual cognitive behavioural therapy and ideal standard care both improved depressive symptoms, but that there was no difference between the two interventions. Limited evidence from one RCT suggests that individual cognitive behavioural therapy may improve postnatal depression in the short term (immediately after treatment) compared with routine primary care. The RCT found no clear longer term benefits (9 months to 5 years post partum) from individual cognitive behavioural therapy in comparison with routine primary care, non-directive counselling, or psychodynamic therapy.

### Interpersonal psychotherapy

One RCT found that interpersonal psychotherapy improved postnatal depression compared with waiting list controls at 12 weeks.

### Non-directive counselling

Limited evidence from two RCTs suggests that in the short term (immediately after treatment) non-directive counselling may improve postnatal depression compared with routine primary care. The one RCT with follow up beyond 12 weeks found no clear longer term benefits (from 9 months to 5 years post partum) from non-directive counselling compared with routine primary care, individual cognitive behavioural therapy, or psychodynamic therapy.

### Psychodynamic therapy

Limited evidence from one RCT suggests that psychodynamic therapy may improve postnatal depression in the short term (immediately after treatment) compared with routine primary care. The RCT found no clear longer term benefits (9 months to 5 years post partum) from psychodynamic therapy compared with routine primary care, non-directive counselling, or cognitive behavioural therapy.

### UNKNOWN EFFECTIVENESS

### Antidepressants other than fluoxetine

We found no RCTs on the effects of antidepressants in women with postnatal depression, and no RCTs that satisfactorily compared antidepressants other than fluoxetine versus psychological treatments.

### Cognitive behavioural therapy (group)

One small RCT in women with a high level of depressive symptoms on screening found that group cognitive behavioural therapy improved symptoms at 6 months compared with routine primary care.

# Postnatal depression

### Hormones

Limited evidence from one small RCT in women with severe postnatal depression suggests that oestrogen treatment may improve postnatal depression at 3 and 6 months compared with placebo.

### Light therapy

We found no RCTs evaluating light therapy.

### Mother–infant interaction coaching

One small RCT found that mother–infant interaction coaching**G** had no significant effect on maternal depression scores compared with usual treatment, but it improved maternal responsiveness to the infant within 10 weeks of starting treatment.

### Psychoeducation with partner

One small RCT found that psychoeducation with partner reduced patients' depression scores and partners' psychiatric morbidity compared with psychoeducation without partner.

### Telephone based peer support (mother to mother)

One small RCT found that telephone based peer support reduced depression scores after 8 weeks compared with usual treatment.

**DEFINITION**    Postnatal depression (PND) is broadly defined as non-psychotic depression occurring during the first 6 months post partum. Puerperal mental disorders have only recently been categorised separately in psychiatric classifications, but both the International Classification of Diseases (ICD-10)[1] and the Diagnostic and Statistical Manual of mental disorders, fourth edition (DSM-IV) require certain qualifications to be met that limit their use: ICD-10 categorises mental disorders that occur post partum as puerperal but only if they cannot otherwise be classified, and DSM-IV allows "postpartum onset" to be specified for mood disorders starting within 4 weeks' post partum.[2] In clinical practice and research the broader definition above is often used, because whether or not PND is truly distinct from depression in general, depression in the postpartum period raises treatment issues for the nursing mother and has implications for the developing infant (see prognosis below).The symptoms are similar to symptoms of depression at other times of life, but in addition to low mood, sleep disturbance, change in appetite, diurnal variation in mood, poor concentration, and irritability, women with postnatal depression also experience guilt about their inability to look after their new baby. In many countries, health visitors screen for PND using the Edinburgh Postnatal Depression Scale**G**,[3,4] which elicits depressive symptoms.

**INCIDENCE/**     The prevalence of depression in women post partum is similar to that found in
**PREVALENCE**     women generally. However, the incidence of depression in the first month after childbirth is three times the average monthly incidence in non-childbearing women.[5] Studies across different cultures have shown a consistent incidence of postnatal depression (10–15%),[6] with higher rates in teenage mothers. A meta-analysis of studies mainly based in the developed world found the incidence of postnatal depression to be 12–13%.[7]

**AETIOLOGY/**      Three systematic reviews have identified the following risk factors for postnatal
**RISK FACTORS**    depression: past history of any psychopathology (including history of previous postnatal depression), low social support, poor marital relationship, and recent life events.[7–9]

Pregnancy and childbirth

**PROGNOSIS** Most episodes of PND resolve spontaneously within 3–6 months,[10] but about one in four affected mothers are still depressed on the child's first birthday.[11] In the developed world, suicide is now the main cause of maternal deaths in the first year post partum,[13] but the suicide rate is lower at this time than in age matched non-postpartum women.[13] PND is also associated with reduced likelihood of secure attachment,[14] deficits in maternal–infant interactions,[15] and impaired cognitive and emotional development of the child, particularly in boys living in areas of socioeconomic deprivation.[15–17] These associations remain significant even after controlling for subsequent episodes of depression in the mother.

Please refer to CD-ROM for full text and references.

# Pre-eclampsia and hypertension

Search date April 2003

*Lelia Duley*

## What are the effects of preventive interventions?

### BENEFICIAL

**Antiplatelet drugs**

One systematic review and one subsequent RCT have found that, in women considered at risk of pre-eclampsia, antiplatelet drugs (mainly aspirin) reduce the risk of pre-eclampsia, death of the baby, and delivery before 37 weeks compared with placebo or no treatment. The RCTs found no significant difference in other important outcomes. The systematic review found no evidence that aspirin increased the risk of bleeding in mother or baby compared with placebo.

**Calcium supplementation**

One systematic review has found that calcium supplementation (mainly 2 g daily) reduces the risk of pre-eclampsia and reduces the risk of having a baby with birth weight under 2500 g compared with placebo. There was no significant effect on the risk of caesarean section, preterm delivery, stillbirth, or perinatal death of the baby before discharge from hospital.

### UNKNOWN EFFECTIVENESS

**Magnesium supplementation**

One systematic review found insufficient evidence about the effects of magnesium supplements on the risk of pre-eclampsia or its complications.

**Other pharmacological agents (atenolol or nitrates)**

We found two small RCTs; one compared atenolol versus placebo and the other compared glyceryl trinitrate patches versus placebo. Both were too small for any reliable conclusions.

**Salt restriction**

Limited evidence from one systematic review found no significant difference in the risk of pre-eclampsia between a low salt diet and a normal diet.

**Vitamins C and E**

One RCT in high risk women found limited evidence that vitamins C and E reduced the risk of pre-eclampsia compared with placebo.

**Fish oil and/or evening primrose oil**

We found six RCTs of fish oil and/or evening primrose oil, which were too small to draw reliable conclusions.

## What are the effects of treatments?

### BENEFICIAL

**Magnesium sulphate for eclampsia**

Systematic reviews have found that magnesium sulphate reduces the risk of further fits in women with eclampsia compared with phenytoin, diazepam, or lytic cocktail⊕. All reviews found trends towards reduced maternal mortality with magnesium sulphate, although the benefit was not significant.

**Prophylactic magnesium sulphate in severe pre-eclampsia**

One systematic review has found that prophylactic magnesium sulphate halves the risk of eclampsia compared with placebo, phenytoin, or nimodipine in women with ▶

severe pre-eclampsia. The trials found no evidence of a difference between magnesium sulphate and placebo for rate of stillbirth or perinatal mortality in babies born to women with severe pre-eclampsia. A quarter of women reported mild adverse effects (mainly flushing).

## LIKELY TO BE BENEFICIAL

### Antihypertensive drugs for very high blood pressure

Consensus opinion is that women with severe hypertension during pregnancy should have antihypertensive treatment. Placebo controlled trials would therefore be unethical. One systematic review and one subsequent RCT in women with blood pressures high enough to merit immediate treatment found no evidence of a difference in the control of blood pressure by various antihypertensive drugs. The studies were too small to draw any further conclusions about the relative effects of different agents. Ketanserin and diazoxide may be associated with more adverse effects than hydralazine and labetalol.

## UNKNOWN EFFECTIVENESS

### Aggressive management for severe early onset pre-eclampsia

One systematic review based on two small RCTs found no evidence that aggressive management reduced stillbirth or perinatal death rates compared with expectant management in babies born to mothers with severe early onset pre-eclampsia. However, it found that aggressive management increased rates of admission to neonatal intensive care and increased the risk of necrotising enterocolitis and respiratory distress in the baby compared with expectant management. We found insufficient evidence about effects of aggressive compared with expectant management in the mother.

### Antihypertensive drugs for mild to moderate hypertension

Two systematic reviews have found that antihypertensive agents may halve the risk of severe hypertension but the effects of antihypertensive agents on other important outcomes are unclear. Systematic reviews found that angiotensin converting enzyme inhibitors used in pregnancy were associated with fetal renal failure, and found that β blockers increased the risk of the baby being small for its gestational age. It remains unclear whether treatment of mild to moderate hypertension during pregnancy is worthwhile with any antihypertensive agent compared with no treatment.

### Antioxidants in severe pre-eclampsia

One RCT found insufficient evidence about the effects of a combination of vitamin E plus vitamin C plus allopurinol compared with placebo.

### Bed rest/hospital admission

We found insufficient evidence about hospital admission or bed rest compared with outpatient or day care.

### Choice of analgesia during labour with severe pre-eclampsia

One RCT found that epidural analgesia during labour reduced mean pain scores compared with patient controlled analgesia given intravenously, but the clinical importance of the difference was unclear.

### Plasma volume expansion in severe pre-eclampsia

One systematic review comparing plasma volume expansion with no expansion found insufficient evidence to draw reliable conclusions.

### Prophylactic diazepam in severe pre-eclampsia

One systematic review found insufficient evidence about effects of diazepam compared with no anticonvulsants in women with severe pre-eclampsia.

# Pre-eclampsia and hypertension

**DEFINITION**  Hypertension during pregnancy may be associated with one of several conditions. **Pregnancy induced hypertension** is a rise in blood pressure, without proteinuria, during the second half of pregnancy. **Pre-eclampsia** is a multisystem disorder, unique to pregnancy, which is usually associated with raised blood pressure and proteinuria. It rarely presents before 20 weeks' gestation. **Eclampsia** is one or more convulsions in association with the syndrome of pre-eclampsia. **Pre-existing hypertension (not covered in this chapter)** is known hypertension before pregnancy or raised blood pressure before 20 weeks' gestation. It may be essential hypertension or, less commonly, secondary to underlying disease.[1]

**INCIDENCE/ PREVALENCE**  Pregnancy induced hypertension affects 10% of pregnancies and pre-eclampsia complicates 2–8% pregnancies.[2] Eclampsia occurs in about 1/2000 deliveries in developed countries.[3] In developing countries, estimates of the incidence of eclampsia vary from 1/100–1/1700.[4,5]

**AETIOLOGY/ RISK FACTORS**  The cause of pre-eclampsia is unknown. It is likely to be multifactorial and may result from deficient placental implantation during the first half of pregnancy.[6] Pre-eclampsia is more common among women likely to have a large placenta, such as those with multiple pregnancy, and among women with medical conditions associated with microvascular disease, such as diabetes, hypertension, and collagen vascular disease.[7,8] Other risk factors include genetic susceptibility, increased parity, and older maternal age.[9] Cigarette smoking seems to be associated with a lower risk of pre-eclampsia, but this potential benefit is outweighed by an increase in adverse outcomes such as low birth weight, placental abruption, and perinatal death.[10]

**PROGNOSIS**  The outcome of pregnancy in women with pregnancy induced hypertension alone is at least as good as that for normotensive pregnancies.[7,11] However, once pre-eclampsia develops, morbidity and mortality rise for both mother and child. For example, perinatal mortality for women with severe pre-eclampsia is double that for normotensive women.[7] Perinatal outcome is worse with early gestational hypertension.[7,9,11] Perinatal mortality also increases in women with severe essential hypertension.[12]

Please refer to CD-ROM for full text and references.

## What are the effects of treatments?

**BENEFICIAL**

### Antenatal corticosteroids

One systematic review found that antenatal corticosteroids significantly reduced respiratory distress syndrome, intraventricular haemorrhage, and neonatal mortality compared with placebo or no treatment.

**LIKELY TO BE BENEFICIAL**

### Antibiotic treatment for premature rupture of the membranes (prolongs gestation and may reduce infection, but unknown effect on perinatal mortality)

One systematic review in women with premature rupture of membranes has found that antibiotics prolong pregnancy and reduce the risk of neonatal morbidity, such as neonatal infection, requirement for treatment with oxygen, and abnormal cerebral ultrasound, compared with placebo. It found that co-amoxiclav (amoxycillin plus clavulanic acid) increased the risk of neonatal necrotising enterocolitis compared with placebo.

### Calcium channel blockers (versus other tocolytics) *New*

We found no systematic review or RCTs comparing calcium channel blockers versus placebo. One systematic review has found that calcium channel blockers significantly reduce deliveries within 48 hours, neonatal morbidity, and withdrawals caused by maternal adverse effects compared with other tocolytics$\mathbf{G}$ (mainly $\beta$ agonists).

### Prophylactic cervical cerclage for women at risk of cervical incompetence where cervical changes have not been identified

Systematic reviews identified five RCTs that found different results for women where cervical changes have not been identified. One large RCT found that cervical cerclage$\mathbf{G}$ at 9 to 29 weeks reduced delivery before 33 weeks' gestation in women with a previous preterm delivery or previous cervical surgery, but doubled the risk of puerperal pyrexia compared with no cerclage. The other four smaller RCTs found no significant difference in preterm delivery before 34 weeks between cerclage at 10 to 30 weeks and no cerclage in women with a variety of risk factors for preterm delivery.

**UNKNOWN EFFECTIVENESS**

### Amnioinfusion for preterm rupture of the membranes

One systematic review found insufficient evidence from one RCT about the effects of amnioinfusion compared with no amnioinfusion in improving neonatal outcomes after preterm rupture of the membranes$\mathbf{G}$.

### Oxytocin receptor antagonists (atosiban) *New*

One systematic review identified two RCTs that compared atosiban with placebo and found different results. The larger RCT found that atosiban prolonged pregnancy compared with placebo but found that atosiban appeared to increase fetal deaths below 28 weeks' gestation. The other RCT found that atosiban increased delivery within 48 hours.

◄ **Prophylactic cervical cerclage for women at risk of cervical incompetence where cervical changes have been identified**

Two RCTs identified by a systematic review found different results for women where cervical changes were present. One RCT found no significant difference in delivery before 34 weeks. The other small RCT found that cerclage plus bed rest reduced delivery before 34 weeks compared with bed rest alone. Neither RCT found a significant difference in perinatal death between cerclage plus bed rest and bed rest alone.

### Prostaglandin inhibitors (indometacin) *New*

One systematic review found limited evidence that indometacin reduced delivery within 48 hours and 7 days and delivery before 37 weeks' gestation compared with placebo. However, it found no significant difference between indometacin and placebo or no treatment in perinatal mortality, respiratory distress syndrome, bronchopulmonary dysplasia, necrotising enterocolitis, neonatal sepsis, or low birth weight. The review may have lacked power to detect a clinically important effect.

## UNLIKELY TO BE BENEFICIAL

### Elective rather than selective caesarean delivery in preterm labour

One systematic review has found that elective caesarean🅖 delivery increases maternal morbidity compared with selective caesarean🅖 delivery, and found no significant difference in neonatal morbidity or mortality. The RCTs may have been underpowered to detect a clinically important neonatal benefit.

### Enhanced antenatal care programmes for socially deprived population groups/high risk groups

RCTs carried out in a range of countries found no significant difference between enhanced antenatal care🅖 and usual care in reducing the risk of preterm delivery.

### Magnesium sulphate *New*

One systematic review found no significant difference between magnesium sulphate and placebo in delivery before 36 weeks; perinatal mortality or respiratory distress syndrome. A second systematic review found no significant difference between magnesium sulphate and other tocolytics (betamimetics, calcium channel blockers, prostaglandin synthetase inhibitors, nitroglycerine, alcohol and dextrose infusion) in delivery within 48 hours, although results were heterogeneous.

## LIKELY TO BE INEFFECTIVE OR HARMFUL

### Antibiotic treatment for preterm labour with intact membranes

One systematic review found that antibiotics do not prolong pregnancy and do not reduce perinatal mortality compared with placebo, but they do reduce the incidence of maternal infection.

### Betamimetics *New*

One systematic review has found no significant difference between $\beta_2$ agonists and placebo or no treatment in perinatal mortality🅖, respiratory distress syndrome or birth weight less than 2500 g. It found that $\beta_2$ agonists increased maternal adverse effects such as chest pain, palpitations, dyspnoea, tremor, nausea, vomiting, headache, hyperglycaemia, hypokalaemia compared with placebo or no treatment.

### Thyrotropin releasing hormone plus corticosteroids before preterm delivery

One systematic review in women at risk of preterm birth has found no significant difference between thyrotropin releasing hormone plus corticosteroids and ►

◀ corticosteroids alone in improving neonatal outcomes. Thyrotropin releasing hormone plus corticosteroids increased maternal and fetal adverse events compared with corticosteroids alone.

**DEFINITION**   Preterm or premature birth is defined by the World Health Organization as delivery of an infant before 37 completed weeks of gestation.[1] There is no set lower limit to this definition, but 23–24 weeks' gestation is widely accepted,[1] which approximates to an average fetal weight of 500 g.

**INCIDENCE/**   Preterm birth occurs in about 5–10% of all births in developed countries,[2–4]
**PREVALENCE**   but in recent years the incidence seems to have increased in some countries, particularly the USA.[5] We found little reliable evidence for incidence (using the definition of premature birth given above) in less developed countries. The rate in northwestern Ethiopia has been reported to vary between 11–22% depending on the age group of mothers studied, and is highest in teenage mothers.[6]

**AETIOLOGY/**   About 30% of preterm births are unexplained and spontaneous.[4,7,8] The two
**RISK FACTORS**  strongest risk factors for idiopathic preterm labour ✚ are low socioeconomic status and previous preterm delivery. Multiple pregnancy accounts for about another 30% of cases.[4,7] Other known risk factors include genital tract infection, preterm rupture of the membranes✚, antepartum haemorrhage, cervical incompetence, and congenital uterine abnormalities, which collectively account for about 20–25% of cases. The remaining cases (15–20%) are attributed to elective preterm delivery secondary to hypertensive disorders of pregnancy, intrauterine fetal growth restriction, congenital abnormalities, trauma and medical disorders of pregnancy.[4,5,7,8]

**PROGNOSIS**   Preterm labour usually results in preterm birth. One systematic review (search date not stated), which compared tocolysis versus placebo, found that about 27% of preterm labours resolved spontaneously and about 70% progressed to preterm delivery.[9] Observational studies have found that one preterm birth significantly raises the risk of another in a subsequent pregnancy.[10]

---

Please refer to CD-ROM for full text and references.

Respiratory disorders (acute)

# Bronchitis (acute)

**Search date September 2003**

*Peter Wark*

---

## What are the effects of treatment in people without chronic respiratory disease?

### TRADE OFF BETWEEN BENEFITS AND HARMS

#### Antibiotics

One systematic review and one subsequent RCT found that antibiotics modestly reduced cough at 1–2 weeks compared with placebo. However, they found no significant difference in quality of life or impairment in normal activity compared with placebo. We found no systematic review or RCTs comparing amoxicillin versus placebo. RCTs found no significant difference in clinical improvement or cure between amoxicillin (amoxycillin) and roxithromycin or cefuroxime. One RCT found that erythromycin reduced the mean number of days of impaired activities compared with placebo. However, RCTs comparing erythromycin versus placebo found no significant difference in other outcomes. RCTs found no significant difference between azithromycin and clarithromycin, among different cephalosporins, or between cefuroxime and amoxicillin plus clavulanic acid. RCTs found that doxycycline significantly reduced the number of people with cough at follow up or the mean number of days of cough compared with placebo. Antibiotics increased the risk of adverse events such as nausea, vomiting, rash, headache, and vaginitis compared with placebo. Two RCTs found that adverse effects were less common with cefuroxime than with amoxicillin plus clavulanic acid. Widespread antibiotic use may lead to bacterial resistance to antibiotics.

### UNKNOWN EFFECTIVENESS

#### Antihistamines

We found insufficient evidence about the effects of antihistamines compared with placebo in people with acute bronchitis.

#### Antitussives

RCTs found no significant difference in cough severity between codeine or dextromethorphan and placebo in children or adults with acute bronchitis. We found limited evidence from one RCT that moguisteine modestly reduced cough severity compared with placebo in adults, but was associated with more adverse gastrointestinal effects.

#### $\beta_2$ Agonists

One systematic review found no significant difference in cough or ability to return to work between inhaled or oral $\beta_2$ agonists and placebo in people with acute bronchitis. It found limited evidence from one small RCT that $\beta_2$ agonists reduced cough compared with erythromycin. The review found that $\beta_2$ agonists are more frequently associated with shaking and tremor in adults compared with placebo.

#### Expectorants

We found insufficient evidence about the effects of expectorants in people with acute bronchitis.

**DEFINITION**   Acute bronchitis is transient inflammation of the trachea and major bronchi. Clinically, it is diagnosed on the basis of cough and occasionally sputum, dyspnoea, and wheeze. This review is limited to episodes of acute bronchitis in people (smokers and non-smokers) with no pre-existing respiratory disease ▶

such as a pre-existing diagnosis of asthma or chronic bronchitis, and/or evidence of fixed airflow obstruction, and excluding those with clinical or radiographic evidence of pneumonia. However, using a clinical definition for acute bronchitis implies that people with either transient/mild asthma or mild chronic obstructive pulmonary disease may have been recruited to some of the reported studies.

**INCIDENCE/ PREVALENCE**  Acute bronchitis affects 44/1000 adults (> 16 years old) a year, with 82% of episodes occurring in autumn or winter.[1] Acute bronchitis was the fifth most common reason to present to a general practitioner in Australia.[2]

**AETIOLOGY/ RISK FACTORS**  Infection is believed to be the trigger for acute bronchitis. However, pathogens have been identified in fewer than 55% of people.[1] Community studies that attempted to isolate pathogens from the sputum of people with acute bronchitis found viruses in 8–23%, typical bacteria (*Streptococcus pneumoniae*, *Haemophilus influenzae*, *Moraxella catarrhalis*) in 45%, and atypical bacteria (*Mycobacterium pneumoniae*, *Chlamydia pneumoniae*, *Bordetella pertussis*) in 0–25%.[1,3,4] It is unclear whether smoking affects the risk for developing acute bronchitis.

**PROGNOSIS**  Acute bronchitis is regarded as a mild self limiting illness but there are few data on prognosis and rates of complications such as chronic cough or progression to chronic bronchitis or pneumonia. One prospective longitudinal study reviewed 653 previously well adults who presented to suburban general practices over a 12 month period with symptoms of acute lower respiratory tract infection.[1] It found that within the first month of the illness 20% of people re-presented to their general practitioner with persistent or recurrent symptoms. One prospective study of 138 previously well adults found that 34% had symptoms consistent with either chronic bronchitis or asthma 3 years after initial presentation with acute bronchitis.[5] It is also unclear whether acute bronchitis plays a causal role in the progression to chronic bronchitis or is simply a marker of predisposition to chronic lung disease. Although smoking has been identified as the most important risk factor for chronic bronchitis,[6,7] it is unclear whether the inflammatory effects of cigarette smoke and infection causing acute bronchitis have additive effects in leading to chronic inflammatory airway changes.

Please refer to CD-ROM for full text and references.

# Community acquired pneumonia

Search date August 2003

*Mark Loeb*

## *What are the effects of treatments?*

### BENEFICIAL

**Antibiotics (amoxicillin, cephalosporins, macrolides, penicillin, quinolones) in hospital**

RCTs that compared different oral or intravenous antibiotics in people admitted to hospital found clinical cure or improvement in 73–96% of people. Four RCTs found no significant difference in clinical cure or improvement among different antibiotics. Two RCTs found that quinolones may increase clinical cure compared with co-amoxiclav (amoxicillin plus clavulanic acid) or cephalosporins. However, most trials were small and were designed to show equivalence between treatments rather than superiority of one over another.

**Antibiotics (amoxicillin, cephalosporins, macrolides, penicillin, quinolones) in outpatient settings**

One systematic review that evaluated different oral antibiotics in outpatient settings has found clinical cure or improvement in over 90% of people regardless of antibiotic taken. Another systematic review found that azithromycin reduced clinical failures over 6–21 days compared with other macrolides, cephalosporins, or penicillin. A third systematic review and a subsequent RCT found no significant difference in clinical cure or improvement between quinolones and amoxicillin, cephalosporins, or macrolides. Most trials were designed to show equivalence between treatments rather than superiority of one antibiotic over another.

### LIKELY TO BE BENEFICIAL

**Prompt administration of antibiotics in people admitted to intensive care with community acquired pneumonia (compared with delayed antibiotic treatment)**

Two retrospective studies found that prompt administration of antibiotics improved survival. It would probably be unethical to perform an RCT of delayed antibiotic treatment.

### UNKNOWN EFFECTIVENESS

**Bottle blowing**

One unblinded RCT in people receiving antibiotics and usual medical care found that bottle blowing physiotherapy plus early mobilisation plus encouragement to sit up regularly and take deep breaths reduced mean hospital stay compared with early mobilisation alone. It found no significant difference in duration of fever.

**Different antibiotic combinations in intensive care settings**

We found no RCTs that compared one combination of antibiotics with another in intensive care units.

**Guidelines for treating pneumonia (for clinical outcomes)**

One systematic review found no significant difference in clinical outcomes between usual care and a guideline based management strategy that incorporated early switch from intravenous to oral antibiotics and early discharge (or both).

▶

◄ **UNLIKELY TO BE BENEFICIAL**

### Intravenous antibiotics in immunocompetent people in hospital without life threatening illness (compared with oral antibiotics)

Two RCTs in immunocompetent people admitted to hospital who did not have life threatening illness found no significant difference in clinical cure or mortality between intravenous and oral antibiotics (co-amoxiclav or cefuroxime). The RCTs found that intravenous antibiotics may increase the length of hospital stay compared with oral antibiotics.

## What are the effects of preventive interventions?

**BENEFICIAL**

### Pneumococcal vaccine in immunocompetent adults

One systematic review found that pneumococcal vaccination reduced pneumococcal pneumonia in immunocompetent people compared with no vaccination.

**LIKELY TO BE BENEFICIAL**

### Influenza vaccine (in elderly people)

We found no RCTs that assessed the effects of influenza vaccine in preventing community acquired pneumonia. Observational studies suggest that influenza vaccine may reduce the incidence of pneumonia and may reduce mortality in the elderly.

**UNKNOWN EFFECTIVENESS**

### Pneumococcal vaccine in chronically ill, immunosuppressed, or elderly people

One systematic review found no significant difference between pneumococcal vaccination and no vaccination in the incidence of pneumonia in elderly people or people likely to have an impaired immune system.

**DEFINITION**  Community acquired pneumonia is pneumonia contracted in the community rather than in hospital. It is defined by clinical symptoms (such as cough, sputum production, and pleuritic chest pain) and signs (such as fever, tachypnoea, and rales), with radiological confirmation.

**INCIDENCE/ PREVALENCE**  In the northern hemisphere, community acquired pneumonia affects about 12/1000 people a year, particularly during winter and at the extremes of age (incidence: < 1 year old 30–50/1000 a year; 15–45 years 1–5/1000 a year; 60–70 years 10–20/1000 a year; 71–85 years 50/1000 a year).[1–6]

**AETIOLOGY/ RISK FACTORS**  Over 100 microorganisms have been implicated in community acquired pneumonia, but most cases are caused by *Streptococcus pneumoniae*❶.[4–7] Smoking is probably an important risk factor.[8] One large cohort study in Finland (4175 people aged ≥ 60 years) suggested that risk factors for pneumonia in the elderly included alcoholism (RR 9.0, 95% CI 5.1 to 16.2), bronchial asthma (RR 4.2, 95% CI 3.3 to 5.4), immunosuppression (RR 3.1, 95% CI 1.9 to 5.1), lung disease (RR 3.0, 95% CI 2.3 to 3.9), heart disease (RR 1.9, 95% CI 1.7 to 2.3), institutionalisation (RR 1.8, 95% CI 1.4 to 2.4), and increasing age (≥ 70 years v 60–69 years; RR 1.5, 95% CI 1.3 to 1.7).[9]

**PROGNOSIS**  Severity varies from mild to life threatening illness within days of the onset of symptoms. One systematic review of prognosis studies for community acquired pneumonia (search date 1995, 33 148 people) found overall mortality to be 13.7%, ranging from 5.1% for ambulant people to 36.5% for people who required intensive care.[10] The following prognostic factors were significantly ►

# Community acquired pneumonia

associated with mortality: male sex (OR 1.3, 95% CI 1.2 to 1.4); pleuritic chest pain (OR 0.5, 95% CI 0.3 to 0.8, i.e. lower mortality); hypothermia (OR 5.0, 95% CI 2.4 to 10.4); systolic hypotension (OR 4.8, 95% CI 2.8 to 8.3); tachypnoea (OR 2.9, 95% CI 1.7 to 4.9); diabetes mellitus (OR 1.3, 95% CI 1.1 to 1.5); neoplastic disease (OR 2.8, 95% CI 2.4 to 3.1); neurological disease (OR 4.6, 95% CI 2.3 to 8.9); bacteraemia (OR 2.8, 95% CI 2.3 to 3.6); leucopenia (OR 2.5, 95% CI 1.6 to 3.7); and multilobar radiographic pulmonary infiltrates (OR 3.1, 95% CI 1.9 to 5.1).

Please refer to CD-ROM for full text and references.

Respiratory disorders (acute)

Search date August 2003

*Abel Wakai*

## What are the effects of treatments?

We found insufficient evidence to determine whether any intervention is more effective than no intervention for spontaneous pneumothorax.

### UNKNOWN EFFECTIVENESS

**Chest tube drainage**

We found no RCTs comparing chest tube drainage versus observation. RCTs provided insufficient evidence to compare chest tube drainage versus needle aspiration.

**Chest tube drainage plus suction**

One RCT and one controlled clinical trial found no significant difference in rate of resolution of pneumothorax whether chest tube drainage bottles were connected to suction or not. However, both trials were too small to rule out a clinically important difference.

**Needle aspiration**

RCTs provided insufficient evidence to compare needle aspiration versus observation or chest tube drainage.

**One way valves on chest tubes**

One RCT found no significant difference in rates of resolution between one way valves and drainage bottles with underwater seals, but it is likely to have been too small to detect a clinically important difference. It found that people treated with one way valves used less analgesia and spent less time in hospital than people treated with drainage bottles.

**Small versus standard sized chest tubes**

We found no RCTs comparing small versus standard sized chest tubes.

## What are the effects of interventions to prevent recurrence?

### TRADE OFF BETWEEN BENEFITS AND HARMS

**Pleurodesis**

Two RCTs have found that adding chemical pleurodesis🅖 to chest tube drainage reduces the rate of recurrence of spontaneous pneumothorax compared with chest tube drainage alone. One of the RCTs found that chemical pleurodesis injection was intensely painful. The RCTs found no significant difference in length of hospital stay. One RCT found that thoracoscopic surgery with talc instillation reduced the rate of recurrence at 5 years compared with chest tube drainage. Two RCTs provided insufficient evidence to compare video assisted thorascopic surgery versus thoracotomy. We found no RCTs comparing chemical versus surgical pleurodesis.

### UNKNOWN EFFECTIVENESS

**Optimal timing of pleurodesis (after first, second, or subsequent episodes)**

We found no RCTs or high quality cohort studies assessing whether pleurodesis should take place after the first, second, or subsequent episodes of spontaneous pneumothorax.

# Spontaneous pneumothorax

**DEFINITION**     A pneumothorax is air in the pleural space. A spontaneous pneumothorax occurs when there is no provoking factor, such as trauma, surgery, or diagnostic intervention. It implies a leak of air from the lung parenchyma through the visceral pleura into the pleural space. This review does not include people with tension pneumothorax.

**INCIDENCE/**     In a survey in Minnesota, USA, the incidence of spontaneous pneumothorax
**PREVALENCE**     was 7/100 000 for men and 1/100 000 for women.[1] In England and Wales, the overall rate of people consulting with pneumothorax (in both primary and secondary care combined) is 24/100 000 a year for men and 9.8/100 000 a year for women.[2] The overall annual incidence of emergency hospital admissions for pneumothorax in England and Wales is 16.7/100 000 for men and 5.8/100 000 for women.[2] Smoking increases the likelihood of spontaneous pneumothorax by 22 times for men and eight times for women.[3] A dose–response relationship was observed.[3]

**AETIOLOGY/**     Spontaneous pneumothorax can be primary (typically in young fit people and
**RISK FACTORS**  thought to be because of a congenital abnormality of the visceral pleura) or secondary (caused by underlying lung disease, typically occurring in older people with emphysema or pulmonary fibrosis).

**PROGNOSIS**     Death from spontaneous pneumothorax is rare. Morbidity with pain and shortness of breath is common. Published recurrence rates vary. One cohort study in Denmark found that, after a first episode of primary spontaneous pneumothorax, 23% of people suffered a recurrence within 5 years, most within 1 year.[4] Recurrence rates had been thought to increase substantially after the first recurrence, but one retrospective case control study (147 military personnel) found that 28% of men with a first primary spontaneous pneumothorax had a recurrence; 23% of the 28% had a second recurrence; and 14% of that 23% had a third recurrence, giving a total recurrence rate of 35%.[5]

Please refer to CD-ROM for full text and references.

### Search date February 2003

*Chris Del Mar and Paul Glasziou*

## What are the effects of treatments?

### BENEFICIAL

**Analgesia/anti-inflammatory drugs for symptom relief**

One systematic review has found that analgesics or anti-inflammatory drugs reduce sore throat at 1–5 days compared with placebo.

**Antibiotics for preventing (rare) complications of β haemolytic streptococcal pharyngitis**

One systematic review has found that antibiotics prevent non-suppurative complications of β haemolytic streptococcal pharyngitis compared with no antibiotics, but in industrialised countries such complications are rare.

### LIKELY TO BE BENEFICIAL

**Antibiotics for reducing time to recovery in people with proven infection with *Haemophilus influenzae, Moraxella catarrhalis,* or *Streptococcus pneumoniae***

In a minority of people, upper respiratory tract infection is found to be caused by *H influenzae, M catarrhalis*, or *S pneumoniae*. One RCT found that, in these people, antibiotics increased recovery at 5 days compared with placebo. However, we have no methods currently of easily identifying this subgroup at first consultation.

**Antihistamines for runny nose and sneezing**

One systematic review has found that antihistamines reduce runny nose and sneezing after 2 days compared with placebo, but the clinical benefit is small.

**Decongestants for short term relief of congestive symptoms**

One systematic review found that a single dose of decongestant reduced nasal congestion over 3–10 hours compared with placebo.

**Vitamin C**

One systematic review found that vitamin C slightly reduced the duration of cold symptoms compared with placebo, but the benefit was small and may be explained by publication bias.

### TRADE OFF BETWEEN BENEFITS AND HARMS

**Antibiotics for reducing time to recovery in people with acute sore throat**

One systematic review has found that antibiotics slightly improve symptoms at 6–8 days compared with placebo. Adverse effects (nausea, vomiting, headache, rash, vaginitis) were more common with antibiotics.

### UNKNOWN EFFECTIVENESS

**Echinacea for prevention**

One systematic review found that, compared with no treatment, echinacea reduced the proportion of people who had one infection episode, but found insufficient evidence about the effects of echinacea compared with placebo.

**Echinacea for treatment**

Systematic reviews found limited evidence that some preparations of echinacea may improve symptoms compared with placebo, but we found insufficient evidence about the effects of any specific product.

▶

# Upper respiratory tract infection

◄ **Steam inhalation**

One systematic review found insufficient evidence about the effects of steam inhalation.

**Zinc (intranasal gel or lozenges)**

Two RCTs found that zinc intranasal gel reduced the mean duration of cold symptoms compared with placebo, but the difference was significant in only one of the RCTs. Two systematic reviews found limited evidence that zinc gluconate or acetate lozenges may reduce duration of symptoms at 7 days compared with placebo.

## LIKELY TO BE INEFFECTIVE OR HARMFUL

### Antibiotics in people with colds

Systematic reviews found no significant difference between antibiotics and placebo in cure or general improvement at 6–14 days.

### Decongestants for long term relief of congestive symptoms

One systematic review found insufficient evidence to assess the effects of longer use of decongestants. One case control study found weak evidence that phenyl-propanolamine may increase the risk of haemorrhagic stroke.

**DEFINITION**     Upper respiratory tract infection involves inflammation of the respiratory mucosa from the nose to the lower respiratory tree, but not including the alveoli. In addition to malaise, it causes localised symptoms that constitute several overlapping syndromes: sore throat (pharyngitis), rhinorrhoea (common cold), facial fullness and pain (sinusitis — see acute sinusitis, p 129), and cough (bronchitis — see acute bronchitis, p 362).

**INCIDENCE/**     Upper respiratory tract infections, nasal congestion, throat complaints, and
**PREVALENCE**     cough are responsible for 11% of general practice consultations in Australia.[1] Each year, children suffer about five such infections and adults two to three infections.[1–3]

**AETIOLOGY/**     Infective agents include over 200 viruses (with 100 rhinoviruses) and several
**RISK FACTORS** bacteria. Transmission is mostly through hand to hand contact with subsequent passage to the nostrils or eyes rather than, as commonly perceived, through droplets in the air.[4] A systematic review of the risk factors for developing prolonged illness (especially tiredness) after infectious mononucleosis of five cohort studies of 531 adults showed that this occurred in 2–56% of people. The best predictor for tiredness was poor physical functioning immediately after the start of the illness; previous psychological factors were identified as unimportant in four studies and predictive in one.[5]

**PROGNOSIS**     Upper respiratory tract infections are usually self limiting. Although they cause little mortality or serious morbidity, upper respiratory tract infections are responsible for considerable discomfort, lost work, and medical costs. Clinical patterns vary and overlap between infective agents. In addition to nasal symptoms, half of sufferers experience sore throat and 40% experience cough. Symptoms peak within 1–3 days and generally clear by 1 week, although cough often persists.[4]

Please refer to CD-ROM for full text and references.

*Respiratory disorders (chronic)*

---

## What are the effects of treatments for chronic asthma?

### BENEFICIAL

**Adding long acting inhaled $\beta_2$ agonists in people with mild, persistent asthma that is poorly controlled by inhaled corticosteroids**

One systematic review and three additional RCTs have found that adding regular doses of long acting inhaled $\beta_2$ agonists improves lung function and symptoms and reduces rescue medication compared with increasing the dose of inhaled corticosteroids. However, one further RCT found that increasing inhaled corticosteroid dose reduced exacerbations compared with adding long acting inhaled $\beta_2$ agonists. We found insufficient evidence about effects of adding long acting inhaled $\beta_2$ agonists on mortality.

**Adding long acting inhaled $\beta_2$ agonists to inhaled corticosteroids in poorly controlled mild to moderate, persistent asthma (for symptom control)**

RCTs have found that, in people with asthma that is poorly controlled with inhaled corticosteroids, adding regular long acting inhaled $\beta_2$ agonists improves symptoms and lung function compared with adding placebo or a leukotriene antagonist. We found insufficient evidence about effects of adding long acting inhaled $\beta_2$ agonists on mortality.

**Low dose, inhaled corticosteroids in mild, persistent asthma**

Systematic reviews and RCTs have found that, in people with mild, persistent asthma, low doses of inhaled corticosteroids improve symptoms and lung function compared with placebo or regular inhaled $\beta_2$ agonists.

**Short acting inhaled $\beta_2$ agonists as needed for symptom relief (as effective as regular use) in adults with mild to moderate, persistent asthma**

One systematic review and one subsequent RCT found no significant difference between regular and as needed short acting inhaled $\beta_2$ agonists for clinically important outcomes.

### LIKELY TO BE BENEFICIAL

**Adding leukotriene antagonists in people with mild to moderate, persistent asthma (likely to be better than adding no treatment, but no clear evidence of benefit over adding inhaled corticosteroids)**

RCTs in people taking $\beta_2$ agonists alone have found that leukotriene antagonists reduce asthma symptoms and $\beta_2$ agonist use compared with placebo. One systematic review and three out of nine subsequent RCTs have found that adding leukotriene antagonists increases exacerbations, reduces lung function, and are less effective for symptom control compared with inhaled corticosteroids. The other six RCTs found no significant difference between adding leukotriene antagonists and adding corticosteroids. Two RCTs have found that an inhaled corticosteroid plus a long acting $\beta_2$ agonist improved symptoms, lung function, and exacerbations compared with a leukotriene antagonist at 12 weeks.

**Adding theophylline in people with mild to moderate, persistent asthma poorly controlled by inhaled corticosteroids** New

One RCT has found that adding theophylline improves peak expiratory flow rate compared with continuing low dose corticosteroids plus placebo after 6 months in people with mild to moderate, persistent asthma that was poorly controlled with ▶

inhaled corticosteroids alone. One small RCT found no significant difference in lung function or symptoms between theophylline and formoterol (a long acting β agonist) or between theophylline and zafirlukast (a leukotriene antagonist) after 3 months.

## UNKNOWN EFFECTIVENESS

### Adding leukotriene antagonists plus inhaled corticosteroids in people with mild to moderate, persistent asthma

One systematic review in people taking inhaled corticosteroids found no significant difference between leukotriene antagonists and placebo for exacerbation rates at 4–16 weeks. However, one subsequent RCT in people taking a stable dose of budesonide found that adding montelukast increased asthma free days and decreased nocturnal waking compared with placebo at 16 weeks. One RCT in people taking inhaled corticosteroids found no significant difference between adding montelukast and doubling budesonide in peak expiratory flow rate, daytime symptoms, nocturnal wakening, days with asthma exacerbations, and quality of life.

## What are the effects of treatments for acute asthma?

### BENEFICIAL

### Inhaled corticosteroids for acute asthma (better than placebo)

One systematic review has found that inhaled corticosteroids given in the emergency department reduced hospital admission rates in adults compared with placebo. One systematic review and one subsequent RCT found no significant difference in relapse rates following emergency department discharge between oral and inhaled steroids at 7–10 days. One systematic review found no significant difference in relapse rates between inhaled plus oral corticosteroids and oral corticosteroids alone up to 24 days.

### Inhaled plus oral corticosteroids for acute asthma (as effective as oral corticosteroid alone)

One systematic review found no significant difference in relapse rates for inhaled plus oral corticosteroid compared with oral corticosteroids up to 24 days.

### Ipratropium bromide added to $\beta_2$ agonists for acute exacerbations

Two systematic reviews and one subsequent RCT have found that ipratropium bromide plus salbutamol⊙ improves lung function compared with salbutamol alone and is likely to reduce hospital admission in people with severe acute asthma.

### Short courses of systemic corticosteroids for acute exacerbations

Two systematic reviews and one subsequent RCT have found that early treatment with systemic corticosteroids reduce admission and relapse rates compared with placebo in people with acute asthma. One systematic review and one small subsequent RCT found no significant difference between oral and inhaled steroids after emergency department discharge in relapse rates at 7–10 days in adults with acute asthma.

### Spacer devices for delivering inhaled medications from pressurised metered dose inhalers in acute asthma (as good as nebulisers)

One systematic review in people with acute, but not life threatening exacerbations of asthma found no significant difference between $\beta_2$ agonists delivered by spacer

◄ device compared with nebulisers in rates of hospital admission, time spent in the emergency department, peak expiratory flow rate⑥, or forced expiratory volume in 1 second⑥.

## LIKELY TO BE BENEFICIAL

### Education about acute asthma

One systematic review and one subsequent RCT provided evidence that education to facilitate self management of asthma in adults reduced hospital admission, unscheduled visits to the doctor, and days off work compared with usual care. One subsequent RCT provided insufficient evidence about effects of asthma education on quality of life or social functioning at 6 months.

### Magnesium sulphate for people with severe acute asthma

We found limited evidence from one systematic review and two subsequent RCTs that intravenous magnesium improved lung function compared with placebo in people with severe acute asthma. One systematic review and three subsequent RCTs found no significant difference between intravenous magnesium sulphate and placebo for hospital admission rates.

### Mechanical ventilation for people with severe acute asthma*

We found no RCTs comparing mechanical ventilation with or without inhaled $\beta_2$ agonists versus no mechanical ventilation in people with severe acute asthma. Evidence from cohort studies support its use, although observational studies suggest that ventilation is associated with a high level of morbidity.

### Oxygen supplementation for acute asthma*

We found no systematic review or RCTs of oxygen in acute asthma. However, consensus opinion and pathophysiology suggest that its role is vital in acute asthma.

### Specialist care for acute exacerbations (more effective than generalist care)

One systematic review found limited evidence that specialist care improved outcomes in people with acute asthma compared with generalist care.

*Highly likely to be effective. RCTs unlikely to be conducted.

## UNLIKELY TO BE BENEFICIAL

### Continuous nebulised short acting $\beta_2$ agonists for acute asthma (no more effective than intermittent nebulised short acting $\beta_2$ agonists)

One systematic review and one subsequent RCT found no significant difference in admission rate between continuous and intermittent nebulised short acting $\beta_2$ agonists for hospital admission rates in adults. The subsequent RCT also found no significant difference between continuous and intermittent nebulised short acting $\beta_2$ agonists in lung function.

### Helium–oxygen mixture for acute asthma

One systematic review found no significant difference between helium–oxygen mixture and air or oxygen in pulmonary function tests at 60 minutes for adults and children.

### Intravenous short acting $\beta_2$ agonists for acute asthma (no more effective than nebulised short acting $\beta_2$ agonists)

One systematic review found that intravenous delivery of short acting $\beta_2$ agonists was no more effective than nebulised delivery in improving peak expiratory flow rate at 60 minutes.

# Asthma

**DEFINITION** Asthma is characterised by variable airflow obstruction and airway hyperresponsiveness. Symptoms include dyspnoea, cough, chest tightness, and wheezing. The normal diurnal variation🅖 of peak expiratory flow rate is increased in people with asthma🅣. Chronic asthma is defined here as asthma requiring maintenance treatment. Asthma is classified differently in the USA and UK🅣. Where necessary, the text specifies the system of classification used.[1,2] Acute asthma is defined here as an exacerbation of underlying asthma requiring urgent treatment.

**INCIDENCE/ PREVALENCE** Reported prevalence of asthma is increasing worldwide. About 10% of people have suffered an attack of asthma.[3–5] Epidemiological studies have also found marked variations in prevalence in different countries.[6,7]

**AETIOLOGY/ RISK FACTORS** Most people with asthma are atopic. Exposure to certain stimuli initiates inflammation and structural changes in airways causing airway hyperresponsiveness and variable airflow obstruction, which in turn cause most asthma symptoms. There are a large number of such stimuli; the more important include environmental allergens, occupational sensitising agents, and respiratory viral infections.[8,9]

**PROGNOSIS** **Chronic asthma:** In people with mild asthma, prognosis is good and progression to severe disease is rare. However, as a group, people with asthma lose lung function faster than those without asthma, although less quickly than people without asthma who smoke.[10] People with chronic asthma can improve with treatment. However, some people (possibly up to 5%) have severe disease that responds poorly to treatment. These people are most at risk of morbidity and death from asthma. **Acute asthma:** About 10–20% of people presenting to the emergency department with asthma are admitted to hospital. Of these, fewer than 10% receive mechanical ventilation.[11,12] Those who are ventilated are at 19-fold increased risk of ventilation for a subsequent episode.[13] It is unusual for people to die unless they have suffered respiratory arrest before reaching hospital.[14] One prospective study of 939 people discharged from emergency care found that 17% (95% CI 14% to 20%) relapsed by 2 weeks.[15]

Please refer to CD-ROM for full text and references.

### Search date September 2003

*Nick ten Hacken, Huib Kerstjens, and Dirkje Postma*

## What are the effects of treatments in people with bronchiectasis but without cystic fibrosis?

### LIKELY TO BE BENEFICIAL

#### Exercise or physical training *New*

One systematic review found that inspiratory muscle training improved quality of life and exercise endurance compared with no intervention or sham training in people with non-cystic fibrosis bronchiectasis.

### UNKNOWN EFFECTIVENESS

#### Inhaled steroids

One systematic review found insufficient evidence from two small RCTs to compare inhaled steroids versus placebo in people with bronchiectasis not due to a specific congenital disease.

#### Long acting $\beta_2$ agonists

One systematic review identified no RCTs comparing long acting $\beta_2$ agonists versus placebo or other treatments in people with non-cystic fibrosis bronchiectasis.

#### Mucolytics (bromhexine or deoxyribonuclease)

One systematic review found insufficient evidence from three RCTs to compare the effects of bromhexine or recombinant human deoxyribonuclease versus placebo in people with non-cystic fibrosis bronchiectasis.

#### Oral steroids

One systematic review found no RCTs comparing steroids versus placebo, no treatment, or any other pharmacological or non-pharmacological treatment in people with non-cystic fibrosis bronchiectasis.

**DEFINITION**  Bronchiectasis is defined as irreversible widening of medium sized airways (bronchi) in the lung. It is characterised by inflammation, destruction of bronchial walls, and chronic bacterial infection. The condition may be limited to a single lobe or lung segment, or it may affect one or both lungs more diffusely. Clinically, the condition manifests as chronic cough and chronic overproduction of sputum (up to about 500 mL daily), which is often purulent.[1] People with severe bronchiectasis may have life threatening haemoptysis and may develop features of chronic obstructive airways disease, such as wheezing, chronic respiratory failure, pulmonary hypertension, and right sided heart failure.

**INCIDENCE/ PREVALENCE**  We found few reliable data. Incidence has declined over the past 50 years and prevalence is low in higher income countries. Prevalence is much higher in poorer countries and is a major cause of morbidity and mortality.

**AETIOLOGY/ RISK FACTORS**  Bronchiectasis is most commonly a long term complication of previous lower respiratory infections such as measles pneumonitis, pertussis, and tuberculosis. Foreign body inhalation and allergic, autoimmune, and chemical lung damage also predispose to the condition.[2] Underlying congenital disorders such as cystic fibrosis, cilial dysmotility syndromes, $\alpha_1$ antitrypsin deficiency, and congenital immunodeficiencies may also predispose to bronchiectasis and may be of greater aetiological importance than respiratory infection in higher income countries. Cystic fibrosis is the most common congenital cause. ▶

# Bronchiectasis

**PROGNOSIS** Bronchiectasis is a chronic condition with frequent relapses of varying severity. Long term prognosis is variable. Data on morbidity and mortality are sparse.[3] Bronchiectasis frequently coexists with other respiratory disease, making it difficult to distinguish prognosis for bronchiectasis alone.

Please refer to CD-ROM for full text and references.

## What are the effects of maintenance drug treatment in stable chronic obsructive pulmonary disease?

We found no evidence about effects of most interventions on progression of chronic obstructive pulmonary disease (measured by decline in lung function). However, we found good evidence from RCTs that inhaled corticosteroids do not prevent decline in lung function.

### BENEFICIAL

**Inhaled anticholinergics (improve exacerbation rate, symptoms, and forced expiratory volume in 1 second)**

RCTs have found that inhaled anticholinergics improve forced expiratory volume in 1 second, exercise capacity, and symptoms compared with placebo. One large RCT found that adding ipratropium to a smoking cessation programme had no significant impact on decline in forced expiratory volume in 1 second over 5 years. RCTs found that inhaled tiotropium (a long acting anticholinergic drug) reduced exacerbation rates compared with placebo or ipratropium

**Inhaled anticholinergics plus $\beta_2$ agonists (improve forced expiratory volume in 1 second more than either drug alone)**

RCTs have found that combining a $\beta_2$ agonist with an anticholinergic drug for 2–12 weeks modestly but significantly improves forced expiratory volume in 1 second compared with either drug alone. One RCT found that, when combined with an anticholinergic drug, a long acting $\beta_2$ agonist improved forced expiratory volume in 1 second and peak expiratory flow rate significantly more than a short acting $\beta_2$ agonist. We found no RCTs of long term treatment comparing anticholinergics plus $\beta_2$ agonists with placebo

**Inhaled $\beta_2$ agonists (improve symptoms and forced expiratory volume in 1 second)**

RCTs have found that inhaled $\beta_2$ agonists for 1 week to 12 months improve forced expiratory volume in 1 second and improve symptoms compared with placebo. One RCT found that long acting inhaled $\beta_2$ agonists reduced exacerbation rates compared with placebo, although two other RCTs did not find a significant difference in exacerbation rates.

**Inhaled corticosteroids plus long acting $\beta_2$ agonists (improve exacerbation rate, symptoms, quality of life, forced expiratory volume in 1 second)** New

RCTs have found that the combination of an inhaled corticosteroid plus a long acting $\beta_2$ agonist in one inhaler reduced exacerbation rates and improved lung function, symptoms, and health related quality of life compared with placebo. In general, the combination was more effective than inhaled corticosteroid alone or long acting $\beta_2$ agonist alone, although this difference was not significant for all outcomes.

### LIKELY TO BE BENEFICIAL

**Inhaled anticholinergics (improve forced expiratory volume in 1 second compared with $\beta_2$ agonists)**

RCTs have found that 3 months of a short acting inhaled anticholinergic improved forced expiratory volume in 1 second compared with short acting $\beta_2$ agonists. RCTs ▶

# Chronic obstructive pulmonary disease

have found inconsistent evidence about effects of short acting inhaled anticholinergics compared with long acting $\beta_2$ agonists for up to 3 months. Two RCTs found that 6 months of a long acting inhaled anticholinergic significantly improved forced expiratory volume in 1 second compared with a long acting inhaled $\beta_2$ agonist.

## Long term domiciliary oxygen (beneficial in people with severe hypoxaemia)

One RCT in people with severe daytime hypoxaemia found that domiciliary oxygen improved survival compared with no domiciliary oxygen. A second RCT in people with severe hypoxaemia found that continuous oxygen reduced mortality compared with nocturnal oxygen. Three RCTs in people with milder hypoxaemia or with nocturnal hypoxaemia only, found no significant difference in mortality between long term domiciliary oxygen and no oxygen.

## Mucolytics (improve exacerbation rates)*

Two systematic reviews found that mucolytics for 3–24 months may reduce the frequency and duration of exacerbations in people with chronic bronchitis compared with placebo. However, it is not clear whether these effects are generalisable to people with chronic obstructive pulmonary disease.

*Extrapolated from studies of different types of pulmonary disease, including chronic obstructive pulmonary disease.

## TRADE OFF BETWEEN BENEFITS AND HARMS

## Inhaled corticosteroids (improve exacerbation rates, but may have long term harms)

RCTs have found no significant difference between inhaled corticosteroids and placebo in lung function (forced expiratory volume in 1 second) over 10 days to 10 weeks. However, one systematic review and subsequent RCTs lasting at least 6 months suggested that inhaled steroids increased forced expiratory volume in 1 second during the first 3–6 months of use, although one RCT found no effect on subsequent decline in lung function. One systematic review and subsequent RCTs found that long term inhaled steroids reduced the frequency of exacerbations compared with placebo. Long term inhaled steroids may predispose to adverse effects, including skin bruising, and oral candidiasis.

## Theophyllines

One systematic review has found that theophyllines slightly improve forced expiratory volume in 1 second compared with placebo after 3 months. One large RCT found that theophyllines improved forced expiratory volume in 1 second compared with placebo after 12 months' treatment. The usefulness of these drugs is limited by adverse effects and the need for frequent monitoring of blood concentrations.

## UNKNOWN EFFECTIVENESS

## $\alpha_1$ Antitrypsin infusion

One RCT in people with $\alpha_1$ antitrypsin deficiency and moderate emphysema found no significant difference between $\alpha_1$ antitrypsin infusion and placebo in the decline in forced expiratory volume in 1 secondG after 1 year.

## Deoxyribonuclease

We found no RCTs comparing the long term effects of deoxyribonuclease with placebo.

◄ **Prophylactic antibiotics**

One systematic review found limited evidence of a small reduction in exacerbation rates and days with disability with prophylactic antibiotics. These benefits probably do not outweigh the harms of antibiotics, especially the development of antibiotic resistance. All the identified RCTs were conducted more than 30 years ago, and the results are unlikely to apply to current practice.

## UNLIKELY TO BE BENEFICIAL

### Oral corticosteroids (evidence of harm but no evidence of long term benefits)

We found no RCTs on long term benefits. One systematic review has found that oral corticosteroids for 2–4 weeks improve forced expiratory volume in 1 second compared with placebo. Long term systemic corticosteroids are associated with serious adverse effects, including osteoporosis and diabetes.

### Oral versus inhaled corticosteroids (evidence of harm but no evidence of long term benefits)

Three RCTs provided insufficient evidence about effects of oral compared with inhaled corticosteroids over 2 weeks. We found no RCTs of long term treatment with oral compared with inhaled corticosteroids. Long term oral corticosteroids are associated with serious adverse effects, including osteoporosis and diabetes.

---

## What are the effects of smoking cessation interventions in stable chronic obstructive pulmonary disease? *New*

## BENEFICIAL

### Psychosocial plus pharmacological intervention

One large RCT in people with mild chronic obstructive pulmonary disease found that nicotine gum plus a psychosocial smoking cessation and abstinence maintenance programme (with or without ipratropium) slowed the decline of forced expiratory volume in 1 second reduced respiratory symptoms and lower respiratory illnesses, but increased weight gain compared with usual care (without psychosocial intervention). The RCT found no significant difference between treatments in all cause mortality at 5 years.

## UNKNOWN EFFECTIVENESS

### Pharmacological interventions alone pharmacological interventions alone

One systematic review found no RCTs in people with chronic obstructive pulmonary disease.

### Psychosocial interventions alone

We found no systematic reviews or RCTs in people with chronic obstructive pulmonary disease.

**DEFINITION**    Chronic obstructive pulmonary disease is characterised by chronic bronchitis or emphysema. Emphysema is abnormal permanent enlargement of the air spaces distal to the terminal bronchioles, accompanied by destruction of their walls and without obvious fibrosis. Chronic bronchitis is chronic cough or mucus production for at least 3 months in at least 2 successive years when other causes of chronic cough have been excluded.[1]

**INCIDENCE/**    Chronic obstructive pulmonary disease mainly affects middle aged and elderly
**PREVALENCE**    people. In 1998, the World Health Organization estimated that chronic obstructive pulmonary disease was the fifth most common cause of death worldwide, responsible for 4.2% of all mortality (estimated 2 249 000 deaths ►

# Chronic obstructive pulmonary disease

in 1998).[2] Both morbidity and mortality are rising. Estimated prevalence in the USA has risen by 41% since 1982, and age adjusted death rates rose by 71% between 1966 and 1985. All cause age adjusted mortality declined over the same period by 22% and mortality from cardiovascular diseases by 45%.[1] In the UK, physician diagnosed prevalence was 2% in men and 1% in women between 1990 and 1997.[3]

**AETIOLOGY/ RISK FACTORS**
Chronic obstructive pulmonary disease is largely preventable. The main cause is exposure to cigarette smoke. The disease is rare in lifelong non-smokers (estimated incidence 5% in 3 large representative US surveys from 1971–1984), in whom "passive" exposure to environmental tobacco smoke has been proposed as a cause.[4,5] Other proposed causes include airway hyperresponsiveness, air pollution, and allergy.[6–8]

**PROGNOSIS**
Airway obstruction is usually progressive in those who continue to smoke, resulting in early disability and shortened survival. Smoking cessation reverts the rate of decline in lung function to that of non-smokers.[9] Many people will need medication for the rest of their lives, with increased doses and additional drugs during exacerbations.

---

Please refer to CD-ROM for full text and references.

## What are the effects of treatments for non-small cell lung cancer?

### BENEFICIAL

#### Palliative chemotherapy in stage 4 non-small cell lung cancer

Systematic reviews in people with stage 4 non-small cell lung cancer have found that adding chemotherapy regimens containing cisplatin to best supportive care increases survival at 1 year compared with supportive care alone. Limited evidence from RCTs suggests that adding chemotherapy to best supportive care may improve quality of life compared with best supportive care alone.

#### Thoracic irradiation plus chemotherapy in unresectable stage 3 non-small cell lung cancer (compared with thoracic irradiation alone)

Systematic reviews and two RCTs in people with unresectable stage 3 non-small cell lung cancer have found that adding chemotherapy to irradiation improves survival at 2–5 years compared with irradiation alone. One RCT found no significant difference in median survival between radical radiotherapy plus chemotherapy and radiotherapy alone. Observational evidence suggests that, in people aged over 70 years with unresectable stage 3 non-small cell lung cancer, chemotherapy plus radiotherapy may reduce quality adjusted survival compared with radiotherapy alone. We found insufficient evidence about effects on quality of life.

### UNKNOWN EFFECTIVENESS

#### Hyperfractionated radiation treatment in unresectable stage 3 non-small cell lung cancer

One systematic review found no clear evidence that altered fractionation regimens, accelerated, hyperfractionated, or hyperfractionated split course🅖 regimens are any more effective than conventional radiotherapy. One RCT identified by the review has found that continuous, hyperfractionated, accelerated radiotherapy🅖 reduces mortality at 2 years compared with conventional radiotherapy in people with stage 3A, 3B, 1, or 2 non-small cell lung cancer.

#### Palliative single drug chemotherapy regimens in stage 4 non-small cell lung cancer (not clearly better that combination chemotherapy)

One systematic review and subsequent RCTs in people with stage 3 and 4 non-small cell lung cancer found inconclusive evidence on the effects of single agent chemotherapy compared with combined chemotherapy. One systematic review and subsequent RCTs provided insufficient evidence to compare first line platinum based versus non-platinum based chemotherapy.

#### Preoperative chemotherapy in people with resectable stage 3 non-small cell lung cancer

One systematic review of small, weak RCTs and one subsequent RCT provided inconclusive evidence about the effects of preoperative chemotherapy in people with resectable stage 3 non-small cell lung cancer.

### UNLIKELY TO BE BENEFICIAL

#### Postoperative chemotherapy in people with resected stage 1–3 non-small cell lung cancer

Systematic reviews and subsequent RCTs in people with completely resected stage 1–3 non-small cell lung cancer found no significant difference in survival at 5 years ▶

# Lung cancer

between postoperative cisplatin based chemotherapy and surgery with or without concomitant radiotherapy, although subgroup analysis in one RCT suggests that postoperative chemotherapy may increase survival in people with stage 3 disease. One systematic review has found that postoperative alkylating agents increase mortality compared with no postoperative chemotherapy.

## *What are the effects of treatments for small cell lung cancer?*

**BENEFICIAL**

### Chemotherapy plus thoracic irradiation in limited stage small cell lung cancer (improves survival compared with chemotherapy alone)

Two systematic reviews in people with limited stage small cell lung cancer have found that adding thoracic irradiation to chemotherapy improves survival at 3 years and local control. However, one of these reviews has found that chemotherapy plus thoracic irradiation increases deaths related to treatment.

**LIKELY TO BE BENEFICIAL**

### Prophylactic cranial irradiation for people in complete remission from limited or extensive stage small cell lung cancer

One systematic review in people with small cell lung cancer in complete remission has found that prophylactic cranial irradiation improves survival at 3 years and reduces the risk of developing brain metastases compared with no irradiation. While long term cognitive dysfunction after cranial irradiation has been described in non-randomised studies, RCTs have not found a cumulative increase in neuropsychological dysfunction.

**UNKNOWN EFFECTIVENESS**

### Dose intensification of chemotherapy (insufficient evidence compared with chemotherapy alone)

One systematic review found limited evidence that intensifying chemotherapy dose by either increasing the number of chemotherapy cycles, increasing chemotherapy dose, or increasing dose intensity per cycle may modestly improve survival compared with standard chemotherapy. However, additional RCTs have found inconclusive evidence about the effects of dose intensification on survival.

**LIKELY TO BE INEFFECTIVE OR HARMFUL**

### Oral etoposide in extensive stage small cell lung cancer (likely to reduce survival compared with combination chemotherapy)

Two RCTs in people with extensive stage small cell lung cancer found that oral etoposide reduced survival compared with combination chemotherapy at 1 year. One RCT, in people with extensive stage small cell lung cancer who had not responded to induction combination chemotherapy, found no significant difference between oral etoposide and no further treatment in mortality at 3 years, although overall mortality was lower in people taking etoposide. RCTs found that etoposide may reduce nausea, alopecia, and numbness in the short term compared with combination chemotherapy. They found no evidence that it offered better quality of life overall.

**DEFINITION**    Lung cancer (bronchogenic carcinoma) is an epithelial cancer arising from the bronchial surface epithelium or bronchial mucous glands. It is broadly divided into small cell and non-small cell lung cancer. For a description of the stages of lung cancer see table 1. ❶

**INCIDENCE/ PREVALENCE**

Lung cancer is the leading cause of cancer death in both men and women annually, affecting about 100 000 men and 80 000 women in the USA, and about 40 000 men and women in the UK. Small cell lung cancer constitutes about 20–25% of all lung cancers, the remainder being non-small cell lung cancers of which adenocarcinoma is now the most prevalent form.[1]

**AETIOLOGY/ RISK FACTORS**

Smoking remains the major preventable risk factor, accounting for about 80–90% of all cases.[2] Other respiratory tract carcinogens have been identified that may enhance the carcinogenic effects of tobacco smoke, either in the workplace (e.g. asbestos and polycyclic aromatic hydrocarbons) or in the home (e.g. indoor radon).[3]

**PROGNOSIS**

Lung cancer has an overall 5 year survival rate of 10–12%.[4] At the time of diagnosis, 10–15% of people with lung cancer have localised disease. Of these, half will have died at 5 years despite potentially curative surgery. Over half of people have metastatic disease at the time of diagnosis. People with non-small cell cancer who have surgery have a 5 year survival of 60–80% for stage 1 disease and 25–50% for stage 2 disease.[4] In people with small cell cancer, those with limited stage disease who have combined chemotherapy and mediastinal irradiation have a median survival of 18–24 months, whereas those with extensive stage disease who are given palliative chemotherapy have a median survival of 10–12 months.[4] About 5–10% of people with small cell lung cancer present with central nervous system involvement, and half develop symptomatic brain metastases by 2 years. Of these, only half respond to palliative radiation, and their median survival is less than 3 months.[4]

---

Please refer to CD-ROM for full text and references.

Sexual health

Search date July 2003

*M Riduan Joesoef and George Schmid*

## What are the effects of different antibacterial regimens in symptomatic non-pregnant women?

Bacterial vaginosis may resolve spontaneously.

### BENEFICIAL

**Antibacterial treatment in symptomatic non-pregnant women**

One systematic review found that antibacterial treatment (intravaginal clindamycin or metronidazole) increased cure rate compared with placebo. One systematic review found no significant difference between oral and intravaginal antibacterial drugs in cure rates after 5–10 days or at 4 weeks. Another systematic review has found that a 7 day course of twice daily oral metronidazole increases cure rates at 3–4 weeks compared with a single 2 g dose. Limited evidence from RCTs found no significant difference in cure rates with oral clindamycin versus oral metronidazole twice daily for 7 days, and no significant difference between once and twice daily dosing with intravaginal metronidazole gel. One RCT found no significant difference in cure rates at 35 days between intravaginal clindamycin ovules for 3 days and intravaginal clindamycin cream for 7 days. We found no evidence on long term outcomes. One small RCT found that more that 50% of women had recurrent bacterial vaginosis 2 months after antibacterial treatment.

## What are the effects of treating pregnant women?

### LIKELY TO BE BENEFICIAL

**Antibacterial treatment (except intravaginal clindamycin) in pregnant women who have had a previous preterm birth**

One systematic review found that antibiotics reduced the risk of low birth weight in women with bacterial vaginosis who had a previous preterm delivery, although results for preterm delivery were heterogeneous. Subgroup analysis of one subsequent RCT found that oral clindamycin given early in the second trimester reduced miscarriages or preterm deliveries compared with placebo.

### UNKNOWN EFFECTIVENESS

**Antibacterial treatment (except intravaginal clindamycin) in low risk pregnancy**

One systematic review in general populations of pregnant women found no significant difference between antibiotics (oral or vaginal) and placebo in the risk of preterm delivery, low birth weight, neonatal sepsis, or perinatal death. However, one subsequent RCT found that oral clindamycin given early in the second trimester reduced miscarriages or preterm deliveries compared with placebo.

### LIKELY TO BE INEFFECTIVE OR HARMFUL

**Intravaginal clindamycin cream**

Three RCTs found that treating pregnant women with intravaginal clindamycin cream was associated with an increased risk of preterm delivery and low birth weight compared with placebo, but the increase was not significant.

◄ ## *What are the effects of treating male sexual partners?*

### Treating a woman's male sexual partner with metronidazole or clindamycin

One systematic review has found that, in women receiving antibacterial agents, and who have one steady male sexual partner, treating the partner with oral metronidazole or clindamycin does not reduce the woman's risk of recurrence.

## *What are the effects of treatment before gynaecological procedures?*

### Oral or intravaginal antibacterial treatment before surgical abortion

Three RCTs consistently found that oral or intravaginal antibacterial treatment in women with bacterial vaginosis about to have surgical abortion was associated with a lower risk of pelvic inflammatory disease compared with placebo, but the difference was only significant in the largest RCT.

### Antibacterial treatment before gynaecological procedures (other than abortion)

We found no RCTs on the effects of antibacterial treatment in women with bacterial vaginosis about to have gynaecological procedures other than abortion.

**DEFINITION**  Bacterial vaginosis is a microbial disease characterised by an alteration in the bacterial flora of the vagina from a predominance of *Lactobacillus* species to high concentrations of anaerobic bacteria. The condition is asymptomatic in 50% of infected women. Women with symptoms have an excessive white to grey, or malodorous vaginal discharge, or both; the odour may be particularly noticeable during sexual intercourse. Diagnosis requires three out of four features: the presence of clue cells; a homogenous discharge adherent to the vaginal walls; pH of vaginal fluid greater than 4.5; and a "fishy" amine odour of the vaginal discharge before or after addition of 10% potassium hydroxide.

**INCIDENCE/ PREVALENCE**  Bacterial vaginosis is the most common infectious cause of vaginitis, being about twice as common as candidiasis.[1] Prevalences of 10–61% have been reported among unselected women from a range of settings.[2] Data on incidence are limited but one study found that, over a 2 year period, 50% of women using an intrauterine contraceptive device had at least one episode, as did 20% of women using oral contraceptives.[3] Bacterial vaginosis is particularly prevalent among lesbians.[4]

**AETIOLOGY/ RISK FACTORS**  The cause of bacterial vaginosis is not fully understood. Risk factors include new or multiple sexual partners[1,3,5] and early age of sexual intercourse,[6] but no causative microorganism has been shown to be transmitted between partners. Use of an intrauterine contraceptive device[3] and douching[5] have also been reported as risk factors. Infection seems to be most common around the time of menstruation.[7]

**PROGNOSIS**  The course of bacterial vaginosis varies and is poorly understood. Without treatment, symptoms may persist or resolve in both pregnant and non-pregnant women. Recurrence after treatment occurs in about a third of women. The condition is associated with complications of pregnancy: low birth weight; preterm birth (pooled OR from 10 cohort studies: 1.8, 95% CI 1.5 to 2.6);[8] preterm labour; premature rupture of membranes; late miscarriage; chorioamnionitis (48% *v* 22%; OR 2.6, 95% CI 1.0 to 6.6);[9] endometritis after normal ►

# Bacterial vaginosis

delivery (8.2% v 1.5%; OR 5.6, 95% CI 1.8 to 17.2);[10] endometritis after caesarean section (55% v 17%; OR 5.8, 95% CI 3.0 to 10.9);[11] and surgery to the genital tract. Women who have had a previous preterm delivery are especially at risk of complications in pregnancy, with a sevenfold increased risk of preterm birth (24/428 [5.6%] in all women v 10/24 [41.7%] in women with a previous preterm birth).[12] Bacterial vaginosis can also enhance HIV acquisition and transmission.[13]

Please refer to CD-ROM for full text and references.

Sexual health

## What are the effects of antibiotic treatment for men and non-pregnant women with uncomplicated genital chlamydial infection?

Short term microbiological cure is the outcome used in most RCTs, but this may not mean eradication of *Chlamydia trachomatis*. Long term cure rates have not been studied extensively because of high default rates and difficulty in distinguishing persistent infection from reinfection due to re-exposure.

### BENEFICIAL

#### Azithromycin (single dose)

A systematic review of 12 blinded and unblinded RCTs found no significant difference in microbiological cure of *C trachomatis* between a single dose of azithromycin and a 7 day course of doxycycline. Rates of adverse effects were similar.

#### Doxycycline, teracycline (multiple dose regimens)

Small RCTs with short term follow up and high withdrawal rates found that multiple dose regimens of tetracyclines (doxycycline, tetracycline) achieve microbiological cure in at least 95% of people with genital chlamydia. A systematic review of 12 blinded and unblinded RCTs found no significant difference in microbiological cure of *C trachomatis* between a 7 day course of doxycycline and a single dose of azithromycin. Rates of adverse effects were similar. Meta-analysis of two RCTs found that doxycycline significantly reduced microbiological failure compared with ciprofloxacin.

### LIKELY TO BE BENEFICIAL

#### Erythromycin (multiple dose regimens)

Three small RCTs found that erythromycin achieved microbiological cure in 77–100% of people, with the highest cure rate with a 2 g compared with a 1 g daily dose.

### UNKNOWN EFFECTIVENESS

#### Amoxicillin, ampicillin, clarithromycin, lymecycline, minocycline, ofloxacin, pivampicillin, rifampicin, rosarimicin, roxithromycin, sparfloxacin, trovafloxacin (multiple dose regimens)

We found limited evidence on the effects of these regimens.

### UNLIKELY TO BE BENEFICIAL

#### Ciprofloxacin (multiple dose regimens)

Two RCTs found that ciprofloxacin cured 63–92% of people. Meta-analysis found that ciprofloxacin significantly increased microbiological failure compared with doxycycline.

▶

# Chlamydia (uncomplicated, genital)

## What are the effects of antibiotic treatment for pregnant women with uncomplicated genital chlamydial infection?

**LIKELY TO BE BENEFICIAL**

### Azithromycin (single dose)

One systematic review found that a single dose of azithromycin significantly increased microbiological cure and decreased the risk of an adverse effect, sufficient to stop treatment, when compared with a 7 day course of erythromycin. Two subsequent unblinded RCTs found no significant difference in cure rate between single dose azithromycin and multiple dose amoxicillin.

### Erythromycin, amoxicillin (multiple dose regimens)

One small RCT identified in a systematic review found that erythromycin versus placebo significantly increased microbiological cure. Other RCTs in the review found high cure rates with erythromycin and amoxicillin and no significant difference in microbiological cure between the two drugs.

**UNKNOWN EFFECTIVENESS**

### Clindamycin (multiple dose regimens)

One small RCT found no significant difference in cure rates between clindamycin and erythromycin.

**DEFINITION**     Genital chlamydia is a sexually transmitted infection of the urethra in men, and of the endocervix, urethra (or both) in women. It is defined as **uncomplicated** if it has not ascended to the upper genital tract. Infection is asymptomatic in up to 80% of cases, but may cause non-specific symptoms, including vaginal discharge and intermenstrual bleeding. Infection in men causes urethral discharge and urethral irritation or dysuria, but may also be asymptomatic in up to half of cases.[1] **Complicated** chlamydial infection includes spread to the upper genital tract (causing pelvic inflammatory disease [see pelvic inflammatory disease, p 401] in women and epididymoorchitis in men) and extra genital sites, such as the eye. Interventions for complicated chlamydial infection are not included in this chapter.

**INCIDENCE/**     Genital chlamydia is the most commonly reported bacterial sexually transmit-
**PREVALENCE**  ted infection in developed countries [1] and reported rates increased by 10% in the UK and USA between 2000 and 2001.[2,3] In women, infection occurs most commonly between the ages of 16 and 19 years. In this age group, about 1000/100 000 new infections are reported each year in the UK,[2] compared with 1900/100 000 in Sweden,[4] and 2536 per 100 000 in the USA.[3] The peak age group for men is 20–24 years, with about 650/100 000 new infections per year in the UK and USA and 1200/100 000 in Sweden.[2–4] Rates decline markedly with increasing age. Reported rates are highly dependent on the level of testing. The population prevalence of uncomplicated genital chlamydia in 18–44 year olds in the UK in 1999 was 2.2% (95% CI 1.5% to 3.2%) in men and 1.5% (95% CI 1.1% to 2.1%) in women.[5]

**AETIOLOGY/**     Infection is caused by the bacterium *C trachomatis* serotypes D–K. It is
**RISK FACTORS** transmitted primarily through sexual intercourse, but also perinatally and through direct or indirect oculogenital contact.[1]

**PROGNOSIS**     In women, untreated chlamydial infection that ascends to the upper genital tract causes pelvic inflammatory disease [see pelvic inflammatory disease, p 401] in an estimated 30–40% of cases.[6] Tubal infertility has been found to occur in about 11% of women after a single episode of pelvic inflammatory disease, and the risk of ectopic pregnancy is increased six- to sevenfold.[7] Ascending infection in men causes epididymitis, but evidence that this causes ▶

male infertility is limited.[8] Maternal to infant transmission can lead to neonatal conjunctivitis and pneumonitis in 30–40% of cases.[1] Chlamydia may coexist with other genital infections and may facilitate transmission and acquisition of HIV infection.[1] Untreated chlamydial infection persists symptomatically in most women for at least 60 days and for a shorter period in men.[9] Spontaneous remission also occurs at an estimated rate of 5% per month.[10]

Please refer to CD-ROM for full text and references.

Sexual health

# Genital herpes

**Search date July 2003**

*Eva Jungmann*

---

## *What are the effects of interventions to prevent transmission?*

### LIKELY TO BE BENEFICIAL

**Male condom use to prevent sexual transmission from infected men to non-infected sexual partners\***

Limited evidence from a prospective cohort study suggests that condom use by men infected with genital herpes may reduce transmission of herpes simplex virus type 2 (HSV-2) to their non-infected sexual partners.

\*Categorisation based on observational evidence.

### UNKNOWN EFFECTIVENESS

**Antiviral treatment to prevent transmission**

We found no systematic review or RCTs on the effects of antiviral treatments to prevent sexual transmission.

**Caesarean delivery in women with genital lesions at term**

We found no systematic review or RCTs on the effects of caesarean delivery on mother to baby transmission of genital herpes in patients with genital lesions at term. The procedure carries the risk of increased maternal morbidity and mortality.

**Daily oral antiviral treatment in late pregnancy (36 or more weeks of gestation) in women with a history of genital herpes**

One systematic review and two subsequent RCTs found that aciclovir reduced the rate of genital lesions at term in women with first or recurrent episodes of genital herpes simplex virus during pregnancy. The review and the RCTs provided insufficient evidence to assess the effect of oral antiviral treatment during pregnancy on neonatal infection.

**Female condoms**

We found no systematic review or RCTs on the effects of female condoms to prevent sexual transmission.

**HSV-2 glycoprotein-D-adjuvant vaccine in HSV-1- and HSV-2-seronegative women**

Limited evidence from one RCT comparing recombinant HSV-2 glycoprotein-D-adjuvant vaccine versus placebo showed protection of the vaccine against new genital herpes infection in women who had been seronegative for HSV-1 and HSV-2 at baseline.

**HSV-2 glycoprotein-D-adjuvant vaccine in men and HSV-1-seropositive women**

Limited evidence from one RCT comparing recombinant HSV-2 glycoprotein-D-adjuvant vaccine versus placebo showed no protection of the vaccine against new genital herpes infection in women who had been seropositive for HSV-1 at baseline or in men.

**Male condom use to prevent transmission from infected women to non-infected men**

Limited evidence from a prospective cohort study suggests that male condom use may provide no protection from transmission of HSV-2 to non-infected men from their infected female partners.

◄ **Other forms of vaccination**

We found no good evidence on other forms of vaccination.

**Serological screening and counselling in late pregnancy**

We found no systematic review or RCTs on the effects of interventions to prevent maternal infection in late pregnancy (such as serological screening and counselling).

**UNLIKELY TO BE BENEFICIAL**

**Recombinant glycoprotein vaccines (gB2 and gD2)**

One RCT found no significant difference between recombinant glycoprotein vaccine (gB2 plus gD2) and placebo in the prevention of HSV-2 infection.

## What are the effects of treatments in people with a first episode of genital herpes?

**BENEFICIAL**

**Oral antiviral treatment versus placebo in first episodes**

RCTs found that oral antiviral treatment versus placebo decreases the duration of lesions, symptoms, and viral shedding, and reduces neurological complications in people with first episode genital herpes. Two small RCTs provided insufficient evidence to assess time to recurrence and frequency of recurrence compared with placebo.

**UNKNOWN EFFECTIVENESS**

**Different routes of antiviral administration in first episodes\*** *New*

We found no systematic reviews or RCTs comparing different routes of administration in antiviral treatment. A non-randomised comparison of results of different trials from one institution suggests that systemic (oral or iv) antiviral treatment may be more effective and associated with fewer reported side effects than topical medication.

**Different types of oral treatment in first episodes\*** *New*

RCTs found no difference in clinical outcomes among oral aciclovir, valaciclovir, and famciclovir in people with a first episode of genital herpes.

## What interventions reduce the impact of recurrence?

**BENEFICIAL**

**Daily oral antiviral treatment in people with high rates of recurrence**

RCTs have found that daily maintenance treatment with oral antiviral agents reduces the frequency of recurrences and improves psychosocial morbidity in people with frequent recurrence compared with placebo.

**Oral antiviral treatment taken at the start of recurrence**

One systematic review and one subsequent RCT found that oral antiviral treatment taken at the start of recurrence reduced the duration of lesions, episode duration, and viral shedding and increased the rate of aborted recurrences compared with placebo in people with recurrent genital herpes. RCTs found no difference among different antiviral agents. All antiviral agents were found to be similarly effective in reducing the duration of symptoms and viral shedding compared with placebo. One RCT found no difference between valaciclovir taken for 3 days versus 5 days. ▶

# Genital herpes

## Psychotherapy to reduce recurrence

One systematic review found insufficient evidence on the effects of psychotherapy on genital herpes recurrence.

---

## What are the eeffects of treatments in people with genital herpes and HIV infection?

## Oral antiviral treatment in people immunocompromised with HIV infection*

We found no systematic review or RCTs evaluating antiviral treatment for genital herpes in people immunocompromised with HIV infection. However, evidence from other settings suggests that antiviral agents may be effective treatments of genital herpes in immunocompromised people.

*Categorisation based on observational or non-randomised evidence in the context of practical and ethical problems of performing RCTs.

| | |
|---|---|
| **DEFINITION** | Genital herpes is an infection with herpes simplex virus type 1 (HSV-1) or type 2 (HSV-2) causing ulceration in the genital area. Herpes simplex virus infections can be confirmed on the basis of virological and serological findings. Types of infection include **first episode primary infection**, which is defined as herpes simplex virus confirmed in a person without prior findings of HSV-1 or HSV-2 antibodies; **first episode non-primary infection**, which is HSV-2 confirmed in a person with prior findings of HSV-1 antibodies or vice versa; **first recognised recurrence**, which is HSV-1 (or HSV-2) confirmed in a person with prior findings of HSV-1 (or HSV-2) antibodies; and **recurrent genital herpes**, which is caused by reactivation of latent herpes simplex virus. HSV-1 can also cause gingivostomatitis and orolabial ulcers; HSV-2 also cause other types of herpes infections, such as ocular herpes; and both virus types can cause infection of the central nervous system (e.g. encephalitis). |
| **INCIDENCE/ PREVALENCE** | Genital herpes infections are among the most common sexually transmitted diseases. Seroprevalence studies showed that 22% of adults in the USA had HSV-2 antibodies.[1] A UK study found that 23% of adults attending sexual medicine clinics and 7.6% of blood donors in London had antibodies to HSV-2.[2] Seroprevalence of HSV-2 increased by 30% (95% CI 15.8% to 45.8%) between the periods 1976–1980 and 1988–1994.[1] However, it should be noted that although antibody levels prove the existence of present or past infections, they do not differentiate between possible manifestations of HSV-2 infections (e.g. genital/ocular). Thus, the figures have to be treated with caution when applied to genital herpes only. |
| **AETIOLOGY/ RISK FACTORS** | Both HSV-1 and HSV-2 can cause a first episode of genital infection, but HSV-2 is more likely to cause recurrent disease.[3] Most people with HSV-2 infection have only mild symptoms and remain unaware that they have genital herpes. However, these people can still pass on the infection to sexual partners and newborns.[4,5] |
| **PROGNOSIS** | Sequelae of herpes simplex virus infection include neonatal herpes simplex virus infection, opportunistic infection in immunocompromised people, recurrent genital ulceration, and psychosocial morbidity. HSV-2 infection is associated with an increased risk of HIV transmission and acquisition.[6] The most common neurological complications are aseptic meningitis (reported in about 25% of women during primary infection) and urinary retention (reported in up to 15% of women during primary infection).[5] The absolute risk of neonatal |

infection is high (41%, 95% CI 26% to 56%) in babies born to women who acquire infection near the time of labour and low (< 3%) in women with established infection, even in those who have a recurrence at term.[7,8] About 15% of neonatal infections result from postnatal transmission from oral lesions of relatives or hospital personnel.[5]

Please refer to CD-ROM for full text and references.

# Genital warts

**Search date May 2003**

*Henry W Buck Jr*

---

## What are the effects of treatments?

### Cryotherapy (as effective in clearing warts as trichloroacetic acid, electrosurgery, or podophyllin)

We found no RCTs comparing cryotherapy versus placebo or no treatment. Two RCTs found no significant difference between cryotherapy and trichloroacetic acid in clearance of warts after 6–10 weeks' treatment. One of the RCTs found no significant difference in recurrence of warts at 2 months after the end of treatment. One RCT found limited evidence that cryotherapy was less effective for clearance than electrosurgery after 6 weeks' treatment. However, follow up of the people with successful wart clearance found no significant difference in the proportion of people who had warts at 3–5 months. Another RCT found no significant difference in wart clearance at 3 months between cryotherapy and electrosurgery. One RCT found that cryotherapy increased clearance after 6 weeks' treatment compared with podophyllin, and follow up of the people with successful wart clearance found that fewer people receiving cryotherapy had warts at 3–5 months.

### Electrosurgery (as effective as cryotherapy or podophyllin, more effective than intramuscular or subcutaneous interferon in clearing warts)

We found no RCTs comparing electrosurgery versus no treatment. One RCT found that electrosurgery improved clearance after 6 weeks' treatment compared with cryotherapy. However, follow up of the people with successful wart clearance found no significant difference in the proportion of people who had warts at 3–5 months after treatment. It also found that electrosurgery improved clearance after 6 weeks' treatment compared with podophyllin, and follow up of the people with successful wart clearance found that the difference was maintained at 3–5 months after treatment. Another RCT found no significant difference in wart clearance at 3 months between electrosurgery and cryotherapy. One RCT found limited evidence that electrosurgery was more effective than intramuscular or subcutaneous interferon in clearing warts at 3 months.

### Imiquimod in people without HIV

One systematic review and one subsequent RCT have found that imiquimod cream increases wart clearance and reduces recurrence compared with placebo in people without HIV. One RCT in women without HIV found that twice daily doses of imiquimod 5% did not increase wart clearance over 20 weeks compared with once daily or three times weekly doses but found that it increased skin erythema.

### Interferon, topical

Three RCTs have found that topical interferon increases wart clearance at 4 weeks after treatment compared with placebo. One of the RCTs also found that topical interferon increased wart clearance at 4 weeks after treatment compared with podophyllotoxin.

### Laser surgery (as effective as surgical excision in clearing warts)

We found no RCTs comparing laser surgery versus no treatment. One RCT found no significant difference in wart clearance or recurrence rates over 36 weeks between laser and surgical excision.

▶

◀ **Podophyllin (as effective as podophyllotoxin or surgical excision in clearing warts but less effective than cryotherapy and electrosurgery, less effective than surgical excision in preventing recurrence)**

We found no RCTs comparing podophyllin versus placebo. RCTs have found that podophyllin resin is as effective in clearing warts as podophyllotoxin and surgical excision. One RCT found that podophyllin was less effective than cryotherapy or electrosurgery in clearing warts at 6 weeks, and follow up of the people with successful wart clearance found that more people receiving podophyllin had warts at 3–5 months. One RCT found that podophyllin was more effective than systemic interferon in clearing warts at 3 months. Another RCT found that podophyllin was less effective than surgical excision in preventing recurrence at 6–12 months. One RCT found no significant difference in wart clearance at 3 months between podophyllin plus trichloroacetic acid and podophyllin alone.

### Podophyllotoxin

RCTs have found that podophyllotoxin increases wart clearance within 16 weeks compared with placebo. They found no significant difference in wart clearance between podophyllotoxin and podophyllin. One RCT found that podophyllotoxin was less effective than topical interferon in clearing warts at 4 weeks.

### Surgical excision (as effective as laser surgery or podophyllin in clearing warts, more effective than podophyllin in preventing recurrence)

We found no RCTs comparing surgical excision versus no treatment. RCTs found no significant difference between surgical (scissor) excision and laser surgery or podophyllin in wart clearance. However, they have found that surgical excision is more effective than podophyllin in preventing recurrence.

### LIKELY TO BE BENEFICIAL

### Bi- and trichloroacetic acid (as effective as cryotherapy in clearing warts)

We found no RCTs comparing bi- and trichloroacetic acid versus placebo. Two RCTs found no significant difference between trichloroacetic acid and cryotherapy in clearance of warts after 6–10 weeks' treatment, and one of the RCTs found no significant difference in recurrence of warts at 2 months after the end of treatment. One RCT found no significant difference in wart clearance at 3 months between trichloroacetic acid plus podophyllin and podophyllin alone.

### UNKNOWN EFFECTIVENESS

### Condoms to prevent transmission of human papillomavirus or external genital warts

Observational studies provided insufficient evidence to assess the effects of condom use on transmission of human papillomavirus. Penetrative intercourse is not required for spread as this can occur with external genital–genital or hand–genital touching. One case control and one cross-sectional study suggested that people who always used condoms were less likely to have genital warts than people who never or occasionally used them.

### Imiquimod in people with HIV

One RCT in people with HIV identified by a systematic review found no significant difference in wart clearance over 16 weeks between imiquimod cream and placebo.

# Genital warts

**UNLIKELY TO BE BENEFICIAL**

## Interferon, systemic

RCTs found that systemic interferon improved wart clearance at 2–3 months compared with placebo but was associated with flu-like symptoms, including blood disorders, headache, chills, fever, nausea, and vomiting. One RCT found that systemic interferon was less effective than podophyllin in clearing warts at 3 months.

| | |
|---|---|
| **DEFINITION** | External genital warts are benign epidermal growths on the external perigenital and perianal regions. There are four morphological types: condylomatous, keratotic, papular, and flat warts. |
| **INCIDENCE/ PREVALENCE** | In 1996, external and internal genital warts accounted for over 180 000 initial visits to private physicians' offices in the USA: about 60 000 fewer than were reported for 1995.[1] In the USA, 1% of sexually active men and women aged 18–49 years are estimated to have external genital warts.[2] It is believed that external and cervical lesions caused by the human papillomavirus (HPV) are the most prevalent sexually transmitted disease among persons 18–25 years of age. In the USA, 50–60% of women aged 18–25 years test positive for HPV DNA, but no more than 10–15% ever have genital warts.[3] |
| **AETIOLOGY/ RISK FACTORS** | External genital warts are caused by HPV and are sexually transmitted. They are more common in people with impaired immune function.[3] Although more than 100 types of HPV have been identified, most external genital warts in immunocompetent people are caused by HPV types 6 and 11.[4,5] |
| **PROGNOSIS** | The ability to clear and remain free of external genital warts is a function of cellular immunity.[6] In immunocompetent people, the prognosis in terms of clearance and avoiding recurrence is good,[7] but people with impaired cellular immunity (e.g. people with HIV and AIDS) have great difficulty achieving and maintaining wart clearance.[3] Without treatment, external genital warts may remain unchanged, may increase in size or number, or may resolve completely. Clinical trials have found that recurrences may occur and may necessitate repeated treatment. External genital warts rarely, if ever, progress to cancer.[8] Juvenile laryngeal papillomatosis, a rare and sometimes life threatening condition, occurs in children of women with a history of genital warts. Its rarity makes it hard to design studies that can evaluate whether treatment in pregnant women alters the risk.[9,10] |

Please refer to CD-ROM for full text and references.

## What are the effects of treatments?

### BENEFICIAL

**Single dose antibiotic regimens using selected cephalosporins or spectinomycin in uncomplicated infection in pregnant women**

One systematic review has found that antibiotic treatment (amoxicillin [amoxycillin] plus probenecid, spectinomycin, ceftriaxone, and cefixime) is effective for curing gonorrhoea in pregnant women. We found no reports of serious adverse effects.

**Single dose antibiotic regimens using selected fluoroquinolones, selected cephalosporins, or spectinomycin in uncomplicated infection in men and non-pregnant women***

One systematic review found limited evidence that single dose regimens (ceftriaxone, ciprofloxacin, gatifloxacin, spectinomycin, azithromycin, ofloxacin, cefixime) achieve cure rates of 95% or higher in urogenital or rectal infection. Cure rates were lower ($\leq$ 80%) for pharyngeal infection. Resistance to penicillins, tetracyclines, and sulphonamides is now widespread, and resistance to fluoroquinolones has become common in some geographic areas.

### LIKELY TO BE BENEFICIAL

**Multidose antibiotic regimens using selected injectable fluoroquinolones or selected injectable cephalosporins in disseminated infection†**

We found no RCTs assessing treatments for disseminated gonococcal infection published, but there is strong consensus that multidose regimens using injectable cephalosporins or quinolones (except where quinolone-resistant *Neisseria gonorrhoeae* have been reported) are the most effective treatment. We found no reports of treatment failures with these regimens.

### UNKNOWN EFFECTIVENESS

**Dual antibiotic treatment for gonorrhoea and chlamydia infections in all people diagnosed with gonorrhoea**

Dual treatment❻ for gonorrhoea and chlamydia infections is based on theory and expert opinion rather than on evidence from RCTs. The balance between benefits and harms will vary with the prevalence of co-infection in each population.

*Based on comparisons of results across arms of different trials.
†Based only on non-RCT evidence and consensus.

**DEFINITION**     Gonorrhoea is caused by infection with *Neisseria gonorrhoeae*. In men, uncomplicated urethritis is the most common manifestation, with dysuria and urethral discharge. Less typically, signs and symptoms are mild and indistinguishable from chlamydial urethritis. In women, the most common manifestation is cervicitis, which produces symptoms (e.g. vaginal discharge, lower abdominal discomfort, and dyspareunia) in only half of the women. Co-infection with chlamydia is reported in 20–40% of people.[1–3]

**INCIDENCE/**     Between 1975 and 1997, the incidence of reported gonorrhoea in the USA
**PREVALENCE**    fell by 74%, reaching a nadir of 122/100 000 people. Since 1997, between 125 and 133 cases have been reported per 100 000 people each year.[4] Rates are highest in younger people. In 2002, the incidence was highest in women aged 15–19 years (676/100 000) and men aged 20–24 years ▶

# Gonorrhoea

(538/100 000). In England, Wales, and Northern Ireland, diagnoses of gonorrhoea have increased since 1994, reaching 296/100 000 for 20–24 year old men and 214/100 000 for 16–19 year old women in 2002.[5]

**AETIOLOGY/ RISK FACTORS** Most infections result from penile–vaginal, penile–rectal, or penile–pharyngeal contact. An important minority of infections are transmitted from mother to child during birth, which can cause ophthalmia neonatorum. Less common are ocular infections in older children and adults as a result of sexual exposure, poor hygiene, or the medicinal use of urine.

**PROGNOSIS** The natural history of untreated gonococcal infection is spontaneous resolution after weeks or months of unpleasant symptoms.[6] During this time, there is a substantial likelihood of transmission to others and of complications developing in the infected individual.[6] In many women, the lack of readily discernible signs or symptoms of cervicitis means that infections go unrecognised and untreated. An unknown proportion of untreated infections causes local complications, including lymphangitis, periurethral abscess, bartholinitis, and urethral stricture; epididymitis in men; and in women involvement of the uterus, fallopian tubes, or ovaries causing pelvic inflammatory disease (see pelvic inflammatory disease, p 401). Gonorrhoea is associated with pelvic inflammatory disease. One review found N gonorrhoeae was cultured from 8–32% of women with acute pelvic inflammatory disease in 11 European studies and from 27–80% of women in eight US studies.[7] The proportion of N gonorrhoeae infections in women that lead to pelvic inflammatory disease has not been well studied. However, one study of 26 women exposed to men with gonorrhoea found that 19 women were culture positive and of these, five women had pelvic inflammatory disease and another four had uterine adnexal tenderness.[8] Pelvic inflammatory disease may lead to infertility (see pelvic inflammatory disease, p 401). In some people, localised gonococcal infection may disseminate. A US study estimated the risk of dissemination to be 0.6–1.1% among women, whereas a European study estimated it to be 2.3–3.0%.[9,10] The same European study found a lower risk in men, estimated to be 0.4–0.7%.[10] When gonococci disseminate, they cause petechial or pustular skin lesions; asymmetrical arthropathies, tenosynovitis or septic arthritis; and, rarely, meningitis or endocarditis.

Please refer to CD-ROM for full text and references.

*Catherine Mathews, Nicol Coetzee, Merrick Zwarenstein, and Sally Guttmacher*

## What are the effects of different partner notification strategies in different groups of people and what are the effects of interventions to improve patient referral?

We found no good evidence on the effects of partner notification on relationships between patients and partners and, in particular, on the rate of violence, abuse, and abandonment of patient or partner.

We found no studies comparing the effects of an intervention across different groups, such as people with different diseases or combinations of diseases, or people from different settings.

### LIKELY TO BE BENEFICIAL

#### Contract referral (as effective as provider referral in people with syphilis)

One systematic review of one large RCT comparing different partner notification strategies in people with syphilis found no significant difference in the proportion of partners notified between provider referral🅖 and contract referral🅖, when people receiving the contract referral option were given 2 days to notify their partners.

#### Offering a choice between provider and patient referral (v patient referral) in people with HIV

One systematic review of one RCT comparing different partner notification strategies found that in people with HIV, offering a choice between provider referral (where the identity of the index patient was not revealed) and patient referral was improved notification rates compared with offering patient referral alone.

#### Provider referral or contract referral (v patient referral) in people with gonorrhoea or non-gonococcal urethritis (mainly chlamydia)

One systematic review, has found that, for people with gonorrhoea, contract referral compared with patient referral increased the rate of partners presenting for treatment. For people with non-gonococcal urethritis, one systematic review found that provider versus patient referral increased the proportion of partners notified and of positive partners detected per patient.

### UNKNOWN EFFECTIVENESS

#### Adding telephone reminders and contact cards to patient referral; educational videos; information pamphlets; patient referral by different types of healthcare professionals; patient referral in HIV

We found insufficient evidence about the effects of these interventions in improving partner notification.

**DEFINITION**    Partner notification is a process whereby the sexual partners of people with a diagnosis of sexually transmitted infection are informed of their exposure to infection. The main methods are patient referral🅖, provider referral🅖, contract referral🅖, and outreach assistance🅖.

# Partner notification

**INCIDENCE/ PREVALENCE**
A large proportion of people with sexually transmitted infections will have neither symptoms nor signs of infection. For example, 22–68% of men with gonorrhoea who were identified through partner notification were asymptomatic.[1] Partner notification is one of the two strategies to reach such individuals, the other strategy being screening. Managing infection in people with more than one current sexual partner is likely to have the greatest impact on the spread of sexually transmitted infections.[2]

**PROGNOSIS**
We found no studies showing that partner notification results in a health benefit, either to the partner or to future partners of infected people. Obtaining such evidence would be technically and ethically difficult. One RCT in asymptomatic women compared identifying, testing, and treating women at increased risk for cervical chlamydial infection versus usual care. It found these reduced incidence of pelvic inflammatory disease (RR 0.44, 95% CI 0.2 to 0.9).[3] This evidence suggests that partner notification, which also aims to identify and treat people who are largely unaware of infection, would provide a direct health benefit to partners who are infected.

Please refer to CD-ROM for full text and references.

## What are the effects of treatments?

### LIKELY TO BE BENEFICIAL

**Antibiotics (for symptoms and microbiological clearance in women with confirmed pelvic inflammatory disease)**

There is consensus that antibiotic treatments are more effective than no treatment for women with confirmed pelvic inflammatory disease (PID). One systematic review of observational studies and RCTs has found that several different antibiotic regimens (including parenteral clindamycin plus parenteral aminoglycoside; parenteral cefalosporin with or without probenecid plus oral doxycycline; and oral ofloxacin) are similarly effective in relieving the symptoms of PID, and achieve high rates of clinical and microbiological cure.

**Oral (versus parenteral) antibiotics**

Two RCTs found no significant difference between oral ofloxacin and parenteral cefoxitin plus doxycycline.

**Outpatient (versus inpatient) antibiotic treatment**

One RCT found no significant difference between outpatient treatment with intramuscular cefoxitin plus probenecid plus oral doxycycline versus inpatient treatment with parenteral antibiotics for outcomes of recurrence of PID, infertility, or ectopic pregnancy at 35 months.

### UNKNOWN EFFECTIVENESS

**Different durations of antibiotic treatment**

We found no good evidence on the optimal duration of treatment.

**Empirical antibiotic treatment versus treatment guided by test results**

We found no RCTs comparing empirical treatment (before receiving results of microbiological tests) versus treatment that is guided by test results.

**Routine antibiotic prophylaxis before intrauterine device insertion in women at high risk**

We found no good evidence about antibiotic prophylaxis before intrauterine device insertion in women at high risk.

### UNLIKELY TO BE BENEFICIAL

**Routine antibiotic prophylaxis before intrauterine device insertion in women at low risk**

One systematic review found no significant difference between routine prophylaxis with doxycycline versus placebo before intrauterine contraceptive device insertion in PID in women at low risk of PID.

**DEFINITION** PID is inflammation and infection of the upper genital tract in women, typically involving the fallopian tubes, ovaries, and surrounding structures.

**INCIDENCE/ PREVALENCE** The exact incidence of PID is unknown because the disease cannot be diagnosed reliably from clinical symptoms and signs.[1-3] Direct visualisation of the fallopian tubes by laparoscopy is the best single diagnostic test, but it is invasive and not used routinely in clinical practice. PID is the most common gynaecological reason for admission to hospital in the USA, accounting for 49/10 000 recorded hospital discharges. A diagnosis of PID is made in 1/62 ▶

# Pelvic inflammatory disease

(1.6%) women aged 16–45 years attending their primary care physician in England and Wales.[4] However, because most PID is asymptomatic, this figure underestimates the true prevalence.[1,5] A crude marker of PID in developing countries can be obtained from reported hospital admission rates, where it accounts for 17–40% of gynaecological admissions in sub-Saharan Africa, 15–37% in Southeast Asia, and 3–10% in India.[6]

**AETIOLOGY/ RISK FACTORS**
Factors associated with PID mirror those for sexually transmitted infections: young age, reduced socioeconomic circumstances, lower educational attainment, and recent new sexual partner.[2,7,8] Infection ascends from the cervix, and initial epithelial damage caused by bacteria (especially *Chlamydia trachomatis* and *Neisseria gonorrhoeae*) allows the opportunistic entry of other organisms. Many different microbes, including *Mycoplasma hominis* and anaerobes, may be isolated from the upper genital tract.[9] The spread of infection to the upper genital tract may be increased by vaginal douching and instrumentation of the cervix, but reduced by the barrier method, levonorgestrel implants, and oral contraceptives compared with other forms of contraception.[10-14]

**PROGNOSIS**
PID has a high morbidity; about 20% of affected women become infertile, 20% develop chronic pelvic pain, and 10% of those who conceive have an ectopic pregnancy.[2] Uncontrolled observations suggest that clinical symptoms and signs resolve in a significant proportion of untreated women.[15] Repeated episodes of PID are associated with a four to six times increase in the risk of permanent tubal damage.[16] One case control study (76 cases and 367 controls) found that delaying treatment by even a few days is associated with impaired fertility (OR 2.6, 95% CI 1.2 to 5.9).[17]

Please refer to CD-ROM for full text and references.

Search date April 2003

*Fay Crawford*

## What are the effects of topical treatments for athlete's foot?
*New*

We found no evidence on recurrence rates in the literature on athlete's foot.

### BENEFICIAL

**Topical allylamines**
One systematic review and four subsequent RCTs have found that allylamines are more effective than placebo for curing fungal skin infections. The review found insufficient evidence comparing different allylamines versus one another. We found no evidence on recurrence rates after clinical cure.

**Topical azoles**
One systematic review has found that azole creams administered for 4–6 weeks increase cure rates compared with placebo. We found no RCTs evaluating differences between individual azoles. We found no evidence on recurrence rates after clinical cure.

### UNKNOWN EFFECTIVENESS

**Improved foot hygiene, including socks, and hosiery**
We found no systematic review or RCTs on the effects of foot hygiene and hosiery.

**DEFINITION**
Athlete's foot is a cutaneous fungal infection caused by dermatophyte infection. It is characterised by itching, flaking, and fissuring of the skin. It may manifest in three ways: the skin between the toes may appear mascerated (white) and soggy; the soles of the feet may become dry and scaly; and the skin all over the foot may become red and vesicular eruptions may appear.[1] It is conventional in dermatology to refer to fungal skin infections as superficial in order to distinguish them from systemic fingal infections.

**INCIDENCE/ PREVALENCE**
Epidemiological studies have produced various estimates of the prevalence of athlete's foot. Studies are usually conducted in populations of people who attend dermatology clinics, sports centres or swimming pools, or who are in the military. UK estimates suggest that athlete's foot is present in about 15% of the general population.[2] Studies conducted in dermatology clinics in Italy[3] and China (1014 people)[4] found prevalences of 25% and 27%, respectively. A population based study conducted in Israel found the prevalence among children to be 30%.[5]

**AETIOLOGY/ RISK FACTORS**
Swimming pool users and industrial workers may be at increased risk of fungal foot infection. However, one survey identified fungal foot infection in only 9% of swimmers, with the highest prevalence (20%) being in men aged 16 years and older.[2]

**PROGNOSIS**
Fungal infections of the foot are not life threatening in people with normal immune status, but in some people they cause persistent itching and, ultimately, fissuring. Other patients are apparently unaware of persistent infection. The infection can spread to other parts of the body and to other individuals.

Please refer to CD-ROM for full text and references.

# Cellulitis and erysipelas

**Search date October 2003**

*Andrew Morris*

## What are the effects of treatments?

**Antibiotics**

We found no RCTs comparing antibiotics versus placebo. RCTs comparing different single antibiotic regimens found clinical cure in 50–100% of people.

**Comparative effects of different antibiotic regimens**

RCTs provided insufficient information on differences between regimens. However, most of the RCTs included only a small number of people with cellulitis or erysipelas, and were designed to test equivalence rather than to detect a clinically significant difference in cure rates between antibiotics.

**Oral versus intravenous antibiotics**

We found no satisfactory RCTs comparing oral antibiotics versus intravenous antibiotics.

**Short versus long courses of antibiotics**

We found no RCTs comparing different durations of antibiotics.

**Treatment of predisposing factors to prevent recurrence**

We found no RCTs or observational studies on the effects of treating predisposing factors for recurrence of cellulitis or erysipelas.

**DEFINITION**
**Cellulitis** is a spreading bacterial infection of the dermis and subcutaneous tissues. It causes local signs of inflammation such as warmth, erythema, pain, lymphangitis, and frequently systemic upset with fever and raised white blood cell count. **Erysipelas** is a form of cellulitis and is characterised by pronounced superficial inflammation. The lower limbs are by far the most common sites, but any area can be affected. The term erysipelas is commonly used when the face is affected.

**INCIDENCE/**
**PREVALENCE**
We found no specific data on the incidence of cellulitis, but cellulitis and abscess infections were responsible for 158 consultations per 10 000 person years at risk in the UK in 1991.[1] In 1985 in the UK, skin and subcutaneous tissue infections resulted in 29 820 hospital admissions and a mean occupancy of 664 hospital beds each day.[2]

**AETIOLOGY/**
**RISK FACTORS**
The most common infective organisms for cellulitis and erysipelas in adults are streptococci (particularly *Streptococcus pyogenes*) and *Staphylococcus aureus*.[3] In children, *Haemophilus influenzae* was a frequent cause prior to the introduction of the HiB vaccination. Several risk factors for cellulitis and erysipelas have been identified in a case control study (167 cases and 294 controls): lymphoedema (OR 71.2, 95% CI 5.6 to 908.0), leg ulcer (OR 62.5, 95% CI 7.0 to 556.0), toe web intertrigo (OR 13.9, 95% CI 7.2 to 27.0), and traumatic wounds (OR 10.7, 95% CI 4.8 to 23.8).[4]

**PROGNOSIS**
Cellulitis can spread through the bloodstream and lymphatic system. A retrospective case study of people admitted to hospital with cellulitis found that systemic symptoms such as fever and raised white blood cell count were present in up to 42% of cases at presentation.[5] Lymphatic involvement can lead to obstruction and damage the lymphatic system that predisposes to recurrent cellulitis. Recurrence can occur rapidly or after months or years. One ▶

study found that 29% of people with erysipelas had a recurrent episode within 3 years.[6] Local necrosis and abscess formation can also occur. It is not known whether the prognosis of erysipelas differs from that of cellulitis. We found no evidence about factors that predict recurrence, or a better or worse outcome. We found no good evidence on the prognosis of untreated cellulitis.

Please refer to CD-ROM for full text and references.

# Chronic plaque psoriasis

**Search date January 2003**

*Luigi Naldi and Bethold Rzany*

---

## What are the effects of treatments?

### Ingram regimen

One large RCT has found that the Ingram regimen⊙ is of similar effectiveness to psoralen plus ultraviolet A in clearing moderate to severe psoriasis.

### Psoralen plus ultraviolet A

We found no systematic review or RCTs that compared psoralen plus ultraviolet A versus no psoralen plus ultraviolet A. One systematic review has found that 40 mg of 8-methoxypsoralen improves psoriasis clearance compared with 10 mg. One RCT found that psoralen plus ultraviolet A was slightly more effective in clearing psoriasis than dithranol. Long term adverse effects include photoaging and skin cancer (mainly squamous cell carcinoma).

### Vitamin D derivatives

Systematic reviews have found that vitamin D derivatives improve plaque psoriasis compared with placebo, are at least as effective as topical steroids, and may be more effective than coal tars and dithranol. One review has found that calcipotriol monotherapy causes more irritation than "potent" topical steroids.

### Dithranol

One systematic review of small RCTs has found that dithranol improves chronic plaque psoriasis after 4–8 weeks compared with placebo. The best evidence relates to its use in the Ingram regimen. One systematic review found that dithranol (short contact therapy) to be less effective than vitamin D derivatives and to cause more adverse effects.

### Topical retinoids (tazarotene)

RCTs have found that tazarotene improves chronic plaque psoriasis in the short term compared with placebo or calcipotriol.

### Ultraviolet B

There is a consensus that ultraviolet B is effective. However, we found insufficient RCT evidence on the effects of ultraviolet B compared with placebo, no treatment or other treatments, or on the effects of narrow band compared with broad band ultraviolet B for either clearance or maintenance treatment. One RCT found limited evidence that ultraviolet B given three times weekly clears psoriasis faster than twice weekly treatment.

### Alefacept

Two RCTs found limited evidence that alefacept improved psoriasis compared with placebo, but increased adverse effects, including chills, nausea, cough, dizziness, and accidents.

### Cyclosporin

One systematic review found that cyclosporin improved clearance compared with placebo. Optimal clearance rates occurred with a cyclosporin dose of 5.0 mg/kg daily. Any advantage of doses greater than 5.0 mg/kg daily may be offset by an ▶

increase in dose related adverse effects, particularly increased renal toxicity. The review found that a cyclosporin dose of 3.0 mg/kg daily was more effective than lower doses or placebo for maintenance.

### Fumaric acid derivatives

One systematic review of four small RCTs found limited evidence that oral fumaric acid esters improved chronic plaque psoriasis after 16 weeks compared with placebo. However, acute adverse effects are common and include flushing and gastrointestinal symptoms. We found no evidence on the effects of fumaric acid derivatives as maintenance treatment.

### Oral retinoids (etretinate, acitretin, liarozole)

We found limited evidence that oral retinoids improved clearance compared with placebo in people with plaque psoriasis. We found little reliable evidence on the effects of oral retinoids as maintenance treatment. Adverse effects led to discontinuation of treatment in 10–20% of people. Teratogenicity renders oral retinoids less acceptable.

### Tacrolimus

One RCT found limited evidence that tacrolimus may improve psoriasis compared with placebo. Adverse effects are reported to be similar to those of cyclosporin.

### Topical steroids

One systematic review and 12 additional RCTs have found that topical steroids, especially "potent" and "very potent" ones, improve psoriasis in the short term. Another systematic review found no difference in effectiveness between potent topical steroids and vitamind D derivatives, but found that vitamin D derivatives caused more irritation. Topical steroids may cause striae and atrophy, which increase with potency and use of occlusive dressings. Continuous use may lead to adrenocortical suppression, and case reports suggest that severe flares of the disease may occur on withdrawal.

### UNKNOWN EFFECTIVENESS

### Emollients, keratolytics, capsaicin, and aloe vera

We found insufficient evidence on the effects of emollients, keratolytics, capsaicin, and herbal extracts of aloe vera.

### Etanercept

We found insufficient evidence about effects of cytokine blocking agents (etanercept and infliximab) in people with plaque psoriasis.

### Goeckerman treatment

We found no good evidence on the effects of the Goeckerman treatment🄖.

### Infliximab

We found insufficient evidence about effects of cytokine blocking agents (etanercept and infliximab) in people with plaque psoriasis.

### Methotrexate

We found insufficient evidence about effects of methotrexate in people with chronic plaque psoriasis. Methotrexate can induce acute myelosuppression. Long term methotrexate carries the risk of hepatic fibrosis and cirrhosis, which is related to the dose regimen employed.

### Pimecrolimus

We found limited evidence from one small RCT that pimecrolimus may improve psoriasis compared with placebo.

# Chronic plaque psoriasis

### ◀ Tars

One systematic review found insufficient evidence from one small RCT for tar compared with placebo. Small RCTs found conflicting results on the effects of tars in combination with ultraviolet B exposure. One systematic review has found that coal tar, alone or in combination with allantoin and hydrocortisone, is less effective than vitamin D derivatives (calcipotriol).

### Acupuncture; anti-CD4 monoclonal antibody; antistreptococcal treatments; balneotherapy; fish oil; heliotherapy; lifestyle changes; oral vitamin D; psychotherapy; sunbeds

We found insufficient evidence on the effects of these interventions.

**DEFINITION** Chronic plaque psoriasis is a chronic inflammatory skin disease that is characterised by well demarcated erythematous scaly patches on the extensor surfaces of the body and scalp. The lesions may itch, sting, and occasionally bleed. Dystrophic nail changes are found in more than a third of people with chronic plaque psoriasis, and psoriatic arthropathy occurs in 1–3%. The condition waxes and wanes, with wide variations in course and severity among individuals. Other varieties of psoriasis include guttate, inverse, pustular, and erythrodermic psoriasis. This review deals with treatments for chronic plaque psoriasis.

**INCIDENCE/ PREVALENCE** Psoriasis affects 1–2% of the general population. It is believed to be less frequent in people from Africa and Asia, but we found no reliable epidemiological data.[1]

**AETIOLOGY/ RISK FACTORS** About a third of people with psoriasis have a family history of psoriasis, but physical trauma, acute infection, and some medications (e.g. lithium salts and β blockers) are believed to trigger the condition. A few observational studies have linked the onset or relapse of psoriasis with stressful life events and personal habits, including cigarette smoking and, less consistently, alcohol consumption. Others have found an association of psoriasis with body mass index◯ and an inverse association with intake of fruit and vegetables.

**PROGNOSIS** We found no long term prognostic studies. With the exceptions of erythrodermic and acute generalised pustular psoriasis (severe conditions that affect < 1% of people with psoriasis and that require intensive hospital care), psoriasis is not known to affect mortality. Psoriasis may substantially affect quality of life.[2] At present there is no cure for psoriasis.

Please refer to CD-ROM for full text and references.

## What are the effects of treatments?

### LIKELY TO BE BENEFICIAL

**Insecticide based pharmaceutical products**

Two RCTs identified by a systematic review found that permethrin and malathion both increased lice eradication rates compared with placebo. Limited evidence from an earlier systematic review suggested that permethrin increased eradication rates compared with lindane. We found inconclusive evidence from three RCTs about the comparative efficacy of insecticides and combing. One RCT found no significant difference between a herbal product and insecticide.

### UNKNOWN EFFECTIVENESS

**Herbal and essential oils**

We found no RCTs that compared herbal treatment with placebo. One RCT found no significant difference in eradication rates between a herbal product (coconut, anise, and ylang ylang) and insecticide (permethrin, malathion, and piperonyl butoxide). However, results may not generalise to different concentrations of these components or to different herbal preparations.

**Mechanical removal of lice or viable eggs by combing**

We found inconclusive evidence from three RCTs about effects of combing instead of or in addition to insecticides.

**Repellents**

We found insufficient evidence on the effects of these interventions.

**DEFINITION**      Head lice are obligate ectoparasites of socially active humans. They infest the scalp and attach their eggs to the hair shafts. Itching, resulting from multiple bites, is not diagnostic but may increase the index of suspicion. Eggs glued to hairs, whether hatched (nits) or unhatched, are not proof of active infection, because eggs may retain a viable appearance for weeks after death. A conclusive diagnosis can only be made by finding live lice.

**INCIDENCE/**      We found no studies on incidence and no recent published prevalence results
**PREVALENCE**   from any developed country. Anecdotal reports suggest that prevalence has increased in the past few years in most communities in the UK and USA.

**AETIOLOGY/**      Observational studies indicate that infections occur most frequently in school
**RISK FACTORS** children, although there is no proof of a link with school attendance.[1,2] We found no evidence that lice prefer clean hair to dirty hair.

**PROGNOSIS**    The infection is almost harmless. Sensitisation reactions to louse saliva and faeces may result in localised irritation and erythema. Secondary infection of scratches may occur. Lice have been identified as primary mechanical vectors of scalp pyoderma Ⓖ caused by streptococci and staphylococci usually found on the skin.[3]

Please refer to CD-ROM for full text and references.

# Herpes labialis

**Search date August 2003**

*Graham Worrall*

---

## What are the effects of preventive interventions?

### LIKELY TO BE BENEFICIAL

**Oral antiviral agents**
Six RCTs provided limited evidence suggesting that prophylactic oral antiviral agents may reduce the frequency and severity of attacks compared with placebo, but the optimal timing and duration of treatment is uncertain.

**Sunscreen**
Two small crossover RCTs provided limited evidence that ultraviolet sunscreen may reduce herpes recurrence compared with placebo.

### UNKNOWN EFFECTIVENESS

**Topical antiviral agents**
We found no RCTs on the effects of topical antiviral agents used as prophylaxis.

## What are the effects treating a first attack of herpes labialis?

### LIKELY TO BE BENEFICIAL

**Oral antiviral agents (aciclovir)**
One small RCT in children found that oral aciclovir reduced the mean duration of pain compared with placebo. Another small RCT in children found that oral aciclovir reduced the median time to healing compared with placebo.

### UNKNOWN EFFECTIVENESS

**Topical antiviral agents**
We found no RCTs on the effects of topical antiviral agents.

---

## What are the effects of treating a recurrent attack?

### LIKELY TO BE BENEFICIAL

**Oral antiviral agents**
Four RCTs found that oral aciclovir and valaciclovir (if taken early in the attack) marginally reduced the duration of symptoms and pain compared with placebo. Two large RCTs found no significant difference between a 1 day and a two course regimen of valaciclovir, and found that a higher proportion of people experienced headaches with valaciclovir compared with placebo.

**Topical antiviral agents**
Twelve RCTs provided limited evidence that topical penciclovir or aciclovir reduced the duration of pain and symptoms compared with placebo, but stronger evidence that healing time is reduced.

### UNKNOWN EFFECTIVENESS

**Topical anaesthetic agents**
One small RCT provided limited evidence that topical tetracaine reduced the mean time to scab loss compared with placebo. However, the clinical importance of this result is unclear.

▶

◀ **Zinc oxide cream**

One small RCT provided limited evidence that zinc oxide cream reduced time to healing compared with placebo, but found that it increased the risk of skin irritation.

| | |
|---|---|
| **DEFINITION** | Herpes labialis is a mild self limiting infection with herpes simplex virus type 1. It causes pain and blistering on the lips and perioral area (cold sores); fever and constitutional symptoms are rare. Most people have no warning of an attack, but some experience a recognisable prodrome. |
| **INCIDENCE/ PREVALENCE** | Herpes labialis accounts for about 1% of primary care consultations in the UK each year; 20–40% of people have experienced cold sores at some time.[1] |
| **AETIOLOGY/ RISK FACTORS** | Herpes labialis is caused by herpes simplex virus type 1. After the primary infection, which usually occurs in childhood, the virus is thought to remain latent in the trigeminal ganglion.[2] A variety of factors, including exposure to bright sunlight, fatigue, or psychological stress, can precipitate a recurrence. |
| **PROGNOSIS** | In most people, herpes labialis is a mild, self limiting illness. Recurrences are usually shorter and less severe than the initial attack. Healing is usually complete in 7–10 days without scarring.[3] Rates of reactivation are unknown. Herpes labialis can cause serious illness in immunocompromised people. |

Please refer to CD-ROM for full text and references.

# Malignant melanoma (non-metastatic)

**Search date February 2003**

*Philip Savage, Thomas Crosby, and Malcolm Mason*

## What are the effects of preventive interventions and treatments?

### LIKELY TO BE BENEFICIAL

#### High dose adjuvant alfa interferon

One RCT has found that high dose alfa interferon extends the time to relapse at median follow up of 6.9 years compared with no adjuvant treatment, and may improve overall survival. However, another RCT found no significant difference in relapse rates or overall survival between high dose interferon and no adjuvant treatment. Toxicity (myelosuppression, hepatotoxicity and neurotoxicity) and withdrawal rates were high.

### UNKNOWN EFFECTIVENESS

#### Adjuvant vaccines in people with malignant melanoma

Four RCTs found no significant difference in survival between adjuvant vaccines and surgery alone or surgery plus placebo vaccine in people with malignant melanoma, but they may have been underpowered to detect a clinically important difference.

#### Low dose adjuvant alfa interferon

RCTs found inconsistent evidence on the effects of low dose alfa interferon compared with no adjuvant treatment or relapse free and overall survival. Toxicity occurred in 10% of people.

#### Sunscreens in prevention

We found no RCTs about the preventive effects of sunscreens. One systematic review of case control studies found inconclusive evidence about the effects of sunscreen for preventing malignant melanoma. However, consensus suggests that the appropriate use of sunscreen (to reduce excessive exposure to sunlight rather than to prolong the time spent in the sun) may reduce the risk of developing melanoma.

#### Surveillance to prevent recurrence

We found no RCTs of surveillance to prevent recurrence of malignant melanoma.

### UNLIKELY TO BE BENEFICIAL

#### Prophylactic lymph node dissection

One systematic review found no significant difference in survival at 5 years between elective lymph node dissection and delayed or no lymph node dissection in people with melanoma without clinically detectable lymph node metastases.

#### Wide excision (no better than narrower excision in people with tumours of <2 mm Breslow thickness)

RCTs found no significant difference in local recurrence rates or overall survival over 4–10 years between more radical local surgery (4–5 cm excision margins) and less radical surgery (1–2 cm excision margins). One RCT found that wide compared with narrow excision increased the need for skin grafting and the length of hospital stay. Only 8.9% of people in the RCTs had tumours of >2 mm thickness, therefore we were unable to draw conclusions about the optimum excision margin in these people.

▶

**DEFINITION**  Cutaneous malignant melanoma is a tumour derived from melanocytes in the basal layer of the epidermis. After undergoing malignant transformation, it becomes invasive by penetrating into and beyond the dermis.

**INCIDENCE/ PREVALENCE**  Incidence in developed countries has increased by 50% in the past 20 years. Incidence varies in different populations❶ and is about 10-fold higher in white than in non-white populations. Despite the rise in incidence, death rates have flattened and even fallen in some populations (e.g. in women and young men in Australia).[1,2] During the same period there has been a sixfold increase in the incidence of melanoma *in situ*, suggesting earlier detection.

**AETIOLOGY/ RISK FACTORS**  The number of common, atypical, and dysplastic naevi on a person's body correlates closely with the risk of developing malignant melanoma. A genetic predisposition probably accounts for 5–10% of all cases. Although the risk of developing malignant melanoma is higher in fair skinned populations living close to the equator, the relation between sun exposure, sunscreen use, and skin type is not clear cut. Exposure to excessive sunlight and severe sunburn in childhood are associated with an increased risk of developing malignant melanoma in adult life. However, people do not necessarily develop tumours at sites of maximum exposure to the sun.

**PROGNOSIS**  The prognosis of early malignant melanoma (stages I–III)❶ relates to the depth of invasion of the primary lesion, the presence of ulceration, and involvement of the regional lymph nodes, with the prognosis worsening with the number of nodes involved.[3] A person with a thin lesion (Breslow thickness❻ < 0.75 mm) and without lymph node involvement has a 3% risk of developing metastases and a 95% chance of surviving 5 years.[4] If regional lymph nodes are macroscopically involved there is a 20–50% chance of surviving 5 years. Most studies have shown a better prognosis in women and in people with lesions on the extremities compared with those with lesions on the trunk.

Please refer to CD-ROM for full text and references.

# Scabies

Search date January 2003

*Godfrey Walker and Paul Johnstone*

## What are the effects of treatments?

### BENEFICIAL

#### Permethrin

One systematic review has found that permethrin increases clinical and parasitic cure after 28 days compared with crotamiton. The systematic review found conflicting results with permethrin versus lindane. One subsequent RCT found limited evidence that permethrin increased clinical cure at 14 days compared with ivermectin.

### LIKELY TO BE BENEFICIAL

#### Crotamiton

One systematic review found that crotamiton was less successful in terms of clinical and parasite cure after 28 days compared with permethrin. One systematic review identified one RCT that found no significant difference between crotamiton and lindane in clinical cure rates at 28 days.

#### Oral ivermectin

One systematic review identified one RCT that found that ivermectin increased clinical cure rates after 7 days compared with placebo. Another small RCT identified by the review found no significant difference between ivermectin and benzyl benzoate in clinical cure rates at 30 days. One subsequent RCT found that, compared with benzyl benzoate, ivermectin increased clinical cure rates at 30 days. One systematic review identified one small RCT that found no significant difference between ivermectin and lindane in cure rates at 15 days. One subsequent RCT found no significant difference between ivermectin and lindane in failed clinical cure rates at 2 weeks, but it found that ivermectin decreased failed cure rates at 4 weeks. One RCT found limited evidence that ivermectin reduced clinical cure rates at 14 days compared with permethrin. Experience suggests oral ivermectin is safe in younger adults being treated for onchocerciasis, but no such experience exists for children, and there have been reports of increased risk of death in elderly people.

### TRADE OFF BETWEEN BENEFITS AND HARMS

#### Lindane

One systematic review identified one RCT that found no significant difference between lindane and crotamiton in clinical cure rates at 28 days. The systematic review found conflicting results between lindane and permethrin after 28 days. Another small RCT identified by the review found no significant difference between lindane and ivermectin in cure rates at 15 days. One subsequent RCT found no significant difference between lindane and ivermectin in failed clinical cure rates at 2 weeks, but it found a higher proportion of people with failed clinical cure between lindane and ivermectin at 4 weeks. We found reports of rare, serious adverse effects such as convulsions.

### UNKNOWN EFFECTIVENESS

#### Benzyl benzoate

One systematic review identified one small RCT that found no significant difference between benzyl benzoate and ivermectin in clinical cure rates at 30 days. One subsequent RCT found that benzyl benzoate reduced clinical cure at 30 days ▶

◀ compared with ivermectin. One systematic review identified one RCT that found no significant difference with benzyl benzoate versus sulphur ointment in clinical cure at 8 or 14 days.

## Malathion

One systematic review found no RCTs on the effects of malathion. Case series have reported cure rates in scabies of over 80%.

## Sulphur compounds

One systematic review identified one RCT that found no significant difference with sulphur ointment versus benzyl benzoate in clinical cure at 8 or 14 days.

**DEFINITION**  Scabies is an infestation of the skin by the mite *Sarcoptes scabiei*.[1] Typical sites of infestation are skin folds and flexor surfaces. In adults, the most common sites are between the fingers and on the wrists, although infection may manifest in elderly people as a diffuse truncal eruption. In infants and children, the face, scalp, palms, and soles are also often affected.

**INCIDENCE/ PREVALENCE**  Scabies is a common public health problem with an estimated prevalence of 300 million cases worldwide, mostly affecting people in developing countries where prevalence can exceed 50%.[2] In industrialised countries, it is most common in institutionalised communities. Case studies suggest that epidemic cycles occur every 7–15 years and that these partly reflect the population's immune status.

**AETIOLOGY/ RISK FACTORS**  Scabies is particularly common where there is social disruption, overcrowding with close body contact, and limited access to water.[3] Young children, immobilised elderly people, people with HIV/AIDS, and other medically and immunologically compromised people are predisposed to infestation and have particularly high mite counts.[4]

**PROGNOSIS**  Scabies is not life threatening, but the severe, persistent itch and secondary infections may be debilitating. Occasionally, crusted scabies develops. This form of the disease is resistant to routine treatment and can be a source of continued reinfestation and spread to others.

---

Please refer to CD-ROM for full text and references.

# Squamous cell carcinoma of the skin (non-metastatic)

Search date May 2003

*Adèle Green and Robin Marks*

## What are the effects of preventive interventions?

### LIKELY TO BE BENEFICIAL

**Sunscreen in prevention (daily v discretionary use)**

One RCT in adults in a subtropical community in Queensland, Australia found that daily compared with discretionary use of sunscreen on the head, neck, arms, and hands reduced the incidence of squamous cell carcinoma after 4.5 years.

**Sunscreens to prevent development of new solar keratoses (v placebo)**

One RCT in people aged over 40 years living in Victoria, Australia who had previous solar keratoses (a risk factor for squamous cell carcinoma) found that daily sunscreen reduced the incidence of new solar keratoses after 7 months compared with placebo.

## What are the effects of treatments?

### UNKNOWN EFFECTIVENESS

**Micrographically controlled surgery (compared with standard surgical excision)**

We found no RCTs or observational studies of sufficient quality comparing the effects of micrographically controlled surgery⊙ versus standard primary surgical excision on local recurrence rates.

**Optimal primary excision margin**

We found no RCTs or observational studies of sufficient quality relating size of primary excision margin to local recurrence rate.

**Radiotherapy after surgery (compared with surgery alone)**

We found no RCTs or observational studies of sufficient quality comparing the effects of radiotherapy after surgery versus surgery alone on local recurrence rates.

**DEFINITION** Cutaneous squamous cell carcinoma is a malignant tumour of keratinocytes arising in the epidermis, showing histological evidence of dermal invasion.

**INCIDENCE/ PREVALENCE** Incidence rates are often derived from surveys because few cancer registries routinely collect notifications of squamous cell carcinoma of the skin. Incidence rates on exposed skin vary markedly around the world according to skin colour and latitude, and range from negligible rates in black populations and white populations living at high latitudes to rates of about 1000/100 000 in white residents of tropical Australia.[1]

**AETIOLOGY/ RISK FACTORS** People with fair skin colour who sunburn easily without tanning, people with xeroderma pigmentosum⊙,[2-4] and those who are immunosuppressed[5] are susceptible to squamous cell carcinoma. The strongest environmental risk factor for squamous cell carcinoma is chronic sun exposure. Cohort and case control studies have found that the risk of squamous cell carcinoma is three times greater in people with fair skin colour, a propensity to burn on initial ▶

exposure to sunlight, or a history of multiple sunburns. Clinical signs of chronic skin damage, especially solar keratoses, are also risk factors for cutaneous squamous cell carcinoma.[3,4] In people with multiple solar keratoses (> 15), the risk of squamous cell carcinoma is 10–15 times greater than in people with no solar keratoses.[3,4]

**PROGNOSIS**  Prognosis is related to the location and size of tumour, histological pattern, depth of invasion, perineural involvement, and immunosuppression.[6,7] A world-wide review of 95 case series, each comprising at least 20 people, found that the overall metastasis rate for squamous cell carcinoma on the ear was 11% and on the lip 14%, compared with an average for all sites of 5%.[7] A review of 71 case series found that lesions less than 2 cm in diameter compared with lesions greater than 2 cm have less than half the local recurrence rate (7% v 15%), and less than a third of the rate of metastasis (9% v 30%).[7]

Please refer to CD-ROM for full text and references.

**Skin disorders**

# Warts

## Search date September 2003

*Mike Bigby, Sam Gibbs, Ian Harvey, and Jane Sterling*

## What are the effects of treatments?

### Topical treatments containing salicylic acid

One systematic review has found that simple topical treatments containing salicylic acid increase complete wart clearance, successful treatment, or loss of one or more warts after 6–12 weeks compared with placebo. The review identified two RCTs comparing salicylic acid versus cryotherapy❻. These found no significant difference in the proportion of people with wart clearance at 3–6 months.

### Cryotherapy

One systematic review of two small RCTs found no significant difference between cryotherapy and placebo or no treatment in the proportion of people with wart clearance after 2–4 months. However, the RCTs may have been too small to detect a clinically important difference. The review identified two RCTs that found no significant difference between cryotherapy and salicylic acid in the proportion of people with wart clearance at 3–6 months. The review found that aggressive cryotherapy increased the proportion of people with wart clearance after 1–3 months compared with cryotherapy.

### Contact immunotherapy (dinitrochlorobenzene)

One systematic review found that contact immunotherapy❻ using dinitrochlorobenzene increased wart clearance compared with placebo.

### Carbon dioxide laser

One systematic review identified no RCTs on the effects of carbon dioxide laser.

### Cimetidine

Three small RCTs provided insufficient evidence to compare cimetidine versus placebo, and one small RCT provided insufficient evidence to compare cimetidine versus local treatments. One small RCT found that cimetidine plus levamisole increased wart clearance at 12 weeks compared with cimetidine alone.

### Distant healing

One RCT provided insufficient evidence to compare distant healing❻ versus no treatment.

### Hypnotic suggestion

We found no RCTs on the effects of hypnotic suggestion in the clearance of warts.

### Inosine pranobex

One RCT provided insufficient evidence about the effects of inosine pranobex on wart clearance.

### Intralesional bleomycin

RCTs found conflicting evidence on the effects of intralesional bleomycin. Two RCTs found that intralesional bleomycin increased the number of warts cured after 6 weeks compared with placebo. One RCT found no significant difference between bleomycin and placebo in the proportion of people with wart clearance after 30 days, and another RCT found weak evidence that bleomycin cured fewer warts ▶

◄ than placebo after 3 months. A fifth RCT found no significant difference between different concentrations of bleomycin in the proportion of warts cured after 3 months.

## Levamisole

Two RCTs and one CCT provided insufficient evidence on the effects of levamisole compared with placebo on the clearance of warts. One RCT found that levamisole plus cimetidine increased wart clearance at 12 weeks compared with cimetidine alone.

## Photodynamic treatment

RCTs provided insufficient evidence on the effects of photodynamic treatment❻ on wart clearance.

## Pulsed dye laser

One RCT provided insufficient evidence on the effects of pulsed dye laser.

## Surgical procedures

One systematic review identified no RCTs on the effects of surgical procedures on wart clearance.

## Systemic interferon α

We found no RCTs of sufficient quality on the effects of systemic interferon α.

### UNLIKELY TO BE BENEFICIAL

## Homeopathy

Two RCTs found no significant difference between homeopathy and placebo in the proportion of people with wart clearance after 8–18 weeks.

**DEFINITION** Non-genital warts (verrucas) are an extremely common, benign, and usually self limiting skin disease. Infection of epidermal cells with the human papillomavirus results in cell proliferation and a thickened, warty papule on the skin. Any area of skin can be infected, but the most common sites involved are the hands and feet. Genital warts are not covered in this review (see chapter on genital warts, p 394).

**INCIDENCE/** There are few reliable, population based data on the incidence and preva-
**PREVALENCE** lence of non-genital warts. Prevalence probably varies widely between different age groups, populations, and periods of time. Two large population based studies found prevalence rates of 0.84% in the USA[1] and 12.9% in Russia.[2] Prevalence is highest in children and young adults, and two studies in school populations have shown prevalence rates of 12% in 4–6 year olds in the UK[3] and 24% in 16–18 year olds in Australia.[4]

**AETIOLOGY/** Warts are caused by human papillomavirus, of which there are over 70 different
**RISK FACTORS** types. They are most common at sites of trauma, such as the hands and feet, and probably result from inoculation of virus into minimally damaged areas of epithelium. Warts on the feet can be acquired from walking barefoot in communal areas where other people walk barefoot. One observational study (146 adolescents) found that the prevalence of warts on the feet was 27% in those that used a communal shower room compared with 1.3% in those that used the locker room.[5] Warts on the hand are also an occupational risk for butchers and meat handlers. One cross-sectional survey (1086 people) found that the prevalence of warts on the hand was 33% in abattoir workers, 34% in retail butchers, 20% in engineering fitters, and 15% in office workers.[6] Immunosuppression is another important risk factor. One observational study in immunosuppressed renal transplant recipients found that at 5 years or longer after transplantation 90% had warts.[7]

# Warts

**PROGNOSIS**   Non-genital warts in immunocompetent people are harmless and usually resolve spontaneously as a result of natural immunity within months or years. The rate of resolution is highly variable and probably depends on several factors, including host immunity, age, human papillomavirus type, and site of infection. One cohort study (1000 children in long stay accommodation) found that two thirds of warts resolved without treatment within a 2 year period.[8] One systematic review (search date 2000, 17 RCTs) comparing local treatments versus placebo found that about 30% of people using placebo (range 0–73%) had no warts after about 10 weeks (range 4–24 weeks).[9]

Please refer to CD-ROM for full text and references.

*Miny Samuel, Rebecca Brooke, and Christopher Griffiths*

## What are the effects of preventive interventions?

**UNKNOWN EFFECTIVENESS**

### Sunscreens; vitamins (vitamin C and vitamin E)

We found no RCTs on the effects of these interventions in preventing wrinkles.

## What are the effects of treatments?

**BENEFICIAL**

### Tazarotene (0.1% strength more beneficial than lower strength or placebo)

Two RCTs in people with moderately photodamaged skin found that tazarotene cream improved fine wrinkling compared with placebo at 24 weeks. One RCT found no significant difference between tazarotene cream and tretinoin in fine wrinkling at 24 weeks.

### Tretinoin (for fine wrinkles after 6 months)

RCTs in people with mild to moderate photodamage found that topical tretinoin applied for up to 48 weeks improved fine wrinkles compared with vehicle cream, but the effect on coarse wrinkles differed among studies. Three RCTs in people with moderate to severe photodamage found that topical tretinoin (0.01–0.02%) applied for 6 months improved fine and coarse wrinkles on the face compared with vehicle cream. Common short term adverse effects with tretinoin included itching, burning, and erythema. Skin peeling was the most common persistent adverse effect, which was most frequent and severe at 12–16 weeks.

**TRADE OFF BETWEEN BENEFITS AND HARMS**

### Isotretinoin

In people with mild to severe photodamage, two RCTs found that isotretinoin cream improved fine and coarse wrinkles after 36 weeks compared with vehicle cream. Severe facial irritation occurred in 5–10% of people using isotretinoin.

**UNKNOWN EFFECTIVENESS**

### Carbon dioxide laser

We found no RCTs comparing carbon dioxide laser versus placebo or no treatment. We found insufficient evidence from small RCTs about the effects of carbon dioxide laser compared with dermabrasion, chemical peel, or other laser treatments.

### Dermabrasion

We found no RCTs comparing dermabrasion versus placebo or no treatment. Three small RCTs in women with perioral wrinkles found no significant difference between dermabrasion and carbon dioxide laser in improvement in wrinkles at 4–6 months. Adverse effects were commonly reported. Erythema was reported in all three RCTs, two of which found that erythema was more common with laser than with dermabrasion.

### Facelift

We found no RCTs on the effects of facelifts.

# Wrinkles

## Oral natural cartilage polysaccharides

One RCT found no significant difference between an oral preparation of cartilage polysaccharide and placebo in wrinkle appearance at 3 months. Smaller RCTs found that oral cartilage polysaccharide reduced fine, moderate, or severe wrinkles compared with placebo. However, these studies were small and of limited reliability. We found limited evidence that some preparations may be more effective than others.

## Retinyl esters

We found no systematic review or RCTs of retinyl esters that evaluated clinical outcomes.

## Topical antioxidants (ascorbic acid)

One poor quality RCT found limited evidence that an ascorbic acid formulation compared with a vehicle cream applied daily to the face for 3 months improved fine and coarse wrinkles. Stinging and erythema were common but were not analysed by treatment group. We were unable to draw reliable conclusions from this study.

## Topical natural cartilage polysaccharides

One small RCT found that a topical commercial preparation of natural cartilage polysaccharide reduced the number of fine and coarse wrinkles at 120 days compared with placebo. However, we were unable to draw reliable conclusions from this study. ❻

**DEFINITION**  Wrinkles, also known as rhytides, are visible creases or folds in the skin. Wrinkles less than 1 mm in width and depth are defined as fine wrinkles and those greater than 1 mm are coarse wrinkles. Most RCTs have studied wrinkles on the face, forearms, and hands.

**INCIDENCE/**  We found no information on the incidence of wrinkles alone, only on the
**PREVALENCE**  incidence of skin photodamage❻, which includes a spectrum of features such as wrinkles, hyperpigmentation, tactile roughness, and telangiectasia. The incidence of ultraviolet light associated skin disorders increases with age and develops over several decades. One Australian study (1539 people aged 20–55 years living in Queensland) found moderate to severe photoageing in 72% of men and 47% of women under 30 years of age.[1] The severity of photoageing was significantly greater with increasing age, and was independently associated with solar keratoses (P < 0.01) and skin cancer (P < 0.05). Wrinkling was more common in people with white skin, especially skin phototypes I and II. One study reported that the incidence of photodamage in European and North American populations with Fitzpatrick skin types I, II, and III❻ is about 80–90%.[2] We found few reports of photodamage in black skin (phototypes V and VI).

**AETIOLOGY/**  Wrinkles may be caused by intrinsic factors (e.g. ageing, hormonal status, and
**RISK FACTORS**  intercurrent diseases) and by extrinsic factors (e.g. exposure to ultraviolet radiation and cigarette smoke). These factors contribute to epidermal thinning, loss of elasticity, skin fragility, and creases and lines in the skin. The severity of photodamage varies with skin type, which includes skin colour and the capacity to tan.[3] One review of five observational studies found that facial wrinkles in men and women were more common in smokers than in non-smokers.[4] It also found that the risk of moderate to severe wrinkles in lifelong smokers was more than twice that in current smokers (RR 2.57, 95% CI 1.83 to 3.06). Oestrogen deficiency may contribute to wrinkles in postmenopausal women.[5]

**PROGNOSIS**  Although wrinkles cannot be considered a medical illness requiring intervention, concerns about ageing may commonly affect quality of life. Such concerns are likely to be influenced by geographical differences, culture, and personal values. In some cases concerns about physical appearance can lead to ▶

difficulties with interpersonal interactions, occupational functioning, and self esteem.[6] In societies in which the ageing population is growing and a high value is placed on the maintenance of a youthful appearance, there is a growing preference for interventions that ameliorate the visible signs of ageing.

Please refer to CD-ROM for full text and references.

# Insomnia

Search date June 2003

*Bazian Ltd*

---

## What are the effects of non-drug treatments in older people?

### UNKNOWN EFFECTIVENESS

**Cognitive behavioural therapy**

One systematic review identified one small RCT, which found that individual or group cognitive behavioural therapy◉ improved sleep quality at 3 months compared with no treatment, although mean sleep quality scores were consistent with continuing insomnia both with and without treatment.

**Exercise programmes**

One systematic review identified one small RCT. It found that sleep quality improved after a 16 week programme of regular, moderate intensity exercise four times a week compared with no treatment. However, mean sleep quality scores were consistent with persisting insomnia both with and without exercise.

**Timed exposure to bright light**

One systematic review found no RCTs comparing the effects of timed bright light exposure with other treatments or no treatment.

| | |
|---|---|
| **DEFINITION** | Insomnia is defined by the US National Institutes of Health as experience of poor quality sleep, with difficulty in initiating or maintaining sleep, waking too early in the morning, or failing to feel refreshed. Chronic insomnia is defined as insomnia occurring for at least three nights a week for 1 month or more.[1] Primary insomnia is defined as chronic insomnia without specific underlying medical or psychiatric disorders such as sleep apnoea, depression, or dementia. This topic only looks at primary insomnia. |
| **INCIDENCE/ PREVALENCE** | Across all adult age groups, up to 40% of people have insomnia.[2] However, prevalence increases with age, with estimates ranging from 31–38% in people aged 18–64 years to 45% in people aged 65–79 years.[3] |
| **AETIOLOGY/ RISK FACTORS** | The cause of insomnia is uncertain. The risk of primary insomnia increases with age and may be related to changes in circadian rhythms associated with age. Psychological factors and lifestyle changes may exacerbate perceived effects of changes in sleep patterns associated with age, leading to reduced satisfaction with sleep.[4] Other risk factors in all age groups include hyperarousal, chronic stress, and daytime napping.[1,5] |
| **PROGNOSIS** | We found few reliable data on long term morbidity and mortality in people with primary insomnia. Primary insomnia is a chronic and relapsing condition.[6] Likely consequences include reduced quality of life and increased risk of accidents owing to daytime sleepiness. People with primary insomnia may be at greater risk of dependence on hypnotic medication, depression, dementia, and falls, and may be more likely to require residential care.[6,7] |

---

Please refer to CD-ROM for full text and references.

## What are the effects of interventions to prevent or minimise jet lag? New

### LIKELY TO BE BENEFICIAL

**Melatonin***

One systematic review found that melatonin reduced mean jet lag scores on eastward and westward flights compared with placebo. The review found case reports of possible adverse effects, and suggests that people with epilepsy or on warfarin (or other oral anticoagulants) should not use melatonin without medical supervision. It concluded that the pharmacology and toxicology of melatonin needs systematic study, and routine pharmaceutical quality control of melatonin products is necessary. One RCT found no significant difference between melatonin plus zolpidem and placebo in alleviating symptoms of jet lag.

*The adverse effects of melatonin have not yet been adequately investigated

### TRADE OFF BETWEEN BENEFITS AND HARMS

**Hypnotics**

One RCT found no significant difference between zopiclone and placebo in subjective jet lag scores, but found that zopiclone increased sleep duration compared with placebo. One RCT found that zolpidem improved sleep quality compared with placebo. One RCT found that zolpidem was more effective in alleviating symptoms of jet lag compared with placebo, but found no significant difference between zolpidem plus melatonin and placebo. Adverse effects reported with hypnotics include headache, dizziness, nausea, confusion, and amnesia. Short term benefits of hypnotics have to be considered in light of potential adverse effects.

### UNKNOWN EFFECTIVENESS

**Lifestyle and environmental adaptations (eating, avoiding alcohol or caffeine, sleeping, daylight exposure, arousal)**

We found no RCTs on the effects of eating, avoiding alcohol or caffeine, sleeping, daylight exposure, or arousal. Such RCTs are unlikely to be performed.

**DEFINITION** Jet lag is a syndrome associated with rapid long haul flights across several time zones, characterised by sleep disturbances, daytime fatigue, reduced performance, gastrointestinal problems, and generalised malaise.[1] As with most syndromes, not all the components have to be present in any one case. It is due to the "body clock" continuing to function in the day–night rhythm of the place of departure. The rhythm adapts gradually under the influence of light and dark, mediated by melatonin secreted by the pineal gland: darkness switches on melatonin secretion, exposure to strong light switches it off.

**INCIDENCE/ PREVALENCE** Jet lag affects most air travellers crossing five or more time zones. The incidence and severity of jet lag increases with the number of time zones crossed.

# Jet lag

**AETIOLOGY/**
**RISK FACTORS**
Someone who has previously experienced jet lag is liable to do so again. Jet lag is worse the more time zones are crossed in one flight, or series of flights, within a few days. Westward travel generally causes less disruption than eastward travel as it is easier to lengthen, rather than to shorten, the natural circadian cycle.[2]

**PROGNOSIS**
Jet lag is worst immediately after travel and gradually resolves over 4–6 days as the person adjusts to the new local time.[2] The more time zones are crossed, the longer it takes to wear off.

Please refer to CD-ROM for full text and references.

Search date December 2002

*Michael Hensley and Cheryl Ray*

## What are the effects of treatments?

### BENEFICIAL

#### Nasal continuous positive airway pressure in moderate to severe obstructive sleep apnoea-hypopnoea syndrome (OSAHS)

Systematic reviews and subsequent RCTs have found that nasal continuous positive airway pressure reduces daytime sleepiness, improves vigilance and cognitive functioning, and reduces depression in people with moderate to severe obstructive sleep apnoea-hypopnoea syndrome after 3–9 months compared with placebo, oral appliances🄖, or no treatment.

### LIKELY TO BE BENEFICIAL

#### Nasal continuous positive airway pressure in mild OSAHS

One systematic review of four RCTs in people with mild OSAHS found no significant difference between nasal continuous positive airway pressure and conservative treatment or placebo tablets in daytime sleepiness, but found significant improvement in some measures of cognitive performance at about 4 weeks. One subsequent RCT found no significant difference between nasal continuous positive pressure plus conservative treatment and conservative treatment alone for daytime sleepiness or functional or cognitive outcomes, but found significant improvement in sleep apnoea-hypopnoea related symptoms at 3 and 6 months.

#### Oral appliance in mild OSAHS

One RCT found that oral appliances that produce mandibular advancement reduced apnoea🄖 and hypopnoea🄖, but had no significant effect on daytime sleepiness or quality of life compared with uvulopalatopharyngoplasty in people with mild OSAHS.

#### Oral appliance in moderate to severe OSAHS

RCTs have found that oral appliances that produce anterior advancement of the mandible reduce daytime sleepiness and sleep disordered breathing🄖 at 1–4 weeks in people with moderate to severe obstructive sleep apnoea-hypopnoea syndrome compared with no treatment or control oral appliances.

### UNKNOWN EFFECTIVENESS

#### Weight loss in mild OSAHS

One systematic review found no RCTs on the effects of weight loss in people with mild OSAHS.

#### Weight loss in moderate to severe OSAHS

One systematic review found no RCTs on the effects of weight loss in people with moderate to severe OSAHS.

**DEFINITION**     Obstructive sleep apnoea-hypopnoea syndrome (OSAHS) is abnormal breathing during sleep that causes recurrent arousals, sleep fragmentation, and nocturnal hypoxaemia. It is associated with daytime sleepiness, impaired vigilance and cognitive functioning, and reduced quality of life.[1,2] Criteria for the diagnosis of significant sleep disordered breathing have not been rigorously assessed, but have been set by consensus and convention.[3,4] Diagnostic criteria have variable sensitivity and specificity. For example, an apnoea/hypopnoea index🄖 of 5–20 episodes an hour is often used to define borderline to mild OSAHS, 20–35 to define moderate OSAHS, and more than ▶

# Sleep apnoea

35 to define severe OSAHS.[5] However, people with upper airway resistance syndrome🄖 have an index below 5 episodes an hour,[6] and many healthy elderly people have an index greater than five episodes an hour.[7] In an effort to obtain an international consensus, new criteria have been proposed but have not been widely used.[8] The most pragmatic test for clinically significant OSAHS is to show clinical improvement in daytime symptoms after treatment for sleep disordered breathing. In this topic, the criteria for OSAHS include apnoeas and hypopnoeas caused by upper airway obstruction. Central sleep apnoea and sleep associated hypoventilation syndromes are not covered here.

**INCIDENCE/ PREVALENCE**
The Wisconsin Sleep Cohort Study of over 1000 people (mean age 47 years) in North America found a prevalence of apnoea/hypopnoea index greater than five episodes an hour in 24% of men and 9% of women, and of OSAHS with an index greater than five plus excessive sleepiness in 4% of men and 2% of women.[9] There are international differences in the occurrence of OSAHS, for which obesity is considered to be an important determinant.[10] Ethnic differences in prevalence have also been found after adjustment for other risk factors.[7,10] Little is known about the burden of illness in developing countries.

**AETIOLOGY/ RISK FACTORS**
The site of the upper airway obstruction in the OSAHS is around the level of the tongue, soft palate, or epiglottis. Disorders that predispose to either narrowing of the upper airway or reduction in its stability (e.g. obesity, certain craniofacial abnormalities, vocal cord abnormalities, and enlarged tonsils) have been associated with an increased risk of OSAHS. It has been estimated that a $1 \text{ kg/m}^2$ increase in body mass index (3.2 kg for a person 1.8 m tall) leads to a 30% increase (95% CI 13% to 50%) in the relative risk of developing abnormal sleep disordered breathing (apnoea/hypopnoea index $\geq$ 5/hour) over a period of 4 years.[10] Other strong associations include increasing age and sex (male to female ratio is 2 : 1). Weaker associations include menopause, family history, smoking, and night time nasal congestion.[10]

**PROGNOSIS**
The long term prognosis of people with untreated severe OSAHS is poor with respect to quality of life, likelihood of motor vehicle accidents, hypertension, and possibly cardiovascular disease and premature mortality.[11] Unfortunately, the prognosis of both treated and untreated OSAHS is unclear.[7] The limitations in the evidence include bias in the selection of participants, short duration of follow up, and variation in the measurement of confounders (e.g. smoking, alcohol use, and other cardiovascular risk factors). Treatment is widespread, making it difficult to find evidence on prognosis for untreated OSAHS. Observational studies support a causal association between OSAHS and systemic hypertension, which increases with the severity of OSAHS (OR 1.21 for mild OSAHS to 3.07 for severe OSAHS).[11] OSAHS increases the risk of motor vehicle accidents three- to sevenfold.[11,12] It is associated with increased risk of premature mortality, cardiovascular disease, and impaired neurocognitive functioning.[11]

---

Please refer to CD-ROM for full text and references.

### Search date September 2003

_Justin Stebbing and Robert Glassman_

## What are the effects of first line hormonal treatment?

BENEFICIAL

### Tamoxifen in oestrogen receptor positive women

RCTs have found that antioestrogens (primarily tamoxifen🅖) increase response rates in women with oestrogen receptor positive metastatic breast cancer. RCTs have found no significant difference in response rates or overall survival between tamoxifen and progestins or ovarian ablation, but tamoxifen is associated with fewer adverse effects. One RCT found that tamoxifen was less effective than medroxyprogesterone in improving bone pain. Two RCTs in women with metastatic postmenopausal breast cancer have found that tamoxifen and the aromatase inhibitor🅖 anastrozole are similarly effective in reducing time to disease progression but that tamoxifen may cause more thromboembolic adverse effects and vaginal bleeding. One RCT found that tamoxifen was less effective than the aromatase inhibitor letrozole in reducing time to disease progression.

### First line hormonal treatment with antioestrogens (tamoxifen) or progestins (no significant difference in survival compared with non-taxane combination chemotherapy so may be preferable in women with oestrogen receptor positive disease)

One systematic review found no significant difference in survival at 12 or 24 months between first line hormonal treatment with progestins or tamoxifen and non-taxane combination chemotherapy. The review suggested that hormonal treatment may be preferable to chemotherapy🅖 as first line treatment in women with oestrogen receptor positive disease unless disease is rapidly progressing. It found that response rates were lower with hormonal treatment than with chemotherapy but it was associated with less nausea, vomiting, and alopecia.

### Selective aromatase inhibitors in postmenopausal women (as effective as tamoxifen in reducing time to disease progression)

Two RCTs have found that the aromatase inhibitor anastrozole as first line treatment in metastatic postmenopausal breast cancer is at least as effective as tamoxifen in reducing time to disease progression and may cause less thromboembolic adverse events and vaginal bleeding. One RCT found that the aromatase inhibitor letrozole was superior to tamoxifen in reducing time to disease progression.

LIKELY TO BE BENEFICIAL

### Combined gonadorelin analogues plus tamoxifen in premenopausal women

RCTs in premenopausal women with oestrogen receptor positive metastatic breast cancer have found that first line treatment with gonadorelin analogues🅖 plus tamoxifen improves response rates, overall survival, and progression free survival🅖 compared with gonadorelin analogues alone.

TRADE OFF BETWEEN BENEFITS AND HARMS

### Ovarian ablation in premenopausal women (no significant difference in response rates or survival compared with tamoxifen but associated with substantial adverse effects)

One systematic review and one subsequent RCT in premenopausal women found no significant difference in response rate, duration of response, or survival ▶

between ovarian ablation (surgery or irradiation) and tamoxifen as first line treatment. Ovarian ablation is associated with substantial adverse effects such as hot flushes and "tumour flare".

### Progestins (beneficial in women with bone pain or anorexia compared with tamoxifen)

RCTs found no significant difference in response rates, remission rates, or survival between medroxyprogesterone and tamoxifen as first line treatment. However, they found that medroxyprogesterone increased nausea, vaginal bleeding, and exacerbations of hypertension. One RCT has found that medroxyprogesterone improved bone pain compared with tamoxifen. Observational evidence suggests that progestins may increase appetite, weight gain, and wellbeing.

## What are the effects of second line hormonal treatment?

**BENEFICIAL**

### Selective aromatase inhibitors in postmenopausal women

RCTs have found that, in postmenopausal women with metastatic breast cancer who have relapsed on adjuvant tamoxifen☉ or progressed during first line treatment☉ with tamoxifen, the selective aromatase inhibitors☉ anastrozole, letrozole, and exemestane prolong survival compared with progestins☉ (megestrol) or non-selective aromatase inhibitors (aminoglutethimide), with fewer adverse effects. Two RCTs found that anastrozole was as effective as fulvestrant for delaying progression. The evidence suggests that selective aromatase inhibitors are better tolerated than previous standard second line treatment☉ with a progestin or aminoglutethimide, and are most effective in oestrogen receptor positive women.

**LIKELY TO BE INEFFECTIVE OR HARMFUL**

### Progestins (less effective than selective aromatase inhibitors and have more adverse effects)

RCTs have found that, in postmenopausal women with metastatic breast cancer who have relapsed on adjuvant tamoxifen or progressed during first line treatment with tamoxifen, progestins are less effective in second line treatment than selective aromatase inhibitors and have more adverse effects.

## What are the effects of first line chemotherapy?

**BENEFICIAL**

### Anthracycline based non-taxane combination chemotherapy regimens (CAF) containing doxorubicin (increase response rates and survival compared with other regimens)

RCTs have found that combination chemotherapy regimens containing an anthracycline, such as doxorubicin (CAF☉) as first line treatment increase response rates, time to progression☉, and survival compared with other regimens.

### Classical non-taxane combination chemotherapy (CMF) (increases response rates and survival compared with modified CMF)

One systematic review has found that classical CMF☉ as first line treatment increases response rate and survival compared with modified CMF regimens.

►

◀ **LIKELY TO BE BENEFICIAL**

**Taxane based combination chemotherapy (may increase response rates compared with non-taxane combination chemotherapy)**

One systematic review found that taxane based combination chemotherapy⑥ as first or second line treatment increased overall survival, time to progression, and overall response compared with non-taxane combination chemotherapy⑥. It found no significant difference in overall survival if the analysis was restricted to RCTs of first line chemotherapy.

**LIKELY TO BE INEFFECTIVE OR HARMFUL**

**High dose chemotherapy (no significant difference in overall survival compared with standard chemotherapy and increased adverse effects)**

One systematic review found no significant difference in overall survival over 1–5 years between high dose chemotherapy (requiring haematopoietic transplant) and standard dose chemotherapy. It found that high dose chemotherapy increased treatment related morbidity and mortality compared with standard chemotherapy.

## *What are the effects of first line chemotherapy in combination with a monoclonal antibody?*

**BENEFICIAL**

**Chemotherapy plus monoclonal antibody (trastuzumab) in women with overexpressed HER2/neu oncogene**

One RCT has found that, in women whose tumours overexpress HER2/neu oncogene, standard chemotherapy plus the monoclonal antibody trastuzumab as first line treatment increased the time to disease progression, objective response, and overall survival compared with standard chemotherapy alone. The most serious adverse effect observed was cardiac dysfunction in women who received an anthracycline plus trastuzumab.

## *What are the effects of second line chemotherapy?*

**LIKELY TO BE BENEFICIAL**

**Taxane based combination chemotherapy (increases response rates in women with anthracycline resistant disease compared with non-taxane combination chemotherapy)**

One systematic review has found that taxane based combination chemotherapy as first or second line treatment increased overall survival, time to progression, and overall response compared with non-taxane combination chemotherapy. The difference remained significant if the analysis was limited to women who had previously received anthracyclines. RCTs found no significant difference in progression or overall survival between docetaxel and 5-fluorouracil plus vinorelbine or between paclitaxel and capecitabine given as second line chemotherapy.

**UNKNOWN EFFECTIVENESS**

**Capecitabine for anthracycline resistant disease**

One RCT found similar response rates and time to disease progression between capecitabine and paclitaxel after anthracycline failure.

**Semisynthetic vinca alkaloids for anthracycline resistant disease**

One RCT found no significant difference in progression or overall survival between 5-fluorouracil plus vinorelbine and docetaxel given as second line chemotherapy. ▶

# Breast cancer (metastatic)

Another RCT has found that second line vinorelbine improved survival and reduced progression compared with melphalan. A third RCT found no significant difference in survival or quality of life between vinorelbine plus doxorubicin and vinorelbine alone.

---

## What are the effects of treatments for bone, cerebral, spinal cord, or choroidal metastases?

### BENEFICIAL

### Radiotherapy for spinal cord compression

We found no RCTs. Spinal cord compression is an emergency. Retrospective analyses found that early radiotherapy improved outcomes. However, fewer than 10% of people walked again if severe deterioration of motor function occurred before radiotherapy.

### Radiotherapy plus appropriate analgesia for bone metastases

We found no RCTs. We found limited evidence from non-randomised studies that persistent and localised bone pain can be treated successfully in over 80% of women with radiotherapy plus concomitant appropriate analgesia (from non-steroidal anti-inflammatory drugs to morphine and its derivatives) and that cranial nerve compression can be treated successfully with radiotherapy in 50–80% of people. RCTs found no evidence that short courses are less effective for pain relief than long courses of radiotherapy. One RCT found that different fractionation schedules can be used to treat neuropathic bone pain effectively.

### Radiotherapy plus high dose steroids in spinal cord compression

One small RCT in women with spinal cord compression suggested that adding high dose steroids to radiotherapy improved the chance of walking 6 months after treatment compared with radiotherapy alone.

### LIKELY TO BE BENEFICIAL

### Bisphosphonates for bone metastases

RCTs in women receiving standard chemotherapy or hormonal treatment for bone metastases secondary to metastatic breast cancer found that bisphosphonates reduced and delayed skeletal complications compared with placebo. None of the RCTs found an impact on overall survival.

### Radiotherapy for cerebral metastases

We found no RCTs. Retrospective studies suggest that whole brain radiation improves neurological function in some women with brain metastases secondary to breast cancer.

### Radiotherapy for choroidal metastases

We found no RCTs. Retrospective studies suggest that radiotherapy benefits some women with choroidal metastases.

### UNKNOWN EFFECTIVENESS

### Intrathecal chemotherapy for cerebral metastases; radiation sensitisers for cerebral metastases; surgical resection for cerebral metastases

We found insufficient evidence to assess these interventions in women with cerebral metastases.

**DEFINITION** Metastatic or advanced breast cancer is the presence of disease at distant sites such as the bone, liver, or lung. It is not treatable by primary surgery and is currently considered incurable. However, young people with good performance status may survive for 15–20 years.[1] Symptoms may include pain from bone metastases, breathlessness from spread to the lung, and nausea or abdominal discomfort from liver involvement.

**INCIDENCE/ PREVALENCE** Breast cancer is the second most frequent cancer in the world (1.05 million people) and is by far the most common malignant disease in women (22% of all new cancer cases). Worldwide, the ratio of mortality to incidence is about 36%. It ranks fifth as a cause of death from cancer overall (although it is the leading cause of cancer mortality in women — the 370 000 annual deaths represent 13.9% of cancer deaths in women). In the USA, metastatic breast cancer causes 46 000 deaths, and in the UK causes 15 000 deaths.[2] It is the most prevalent cancer in the world today and there are an estimated 3.9 million women alive who have had breast cancer diagnosed in the past 5 years (compared, for example, with lung cancer, where there are 1.4 million alive). The true prevalence of metastatic disease is high because some women live with the disease for many years. Since 1990, there has been an overall increase in incidence rates of about 1.5% annually.[3]

**AETIOLOGY/ RISK FACTORS** The risk of metastatic disease relates to known prognostic factors in the original primary tumour. These factors include oestrogen receptor negative disease, primary tumours 3 cm or more in diameter, and axillary node involvement — recurrence occurred within 10 years of adjuvant chemotherapy for early breast cancer🝆 in 60–70% of node positive women and 25–30% of node negative women in one large systematic review.[4]

**PROGNOSIS** Prognosis depends on age, extent of disease, and oestrogen receptor status. There is also evidence that overexpression of the product of the HER2/neu oncogene, which occurs in about a third of women with metastatic breast cancer, is associated with a worse prognosis.[5] A short disease free interval🝆 (e.g. < 1 year) between surgery for early breast cancer and developing metastases suggests that the recurrent disease is likely to be resistant to adjuvant treatment🝆.[6] In women who receive no treatment for metastatic disease, the median survival from diagnosis of metastases is 12 months.[7] The choice of first line treatment (hormonal or chemotherapy) is based on a variety of clinical factors🝆.[8–11] In many countries, such as the USA, Canada, and some countries in Europe, there is evidence of a decrease in death rates in recent years. This probably reflects improvements in treatment (and therefore improved survival) as well as earlier diagnosis.[2,12]

---

Please refer to CD-ROM for full text and references.

# Breast cancer (non-metastatic)

Search date June 2003

*J Michael Dixon, Alan Rodger, and Justin Stebbing*

## What are the effects of treatments for ductal carcinoma in situ?

### Radiotherapy after breast conserving surgery (reduces recurrence)

Two RCTs have found that radiotherapy🅖 after breast conserving surgery for ductal carcinoma *in situ* reduces local recurrence and invasive carcinoma compared with no radiotherapy after 4 and 8 years. However, they found no evidence of an effect on survival. One RCT in women having local excision found no significant difference between tamoxifen🅖 plus radiotherapy and radiotherapy alone in total invasive or ductal carcinoma *in situ* events after median follow up of 1 year.

### Tamoxifen plus radiotherapy after breast conserving surgery (reduces recurrence)

One RCT found that adjuvant🅖 tamoxifen reduced breast cancer events in women who have had wide excision and radiotherapy after median follow up of 6 years, although subgroup analysis suggested that benefit may be limited to people with oestrogen receptor positive tumours. It found no evidence of an effect on survival. One RCT in women having local excision found no significant difference between tamoxifen plus radiotherapy and radiotherapy alone in invasive or ductal carcinoma *in situ* events after median follow up of 1 year.

## What are the effects of treatments for operable breast cancer?

### Adjuvant chemotherapy

One systematic review has found that adjuvant chemotherapy reduces recurrence and improves survival at 10 years compared with no chemotherapy. The benefit seems to be independent of nodal or menopausal status, although the absolute improvements are greater in women with node positive disease, and probably greater in younger women.

### Adjuvant tamoxifen

One systematic review has found that adjuvant tamoxifen taken for up to 5 years reduces the risk of recurrence and death in women with oestrogen receptor positive tumours irrespective of age, menopausal status, nodal involvement, or the addition of chemotherapy. Five years of treatment seems better than shorter durations, but available evidence does not find benefit associated with prolongation beyond 5 years. Tamoxifen slightly increases the risk of endometrial cancer, but we found no evidence of an overall adverse effect on non-breast cancer mortality.

### Anthracycline regimens as adjuvant chemotherapy

One systematic review has found that adjuvant regimens containing an anthracycline🅖 reduce recurrence, and improve survival compared with a standard multidrug chemotherapy (CMF🅖) regimen at 5 years.

◄ **Breast conserving surgery (similar survival to more extensive surgery)**

Systematic reviews and long term results of included RCTs have found that, providing all local disease is excised, more extensive surgery does not increase survival up to 20 years. More extensive local resection in breast conserving surgery◉ gives worse cosmetic results.

## Combined chemotherapy plus tamoxifen

One RCT found that adding chemotherapy (CMF) to tamoxifen improves survival at 5 years in women with lymph node negative, oestrogen receptor positive early breast cancer.

## Ovarian ablation in premenopausal women

One systematic review has found that in women less than 50 years of age, ovarian ablation◉ improves survival for at least 15 years compared with no ablation.

## Radiotherapy after breast conserving surgery (reduces local recurrence; no evidence of effect on survival)

One systematic review has found that adding radiotherapy to breast conserving surgery reduces the risk of isolated local recurrence and loss of a breast. However, it does not increase survival at 10 years. Rates of survival and local recurrence are similar with radiotherapy plus either breast conserving surgery or mastectomy. One RCT found that radiotherapy (with and without tamoxifen) reduced ipsilateral breast cancer recurrence compared with tamoxifen alone after median follow up of 87 months. It found no significant difference in survival.

## Radiotherapy after mastectomy in women at high risk of local recurrence

One systematic review has found that radiotherapy to the chest wall after mastectomy reduces the risk of local recurrence by about two thirds and the risk of death from breast cancer at 10 years. It found no evidence of effect on overall 10 year survival. Radiotherapy may be associated with late adverse effects, which are rare, including pneumonitis, pericarditis, arm oedema, brachial plexopathy, and radionecrotic rib fracture.

---

**LIKELY TO BE BENEFICIAL**

## Neoadjuvant chemotherapy (reduces mastectomy rates more effectively than adjuvant chemotherapy; no evidence of effect on survival)

RCTs have found that neoadjuvant chemotherapy◉ reduces mastectomy rates compared with adjuvant chemotherapy. However, it found no significant difference in survival at 4–10 years.

## Total nodal radiotherapy in high risk disease

RCTs have found that, in women with high risk disease, total nodal irradiation◉ improves survival compared with no irradiation. An earlier systematic review found reduced locoregional recurrence, but no evidence of improved survival.

---

**TRADE OFF BETWEEN BENEFITS AND HARMS**

## Axillary clearance (no evidence of survival benefit and increased morbidity compared with axillary sampling)

RCTs found no significant difference in survival at 5–10 years between axillary clearance◉ and axillary sampling◉, axillary radiotherapy◉, or sampling plus radiotherapy combined. One systematic review of mainly poor quality evidence found that the risk of arm lymphoedema was highest with axillary clearance plus radiotherapy, lower with axillary sampling plus radiotherapy, and lowest with sampling alone.

# Breast cancer (non-metastatic)

### Axillary radiotherapy

One systematic review has found that axillary radiotherapy reduces isolated local recurrence compared with axillary clearance. It found no significant difference in mortality or overall recurrence at 10 years. One systematic review of mainly poor quality evidence found that radiotherapy plus axillary surgery was associated with arm lymphoedema.

### Radiotherapy after mastectomy in women not at high risk of local recurrence

One systematic review has found that radiotherapy to the chest wall after mastectomy reduces the risk of local recurrence by about two thirds and the risk of death from breast cancer at 10 years. However, it found no evidence of effect on overall 10 year survival. Radiotherapy may be associated with late adverse effects, which are rare, including pneumonitis, pericarditis, arm oedema, brachial plexopathy, and radionecrotic rib fracture. There is, therefore, a trade off between absolute benefits and harms in women not at high risk of local recurrence.

## UNKNOWN EFFECTIVENESS

### Radiotherapy to the internal mammary chain

One RCT found no significant difference in relapse or survival at 2–3 years between radiotherapy and no radiotherapy to the internal mammary chain. Treatment may increase radiation induced cardiac morbidity.

### Radiotherapy to the ipsilateral supraclavicular fossa

We found insufficient evidence about the effects of irradiation of the ipsilateral supraclavicular fossa on survival. RCTs have found that radiotherapy reduces the risk of supraclavicular fossa nodal recurrence.

## UNLIKELY TO BE BENEFICIAL

### Enhanced dose regimens of adjuvant chemotherapy

RCTs found no significant improvement from enhanced dose regimens.

### Prolonged chemotherapy (8–12 months v 4–6 months)

One systematic review found no additional benefit from prolonging adjuvant chemotherapy from 4–6 to 8–12 months.

### Radical mastectomy (no greater survival than less extensive surgery)

Systematic reviews and long term follow up of one RCT found no significant difference between radical, total, supraradical❺, or simple mastectomy in survival up to 25 years. More extensive surgery results in greater mutilation.

## LIKELY TO BE INEFFECTIVE OR HARMFUL

### High dose chemotherapy plus bone marrow or peripheral blood stem cell autograft

One systematic review found no significant difference between high dose chemotherapy plus autograft and conventional chemotherapy in 5 year survival for women with early, poor prognosis breast cancer. The review found that high dose chemotherapy increased treatment related and non-cancer related deaths compared with conventional chemotherapy.

◄ **What are the effects of treatments for locally advanced breast cancer?**

### Radiotherapy

For locally advanced breast cancer❸ that is rendered operable, small RCTs found that radiotherapy or surgery as sole local treatments have similar effects on response rates, duration of response, and overall survival.

### Radiotherapy after attempted curative surgery

One RCT found weak evidence that radiotherapy after attempted curative surgery may reduce local and regional recurrence compared with no further local treatment.

### Surgery

For locally advanced breast cancer that is rendered operable, small RCTs found that surgery or radiotherapy as sole local treatments have similar effects on response rates, duration of response, and overall survival.

### Tamoxifen plus radiotherapy (improves survival compared with radiotherapy)

One RCT found that hormone treatment plus radiotherapy improved locoregional recurrence at 6 years and improved median survival at 8 years compared with radiotherapy alone.

### Chemotherapy (cyclophosphamide/methotrexate/fluorouracil or anthracycline based regimens)

We found no evidence that the cytotoxic, multidrug chemotherapy regimen (CMF) improves survival, disease free survival❸, or long term locoregional control.

**DEFINITION** **Ductal carcinoma in situ** is a non-invasive❸ tumour characterised by the presence of malignant cells in the breast ducts but with no evidence that they breach the basement membrane and invade into periductal connective tissues. **Invasive breast cancer** can be separated into three main groups: early❸ or operable breast cancer, locally advanced disease, and metastatic breast cancer (see metastatic breast cancer, p 429). **Operable breast cancer** is apparently restricted to the breast and sometimes to local lymph nodes and can be removed surgically. Although these women do not have overt metastases at the time of staging❸, they remain at risk of local recurrence and of metastatic spread. They can be divided into those with tumours greater than 4 cm with multifocal cancers that can be treated by mastectomy, and those with tumours less than 4 cm with unifocal cancers that can be treated by breast conserving surgery. **Locally advanced breast cancer** is defined according to the TNM staging system❸ of the UICC TNM system❸[1] as stage III B (includes T4 a–d; N2 disease, but absence of metastases). It is a disease presentation with evidence (clinical or histopathological) of skin, or chest wall involvement, or axillary nodes matted together by tumour extension, or a combination of these features. **Metastatic breast cancer** is presented in a separate topic (see metastatic breast cancer, p000).

**INCIDENCE/** Breast cancer affects 1/10–1/11 women in the UK and causes about 21 000
**PREVALENCE** deaths a year. Prevalence is about five times higher, with over 100 000 women living with breast cancer at any one time. Of the 15 000 new cases of breast cancer a year in the UK, most will present with primary operable disease.[2]

▶

# Breast cancer (non-metastatic)

**AETIOLOGY/ RISK FACTORS**  The risk of breast cancer increases with age, doubling every 10 years up to the menopause. Risk factors include an early age at menarche, older age at menopause, older age at birth of first child, family history, atypical hyperplasia, excess alcohol intake, radiation exposure to developing breast tissue, oral contraceptive use, postmenopausal hormone replacement therapy, and obesity. Risk in different countries varies fivefold. The cause of breast cancer in most women is unknown. About 5% of breast cancers can be attributed to mutations in the genes *BRCA1* and *BRCA2*.[3]

**PROGNOSIS**  **Primary carcinoma** of the breast is potentially curable. The risk of relapse depends on various clinicopathological features, including axillary node involvement, oestrogen receptor status, and tumour size. Tumour size, axillary node status, histological grade, and oestrogen receptor status provide the most significant prognostic information. Of women with operable disease 70% are alive 5 years after diagnosis and treatment (adjuvant drug treatment is given to most women after surgery). Risk of recurrence is highest during the first 5 years, but the risk remains even 15–20 years after surgery. Those with node positive disease have a 50–60% chance of recurrence within 5 years, compared with 30–35% for node negative disease. Recurrence at 10 years, according to one large systematic review,[4] is 60–70% compared with 25–30% of node negative women. The prognosis for a free survival at 5 years is worse for stage III B (33%) than that for stage III A (71%). Five year overall survival is 44% for stage III B and 84% for stage III A.[5] Poor survival and high rates of local recurrence characterise locally advanced breast cancer.

Please refer to CD-ROM for full text and references.

## What are the effects of treatments?

### LIKELY TO BE BENEFICIAL

**Diet (low fat, high carbohydrate)**

One small RCT found limited evidence that advice to follow a low fat, high carbohydrate diet reduced self reported breast swelling and breast tenderness at 6 months compared with general dietary advice.

### TRADE OFF BETWEEN BENEFITS AND HARMS

**Danazol**

One RCT found that danazol reduced cyclical breast pain after 12 months compared with placebo, but increased adverse effects (weight gain, deepening of the voice, menorrhagia, and muscle cramps). It found no significant difference in pain relief between danazol and tamoxifen.

**Gestrinone**

One RCT found that gestrinone reduced breast pain after 3 months compared with placebo, but increased adverse effects (greasy skin, hirsutism, acne, reduction in breast size, headache, and depression).

**Tamoxifen**

Three RCTs found limited evidence that tamoxifen is more effective than placebo at reducing breast pain. Two of the RCTs found more hot flushes and vaginal discharge with tamoxifen compared with placebo, although differences between groups did not reach significance. The third RCT did not report on adverse events. One RCT found similar efficacy but fewer adverse effects with a lower dose of 10 mg compared with 20 mg. One RCT found no significant difference in pain relief between tamoxifen and danazol. One meta-analysis of four large breast cancer prevention trials found that tamoxifen used long term was associated with an increased risk of venous thromboembolism.

### UNKNOWN EFFECTIVENESS

**Lisuride maleate**

One RCT with weak methods found limited evidence that lisuride maleate (a dopamine agonist) reduced breast pain over 2 months compared with placebo.

**Tibolone**

We found no placebo controlled RCTs of tibolone. One small RCT found limited evidence that tibolone reduced breast pain after 1 year compared with hormone replacement therapy.

**Antibiotics; diuretics; evening primrose oil; gonadorelin analogues (luteinising hormone releasing hormone analogues); progestogens; pyridoxine; vitamin E**

We found no RCTs of sufficient quality on the effects of these interventions.

### UNLIKELY TO BE BENEFICIAL

**Bromocriptine**

One RCT with high withdrawal rates and one small crossover RCT reporting post crossover results found limited evidence that bromocriptine (a dopamine agonist) reduced breast pain compared with placebo. However, both RCTs found a higher ▶

# Breast pain

incidence of adverse effects with bromocriptine compared with placebo. Adverse events included nausea, dizziness, postural hypotension, and constipation. One of the RCTs found that withdrawals related to adverse effects were more frequent with bromocriptine compared with placebo, although differences between groups did not reach significance.

## Hormone replacement therapy

We found no placebo controlled RCTs of hormone replacement therapy. One small RCT found limited evidence that women taking hormone replacement therapy had more breast pain after 1 year than women taking tibolone.

## Progesterones

Two small crossover RCTs found no significant difference between progesterones and placebo in breast pain.

| | |
|---|---|
| **DEFINITION** | Breast pain can be differentiated into cyclical mastalgia (worse before a menstrual period) or non-cyclical mastalgia (unrelated to the menstrual cycle).[1,2] Cyclical pain is often bilateral, usually most severe in the upper outer quadrants of the breast, and may be referred to the medial aspect of the upper arm.[1-3] Non-cyclical pain may be caused by true breast pain or chest wall pain located over the costal cartilages.[1,2,4] Specific breast pathology and referred pain unrelated to the breasts are not included in this chapter. |
| **INCIDENCE/ PREVALENCE** | Up to 70% of women develop breast pain in their lifetime.[1,2] Of 1171 US women attending a gynaecology clinic, 69% suffered regular discomfort, which was judged as severe in 11% of women, and 36% had consulted a doctor about breast pain.[2] |
| **AETIOLOGY/ RISK FACTORS** | Breast pain is most common in women aged 30–50 years.[1,2] |
| **PROGNOSIS** | Cyclical breast pain resolves spontaneously within 3 months of onset in 20–30% of women.[5] The pain tends to relapse and remit, and up to 60% of women develop recurrent symptoms 2 years after treatment.[1] Non-cyclical pain responds poorly to treatment but may resolve spontaneously in about 50% of women.[1] |

Please refer to CD-ROM for full text and references.

Search date March 2003

*Des Spence*

## What are the effects of treatments for acute vulvovaginal candidiasis in non-pregnant women?

### BENEFICIAL

**Intravaginal imidazoles**

RCTs found that intravaginal imidazoles (butoconazole, clotrimazole, miconazole, or terconazole) reduced persistent symptoms of vulvovaginal candidiasis after 9–38 days compared with placebo, and found no clear evidence that effects differ among the various intravaginal imidazoles. RCTs found no clear evidence of any difference in persistent symptoms between shorter and longer durations of treatment (1–14 days). RCTs found no significant difference in symptoms between and intravaginal imidazoles and oral fluconazole, itraconozole or ketoconazole. RCTs found that intravaginal imidazoles were associated with less nausea, headache, and abdominal pain but more vulvar irritation and vaginal discharge, than oral fluconazole or oral ketoconazole. Two RCTs provided insufficient evidence to compare intravaginal imidazoles versus intravaginal nystatin.

**Oral fluconazole**

We found no RCTs comparing oral fluconazole versus placebo or no treatment. One systematic review found no significant difference in persistent symptoms of vulvovaginal candidiasis over 1–12 weeks between oral fluconazole or oral itraconazole and intravaginal imidazoles, and found that oral fluconazole was associated with more nausea, headache, and abdominal pain but less vulvar irritation and vaginal discharge than intravaginal imidazoles. Two weak RCTs provided insufficient evidence to compare oral fluconazole versus oral itraconazole. One systematic review found no significant difference in persistent symptoms of vulvovaginal candidiasis or adverse effects between oral fluconazole and oral ketoconazole.

**Oral itraconazole**

One RCT found that oral itraconazole reduced persistent symptoms of vulvovaginal candidiasis at 1 week after treatment compared with placebo. One systematic review found no significant difference in persistent symptoms over 1–12 weeks between oral itraconazole or oral fluconazole and intravaginal imidazoles. One weak RCT provided insufficient evidence to compare oral itraconazole versus oral fluconazole.

### LIKELY TO BE BENEFICIAL

**Intravaginal nystatin**

One RCT found that intravaginal nystatin reduced the proportion of women with a poor symptomatic response after 14 days' treatment compared with placebo. Two RCTs provided insufficient evidence to compare intravaginal nystatin versus intravaginal imidazoles. We found no RCTs comparing intravaginal nystatin versus oral fluconazole, itraconazole, or ketoconazole.

### UNLIKELY TO BE BENEFICIAL

**Oral ketoconazole**

We found no RCTs comparing oral ketoconazole versus placebo or versus no treatment. RCTs found no significant difference between oral ketoconazole and intravaginal imidazoles in persistent symptoms of vulvovaginal candidiasis and found that oral ketoconazole may cause more nausea, fatigue and headaches but ▶

# Candidiasis (vulvovaginal)

less vulvar irritation. One systematic review found no significant difference in persistent symptoms or adverse effects between oral ketoconazole and oral itraconazole. Case reports have associated ketoconazole with a low risk of fulminant hepatitis (1/12 000 courses of treatment with oral ketoconazole).

## What are the effects of treatments for recurrent vulvovaginal candidiasis in non-pregnant women?

### LIKELY TO BE BENEFICIAL

### Regular prophylaxis with oral itraconazole

One RCT found that regular prophylaxis with oral itraconazole reduced the rate of symptomatic recurrence of vulvovaginal candidiasis over 6 months compared with placebo.

### TRADE OFF BETWEEN BENEFITS AND HARMS

### Intermittent or continous prophylaxis with oral ketoconazole

One RCT found that oral ketoconazole, reduced symptomatic recurrence of vulvovaginal candidiasis over 6 months compared with placebo. This benefit is associated with an increased risk of harms, including rare cases of fulminant hepatitis (1/12 000 courses of treatment with oral ketoconazole).

### UNKNOWN EFFECTIVENESS

### Regular prophylaxis with intravaginal imidazoles

Two RCTs provided insufficient evidence about the effects of regular prophylaxis with intravaginal clotrimazole versus placebo in preventing recurrence of vulvovaginal candidiasis. One RCT found no significant difference in the number of episodes of symptomatic vaginitis over 6 months between regular prophylaxis with intravaginal clotrimazole and treatment as required, although women taking regular prophylaxis had fewer episodes. The RCT was too small to exclude a clinically important difference. More women preferred treatment as required. One RCT found insufficient evidence about the effects of regular prophylaxis with intravaginal clotrimazole versus oral itraconazole.

### Regular prophylaxis with oral fluconazole

We found no RCTs about the effects of regular prophylaxis with oral fluconazole in preventing symptomatic recurrence of vulvovaginal candidiasis.

### Treating a male sexual partner

Two RCTs found no significant difference between treating and not treating a woman's male sexual partner in the resolution of the woman's symptoms of vulvovaginal candidiasis over 1–4 weeks or in the rate of symptomatic recurrance. The women in the RCTs were not selected because of a history of recurrent vulvovaginal candidiasis.

DEFINITION   Vulvovaginal candidiasis is symptomatic vaginitis (inflammation of the vagina), which often involves the vulva, caused by infection with a *Candida* yeast. Predominant symptoms are vulvar itching and abnormal vaginal discharge (which may be minimal, a "cheese like" material, or a watery secretion). Differentiation from other forms of vaginitis requires the presence of yeast on microscopy of vaginal fluid. The definition of recurrent vulvovaginal candidiasis varies among RCTs, but it is commonly defined as four or more symptomatic episodes a year.[1] This review excludes studies of asymptomatic women with vaginal colonisation by *Candida* species.

| | |
|---|---|
| **INCIDENCE/ PREVALENCE** | Vulvovaginal candidiasis is the second most common cause of vaginitis (after bacterial vaginosis). Estimates of its incidence are limited, and often derived from women attending hospital clinics. At least one episode of vulvovaginal candidiasis occurs during the lifetime of 50–75% of all women. Vulvovaginal candidiasis is diagnosed in 5–15% of women attending sexually transmitted disease and family planning clinics.[1] About half of the women who have an episode develop recurrent vulvovaginal candidiasis.[2] |
| **AETIOLOGY/ RISK FACTORS** | *Candida albicans* accounts for 85–90% of cases of vulvovaginal candidiasis. Development of symptomatic vulvovaginal candidiasis probably represents increased growth of yeast that previously colonised the vagina without causing symptoms. Risk factors for vulvovaginal candidiasis include pregnancy (RR 2–10), diabetes mellitus, and systemic antibiotics. The evidence that different types of contraceptives are risk factors is contradictory. The incidence of vulvovaginal candidiasis rises with initiation of sexual activity, but we found no direct evidence that vulvovaginal candidiasis is sexually transmitted.[3–5] |
| **PROGNOSIS** | We found few descriptions of the natural history of untreated vulvovaginal candidiasis. Discomfort is the main complication and can include pain while passing urine or during sexual intercourse. Balanitis🅖 in male partners of women with vulvovaginal candidiasis can occur, but it is rare. |

Please refer to CD-ROM for full text and references.

# Domestic violence towards women

**Search date July 2003**

*Joanne Klevens and Laura Sadowski*

## What are the effects of interventions initiated by healthcare professionals, aimed at female victims of domestic violence?

### LIKELY TO BE BENEFICIAL

#### Advocacy

One RCT and one non-randomised controlled trial found that advocacy reduced reabuse compared with no treatment. The RCT also found an improvement in women's quality of life with advocacy compared with no treatment. One controlled trial in pregnant Hispanic women found no significant difference in rates of reabuse between combined counselling plus mentoring (similar to advocacy) and a resource card, but found that counselling plus mentoring slightly reduced rates of reabuse compared with unlimited counselling.

#### Safety planning

One RCT found that providing telephone sessions on safe behaviour in addition to usual care increased safe behaviour at 6 months compared with usual care alone. We found limited evidence from one non-randomised controlled trial in pregnant women that helping participants to make a safety plan reduced spouse abuse and increased safe behaviour at 12 months.

### UNKNOWN EFFECTIVENESS

#### Cognitive behaviour orientated counselling

One controlled trial found that cognitive behaviour orientated therapy improved women's assertiveness and reduced their exposure to abuse compared with baseline levels, whereas non-specific support did not. However, the study did not directly compare effects of interventions.

#### Couple counselling

Controlled trials found that both gender specific counselling and couple counselling reduced physical aggression, psychological aggression and depression in wives from baseline levels, but they found no significant differences between treatments. One controlled trial found no significant difference between group and individual couple counselling on reduction in physical violence or on psychological wellbeing.

#### Grief resolution orientated counselling

One controlled trial found that grief resolution orientated counselling improved self esteem and self efficacy from baseline, whereas feminist orientated counselling did not. However, the study did not directly compare effects of interventions.

#### Peer support groups

We found no systematic reviews or controlled trials on the effect of peer support groups.

#### Shelters

We found no reliable controlled trials. One cohort study found a reduced incidence of violence in the weeks following shelter stay for women choosing to use the shelter when they were also engaged in other types of help seeking behaviour compared with women not choosing to stay at the shelter. Women choosing to stay at the shelter who had not sought help elsewhere experienced an increase in violence.

## Non-specific counselling

Two controlled trials and one comparative cohort study found no effect of counselling compared with no treatment on medical care utilisation rates, reported exposure to violence and threats of violence, or depression, anxiety, and self esteem.

**DEFINITION**  Domestic violence, also called intimate partner violence, is actual or threatened physical or sexual violence, or emotional or psychological abuse (including coercive tactics) by a current or former spouse or dating partner (including same sex partners).[1] Other terms commonly used to describe domestic violence include domestic abuse, spouse abuse, marital violence, and battering.

**INCIDENCE/ PREVALENCE**  Between 10–69% of women participating in population based surveys in 48 countries from around the world reported being physically assaulted by a partner during their lifetime.[2] Rates of assault by a partner are 4.3 times higher among women than men.[3] Nearly 25% of surveyed women in the USA reported being physically and/or sexually assaulted by a current or former partner at some time during their lives, and 1.5% were victimised during the previous 12 months.[3] Rates of violence against pregnant women range from 0.9–20%.[4] Between 11.7–24.5% of women in prenatal clinics[5–8] and 5.5–17% of women in primary or ambulatory care reported being abused by a partner in the past year.[9–12]

**AETIOLOGY/ RISK FACTORS**  A recent systematic review found that physical domestic violence toward women is associated with lower levels of education and unemployment, low family income, marital discord, and with the partner's lower level of occupation, childhood experiences of abuse, witnessing interparental violence, higher levels of anger, depression, heavy or problem drinking, drug use, jealousy, and lack of assertiveness with spouse.[13] A similar review of research on psychological aggression found that the few demographic and psychological variables assessed were either inconsistently associated with psychological domestic violence or were found to be associated with psychological domestic violence in studies with serious methodological limitations.[14]

**PROGNOSIS**  There are few prospective studies documenting the course of domestic violence and its outcomes. Cross sectional surveys suggest that domestic violence persists for at least two thirds of women.[15,16] Among black and Hispanic people persistence of domestic violence seems to be dependent on initial severity.[17] For all ethnic groups, half of those reporting moderate domestic violence did not report occurrences of domestic violence at the 5 year follow up, but for people of black or Hispanic origin reporting severe domestic violence only a third did not report occurrences of domestic violence at the 5 year follow up. A case control study conducted in middle class working women found that, compared with non-abused women, women abused by their partners during the previous 9 years were significantly more likely to have or report headaches (48% v 35%), back pain (40% v 25%), sexually transmitted diseases (6% v 2%), vaginal bleeding (17% v 6%), vaginal infections (30% v 21%), pelvic pain (17% v 9%), painful intercourse (13% v 7%), urinary tract infections (22% v 12%), appetite loss (9% v 3%), digestive problems (35% v 19%), abdominal pain (22% v 11%), and facial injuries (8% v 1%).[18] After adjusting for age, race, insurance status, and cigarette smoking, a cross sectional survey found that women experiencing psychological abuse are also more likely to report poor physical and mental health, disability preventing work, arthritis, chronic pain, migraine and other frequent headaches, sexually transmitted infections, chronic pelvic pain, stomach ulcers, spastic colon, frequent indigestion, diarrhoea, or constipation❶.[19]

Please refer to CD-ROM for full text and references.

# Dysmenorrhoea

### Search date February 2003

*Michelle Proctor and Cynthia Farquhar*

## What are the effects of treatments?

BENEFICIAL

### Non-steroidal anti-inflammatory drugs (other than aspirin)

Two systematic reviews have found that naproxen, ibuprofen, mefenamic acid, valdecoxib, and rofecoxib reduce pain compared with placebo. It remains unclear from direct comparisons which non-steroidal anti-inflammatory drugs have better efficacy or safety. One systematic review found that naproxen reduced pain more and was associated with fewer adverse effects than co-proxamol. It also found that mefenamic acid reduced symptoms more than co-proxamol.

LIKELY TO BE BENEFICIAL

### Aspirin, paracetamol, and compound analgesics

One systematic review found that aspirin was more effective for pain relief than placebo, but less effective than naproxen or ibuprofen. The review found no significant difference between paracetamol compared with placebo, aspirin, or ibuprofen in pain relief, although some of the RCTs may have been too small to rule out clinically important differences. It found limited evidence that co-proxamol❻ reduced pain compared with placebo.

### Magnesium

One systematic review found limited evidence from two out of three small RCTs that magnesium reduced pain after 5–6 months compared with placebo. A third RCT found no significant difference.

### Thiamine

One large RCT identified by a systematic review found that thiamine reduced pain after 60 days compared with placebo.

### Toki-shakuyaku-san (herbal remedy)

One systematic review found limited evidence that toki-shakuyaku-san reduced pain after 6 months compared with placebo and that it reduced the need for additional medication with diclofenac.

### Topical heat (about 39 °C)

One RCT found topical heat (about 39 °C) treatment to be as effective as ibuprofen and more effective than placebo in reducing pain.

### Transcutaneous electrical nerve stimulation

One systematic review found limited evidence from small RCTs that high frequency transcutaneous electrical nerve stimulation❻ reduced pain compared with placebo transcutaneous electrical nerve stimulation. We found insufficient evidence from small RCTs to assess effects of low frequency transcutaneous electrical nerve stimulation compared with other or no treatment.

### Vitamin E

One RCT found limited evidence that vitamin E reduced pain compared with placebo.

## UNKNOWN EFFECTIVENESS

### Acupuncture

One systematic review of one small RCT found insufficient evidence to compare acupuncture with placebo or no treatment.

### Behavioural interventions

We found insufficient evidence from two poor quality RCTs about the effects of behavioural interventions🄖.

### Combined oral contraceptives

One systematic review found insufficient evidence about the effects of combined oral contraceptives versus placebo for pain relief.

### Fish oil

One small RCT identified by a systematic review and one additional RCT found limited evidence that fish oil reduced pain and symptoms after 1–3 months compared with placebo.

### Herbal remedies (other than toki-shakuyaku-san)

We found no RCTs of other herbal remedies.

### Surgical interruption of pelvic nerve pathways

One small RCT found limited evidence suggesting that laparoscopic uterine nerve ablation🄖 increased pain relief compared with diagnostic laparoscopy. Another RCT found that laparoscopic uterine nerve ablation reduced pain at 12 months compared with laparoscopic presacral neurectomy🄖. It found no significant difference in pain relief between treatments at 3 months. It also found increased constipation with laparoscopic uterine nerve ablation.

### Vitamin B$_{12}$

We found no RCTs that compared vitamin B$_{12}$ with placebo. One small RCT found insufficient evidence for vitamin B$_{12}$ compared with advice to follow a low fat vegetarian diet.

## UNLIKELY TO BE BENEFICIAL

### Spinal manipulation

One systematic review has found inconclusive evidence on the effects of spinal manipulation compared with placebo or no treatment in pain relief.

**DEFINITION**   Dysmenorrhoea is painful menstrual cramps of uterine origin. It is commonly divided into primary dysmenorrhoea (pain without organic pathology) and secondary dysmenorrhoea (pelvic pain associated with an identifiable pathological condition, such as endometriosis [see endometriosis p 449] or ovarian cysts). The initial onset of primary dysmenorrhoea is usually shortly after menarche (6–12 months) when ovulatory cycles are established. Pain duration is commonly 8–72 hours and is usually associated with the onset of menstrual flow. Secondary dysmenorrhoea can also occur at any time after menarche, but may arise as a new symptom during a woman's fourth and fifth decade, after the onset of an underlying causative condition.[1]

**INCIDENCE/**   Variations in the definition of dysmenorrhoea make it difficult to determine
**PREVALENCE**   prevalence precisely. However, various types of study have found a consistently high prevalence in women of different ages and nationalities. One systematic review (search date 1996) of the prevalence of chronic pelvic pain, summarising both community and hospital surveys, estimated prevalence to be 45–95%.[2] Reports focus on adolescent girls and generally include only primary dysmenorrhoea, although this is not always specified🄣.

# Dysmenorrhoea

**AETIOLOGY/**
**RISK FACTORS**
A longitudinal study of a representative sample of women born in 1962 found that severity of dysmenorrhoea was significantly associated with duration of menstrual flow (average duration of menstrual flow was 5.0 days for women with no dysmenorrhoea and 5.8 days for women with severe dysmenorrhoea; where severe dysmenorrhoea was defined as pain that did not respond well to analgesics and clearly inhibited daily activity; P < 0.001; WMD –0.80, 95% CI –1.36 to –0.24); younger average menarcheal age (13.1 years in women without dysmenorrhoea v 12.6 years in women with severe dysmenorrhoea; P < 0.01; WMD 0.50, 95% CI 0.09 to 0.91); and cigarette smoking (41% of smokers and 26% of non-smokers experienced moderate or severe dysmenorrhoea).[9] There is also some evidence of a dose-response relationship between exposure to environmental tobacco smoke and increased incidence of dysmenorrhoea.[10]

**PROGNOSIS**
Primary dysmenorrhoea is a chronic recurring condition that affects most young women. Studies of the natural history of this condition are sparse. One longitudinal study in Scandinavia found that primary dysmenorrhoea often improves in the third decade of a woman's reproductive life, and is also reduced after childbirth.[9] We found no studies that reliably examined the relationship between the prognosis of secondary dysmenorrhoea and the severity of underlying pathology such as endometriosis.

---

Please refer to CD-ROM for full text and references.

## *What are the effects of treatments in women with pain attributed to endometriosis?*

We found no RCTs comparing medical versus surgical treatments.

### BENEFICIAL

### Hormonal treatment at diagnosis (combined oral contraceptives, medroxyprogesterone)

RCTs have found that hormonal treatments at diagnosis (except for dydrogesterone) reduce pain attributed to endometriosis over 3-6 months of treatment and are all similarly effective. One systematic review found that combined low dose oral contraceptives reduced dysmenorrhoea compared with goserelin during 6 months of treatment, but all women improved 6 months after stopping treatment. Two RCTs found no significant difference in overall pain relief between combined oral contraceptives and gonadorelin analogues. Adverse effects of hormonal treatments are common. One RCT found that combined oral contraceptives are associated with less insomnia and vaginal dryness than gonadorelin analogues.

### LIKELY TO BE BENEFICIAL

### Combined laparoscopic ablation of endometrial deposits and uterine nerve

One RCT found limited evidence that laparoscopic ablation of deposits plus laparoscopic uterine nerve ablation reduced pain at 6 months compared with diagnostic laparoscopy, and that pain reduction persisted for several years in more than 50% of the women. One systematic review of two small RCTs provided insufficient evidence to compare laparoscopic ablation of endometrial deposits plus laparoscopic uterine nerve ablation versus laparoscopic ablation alone.

### Hormonal treatment after conservative surgery

RCTs have found that, compared with placebo or expectant management, hormonal treatment with danazol or medroxyprogesterone for 6 months after surgery reduces pain and delays the recurrence of pain at 12 and 24 months. Treatment for 3 months or treatment with combined oral contraceptives for 6 months does not seem to be effective. Adverse effects of hormonal treatment are common and include hot flushes and bone loss with gonadorelin analogues and androgenic adverse effects with danazol.

### Laparoscopic cystectomy for ovarian endometrioma

One RCT found that cystectomy reduced pain caused by ovarian endometrioma at 2 years compared with laparoscopic drainage. Complication rates were similar.

### TRADE OFF BETWEEN BENEFITS AND HARMS

### Hormonal treatment at diagnosis (danazol, gestrinone, gonadorelin analogues)

RCTs have found that hormonal treatments at diagnosis (except for dydrogesterone) reduce pain attributed to endometriosis over 3–6 months of treatment and are all similarly effective. Adverse effects of hormonal treatments are common and include hot flushes and bone loss with gonadorelin analogues or gestrinone and androgenic adverse effects with danazol.

# Endometriosis

## UNKNOWN EFFECTIVENESS

### Hormonal treatment after oophorectomy

One RCT in women who previously had an oophorectomy found insufficient evidence on the effects of hormone replacement therapy in recurrence of endometriosis compared with no treatment.

### Hormonal treatment at diagnosis (dydrogesterone)

One small RCT provided insufficient evidence to compare dydrogesterone versus placebo.

### Hormonal treatment before surgery

Two RCTs provided insufficient evidence on the effects of hormonal treatments before surgery in women with pain attributed to endometriosis.

### Laparoscopic ablation of endometrial deposits without laparoscopic uterine nerve ablation

We found no RCTs evaluating laparoscopic ablation of endometrial deposits alone in women with pain attributed to endometriosis.

### Laparoscopic uterine nerve ablation without laparoscopic ablation of endometrial deposits

We found no RCTs evaluating laparoscopic uterine nerve ablation alone in women with pain attributed to endometriosis.

**DEFINITION** Endometriosis is characterised by ectopic endometrial tissue, which can causes dysmenorrhoea, dyspareunia, non-cyclical pelvic pain, and subfertility. Diagnosis is made by laparoscopy. Most endometrial deposits are found in the pelvis (ovaries, peritoneum, uterosacral ligaments, pouch of Douglas, and rectovaginal septum). Extrapelvic deposits, including those in the umbilicus and diaphragm, are rare. Severity of endometriosis Ⓖ is defined by the American Fertility Society: this review uses the terms mild (stage I and II), moderate (stage III), and severe (stage IV).[1] Endometriomas are cysts of endometriosis within the ovary. This review assesses dysmenorrhoea, dyspareunia, and non-cyclical pelvic pain associated with endometriosis. For subfertility associated with endometriosis see infertility and subfertility, p000.

**INCIDENCE/ PREVALENCE** In asymptomatic women, the prevalence of endometriosis is 2–22%, depending on the diagnostic criteria used and the populations studied.[2–5] In women with dysmenorrhoea, the incidence of endometriosis is 40–60%, and in women with subfertility is 20–30%.[3,6,7] The severity of symptoms and the probability of diagnosis increase with age.[8] Incidence peaks at about 40 years of age.[9] Symptoms and laparoscopic appearance do not always correlate.[10]

**AETIOLOGY/ RISK FACTORS** The cause of endometriosis is unknown. Risk factors include early menarche and late menopause. Embryonic cells may give rise to deposits in the umbilicus, whereas retrograde menstruation may deposit endometrial cells in the diaphragm.[11,12] Use of oral contraceptives reduces the risk of endometriosis, and this protective effect persists for up to 1 year after their discontinuation.[9]

**PROGNOSIS** We found two RCTs in which laparoscopy was repeated after treatment in women given placebo.[13,14] Over 6–12 months, endometrial deposits resolved spontaneously in up to a third of women, deteriorated in nearly half, and were unchanged in the remainder.

Please refer to CD-ROM for full text and references.

# Fibroids (uterine myomatosis, leiomyomas)

Search date April 2003

*Anne Lethaby and Beverley Vollenhoven*

## What are the effects of medical treatment alone?

### LIKELY TO BE BENEFICIAL

**Gonadorelin analogues (GnRHa) plus progestogen (reduced heavy bleeding and hot flushes associated with GnRHa compared with GnRHa alone)**

One small RCT found that leuprorelin (leuprolide) acetate plus progesterone reduced heavy bleeding compared with leuprorelin acetate alone, and reduced the proportion of women who had hot flushes.

**Gonadorelin analogues plus tibolone (no significant difference in fibroid symptoms compared with GnRHa alone but adding tibolone reduces hot flushes and prevents loss in bone mineral density associated with GnRHa)**

Two small RCTs found no significant difference between GnRHa alone and GnRHa plus tibolone in fibroid related symptoms or uterine and fibroid size. They found that adding tibolone reduced hot flushes, vaginal dryness, and night sweats and prevented loss in bone mineral density.

### TRADE OFF BETWEEN BENEFITS AND HARMS

**Gonadorelin analogues alone**

RCTs have found that GnRHa reduce fibroid related symptoms compared with placebo, but are associated with important adverse effects. One RCT found that nafarelin increased amenorrhoea at 12 weeks compared with placebo. One RCT provided insufficient evidence to compare nafarelin versus buserelin. One RCT found that higher doses of nafarelin increased amenorrhoea at 16 weeks compared with lower doses. Two RCTs found that nafarelin reduced bone density from baseline after 16 weeks' treatment compared with placebo, but that bone density returned to pretreatment levels 6 months after treatment was stopped. Two RCTs found that hot flushes were more common with nafarelin than with placebo or buserelin.

### UNKNOWN EFFECTIVENESS

**Gonadorelin analogue plus raloxifene (insufficient evidence on effects compared with GnRHa alone)**

One RCT found that adding raloxifene to GnRHa reduced fibroid size compared with GnRHa alone. It found no significant difference in fibroid related symptoms or hot flushes.

**Gonadorelin analogues plus combined oestrogen–progestogen (insufficient evidence on effects compared with GnRHa plus progesterone)**

One RCT provided insufficient evidence to compare GnRHa plus oestrogen–progestogen hormone replacement therapy versus GnRHa plus progesterone hormone replacement therapy.

**Non-steroidal anti-inflammatory drugs**

Two small RCTs provided insufficient evidence to assess non-steroidal anti-inflammatory drugs in women with fibroids.

**Gestrinone; levonorgestrel intrauterine system; mifepristone**

We found no RCTs on the effects of these interventions.

# Fibroids (uterine myomatosis, leiomyomas)

## *In women scheduled for fibroid surgery, what are the effects of preoperative medical treatments?*

### LIKELY TO BE BENEFICIAL

#### Gonadorelin analogues

One systematic review has found that GnRHa for at least 3 months before fibroid surgery improve preoperative haemoglobin concentration and haematocrit, and reduce uterine and pelvic symptoms compared with placebo or no pretreatment. Preoperative gonadorelin also reduced blood loss and the rate of vertical incisions during laparotomy. Women having hysterectomy were more likely to have a vaginal rather than an abdominal procedure after GnRHa pretreatment compared with placebo or no pretreatment. Another small RCT found that GnRHa combined with endometrial resection☉ reduced the need for further treatment (either medical or surgical) over 1 year compared with GnRHa alone. However, women were more likely to experience adverse hypo-oestrogenic effects from preoperative treatment, such as hot flushes, vaginal symptoms, and sweating, and were more likely to withdraw from treatment because of adverse effects.

## *What are the effects of surgical treatments?*

### BENEFICIAL

#### Laparoscopic myomectomy (reduces recovery time and postoperative pain compared with abdominal myomectomy)

One RCT found that laparoscopic myomectomy☉ resulted in lower postoperative pain, and a shorter recovery time compared with abdominal myomectomy.

### LIKELY TO BE BENEFICIAL

#### Laparoscopically assisted vaginal hysterectomy (reduces recovery time and postoperative pain but increases operating time and blood loss compared with total abdominal hysterectomy)

We found no RCTs comparing long term effects of laparoscopic assisted vaginal hysterectomy versus other treatments. Two RCTs found that women having laparoscopically assisted vaginal hysterectomy☉ had shorter recovery times and less postoperative pain compared with women having total abdominal hysterectomy☉.One RCT found that women having laparoscopically assisted vaginal hysterectomy had longer operating time and more blood loss than women having total vaginal hysterectomy.

#### Total abdominal hysterectomy

We found no RCTs and an RCT is unlikely to be conducted. There is consensus that total abdominal hysterectomy is superior to no treatment in reducing fibroid related symptoms.

#### Total laparoscopic hysterectomy (reduces postoperative fever, hospital stay, and recovery time compared with total abdominal hysterectomy) *New*

One RCT found that women having total laparoscopic hysterectomy☉ had less postoperative fever, shorter hospital stay, and shorter recovery times compared with women having total abdominal hysterectomy.

#### Total vaginal hysterectomy (reduces operation time, less blood loss, pain, fever, and hospital stay compared with total abdominal hysterectomy and increases satisfaction with operation) *New*

Two RCTs found that women having total vaginal hysterectomy☉ had shorter operation time, less blood loss, pain and fever, shorter hospital stay, earlier return ▶

◀ to work, and greater satisfaction than women having total abdominal hysterectomy. One RCT found that women having total vaginal hysterectomy had shorter operation times and less blood loss than women having laparoscopically assisted vaginal hysterectomy.

## UNKNOWN EFFECTIVENESS

### Thermal balloon endometrial ablation

We found no RCTs comparing thermal balloon ablation🅖 versus non-surgical treatment or hysterectomy. One RCT compared thermal balloon ablation versus rollerball endometrial ablation🅖 in women with fibroids smaller than the average size of a 12 week pregnancy, all of whom had been pretreated with gonadorelin analogues. It found no significant difference between thermal balloon and rollerball ablation in amenorrhoea rates, pictorial bleeding assessment chart🅖 score, haemoglobin, or hysterectomy rates at 12 months. It found that thermal balloon ablation reduced operation time and intraoperative complication rate compared with rollerball ablation. About one third of women reported being "not very satisfied" with either operation.

**DEFINITION**  Fibroids (uterine leiomyomas) are benign tumours of the smooth muscle cells of the uterus. Women with fibroids can be asymptomatic or may present with menorrhagia (30%), pelvic pain with or without dysmenorrhoea or pressure symptoms (34%), infertility (27%), and recurrent pregnancy loss (3%).[1] Much of the data describing the relationship between the presence of fibroids and symptoms are based on uncontrolled studies that have assessed the effect of myomectomy🅖 on the presenting symptoms.[2] The prevalence of fibroids in infertile women can be as high as 13%, but no direct causal relationship between fibroids and infertility has been established.[3]

**INCIDENCE/**  The reported incidence of fibroids varies from 5.4–77.0% depending on the
**PREVALENCE**  method of diagnosis (the gold standard is histological evidence). A random sample of 335 Swedish women aged 25–40 years was reported to have an incidence of fibroids of 5.4% (95% CI 3.0% to 7.8%) based on transvaginal ultrasound examination.[4] The prevalence of these tumours increased with age (age 25–32 years: 3.3%, 95% CI 0.7% to 6.0%; 33–40 years: 7.8%, 95% CI 3.6% to 12.0%).[4] Another large case control study found that the rate of fibroids was higher in women aged less than 50 years; it found a rate of pathologically confirmed fibroids of 4.24/1000 woman years in women aged 50 years or more compared with 6.20/1000 in women aged 45–50 years, 4.63/1000 in women aged 40–45 years, 2.67/1000 in women aged 35–40 years, 0.96/1000 in women aged 30–35 years and 0.31/1000 in women aged 25–30 years.[5] Based on postmortem examination, 50% of women were found to have these tumours.[6] Gross serial sectioning at 2 mm intervals of 100 consecutive hysterectomy specimens revealed the presence of fibroids in 50/68 [73%] premenopausal women and 27/32 [84%] postmenopausal women. These women were having hysterectomies for reasons other than fibroids.[7] The incidence of fibroids in black women is three times greater than that in white women, based on ultrasound or hysterectomy diagnosis.[8] Submucosal fibroids have been diagnosed in 6–34% of women having a hysteroscopy for abnormal bleeding, and in 2–7% of women having infertility investigations.[9]

**AETIOLOGY/**  The cause of fibroids is unknown. It is known that each fibroid is of monoclonal
**RISK FACTORS**  origin and arises independently.[10,11] Factors thought to be involved include the sex steroid hormones oestrogen and progesterone as well as the insulin-like growth factors, epidermal growth factor and transforming growth factor. Risk factors for fibroid growth include nulliparity and obesity. There is a risk reduction to a fifth with five term pregnancies, compared with nulliparous women (P < 0.001).[5] Obesity increases the risk of fibroid development by 21% with ▶

# Fibroids (uterine myomatosis, leiomyomas)

each 10 kg weight gain (P = 0.008).[5] The combined oral contraceptive pill also reduces the risk of fibroids with increasing duration of use (women who have taken oral contraceptives for 4–6 years compared with women who have never taken oral contraceptives: OR 0.8, 95% CI 0.5 to 1.2; women who have taken oral contraceptives ≥ 7 years compared with women who have never taken oral contraceptives: OR 0.5, 95% CI 0.3 to 0.9).[12] Women who have had injections containing 150 mg depot medroxyprogesterone acetate also have a reduced incidence compared with women who have never had injections of this drug (OR 0.44, 95% CI 0.36 to 0.55).[13]

**PROGNOSIS** There are few data on the long term untreated prognosis of these tumours, particularly in women who are asymptomatic at diagnosis. One small case control study reported that in a group of 106 women treated with observation alone over 1 year there was no significant change in symptoms and quality of life over that time.[14] Fibroids tend to shrink or fibrose after the menopause.[5]

Please refer to CD-ROM for full text and references.

## What are the effects of treatments for infertility caused by ovulation disorders?

### LIKELY TO BE BENEFICIAL

#### Clomifene

One systematic review has found that clomifene (clomiphene) increases pregnancy rate compared with placebo in women who ovulate infrequently. Four other studies, including two RCTs, have found no significant difference in ovulation or pregnancy rates between clomifene and tamoxifen. One RCT found that clomifene plus metformin increased pregnancy rates after 6 months' treatment compared with clomifene alone.

### TRADE OFF BETWEEN BENEFITS AND HARMS

#### Gonadotrophins

We found no RCTs comparing gonadotrophins versus placebo or clomifene. One systematic review found that pregnancy rates with human menopausal gonadotrophins or urofollitropin (urofollitrophin, urinary follicle stimulating hormone) ranged from 10–12%. The review found no significant difference in pregnancy rates between treatments. Two RCTs found that pregnancy rates with follitropin (recombinant follicle stimulating hormone) or urofollitropin ranged from 24–27%. It found no significant difference between treatments. The review found that urofollitropin reduced the risk of ovarian hyperstimulation syndrome❻ compared with human menopausal gonadotrophins, although this was confined to women who were not treated with concomitant gonadotrophin releasing hormone analogues. One systematic review and one subsequent RCT found no significant difference in pregnancy rates between gonadotrophins and laparoscopic ovarian drilling, but found that gonadotrophins increased rates of multiple pregnancies. Observational evidence suggests that gonadotrophins may be associated with an increased risk of non-invasive ovarian tumours and multiple pregnancies.

### UNKNOWN EFFECTIVENESS

#### Cyclofenil

One RCT provided insufficient evidence about the effects of cyclofenil in women with ovulatory disorders.

#### Laparoscopic ovarian drilling

We found no RCTs comparing laparoscopic ovarian drilling❻ versus no treatment. One systematic review and one subsequent small RCT found no significant difference in pregnancy rates between laparoscopic ovarian drilling and gonadotrophins. They found that laparoscopic ovarian drilling reduced rates of multiple pregnancies.

#### Pulsatile gonadotrophin releasing hormone

One systematic review of small, weak RCTs provided insufficient evidence to assess pulsatile gonadotrophin releasing hormone treatment.

## What are the effects of treatments for tubal infertility?

### In vitro fertilisation

We found no RCTs comparing in vitro fertilisation versus no treatment. RCTs are unlikely to be conducted. Observational evidence in the UK and the USA suggests an average live birth rate of 22–25% per in vitro fertilisation cycle if intracytoplasmic sperm injection is taken into account. One RCT found that immediate❻ compared with delayed in vitro fertilisation❻ increased pregnancy and live birth rates. Three RCTs found no significant difference in numbers of live births between in vitro fertilisation and intracytoplasmic sperm injection. Observational evidence suggests that adverse effects associated with in vitro fertilisation include multiple pregnancies and ovarian hyperstimulation syndrome.

### Tubal flushing with oil soluble media

One systematic review found that tubal flushing with oil soluble media increased pregnancy rates compared with no intervention. It found that tubal flushing with oil soluble media increased the live birth rate compared with flushing with water soluble media.

### Tubal surgery before in vitro fertilisation

One systematic review in women with hydrosalpinges undergoing in vitro fertilisation has found that tubal surgery increases pregnancy and live birth rates compared with no treatment or medical treatment. One systematic review found no significant difference in pregnancy rates among different types of tubal surgery. One systematic review found no significant difference in pregnancy rates between tubal surgery plus additional treatments to prevent adhesion formation (steroids, dextran, noxytioline) and tubal surgery alone. Another systematic review provided insufficient evidence to assess postoperative hydrotubation❻ or second look laparoscopy❻.

### Selective salpingography plus tubal catheterisation

We found no RCTs on the effects of selective salpingography plus tubal catheterisation.

### Tubal flushing with water soluble media

One systematic review identified no RCTs comparing tubal flushing with water soluble media versus no intervention. It found that tubal flushing with water soluble media decreased live birth rate compared with flushing with oil soluble media.

## What are the effects of treatment for infertility associated with endometriosis?

### Intrauterine insemination plus gonadotrophins

One RCT found that intrauterine insemination plus gonadotrophins increased live birth rates compared with no treatment. A second RCT found no significant difference in birth rates between intrauterine insemination plus pituitary down regulation plus gonadotrophins and expectant management, but it is likely to have been underpowered to detect a clinically important difference. A third RCT found that intrauterine insemination plus gonadotrophins increased pregnancy rates after the first treatment cycle compared with intrauterine insemination alone.

◀ **In vitro fertilisation**

We found no RCTs comparing in vitro fertilisation versus no treatment in women with endometriosis related infertility. RCTs are unlikely to be conducted. Observational evidence in the UK and the USA suggests an average live birth rate of 22–25% per in vitro fertilisation cycle if intracytoplasmic sperm injection is taken into account. Observational studies found inconclusive evidence about whether in vitro fertilisation is as effective in women with endometriosis as in women with tubal infertility.

**Laparoscopic ablation of endometrial deposits**

We found no RCTs comparing laparoscopic surgery versus no treatment or versus ovarian suppression. One systematic review has found that laparoscopic resection or ablation of endometrial deposits increases live birth rates and ongoing pregnancy rates compared with diagnostic laparoscopy. Operative complications were not increased with laparoscopic surgery.

### LIKELY TO BE INEFFECTIVE OR HARMFUL

**Drug induced ovarian suppression**

One systematic review found no significant difference in pregnancy rates between drugs that induce ovarian suppression and placebo. The review found that ovulation suppression agents (medroxyprogesterone, gestrinone, combined oral contraceptives, and gonadotrophin releasing hormone analogues) cause adverse effects, including weight gain, hot flushes, and osteoporosis, and that danazol may cause dose related weight gain and androgenic effects.

## What are the effects of treatments for male factor infertility?

### BENEFICIAL

**Intracytoplasmic sperm injection plus in vitro fertilisation**

We found no RCTs of intracytoplasmic sperm injection plus in vitro fertilisation that assessed pregnancy and live birth rates. Observational evidence in the UK suggests an average live birth rate of 22% per in vitro fertilisation cycle if intracytoplasmic sperm injection is taken into account.

**Intrauterine insemination**

Two systematic reviews have found that intrauterine insemination increases pregnancy rates per cycle compared with intracervical insemination or timed intercourse.

### UNKNOWN EFFECTIVENESS

**Donor insemination**

We found no RCTs on the effects of donor insemination. Observational evidence suggests an average live birth rate of 11%, but it is sometimes unclear whether ovarian stimulation was used in addition to donor insemination.

**In vitro fertilisation versus gamete intrafallopian transfer**

One small RCT provided insufficient evidence to compare in vitro fertilisation versus gamete intrafallopian transfer.

▶

# Infertility and subfertility

## *What are the effects of treatments for unexplained infertility?*

### BENEFICIAL

#### Intrauterine insemination plus gonadotrophins

Two systematic reviews and one subsequent RCT have found that intrauterine insemination plus gonadotrophins increases pregnancy rates compared with timed intercourse or intracervical insemination. One systematic review found no significant difference between intrauterine insemination and timed intercourse or intracervical insemination in pregnancy rates. However, it found that adding gonadotrophins to any of the three interventions increased pregnancy rates per cycle. One systematic review and one subsequent RCT have found that fallopian tube sperm perfusion⊖ increases pregnancy rates compared with intrauterine insemination. One systematic review found no significant difference in live birth rate between intrauterine insemination with or without ovarian stimulation and in vitro fertilisation.

### LIKELY TO BE BENEFICIAL

#### Clomifene

One systematic review found limited evidence that clomifene (clomiphene) increased rates of pregnancy per cycle compared with placebo.

#### Fallopian tube sperm perfusion

One systematic review and one subsequent RCT have found that fallopian tube sperm perfusion increases pregnancy rates compared with intrauterine insemination.

### UNKNOWN EFFECTIVENESS

#### Gamete intrafallopian transfer

We found no RCTs comparing gamete intrafallopian transfer versus no treatment. RCTs found conflicting effects on pregnancy rates of gamete intrafallopian transfer versus other treatments (intrauterine insemination, timed intercourse, and in vitro fertilisation).

#### In vitro fertilisation

Observational evidence in the UK and the USA suggests an average live birth rate of 22–25% per in vitro fertilisation cycle. However, one systematic review identified one RCT in couples with unexplained infertility that found no significant difference in pregnancy rates between in vitro fertilisation and expectant management. RCTs included in the review found no significant difference in live birth rate between in vitro fertilisation and either gamete intrafallopian transfer or intrauterine insemination with or without ovarian stimulation.

**DEFINITION** Normal fertility has been defined as achieving a pregnancy within 2 years by regular sexual intercourse.[1] However, many define infertility as the failure to conceive after 1 year of unprotected intercourse. Infertility can be primary, in couples who have never conceived, or secondary, in couples who have previously conceived. Infertile couples include those who are sterile (who will never achieve a natural pregnancy) and those who are subfertile (who could eventually achieve a natural pregnancy).

**INCIDENCE/ PREVALENCE** Although there is no evidence of a major change in the prevalence of infertility, many more couples are seeking help than previously. Currently, about 1/7 couples in industrialised countries will seek medical advice for infertility.[2] Rates of primary infertility vary widely between countries, ranging from 10% in Africa to about 6% in North America and Europe.[1] Reported rates of secondary infertility are less reliable.

**AETIOLOGY/ RISK FACTORS**  In the UK, nearly a third of infertility cases are unexplained.[3] The rest are caused by ovulatory failure (27%), low sperm count or quality (19%), tubal damage (14%), endometriosis (5%), and other causes (5%).[3]

**PROGNOSIS**  In developed countries, 80–90% of couples attempting to conceive are successful after 1 year and 95% after 2 years.[3] The chances of becoming pregnant vary with the cause and duration of infertility, the woman's age, the couple's previous pregnancy history, and the availability of different treatment options.[2,4] For the first 2–3 years of unexplained infertility, cumulative conception rates remain high (27–46%) but decrease with increasing age of the woman and duration of infertility.[4] The background rates of spontaneous pregnancy in infertile couples can be calculated from longitudinal studies of infertile couples who have been observed without treatment.[4]

Please refer to CD-ROM for full text and references.

# Menopausal symptoms

Search date July 2003

*Edward Morris and Janice Rymer*

## What are the effects of medical treatments?

### BENEFICIAL

#### Progestogens (but serious adverse effects of used with oestrogens)

One systematic review and four additional RCTs have found that progestogen with or without oestrogen reduces vasomotor symptoms compared with placebo. One RCT found no significant difference in vasomotor symptoms between progesterone alone and placebo. Two RCTs found that reduction in vasomotor symptoms was similar with progesterone with or without oestrogen compared with oestrogen alone. Two RCTs found no significant difference in psychological symptoms or quality of life between progesterone with or without oestrogen and placebo or oestrogen alone. The combination of oestrogen and progestogen is associated with an increased risk of breast cancer, stroke, and venous thromboembolic disease.

#### Tibolone

Three RCTs have found that tibolone improves vasomotor symptoms and sexual function compared with placebo. Two RCTs provided limited evidence that tibolone was not as effective for reducing vasomotor symptoms compared with oestrogen plus progestogen. Two RCTs found that tibolone improved sexual function compared with oestrogen plus progestogen.

### LIKELY TO BE BENEFICIAL

#### Phyto-oestrogens

We found limited evidence from seven RCTs that phyto-oestrogens reduced vasomotor symptoms compared with placebo.

### UNKNOWN EFFECTIVENESS

#### Antidepressants

We found no RCTs on the effects of antidepressants on menopausal symptoms.

#### Clonidine

One small RCT found that transdermal clonidine reduced the number and intensity of hot flushes after 8 weeks compared with placebo. However, we were unable to draw reliable conclusions from that study.

#### Testosterone

We found no RCTs comparing testosterone versus placebo. Small RCTs provided no consistent evidence about the effects of testosterone plus oestrogens on vasomotor symptoms or sexual function compared with oestrogen alone.

### TRADE OFF BETWEEN BENEFITS AND HARMS

#### Oestrogens (improved menopausal symptoms but increased risk of breast cancer, endometrial cancer*, stroke, and venous thromboembolism after long term use)

Systematic reviews and subsequent RCTs provided evidence that oestrogen with or without progestogens improves vasomotor symptoms, urogenital symptoms, psychological symptoms, and quality of life in the short term compared with placebo. ▶

◄ However, important adverse effects include increased risk of breast cancer, endometrial cancer, stroke, and venous thromboembolic disease. Adding progestogen reduces the risk of endometrial cancer.

*Should therefore be given with progesterone in women who have not had a hysterectomy.

**DEFINITION**    Menopause is defined as the end of the last menstrual period. A woman is deemed to be postmenopausal 1 year after her last period. For practical purposes most women are diagnosed as menopausal after 1 year of amenorrhoea. Menopausal symptoms often begin in the perimenopausal years.

**INCIDENCE/**    In the UK, the mean age for the start of the menopause is 50 years and 9
**PREVALENCE**    months. The median onset of the perimenopause is 45.5–47.5 years. One Scottish survey (6096 women aged 45–54 years) found that 84% of women had experienced at least one of the classic menopausal symptoms, with 45% finding one or more symptoms a problem.[1]

**AETIOLOGY/**    Urogenital symptoms of menopause are caused by decreased oestrogen
**RISK FACTORS** concentrations, but the cause of vasomotor symptoms and psychological effects is complex and remains unclear.

**PROGNOSIS**    Menopause is a physiological event. Timing of the natural menopause in healthy women may be determined genetically. Although endocrine changes are permanent, menopausal symptoms such as hot flushes, which are experienced by about 70% of women, usually resolve with time.[2] Some symptoms, however, such as genital atrophy, may remain the same or worsen.

Please refer to CD-ROM for full text and references.

# Menorrhagia

**Search date February 2003**

*Kirsten Duckitt and Keri McCully*

## What are the effects of treatments?

### BENEFICIAL

**Endometrial thinning before hysteroscopic surgery**

One systematic review has found that preoperative gonadorelin (gonadotrophin releasing hormone) analogues reduce moderate or heavy periods and increase amenorrhoea compared with placebo, no preoperative treatment, or preoperative danazol. We found insufficient evidence about effects of preoperative danazol or progestogens compared with placebo or no preoperative treatment.

**Hysterectomy (v endometrial destruction) after medical failure**

Systematic reviews have found that hysterectomy reduces menstrual blood loss and the number of women requiring further operations, and increases satisfaction compared with endometrial destruction. RCTs found no differences in effectiveness between different types of hysterectomy. One large cohort study reported major or minor complications in about a third of women undergoing hysterectomy.

**Non-steroidal anti-inflammatory drugs**

One systematic review has found that non-steroidal anti-inflammatory drugs reduce mean menstrual blood loss compared with placebo. One systematic review found no significant difference in menstrual blood loss between mefenamic acid and naproxen, or between non-steroidal anti-inflammatory drugs and oral progestogens, oral contraceptives, or progesterone releasing intrauterine devices.

**Tranexamic acid**

Systematic reviews have found that tranexamic acid reduces menstrual blood loss compared with placebo or other drugs (oral progestogens, mefenamic acid, etamsylate, flurbiprofen, and diclofenac). Adverse effects of tranexamic acid include leg cramps and nausea, which occur in about a third of women using this drug. One long term population based observational study found no evidence that tranexamic acid increases the risk of thromboembolism.

### LIKELY TO BE BENEFICIAL

**Hysteroscopic versus non-hysteroscopic destruction after medical failure**

One systematic review found that hysteroscopic methods of endometrial destruction increased amenorrhoea at 12 months compared with non-hysteroscopic methods. We found no consistent evidence of a difference in amenorrhoea or satisfaction rates among different types of hysteroscopic procedure. RCTs found that complications, such as infection, haemorrhage, or uterine perforation occurred in up to 15% of women undergoing endometrial destruction.

### TRADE OFF BETWEEN BENEFITS AND HARMS

**Danazol**

Systematic reviews found limited evidence that danazol reduced blood loss compared with placebo, luteal phase oral progestogens, mefenamic acid, naproxen, or oral contraceptives, but found that danazol increased adverse effects compared with either non-steroidal anti-inflammatory drugs or oral progestogens. ▶

### UNKNOWN EFFECTIVENESS

**Combined oral contraceptives**

One systematic review found insufficient evidence about effects of oral contraceptives in women with menorrhagia.

**Endometrial resection versus medical treatment**

One systematic review and one additional RCT found no consistent evidence of a difference in blood loss or satisfaction between transcervical endometrial resection◑ and medical treatment. RCTs found that complications, such as infection, haemorrhage, or uterine perforation occurred in up to 15% of women undergoing endometrial destruction.

**Etamsylate**

We found insufficient evidence from one systematic review about effects of etamsylate compared with placebo, mefenamic acid, aminocaproic acid, or tranexamic acid.

**Intrauterine progestogens**

We found no systematic review or RCTs comparing intrauterine progestogens versus placebo. Two systematic reviews and three subsequent RCTs found conflicting evidence about menstrual blood loss, satisfaction rates, and quality of life scores with levonorgestrel releasing intrauterine devices compared with other treatments (endometrial resection, thermal balloon ablation◑, norethisterone, medical treatment, non-steroidal anti-inflammatory drugs, and hysterectomy).

**Dilatation and curettage after medical failure; gonadorelin (gonadotrophin releasing hormone) analogues; myomectomy after medical failure**

We found no RCTs on the effects of these interventions.

### UNLIKELY TO BE BENEFICIAL

**Oral progestogens (longer cycle)**

We found no RCTs comparing oral progestogens versus placebo. One RCT identified by a systematic review found no significant difference in menstrual blood loss between a longer treatment cycle of oral progestogen and a levonorgestrel releasing intrauterine device.

### LIKELY TO BE INEFFECTIVE OR HARMFUL

**Oral progestogens in luteal phase only**

We found no RCTs comparing oral progestogens versus placebo. One systematic review has found that luteal phase oral progestogens increase mean menstrual blood loss compared with danazol, tranexamic acid, or a progesterone releasing intrauterine device.

**DEFINITION** Menorrhagia is defined as heavy but regular menstrual bleeding. Idiopathic ovulatory menorrhagia is regular heavy bleeding in the absence of recognisable pelvic pathology or a general bleeding disorder. Objective menorrhagia is taken to be a total menstrual blood loss of 80 mL or more in each menstruation.[1] Subjectively, menorrhagia may be defined as a complaint of regular excessive menstrual blood loss occurring over several consecutive cycles in a woman of reproductive years.

**INCIDENCE/ PREVALENCE** In the UK, 5% of women (aged 30–49 years) consult their general practitioner each year with menorrhagia.[2] In New Zealand, 2–4% of primary care consultations by premenopausal women are for menstrual problems.[3]

# Menorrhagia

**AETIOLOGY/ RISK FACTORS**  Idiopathic ovulatory menorrhagia is thought to be caused by disordered prostaglandin production within the endometrium.[4] Prostaglandins may also be implicated in menorrhagia associated with uterine fibroids, adenomyosis, or the presence of an intrauterine device. Fibroids have been reported in 10% of women with menorrhagia (80–100 mL/cycle) and 40% of those with severe menorrhagia (≥ 200 mL/cycle).[5]

**PROGNOSIS**  Menorrhagia limits normal activities and causes iron deficiency anaemia in two thirds of women proved to have objective menorrhagia.[1,6,7] One in five of all women in the UK and one in three women in the USA have a hysterectomy before the age of 60 years; menorrhagia is the main presenting problem in at least 50% of these women.[8–10] About 50% of the women who have a hysterectomy for menorrhagia are found to have a normal uterus.[11]

Please refer to CD-ROM for full text and references.

**Search date June 2003**

*Richmal Oates-Whitehead*

We found insufficient evidence on the effects of any treatments on quality of life.

---

## What are the effects of surgical treatments for ovarian cancer that is advanced at first presentation?

### UNKNOWN EFFECTIVENESS

**Primary surgery versus no surgery; primary surgery plus chemotherapy versus chemotherapy alone**

We found no RCTs.

**Routine interval debulking after primary surgery plus chemotherapy**

One RCT found that interval debulking🅖 after primary surgery plus chemotherapy improved overall survival over about 3.5 years compared with chemotherapy alone. A second RCT found that interval debulking had no effect on survival, but it was probably underpowered to detect a clinically important effect.

### UNLIKELY TO BE BENEFICIAL

**Routine second look surgery**

Two RCTs found no evidence that routine second look surgery🅖 improved overall survival compared with watchful waiting in women undergoing chemotherapy after primary surgery for advanced ovarian cancer.

---

## What are the effects of cytotoxic chemotherapy for ovarian cancer that is advanced at first presentation?

### BENEFICIAL

**Adding a single platinum agent to a non-platinum combination regimen**

One systematic review (4 RCTs, 1024 women) found that adding a platinum agent to a non-platinum combination regimen reduced mortality compared with the non-platinum regimen alone.

**Adding a taxane (paclitaxel) to a platinum regimen**

One systematic review and one additional RCT have found that adding paclitaxel to platinum based chemotherapy significantly improves progression free survival and overall survival after primary surgery for advanced ovarian cancer.

**Platinum based chemotherapy (at least as effective as non-platinum regimens)**

A systematic review and subsequent RCTs have found that platinum based regimens are at least as effective as non-platinum regimens, and that adding a platinum compound to a non-platinum combination regimen improves survival.

### LIKELY TO BE BENEFICIAL

**Single agent platinum regimens (as effective as combination platinum chemotherapy, but with fewer adverse effects and better than single agent non-platinum regimens)**

One systematic review and three subsequent RCTs found that single agent platinum based regimens were at least as effective for progression free or overall ▶

survival as combination platinum regimens, and had fewer adverse effects. One RCT found that cisplatin improved progression free survival but not overall survival compared with thiotepa.

## UNKNOWN EFFECTIVENESS

### Relative eficiacy of different platinum agents (cisplatin versus carboplatin) added to a taxane (paclitaxel)

One RCT found no significant difference in progression free or overall survival between adding cisplatin and adding carboplatin to paclitaxel, although it may have lacked power to detect clinically important effects.

### Relative efficiacy of different taxanes (paclitaxel versus docetaxel) added to a platinum agent docetaxel

We found no reliable RCTs comparing the effects of carboplatin plus paclitaxel versus those of carboplatin plus docetaxel.

**DEFINITION** Ovarian tumours are classified according to the assumed cell type of origin (surface epithelium, stroma, or germ cells). Most malignant ovarian tumours (85–95%) are derived from the epithelium of the ovarian surface, and thus are termed epithelial.[1] These can be further grouped into histological types (serous, mucinous, endometroid, and clear cell). Epithelial ovarian cancer is staged using the FIGO classification (see table A on web extra). This review concerns only advanced epithelial ovarian cancer, which is regarded as FIGO stages II–IV.

**INCIDENCE/ PREVALENCE** The worldwide annual incidence of ovarian cancer exceeds 140 000.[2] Rates vary between countries. Differences in reproductive patterns, including age of menarche and menopause, gravidity, breast feeding, and use of the oral contraceptive pill, may contribute to this variation. Rates are highest in Scandinavia, northern America, and the UK; and lowest in Africa, India, China, and Japan.[3] In the UK ovarian cancer is the fourth most common malignancy in women and is the leading cause of death from gynaecological cancers, with a lifetime risk of about 2%.[4] In the UK the incidence was 5174 in 1988[5] and 6880 in 1998.[6] The incidence of ovarian cancer appears to be stabilising in some other countries, and in some affluent countries (Finland, Denmark, New Zealand, and the USA) rates are declining.

**AETIOLOGY/ RISK FACTORS** Risk factors include increasing age, family history of ovarian cancer, low fertility, use of fertility drugs, and low parity.[7–11] Case control studies found that using the combined oral contraceptive pill for more than 5 years was associated with a 40% reduction in the risk of ovarian cancer.[3,7,12,13]

**PROGNOSIS** More than 80% of women present with advanced disease, and the overall 5 year survival rates are poor (< 30%).[6] For advanced disease the major independent prognostic factors appear to be stage, and residual tumour mass after surgery.

Please refer to CD-ROM for full text and references.

## What are the effects of treatments?

### BENEFICIAL

**Diuretics**

RCTs have found that spironolactone improves symptoms of premenstrual syndrome including breast tenderness and bloating, compared to placebo. Two RCTs have found that metolazone or ammonium chloride versus placebo reduce premenstrual swelling and weight gain.

**Non-steroidal anti-inflammatory drugs**

RCTs found that prostaglandin inhibitors significantly improved a range of premenstrual symptoms but did not reduce premenstrual breast pain, compared to placebo.

**Selective serotonin reuptake inhibitors**

One systematic review and subsequent RCTs have found that selective serotonin reuptake inhibitors significantly improve premenstrual symptoms, but cause frequent adverse events compared to placebo.

### LIKELY TO BE BENEFICIAL

**Cognitive behavioural therapy**

RCTs found that cognitive behavioural therapy significantly reduced premenstrual symptoms compared to control treatments, but the evidence is insufficient to define the size of an effect.

**Exercise**

One RCT has found that aerobic exercise significantly improves premenstrual symptoms compared to placebo. Another RCT has found that high intensity aerobic exercise improves symptoms significantly more than low intensity.

**Oestrogens**

Limited evidence from small RCTs suggests that oestradiol improves symptoms compared to placebo, but the magnitude of any effect remains unclear.

**Oral contraceptives**

RCTs found limited evidence that oral contraceptives improved premenstrual symptoms compared to placebo.

### TRADE OFF BETWEEN BENEFITS AND HARMS

**Bromocriptine (breast symptoms only)**

RCTs have found limited evidence that bromocriptine relieves breast tenderness compared to placebo, although adverse effects are common.

**Danazol**

RCTs have found that danazol significantly reduces premenstrual symptoms compared to placebo, but has important adverse effects associated with masculinisation when used continuously in the long term.

**Gonadorelin analogues**

RCTs have found that gonadorelin analogues (GnRH in previous nomenclatrues) significantly reduce premenstrual symptoms compared to placebo. RCTs have found that gonadorelin plus oestrogen plus progestogen (addback treatment) improves symptom scores less than that gonadorelin analogue alone but more ▶

# Premenstrual syndrome

than placebo. One small RCT found a similar reduction in symptom scores with gonadorelin analogue plus tibolone compared to gonadorelin analogue plus placebo. Treatment with gonadorelin analogues for more than 6 months carries a significant risk of osteoporosis, limiting their usefulness for long term treatment.

### Non-selective serotonin reuptake inhibitor antidepressants/anxiolytics

RCTs have found that non-selective serotonin reuptake inhibitor antidepressants and anxiolytic drugs significantly improve at least one symptom of premenstrual syndrome compared to placebo, but a proportion of women stop treatment because of adverse effects. We found insufficient evidence from small RCTs about effects of β blockers and lithium.

## UNKNOWN EFFECTIVENESS

### Hysterectomy with or without bilateral oophorectomy

We found no RCTs. Observational studies have found that hysterectomy plus bilateral oophorectomy is curative. Hysterectomy alone may reduce symptoms, but evidence is limited because of the difficulty in providing controls. The risks are those of major surgery. Infertility is an irreversible consequence of bilateral oophorectomy.

### Progestogens

We found insufficient evidence from one small RCT about the effects of progestogens compared to placebo.

### Pyridoxine

One systematic review of poor quality RCTs found insufficient evidence about the effects of pyridoxine (vitamin $B_6$). In the review, an analysis of weak RCTs suggested that pyridoxine significantly reduced symptoms compared to placebo. Additional RCTs with weak methods found conflicting evidence on the effects of pyridoxine.

### Tibolone

One small RCT found limited evidence that tibolone improved premenstrual symptom score compared to placebo (multivitamins).

### Chiropractic treatment; dietary supplements; endometrial ablation; evening primrose oil; laparoscopic bilateral oophorectomy; reflexology; relaxation treatment

We found insufficient evidence about the effects of these interventions.

## LIKELY TO BE INEFFECTIVE OR HARMFUL

### Progesterone

One systematic review of progesterone has found a small but significant improvement in overall premenstrual symptoms and no increase in the frequency of withdrawals caused by adverse effects, compared to placebo. However, the improvement is unlikely to be clinically important. It remains unclear whether the route or timing of administration of progesterone is important.

| | |
|---|---|
| **DEFINITION** | A woman has premenstrual syndrome if she complains of recurrent psychological or somatic symptoms (or both) occurring specifically during the luteal phase of the menstrual cycle and resolving by the end of menstruation❶.[1] |
| **INCIDENCE/ PREVALENCE** | Premenstrual symptoms occur in 95% of all women of reproductive age; severe, debilitating symptoms (premenstrual syndrome)❻ occur in about 5% of those women.[1] |

**AETIOLOGY/** The aetiology is unknown, but hormonal and other (possibly neuroendocrine)
**RISK FACTORS** factors probably contribute.[2,3] There may be enhanced sensitivity to progesterone, possibly caused by a deficiency of serotonin.[2]

**PROGNOSIS** Except after oophorectomy, symptoms usually recur when treatment is stopped.

Please refer to CD-ROM for full text and references.

# Pyelonephritis in non-pregnant women

**Search date July 2003**

*Adriana Wechsler*

## What are the effects of treatments?

### LIKELY TO BE BENEFICIAL

**Intravenous antibiotics in women admitted to hospital with uncomplicated infection\***

We found no RCTs comparing intravenous antibiotics versus no antibiotics. Consensus holds that intravenous antibiotics are effective, and it is unlikely that a placebo controlled RCT would now be performed. One RCT found no significant difference between intravenous ampicillin plus intravenous gentamicin and intravenous co-trimoxazole plus intravenous gentamicin for relief of symptoms and recurrence of bacteriuria at 28 days. We found insufficient evidence to compare clinical effects of different intravenous regimens.

**Oral antibiotics for women with uncomplicated infection\***

We found no RCTs comparing oral antibiotics with no antibiotics. However, consensus holds that these drugs are effective, and it is unlikely that such an RCT would now be performed. One systematic review and one subsequent RCT in women with uncomplicated pyelonephritis (none of whom were admitted to hospital) have found no consistent differences between co-amoxiclav, or quinolones (ciprofloxacin, norfloxacin, levofloxacin, or lomefloxacin) in bacteriological or clinical cure rates. However, observational data suggest that broader spectrum antibiotics, such as quinolones, are more effective than narrow spectrum antibiotics such as amoxicillin and trimethoprim–sulphamethoxazole in areas with high prevalence of resistance to these drugs.

### UNKNOWN EFFECTIVENESS

**Relative effectiveness of different oral and antibiotic regimens, inpatient versus outpatient management, intravenous versus oral antibiotics**

We found no RCTs in women with acute uncomplicated pyelonephritis.

\*This categorisation is not based on placebo controlled RCTs. Such studies are likely to be considered unethical.

**DEFINITION**  Acute pyelonephritis, or upper urinary tract infection, is an infection of the kidney characterised by pain when passing urine, fever, flank pain, nausea, and vomiting. White blood cells are almost always present in the urine and occasionally white blood cell casts are also seen on urine microscopy. There is no real consensus on the definitions for grades of severity. However, people with acute pyelonephritis may be divided into those able to take oral antibiotics and without signs of sepsis, who may be managed at home, and those requiring intravenous antibiotics in hospital. There is little difference in the application of treatments between men and non-pregnant women.

**INCIDENCE/ PREVALENCE**  In the USA, there are 250 000 cases of acute pyelonephritis a year.[1] Worldwide prevalence and incidence are unknown.

**AETIOLOGY/ RISK FACTORS**  Pyelonephritis is most commonly caused when bacteria in the bladder ascend the ureters and invade the kidneys. In some cases, this may result in bacteria entering and multiplying in the bloodstream. People with structural or functional urinary tract abnormalities are more prone to pyelonephritis that is refractory to oral therapy or complicated by bacteraemia. Repeated urinary tract infections also predispose them to drug resistant organisms.

**Women's health**

**PROGNOSIS**   Complications include urosepsis, renal impairment, and renal abscess. Conditions such as underlying renal disease, diabetes mellitus, and immunosuppression may worsen prognosis, but we found no good long term evidence about rates of sepsis or death among people with such conditions.

---

Please refer to CD-ROM for full text and references.

# Recurrent cystitis in non-pregnant women

**Search date April 2003**

*Adriana Wechsler*

---

## *What are the effects of interventions to prevent further recurrence of cystitis?*

### BENEFICIAL

#### Continuous antibiotic prophylaxis (trimethoprim, co-trimoxazole, nitrofurantoin, cefaclor, or a quinolone)

RCTs have found that continuous antibiotic prophylaxis for 6–12 months with trimethoprim, co-trimoxazole, nitrofurantoin, cefaclor, or a quinolone reduces rates of recurrent cystitis compared with placebo❶, and have found no consistent difference in recurrence rates among different continuous regimens. One RCT comparing continuous daily antibiotic prophylaxis versus postcoital antibiotic prophylaxis found no significant difference in rates of positive urine culture after 1 year.

#### Postcoital antibiotic prophylaxis (co-trimoxazole, nitrofurantoin, or a quinolone)

Four RCTs have found that co-trimoxazole, nitrofurantoin, or a quinolone up to 2 hours after sexual intercourse reduces the rates of cystitis compared with placebo❶. One RCT comparing continuous daily antibiotic prophylaxis versus postcoital antibiotic prophylaxis found no significant difference in rates of positive urine culture after 1 year.

### UNKNOWN EFFECTIVENESS

#### Cranberry juice and cranberry products

One systematic review of two weak RCTs provided insufficient evidence on the effects of cranberry juice and other cranberry products in women with recurrent cystitis.

#### Prophylaxis with methenamine hippurate

One systematic review of weak RCTs provided insufficient evidence to assess methenamine hippurate (hexamine hippurate) in women with recurrent cystitis.

#### Single dose self administered co-trimoxazole

One small RCT found single dose, self administered co-trimoxazole started at the onset of cystitis symptoms was less effective in reducing recurrence rates over 1 year than continuous co-trimoxazole prophylaxis. However, evidence was too limited to draw firm conclusions.

**DEFINITION**  Cystitis is an infection of the lower urinary tract, which causes pain when passing urine, and causes frequency, urgency, haematuria, or suprapubic pain not associated with passing urine. White blood cells and bacteria are almost always present in the urine. The presence of fever, flank pain, nausea, or vomiting suggests pyelonephritis (upper urinary tract infection) (see pyelonephritis in non-pregnant women, p 000). Recurrent cystitis may be either a reinfection (after successful eradication of infection) or a relapse after inadequate treatment.

**INCIDENCE/ PREVALENCE**  The incidence of cystitis among premenopausal sexually active women is 0.5–0.7 infections per person year,[1] and 20–40% of women will experience cystitis during their lifetime. Of those, 20% will develop recurrence, almost always (90% of cases) because of reinfection rather than relapse. Rates of infection fall during the winter months.[2]

**AETIOLOGY/ RISK FACTORS** Cystitis is caused by uropathogenic bacteria in the faecal flora that colonise the vaginal and periurethral openings, and ascend the urethra into the bladder. Prior infection, sexual intercourse, and exposure to vaginal spermicide are risk factors for developing cystitis.[3,4]

**PROGNOSIS** We found little evidence on the long term effects of untreated cystitis. One study found that progression to pyelonephritis was infrequent, and that most cases of cystitis regressed spontaneously, although symptoms sometimes persisted for several months.[5] Women with a baseline rate of more than two infections a year, over many years, are likely to have ongoing recurrent infections.[6]

Please refer to CD-ROM for full text and references.

# Stress incontinence

Search date April 2003

*Bazian Ltd*

---

### *What are the effects of non-surgical treatments for women with stress urinary incontinence?* New

#### Pelvic floor electrical stimulation

RCTs have found that pelvic floor electrical stimulation reduces symptoms compared with no treatment or sham pelvic floor electrical stimulation. One systematic review found no significant difference in cure or improvement rates at 12 months between pelvic floor electrical stimulation and pelvic floor muscle exercises. It found that pelvic floor electrical stimulation was associated with a small number of cases of vaginal irritation and difficulties in maintaining motivation for treatment. RCTs found no significant difference in self reported cure or improvement rates or urinary leakage between pelvic floor electrical stimulation and vaginal cones, but they may have lacked power to detect a clinically important difference.

#### Pelvic floor muscle exercises

One systematic review has found that pelvic floor muscle exercises increase rates of cure or improvement and reduce the number of leakages over 3–6 months compared with no treatment or placebo. It found no significant difference in cure or improvement rates at 12 months between pelvic floor muscle exercises and pelvic muscle electrical stimulation. It found that pelvic floor muscle exercises reduced the number of leakage episodes at 6 months compared with vaginal cones. There was no significant difference in rates of cure or improvement at 12 months.

#### Vaginal cones

One systematic review found that vaginal cones increased self reported cure or improvement rates compared with control over 6–12 months. It found no significant difference in leakage episodes. RCTs found no significant difference in self reported cure or improvement rates over 12 months between vaginal cones and pelvic floor muscle exercises. It found that vaginal cones were less effective than pelvic floor muscle exercises in reducing the number of leakage episodes over 6 months. RCTs also found no significant difference between vaginal cones and pelvic floor electrical stimulation in self reported cure or improvement rates, or urinary leakage over 4 weeks to 12 months, but they may have lacked power to detect a clinically important difference. The most common adverse effect associated with vaginal cones was difficulty maintaining motivation for use but a small number of more serious events such as vaginitis and abdominal pain were reported.

#### Oestrogen supplements

RCTs provided insufficient evidence to assess oestrogen supplements in women with stress urinary incontinence.

◀ *What are the effects of surgical treatments for women with stress urinary incontinence?* New

### Laparoscopic colposuspension

We found no RCTs comparing laparoscopic colposuspension versus no treatment, non-surgical treatment, anterior vaginal repair, suburethral slings, or needle colposuspension. One systematic review found that laparoscopic colposuspension was less effective than open retropubic colposuspension in improving objective cure rates at 1 year. It found no significant difference in objective cure rates at 5 years, or in subjective cure rates at 1 or 5 years.

### Open retropubic colposuspension

We found no RCTs comparing open retropubic colposuspension versus no treatment or sham treatment. One systematic review found that open retropubic colposuspension increased cure rates at 1–5 years compared with non-surgical treatment, anterior vaginal repair, or needle colposuspension but was associated with more adverse effects than non-surgical treatment or needle colposuspension. It found that open retropubic colposuspension improved objective cure rates at 1 year compared with laparoscopic colposuspension. It found no significant difference in objective cure rates at 5 years, or in subjective cure rates at 1 or 5 years. It also found no significant difference in cure rates at 1 year between open retropubic colposuspension and suburethral slings. The review found that open retropubic colposuspension was associated with fewer perioperative complications than anterior vaginal repair or suburethral slings but more than needle colposuspension.

### Needle colposuspension

We found no RCTs comparing needle colposuspension versus no treatment, non-surgical treatment, or laparoscopic colposuspension. One systematic review found no significant difference in cure or improvement rates between needle colposuspension and anterior vaginal repair or suburethral slings, but found that needle colposuspension was associated with fewer perioperative complications than suburethral slings. Another systematic review found that open retropubic colposuspension improved cure rates compared with needle colposuspension at 5 years but that needle colposuspension was associated with fewer perioperative complications.

### Suburethral slings

We found no RCTs comparing suburethral slings versus no treatment, non-surgical treatment, anterior vaginal repair, or laparoscopic colposuspension. One systematic review found no significant difference in cure or improvement rates at 1 year between suburethral slings and open retropubic colposuspension but found that slings may increase the risk of bladder perforation. One small RCT identified by the review found no significant difference in cure rates at 1 year between suburethral slings and needle colposuspension, but it may have been underpowered to detect a clinically important difference in cure rates. The RCT found that suburethral slings increased perioperative complications compared with needle colposuspension.

### Anterior vaginal repair

We found no RCTs comparing anterior vaginal repair (anterior colporrhaphy) versus no treatment, suburethral slings, or laparoscopic colposuspension. One RCT ▶

# Stress incontinence

provided insufficient evidence to compare anterior vaginal repair versus non-surgical treatment. One systematic review found that anterior vaginal repair was less effective than open retropubic colposuspension in increasing cure rates at 12 months or 5 years. It found no significant difference in overall operative complications between the two procedures. It found no significant difference in cure rates at 12 months between anterior vaginal repair and needle colposuspension.

**DEFINITION** Stress incontinence is the involuntary loss of urine on laughing, coughing, sneezing, or straining, which causes a social or hygiene problem. It predominantly affects women. Typically, there is no anticipatory feeling of needing to pass urine. Physiologically, stress incontinence is defined as intravesical pressure that exceeds urethral pressure in the absence of a detrusor contraction.

**INCIDENCE/ PREVALENCE** Stress urinary incontinence is a common problem. Prevalence has been estimated at 17–45% of adult women in the setting of a high income country.[1] During 2000/2001, about 10 000 operations on the outlet of the female bladder were carried out in England.[2] About 4000 were open abdominal operations, about 3000 were vaginal, about 1500 were endoscopic, and the rest were categorised as "other".

**AETIOLOGY/ RISK FACTORS** Aetiological factors include pregnancy and vaginal delivery, obesity, and cigarette smoking.[3–5] We found no reliable data measuring the risks associated with these factors.

**PROGNOSIS** We found no reliable data about the natural history of stress incontinence. Untreated stress incontinence is believed to be a persistent, lifelong condition.

Please refer to CD-ROM for full text and references.

### Search date March 2003

*Iara Marques de Medeiros and Humberto Saconato*

## What are the effects of interventions to prevent mammalian bites?

### LIKELY TO BE BENEFICIAL

**Education**

We found no RCTs of the effect of education programmes on the incidence of mammalian bites. One RCT in school children found that an educational programme increased precautionary behaviour around dogs compared with no education.

### UNKNOWN EFFECTIVENESS

**Education in specific occupational groups**

We found no RCTs of education to prevent bites in specific occupational groups.

## What are the effects of measures to prevent complications from mammalian bites?

### LIKELY TO BE BENEFICIAL

**Antibiotic prophylaxis**

The effects of antibiotic prophylaxis in preventing complications of mammalian bites remain unclear. Limited evidence from one systematic review found that, when all causes and sites of mammalian bite were combined, there was no evidence of a difference in infection rate between antibiotics and placebo. Meta-analysis according to the site of the wound found that antibiotics reduced infections of the hand only. One small RCT in the review found that in people with human bites, antibiotics reduced the rate of infection compared with placebo.

**Debridement, irrigation, and decontamination**

We found no reliable studies assessing debridement, irrigation, decontamination measures, or serum infiltration in the wound. However, there is consensus that such measures are likely to be beneficial.

### UNKNOWN EFFECTIVENESS

**Primary wound closure**

One poor quality RCT comparing primary wound closure with no closure in people with dog bites found no significant difference in the incidence of infection, but the RCT was too small to exclude clinically important effects.

**Tetanus immunisation after mammalian bites**

We found no evidence on the effects of tetanus toxoid or tetanus immunoglobulin in preventing tetanus after human or animal bites.

# Bites (mammalian)

## *What are the effects of treatments for infected mammalian bites?*

### LIKELY TO BE BENEFICIAL

#### Antibiotics for treatment of infected mammalian bites

We found no RCTs of antibiotics compared with placebo for infected mammalian bites. However, there is consensus that antibiotics are likely to be beneficial

### UNKNOWN EFFECTIVENESS

#### Comparative effectiveness of different antibiotics for treatment of infected mammalian bites

One RCT in people with infected and uninfected animal and human bites found no significant difference in failure rate (which was undefined) with penicillin, with or without dicloxacillin, compared with amoxicillin/clavulanic acid.

**DEFINITION**   Bite wounds are mainly caused by humans, dogs, or cats. They include superficial abrasions⊙ (30–43%), lacerations⊙ (31–45%), and puncture wounds⊙ (13–34%).[1]

**INCIDENCE/**   In areas where rabies is poorly controlled among domestic animals, dogs
**PREVALENCE**   account for 90% of reported mammalian bites compared with less than 5% in areas where rabies is well controlled. In the USA, an estimated 3.5–4.7 million dog bites occur each year.[2] About 1 in 5 people bitten by a dog seek medical attention, and 1% of those require admission to hospital.[3,4] Between a third and half of all mammalian bites occur in children.[5]

**AETIOLOGY/**   In over 70% of cases, people are bitten by their own pets or by an animal known
**RISK FACTORS**   to them. Males are more likely to be bitten than females, and are more likely to be bitten by dogs, whereas females are more likely to be bitten by cats.[2] One study found that children under 5 years old were significantly more likely than older children to provoke animals before being bitten.[6] One study of infected dog and cat bites found that the most commonly isolated bacteria was *Pasteurella*, followed by *Streptococci*, *Staphylococci*, *Moraxella*, *Corynebacterium*, and *Neisseria*.[7] Mixed aerobic and anaerobic infection was more common than anaerobic infection alone.

**PROGNOSIS**   In the USA, dog bites cause about 20 deaths a year.[8] In children, dog bites frequently involve the face, potentially resulting in severe lacerations and scarring.[9] Rabies, a life threatening viral encephalitis, may be contracted as a consequence of being bitten or scratched by a rabid animal. More than 99% of human rabies is in developing countries where canine rabies is endemic.[10]

Please refer to CD-ROM for full text and references.

## What are the effects of preventive interventions?

### BENEFICIAL

**Foam alternatives (compared with standard foam mattresses)**

One systematic review has found that foam alternatives to the standard hospital foam mattress reduces the incidence of pressure sores over 10–14 days in people at high risk. We found no evidence of a "best" foam alternative.

**Pressure relieving overlays on operating tables**

One systematic review has found that the use of pressure relieving overlays on operating tables reduces the incidence of pressure sores.

### LIKELY TO BE BENEFICIAL

**Low air loss beds in intensive care (compared with standard beds)**

One RCT in people in intensive care found that low air loss beds☺ reduced the risk of new pressure sores compared with standard intensive care beds.

**Medical sheepskin overlays**

One RCT found that medical sheepskin overlays reduced the incidence of pressure sores compared with standard treatment in people aged 60 years or more who underwent orthopaedic surgery.

### UNKNOWN EFFECTIVENESS

**Alternating pressure surfaces☺; different seat cushions; electric profiling beds; low air loss hydrotherapy beds; low tech constant low pressure supports☺; repositioning (regular "turning"); topical lotions and dressings**

We found insufficient evidence about the effects of these interventions in preventing pressure sores.

### LIKELY TO BE INEFFECTIVE OR HARMFUL

**Air filled vinyl boots with foot cradle**

One small RCT found that air filled vinyl boots with foot cradles were associated with more rapid development of pressure sores compared with hospital pillows.

## What are the effects of treatments?

### LIKELY TO BE BENEFICIAL

**Air fluidised supports (compared with standard care)**

We found limited evidence from three RCTs that air fluidised supports☺ healed more established sores than standard care.

### UNKNOWN EFFECTIVENESS

**Alternating pressure surfaces; debridement; electrotherapy☺; hydrocolloid dressings (compared with gauze soaked in saline or hypochlorite); low air loss beds☺; low level laser therapy☺; low tech constant low pressure supports; nutritional supplements; other dressings; seat cushions; surgery; therapeutic ultrasound☺; topical negative pressure; topical phenytoin**

We found insufficient evidence on the effects of these interventions in healing pressure sores.

▶

# Pressure sores

**DEFINITION**  Pressure sores (also known as pressure ulcers, bed sores, and decubitus ulcers) may present as persistently hyperaemic, blistered, broken, or necrotic skin and may extend to underlying structures, including muscle and bone. Whether blanching or non-blanching erythema constitute pressure sores is controversial.

**INCIDENCE/ PREVALENCE**  The most comprehensive data on prevalence and incidence come from hospital populations. Studies have found a prevalence of 6–10% in National Health Service hospitals in the UK,[1] and 8% in a teaching hospital in the USA.[2]

**AETIOLOGY/ RISK FACTORS**  Pressure sores are caused by unrelieved pressure, shear, or friction; they are most common below the waist and at bony prominences, such as the sacrum, heels, and hips. They occur in all healthcare settings. Increased age, reduced mobility, and impaired nutrition emerge consistently as risk factors;[3] however, the relative importance of these and other factors is uncertain.

**PROGNOSIS**  The presence of pressure sores has been associated with a twofold to fourfold increased risk of death in elderly people and people in intensive care.[4,5] However, pressure sores are a marker for underlying disease severity and other comorbidities rather than an independent predictor of mortality.[4]

---

Please refer to CD-ROM for full text and references.

Search date March 2003

*E Andrea Nelson, Nicky Cullum, and June Jones*

## What are the effects of treatments?

### BENEFICIAL

**Compression**

One systematic review has found that compression heals more venous leg ulcers than no compression. We found insufficient evidence from RCTs to compare the effects of different types of multilayer compression, or multilayer high compression versus short stretch bandages. One systematic review found that multilayer compression increased ulcer healing compared with single layer bandages.

**Pentoxifylline**

One systematic review and two subsequent RCTs have found that oral pentoxifylline increases the proportion of ulcers healed over 6–12 months compared with placebo.

### LIKELY TO BE BENEFICIAL

**Cultured allogenic bilayer skin replacement**

One RCT found that cultured allogenic bilayer skin replacement◉ increased the proportion of ulcers healed after 6 months compared with a non-adherent dressing.

**Flavonoids**

Two RCTs found that flavonoids increased ulcer healing compared with placebo or standard care.

**Peri-ulcer injection of granulocyte–macrophage colony stimulating factor (GM-CSF)**

One RCT found that peri-ulcer injection of GM-CSF increased the proportion of ulcers healed after 13 weeks' treatment compared with placebo.

**Sulodexide**

Two RCTs found that sulodexide plus compression increased the proportion of ulcers healed after 60–90 days' treatment compared with compression alone.

**Systemic mesoglycan**

One RCT found that systemic mesoglycan plus compression increased the proportion of ulcers healed after 24 weeks' treatment compared with compression alone.

### UNKNOWN EFFECTIVENESS

**Antimicrobial agents; aspirin; debriding agents; foam, film, or alginate (semi-occlusive) dressings versus simple dressings in the presence of compression; intermittent pneumatic compression; low level laser treatment; oral rutosides; oral zinc; skin grafting; thromboxane $\alpha_2$ antagonists; topical calcitonin gene related peptide plus vasoactive intestinal polypeptide; topical keratinocyte growth factor 2; topical mesoglycan; topical negative pressure; ultrasound; vein surgery**

We found insufficient evidence about the effects of these interventions on ulcer healing.

# Venous leg ulcers

### UNLIKELY TO BE BENEFICIAL

**Hydrocolloid dressings versus simple low adherent dressings in the presence of compression**

One systematic review found that, in the presence of compression, hydrocolloid dressings did not heal more venous leg ulcers than simple, low adherent dressings.

**Topically applied autologous platelet lysate**

One RCT found no significant difference in time to healing of ulcers after 9 months between topically applied autologous platelet lysate and placebo.

---

## What are the effects of interventions to prevent recurrence?

### BENEFICIAL

**Compression**

We found limited evidence that compression reduced recurrence, and that non-compliance with compression is a risk factor for recurrence.

### UNKNOWN EFFECTIVENESS

**Rutoside; stanozolol; vein surgery**

We found insufficient evidence about the effects of these interventions on ulcer recurrence.

**DEFINITION**  Definitions of leg ulcers vary, but the following is widely used: loss of skin on the leg or foot that takes more than 6 weeks to heal. Some definitions exclude ulcers confined to the foot, whereas others include ulcers on the whole of the lower limb. This review deals with ulcers of venous origin in people without concurrent diabetes mellitus, arterial insufficiency, or rheumatoid arthritis.

**INCIDENCE/ PREVALENCE**  Between 1.5 and 3/1000 people have active leg ulcers. Prevalence increases with age to about 20/1000 in people aged over 80 years.[1]

**AETIOLOGY/ RISK FACTORS**  Leg ulceration is strongly associated with venous disease. However, about a fifth of people with leg ulceration have arterial disease, either alone or in combination with venous problems, which may require specialist referral.[1] Venous ulcers (also known as varicose or stasis ulcers) are caused by venous reflux or obstruction, both of which lead to poor venous return and venous hypertension.

**PROGNOSIS**  People with leg ulcers have a poorer quality of life than age matched controls because of pain, odour, and reduced mobility.[2] In the UK, audits have found wide variation in the types of care (hospital inpatient care, hospital clinics, outpatient clinics, home visits), in the treatments used (topical agents, dressings, bandages, stockings), in healing rates, and in recurrence rates (26–69% in 1 year).[3,4]

---

Please refer to CD-ROM for full text and references.

**Note**

When looking up a class of drug, the reader is advised to also look up specific examples of that class of drug where additional entries may be found. The reverse situation also applies. Abbreviations used: CVD, cardiovascular disease; HRT, hormone replacement therapy; IVF, in vitro fertilisation; MI, myocardial infarction; NSAIDs, non-steroidal anti-inflammatory drugs; STD, sexually transmitted disease.

# INDEX

© BMJ Publishing Group Ltd 2004

# Subject index

# Clinical evidence
## *concise* comments

*Clinical Evidence* is an evolving resource and we welcome any feedback on the content of this issue and suggestions for future issues.

Please photocopy and complete this form, then return it to us.

For UK and rest of world - Fax: + 44 (0) 20 7383 6242, mail: BMJ Clinical Evidence, BMJ Publishing Group, BMA House, Tavistock Square, London WC1H 9JR, UK

For North and South America - Fax: 1-240-646-7005, mail: BMJ Clinical Evidence, PO Box 512, Annapolis Jct, MD20701-0512, USA

### Alternatively, email us at CEfeedback@bmjgroup.com

Name: ............................................................................................

Address: ........................................................................................

..........................................................................................................

..............................................................Email: ............................

## Position

- [ ] GP/Primary Care Physician
- [ ] Hospital Doctor/ Specialist Physician
- [ ] Pharmacist
- [ ] Resident/Registrar
- [ ] Nurse
- [ ] PAM
- [ ] Manager
- [ ] Press
- [ ] Researcher
- [ ] Administrator
- [ ] Librarian
- [ ] Medical Student
- [ ] Member of Public/ Patient Support Group
- [ ] Other.......................

### 1. Comments concerning the selection of studies

Section.............................................................................................

Topic ...............................................................................................

Reference ........................................................................................

Comment..........................................................................................

..........................................................................................................

..........................................................................................................

### 2. Suggestions for future issues

..........................................................................................................

..........................................................................................................

..........................................................................................................

### 3. Other comments/questions

..........................................................................................................

..........................................................................................................

..........................................................................................................

# Estimating cardiovascular risk and treatment benefit

*Adapted from the New Zealand guidelines on management of dyslipidaemia[1] and raised blood pressure[2] by Rod Jackson*

## How to use these colour charts

The charts help the estimation of a person's absolute risk of a cardiovascular event and the likely benefit of drug treatment to lower cholesterol or blood pressure. For these charts, cardiovascular events include: new angina, myocardial infarction, coronary death, stroke or transient ischaemic attack (TIA), onset of congestive cardiac failure, or peripheral vascular syndrome.

There is a group of patients in whom risk can be assumed to be high (>20% in 5 years) without using the charts. They include those with symptomatic cardiovascular disease (angina, myocardial infarction, congestive heart failure, stroke, TIA, and peripheral vascular disease), or left ventricular hypertrophy on ECG.

To estimate a person's absolute 5 year risk:
■ Find the table relating to their sex, diabetic status (on insulin, oral hypoglycaemics, or fasting blood glucose over 8 mmol/L), smoking status, and age. The age shown in the charts is the mean for that category, i.e. age 60 = 55 to 65 years.
■ Within the table find the cell nearest to the person's blood pressure and total cholesterol : HDL ratio. For risk assessment it is enough to use a mean blood pressure based on two readings on each of two occasions, and cholesterol measurements based on one laboratory or two non-fasting Reflotron measurements. More readings are needed to establish the pre-treatment baseline.
■ The colour of the box indicates the person's 5 year cardiovascular disease risk (see below).

Notes: (1) People with a strong history of CVD (first degree male relatives with CVD before 55 years, female relatives before 65 years) or obesity (body mass index above 30 kg/m$^2$) are likely to be at greater risk than the tables indicate. The magnitude of the independent predictive value of these risk factors remains unclear — their presence should influence treatment decisions for patients at borderline treatment levels. (2) If total cholesterol or total cholesterol : HDL ratio is greater than 8 then the risk is at least 15%. (3) Nearly all people aged 75 years or over also have an absolute cardiovascular risk over 15%.

Charts reproduced with permission from The National Heart Foundation of New Zealand. Also available on http://www.nzgg.org.nz/library/gl_complete/bloodpressure/table1.cfm.

## REFERENCES

1. Dyslipidaemia Advisory Group. 1996 National Heart Foundation clinical guidelines for the assessment and management of dyslipidaemia. *NZ Med J* 1996;109:224–232.
2. National Health Committee. Guidelines for the management of mildly raised blood pressure in New Zealand: Ministry of Health National Health Committee Report, Wellington, 1995.

| RISK LEVEL | | BENEFIT (1) | BENEFIT (2) |
|---|---|---|---|
| 5 year CVD risk (non-fatal and fatal) | | CVD events prevented per 100 treated for 5 years* | Number needed to treat for 5 years to prevent one event* |
| Very High | >30% | >10 per 100 | <10 |
| | 25–30% | 9 per 100 | 11 |
| | 20–25% | 7.5 per 100 | 13 |
| High | 15–20% | 6 per 100 | 16 |
| Moderate | 10–15% | 4 per 100 | 25 |
| Mild | 5–10% | 2.5 per 100 | 40 |
| | 2.5–5% | 1.25 per 100 | 80 |
| | <2.5% | <0.8 per 100 | >120 |

*Based on a 20% reduction in total cholesterol or a reduction in blood pressure of 10–15 mm Hg systolic or 5–10 mm Hg diastolic, which is estimated to reduce CVD risk by about a third over 5 years.

# Estimating cardiovascular risk and treatment benefit

**RISK LEVEL: MEN**

## NO DIABETES

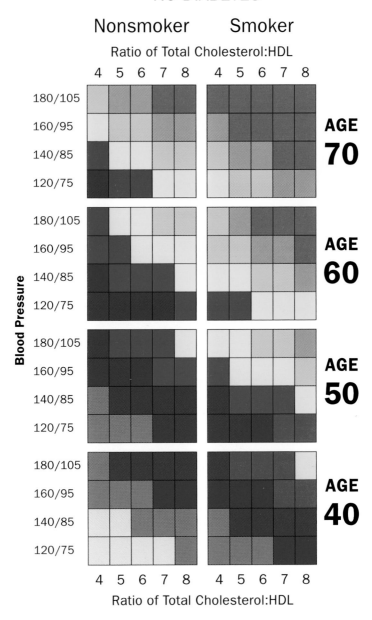

Nonsmoker　　　Smoker

Ratio of Total Cholesterol:HDL

AGE 70

AGE 60

AGE 50

AGE 40

Blood Pressure

Ratio of Total Cholesterol:HDL

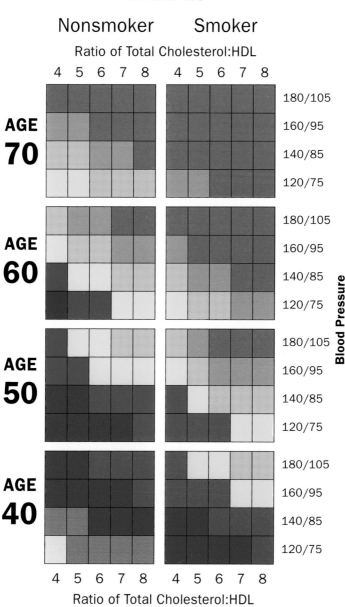

## DIABETES

Nonsmoker      Smoker

Ratio of Total Cholesterol:HDL

# Estimating cardiovascular risk and treatment benefit

**RISK LEVEL: WOMEN**

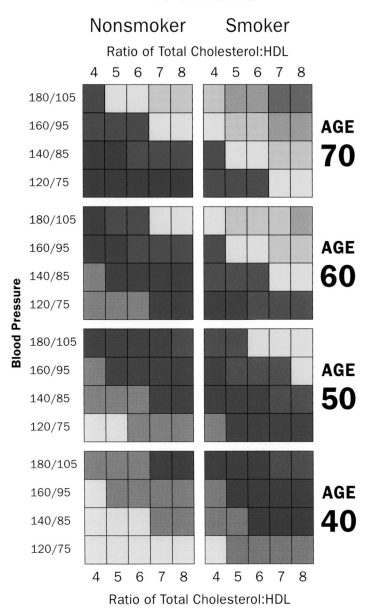

## DIABETES

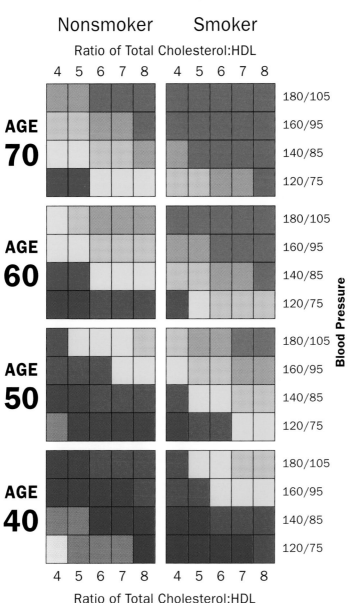

Nonsmoker     Smoker

Ratio of Total Cholesterol:HDL

AGE 70

AGE 60

AGE 50

AGE 40

Blood Pressure

Ratio of Total Cholesterol:HDL

# The number needed to treat: adjusting for baseline risk

*Adapted with permission from Chatellier et al, 1996[1]*

## BACKGROUND

The number needed to treat (NNT) to avoid a single additional adverse outcome is a meaningful way of expressing the benefit of an active treatment over a control. It can be used both to summarise the results of a therapeutic trial or series of trials and to help medical decision making about an individual patient.

If the absolute risk of adverse outcomes in a therapeutic trial is ARC in the control group and ART in the treatment group, then the absolute risk reduction (ARR) is defined as (ARC − ART). The NNT is defined as the inverse of the ARR:

$$NNT = 1/(ARC - ART)$$

Since the Relative Risk Reduction (RRR) is defined as (ARC − ART)/ARC, it follows that NNT, RRR, and ARC are related by their definitions in the following way:

$$NNT \times RRR \times ARC = 1$$

This relationship can be used to estimate the likely benefits of a treatment in populations with different levels of baseline risk (that is different levels of ARC). This allows extrapolation of the results of a trial or meta-analysis to people with different baseline risks. Ideally, there should be experimental evidence of the RRR in each population. However, in many trials, subgroup analyses show that the RRR is approximately constant in groups of patients with different characteristics. Cook and Sackett therefore proposed that decisions about individual patients could be made by using the NNT calculated from the RRR measured in trials and the baseline risk in the absence of treatment estimated for the individual patient.[2]

The method may not apply to periods of time different to that studied in the original trials.

## USING THE NOMOGRAM

The nomogram shown on the next page allows the NNT to be found directly without any calculation: a straight line should be drawn from the point corresponding to the estimated absolute risk for the patient on the left hand scale to the point corresponding to the relative risk reduction stated in a trial or meta-analysis on the central scale. The intercept of this line with the right hand scale gives the NNT. By taking the upper and lower limits of the confidence interval of the RRR, the upper and lower limits of the NNT can be estimated.

## REFERENCES

1. Chatellier G, Zapletal E, Lemaitre D, *et al*. The number needed to treat: a clinically useful nomogram in its proper context. *BMJ* 1996;312:426–429.
2. Cook RJ, Sackett DL. The number needed to treat: a clinically useful measure of treatment effect. *BMJ* 1995;310:452–454.

# The number needed to treat

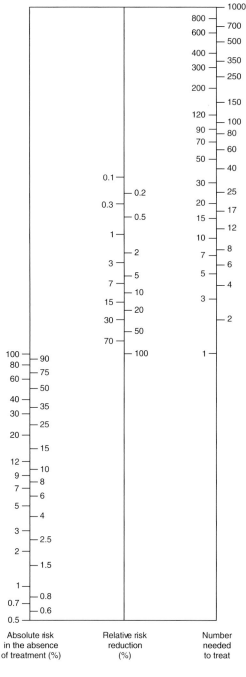

**FIGURE** Nomogram for calculating the number needed to treat.
Published with permission.[1]

# Clinical Evidence mini CD-ROM

The *Clinical Evidence* mini CD-ROM allows you to:
- Refer to the full *Clinical Evidence* content, including clinical questions, summary, and background information, evidence detail, figures, tables and appendices
- Choose the method of navigation you prefer, through the table of contents, topic sections, or the search engine
- Hyperlink references to abstracts where they appear on PubMed and Cochrane (Internet access required)
- Hyperlink to the glossary, figures, tables, and references
- Print the full text of the topics

**To access *Clinical Evidence* help:**
- From within the *Clinical Evidence* CD-ROM, simply click on the link at the top of the screen or from within Windows, select Programs > Clinical Evidence > Help (if you have already installed *Clinical Evidence*)
- For technical help, please go to the FAQs at www.clinicalevidence.com
- For damaged CD-ROMs please contact:
  BMJ Publishing Group • Tel: +44(0) 207 383 6270 • subscriptions@bmjgroup.com (UK/ROW)
  For individual subscriptions • Tel: +1 800 373 2897/+1 240 646 7000 • clinevid@pmds.com (USA)
  For individuals receiving *Clinical Evidence* courtesy of United Health Foundation:
  ce@unitedhealthfoundation.org

## To install *Clinical Evidence*

(i) Exit from any programs you have running.

(ii) Insert the *Clinical Evidence* Installation CD-ROM into the CD-ROM drive. The installation starts automatically (if it does not, select Run from the Start menu and enter d:\setup (where d: is your CD-ROM drive letter).

(iii) Follow the on-screen instructions. As part of this process, you can install Adobe Acrobat Reader so you can efficiently print *Clinical Evidence* topics — this can also be installed later by following the instructions below. An additional 20 Mbytes of hard disk space is required for this.

## Minimum system requirements

An IBM compatible PC with at least this specification:
- 60 MBytes hard disk space
- 90 MHz processor
- 32 MBytes of RAM
- CD-ROM drive
- Modem, if you want to access the Internet for updates, etc.
- SVGA monitor recommended

## Operating systems

This software has been tested with the following operating systems:
- Microsoft Windows 95
- Microsoft Windows 98
- Microsoft Windows 2000 Professional
- Microsoft Windows XP Professional
- Microsoft Windows NT SP6
- Microsoft Windows 2000 Server

### *Please note*

Windows XP Home Edition may require special handling. Please refer to the appropriate section in the Readme file, or access the full text at www.clinicalevidence.com. The Readme file is located at:
Start > Programs > Clinical Evidence > Readme (if you have already installed *Clinical Evidence*) or contact technical help.

## Browsers

Microsoft Internet Explorer 5.5 is the recommended browser, and should be your default browser when installing *Clinical Evidence*.
This software has been tested with the following browsers:
- Microsoft Internet Explorer 5.0 (English)
- Microsoft Internet Explorer 5.5 (English)
- Microsoft Internet Explorer 6.0 (English)
- Netscape 4.7 (English)
- Netscape 6.0 (English)

### *Please note*

Microsoft Internet Explorer 4 is not a supported browser.
Microsoft Internet Explorer 6 is not compatible with Windows 95.
Internet Explorer 5.5 and 6.0 are available on the installation CD-ROM — see below for details.

## To install Microsoft Internet Explorer v5.5

(i) With the *Clinical Evidence* Installation CD-ROM in the CD-ROM drive, select Run from the Start menu.

(ii) Type d:\other\ie5.5\ie5setup and click OK (where d: is your CD-ROM drive letter).

(iii) Follow the on-screen instructions. The typical installation requires approximately 17 Mbytes of hard disk space.

## To install Microsoft Internet Explorer v6.0

(i) With the *Clinical Evidence* Installation CD-ROM in the CD-ROM drive, select Run from the Start menu.

(ii) Type d:\other\ie6.0\ie6setup and click OK (where d: is your CD-ROM drive letter).

(iii) Follow the on-screen instructions. The typical installation requires approximately 25 Mbytes of hard disk space.

## To install Adobe Acrobat Reader v5.0.5

(i) With the *Clinical Evidence* Installation CD-ROM in the CD-ROM drive, select Run from the Start menu.

(ii) Type d:\Adobe\ar505enu and click OK (where d: is your CD-ROM drive letter).

(iii) Follow the on-screen instructions.

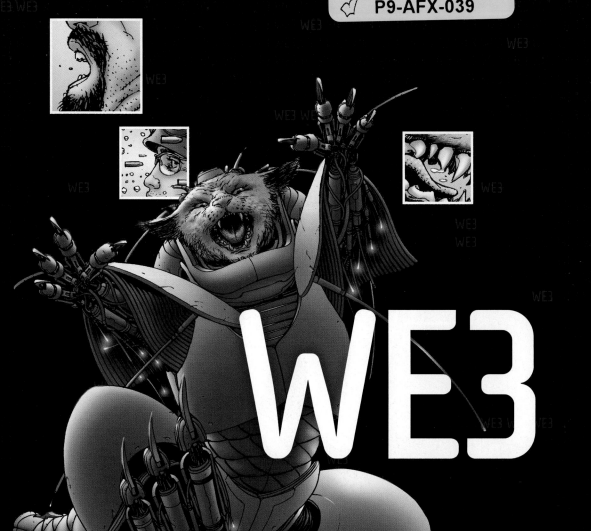

**GRANT MORRISON**
writer

**FRANK QUITELY**
artist

**JAMIE GRANT**
colorist and digital inker

**TODD KLEIN**
letterer

WE3 created by
**GRANT MORRISON AND FRANK QUITELY**

RGER Editor – Original Series WE3 PORNSAK PICHETSHOTE Assistant Editor – Original Series WE3 SCOTT NYBAKKEN Editor
BIN BROSTERMAN Design Director – Books WE3 ROBBIE BIEDERMAN Publication Design

OND Executive Editor – Vertigo
ALZ Senior VP – Vertigo and Integrated Publishing

LSON President WE3 DAN DIDIO and JIM LEE Co-Publishers WE3 GEOFF JOHNS Chief Creative Officer
O Executive VP – Sales, Marketing and Business Development WE3 AMY GENKINS Senior VP – Business and Legal Affairs
RDINER Senior VP – Finance WE3 JEFF BOISON VP – Publishing Planning WE3 MARK CHIARELLO VP – Art Direction and Design
NINGHAM VP – Marketing WE3 TERRI CUNNINGHAM VP – Editorial Administration WE3 ALISON GILL Senior VP – Manufacturing and Operations
N VP – Business and Legal Affairs, Publishing WE3 JACK MAHAN VP – Business Affairs, Talent WE3 NICK NAPOLITANO VP – Manufacturing Administration
A VP – Book Sales WE3 COURTNEY SIMMONS Senior VP – Publicity WE3 BOB WAYNE Senior VP – Sales

gn by Frank Quitely and Brainchild Studios/NYC.

adway, New York, NY 10019. A Warner Bros. Entertainment Company.
the USA. First Printing.  ISBN: 978-1-4012-4302-9

SUSTAINABLE
FORESTRY
INITIATIVE

ed Chain of Custody
20% Certified Forest Content

www.sfiprogram.org
SFI-01042
PPLIES TO TEAT STOCK ONLY

f Congress Cataloging-in-Publication Data

Grant.
ant Morrison, Frank Quitely.

lly published in single magazine form as We3 1-3."
3-1-4012-4302-9 [alk. paper]
gs--Comic books, strips, etc. 2.  Graphic novels.  I. Quitely, Frank, 1968- II. Title. III. Title: We 3. IV. Title: We three.
M677W44 2012
311--dc23
                        2012037331

# MISSING
MEDIUM SIZE DOG - BROWN LABRADOR MIXED
FRIENDLY & APPROACHABLE
ANSWERS TO 'BANDIT'
REWARD OFFERED FOR ANY INFORMATION
PHONE: 555-2314

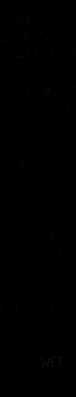

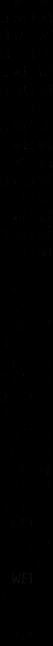
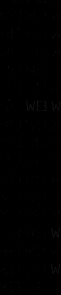

CHAPTER 1

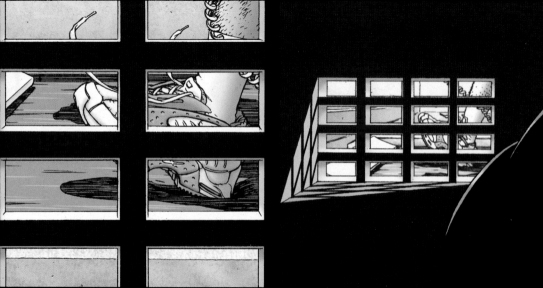

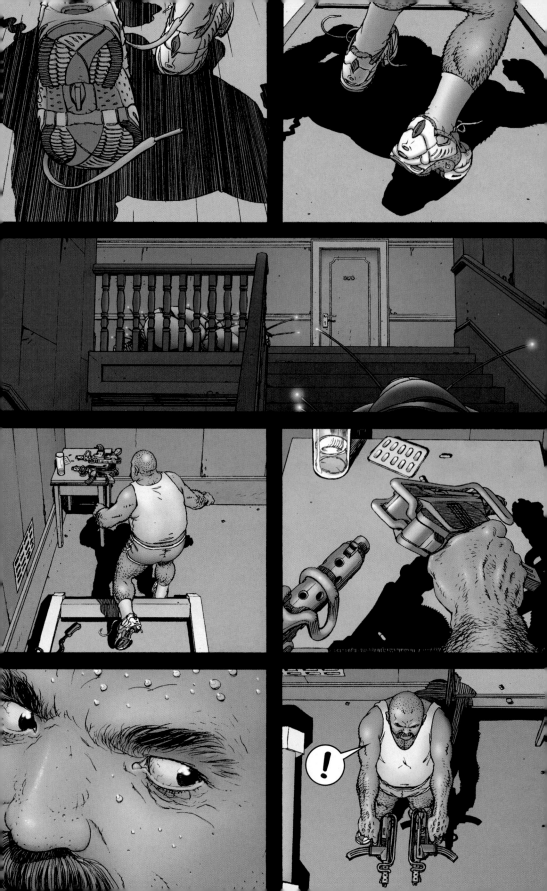

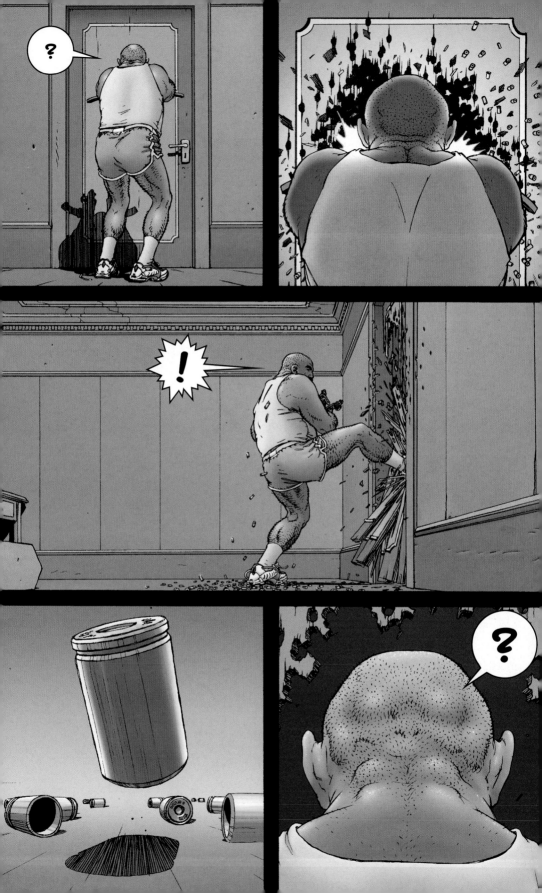

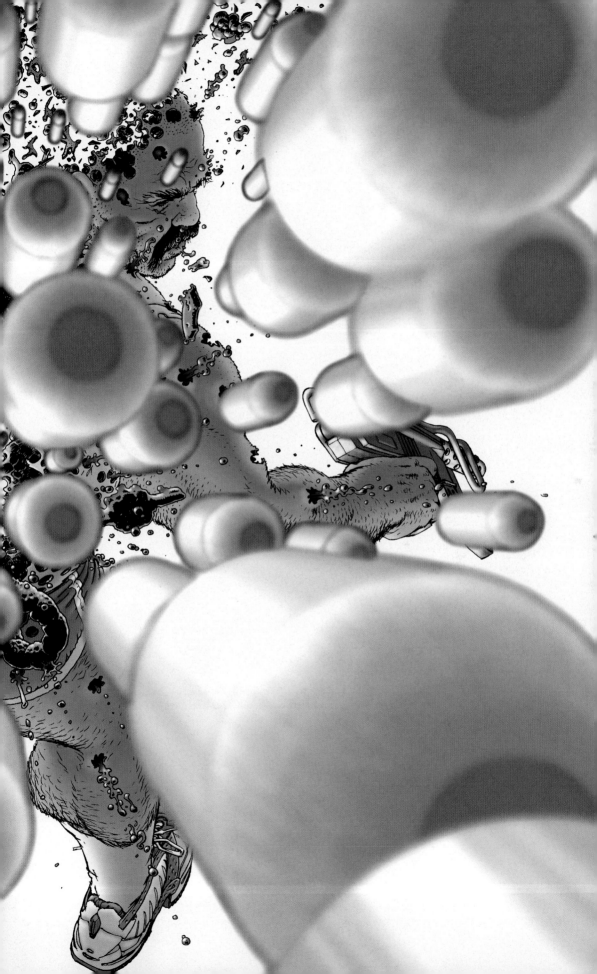

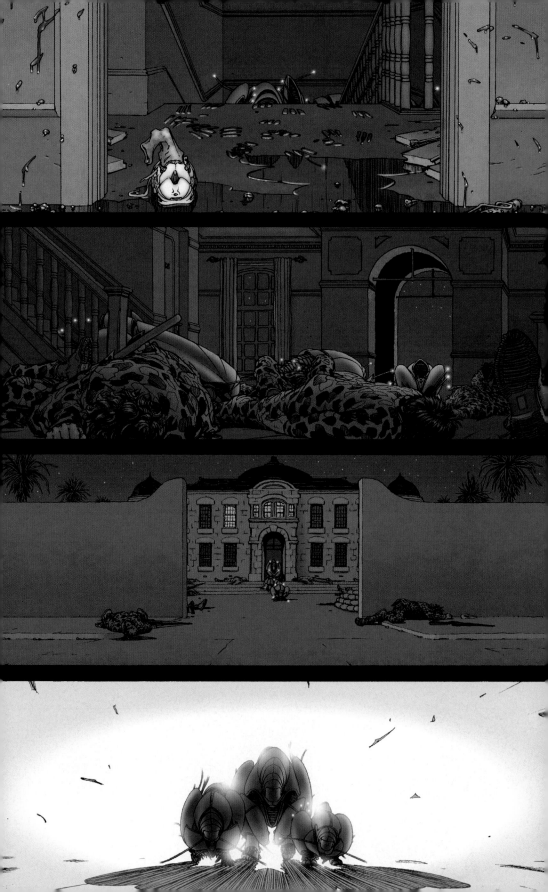

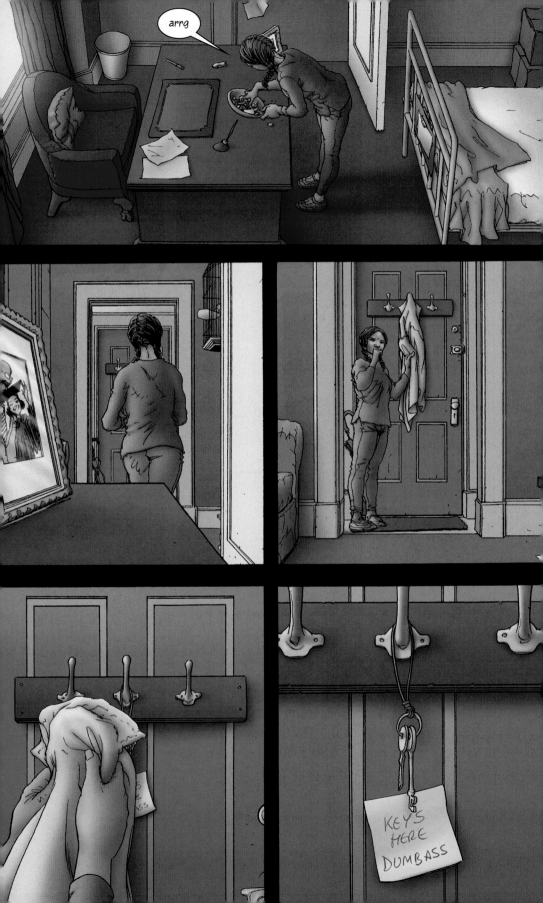

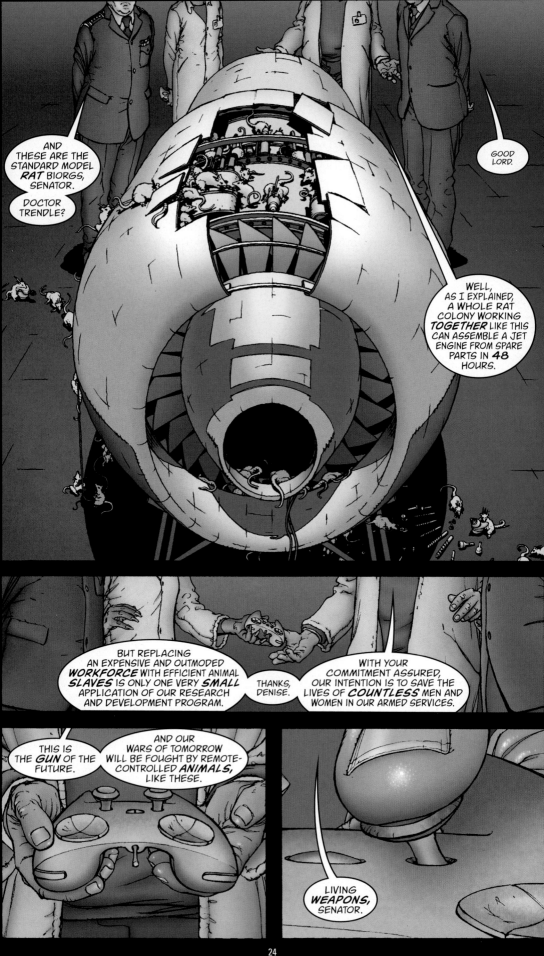

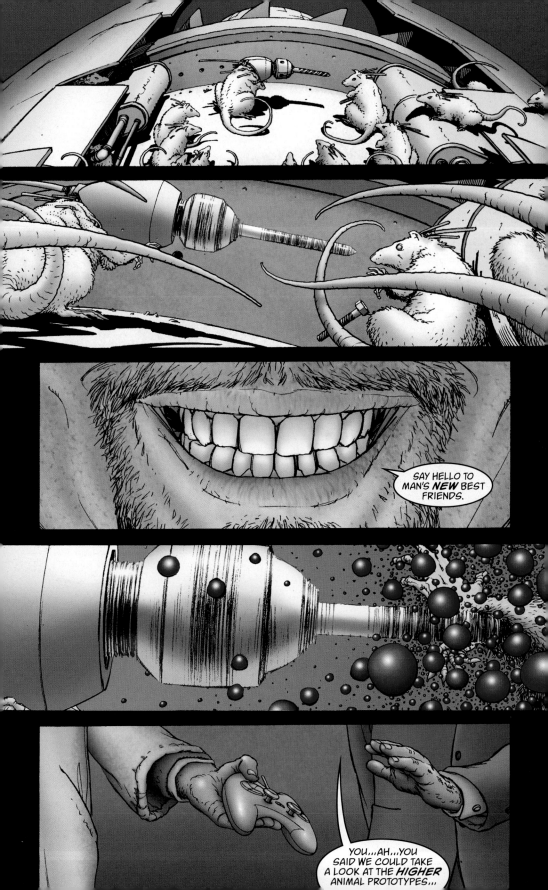

THIS IS **ROSEANNE BERRY,** OUR VERY OWN "DOCTOR DOLITTLE."

THE **ANIMALS** KEEP HER ENTERTAINED FOR **HOURS,** BUT SHE OFTEN HAS A HARD TIME COMMUNICATING WITH US MERE **HUMANS...**

...**DON'T** YOU, ROSEANNE?

...AS I WAS SAYING, GENTLEMEN; OUR **RABBIT** BIORG WAS DESIGNED AND TRAINED TO DELIVER MINES AND POISON GAS.

YOU CAN THINK OF THE DOG AS A SMALL **TANK,** THE CAT, A LETHAL STEALTH MACHINE.

ANIMAL WEAPON 3

OF COURSE, IT'S THE HARDWARE THAT DOES THE **REAL** WORK.

AND SHOULD THEY EVER FALL INTO ENEMY HANDS, AND ANY ATTEMPT IS MADE TO **REMOVE** THE TECHNOLOGY...

IMMEDIATE SELF-DESTRUCT.

THE ANIMALS **ARE** THE HARDWARE, SIR.

3

1! MR. WAH-SHING-TON WD LIK 2 MEET U.

HA.

HELLO, BOY.

AND HOW ARE **YOU** TODAY?

I. M. GUD.

R. GUD

"MR. WAH-SHING TON."

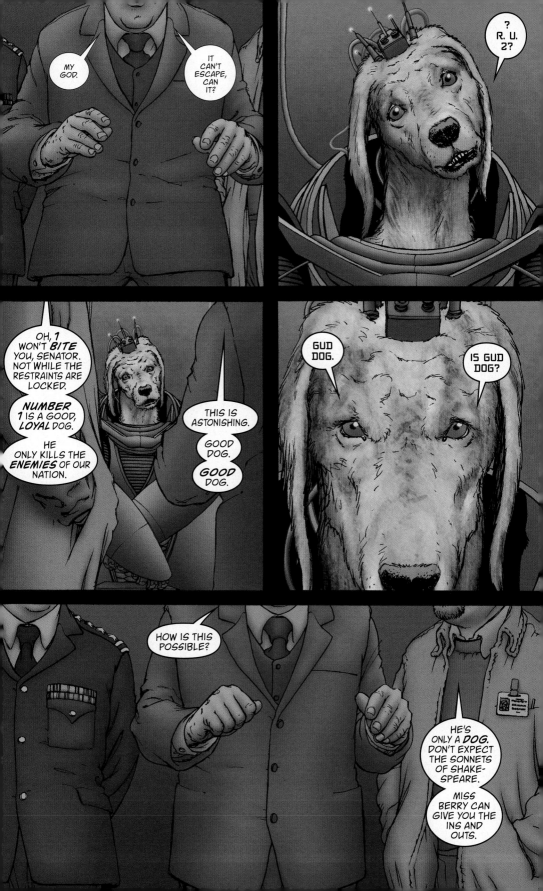

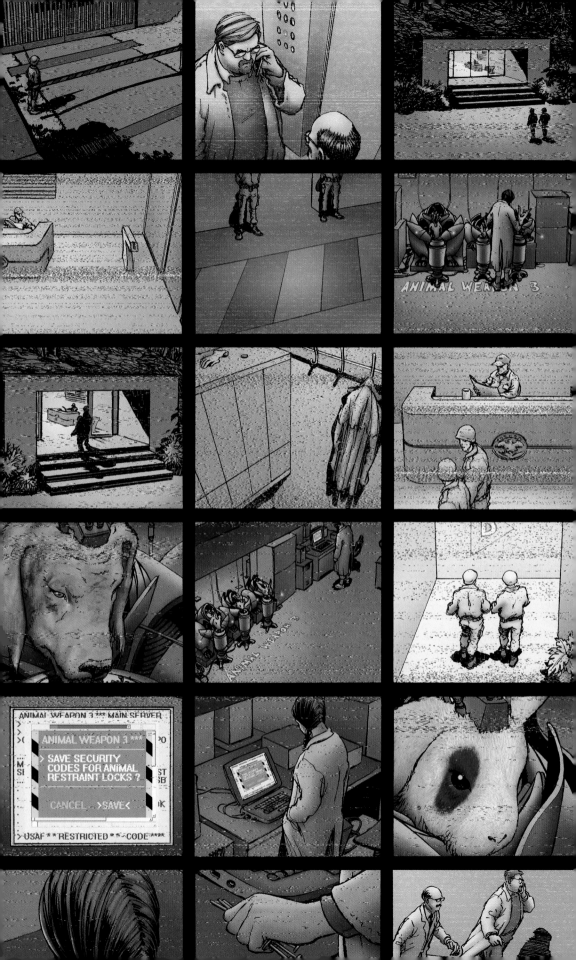

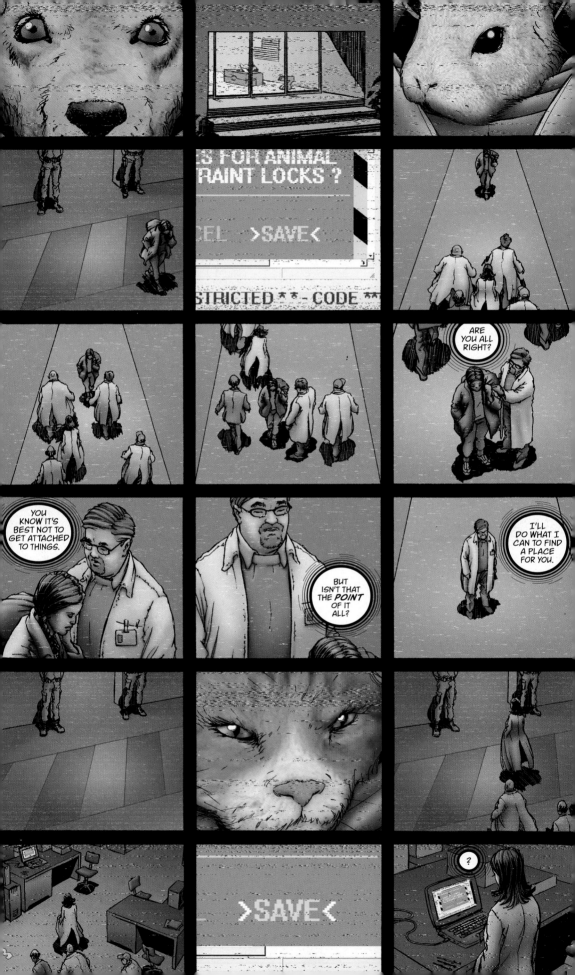

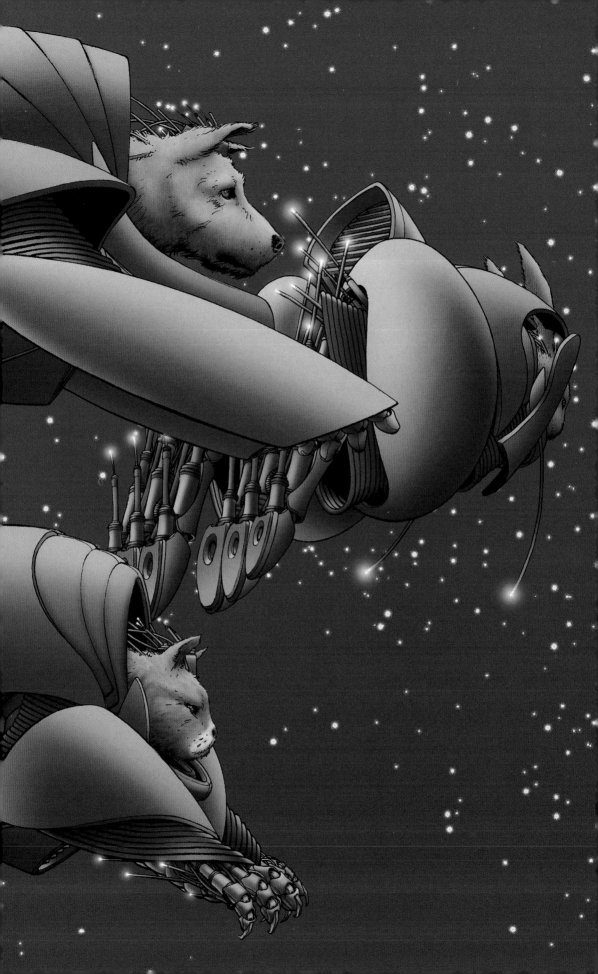

# L◦ST

**TINKER** IS A GINGER-STRIPED CAT WITH A WHITE NOSE & WHITE TIP OF HER TAIL. LAST SEEN OUTSIDE THE LAUNDROMAT ON BELLTOWER STREET. PLEASE CALL **CARLA** WITH ANY INFO AT 555-3899. THANKS.

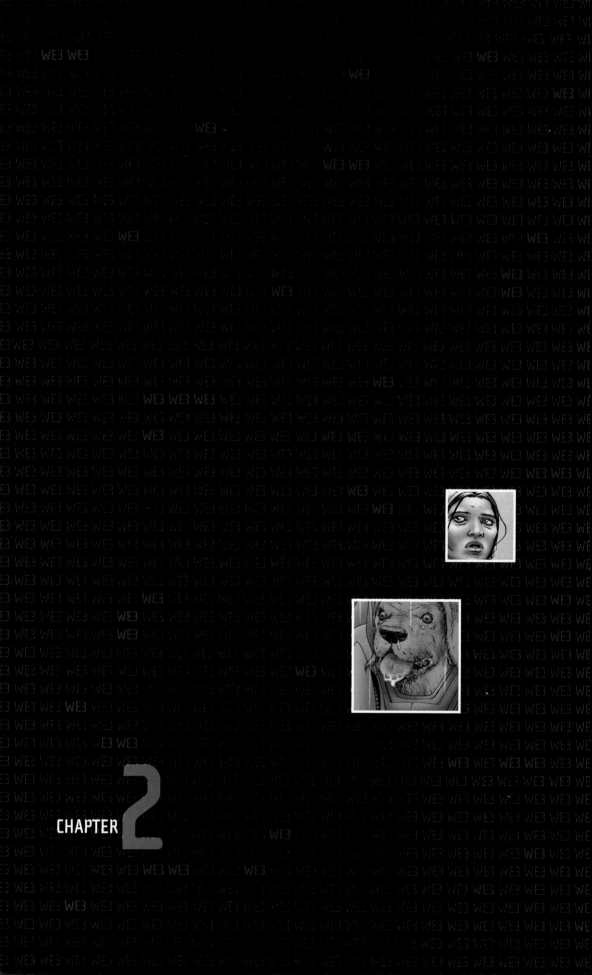

CHAPTER 2

THEY JUST DON'T UNDERSTAND WHAT WE'VE MADE HERE.

THOSE POOR MEN.

SEE WHAT YOU'VE DONE?

OH, THOSE POOR MEN.

AIM FOR THE HEADS!

AIM FOR--

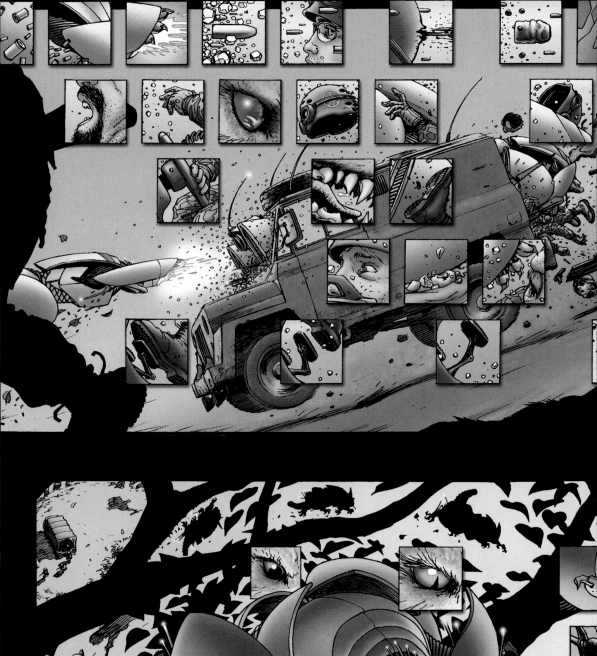
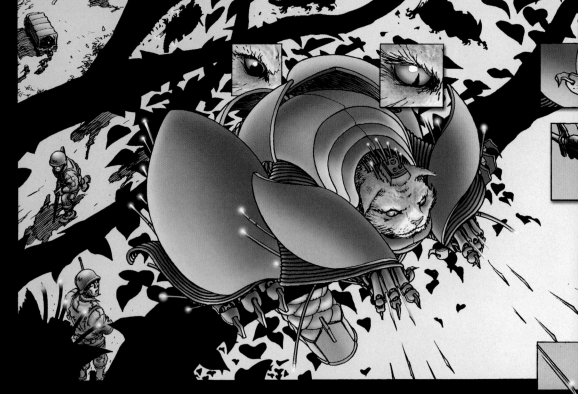

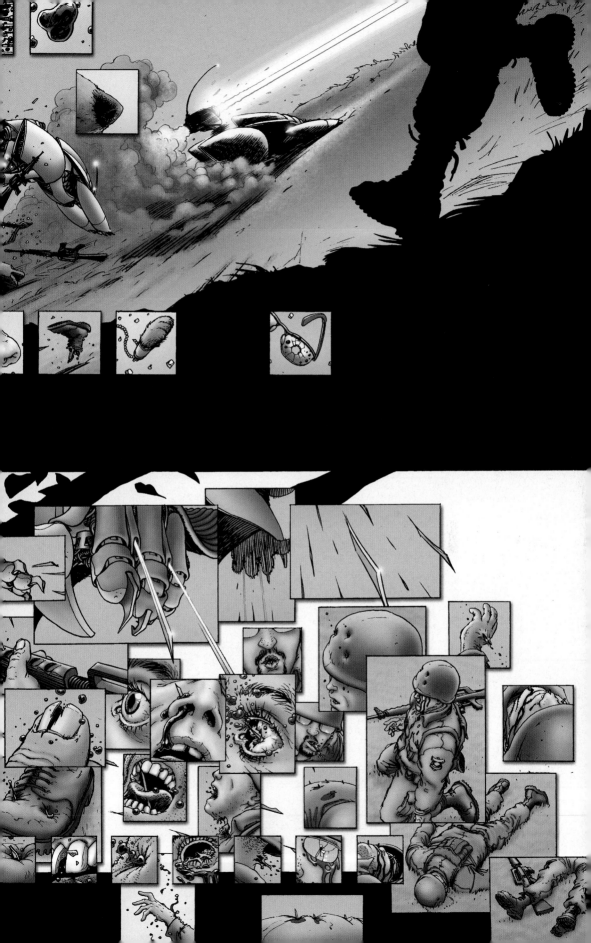

MIAAAAAUUU!

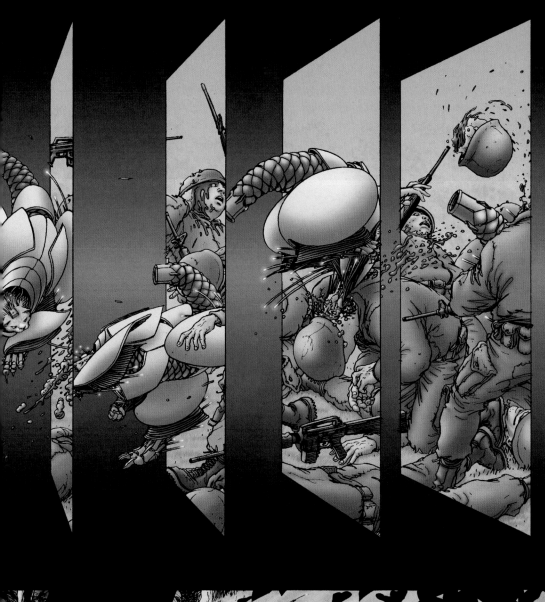

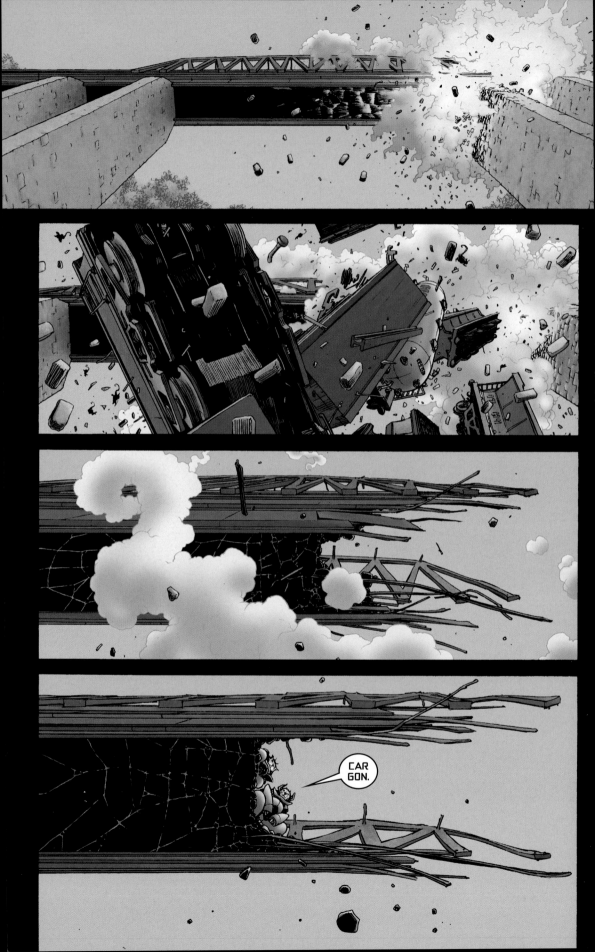

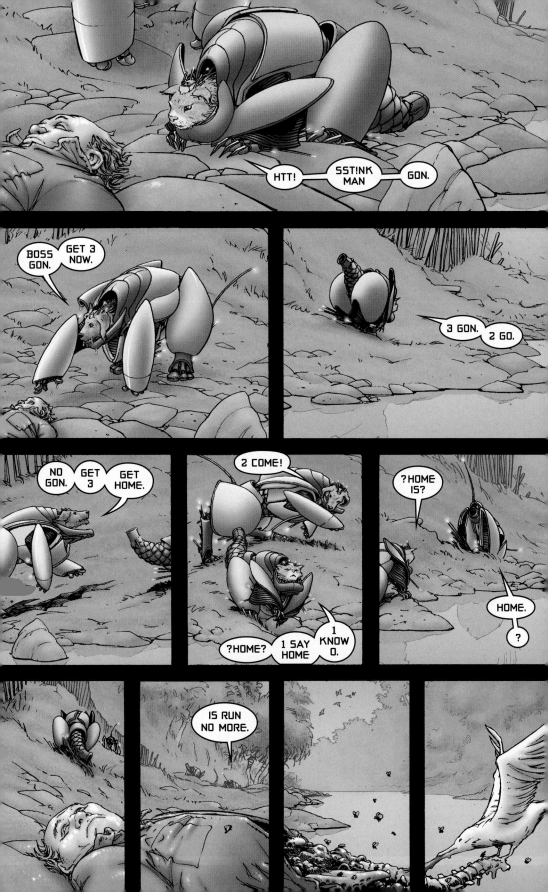

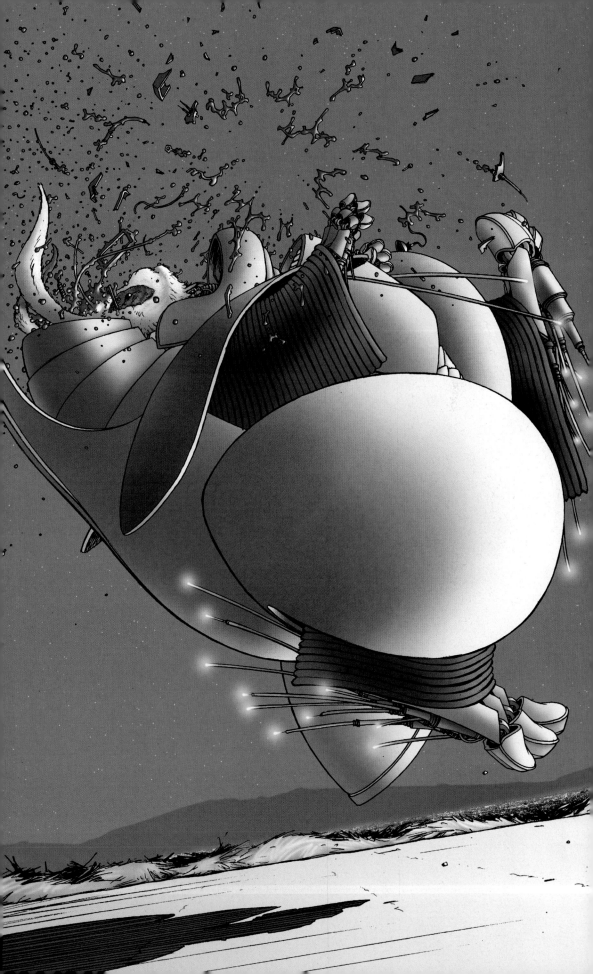

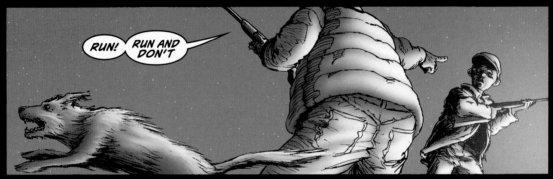

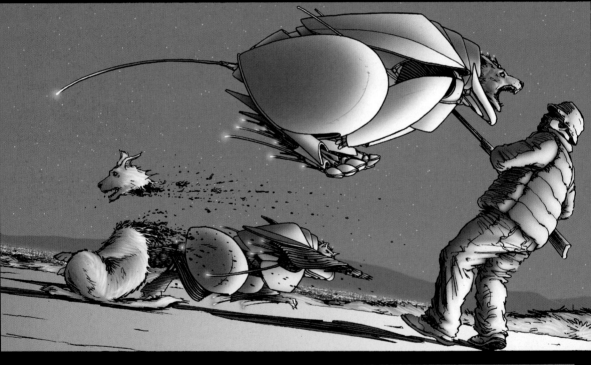

## Lost Rabbit

Can you help us find Pirate? He is white with a brown patch over his eye. He likes lettuce and carrots.
Thank you Johnny and Claire

(PLS PHONE - MRS MORTIMER : 555 6783)

CHAPTER 3

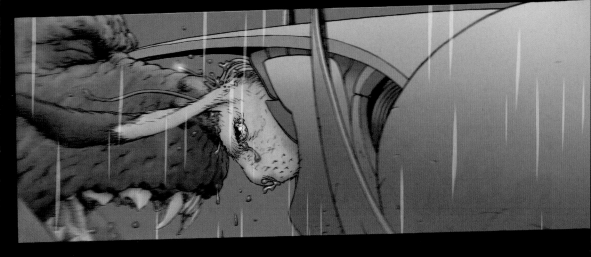

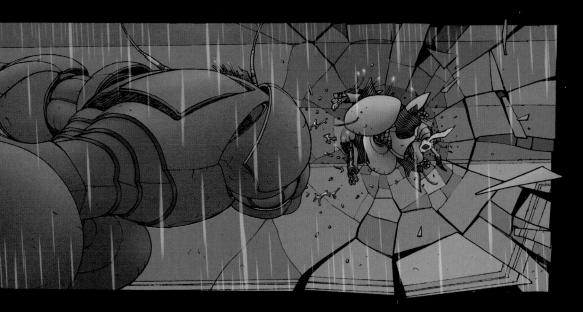

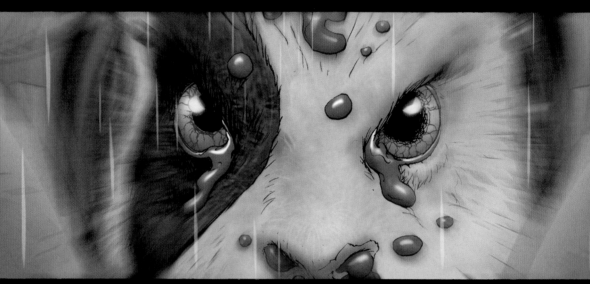

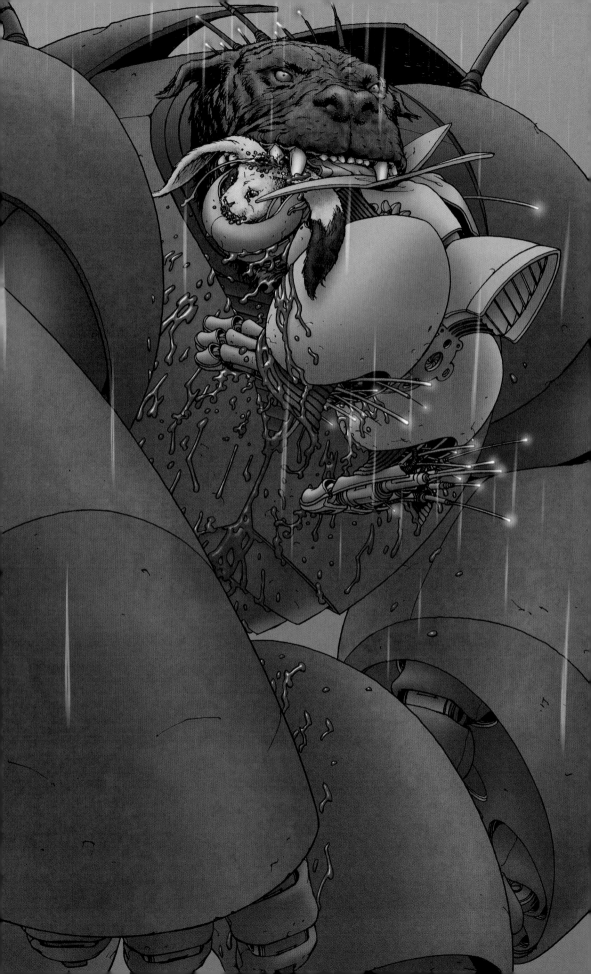

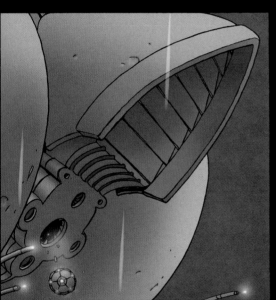

UH-OH.

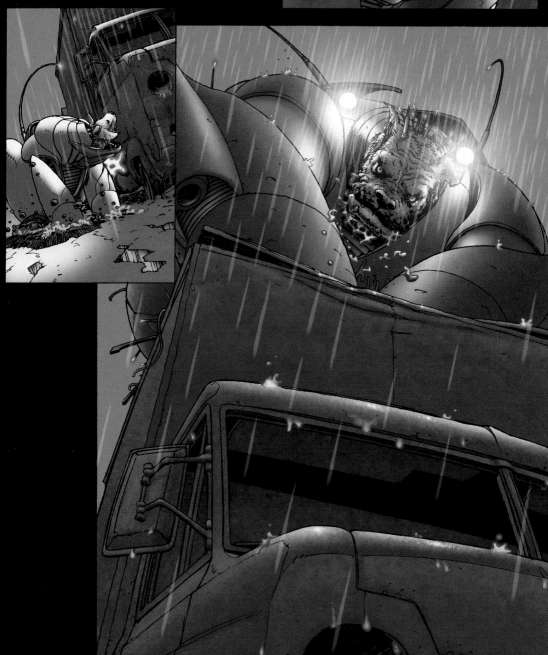

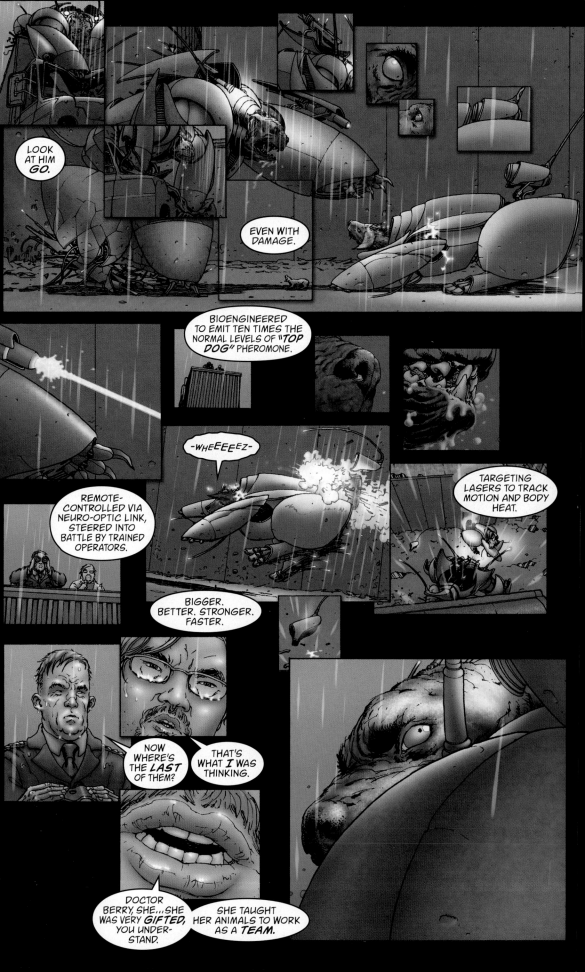

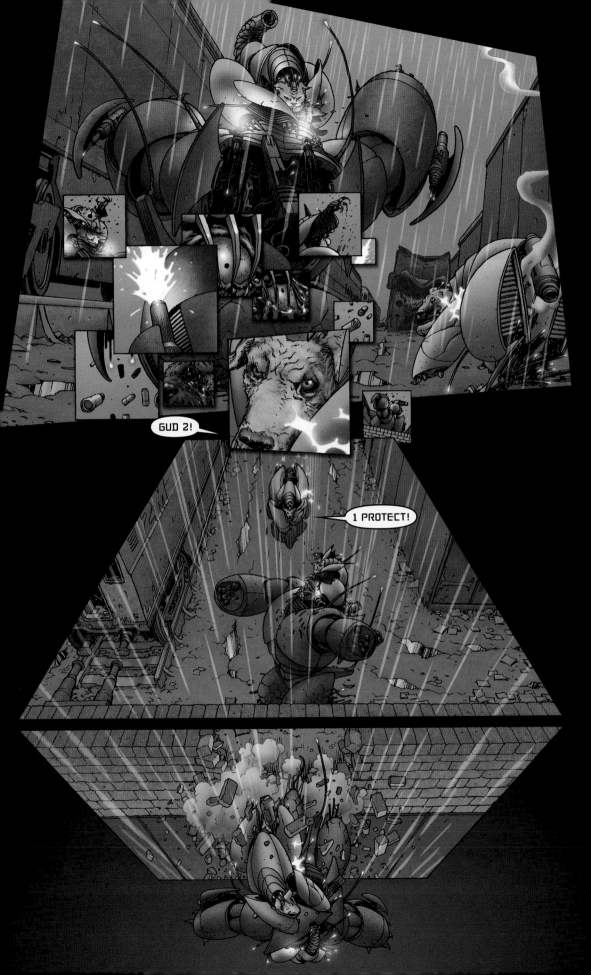

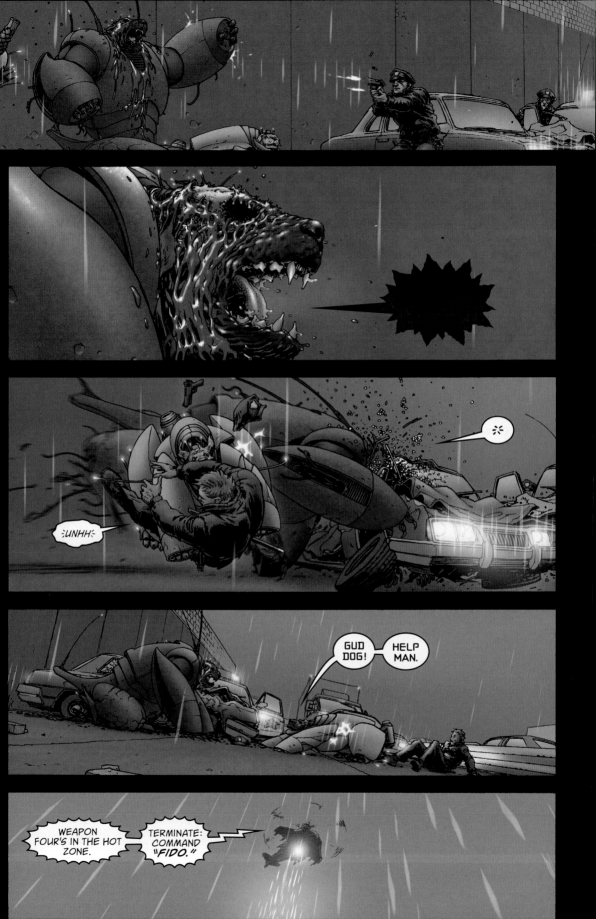

DAMN THING ALMOST ATE A POLICE OFFICER.

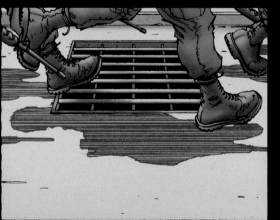

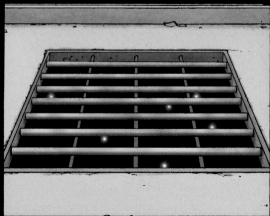

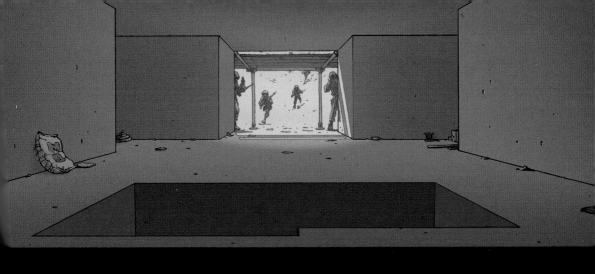

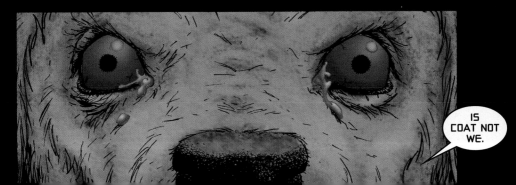

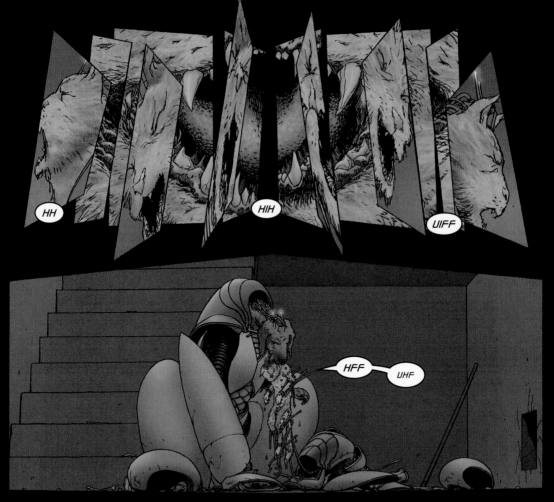

HH

HIH

UIFF

HFF

UHF

IS COAT.

RRAOWWR

NOT WE.

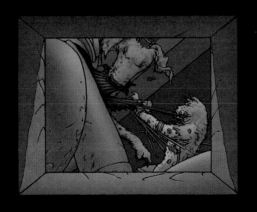

BE CAREFUL DOWN THERE.

THE DOG MAY STILL BE *ARMED,* AND THE *CAT'S* A KILLER. TAKE YOUR TIME.

PROCEED WITH *UTMOST* CAUTION.

THERE WAS A LOT OF *NOISE* BUT IT JUST *STOPPED.*

PIECES OF ARMOR EVERY-WHERE.

AND ALL I CAN HEAR NOW IS...A *BLEEPING* NOISE.

WHAT *KIND* OF A BLEEPING NOISE?

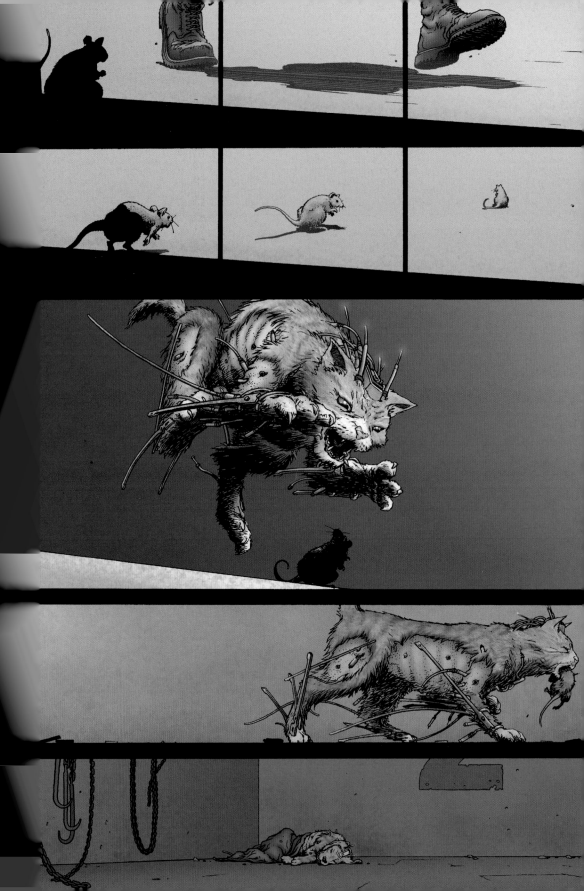

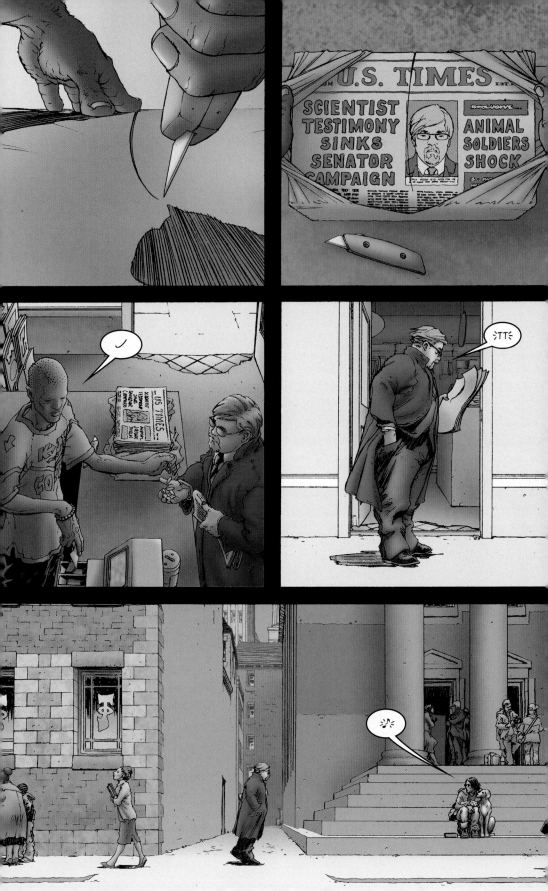

# STINK BOSS!

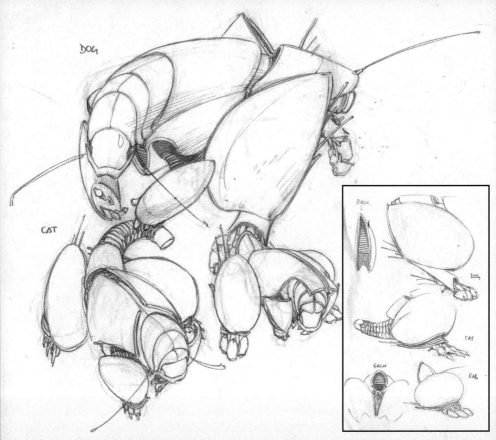

**Building the world of WE3 with** FRANK QUITELY **and** GRANT MORRISON

# CHARACTER DESIGNS

**GRANT** I originally had the animals in biped robot suits that made them look more like bulky humans with animal heads, but it just didn't work and we decided instead to make the armor conform more closely to the shape of the animal underneath, which was much more visually appealing and allowed Frank to create some truly original animal action sequences.

FRANK: The animals' armor was designed from the ground up and began with practical considerations rather than aesthetic ones, as though I was designing something that could conceivably be made and used. I looked closely at fleas, roaches, pangolins and other naturally armored creatures; robots, sports watches, American cars and Italian and Japanese mopeds also helped to inform the styling. We decided against camouflaged finishes in the interest of clarity, and instead settled on a two-tone scheme using color and grey that is typical of many mammals in the natural world.

FRANCIS
LAYDIER
ALHAMBRA
BRADFORD?

NO
EARS.

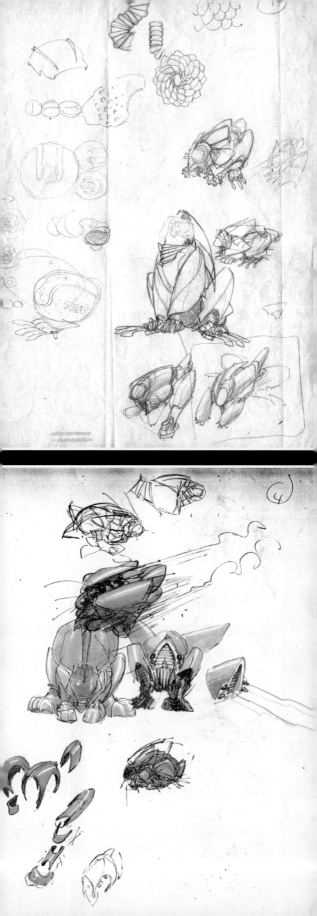

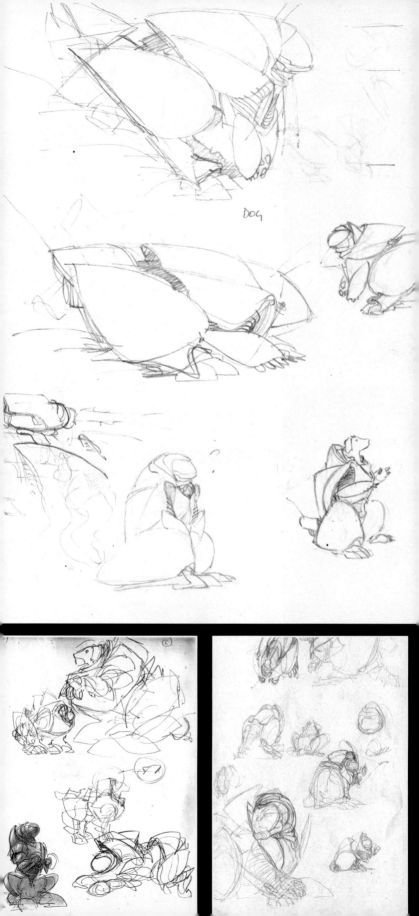

DOG

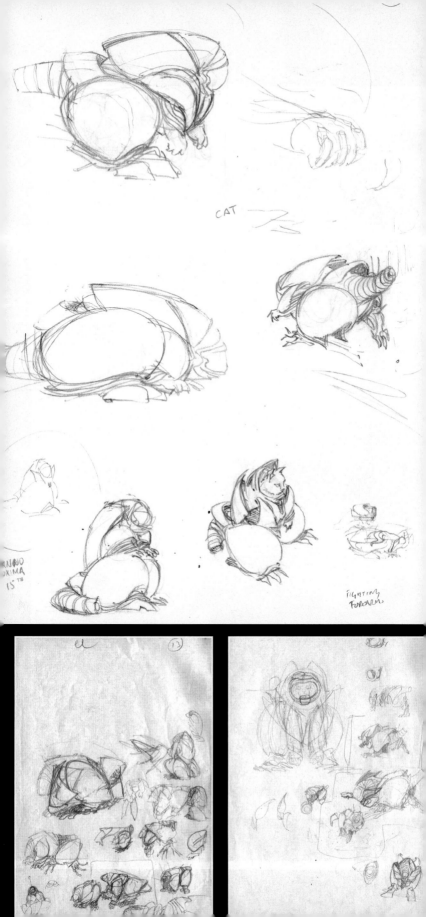

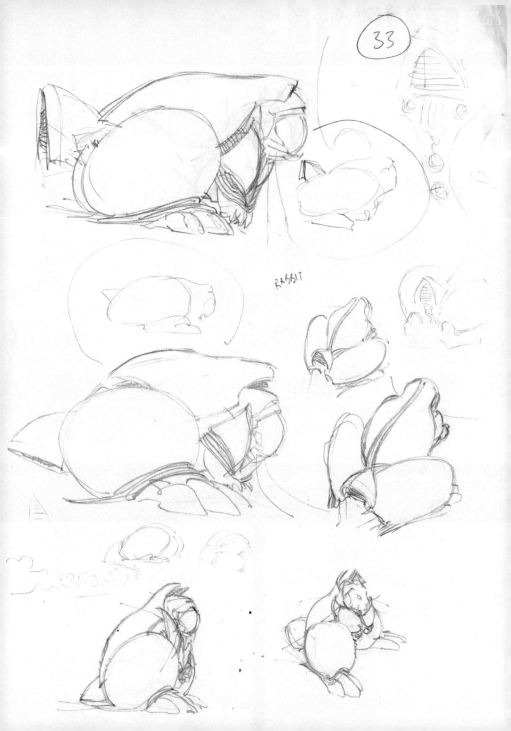

33

RABBIT

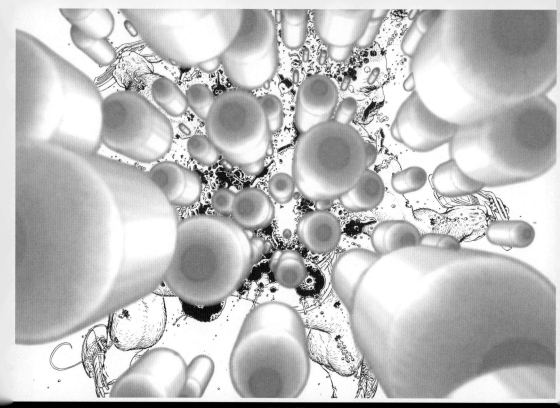

FRANK: I drew preliminary roughs for "shooting" this scene from two different angles — side-on, and from behind. In retrospect, I'm glad that Grant chose behind.

**GRANT:** This was the first big action shot in the book and an eye-popping demonstration of the "3-D page space" effects we'd developed — of which more later. Additionally, the explosive death of Señor Guerrera left readers in no doubt as to the levels of gore they would have to expect from this heartwarming tale of fluffy animals.

The visceral, forensic detail of the blood and guts in this book has often raised eyebrows, but we felt it was a necessary "red in tooth and claw" counterbalance to the sentimentality that's always hard to avoid in tales of plucky animal pals. Parents who may feel uncertain about exposing their little angels to anatomically detailed drawings of entrails and punctured eyeballs may not necessarily be surprised to discover that Quitely was relentlessly goaded to each fresh crescendo of grand guignol by his sons Vinnie and Joe, both under ten years old at the time.

# CCTV
# SEQUENCE

**FRANK:** All 108 panels for this 6-page sequence were drawn and cut out individually and color-coded for each camera involved — that way I could lay it out as per my roughs, and then easily see how any changes made would affect the sequence as a whole.

It took a lot of time to prepare, but it really made it easier to get the storytelling right. The cards can be arranged linearly, like dominoes, intersecting like a crossword, or concurrently but in separate sequences, like musical tracks.

I kept them in a small cardboard box, which became really beaten up after a while, and someone put it in the bin by mistake, but fortunately I rescued it before the bin was emptied.

**GRANT:** That little cardboard box is a genuine wonder of the world. It allows an entire sequence of events to be experienced in any order including backwards, forwards and sideways. You can even play the scene as a card game if you like! The original idea was to use CCTV screen images to create a kind of "cubist" version of an unfolding event as it might be seen from multiple fixed camera angles. Close study of the sequence will cause a curious 4-D object or map to appear in one's head! The tight repeated rhythm of the 18-panel grids creates a sense of tension and claustrophobia that is released by the lovely 2-page escape spread.

# ATTACK SEQUENCE

GRANT: At the beginning of the process of writing WE3, I described it as a story of "meat and motion." Structured around the direct desires of three animals, it was intended as a very straightforward linear narrative. The simplicity of the story freed us up to make the page layouts somewhat experimental, so Frank Quitely and I set about devising a different approach to the comics page that we hoped might suggest non-human perception of time and space.

We chose to treat the page not as a flat 2-D surface upon which panels were "pasted" down flat but as a virtual 3-D space in which panels could be "hung" and "rotated" or stacked one on top of the other. According to scientists, small animals experience time more slowly, and we liked the idea of extending the gutters around the panels to suggest the immense amounts of still "zen" time a cat might pass through between the micro-seconds of human awareness.

Written before Frank and I worked out how this might actually look on the page, the following script excerpt shows the first attempts to articulate the idea to editor Karen Berger and ends with a hopeful "... trust us, it'll look unbelievable." Fortunately, it did.

WE3: ISSUE 2

PAGES 6/7

Frame 1

This is the first of two big special effects action spreads which attempt to show time, space and motion from an animals' POV instead of emphasizing human senses. To do this Frank and I are creating what I'm calling the "Pop-Out" effect which is all about thinking past the apparent "flatness" of the 2-D page surface and instead visualizing the page surface as having infinite white DEPTH — this allows for a new kind of "camera-eye" for comics — panels can "pop" out of the page or sink into the page etc. It's all worked out visually and will change comics forever but beyond that to explain more would be to spoil the surprise of seeing the pages. This is a completely new way of depicting high-speed action which only comics can do.

Rapid cut to super-cool feline ultra-violence. The cats up in the topmost branches firing insane amounts of ammo. Close up pop out panels showing microscopic 3-D detail on the needles. Or heat images. Pheromone frequencies. Flash cut with receding panels of snarling animal faces. Dying men.

The dog leaps at the windscreen of the second jeep. We're right in there with the men as the monstrous cyborg comes straight at us. Firing a single missile from its back cannon. These are not cuddly animals to fuck with, no sir! Pop-out panels show impact wounds in forensic close up. Sound bursts. Close up animal reactions, sniffing noses. Fumes etc. All sliding and shuttling around in the white depths of the page. Let Hollywood try to copy THIS stuff...

CAT:     SSSTINK
CAT:     BOSS
CAT:     DIE!

PAGE 10/11

Frame 1

The second of the "this is what you pay for..." super-effects "POP-OUT" effects spreads, this time with the pop-out panels arranged on a different plane in page space... trust us, it'll look unbelievable. The big images here show the Cat in super-strobe lapse slinking down and around a flaming tree, back onto the ground... shooting down the final opponents. The Dog leaps from the second jeep as it crashes. The animals tumble down the bank. Flames take control.

Frame 2

DOG:      !?!
DOG:      GUD 2
DOG:      COME
RABBIT:   TAIL
RABBIT:   BAD
RABBIT:   TAIL

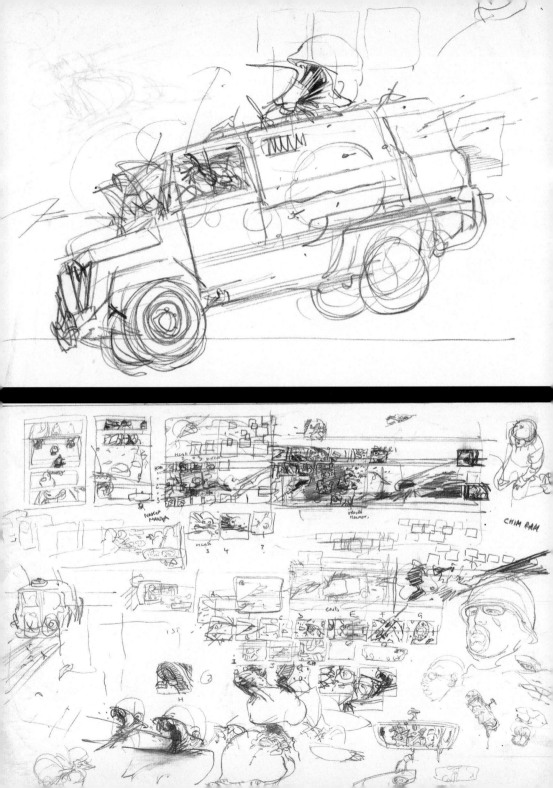

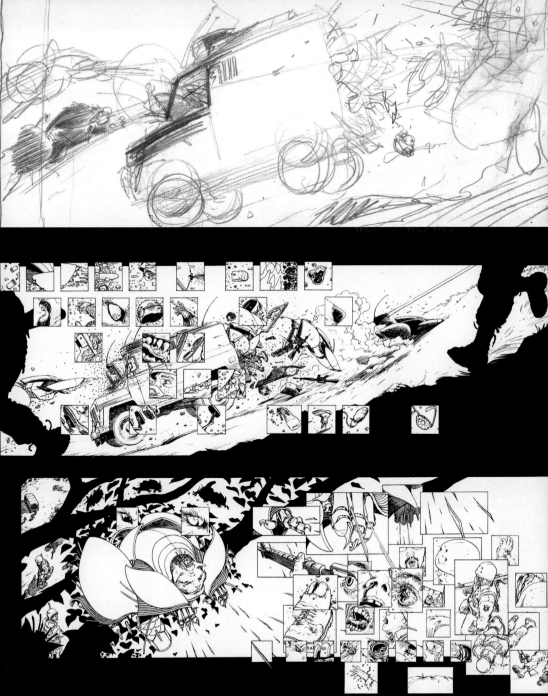

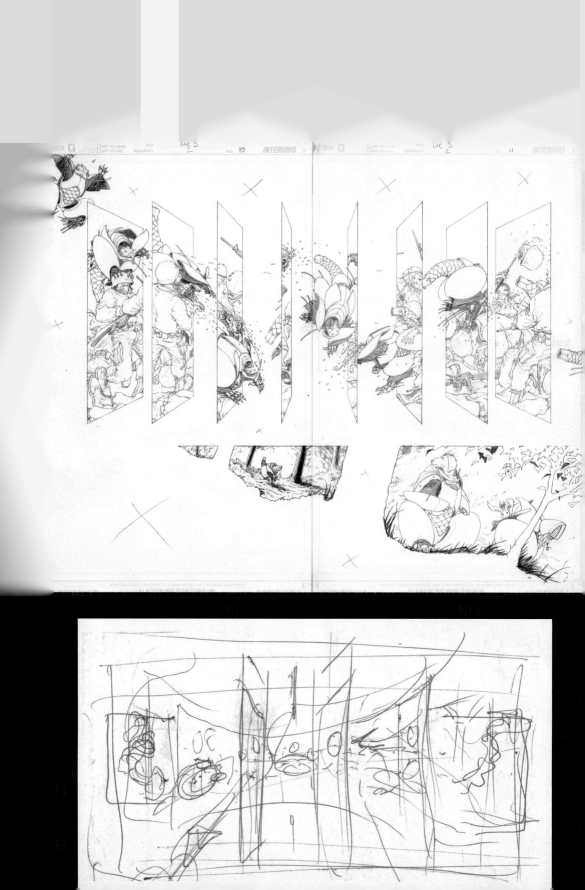

# ORIGINAL MINISERIES COVER ART

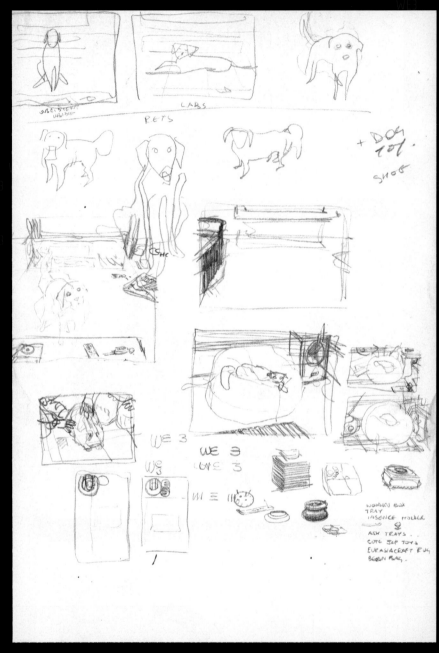

FRANK: The first cover for the original miniseries has an array of props from my own house at the time; the second has half the stuff I had in my bedroom as a teenager; and the writing on the third was done by my family — Johnny and Claire's by my kids, and Mrs. Mortimer's by my wife.

GRANT: The three covers were one of the first story elements that occurred to me. If we have hearts at all we've all had them broken by those sad, hopeful "pet missing" posters; those personal photos of beloved pets taken in happier times; the reward offers; the gut-wrenching fear and worry that haunts every handwritten, home-printed line. We wanted to emphasize what kind of story this was by engaging our readers' emotions straight away, and I think these covers do the job of not only introducing the three animals but making them immediately vulnerable and relatable.

# LOGO DESIGN

This one page of logo ideas represents the entire process from initial discussion to enlisting Bra NYC to do the finished art.

We liked the idea of the logo being a literal dog tag, which would play with the double mea and animals. The melting tag also suggested the way that the hard shell of military armor and t eak down into more free-flowing unconfined natural shapes and responses after the animals e tivity. And we wanted, I seem to remember, something that recalled the metallic logos on bloc ovies.

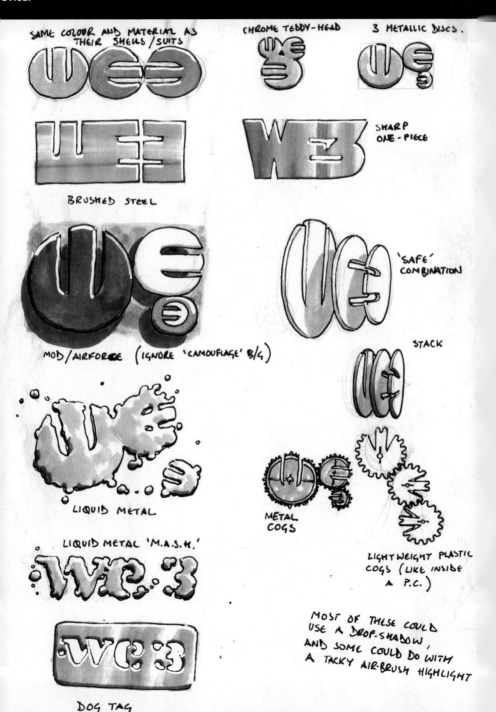

SAME COLOUR AND MATERIAL AS THEIR SHELLS / SUITS

CHROME TEDDY-HEAD

3 METALLIC DISCS.

BRUSHED STEEL

SHARP ONE-PIECE

MOD/AIRFORCE (IGNORE 'CAMOUFLAGE' B/G)

'SAFE' COMBINATION

STACK

LIQUID METAL

METAL COGS

LIGHTWEIGHT PLASTIC COGS (LIKE INSIDE A P.C.)

LIQUID METAL 'M.A.S.H.'

MOST OF THESE COULD USE A DROP-SHADOW, AND SOME COULD DO WITH A TACKY AIR-BRUSH HIGHLIGHT

DOG TAG

# DELUXE EDITION
# COVER ART

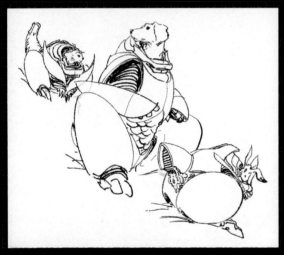

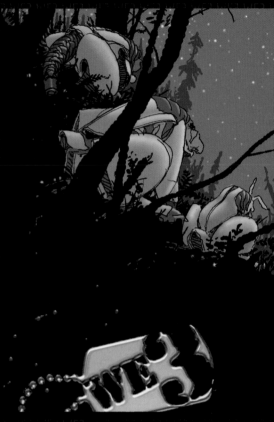